PEASANTS UNDER SIEGE

PEASANTS UNDER SIEGE

THE COLLECTIVIZATION OF ROMANIAN AGRICULTURE, 1949–1962

Gail Kligman and Katherine Verdery

PRINCETON UNIVERSITY PRESS PRINCETON AND OXFORD

Published by Princeton University Press, 41 William Street,
Princeton, New Jersey 08540
In the United Kingdom: Princeton University Press, 6 Oxford Street,
Woodstock, Oxfordshire OX20 1TW

press.princeton.edu

Cover art: *Establishing the Collective Farm* (*Constituirea Gospodăriei Colective*), painting by Corneliu Baba, 1950. Courtesy of City Museum of Bucharest (Muzeul Municipiului Bucureşti).

Library of Congress Cataloging-in-Publication Data

Kligman, Gail.
Peasants under siege : the collectivization of Romanian agriculture, 1949-1962 / Gail Kligman, Katherine Verdery.
p. cm.
Includes bibliographical references and index.
ISBN 978-0-691-14972-1 (hardcover :alk. paper) – ISBN 978-0-691-14973-8 (pbk. : alk. paper)
1. Collectivization of agriculture—Romania—History—20th century. 2. Agriculture and state—Romania—History—20th century. 3. Romania—Politics and government—1944–1989. I. Verdery, Katherine. II. Title.
HD1492.R8K55 2011
338.1'849809045—dc22 2011012452

British Library Cataloging-in-Publication Data is available

This book has been composed in Sabon and ITC Fenice

Printed on acid-free paper. ∞

Printed in the United States of America

10 9 8 7 6 5 4 3 2 1

We dedicate this work with love to our siblings and their families

Douglas Kligman

Michael Kligman

Margaret Verdery Little

and in loving memory of

Albert M. Kligman

Beatrice H. Verdery

Contents

Illustrations

Tables

Preface

Peasants have been under siege since time immemorial by those intent on prying from them agricultural surpluses or the means of agricultural production. Sometimes the weapons used against them were tithes and taxes, sometimes agrarian reforms, sometimes enclosures and privatization. This book concerns a form of siege warfare specific to the twentieth century: the collectivization of agriculture. Invented in Stalin's Soviet Union in the late 1920s, it entailed wrenching from peasants' control the land, animals, and implements with which Russian and other Soviet villagers, as well as those in Eastern Europe, China, and elsewhere, had sustained their households across generations. We ask how that was accomplished, and with what effects, in Romania between 1949 and 1962, but our ambition is much greater: to illuminate a policy experienced by millions of peasants worldwide.

The book thus deals with two immense themes: communism and property. Although the communist idea lost some of its power to frighten (or inspire) in 1989, its impact on property will not soon be forgotten. We turn to Romania for our investigation because its form of collectivizing was very similar to that of the Soviet Union, yet importantly different: somewhat less violent, more protracted, and, in a country dominated by smallholders rather than communal villages, more individualized. To the extent that there was anything to be said for collectivization—and in principle there was, though the devastating manner of its execution largely nullified its benefits—the comparisons are worth exploring. We find that when applied in a context where the Communist Party was weak, the policy imported from the Soviet Union resulted in complex patterns of bargaining and negotiation that—especially in the formative years—change our picture of communist dictatorship. That is the story we tell here.

This book has been long in the making, almost as long as the collectivization campaign itself. It is the fruit, on the one hand, of our individual research in Romania, and, on the other, of a multidisciplinary collaborative project entitled *Transforming Property, Persons, and State: Collectivization in Romania, 1949–1962*, which we initiated in 1998 with a group of Romanian and other scholars. Each of us had worked with Romanian villagers under socialism and developed deep attachments to them, inspiring our interest in joining efforts to recover some of their "hidden histories" after 1989. We had no thought of writing a comprehensive history of collectivization—it is too early for that—but only of offering our own perspective on the process, based on a combination of archival and ethnographic research and on social science notions concerning person, property, and state. By inquiring into what collectivization reveals about the nature of the Party-state, we hoped to contribute some perhaps novel ways of thinking about it as a stimulus to further work. Because we are also writing for English-speaking audiences, however, we found we had to provide extensive background on the process, making this book bigger than we had at first imagined it.

We embarked upon the research from two different angles. In the late 1990s, Kligman returned to the site of her long-term fieldwork in Romania, doing oral history interviews and collecting oral poetry that elderly informants had preserved in written form to chronicle the tumultuous years of collectivization. When she had begun her work there in 1978, the Securitate (Romanian secret police), seeking to silence any reference to that process, had prohibited villagers from discussing it with her. Nonetheless, at the end of her stay, an elderly woman who had avoided all contact with her decided to reveal this hidden history, singing it to her in a ritualized form through which peasants often expressed conflict and dissent (see Kligman 1988). This bombshell set the stage for Kligman's post-1989 interest in the topic. In 1998, Kligman approached Verdery, who was completing a project on postsocialist decollectivization and had been learning about the earlier formation of collectives, a topic she too had been explicitly instructed to avoid during her work in the 1970s. She had now become intrigued with studying both sets of property transformation, *to* socialism as well as *from* it. After years of working separately in Romania, we were eager to do a project together and settled on this one.

To pursue it, we formed an international interdisciplinary research team and held a preliminary workshop at UCLA in 1999. Once we obtained funds for the project we expanded the team, which finally consisted of nineteen researchers altogether; their names appear at the head of the acknowledgments, and more information about them is found in appendices 1 and 2. Our main objectives in assembling the team were to foster multidisciplinary, international, and intergenerational cooperation. We selected as our colleagues scholars from the United States (two), the United Kingdom (one), and Romania (fourteen), spanning a variety of fields (history, anthropology, sociology, ethnography, law, and literary criticism) as well as four scholarly generations. Five participants focused on macro-level issues of state policy, exploring property law, propaganda through literature, and Party debates and policies on collectivization. Everyone else would carry out a combination of interviewing and archival research in communities in which they had already been working. Because we view collectivization as variable across space and time, we selected researchers who could cover a broad sample of research sites. To gain a variety of perspectives, researchers all conducted interviews across a wide spectrum that included people of differing social positions, local and regional Party leaders, heads of collective farms, and so on. They provided us with their results in lengthy reports, upon which we have drawn extensively (along with our own data) in constructing our arguments. Because of our collaboration, this is a multiauthored work in several senses. Not only did the two of us write it together, and not only did we draw on the reports of our project participants, but we include extensive quotations from our own and our collaborators' respondents and the documents we all consulted. Our goal has been to create as "experience-near" an account as we can, concerning both the events of collectivization and the research process itself.

* * *

The magnitude of our themes and of the material at our disposal, as well as the difficulty of interpreting it, have often seemed overwhelming to us. Each of our chapters could easily have become its own book. Moreover, ongoing research by Romanian scholars continues to illuminate the collectivization process. We nonetheless hope the questions and arguments we pose in this volume will prove fruitful for those who take up these issues in the future, whether in Romania or elsewhere, and will contribute productively to ongoing analyses of the communist period. In a world context whose property order has spun out of control, seeking to understand the alternatives remains an urgent task.

Acknowledgments

OUR FIRST AND most indispensable acknowledgment is to the members of our research team: Julianna Bodó, Liviu Chelcea, Dorin Dobrincu, Călin Goina, Constantin Iordachi, Daniel Puiu Lățea, Robert Levy, Linda Miller, Eugen Negrici, Sándor Oláh, Marius Oprea, Octavian Roske, Dumitru Şandru, Michael Stewart, Cătălin Stoica, Virgiliu Ţărău, and Smaranda Vultur. Without these superb colleagues, this book could not exist. Each of them contributed unstintingly their time, intelligence, talent, and goodwill to make our project a success. The data they provided in extensive project reports (cited in our bibliography) form a large part of our material; many of them read some or all of this manuscript and gave us precious advice; they responded to an endless succession of queries over several years, long after they had thought the project complete. We owe an especially great debt to Dorin Dobrincu and Constantin Iordachi, who not only read multiple drafts, offered frequent archival and bibliographic assistance, provided photographs, and responded readily to an unending stream of questions and calls for help, but also took on the responsibility of editing the volume of case studies from the project, in both Romanian and English versions (see our bibliography). *Mulţumim din suflet!* Robert Levy provided us not only with his research results but also with his entire document collection from his dissertation research. Michael Stewart secured funds from the British Academy for all three of our workshops, and Smaranda Vultur and the Fundaţia A Treia Europă (Third Europe Foundation) of Timişoara hosted the first of our meetings.

Aside from our team members, throughout the several years of its operation our project benefited from the generous and varied assistance of many persons and institutions. We are indebted above all to the people in the settlements covered by our research who granted us interviews on this often-disturbing subject, frequently across multiple meetings that lasted several hours. Even while sometimes interpreting their words in a light they might find surprising, we hope we have rendered them with appropriate sensitivity. We wish in addition to thank the funding agencies whose support was essential to our work. The U.S. National Science Foundation (NSF) awarded us contract no. BCS 0003891, and the National Council for Eurasian and East European Research (NCEEER), funded by the Title VIII congressional appropriation to the U.S. Department of State, awarded us contract no. 816-12g. These grants were administered through the University of Michigan; we thank not only those two organizations but also Patti Ferullo and Linda Bardeleben at the University of Michigan as well as Mary Jane Pica and Linda Schulman at UCLA for their invaluable assistance. A Woodrow Wilson International Center for Scholars

Short-Term Fellowship brought Gail to the east coast in fall 2008, enabling us to work together more closely. We also received funds for various aspects of the project from the National Endowment for the Humanities, the Center for European and Eurasian Studies and Department of Sociology at UCLA, and the departments of Anthropology at the University of Michigan and the Graduate Center of the City University of New York. We are thankful to the British Academy for its grant to Michael Stewart in support of our three workshops. Finally, fellowships to each of us at the Russell Sage Foundation (2004–5) made it possible for us to begin writing; as we struggled to finish the book without additional extended time together, we were even more grateful for that initial year. Their assistance notwithstanding, these organizations bear no responsibility for our views in this book.

In Romania, all team members benefited from the use of their respective County branches of the Romanian National Archives, whose directors and staff we acknowledge here; some also made use of the central repository in Bucharest. In addition, several of us were granted access to the secret police archives, through the National Council for the Study of the Securitate Archives (CNSAS). We are especially grateful to Andrei Pleşu, Gheorghe Onişoru, and Florica Dobre for their assistance, as we are generally to the Council's Archival Directorate. We additionally thank István Rév, director of the Open Society Archive in Budapest, and Pavol Salamon, then senior supervisory archivist, for their help with documents from this collection. The New Europe College in Bucharest provided us with a number of services, hosting our third meeting and administering other project-related matters. Our special thanks to its rector, Andrei Pleşu, and to Anca Oroveanu and Marina Hasnaş for their generous assistance.

We also thank Mihai Oroveanu for his help in providing visual material. Other Romanian friends and colleagues also contributed importantly to one or another aspect of the project and we acknowledge them here: Sorin Antohi, Adriana Băban, Suzana Balea, Gabriel Catalan, Silvia Colfescu, Maricuţă Dăncuş, Mihai and Ioana Dăncuş, Robert Fürtös, Silviu Lupescu, Lia Pop, Andrei and Iriana Pop-Jora, Marius Uglea, Cristian Vasile, and Alexandru Zub.

In the United States, we benefited from the comments of numerous colleagues, either on parts of the manuscript or on papers from it presented to various audiences; among them are Rene Almeling, Pamela Ballinger, Ivan Berend, Rogers Brubaker, Jane Burbank, Sheila Fitzpatrick, J. Arch Getty, Bruce Grant, Martha Lampland, Phyllis Mack, Michael Mann, Emily Martin, Terry Martin, Veena Oldenburg, Jane Schneider, James Scott, Ann Stoler, Iván Szelényi, Ron Suny, Lynne Viola, Mark von Hagen, Susan Woodward, and participants in seminars at the many universities and research institutions where we have presented parts of this work. We thank them all and wish we could have incorporated even more of their comments. We have been very fortunate in our research assistants, especially Liana Grancea, Yossi Harpaz, and Ana Vinea, as well as Dan David, Jon Fox, Robert Levy, and Jon Sigmon. Finally, we acknowledge with thanks the inspiration we have found in the work and encouragement of Ken Jowitt, whose ideas about collectivization have informed many of our arguments.

At Princeton University Press, we are deeply grateful to Eric Schwartz for his support of this project, to Kathleen Cioffi for shepherding it through the production process, and to our copy editor, Robert Demke

A project of this duration rests as well on the sustenance provided by our families and friends—many more than we can name. Heartfelt appreciation to Andrew Abbott, Iván Berend, Rogers Brubaker, Charles Camic, Gillian Feeley-Harnik, Ashraf Ghani, Sandra Harding, David Harvey, Ken Jowitt, Robert Levy, Linda Miller, Nancy Scheper-Hughes, Iván Szelényi, the late G. William Skinner, and Sidney Mintz, for their many contributions and ongoing support. Lori Kligman and the late Albert M. Kligman generously offered us their home for intensive work meetings; thanks from us both, and from Gail special appreciation for their steadfast love and encouragement. Loving gratitude from Katherine to Phyllis Mack, for putting up with work-filled vacations and offering constant nourishment for the soul, and to Victoria Mack, for making me a proud stepmother. Most especially, each of us is deeply indebted to the other for the inspiring collegiality and enduring friendship that have sustained our work on this project.

Abbreviations

ACNSAS *Arhiva Consiliului Național pentru Studierea Arhivelor Securității*, The National Council for the Study of the Securitate Archives, Bucharest.

ANIC *Arhivele Naționale Istorice Centrale*, National Central Historical Archives, Bucharest.

ASRI *Arhiva Serviciului Român de Informații*, Archive of the Romanian Information Service, Bucharest.

ARO *Arhivele Raionului Odorhei*, Archive of Odorhei District.

CAP *Cooperativă Agricolă de Producție*, Agricultural Production Cooperative, socialist collective farm.

C.C. al P.C.R./P.M.R. Central Committee of the Romanian Communist/ Workers Party.

DJAN *Direcția Județeană a Arhivelor Naționale*, County Branch of the National Archives. We use the following county abbreviations for frequently cited archives: AB (Alba), BT (Botoşani), CJ (Cluj), CS (Caraş-Severin), HA (Harghita), HD (Hunedoara), MM (Maramureş), MU (Mureş).

Fond Archival fond.

Fond "D" Fond "Documentar," Documentary Fond (ASRI); FD (ACNSAS).

Fond "I" Fond "Informativ," Informative Fond; FI (ACNSAS).

Fond "P" Fond "Penal," Penal Fond; FP (ACNSAS).

Fond "R" Fond "Rețea," Network Fond; FR (ASRI and ACNSAS).

GAC *Gospodărie Agricolă Colectivă*, Agricultural Collective Farm (later CAP).

MNAC *Muzeul Național de Artă Contemporană*, National Museum of Contemporary Art.

PCR *Partidul Comunist Român*, the Romanian Communist Party (RCP).

PMR *Partidul Muncitoresc Român*, the Romanian Workers' Party (RWP).

RAM *Regiunea Autonomă Maghiară*, the Hungarian Autonomous Region (HAR).

Reg. *Regiune*, region.

RLA Robert Levy Archives.[1]

RPR *Republica Populară Română*, the Romanian People's Republic.

A list of initials for the people interviewed appears in appendix 3.

[1] (RLA) at the end of a citation indicates our use of Party documents found in the Robert Levy archive, located at the UCLA Young Research Library. Some page numbers may differ from documents now available in the Romanian National Archives.

PEASANTS UNDER SIEGE

Introduction

Collectivization, in my opinion, was a kind of chaos. It was the sort of thing where they turned people into serfs, slaves, they took away their land, they took away their rights, and even the dirt under the hearth belonged to the *kolkhoz*. . . . You don't have any rights, only . . . that's it. You have nothing.[1]

[The collective] was really great while it worked. . . . I tell you, I brought home 2,400 kilos of wheat. I had flax, I had hemp, I had beets, two freight cars full of sheep. . . . And I got 2,400 kilos, brought it home with this trailer, here. I worked. Those who didn't want to, didn't. And it really saved me, 'cause then I sold that wheat. I sold it and got corn.[2]

They came at night and took me away. . . . and just the way my mother made me they took off my clothes and took them from there. . . . No, they didn't beat me, just every couple of hours they came and asked if I'd work in the collective, 'cause then they'd let me go. I told them, yes, of course I'll work, but how can I leave the house with these little kids?[3]

For us shepherds, it was different [from the peasants]. We made agreements among ourselves: "If they come to count yours"—they were counting the sheep right there, where you were with them, you know—"then you tell them that 50 are mine." . . . And they checked in their files: "Yes, 50 sheep." But the guy had more. And when they came to count my sheep, I told them that part of the sheep belonged to the other guy. That's how it worked. There was no way they could catch you.[4]

I ask[ed] myself: "Oh, how can you sign on a piece of paper that you give away your property right? I always bought land, I scraped it together little bit by little bit, I had my wife wear felt shoes, and we scrimped and saved, and now I'm going to give it away on a piece of paper? I'm not giving it anywhere!" . . . And why should I join? How can you give away your right? After all, . . . you bought it and have it from your parents. How could you just give it away like that, for nothing?[5]

[1] V. T. T., Dobrincu interview, Darabani. Throughout this book, quotations from our respondents are noted by their initials (or other numbering systems, different for each interviewer), keyed to the interviewer list in appendix 3, which gives data about the respondent.

[2] P. N., Budrală interview for M. Stewart, Apoldu de Jos.

[3] M. G., Vultur interview, Domaşnea.

[4] D. I., R. Stan interview for M. Stewart, Poiana Sibiului.

[5] I. F., Dobrincu interview, Darabani, concerning the decision to join the collective in 1962.

"THE THEORY OF the Communists," Marx and Engels wrote in the *Communist Manifesto*, "may be summed up in the single sentence: Abolition of private property." Their Bolshevik disciples who gained power and founded the Soviet Union followed this theory in full, confiscating most of the country's wealth by various means and using it to set up a new property regime: socialist property. Not that what it replaced was entirely *private* property, for what then prevailed in the Russian countryside was communal tenure. The dissolution of the previous forms did not take long: some nationalization decrees, a few years of constant assault on the peasantry, and people renounced their ownership prerogatives. The 125 million peasants of the Soviet Union were largely "collectivized" in the course of four years (1929–33); those in Eastern Europe, beginning in 1948, followed suit in the course of ten to fourteen (1948–62). Although a *sense* of private ownership may have lingered, the *rights* associated with it passed over to the planning ministries and bureaucratic apparatus of Soviet-style communism.

The collectivization of agriculture was the first mass action, in largely agrarian countries like the Soviet Union, Bulgaria, and Romania, through which the new communist regime initiated its radical program of social, political, cultural, and economic transformation. Collectivizing agriculture was not merely an aspect of the larger policy of industrial development but an attack on the very foundations of rural life. That is the process we illuminate in this book, for one East European country, Romania, in the years 1949 to 1962. The Romanian villagers we quoted above provide its coordinates.

In every country where communist parties came to power in the twentieth century, they soon moved to transform property arrangements, for property was fundamental to both the policies and the self-conception of communists. In consequence, private property came under immediate and sustained attack. Communist parties nationalized factories and trades establishments, which, like the new industrial and commercial units then set up, were to be run in the interests of "the whole people" rather than for the profit of a wealthy few. Land was either nationalized and grouped into state farms (Russian: *sovkhozy*) or gradually pried from the clutches of its owners, who "donated" it to collective farms (*kolkhozy*). This is the process known as "collectivization"; accomplishing it was the subject of fierce debate within communist parties everywhere.

The Romanian Communist Party was no exception. From the outset, collectivization there was controversial: stenographs of Central Committee meetings reveal a bitter struggle between those who advocated pushing it at all costs and those who preferred a more gradual approach that would rely on persuasion only, not on coercion (see Levy 2001). The former faction won out, unleashing an intense, often violent campaign to collectivize. From the earlier Soviet experience, Romania's leaders knew that the policy would be difficult to implement and that the widespread negative image of the Soviet kolkhoz would be a major obstacle. Party cadres went into every village to talk up the collectives as the most "modern" form of agriculture. They sought to persuade potential collective farmers that socialist farming would be successful, even taking delegations of Romanian cultivators to visit "model" Soviet kolkhozy as evidence. Most peasants, however, proved difficult to convince and were at length driven into the collectives mainly by force.

Contrary to popular belief, collectivization in Romania did not involve a powerful Communist Party imposing its will on the countryside, for Party rule itself was in a process of being created. To see the Party-state as a fully formed social actor at the time of collectivizing—in *any* of these countries—would be an error (see, e.g., Câmpeanu 1988, 1990; Gross 1988; Kotkin 1995). Communist parties had barely consolidated control, and officials at all levels were struggling to devise what would become the mechanisms of Party domination: simply put, they lacked the power to enforce their will over a resistant populace (Jowitt 1978). The various Party apparatuses in Eastern Europe, while largely modeled on the Soviet one, were creating themselves through the policies they implemented at Soviet urging. A process as all-encompassing as collectivization, which in most cases affected half or more of the populace of these countries, was clearly central to this "self-creation." What makes this even more true is that in modern times, property has been basic to how political regimes define themselves and their subjects.

Collectivization brought undeniable benefits to some rural inhabitants, especially those who had owned little or no land. It freed them from laboring on the fields of others, and it increased their control over wages, lending to their daily existence a stability previously unknown to them. For many, however, collectivization was the major trauma of the socialist period.[6] Because 77 percent of the population resided in rural areas as late as 1948,[7] this one traumatic policy was more far-reaching and affected more Romanian citizens—twelve million out of sixteen million—than any other single act of the entire communist period. By leaving rural inhabitants without their own means of livelihood, it radically increased their dependence on the Party-state. It both prepared and compelled them to be the proletarians of new industrial facilities. It destroyed or at least frayed both the vertical and the horizontal social relations in which villagers were embedded and through which they defined themselves and pursued their existence. It forcibly stripped those who had land—howsoever little—of their relationship to something many of them considered an integral part of their relations to ancestors, other kin, and neighbors, rather than just an

[6] Following our practice in earlier publications, we use the terms "communist" and "socialist" more or less interchangeably, preferring the latter term as closer to the realities claimed by communist-party regimes in the former Soviet bloc.

[7] Figure from *Republica Socialistă România* (1984: 12). Residing in rural areas does not, of course, mean full dependence upon agriculture for livelihood, but it does indicate the number of people collectivization was likely to affect.

object external to themselves. For those people, collectivization was a grievous assault on their very conceptions of themselves as human beings.

Main Themes

We approach collectivization not simply as an adjunct to industrial development, as is common in the literature, but as part of a broader set of modernizing technologies that include mass education, improved public health, industrialization (which collectivization helped to enable), and so on. In its Soviet form, these modernizing technologies resembled those in western Europe only in certain respects: the Soviet version represented an alternative modernity, which transformed production in system-specific ways, of which eliminating "bourgeois" property forms was but one. Displacing the modernizing efforts of previous Romanian elites, the Soviets exported their technologies to Romania and other East European countries. Soviet-style modernization as a form of technology transfer involved a double movement: first the Bolsheviks imitated western capitalist production technologies, modifying them in the process, then they transferred the results to Eastern Europe.[8] The Soviets exported an ideology, institutions, and sets of practices that their recipients, in turn, modified again.

What they exported was not, however, simply a way of modernizing production but a transformation of rule, a change in the technologies of government and power. The change was not total: with the possible exception of Pol Pot's Cambodia, no new regime can survive if it completely destroys the institutions it replaces—nor, in general, has it the capacity to do that, as we indicate in this book. Nonetheless, the forms of rule the Soviet Union exported had their specificities, and collectivization was a fundamental means of installing them in its largely agrarian satellites.[9] Because property involves not just rights but cultural, social, and political relationships as well, collectivization changed rural people's connections to land and also to themselves, to one another, to the state, and to the cosmos. They became new kinds of subjects, new kinds of persons.

At least as significant, the process of implementing collectivization transformed rule for the rulers. It created Party cadres as certain kinds of subjects

[8] Lampland observes, for instance, that the notion of the *work unit* central to Soviet remuneration systems was imported from Germany and then modified by incorporating a measure of property ownership (n.d.: 32).

[9] Eastern European countries differed in the degree to which they were dependent on agriculture and therefore in the extent to which collectivization occupied a central place in transforming rule. For instance, the percent of the population employed in agriculture as of the late 1940s varied from 88 percent in Albania to 29 percent in eastern Germany and 38 percent in Czechoslovakia. By this measure, Romania, Bulgaria, and Yugoslavia ranged from 74 percent to 80 percent agrarian, Poland and Hungary from 53 percent to 57 percent.

and consolidated the Party-state itself as a Soviet-Romanian hybrid. As we examine the process of collectivizing from this angle using the methods of historical ethnography, we contribute to understanding how a particular kind of state configuration—the Romanian Communist Party-state—was constituted, with its accompanying subjectivities and social relationships. That is, we help to build a historical ethnography of state formation. We focus on political, cultural, and social-relational issues rather than questions about how collective farms worked, how they transformed agricultural production, or whether they contributed to socialism's economic failings. Such questions, although important, pertain to a different story from the one we tell, a story that begins where ours ends, in 1962 with the campaign's conclusion. Nonetheless, what we say here about how collective farms took shape is crucial to assessing their subsequent operation, for those who would assume that task.

Making the Party-State

Research into collectivization in the Soviet Union is well advanced, compared with that in Eastern Europe, having benefited from earlier access to archives as well as from the outstanding work of pioneers of this topic, such as Robert Conquest (1986), R. W. Davies (1980), Sheila Fitzpatrick (1994), Moshe Lewin (1968, 1985), and Lynne Viola (1987, 1996, 2005, 2007). Much of this work contested the "totalitarian" assumption that Stalinism meant imposing policy from the top down and suppressing all resistance. Their view became a consensus among subsequent scholarly generations, in the work of such people as Jochen Hellbeck (2006), Stephen Kotkin (1995), Terry Martin (n.d.), and others (see Fitzpatrick 2000).[10] We too subscribe to this view, regarding collectivization as a long, dynamic process of becoming, in which parts of the apparatus took on specific characteristics not just from an initial program but as practices developed over time. For example, we agree with Kotkin (1995), Viola (2000), and Tănase (1998) that the strength and capacity of the early secret police organizations such as the Soviet OGPU (precursor to the NKVD), the East German Stasi, and the Romanian Securitate did not *antedate* the major tasks assigned to them—collectivization, the verification of Party members, and the deportation of the rural bourgeoisie (called *kulaks* in Russian and *chiaburs* in Romanian). Rather, these organizations were *formed with and by* those tasks. Similarly, Viola argues that collectivization was crucial in preparing the ground of the Great Purge, for the OGPU/NKVD gained extensive experience from crushing peasant rebellions in 1929–30, deporting the kulaks, and administering a far-flung kulak diaspora, all of which served it well in its work in the 1937 purges (Viola 1996: 234; see also Viola 2007; Shearer 2009). We would go even further,

[10] This consensus view was to some extent anticipated by Fainsod (1953, 1958).

proposing that the inability of the Party-state to control its collectivization cadres shaped a particular kind of state-society relation as well as behavioral habits that would, in our case, mark the Romanian Communist Party throughout its tenure.

Therefore, we treat the collectivization process as instrumental in establishing the nature of the new Party-state itself and of its subjects. It was a defining moment both for the apparatus that initiated it and for the peasantry who suffered its consequences, with the introduction of new relations among Party cadres at various levels and between them and the rural population. In what ways did the new regime *in statu nascendi* take on certain characteristics precisely because collectivization was among its first major tasks? Would central directives repeatedly override policies adopted locally in response to local problems, and would local resistance cause central authorities to modify their directives, thus modifying how collective property was being made? How did collectivization change people's self-conceptions and social entanglements, replacing longstanding village communities with a completely different kind of social structure—a formal organization that spilled far beyond village borders? The collective nature of our project enables us to ask comparative questions as well. Was resistance more marked in some parts of the country than others—thus, did certain locales affect the national outcome disproportionately? Are there discernible differences in the process according to the ethnonational or religious composition of different villages and regions? Answers to these questions will enable us to ask how a policy instigated in obedience to the Stalinist model took specific shape in Romania and helped to form there a particular configuration of interbureaucratic and state-subject relations, the essence of which lay in the specificity of its connections between Party and state, Party and society.

To speak of making the Party-state through a process of technology transfer suggests an image of power that we hasten to modify. We are interested in how Romanian communists tried to follow the Soviet example and what countercurrents this aroused; they imported policies from the Soviet Union but applied them to a very different case, and without sufficient political capacity to enforce them. Because the political center could not control what was happening below, Romania's Party-state took shape in the space between *receiving* Soviet directives and *implementing* them. Especially in the formative years during which collectivization occurred, the result was a complex process of negotiation, not a direct replication of dictatorship. (After all, Stalin himself urged Eastern Europe's leaders not to repeat the violence of the Soviet experience.) Even if Romania's top leaders had been in agreement about how to collectivize, the farther out the policy moved the less they could manage it. As it entered daily life in the regions and districts, it encountered recalcitrant peasants and practices, other modes of power flowing in the opposite direction—social-organizational forms and relationships that constituted alternative power sources, alternative "technologies." It occurred in a diverse field of forces.

Therefore, we emphasize how collectivization was localized in village social relations, working upward as well as downward, and we reject the assumption that the center was always directing outcomes. The technology transfer may have been top-down, but its execution was not. This perspective affects our treatment of resistance. Although peasant resistance figures prominently in our account, celebrating it is not our main goal. We hope, rather, to show the complexity of the relations that developed between the peasantry and the Party-state—sometimes oppositional, sometimes pedagogical, sometimes symbiotic. The omnibus category of "resistance" does not do justice to this complexity. Nor does a concentration on *peasant* resistance, for cadres too engaged in multiple forms of it, including avoidance, noncompliance, and bending higher directives to their own purposes.

Such a perspective, we believe, gives us the best ethnographic purchase on studying the Party-state to combine with our use of material from archives. Because Romania was collectivized much more recently than the Soviet Union, we have a methodological possibility less available to scholars such as Davies, Fitzpatrick, and Viola: we can conjoin documents with living memory—though we recognize the limitations of both kinds of source (see "Methods and Sources" section below and appendix 2). Alongside reading Central Committee meeting stenograms or the speeches of Party leaders, we can gain some access to the everyday experience of the activists and the rural populace through whom collectivization actually took place. We look for relationships formed among activists themselves and between them and the peasantry and then examine the practices and technologies activists employed, thus gaining a glimpse of the sites at which peasants encountered "the Party-state" directly. Using this formulation, we see more precisely how practices and technologies evoked counter-practices among the peasantry, which perhaps modified the operation of the Party-state in turn (see Iordachi and Dobrincu 2009; MacLean 2007; Sharma and Gupta 2005; Viola 1996). In this way we can offer views unlike those of the usual political history, illuminating both collectivization and the Party-state as they developed and were experienced in daily life.

Collectivization is a particularly revealing policy because of the magnitude of its effects (given the size of the rural population) and also because of the multiple themes inherent in the concept of property, which lies at its core. Property is about rights and obligations, about economic access, about citizenship and political status, about social relationships, and about notions of personhood. All of these entered into collectivization. Leaving its legal, economic, and political aspects to other disciplines, our discussion emphasizes primarily the social relations and persons of this momentous change in property forms.

Property and Persons

Property has long been a central topic of interest to many disciplines, anthropology among them. We use an anthropological conception of it here, finding that view the most flexible and enlightening for our purposes. In over a century of work, anthropologists have inquired into what property means cross-culturally and what other social forms it is linked with.[11] They understand property not as a thing or a relation of persons to things but as a relationship between or among persons with respect to things or values. Anthropological research has pointed to a wide variety of property arrangements, of which individual ownership is only one possible form. This sort of work reveals the complexity of property rights, far beyond the flat dichotomy between exclusive individual or state/collective ownership rights that appears in comparisons with the former Soviet bloc (e.g., Poznanski 1992). It also asks how *persons* are made through their relation to things.[12] What is the relation of property and persons? How is property a "person-making" cultural form?

If people's embeddedness in social relations and the definition of what constitutes a "person" are fundamental to any property system, then social embeddedness and personhood are basic to understanding collectivization, a process that tore people from their accustomed relations, forcibly constituted new ones, and in so doing transformed their conception of themselves. Our book aims to show how collectivization accomplished this and how its targets reacted. Making collective property involved a colossal struggle between the utopian property vision of the communist regime, on the one hand, and the peasants' notions of personhood and their universe of social relations, on the other.

For example, the Party stigmatized and derided well-to-do families, labeling them "exploiters." Cadres strove in this way to foment class war and divide villagers against one another, thereby breaking up local solidarities to facilitate forming collectives. In many cases, however, villagers refused to take up the cudgel against these "exploiters," who might be their godparents or neighbors (see Kideckel 1982, 1993). Instead, they often protected them, hid food for them, lent them money, and refused to participate in confiscating their goods. In these communities, peasants defined themselves through a property-based status order, which was not easily overthrown. Countless small resistances of this kind led István Rév to conclude, for Hungary, that the peasantry won the first round of the collectivization wars against the Party-state (Rév 1987).

In pointing to the connections between property and persons and to the devastating consequences of revising them, we do not mean to imply that private property is the normative centerpiece of social order, and that our goal thus

[11] The discipline's investigation of this topic begins with the work of Lewis Henry Morgan (1877) and Henry Maine (1863), continuing on to the influential contributions of Malinowski (1935), Gluckman (1943, 1965), and Hallowell (1955), and in later scholarship as well (e.g., M. Brown 2003; Ferry 2005; Hann 1998; Verdery 2003; Weiner 1992).

[12] See, for example, Appadurai 1986; Carrithers 1985; Strathern 1988; Weiner 1992. This line of inquiry began, of course, with Mauss's celebrated *The Gift*, although Mauss was far from the first to pose questions about property and persons; we find them in ancient Greek philosophy, in Hegel, and in Locke, among others.

should be to reveal the horrors of attempting its opposite. On the contrary: we are well aware of the equally devastating ways private property was made in early modern times, and of how unequal property endowment has crippled the lives of people everywhere, including precommunist Eastern Europe. Our aim is not to tout one property form above another but to try to understand how property regimes are made, and in particular how their making connects notions of personhood with the kind of state that is taking shape. In selecting the history of collectivization in Romania as our vehicle for this, we encounter another set of literatures, dealing with the production of history and its relation to memory.

Revisiting Collectivization: History and Memory

> [I]t is in society that people normally acquire their memories. It is also in society that they recall, recognize, and localize their memories.
> —*Halbwachs [1925] 1992: 38*

> Neither memories nor histories seem objective any longer. In both cases we are learning to take account of conscious or unconscious selection, interpretation and distortion. In both cases this selection, interpretation and distortion is socially conditioned.
> —*Burke 1989: 98*

All shifts of power generate a reconfiguration of the "known past." In Romania, as in the rest of the postsocialist region after 1989, memory work and historical re-visioning saturated politics as the collapse of communist regimes created political openings for civil society organizations and scholars to probe silenced or hidden histories.[13] Rather than being a "thing of the past" or "a distant memory," the past became grist for the mill, as scholars, politicians, and ordinary citizens battled not only over the postsocialist present but over the socialist past—how to represent it, and what claims to lay upon it (e.g., Judt 2002; Müller 2002; Tismăneanu 2008; Tismăneanu et al. 2007; Wertsch 2002). As John Keane observed, "crisis periods . . . prompt awareness of the crucial political importance of the past for the present" (in Müller 2002: 3).[14]

In Romania after 1989, a number of scholars began excavating the history of collectivization, stimulated by both personal and academic concerns. Motivating many of them was an urge to understand how the process unfolded in their

[13] The legacies of dictatorships in Western and Eastern Europe (e.g., Nazi, Fascist, Soviet) and of Soviet colonization in Eastern Europe and the former Soviet republics have provoked unrelenting soul-searching among and about Germans, but also among and about Italians, Spaniards, East Europeans, and post-Soviet peoples. See, for instance, Kopeček 2008.

[14] Keane further observed: "As a rule, crises are times during which the living do battle for the hearts, minds and souls of the dead" (in Müller 2002: 3). See also Gal and Kligman 2000; Müller 2002; Verdery 1999.

own communities or regions; for some, a desire to expose and valorize personal or familial trauma gave their research added impetus.[15] Valuable collections of documents were published, along with a number of works of historical synthesis, as well as village-level studies.[16] Complementing document-based research was a growing interest in oral history, with some scholars making explicit claims to memory as the source of a new, more correct historical truth.[17] For the most part, the aim of all this work was to extend knowledge of the collectivization process across Romania and to recuperate formerly hidden sources, rather than to raise contentious questions about how history is made and what role memory plays in that process.

In contrast to these recuperative efforts, our own research on collectivization began in the late 1990s amid heated debates about the "production of history" (e.g., Cohen 1994; Trouillot 1995), forcing us to confront questions about who "owns" the past and has the authority and legitimacy to assess or (re)write it. How is collectivization to be chronicled and understood? Is it, like the communist period of which it is an essential feature, to be repudiated fully, thereby

[15] An early work was Octavian Roske's (1992) volume of interviews and documents, commissioned by the Romanian Parliament as property restitution was beginning in 1991.

[16] Dan Cătănuş and Octavian Roske (e.g., 2000, 2004, 2005) embarked upon a large project to publish documents on collectivization, including stenograms of Politburo, Secretariat, and Central Committee meetings and secret police reports (see also Roske et al. 2007). This and much other work was published under the auspices of the National Institute for the Study of Totalitarianism, founded in 1993, and its journal *Arhivele Totalitarismului.* Numerous similar projects emerged, bringing out documents both from the Party leadership and from particular regions or locales. (See, e.g., Ciuceanu et al. 2003; Iancu et al. 2000; Cojoc 2001 [for Dobrogea]; Damian et al. 2002 [for Vlaşca]; Dobeş et al. 2004 [for Maramureş]; Márton 2003 and Oláh 2001 [for Odorhei district]; Moisa 1999 [for western Romania].) Of signal importance were the publications of the National Council for the Study of the Securitate Archives (CNSAS), the Civic Academy (Academia Civică), and the Romanian Institute for Recent History (IRIR), which include both document collections and analytic-interpretive essays on a variety of topics, collectivization among them. Works of historical synthesis include Ionescu-Gură's on the stalinization of Romania (2005) and Tănase's on the Gheorghiu-Dej regime (1998); village studies include Liiceanu's (2000) and Mungiu-Pippidi's (2010). An increasing number of articles on collectivization began appearing in edited volumes about the communist era (e.g., Cesereanu 2006; Dăncuş 2005; Iordachi and Dobrincu 2009) and in several journals (especially *Analele Sighet*, *Arhivele Totalitarismului*, *Anuarul Institutului de Istorie Orală*, *Anuarul Institutului Român de Istorie Recentă*, and *Institutul de Investigare a Crimelor Comunismului în România*, alongside the more academic journals of the history institutes in Bucharest, Cluj, Iaşi, Timişoara, and so on). These studies, too numerous to list here, range from annotated publications of selected documents to case studies of specific communities.

[17] Smaranda Vultur, for example, in conjunction with the Anthropology–Oral History Group of the "Third Europe" Foundation in Timişoara, edited several volumes of life-history interviews, many of which contain reminiscences about collectivization (e.g., 1997, 2000, 2002a, 2002b, 2009a). University programs emerged such as the Institute for Oral History in Cluj, coordinated by Doru Radosav, with its associated journal (*Anuarul Institutului de Istorie Orală*) and numerous volumes concerning the anticommunist resistance (see, e.g., Budeanca et al. 2006; Radosav et al. 2003). Similar recuperative activities exist in several counties, through their museums or other institutions (see publications such as *Analele Sighet* and *Crisia*).

fulfilling one goal of both scholars and civil society representatives to pass moral judgment on communism? And, if so, on what is the historical record to be based: Documents from that same discredited regime? The recollections of people whose voices were silenced during that period and whose memories today may or may not be reliable? How do we weigh these different evidentiary sources? How do we assess the weight of the past on the present, and, conversely, that of the present on the past? These concerns led us to consider further the complex relationship between memory and history that permeates contemporary historiography about socialism and its aftermath as well as our use and assessment of both written and oral sources. We offer a brief review of the ever-expanding literature on memory studies,[18] in part to situate better our own use of oral histories and their relationship to the archival data from which we also draw. Discussion of such interdisciplinary approaches to memory and history will illuminate our analytic strategy.

Contemporary scholarship has moved in the direction of seeing memory as a distinct form of "social action" (see Berdahl 2010; Lee and Yang 2007; White 2006), problematically related to "what actually happened." By the turn of the millennium, "memory" had joined or, some argue, supplanted other key conceptual categories such as culture, history, and identity (e.g., Confino 1997; Klein 2000), forming what may be viewed as a veritable "memory industry."[19] Memory has been studied under varied rubrics such as individual, collective, social, mythic, official, popular, vernacular, oppositional—the differences or boundaries separating them often unclear.[20] Particularly debated was the relationship between individual and collective memory, partly in response to Halbwachs's assertion in the 1920s regarding memory's social construction (see epigraph for this section). Kansteiner critically observes:

> But the fact that individual memory cannot be conceptualized and studied without recourse to its social context does not necessarily imply the reverse, that is, that collective memory can only be imagined and accessed through its manifestations in individuals. At the very least, we have to differentiate between different types of "so-

[18] We review but cursorily the literature on memory and history, as well as memory studies in the social sciences and humanities, confining some of our observations to the footnotes. Memory studies have exploded, supplementing the extensive testimonials and scholarly analyses of the Holocaust with more recent witness accounts and analyses of the abuses of communist regimes, apartheid, and many other cases of people's inhumanity.

[19] Kansteiner attributes the popularity of studying memory to a combination of its "social relevance and intellectual challenge" (2002: 180), regretting (as do others, such as Olick and Robbins 1998; Klein 2000; Ten Dyke 2001) that conceptual clarity did not necessarily accompany the heightened attention to memory or to its relationship with history.

[20] In this respect, the variety of "memories" studied mirrors the introduction of popular, vernacular, and everyday histories that challenged the authorial conventions of History writ large. In postsocialist societies, and in other postauthoritarian contexts, memory work and historical recovery have been managed through analysis, for example, of official, public, and collective memories, on the one hand, and popular, vernacular, and individual memories, on the other.

cial" memory, autobiographic memory on the one hand and collective memory on the other. (2002, 185)

Trouillot too criticizes the easy recourse to notions of collective memory, noting the failure to problematize both the collective subject that does the remembering and who in the collectivity decides what to include or exclude in its history (1995: 15–16). To reconcile these distinctions and clarify the relationship between individual and collective memory, Olick (1999) has proposed an "integrated paradigm" that evaluates the impact of the social on what he aptly calls "collected" (rather than collective) memory, a term we find compelling, for it avoids the homogeneity that "collective memory" assumes.

The manifestations of memory referred to above point to another important dimension of memory study that builds on Halbwachs's distinction between memory and history, on the one hand, and "the materiality of memory" in history, on the other. Pierre Nora (1984–92, 1989) posits that modernity, distinguished by an accelerated pace of change, brought about both the loss of memory and the loss of tradition, thereby replacing what he labeled *milieux de memoire,* "[living] contexts of memory," with *lieux de memoire*, "memory sites" (e.g., museums, commemorations, archives). He claims that "what we call memory today is therefore not memory but history" (1989: 13), rendered through the "materiality of the past" and the materialization of memory. In effect, modern memory is "archival."[21] In analyzing our data, we have drawn on archival sources and other print media (e.g., memoirs, novels, academic and popular books) that form the selective materiality of memory, noting how these sources may have jogged individual memory, reshaping it in the process of "remembering."

In addition to memory's materiality are its social and processual features, such as those pointed to by Zerubavel (2003; see also Connerton 1989). Focusing on how things are remembered, he—like others—has fruitfully elaborated on memory as "mnemonic socialization" in "mnemonic communities," which

[21] In a useful summary of Nora's conceptual work, Ten Dyke (2001: 31) notes that it signals that "memory . . . exists in interactions between people and things such as monuments and places such as museums," taking up the theme of the reciprocal shaping at work in the construction of individual and collective memories—a theme echoed throughout the literature, and one that guides our overall analytic strategy. For example, during our research, we found that archival material opened up avenues for exploration in our interviews, just as oral accounts alerted us to issues to explore in the archives. (Ten Dyke also emphasizes Nora's historization of memory practices and representations of the past in relation to processes of social change and changes in such practices; see also Yates 1966; Le Goff 1992; Huyssen 1995; and Rappaport 1998.) Assmann (1995) examines the materialization of memory in terms of "cultural memory," differentiating between "everyday communications about the meaning of the past" (akin to oral history) and "cultural memory" as objectified culture. The latter endures and encompasses what most consider collective memory. See Kansteiner on Assmann and cultural memory (2002), from which we draw. Also see Ten Dyke (2001) for a useful summary of Nora's conceptual contributions and Lee and Yang (2007) on the culture of memory.

circumscribe what individuals should remember or forget. Furthermore, because memory is formed through a social process, Zerubavel also addresses intergenerational transmission between individuals and collectivities. Attention to memory and temporality allows him to discuss historical continuities and discontinuities, the latter readily marked through "periodizing the past" (Zerubavel 2003: 87).

Mnemonic practices realized through different expressive genres (e.g., monuments, memoirs, pictures) both serve as "vehicles of memory" and give form to it (Confino 1997). In so doing, they call attention to the relationship between memory and culture. Lee and Yang (2007: 11) refer to a "'poetics' of memory, that is, the use of cultural tools and resources for the constitution and articulation of memory." The cultural dimensions of memory production—like those of history—point to an issue about which scholars interested in culture and communication have cautioned (e.g., Confino 1997; Kansteiner 2002): a tendency to conflate the representations of memory with their meaning and reception.[22] Meaning and reception are particularly salient in socialist and post-socialist contexts in which memory and history have been and remain highly politicized.

A variant of the meaning-reception problem is the relation of official to everyday versions of experience. Wertsch (2002), studying history and memory in the Soviet Union, tempered this distinction, maintaining that the regime's tight control over the production of textual resources shaped not only a univocal account of the past but also its citizens' collective memory. As political control over authoritative texts diminished, however, collective memory became more heterogeneous. While we appreciate Wertsch's emphasis on the dynamic interplay between official and unofficial versions of memory and history production, we nonetheless take issue with the deterministic force he accords to the Party's control over cultural production and its impact on shaping citizens' memories. On the one hand, during socialism political elites struggled over discursive control of the "message" (e.g., Verdery 1991; Levy 2001); on the other, even though the Party shaped individual memories, they were refracted through personal, family, and community memories and experiences as well. The permeation of the environment with communism's political symbols and propaganda affected how people understood the world around them, whether or not they agreed with the purported claims about it. The disjuncture between "public" and "private," or "official" and "popular," was not as stark as many thought (see Gal and Kligman 2000; Getty and Naumov 1999; Hellbeck 2006;

[22] It is beyond our scope to review the literature on representation, meaning, intention, and reception. Nor do we delve into the complex link between memory and narrative, the latter rendering events meaningful through their selective structuring. See, for example, Somers 1992; Eyal 2004. Stewart (2003) assesses an oral account about the death of a partisan in terms of its narrative structure, which he suggests calls into question the account's reliability as recollection. Because memory is generally accessed through language, it is often uncritically treated as narrative.

Yurchak 2006). Our project's data contain countless examples of people's performative use of the Party's categories and language. In writing petitions, for example, they invoked the Party's class-based terms in their attempts to refashion themselves in their own self-interest. That they did so instrumentally does not mean, however, that such terms were any less a part of everyday communication and of how people came to understand themselves in relation to others.

Our final point concerns the political context of research into memory in its relation to history making. In discussing collective memories in China, Lee and Yang (2007) explicitly address the "politics of memory" through an analysis of the relationships between "the power of memory" and "the memory of power."[23] For them, this entails understanding:

> First, . . . contentions over interpretations of historical experiences between official history and social memory, and among different versions of popular memories. Second, . . . the appropriation of these interpretations for political action, critique, and consent. Third, . . . the formation of political subjects *through* remembering and forgetting, a process that contributes to the microfoundation of the state and its challenges from society. (2007: 3)[24]

As many have observed, "official" or Party history—that which fills the public record—is itself the result of intense internal contestations among rival factions (see Levy 2001). We find Lee and Yang's emphasis on the *political* mediation of memory an essential complement to the usual focus on the narrative and *social* mediation of memory and history (whether "official" or "popular," oral or written) in creating selectively "usable" elements. As Müller puts it, "Memory matters *politically*" (2002: 2). This is especially true of contexts such as ours in this book, where the process of social mediation was politically overdetermined during both socialist and postsocialist periods, although quite differently. In both times, the rewriting of history and reshaping of memory were expressly meant to legitimate a new political regime.

In short, the political-cultural context of research bears on its findings and their interpretation. For many scholars, postsocialist historical work is a recuperative act intended to create new truths and a new collective imaginary to replace those of the communist era. Sometimes the recuperation is deeply personal, as researchers bring to light suffering like that of their own families. This is the position of some in our research team—a position with which we sympathize and which we respect. Our own view is somewhat different, however. Rather than seeing the new historiography as uncovering the "truth" about the past, including collectivization, we see it as part of a process of recovering and reconstructing usable pasts—plural because of the widely divergent interpreta-

[23] On memory and power, see also Müller 2002.

[24] While this analytic strategy is helpful, it nonetheless illustrates a tendency to reify the distinction between official history and popular memories and to view official history in monolithic terms.

tions (ranging from anticommunist to communist-nostalgic) that are competing for the power both to reclaim and to rewrite history.[25] We believe that by exploring the diversity of pasts that our research has yielded, we are able to present a more fully representative, more nuanced picture of the communist era, thereby shedding light not only on the relationship between communist rule, community, and everyday life, but on memory and history as well. To that end, we now turn to a discussion of our use of archival and oral sources, a discussion we continue in greater detail in appendix 2.

Researching Collectivization: Methods and Sources

Our research focused on the years from collectivization's beginnings in 1948 to its officially declared successful conclusion in 1962. Yet its significance extends into the present and is of considerable interest to many people besides scholars. After 1989, the politics of postsocialist agriculture was fraught with problems, ranging from the privatization of property to the thorough reorganization of agricultural production to the negotiation of conditions for Romania's entrance into the European Union. For the families dispossessed of their land in the 1950s, attempts to reclaim it in the 1990s through the tangled process of property restitution underscored collectivization's ongoing salience (see Verdery 2003). And, as we will see in the following chapters, for some whose lives collectivization deeply marked, giving voice to their sufferings made revisiting the period crucial to reclaiming not only their land and possessions, but their senses of self and dignity.

Studying a relatively recent past that had been buried under the historical edifice erected by the Communist Party has been laden with both daunting challenges and unanticipated opportunities. Unlike most scholars of collectivization in the Soviet Union, we have been able to interview people who lived through this experience.[26] Yet because the past is so alive in the present, gaining access to varied kinds of data has posed frustrations and concerns—ranging from archival material that has not been catalogued, has been lost, or is only selectively available, to individuals either eager or reluctant to share their recollections or too infirm to do so.[27] Moreover, respondents' accounts recorded in 2000–4 were inevitably affected by the near-universal condemnation of com-

[25] We do not review the seminal works of postmodernist thinkers such as Foucault and Habermas on the relativization of truth, nor Derrida's contributions to debates on relativism and nihilism.

[26] Most scholars working on collectivization in the Soviet Union have generally had to rely on archival sources. The age of our interlocutors for this project lent urgency to our research. Several of us learned of a key respondent's death just before or during the course of our research.

[27] Selectivity pertains to memory, oral-historical, and archival sources. See Climo and Cattell (2002) on remembering and ethnography as methodological practice; see also Tonkin (1992).

munism that emerged worldwide after its collapse, even though by the late 1990s some began to express a certain nostalgia. In Romania as elsewhere, 1989 unleashed a "return of the repressed," as people articulated what had been publicly silenced for several decades. The previously extolled "radiant future" was tarred by an explosion of oral histories, confessional autobiographies, memoirs, literary works, television documentary series such as the *Memorialul Durerii* (Memorial to Suffering),[28] and publications, as well as the *Final Report* of Romania's Presidential Commission charged with analyzing and condemning the communist dictatorship and its crimes[29]—all of which have exposed, however unevenly, the once-unacknowledged abuses of Communist Party rule. Not surprisingly, such revelations have had their own silencing effects, discouraging those Romanians who hold more positive, even nostalgic memories of the socialist period from expressing them, and, in turn, further affecting the subsequent historiography of the communist period.[30]

Hence, in examining collectivization between 1949 and 1962, we have had to consider our project's contemporary conditions as well as the implications of our multimethodological strategy, entailing both oral-historical and archival research.[31] Even though scholars generally acknowledge memory to be highly selective, often distorted or repressed, they readily consider it a "distinctive method of truth production."[32] But in our case, our research took place when collectives no longer existed, and forty to fifty years after collectivization occurred. What effects might that have on memory as a source of truth? People's accounts, retrospectively produced, were influenced by memory's vicissitudes over the preceding decades; their recollections varied widely—from acutely vivid to vague or sketchy. Moreover, after 1989, scholars and others often car-

[28] In 2003, the Sighet Memorial Museum was inaugurated as a Memorial to the Victims of Communism and the Anticommunist Resistance. Housed in the infamous prison in Sighetu Marmației (in northern Romania) in which many of Romania's notables died, the Memorial includes extensive museum exhibits aimed at educating the public about this dark history. It also promotes research and teaching. For additional works on the abuses of communism, see Tismăneanu et al. 2007 and Iordachi and Dobrincu 2009.

[29] In 2006, President Traian Băsescu authorized the formation of a Presidential Commission for the Analysis of the Communist Dictatorship in Romania. On the basis of the ensuing report, he officially condemned communism in Romania at a Parliamentary session on December 18, 2006. See Tismăneanu et al. 2007.

[30] In a six-country project on Poverty, Gender, and Ethnicity in Transitional Societies, initiated by Iván Szelényi (Yale University), researchers found that people's experiences after 1989 contributed to reshaping their perceptions about the socialist period. In an unpublished report from the study, more Romanians remembered themselves as having been better off in 1988 than they were in 2000, a notable shift from pre-1989 reports about living conditions in Romania (see tables 3.1, 3.2, and 3.4).

[31] All the members of our team doing case studies used archives, but not all had the same kind of access to them; see appendix 2. All members also did interviews, and like the archival research, our experiences varied considerably; see appendix 2.

[32] We thank Jon Sigmon, from whose unpublished notes we quote. On memory as factual record of past experience, see, for example, Prager 1998.

ried out oral histories and in-depth interviews without sufficient regard for the fact that memory was being solicited after the collapse of the system being remembered.

Archival research proved no less challenging. Although the situation improved in the mid-2000s, access to Romania's archives was highly problematic at the time of our research (see appendix 2). To the extent that we were able to overcome the myriad problems of access, we wrestled with persistent public skepticism about the utility of the Party and Securitate archives, which often diverts attention from the wealth of information they contain. Like oral histories, archival sources raise major questions of reliability. Despite a superficial inclination to think that archives are of unquestioned veracity as repositories of the written word, historians will be the first to acknowledge that nowhere is this the case. One has to learn to read them—and how to read documents against one another—in order to squeeze anything of value from them. We believe that for socialist countries in particular, written sources that might be reliable in other contexts are often of questionable validity—a fact that places them on a footing similar to oral histories, which are also problematic.[33] Furthermore, rather than opposing oral to written sources, historians now recognize that the former have often been used in creating the latter, and that written documents were often produced well after the fact, sometimes by nonwitnesses to the events described (Lummis 1987; Portelli 1991). For this reason, our methods purposely cut across the division between oral and written.

In our research, we pursued history as recorded both by the official "biographers" of collectivization (such as Party activists and historians and Securitate agents) and by its unofficial ones (peasants and local intellectuals who recorded their own experiences either at the time or soon after 1989), along with history as recollected in oral-historical and interview accounts of Party activists, intellectuals, and peasants whose "collected memories" represent a broad spectrum of experiences. Using such diverse resources has enabled us to explore more amply how competing groups struggled to promote their interests and to make sense of their everyday lives in the midst of collectivization's radical social engineering project.

In analyzing these different kinds of sources, we underscore that the "memory practices" of the Party-state permeated collectivization and affected the relation among the various sources. Romania's authorities—like others throughout the former socialist bloc, especially during the 1950s—considered the memory of bourgeois times an intrinsic threat to the new order, and their con-

[33] We use "oral history" for simplicity's sake although the term does not capture the variety of oral research methods employed, including in-depth interviews and in-depth discussions in the context of ethnographic research. We also take note of the distinction between life histories and life stories (Bertaux 1981: 8). Although oral history has been the subject of intense debate on the reliability of memory (Benison 1971; Cutler 1970; Grele 1985), it long ago achieved a respectable place in mainstream historiography (e.g., Storm-Clark 1971; Tonkin 1992; Vansina 1965).

trol over the public sphere generally confined memory's expression to the recesses of personal thought.[34] Through techniques that would become standard, Party officials deliberately rewrote history and mythologized it (Sherbakova 1992; Watson 1994), endeavoring to supplant all memories but its own and thus to erase forms of self that depended on localized practices of remembering. Here, it is important to keep in mind that the often-invoked injunction against forgetting became publicly possible through critical personal accounts (e.g., memoirs, oral histories) only after the collapse of communism, which opened the way for social and cultural remembering to emerge from politically induced public amnesia.

Throughout the communist period, political documentation for and about its elites suppressed everyday forms of historical evidence, although the inverse was often true in the Securitate archives, which often documented actions against the regime by its "enemies." In this context, we found it doubly important to retrieve oral as well as local written accounts that the Party viewed as subversive but that can enrich the historical record. This made our project a kind of "salvage history," giving it special urgency, since the number of those who experienced collectivization firsthand as adults was already dwindling as we began.

On Official Written Sources

> The ethnographic space of the archive resides in the disjuncture between prescription and practice, between state mandates and the maneuvers people made in response to them, between normative rules and how people actually lived their lives.
>
> —*Stoler 2009: 32*

Although archival and other written sources of the communist era challenge assumptions regarding their reliability, our aim is not to repudiate their use. To the contrary, the archives contain a profusion of information as illuminating as it can be distorting.[35] These regimes were famous for their "graphomania" (to use Milan Kundera's felicitous term [1981]), recording their practices in abundance. In line with Claude Lefort's comments about the loquaciousness of the Stalinist state (1986: 297–302), Stephen Kotkin asserts in *Magnetic Mountain*, "Stalinism could not stop speaking about itself. . . . The advent of Stalinism brought one of the greatest proliferations of documents the world has ever

[34] There is a large literature, scholarly and literary, on public and private memory under socialism, of which Miłosz 1953 is exemplary.

[35] Some other researchers also give these sources a fair amount of credence: for instance, Ross (2000) writes that lower-level East German officials were inclined to spruce up their reports so they would not be cast in an unfavorable light, yet he concludes, "Despite the tendency towards 'beautification,' most reports seem to attempt to describe the situation on the ground more or less soberly or even pessimistically" (2000: 11).

seen" (1995: 367).[36] Getty and Naumov (1999: xi) further suggest, "The directors of the terror machine were unashamed and unafraid of a negative historical verdict. They recorded and documented almost everything they did." Because members of the Soviet Communist Party believed that the Party would be eternal and of world-historical significance, they wanted to document its actions. When events sometimes turned out poorly, participants would make the documents look the way a model should. In consequence, as many historians would agree, the archives are not always very useful as a record of history "*wie es eigentlich gewesen war*"; nonetheless, we emphasize their value and urge their exploration. In what follows, we review some of the key issues we confronted in gaining "literacy" with archival materials and suggest some of the ways we have "read" them.

The voluminous holdings in Romania's archives reveal what issues Party leaders worried about, the categories in which they operated, what they saw as problems, and ways to address them.[37] In reading the documents, then, we should be looking for these kinds of things rather than for the literal truth-value of their contents. They reveal discursive frames and culturally significant categories of communicative action between the Party and "the people" (e.g., food requisitions, joining the collectives, resistance, and so on), as well as the new vocabulary through which everyone up and down the bureaucratic hierarchy was learning to think and act (e.g., class- rather than status-inflected terms, new ways of othering people as enemies). These, in turn, shed light on the structural mirroring found in the content of official and unofficial sources. Reading across them illuminates the kinds of relationships being created, negotiated, and contested between the Party and its citizens.[38]

The archives reflect the very architecture of the Party-state: in them, we can begin to trace the complexly interlinked paper trails that reveal the enormous bureaucratic and administrative apparatus put in place to facilitate centralized control, as well as the elaborate reporting system by which Party and state functionaries at local, regional, and national levels had to produce all manner of reports at regular and frequent intervals. Reports came in many different forms, ranging from general informational ones to responses to questionnaires; their distinctive genres were indicated in each report's heading.[39] These myriad re-

[36] This excess might surprise a reader who believes that these regimes worked only according to *diktat* and arbitrariness attended by pervasive secrecy. Ross (2000), writing about East German archival reports, petitions, complaints, and so on, also commented on their "sheer and overwhelming profusion" (2000, 12).

[37] On the various archives, see Oprea 2001 and Iordachi and Dobrincu 2009.

[38] "The Party and its citizens" reifies a standard dichotomy that masks the overlap between "them" and "us."

[39] Among the types were "note" or "informative note," "synthesis," "memorandum," several kinds of "report" (*dare de seamă*, *referat*, and *raport*), "minutes" (*proces verbal*), "receipt," "certification," "instruction," "nominal table," "declaration," "situation," "notice," "plan of action," "schema," "decision," "confirmation," "communication," "decree," "order," as well as miscellaneous correspon-

ports addressed myriad issues, from statistics on the number of collective farms and members, crops and yields, soil quality, and finances, to the number of Party members, rumors, lists of enemies, abuses by cadres, and so on. In view of their variety, mastering how to prepare them was an education in itself, for each genre of document had its own conventions as well as rules pertaining to its reporting channel(s).[40] Without understanding these conventions, one can miss clues that lie buried in each kind of document. Alongside all the reports were petitions from ordinary citizens and accompanying correspondence (see chapter 4). Yet another chain of documents linked together the different branches of the Securitate (secret police), which received and sent reports both within the hierarchy of its own organization and into other branches; it documented all citizens who for one or another reason were being followed, took down informers' verbatim reports, recorded the new tasks these informers were given, responded to requests for information, and wrote regular reports on the popular "mood" (see below and chapter 1)

A good many reports were typed[41] and submitted in multiple copies, with an

---

dence not otherwise identified. (In this book, we use text, report, minutes, and documents generically unless noted otherwise.) Three historians explained to us some of the distinctions among these. For example, the *dare de seamă* was the most general and comprehensive kind of report, such as an account of propaganda activity over time or a response to an inspection. It was usually solicited by a superior, even if implicitly. It had substantial informational value and was the main ideological and practical basis for decision making. The *proces verbal* referred to a specific event—a meeting on a specific date, discussions on a particular theme—and was always written on the spot, specifying the date, the attendees, and the number of copies. It had the value of a stenogram and underwrote resolutions or decisions. A *notă* or *notă informativă* referred to a very specific matter and was short, capturing for instance something that happened in a meeting of the local Party cell. Its goal was very precise, and it was usually done at the initiative of the person writing it. A *minută* was something agreed to between two parties (I engage to resolve a problem in X time period, you agree to do Y); it was like a contract. Other forms included the *referat*, a document presenting and analyzing facts on a given subject and making recommendations; the *sinteză*, a synthetic report on a large issue or problem from a given administrative unit, such as a region or district; a *circulară* (circular), which informed subordinate structures of decisions that were immediately in effect; and *instrucțiune* (instructions), which informed them how to implement various decisions, policies, and so on. A *hotărâre* (decision) could be issued from Party or state bodies, at central or local levels. See Fitzpatrick (1990) for a discussion of genres in the Soviet archives.

These various documents had certain regular features that developed over time. In the early years, changes in the kind of information the center wanted precluded publishing a handbook, but at various times instructions would be circulated explaining the content proper to each form (for example, how many chapters a report should have, how many subchapters, what problems they should treat, and so on).

[40] For example, in the Soviet Union, because bureaucratic officials might hesitate to pass bad news upward, certain NKVD/KGB reports existed solely for this purpose; similar purveyors of bad news were the petitions and denunciations that individual citizens sent to higher officials (Fitzpatrick 1994a: 327). (Countering these, of course, were the rosy reports produced by the propaganda machine for newspapers, agitprop, and many official speeches.) From our own research, one former collective farm chairman from Transylvania recollected that during the ten months he spent at Party school in Bucharest, he had learned to write reports (186, Verdery interview).

[41] Some files contain both original copies written by hand and typed copies. Also some of these

indication where the copies had been sent. Quite a number of them were sent unsigned, perhaps signaling just sloppiness or haste, or, in a culture in which blame was so readily assigned, anxiety about taking responsibility for the content. Signed or not, many reports had handwritten notes scribbled across their margins, underlinings, circles, and the like penciled in. These markings, as well as marginal notes (sometimes in several different handwritings) that indicate a passage back to some subordinate with his superior's disposition of the case or guidance on how to write better reports, show that reports were read and offer a window onto the tracks of power.

Submitting a report (as well as a petition or complaint) necessitated learning to communicate in what we call "officialese," often labeled "wooden language" (*limbă de lemn* in Romanian, or *dubovîi iazîk*, literally "oaken language," in Russian); awareness of its linguistic and stylistic features is important for interpreting the different kinds of documents. The original model for officialese was the style favored by the tsarist bureaucracy, which the Bolsheviks took over and passed along to their client states.[42] There were other, "quasi-official" styles that did not use the formulas of officialese, such as reports written by lower-level authorities who had not yet mastered it, or Securitate reports that fabricated reported speech.[43] We also found a register that we call "lay officialese," such as in documents written by peasants with the assistance of a more-educated person, perhaps a Party member. The writer knows some of the concepts and tropes of officialese but not the syntactic or stylistic conventions for stringing them together (producing, say, a document that mentions the class struggle and the proletariat and that signs off with "Long live the Communist Party!" but otherwise uses normal vernacular style). Yet another important characteristic of official documents was a writing style that effaced authorship, even when the signatory was given, by devices such as the widespread use of subjunctive or passive constructions and of plural rather than singular pronouns, as when file producers regularly referred to the Party as "we" or "our organs." In this manner, individuality was subordinated to the collective as individuals were socialized into it.[44]

---

reports are written on the backs of forms and reports from the prewar period—in Transylvania, as far back as Hungarian documents from before World War I—a possible sign of financial or paper shortages or distribution problems in the newly established regime.

[42] See Stere 2005–6, 337–38. Both outside observers and citizens of socialist countries have characterized the style of writing and of formal political address as "wooden language." A classic work is Thom 1987; on Russia, see Yurchak 2006; on Romania, see also Slama-Cazacu 1991, 2000. Bakhtin writes of "authoritative discourse," of which officialese is clearly an instance (1981, 342–48). See also Orwell's *1984*.

[43] Reported speech, quotes attributed to specific individuals or to unidentified groups of people, can be found in minutes of Party meetings, reports produced by or for the secret police, and in oral accounts. In whatever form, reported speech is invoked to lend increased legitimacy or weight to the information provided.

[44] For more on linguistic forms, see, among others, Seriot 2002 and Yurchak 2006. Clearly, requiring cadres to write reports at regular and frequent intervals had important pedagogical effects,

The sheer volume of reports circulating served the Party-state in its effort to create a centralized system of information that could be controlled, compared, and generalized. Yet those charged with furnishing a never-ending stream of reports were often overwhelmed by the large number of documents they both received and were expected to submit, resulting in their not paying sufficient attention to what they read or wrote.[45] This, in turn, affected the quality of the data submitted. An entire file, "Bureaucratic Methods and Superficiality in Party Work," dated June 12, 1951, included damning assessments such as: "Having been asked for diverse information, tables with tens of columns, questionnaires on which they work weeks on end, the Secretaries of the Party cells, not being familiar with all of the data, provide formal responses, inexact data, or, not knowing what to do with so many tables, don't respond at all."[46] Statements such as this also indicate the authorities' inability to control their subordinates sufficiently to guarantee the production and submission of reliable data.

Moreover, as Horváth and Szakolczai have written about Hungary (in comments as applicable to Romania and to different kinds of reports as well), reports inadequately reflect what they document: "It is very rare that an information report sums up what has really happened at the meeting . . . it is such a compressed summary that it really doesn't even reflect what has happened there" (1992: 114). Making matters worse, and especially in the early years, many of those producing reports were themselves barely literate. Şandru found that such basic literacy problems were compounded by basic sloppiness: "Many reports or minutes contain contradictory information. Sometimes, the same Report or Note includes different data for the same circumstance; at other times, information is missing, replaced with dots or penciled in by the person who wrote the text, making it virtually unusable" (2003: 2). In addition, the data contained in these reports were too often not just incomplete but inaccurate to boot. Statistics were manipulated and falsified: production figures were routinely inflated, and animals, land, and other objects disappeared.[47] For in-

---

helping them learn the system's hierarchy, rules, values, and language through their constant reproduction. They were provided instructions with how to fill out forms—what kind of information to include and so on. See, for example, ANIC, Fond C.C. al P.C.R.–Agrară, file 90/1950, 41, 42; ANIC, Fond C.C. al P.C.R.–Organizatorică, file 36/1954. At the same time, tracking the different trails of paper sent up and across the Party or state hierarchy enables researchers "to study the relationships between the local and central levels of power, as well as the strategies used by the Party and the Securitate to strengthen their control over society and to prevent or repress any form of opposition" (Vultur 2009b: 148).

[45] See ANIC, Fond C.C. al P.C.R.–Organizatorică, file 26/1951, 14.

[46] See Fond C.C. al P.M.R.–Organizatorică, file 26/1951, 16. To counteract the submission of "inexact data," one questionnaire—with ninety-three questions to be completed—stated at the top: "Respond to the questions below using 'absolutely real' data!" (109, in the Anexa documentară of this large file). Our translation reproduces the verbal confusion of the original.

[47] The literature on the political economy of socialism is rife with instances of how and why statistics were falsified and other kinds of information distorted through various forms of self-

stance, Oláh found that the grain yields reported for two villages situated in a mountainous area with poor-quality soil far exceeded both the national average per hectare and the highest regional average.[48] Information was produced after the fact or simply made up.[49] Stoica learned from a former Party Secretary that in the 1970s and 1980s, the "verbal reports" that allegedly served as an official record of regularly held local Party meetings had in fact been fabricated: for a variety of reasons, including lack of time, the meetings had not taken place.[50] Distorting the information sent upward could be a life or death matter; Fitzpatrick observes of the 1930s under Stalin, "messengers bearing bad news really were in danger of being shot" (1994b: 327). While the consequences in Romania were not usually as dire, it would nonetheless be unwise for us to take literally the reports on how many food requisition quotas had been filled, how many peasants had been arrested, what percentage of them had been collectivized by particular dates, and so on.

In response to the kinds of information solicited, over time bureaucrats and cadres increasingly furnished standardized data, often superficially prepared. Responses to standardized questions tended to include short comments, numbers, and a "yes" or "no." In perusing the Party archives for our two counties—Hunedoara and Maramureş—we noted that in the early 1950s, the ratio of documents written in officialese to those in less formal, often more colorful language was heavily weighted toward the latter; by the end of the 1950s, formal language dominated, along with preprinted questionnaires that took the place of freely composed written reports. Vultur (2003a) also found an increasing codification over time as the language became less transparent and more cumbersome. This is not a uniform finding, however, for Bodó (2003), who conducted field research in two Hungarian villages in Transylvania, instead found that they were standardized from the outset; she attributes this to cultural practices inherited from the Austro-Hungarian period. Noting a remarkable similarity between the structure and language used in documents then and in the communist era, she argues that they reflect local responses to and interactions

---

censorship and self-aggrandizement at all levels of the Party and bureaucracy. See, for example, Horváth and Szakolczai 1992; Kligman 1998; Rév 1987; Verdery 1994. Also see ANIC, Fond C.C. al P.C.R.–Agrară, file 70/1953, 31, about identifying hidden land holdings.

[48] Oláh (2003: 66) reports that documents showed 2,028 kilograms per hectare and 2,571 kilograms per hectare for the two villages, against a national mean of 849 kilograms per hectare and a regional mean of 1,200 kilograms per hectare in the Stalin region.

[49] See ACNSAS, FD, file 5, 196, which notes that those doing the collective's inventory were prevented from entering so they fabricated the inventory in their office.

[50] Regardless, official reports had to be deposited in the regional archive, which a regional commission later used in its quinquennial assessment of the activities of all Party organizations within its purview. To cover themselves, the local Party representatives virtually had to bribe the regional archivists to return the (made up) records in order to modify or simply copy them prior to the control. See Stoica (2003), on using oral and written sources.

with "foreign" power structures (whether Austro-Hungarian or communist rule), to which as little information as possible was to be conveyed (71–74).

Different documents, then, warrant different readings. Sometimes we take the contents of a report or the minutes of a meeting at face value, such as when an official writes that he can make little sense of the information sent up by lower-level cadres who are illiterate. However, we see a table with numbers as telling us less about true figures than about the categories officials used to organize information; for example, a table giving the Party elite of one region has "numbers of cadres: actual, and needed," a distinction much more revealing than the actual numbers in those two rows. Or, we view the repeated mention of activists being "drunks" as an indication not that they all *were* drunks but that the mention of drinking was a significant way of characterizing another person (negatively) and was thus a likely weapon in power struggles among cadres. As Oláh suggests, "Some archival materials cannot be interpreted strictly as documents of the events or processes to which they refer, but rather as documents about the persons who created them" (2003: 67; see also Levy 2001: 12–13). They also provide valuable information about a certain mentality, culturally significant categories, behavioral templates or possibilities for action within the system, and likely practices by its agents. Interrogations, renowned for being forced or prefabricated, nonetheless show what the authorities were concerned to know about.[51] These ways of reading the documents enable us to make use of Romania's Party, administrative, and police archives without assuming that their content tells us the truth about how things happened.

Sometimes the contents of these archives are valuable in themselves, without resort to complex ways of reading them. For example, the lengthy and detailed minutes of Romania's Communist Party Secretariat, Politburo, and Central Committee meetings, collected by Robert Levy and increasingly available in the publications of Romania's National Archive and National Council for the Study of the Securitate Archives, provide remarkable access to the arguments of Romania's leaders over fundamental questions of strategy. Even the archives of the secret police (partially accessible to scholars in Romania, although less so in the Soviet case) can prove revealing despite—or because of—that organization's

[51] Kotkin makes several further observations on how to use various additional sources for writing Soviet history, which are also relevant to our purposes. For instance, concerning agitprop writings—often considered useless to scholars—he notes that they told a great deal about the values the regime stood for and the political struggles to realize them. Newspapers, another major source, were not meant for simply reporting events but for active interventions into society, and they should be read in that way. In addition, although we cannot count on their veracity, they often tell us something by their omissions and juxtapositions; he gives the example of a newspaper that says nothing of a bad harvest but has multiple stories about hoarding and reselling bread (Kotkin 1995: 368). Kligman recalls researchers at the Institute of Ethnography and Folklore listening attentively to the radio broadcasts of important Ceaușescu speeches to glean which institutes would come under stricter surveillance. The practice of "reading between the lines" was an essential feature of what it meant to be literate in socialist societies, a practice that extended beyond reading itself.

penchant for secrecy. Here are two examples. First, we found these files useful in extending the network of people we might interview, as Kligman was able to do. In the penal files of persons from the village where she worked, she found an organizational chart of anticommunist resistance or "terrorist" groups operating in the region, which listed the names of suspected members in each village, including each group's "political" and "spiritual" leaders.[52] While the Securitate's presumptions about who was doing what, when, and why ranged from contestable to wrong, the list proved invaluable for filling out the history of that period, enabling her to track down villagers who had been imprisoned but had not returned to the village after their release in the 1960s. Without the files, it is doubtful that Kligman would have learned several decades later about most of the names recorded in them, but using the organizational chart she made inquiries and interviewed most of those still alive.[53] Access to these archival sources saved considerable time, opening up unanticipated and crucial avenues of inquiry.[54] This example shows our methodological strategy of reading oral accounts against archival sources to arrive at proximate "truths" and uncover omissions and silences.

Second, the Securitate prepared regular reports on the popular "mood" (*starea de spirit*), a vital source of information for Party elites, which reveal not only something of what informers reported about people's attitudes but also the sources of anxiety for Party leaders (as evident in the categories for which they requested information).[55] Such reports enabled them to respond to problems and complaints, introduce new policies, modify others by tightening or loosening control, raise salaries, lower quotas, or increase the availability of basic foodstuffs and supplies to increase popular satisfaction. (One mood report addressed the lack of petrol and of matches in rural areas.) Securitate officers

[52] See ACNSAS, FP, file 84/v. 11, 86: "Schiță de organizare a bandei teroriste Popșa."

[53] See also Kligman 2009. Not only did Ieudeni not discuss that period with Kligman in the 1970s, but most of those eventually released from prison moved elsewhere in the region or stayed where they had lived under house arrest, in part to spare their relatives from the stigma associated with them. Villagers' failure to mention those who no longer lived there was not a deliberate omission but was usually due to their absence from daily life. Once Kligman inquired, Ieudeni helped her locate them and arrange interviews.

[54] For some Soviet examples, the Soviet OGPU/NKVD reports gave a great deal of information and analysis about the place of women in anticollectivization riots, as well as about peasants' selling or slaughtering livestock to prevent having to give them to collectives for free. See, for example, Viola et al. 2005, documents 47, 67, and 78. Reports of the December Politburo Commission on Soviet collectivization, while not providing the full picture, offer a fascinating glimpse into the personal and political dynamics of Soviet high politics. (Lynne Viola, personal communication, and Viola et al. 2005: chapter 4.)

[55] Our efforts to obtain mood reports were repeatedly rebuffed during the time of our research. At least one member of our team, Vultur, received some, and in 2006, Kligman was given a more substantial sample for her work on the Presidential Commission. Top secret documents can be found in ANIC, Fond C.C. al P.C.R. at the State Archives, or at the National Council for the Study of Securitate Archives (CNSAS). We especially thank Florica Dobre for her assistance.

could also trace rumors attributed to "enemies of the people" and respond to them, or float other rumors to "test the waters" or to provide additional fodder against enemies.[56] Reading Securitate documents, then, gives us a sense of what the leaders were likely to know. As one regional Party Secretary (in the 1950s) observed in an interview, "The Party was aware of the overall situation in the country and kept it under control. But things did happen, in one region or another, that were in total contradiction with all directives."[57] The issue of what Party leaders did or did not know, order, or control has been a major preoccupation in our analysis, particularly concerning the use of violence against peasants. Although the central authorities did not order all such excesses, information contained in Central Committee and "top secret" documents makes it clear that they were hardly ignorant. In the following chapters, we explore the complex relationships between the Party and the population; our point here is to underscore the enormous value of access to the documents that shed light on these relationships—despite the problems we have thus far signaled.

On Unofficial Written Sources

We have been discussing archival materials, but not all written sources are archived nor are they necessarily forms of official communication. While even more haphazardly obtained, what are often labeled "popular histories" offer another illuminating lens on collectivization. Their contents shed light on the lived experiences of what official documents reveal, providing local, everyday contextualization and sometimes corroborating what archives contain about the same events. Authors of such localized chronicles include teachers, priests, former political prisoners, and literate peasants alike. Although generally written in narrative style, some also take poetic form.[58] They may review events that generally affected an entire community, or they may be autobiographical or represent a combination of forms. Their authors' life perspectives typically colored what they wrote when they set pen to paper. For example, a history of local events written by a Greek-Catholic priest was less likely to gloss over the dramatic changes of 1948 that banned the Greek-Catholic Church than one written by an Orthodox priest; a wealthy peasant's local history of collectivization would dwell more on the blows dealt the "class enemy" than would a poor peasant's version.[59]

[56] On increasing salaries to quell revolts, see, for example, Fond C.C. al P.C.R.–Organizatorică, file 43/1956, 11. On petrol and matches, see ACNSAS, FD, file 5, 16. On concerns about Hungary's 1956 revolution, see, for example, ANIC, Fond C.C. al P.C.R.–Organizatorică, file 43/1956.

[57] P. G., Kligman interview.

[58] Some are found in penal files as examples of subversive beliefs. See ACNSAS, FP, file 84/v. 5, 225, "Poezie scrisă de numitul . . . com. Şieu, Cântec de Suferinţă."

[59] The peasant histories we have come across are not typically written by poor peasants. Kligman

Generally, these local histories include a wealth of information not available elsewhere and can guide interview strategy. Şandru, for example, extracted useful data he had not found otherwise, including statistics, from a seventy-five-page monograph written by a former mayor of the community Pechea.[60] Such memoirs might even be published and enter into the subsequent production of local history, as occurred with a former political prisoner who had participated in the 1957 revolt in Vadu Roşca. Stoica, researching this revolt, received the book from a respondent who suggested he read it to learn "exactly" what had happened there.[61] In assessing this book and others like it, we should keep in mind that what is reported was retrospectively produced and is subject to the same issues we raise below about retrospective interviews.

Not all popular histories that have emerged since the collapse of communism were created after 1989, however. Some peasants, for example, kept notebooks in which they recorded events and their thoughts about them safely hidden in their houses, aware of the risks they assumed in so doing. One of Kligman's key respondents had such a "secret" set of poems, which he shared with a very few trusted confidants in the village. Unlike his other poems that earned him the title of Poet Laureate in Ceauşescu's time, these were not meant for public consumption; they contained titles on silenced topics such as collectivization and persuasion work. This same man was among several who chronicled Ieud's transformation under communism in narrative form as well. Others composed oral poetic "laments" in rhymed couplets about the events that befell them and their community (e.g., collectivization, class war, excessive requisitions), which they privately rehearsed over the years of communist rule as "memory markers" of their experiences and committed to paper after the collapse of the Ceauşescu regime.[62]

---

collected a number of these histories, such as Ştefan Balea's *Memorie* and Gavrilă Pleş-Chindriş's *Colectivizaria la Ieud, Mărturisiri din celea petrecute*. Both authors were from wealthier peasant families.

[60] See Şandru 2003, on oral and written sources. The statistical data were later confirmed in archival sources he found. Needless to say, popular histories, like archival documents, must be evaluated with care. One should pay attention to when they were penned: while some were written at the time of the events they review and others at some point prior to the collapse of communism, many were authored after 1989 when people felt safer keeping written records among their possessions. (Before then, any written criticism of the regime could result in harassment by the Securitate as well as imprisonment.) In the very first years after the regime fell, ordinary citizens still kept their authorial efforts to themselves, fearful that things might again change. During a four-hour interview in 2002 with a former "enemy of the people," Kligman asked whether he had ever considered writing his memoirs. With his closest family and friends present, he confessed—to their amazement—that he had already written some five hundred pages! (See Dunca 2004.) Lena Constante, in the early 1990s, was one of the few living survivors of the Pătrăşcanu trial. The original draft of her award-winning memoir, *L'evasion silencieuse* (1990), was handwritten in tiny script. (See also 1995.)

[61] Stoica 2003: 7. The book in question is *Rezistenţa armată anticomunistă din munţii României: 1946–1958* by Cicerone Ioniţoiu.

[62] We discuss memory markers in more detail later in this chapter. Prison memoirs often re-

We were fortunate in our project to have access to multiple sources, enabling us to read intertextually, corroborating our material as broadly as possible against the problems of falsified data and source credibility. Because of these problems, we agree with Bodó, who views the possibility of reconstituting what happened on the basis of written sources as limited, requiring us to supplement them with oral ones (Bodó 2003: 69–70). We now turn to a discussion of this second category of sources.

On Oral Sources

Oral histories and in-depth retrospective interviews (terms we use interchangeably unless otherwise specified) shed light on how people who lived under now-defunct regimes attempt to reconstruct their life stories and make sense of them. Passerini observed that in the former Soviet Union, people "who now feel free to narrate their experiences under Stalinism do face the problem of justifying themselves, and at the same time of establishing some sort of continuity in their life stories" (1992: 12).[63] So too in Romania, where oral accounts enable us to explore how collectivization lives on in the memories of Romanians alive at the time. They also serve to integrate the voices and experiences of those previously "hidden from history" (Rowbotham 1973) into the historical record of communism and collectivization.

Like written accounts, oral ones raise myriad problems. Memories are notoriously malleable and selectively shaped by the social conditions and motivations of those interviewed. They are not fixed in quantity or quality but vary over time, re-formed in the present of their rendition through an interpretive process of (re)collecting.[64] Passerini emphasizes that "Remembering has to be conceived as a highly inter-subjective relationship" (1992: 2). What emerges can be affected by intervening events, by the passage of time, by the relationship

---

count the kinds of memory markers that sustained their authors through the hardships of incarceration. For Romania, see, for example, Brauner 1979 and Constante 1995.

[63] Khubova et al. (2005: 96) suggest in a related vein that without an "overall public historical story to which to relate [their personal memories]" since the collapse of the Soviet Union, people find it "very difficult to make sense of their own memories." See also Bodó on producing a collective history, in our concluding chapter. We argue for producing usable pasts, in the plural, to reflect diverse perspectives.

[64] We reiterate that oral accounts are retrospectively produced, with the exception of interviews done for RFE/RL during the period. In these, Romanian-speaking reporters talked to Romanians who had escaped or were refugees to the West. We rarely cite them, although we note that the general information in them tends to corroborate our own. Each interview was transcribed and reported in Romanian and summarized in English. Sources are described generically: for example, a student, former teacher, intelligent, competent, mostly reliable; their age and gender are not consistently given. See, for example, HU OSA 300-1-2. These materials are housed at the Open Society Archive, Budapest. We especially thank its director, István Rév, and Pavol Salamon, then senior supervisory archivist.

between the interviewer and respondent, by the latter's desire to be seen in a favorable light, and by many other factors, some of which we will explore below.[65] Moreover, after 1989 remembering as a process was enhanced by media attention to the hidden histories of the past, made public in television series focused on oral histories, documentaries, and publications. Not surprisingly, mass-mediated accounts themselves became reference points or memory markers for some and, following Nora (1989), contributed to formalizing and codifying memory (as with Stoica's respondent who invoked a published version of "exactly" what had happened).

This kind of interplay between oral and mass-mediated sources points to another form of intertextuality to which researchers must be sensitive: what we might call "assisted memory."[66] Khubova and her colleagues (1992) revisited villages in the Kuban area of the former Soviet Union where they had worked four years earlier. Their second visit occurred in the context of perestroika, when the media were filled with recollections of Stalinist-era repression. Among those they reinterviewed, they found:

> Their historical consciousness seemed to have changed. Not only were they now very willing to talk, but a good many of them . . . now also included recollections of real personal experiences as well as "memories" which they clearly had picked up from the media—perhaps they genuinely believed these had happened to them, enabling them to present a new self image. (1992: 95)

This example also underscores the impact of the present on renditions of the past. In using oral accounts, then, we do not claim that people's memories of how collectivization occurred are necessarily "accurate," or more so than the problematic documents we have discussed above.

That few people during our research openly expressed positive views about collectivization, even if they held them, might seem an effect of the postsocialist climate. Nevertheless, we remind readers that many archival documents from the period are themselves often quite negative, countered primarily by the rosy representations promulgated in propaganda and socialist realist arts. But, unlike documents, oral accounts allow us to gain entry into what people remember their experiences to have been, which ones they found to be the most

[65] Khubova et al. (2005, 96) observe that respondents "are grasping for stories to make sense of their own lives."

[66] Arch Getty (personal communication) related Mary McCauley's experience when interviewing Leningraders years ago about Stalin's terror. Their memories had been "assisted" by post-Khrushchev anti-Stalin culture in which "everyone was arrested." But when pressed to note exactly who was arrested, they admitted that few people they knew had actually been arrested. Prager (1998), a sociologist and lay psychoanalyst, discussed a related process that is helpful to our analytic endeavor. One of his clients who sought explanatory frames for her suffering concluded that she had been the victim of childhood sexual abuse. Prager notes that her interpretation coincided with and was influenced by the "recovered memory" movement and that careful analysis of the corpus of her memories of abuse and nonabuse did not support her claim.

trying or the most appreciated, and so on. Many things shape what they remember, to whom, and when. In the next sections, we first discuss key issues in oral-historical research, focusing on people's willingness to talk about the past and how we interpret what they share; we then reflect briefly on multiple-source interpretation.

INTERVIEWS, INTERVIEWER EFFECTS, AND TEMPORALITY

Our project sought out a wide range of people, most of whom were young or middle-aged adults during the collectivization campaign; some were children. The majority of those we interviewed had been peasants, a good number of whom became salaried workers in factories or Party offices; some held positions of considerable authority, including regional Party secretaries, district functionaries, heads of collective farms, and village mayors. As we shall see below, not everyone was disposed to enter into a dialog with our team, although many were. Some people refused to talk in case things changed, noting that "the times are unstable," and they feared being held accountable should the political situation shift again.[67] Khubova et al. (1992: 100) encountered the same reasoning during their research in the Kuban. Several of our team members (e.g., Dobrincu, Stoica, and Verdery) found respondents willing to talk but unwilling to have the interviews taped, also out of fear. Still others refused in a more subtle manner, saying there was no point to an interview: "Let it be—when I have time, I'll write my own memoir" (Stoica 2003: 8). There were undoubtedly people who found it too painful to revisit those times; however, that was not primarily our experience.

A critical variable in any kind of interviewing concerns characteristics of the researcher and the nature of his or her relationships with the people being interviewed. These relationships vary in many respects, such as by the researcher's age, sex, and place of origin. We provide detail in appendix 2 but will make a few brief points here to show the complexity of interviewer effects. Although all of the Romanians and Hungarians on our team had had some previous field experience in the places they studied, several of them (Dobrincu, Bodó, Goina, and Lățea) were themselves born in the locales where they did their research or had family members living there. The consequences of their familiarity were complicated. They did not have to spend the long time that good ethnographers need to build trust, but they might be hampered by their family members' positions (see appendix 2). As for other characteristics, an interviewer's greater age is generally a plus in garnering cooperation from Romanian villagers, although sometimes the lower status of graduate students makes respondents less guarded with them. We believe that female interviewers tend to have better access to both sexes than male interviewers, even though (perhaps *because*) they

[67] Dobrincu (2003a) commented that the success of former communists in the elections of 2000 was the basis of their fear of a return to the recent (socialist) past.

carry less authority; this said, however, among our team's most successful ethnographers were male graduate students. Other differences might not prove as significant as we would expect, such as that between foreigners and Romanians. One might think that Romanian villagers would be more suspicious of foreigners like us than of interviewers who are Romanian, or more likely to feed us anticommunist views. This might be true of foreigners new to Romania, but our lengthy association with our two villages (Vlaicu and Ieud) made it more difficult for locals to lie to us or to present selves discordant with what we already knew of them. Our close friendships more readily invited conversations on difficult subjects than would have been true for the Romanian researchers who lacked such extended experience. In Kligman's case, it was her long-term fieldwork that enabled her to uncover "hidden histories" in both poetic and impassioned narrative form; others have interviewed in her site since 1989 without comparable results. Here we see the crucial difference between simply carrying out interviews and doing so in the context of extended ethnographic research. In brief, then, interviewer effects, while critical ingredients of ethnography, are too multifarious to be systematically included in our interpretation.

Additional variables affecting the value of oral sources concern traits of the respondents—whether in specific relation to the interviewer (e.g., relative age and sex) or not. For instance, Chelcea observed significant differences in what respondents recollected or were disposed to recollect (2009: 400). Formerly poor peasants remembered much less about collectivization and had at best a vague sense of the dates at which specific things had happened, whereas the wealthier spoke at much greater length, with much more precise dates and many details.[68] Although others in our team did not find the same pattern, the example nonetheless reminds us that respondents' social origins and trajectories inevitably affect what they recollect—a point to which we return in chapter 8.

Another important variable is generation, for where one is positioned in the life cycle bears significantly on how one remembers or views both past and present.[69] As we hope our discussions in subsequent chapters will demonstrate, we do not mean to imply that such factors as gender, religion, nationality, or geographical location are any less significant. Nevertheless, in times of rupture, generation anchors memory in fundamental ways (see, e.g., Vultur 2002a). Generational differences have long been recognized in the study of revolutionary regimes, often fueled by youthful zeal (think of Maoist China's revolutionary guards in the Cultural Revolution). With age, that zeal may be radically transformed into full disillusionment, as was the case for many true believers following Khrushchev's revelations about Stalin's crimes. Or, as we saw above,

[68] Among the possible explanations for these differences is that the former poor may have been more intimidated by the interview situation; another is that the richer memories of the wealthy perhaps reflected their having lost more and having suffered the effects of collectivization more gravely.

[69] In Vultur (2002b), two chapters on memories of the Jews in Banat are organized by generation (seniors and middle-aged, respectively).

with wisdom gained from age and the passage of time, some may critique their memories of their pasts.

Following Mannheim's suggestion that generations are marked by the events individuals experience in adolescence and early adulthood, Schuman and Scott posit a collective memory formed through a process of "generational imprinting" (1989: 378). We find this notion useful more broadly across the age spectrum. Here is an example of embodied memory seared into the consciousness of a child at the time of collectivization:

> My father spent eight years as a prisoner in Russia, so he knew what a kolkhoz was. He barely got back and it was starting here, but he said he'd never join. The teacher in my second-grade class would make me and one other girl stand up in front of everyone because our families still hadn't joined the GAC. They were mean to us. I remember at Christmas time they would line everyone up to get candies, but they pulled us two out of the line, so we couldn't get any. . . . I despised that teacher and I'd get revenge whenever I had a chance. She was the priest's wife; any time I went to the priest's house, like for a children's birthday party, I'd throw some cake on the rug and stomp it in, or I'd get into the cellar and throw things around. Many years later I saw this teacher on the street. She came up to me and said hello, but I walked right past her.[70]

Yet, we also note that some memories of those who were children at the time of collectivization are not generationally distinctive. Torture or physical abuse is embodied in memory regardless of the age at which it was experienced. One of Kligman's respondents recounted how the Securitate had abused him when he was ten years old during their search for his "enemy" father (whom they later fatally shot):

> They beat me and they pierced my tongue with a needle. I was unable to eat anything for four weeks except I could drink milk! They said they were going to give me candies [to make him open his mouth]; they grabbed my tongue and held it while they stuck it many times with the needle, taunting me with: "Offspring of a reactionary! Offspring of a chiabur." And how many times they kicked me! . . . To this day, you see the marks from the beatings I took from them.[71]

With such exceptions in mind, the generation of these respondents' parents typically remembers a different set of (adult) concerns about the collectivization campaign, such as forced collections, the expropriation of property, and so on. But wherever they were in the life cycle at the time of that campaign, their memories and what they recount are marked or imprinted accordingly.[72]

[70] 213n, Verdery interview. The comment has been reconstructed from notes. The literature on Stalinism is filled with memories seared into the existence of those who were children at the time.

[71] P. G. R., Kligman interview.

[72] We do not address the related issue of nostalgia, also generationally marked. For the elderly, nostalgia for the communist period—which some may categorize as strategic forgetting—is often

Still another variable affecting memory involves the timing of the interviews. Verdery conducted some research in 1991–94 (before our project began), when the process of *de*collectivization was in full swing. She found that people talking about collectivization at that time emphasized the 1950s confiscations and land exchanges that were then causing them problems in getting their land back, but these themes were less common after 2000. The most serious obstacle for us, interviewing after 1989 about the socialist period, was the tendency for respondents to have "teleological" recollections: they knew the end of the story. The collapse of the communist system and its collective farms colored how respondents would recall painful experiences from those times. For some, the public repudiation of that system encouraged forgetting what might have been good about collective farms and provided an incentive (especially in the case of former authorities) to distance themselves retrospectively from their previous actions. Yet for others, the shortcomings of postsocialist life also encouraged nostalgia for certain aspects of the old regime. Thus, one must scrutinize these recollections closely.

Another aspect of recollected temporalities concerns the kinds of events that people experienced. Stoica (2003), like others in our team, found that most accounts were event-oriented: what people remembered, or what they wanted to talk about, were specific, often highly selective situations rather than broader generalities (see Schuman and Scott 1989). Most of his respondents in Vadu Roşca focused on the revolt of 1957, even though he was interested in the broader process of collectivization, not only the role of the revolt in it. Sometimes a respondent's focus on particular moments compressed the temporality of the process, glossing over the social complexity of what had taken place. This was especially true where there had been considerable opposition and repression, which some respondents tended to forget in characterizing the process as rapidly completed. These examples again call our attention to the analytic necessity of situating what is said in the fullest temporal field.

MEMORY AND TRAUMA, SPEECH AND SILENCE

Those willing to be interviewed engaged in dialog to differing degrees. Some were eager to talk with anyone who would listen, gaining satisfaction from the public airing of long-held grievances as they reconstructed usable pasts from their lives.[73] Lăţea views this as a linguistic form of "settling accounts."[74] Many others were neither excited by the "sheer novelty of talking" (Khubova et al.

linked to their more precarious circumstances since its collapse. Young people who were not alive during communism, by contrast, can be staunchly anticommunist because of what their families suffered, or, as in Russia, they may register nostalgia for Stalin (see Mendelson and Gerber 2006).

[73] There is a large literature on repressed memory due to traumatic experience, which we do not examine here.

[74] See Lăţea (2009: 349), for a discussion of peasants' willingness to "forget, but never forgive."

1992: 96) nor reticent about doing so. Instead, they had suffered greatly and welcomed the opportunity to "give voice" to their silenced autobiographies.[75] For them, such recountings could be personally cathartic and open up ways to talk with family members about things they had never mentioned.[76] A peasant woman, upon learning about the project, shyly informed Kligman that she wanted to share her family's tragic story from the collectivization period, which we recount in chapter 6, that left her mother dead. At the time of the interview, Kligman had known this peasant woman for over two decades yet had heard nothing of her traumatic past. Certainly, such cases—which are legion—lend urgency to uncovering these hidden histories and simultaneously draw attention to the problems of rewriting histories of the communist period.

So far we have been writing of those who entered willingly into dialog with us. What about those who give us very little, perhaps shrugging off our questions about the campaign with, "We didn't have any choice, they made us join, and we got used to it." What is an interviewer to do in the face of such a reply? Do the respondents genuinely not remember, or are they refusing to remember because of actions or compromises they might not now wish to acknowledge publicly? Should we try to draw out their recollections or is there a dark hole where recollection might lie, a hole that may be the product of repressed trauma? This leads to an important aspect of our conversations: the relation of trauma to memory. Among the long-silenced histories that have come into the open since 1989 are numerous accounts from people who experienced physical abuse and public humiliation at the hands of the communist regime. As we learn from debates on "recovered memory" and the nature of trauma, there is a very problematic relation between "what actually happens" to people and how those happenings appear in memory. Against those experts who argue that retrospective memory always grasps a real past event, others see trauma as consisting precisely in the victim's *incapacity* to represent what has happened, for traumatic experience evades the brain centers responsible for narrative capacity and verbal representation (see discussion in Leys 2000 and Daniel 1996). Others caution against taking accounts of traumatic pasts at face value, noting that the "agentic self constitutes itself in time" (Prager 1998: 82) and can be heavily influenced by contemporary frames of meaning when reconstructing past memories.

How then might we look at the complicated relationship between trauma and memory in our own interviews? Is there something about the nature of people's past experiences that shapes the form of their present expression? Kligman was consistently surprised by the detailed accounts offered by respondents who had spent long years resisting the regime, hiding in the mountains, and were then incarcerated in prison and tortured. Their recollections were acutely

[75] We distinguish these from the scripted autobiographies written for or by the Party, particularly of prisoners or for verification of Party members.

[76] The history of collectivization is filled with such silences between kin.

vivid, as though their experiences had happened yesterday,[77] reminding us of the role of the performative discussed previously and of Nietzsche's claim that for something to stay in memory, "it must be burned in; only that which never ceases to hurt stays in the memory" ([1887] 1989: 61). Indeed, the Party-state recognized the pedagogical "virtues" of memory written on the body, or what we refer to as "embodied memory." For those whose experiences were imprinted on their bodies through torture, enduring forms of physical deprivation, or repeated humiliation, the memories were literally embodied; their bodies serve as memory sites, in Nora's sense, or *mnemotechnic* vehicles, in Nietzsche's.[78] Although these are complicated issues, we tend to accord special truth-value to the recollections of those who suffered bodily harm through forms of torture.

Lățea, on the other hand, found that many of his respondents, especially men, took advantage of "strategic forgetting," which he views counterintuitively as a constructive form of memory practice that enables people *not* to see themselves as victims. He notes insightfully:

> Men were more exposed to violence and dishonor and thus it is not surprising that they would be more tempted than women to euphemize or simply "forget" the ugliest episodes of collectivization. . . . "forgetting" can be understood positively, as a form of "memory," and not as its antithesis. People "forget" the violence that contradicts the categories of ordinary thinking, or they refuse to integrate what would otherwise destroy them socially (extreme examples are slaves, Gulag and Holocaust survivors, as well as victims of torture and rape). . . . in cases such as collectivization, forgetting is as much a favor to oneself as a strategic positioning towards the agents of violence. (2009: 348)

Strategic forgetting may help to explain memories that seem fuzzy in terms of narrative detail and dates. In the political climate of our research, some respondents may not have been proud of their actions in the 1950s, having perhaps turned a blind eye to the travails of others. Their reticence may manifest self-interested strategic forgetting, for which an interviewer must be on guard, so as to uncover the silences that strategic forgetting creates.

How might "embodied memories" and "strategic forgetting" be similar? In each, the passage of time enables individuals as agents of their own pasts to engage their memories, thus making sense of their personal histories, then and now. Strategic forgetting, in Lățea's view, is a condition of social survival that

[77] One respondent, answering questions that grew out of a reading of his prison file, virtually reenacted the scenario of his arrest in the mountains, demonstrating who was where, and so on. C. V., Kligman interview.

[78] We thank Jon Sigmon for reminding us of Nietzsche's essay. Connerton looked at embodied memory in a more collective sense in what he views as habit memory, itself "passed on in non-textual and non-cognitive ways" (1989: 102–3). See also Ten Dyke (2001: 67–69). Embodied memories in this sense differ from individuals' having been betrayed by their own bodies, to which we return in subsequent chapters.

allows people to live with their pasts in the present as survivors (to draw on a contemporary trope), rather than as victims. Embodied memories do the same, allowing those who suffered such trials to highlight today the positive aspects of their past resistance and endurance rather than the negative, for which they had suffered greatly and been stigmatized for so long.

Interpreting the meaning of embodied memories and strategic forgetting, as well as drawing from the ethnographic encounter meanings that are invisible in official documents, requires unusual skill. Here are some techniques our team members used toward these ends; all involve ways of reading silences or uses of language. We begin with Julianna Bodó, whose two decades of experience in her field area enriched her work for our project. Initially her respondents claimed that nothing out of the ordinary had happened during collectivization, and they seemed to have few memories of the events. Based on small cues in the way they spoke, however, she concluded that a great deal happened, but it was out of sight: "For instance, the voices of people interviewed still trembled when they referred to collectivization, forty years later. . . . How is it possible that those 'insignificant' events triggered such a profound reaction?" (Bodó 2009: 355). Part of her answer, which we will take up in chapter 8, concerns the effects of overturning status hierarchies; additionally, she invokes the silencing of public discourse about collectivization while it took place and after. The absence of talk, she suggests, led to the community's failure to shape collective versions of what had happened. Thus, any one person asked about it is unsure of what to say, not knowing what *others* would say.[79] The silence around collectivization, in this context, is preeminently social, rather than individual.

Our colleague Smaranda Vultur (2003a, 2009b) read not silences but metaphors, examining written and oral sources from a linguistic standpoint. In her research she read published speeches and compared their metaphors with those of unpublished minutes from meetings; additionally, she compared through both time and space the language of documents from two villages whose collectivization fates differed significantly. Among her findings were not only the specific contexts for the military metaphors so common to the entire communist period (e.g., campaign, enemy, battle; see discussion in chapter 1), but also contrasts between time periods. Comparing two villages—one collectivized earlier, the other later—she found in the former a grim language of "bitter struggle against the class enemy," as opposed to a language of light and optimism ("lively, intense, and enthusiastic work") in the latter. The timing suggested a shift from an emphasis on repression to one on persuading and stimulating; the comparison mirrors the collectivization process itself, which in many places moved from initial repression to less coercive forms of persuasion later. Vultur's intertextual analysis illustrates how much we can learn from the ways language—and especially metaphor—is used.

[79] This argument appears in her longer report (2003). See Kligman 2009, on silenced histories in Ieud.

Puiu Lățea (2003, 2009) employed the strategies of both Bodó and Vultur, attending to metaphors and to other "textual" registers including his respondents' mimicry, gestures, bodily postures, and tonal variation. Earlier, we noted that the body itself serves as a memory site; both Bodó and Lățea paid careful attention to body language in relation to what their respondents were saying. Lățea closely explored the use of certain words as well, such as "understanding," "bargaining," "negotiation," or "haggling" (in contrast to "imposition" or "constraint"). He attended to the complex practices these words indicated—avoidance strategies, indirect speech, rhetorics of imprecision, deliberate delaying tactics, and so on. For instance, he examined the way his interlocutors used tenses, which showed some of their strategies for using time against the activists who had come to persuade them to join the collective. "[T]ense manipulation," he observes, "was one of the most felicitous strategies used by the villagers who tried to postpone, as long as possible, joining the collective" (2009: 241). With this analysis he aims to demonstrate that despite heavy repression, people retained some capacity for action and could even tame or transform power, in small ways, to their advantage. Bargaining or negotiation, then, was a frequent strategy, a way of corrupting local officials by compromising them.

Even if we cannot take as "truth" everything an interviewee says, then, to discover information unavailable in the archives, we can read their tones of voice, note their moments of distress, and listen to their language and the metaphors they use. We advocate precisely this kind of mixed analytic methodology, involving the dialogic interplay of written and oral sources—a strategy that is admittedly more available to scholars of Eastern European collectivization than to Soviet specialists, who lack living peasant respondents.[80]

Multiple Source Interpretation

Thus far, we have been discussing the respective possibilities and limitations of written and oral sources, which make clear that both are inadequate in and of themselves for making usable pasts that better approximate the complexity of the times. Elaborating on this point, Bodó comments that written documents "can only be deciphered with knowledge of the interpersonal relations among local actors" (2003: 73)—a view with which we concur. To conclude our discussion, we offer three examples that illustrate the virtues of working intertextually across as many different sources as possible—written, oral, and bodily—to corroborate information or claims. This expanded approach to intertextuality can enrich research and analysis in unexpected ways, helping us to meet the chal-

[80] This is not to say that Soviet specialists cannot use interviews: Sheila Fitzpatrick (personal communication), for example, has often used them to clarify her reading of documents, but not even she was able to rouse peasants from the dead.

lenge of analyzing fluid categories in a dynamic process that contains many variables.

We have already given one example from Kligman's research concerning her use of the Securitate archive to extend her network of interviewees. A second example demonstrates how oral sources can expose the pitfalls of literal readings of official written sources, especially penal files. In the Securitate files, she came across a list of punishments meted out to alleged members of the "Popşa terrorist gang," one of which was for a person listed as "missing" and tried in absentia.[81] After interviewing this man's sister, Kligman went on to find official confirmation that the security forces had "mortally wounded" him.[82] At the time of his sentencing, then, he was not actually missing but dead and buried. While a seeming detail, the difference between "missing" and "dead" is significant for the historical record: the regime's cynicism and brutality were effaced under the ubiquitous category of "missing."[83] Had it not been for the interviews, Kligman would have read "missing" as just that, a name attached to a statistical category. In cases like this, the dialogic interplay between oral and archival knowledge transforms our understanding of what is represented in the official register in relation to what actually happened.

A second example of multiple source interpretation comes from Verdery's research. In the Securitate archives she found an anonymous denunciation written in 1984 by "a group of workers," claiming that one G. C. from Vlaicu had "renewed his anticommunist calumnies."[84] District authorities investigated the charges and solicited handwritten notes about them from various villagers, in hopes of identifying the handwriting on the document. One such note was signed by a man with whom Verdery was on particularly close terms. In subsequent conversation with him, she asked him in a general way if he had ever heard of people writing letters concerning a denunciation; he replied that he himself had written such a supporting note, about G. C., but not (as she had assumed) in response to an officer's dictation. Then he voluntarily explained who had initiated the denunciation (one of G. C.'s rivals, ticked off with him for some minor matter or a quarrel over women), who else had been involved (several friends of the instigator and neighbors of G. C., all annoyed with him for various reasons), and who had formulated it (the instigator's nephew, employed by the Securitate in Bucharest). Without the stimulus of the archive, Verdery would not have known whom to ask for concrete information on denunciatory practices, and only her long relation with her respondent enabled her to learn how in this case, at least, Securitate members were feeding those very practices themselves.

[81] See ACNSAS, FP, file 84/v. 5, 334, for the sentence issued on February 20, 1950.

[82] See ACNSAS, FP, file 84/v. 1, 335, telegram of January 3–4, 1950.

[83] Certainly, this is but one of the far too many deaths at the hands of the Securitate that have been "hidden."

[84] ACNSAS, FI, file 3935/2, 26ff.

A third example, from Smaranda Vultur, deepens our sense of the silences around collectivization. In Domaşnea, she interviewed people whose names she had found in two Securitate files from 1960–62, comparing what they themselves said after 2000 with what the Securitate officer following them reported they had said at the time. According to the files, the Securitate had interrogated most of the people she was interviewing, holding them for a day or more and then having them sign a declaration that they would never tell anyone anything about the interrogation.[85] Of all the people she interviewed, only one woman confirmed this; the others said not a word, presumably being afraid to contravene what they had signed forty or fifty years earlier. Partisans from this village had fiercely resisted collectivization, and in 1958–59 some of them were caught, shot, and left in the center of the village for three days so everyone could see what might happen to people who behaved like them. Perhaps that helps to explain their silence so many years later. It was only the combination of interviews with material from the files of people interrogated that enabled Vultur to hear the silence.[86]

In all these examples, our archival data opened up aspects of the past that had long been suppressed, not only offering information but also serving as methodological tools for ethnographic research.[87] We have dwelt on the methodological strengths and weaknesses of the sources we have used both to enhance readers' understanding of them as analytic resources and to shed critical light on the tangled relationship between history and memory. In so doing, we hope to have shown some of the ways in which attention to the interplay between diverse sources—oral, written, the body—through time and space enables a more nuanced, complex excavation and interrogation of those pasts.

Plan of the Book

In the chapters to follow, we will describe the collectivization process in Romania in detail. Part 1 lays the groundwork for that process. We begin in chapter 1 with the Soviet blueprint, which established the technology of collectivization that East European leaders followed, with variations, during the 1950s. Briefly

[85] The following is a typical example of these declarations signed before release from prison: "I understand that I am not allowed to divulge to anyone anything that I have seen in the detention sites where I have been, nor about anyone I have seen in them, and, relatedly, I will not, in writing or verbally, communicate with relatives or others anything about those who remain imprisoned," subject to legal action for violation of these terms. See ACNSAS, FP, file 160/7, 88.

[86] The reports are found in DJAN CS, Fond Inspectoratul Judeţean de Securitate Caraş-Severin (FD 116 vols. I and II). Interviews conducted in August 2001 and September 2002.

[87] Lăţea (personal communication) found that starting first with archival research, then supplementing it with discussions with his closest relatives, made him "competent" or literate in local collectivization matters. In turn, when he began talking with a broader circle of people, they were positively inclined to enter into dialogue with him.

summarizing how collectivization occurred in the Soviet Union, we sketch some of the major departures from that model in Eastern Europe. In chapter 2 we describe the object of collectivization in Romania—the "traditional" Romanian village, organized by kinship and social status—indicating critical points at which this organization conflicted with the plans for collectivizing; we then summarize the process as a whole in Romania between 1948 and 1962 to facilitate the more detailed discussion in subsequent chapters. Chapter 3 focuses on the Party cadres who implemented collectivization, describing aspects of their recruitment, their work, and their life as activists. What kinds of people were they, what was it like to be one, and what sorts of social relations developed among them? We argue that because the Party achieved power without an adequate number of prepared and ideologically committed cadres, certain compromises followed. First, their work would rely more on force than on persuasion, and therefore peasants would end by joining collectives only pro forma rather than from conviction. Second, the exigencies of cadres' work led them to develop networks, which protected them while making the bureaucratic apparatus more personalistic.

The three chapters in part 2 describe some of the pedagogical techniques used to draw people into the collectives. Chapter 4 presents some of the language the Party created to carry out its mission—including categories that named classes, types of "enemies" and political insurgents, acceptable vs. suspect religions, and ethnonational groups—as well as some of the techniques employed: various forms of propaganda, modeling by example, denunciation and unmasking, and petition writing. Many of these forms compelled peasants to enter a relationship with the Party and to adopt its terms even when contesting them. In chapter 5, we continue this discussion of techniques with a look at "persuasion work," explaining aspects of village social organization upon which it hinged and arguing that unpersuasive cadres secured not commitment to the collective project but the performance of consent. Chapter 6 describes how "class war" that aimed to decapitate the village elite, turn other villagers against them, and raise up the village poor was brought to a countryside lacking classes. Last, part 3 presents some outcomes of collectivization. In chapter 7 we show how collectives were finally formed—in part through using that same village elite—and how different variables affected the process. Chapter 8 describes new chances for social mobility and how village life was bureaucratized and politicized, along with the transformation of the earlier organizational forms involving kinship and social status.

Throughout our discussion, we present data from all the research sites included in our project, even if material from our own research in Hunedoara and Maramureş counties predominates. We selected the project sites to differ in ethnonational and religious composition (both of which might influence personhood and relations with the Romanian Party-state), economic and ecological adaptation (influencing an area's suitability for collective farms), major historical or strategic region (reflecting different historical influences, population composition, and development potential), and the date of collectivization. Map 1 shows the distribution of all the sites, using the administrative boundaries of 1960; table 0.1 presents the sites in greater detail. In our text, we refer to the principal study sites without further specification; additional settlements that we mention, from archival or other sources, are followed by the names of the counties in which they are presently located.

* * *

All historical narratives, Trouillot observes (1995), could have been told differently. What distinguishes this one from other possible tellings? First, like others, we see collectivization as a story about an Enlightenment project for modernizing a "backward" country on a model from the Soviet Union, but we emphasize departures from the model as well as its imposition. Second, more unusually, we emphasize the coming-into-being of the political organization that is often unproblematically seen as collectivization's author—the Communist Party-state—underscoring instead the ways in which collectivization created it, as much as the other way around. Third, we explore in detail the "technology transfer" involved in this process, whereby the peasantry was tied in place differently from before, by transforming their relations to land and one another and by bureaucratizing their daily life. In place of a largely political history, we foreground the social and cultural relations of the process that attempted to substitute—for both peasants and cadres alike—a formal bureaucratic organization for one based on kinship relations. It was a monumental uprooting, carried out with remarkable speed and fraught throughout with unintended consequences that vitiated the plans of its architects, in ways we will describe in the pages to follow.

Table 0.1
Project Research Sites

Name of Village (Hungarian/ German)/ Commune (Researcher)	*District/ Region 1950*	*Relief*	*Soil Fertility*	*Primary Economic Activity*
Armăşeni (Csíkmenaság)/ Armăşeni *(Bodó)*	Ciuc/ Stalin	Hilly, mountainous	Poor	Agriculture, especially animal husbandry
Aurel Vlaicu/Şibot *(Verdery)*	Orăştie/ Hunedoara	Plains	Medium	Agriculture, animal husbandry
Corund (Korond)/ Corund *(Bodó)*	Odorhei/ Stalin	Hilly, mountainous	Poor	Agriculture, crafts (pottery)
Darabani/Darabani *(Dobrincu)*	Dorohoi/ Botoşani	Hilly area	Medium	Agriculture, crafts
Dobrosloveni/ Dobrosloveni *(Lăţea)*	Caracal/ Dolj	Plains	Superior	Agriculture, vegetable production
Domaşnea/ Domaşnea *(Vultur)*	Caransebeş /Severin	Mountainous	Medium	Animal husbandry, agriculture orchards,
Ieud/Ieud *(Kligman)*	Sighet/ Baia Mare	Mountainous area, with some Plains	Poor	Animal husbandry, agriculture, orchards
Jurilovca/Jurilovca *(Iordachi)*	Baia/ Constanţa	Plains	Poor	Fishing, agriculture
Lueta (Lövéte)/Lueta *(Olah)*	Odorhei/ Stalin	Mountainous area	Poor	Agriculture, animal husbandry, forestry
Măgina/Cacova *(Ţârău)*	Turda/ Cluj	Hilly area	Medium	Agriculture, orchards, viticulture
Mircea/Reviga *(Chelcea)*	Slobozia/ Ialomiţa	Plains	Superior	Agriculture

Population in 1956	*Ethnic Composition*	*Religious Composition*	*When Collectivized (Beginning–End)*	*Extent Collectivized*
1,664	Hungarian	Roman Catholic	1962	Total
812	Romanian, German (Swabian)	Romanian Orthodox, Lutheran	1958–59	Total
3,629	Hungarian	Roman Catholic, Unitarian	1962	Total
5,281	Romanian Jewish	Romanian Orthodox, Neo-Protestants, Jews	1950–March 1962	Total
1,298	Romanian	Romanian Orthodox	June 1958–March 1961	Total
1,783	Romanian	Romanian Orthodox	March–April 1962	Quasi-total
3,715	Romanian	Romanian Orthodox, Greek Catholic	March 1950–62	Partial
3,489	Russian-Old Believer, Romanian	Old Believers, Romanian Orthodox	1950–October 1957	Quasi-total
3,066	Hungarian	Roman Catholic, Protestants	1955–	Partial
790	Romanian	Romanian Orthodox	January–March 1961	Total
618	Romanian	Romanian Orthodox	1959	Total

Table 0.1 (*continued*)

Name of Village (Hungarian/ German)/ Commune (Researcher)	*District/ Region 1950*	*Relief*	*Soil Fertility*	*Primary Economic Activity*
Nănești/Nănești *(Stoica)*	Focșani/ Galați	Plains	Medium	Agriculture
Pechea/Pechea *(Șandru)*	Galați/ Galați	Plains	Superior	Agriculture
Poiana Sibiului/ Poiana Sibiului *(Stewart/Stan)*	Sebeș/ Sibiu	Mountainous	Poor	Sheep husbandry, seasonal migration
Reviga/Reviga *(Chelcea)*	Slobozia/ Ialomița	Plains	Superior	Agriculture
Rimetea/Rimetea *(Țărău)*	Turda/ Cluj	Mountainous	Poor	Mining, stone in-dustry, agriculture
Rovine/Reviga *(Chelcea)*	Slobozia/ Ialomița	Plains	Superior	Agriculture
Sânpaul (Homoród-szentpál)/Sânpaul *(Olah)*	Odorhei/ Stalin	Hilly area	Good	Agriculture, animal husbandry, forestry
Sântana/Sântana *(Goina)*	Criș/ Arad	Plains	Superior	Agriculture
Tomnatic (Triebswetter)/ Tomnatic *(Vultur)*	Sânnicolau Mare/ Timișoara	Plains	Superior	Agriculture, viticulture
Vadu Roșca/Vultur *(Stoica)*	Focșani/ Galați	Plains	Medium	Agriculture, crafts

Population in 1956	*Ethnic Composition*	*Religious Composition*	*When Collectivized (Beginning–End)*	*Extent Collectivized*
1,982	Romanian	Romanian Orthodox, Evangelical movement "The Lord's Army"	1959–62	Total
7,585	Romanian	Romanian Orthodox	1949–57	Total
4,084	Romanian (92%) Roma (8%)	Romanian Orthodox		Not collectivized
2,301	Romanian	Romanian Orthodox	1959–62	Total
1,135	Hungarian	Unitarian	1952–61	Total
1,852	Romanian	Romanian Orthodox	1956–57	Total
835	Hungarian	Unitarian	1952–62	Total
11,846	German (88%) Romanian (4.6%) Hungarian (7%)	Roman Catholic, Romanian Orthodox	1949–62	Total
3,501	German (Swabian) Romanian Hungarian	Roman Catholic, Romanian Orthodox	1950–57	Total
1,089	Romanian	Romanian Orthodox	1959–62	Total

Map 1. Romania, showing project research sites (in 1960 administrative boundaries).
Note: The map uses pre- and postsocialist orthography: â in place of î.

Part I

LAYING THE GROUNDWORK

Chapter 1

The Soviet Blueprint

The successes of our collective-farm policy are due, among other things, to the fact that it rests on the *voluntary character* of the collective-farm movement and on *taking into account the diversity of conditions* in the various regions of the USSR. Collective farms must not be established by force. That would be foolish and reactionary.
—*Stalin, "Dizzy with Success" speech, 1930*[1]

Information about mass disturbances of peasants . . . coming into the CC in February [1930] cannot be anything but threatening. If we had not immediately taken measures against the violations of the party line, we would have had a vast wave of insurrectionary peasant uprisings, a good part of our lower-level officials would have been slaughtered by the peasantry, . . . and our internal and external situation would have been threatened.
—*Closed letter of C.C. of C.P.S.U., April 2, 1930, concerning the situation in the countryside*[2]

We asked Moscow two or three times how we should proceed. We were told to proceed bearing in mind our situation, that our Party is young, that the level of training is insufficient, that we still have a small commodity-producing sector, that we have the remnants of the former exploiting classes who have not died and physically exist.
—*Gheorghiu-Dej, Romania's First Party Secretary, 1958*[3]

We have the good fortune of the Soviet experience.
—*Leonte Răutu, Romania's Minister of Propaganda, 1950*[4]

As THE FIRST country in the world to be founded on Marxist-Leninist principles, the Soviet Union had myriad problems to solve. They included establishing control over vast areas and diverse populations, developing a new political form (the "Party-state"), creating sufficient numbers of cadres who would promote the Party's goals, verifying the loyalty of those cadres, securing a police force to ensure internal and external security, and finding sources of accumulation that would enable the country to industrialize; collectivization would be the principal means. In addition, the leaders' ambitious program of social engi-

[1] Cited in Viola et al. 2005: 277.

[2] Ibid., 320.

[3] ANIC, Fond C.C. al P.C.R.–Cancelarie, file 23/1958. Cited in Ionescu-Gură 2005: 484.

[4] ANIC, Fond C.C. al P.C.R.–Propagandă și Agitație, file 3/1950, 116.

neering required developing a variety of techniques for carrying out specific tasks, such as obtaining food requisitions, collectivizing agriculture, and so on. These techniques formed the basis for creating "replica" regimes (Jowitt 1992: 176) in Eastern Europe following World War II, in a process of technology transfer of almost unparalleled scope.[5] We might call that technological package "the Soviet blueprint," of which collectivization was a major part. Although the results varied considerably, each East European country was pressed into adopting more or less the same package.[6] Nowhere, however, did the blueprint fully succeed against recalcitrant local realities—not even in the Soviet Union itself. Although our overarching narrative structure in this book parallels Soviet efforts to organize Romanian communism, the details of the story show the fragmenting and reactive effects of those efforts.

Romania proved a more successful replica than most, emerging in the 1960s as the prime instance of "Stalinism after Stalin." In this chapter we will briefly describe the two main mechanisms for ensuring conformity to the Soviet blueprint—the Soviet councilors and the Romanian secret police (henceforth, Securitate)—and the main political form that was imitated under the Soviets' watchful eye: that signature of Soviet socialism, the dual Party-state organization.[7] Through the operation of these structures and mechanisms were realized a number of other policies that followed Soviet practice closely, including rapid industrialization on the backs of the peasantry together with the full collectivization of agriculture, which we discuss for the Soviet Union later in this chapter and for Romania in chapter 2.

Ensuring Compliance: Soviet Councilors and the Secret Police

Between 1945 and 1948, the Romanian Communist Party (or RCP)—the name we will use in this book, although from 1948 to 1965 it was technically the Romanian Workers' Party (RWP)—gradually gained a political toehold and then secured full control over all major political institutions, eliminating other centers of power.[8] The path was cleared by Soviet policy that cut the Romanian army to one-third of its former size between 1944 and 1947, substituting Soviet

[5] Similar in scope was the attempt to create market democracies based on private property following the collapse of the socialist bloc in 1989.

[6] For more on the Soviet model, see Degeratu and Roske 1994a, 1994b, and 1994c, and Cătănuş and Roske 2000: 13–14.

[7] This chapter benefits greatly from the assistance of Constantin Iordachi and Dorin Dobrincu, who clarified many details of Romanian political life in the 1940s and '50s—too many for us to include them all here.

[8] The Party had a number of different names throughout its history, including Communist Party of Romania, a separate Socialist Party of Romania that was joined to the Communist Party in 1948, Romanian Communist Party, and Romanian Workers' Party. In addition to the term Romanian

troops as guarantors of order (Deletant 1998: 50–51). Among the steps taken to consolidate communist power were gaining full control of the government (March 1946); falsifying elections to achieve a greater communist political presence (November 1946); banning the largest opposition party, the National Peasant Party (July 1947); forcing the abdication of Romania's king (December 1947); compelling the Social Democratic Party into union with the Communist Party to form the Romanian Workers' Party (February 1948); and adopting a new constitution based on the Soviet one (April 1948).

From this point on, although formally it was possible for some other political formations to exist, in practice Romania was a one-party state. Its leadership enacted further fundamental transformations, such as nationalizing and centralizing the economy, expropriating landholdings over twenty hectares,[9] overhauling the country's administrative organization, transforming the military and the system of justice, subordinating both the judiciary and the legislature to the executive power, and reorganizing relations between government and religion.[10] In a word, the Party reconfigured the entire field of social, cultural, political, and economic relations. At every step it received the "fraternal assistance" of the Red Army and other Soviet personnel.

Following World War II, Soviet leaders faced a significant problem in bringing Romania into their orbit, for Romania's Communist Party was weak. Internal support for it was low prior to World War II: partly because of its illegal status during the interwar years and its deeply unpopular stance on the national question,[11] in 1944 it had only one thousand members, the smallest per-capita membership of any country in the region (Tismăneanu 2003: 279n37).[12] In addition, the urban proletariat was minuscule and had been heavily recruited by the interwar fascist party, the Iron Guard.[13] This indigenous movement, preach-

Communist Party, we use Party except when citing files pertaining to a specific name (RWP, RCP, PMR).

[9] A hectare, the standard unit of areal measurement in the metric system, is 10,000 square meters, or about 2.5 acres.

[10] These changes included—especially important for this book—forcibly merging the Greek Catholic and Orthodox churches, persecuting and jailing Greek Catholic clergy who refused to switch to Orthodoxy, and turning Greek Catholic church properties over to the Orthodox Church.

[11] The industrial labor force constituted only 10 percent of the employed population; the RCP was banned in 1924; and following the internationalist line of the worldwide communist movement, the RCP opposed the multinational Romanian state formed after World War II, calling it a "multinational empire" (see Tismăneanu 2003: 24). This was a suicidal position to be taking at the time, for to create a monoethnic state would entail significant transfers of either territory or population.

[12] He notes further, "In absolute terms, it equaled the membership of the Albanian communist party" (279n37). The early membership was heavily non-Romanian (particularly Hungarian and Jewish), though precise figures are hard to come by (see King 1980: 82). For further information on the history of the Romanian Communist Party, see King 1980; Levy 2001; Stoica 2006.

[13] Several organizations were linked in this mass movement, as one succeeded another. First formed was the Legion of the Archangel Michael, hence the name "legionaries" to refer to its mem-

Figure 1.1. Celebrating the Soviet blueprint. The banner in Romanian and Russian reads: "Long Life to the Romanian People's Republic." Courtesy of Artexpo Foundation.

ing a message antithetical to that of the Communists, attracted both workers and peasants (the latter mostly sympathizers of the center-right National Peasant Party) to a radical alternative more successfully than the Communists were able to do. Although recruitment efforts brought the Communist Party's numbers in 1948 up to one million, the vertiginous increase indicates primarily that many of these people were "communists" in name only. Thus, Romania's top political elite was highly dependent on the Soviet Union, without whose presence they would never have achieved power. Effectively vassals of the Soviet Communist Party (Tănase 1998: 34), their servility to the Soviet leadership further reduced popular support for them and thus aggravated their dependency, in an ongoing negative spiral.

A result of this dependency was that for almost two decades, Romania's Party leaders offered minimal resistance to adopting central features of the Soviet blueprint. Ritual references to it permeate their speeches and discussions, both public and secret. For several of myriad examples: when a "verification" of Party members was completed in 1950 (see below), Politburo member Iosif

bers. This morphed into the Iron Guard, which formed a party, *Totul pentru Țară* (All for the Fatherland) that came in third in national elections in 1937, with 16 percent of the vote. For more on the Iron Guard, see Heinen 1986.

Figure 1.2. Soviet soldiers help with plowing (1945). Courtesy of *Fototeca online a comunismului românesc*, photograph #W030, *cota* 22/1945.

Chişinevski observed, "To bring this great action to a successful end, almost all possible Soviet documents were studied," adding that "in all its activity, our party was inspired by Lenin's and Stalin's teachings about the party and by the great experience of the Bolshevik Party" (cited in Ionescu-Gură 2005: 207). As Ana Pauker said in 1952, "We know what advice from the Soviet comrades means; I won't even talk about advice from comrade Stalin. We know that these people are basing themselves on science and on the experience of the Bolshevik Party of the USSR, and we take their advice—as well we should."[14] Specifically concerning collectivization, Soviet documents were translated into Romanian so they could be read and followed.[15] In closed discussions, the leaders repeatedly compared their progress with the Soviet model—and found themselves wanting. (See figure 1.1.)

It is not, of course, surprising to see the Soviet Union so often invoked, since its representatives were present at most high-level meetings. These included the so-called Soviet councilors or advisors, who over the course of twenty years were deployed to Bucharest (and other East European capitals) in large numbers, joining the Soviet troops already present by the terms of the armistice. The

[14] ANIC, Fond C.C. al P.C.R.–Cancelarie, file 12/1952, 20 (RLA). Dej immediately interjected: "When they [the Soviet comrades] were sent, they didn't come without directives. The Soviet Communist Party doesn't send people without telling them what they have to do."

[15] ANIC, Fond C.C. al P.C.R.–Agrară, file 46/1953. In an interview with Kligman, an agronomist with the State Planning Commission reported being told "how to prepare all the documentation and so forth, by reading the Soviet materials that they translated into Romanian for us so we could follow it" (H. D., Kligman interview).

presence of these councilors was Moscow's response to the fact that it did not have a sufficiently powerful partner in Romania (or the other East European states) to whom it could entrust governance, owing to the Party's weakness and the divisions within its leadership. Most of the councilors were in the army, the Ministry of the Interior, and the Securitate, but they were to be found in all central administrative bodies as well as in the cultural bureaucracy.[16] Their task was to see that the Soviet Union was more than just a model but actually exercised power in Romania in its own right (Dobrincu 2000–01: 211–12). Romanian political analyst Tănase states, "Here more than anywhere else and in a less camouflaged way, the Soviets were present in the army, the police, the administration, and economic life, of which they directly controlled an important part. As early as 1947 in communist circles of the other People's Democracies, Romania was regarded as the seventeenth Soviet Republic" (1998: 36).[17]

There is very little documentary evidence available on the activities of these councilors in the countries to which they were sent. Nevertheless, scholars working in the Soviet archives have been finding new information (see Tismăneanu et al. 2007: 155–65), and there is still much more to learn about this crucial institution.[18] At least some of the councilors came at the explicit request of Romania's Party leaders. In 1949 Gheorghiu-Dej asked for the assistance of "one or two specialists" to help with the verification of cadres, and in 1950 a convention between the two countries regularized their presence (155–56). There are records of further requests, such as by Defense Minister Bodnaraş (for forty-nine councilors in 1951) and by Dej (for seventy-nine more in 1952)—both serving only the army[19]—and by various agricultural bodies asking to extend their councilor's stay for another year.[20] It is likely that the Soviets sent many more without being asked. In 1957 they proposed reducing the number and Gheorghiu-Dej agreed, though he continued to request new advisors for the next few years. In 1964, however, when he asked that all the councilors leave and tried to remove the Securitate from KGB control, Soviet leaders protested vigorously.

The Soviet councilors wielded enormous and sometimes decisive influence over Romania's leaders, even though their advice was not always unanimous: there were power struggles among them, paralleling those in the Soviet Union,

[16] One of our respondents recalled that when he was in university in 1955, an area of his dormitory was roped off with a sign saying "Restricted area": it was the apartment of the Soviet councilor. There was one in every university, he recalled. (R. A., Verdery interview)

[17] From 1940 to 1956 the Soviet Union contained sixteen republics, the sixteenth being the Karelo-Finnish SSR.

[18] Useful sources include Barany 1995; Chiper and Constantiniu 1995; Constantiniu and Ionescu 1993; Dobrincu 2000–1; Muraşko 1998. Barany (1995) indicates something of the range of variation in the extent of the work of Soviet councilors in the different countries—much more extensive in Poland, for example, than in Hungary, which was regarded as a less important satellite.

[19] Tismăneanu et al. 2007: 155, 160.

[20] ANIC, Fond C.C. al P.C.R.–Agrară, file 10/1952, 6, 12.

which meant that factions in Romanian politics would each have their Soviet backers.[21] Here is a small sampling of their activities. They assisted with (perhaps even precipitated) the purge of Gheorghiu-Dej's chief rivals, helping to write the resolution that would bring them down as well as the questions for the interrogations; they directed reorganizations of the Party toward closer conformity with the Soviet model; they controlled the instruction of cadres, approved all measures taken in the Interior Ministry, drew up the first Five-Year Plan (to Soviet advantage), and advised on the Danube Canal, Romania's gulag, which was central to the Soviet industrial program. It was they who insisted on forced industrialization for Romania, as well as on high levels of food requisitions (despite extensive rural opposition) to facilitate the currency reform they were instrumental in creating (Levy 2001: 121, 127). They were active in planning and executing the collectivization of agriculture, insisting that it be tried first in Constanța region, where the Soviet army was stationed,[22] and they prevailed in excluding wealthy peasants from the collectives, as in the Soviet Union, until late in the process.[23]

Above all, they oversaw the creation of Romania's repressive apparatus—particularly its espionage division and the Securitate, a direct offshoot of the KGB.[24] The Securitate was formed in 1948 to replace the Siguranța (Security Police) and Special Information Service of the bourgeois era. Among its declared missions were to defend the gains of the Romanian working class and to "cleanse society of the 'impure'" (Anisescu 2002: 12)—such as members of earlier bourgeois political parties and other "antidemocratic" organizations, holders of wealth, persons resisting policies like collectivization, and so on.[25] Soviet design

[21] Robert Levy, personal communication. Much of the information in this paragraph comes from Tismăneanu et al. 2007: 155–65.

[22] See Liuba Chișinevski's remark in an Orgburo meeting: "I think it will be a decision, perhaps a special one, in favor of Constanța, to gain experience—this is what the Soviet councilors are teaching us—to try this thing in Constanța" (Cătănuș and Roske 2000: 299).

[23] In the work of the Agrarian Commission one finds frequent references to Soviet councilor Veretnikov (also spelled Veretenicov and Veretelnicov in the documents), assigned to oversee collectivization. According to Pauker, Moghioroș, filling in for her, "asked that comrade Veretnikov and those from the Agriculture Ministry and the Leading Organizational Section be called in" (ANIC, Fond C.C. al P.C.R.-Cancelarie, file 59/1950, 12 [RLA]). The Ministry of Agriculture praised the councilors, who "through their exceptional professional training and their vast experience in the area of the socialist construction of agriculture help us greatly in the organization and consolidation of the socialist sector in agriculture" (Tismăneanu et al. 2007: 162).

[24] The Soviet secret police were initially known by the acronym OGPU, then NKVD, and finally (as of 1954) KGB. We will generally use KGB because of its familiarity to readers, except when to do so would be grossly anachronistic.

[25] Initially, the Securitate was divided into ten directorates, subdivided in turn into regional, district, municipal, and commune bureaus, with the lower-level bureaus having to write monthly reports to the higher directorates in Bucharest (Deletant 1995: 21). Following several changes, the Interior Ministry was reorganized in 1956, creating a separate Department for the Securitate; further modifications followed in the 1960s. (Information from Deletant 1995: 65–67; see also Dobre 2006.)

of the repressive institutions helped to ensure, however, that the interests of Moscow were the main ones served (Dobrincu 2000–1: 223). In 1949 a new police force (*miliţie*) and a force of Securitate troops (supplied with weapons from the USSR) were also set up (Neagoe 2002: 138–39). A former Securitate general observed in 1998 that under the early directors of the Securitate "there were hundreds of other NKVD-ists, who occupied all the decision-making posts and many of the implementation functions of the repressive organs of that time."[26] The ubiquity and critical placement of Soviet councilors, then, gives an incontrovertible foundation to the idea of a Soviet blueprint imposed on Romania.

A key Securitate activity was issuing periodic reports on the population's state of mind (*starea de spirit*) or "mood." This practice, variants of which in Europe can be traced back at least to the Napoleonic state, had also been followed by the tsarist secret police with its mood (*nastroenie*) reports and was central to the Soviet KGB in its various incarnations. According to an Instruction issued in 1922 concerning intelligence gathering, "the most important task of state information is casting light on the mood of every population group and the factors surrounding changes in that mood" (Martin n.d.: chapter 1). It was especially important to monitor "bad" moods, owing to the key policing concept that a negative mood in a major population category could open that category to counterrevolutionary influence. To forestall further organization, the political police must signal any such bad moods so the leadership could take appropriate action—propaganda, repression, or changes in policy (Martin n.d.: chapter 2). The categories around which Securitate mood reports were organized were identical to those Martin reports for the Soviet ones (n.d.: chapter 1), reflecting Soviet influence and perhaps a common French source for both systems.[27]

In its first year, the Securitate was assigned the huge task of verifying all Party members, so as to ensure a corps of Party cadres who were reliable. Soviet advice was useful here, for the Soviet Communist Party had carried out precisely this kind of verification and "purification" in 1929. Such purification was essential, owing to the manner of the Romanian Party's growth after 1944: a one thousandfold increase in just four years. People had joined it in four waves, beginning in 1945 with the incorporation—at the government's express invitation—of many from the fascist Iron Guard. A second wave came in 1946–47 from units of the army and administrative personnel who had been working with the Soviet administration; the forced merger of the Social Democrats with the Communist Party in 1948 produced a third wave; and a fourth came from people brought into the new bureaucracy (Deletant 1998: 80). In conducting a

[26] See Dobre 2006: xx.

[27] Notably, the prewar Romanian Siguranţa also used mood reports, though those we have found were much less detailed than their communist counterparts. See, for example, DJAN HD, Fond Chestura de Poliţie Deva, file 6/1927, 14, 19; file 72/1937, 7–8.

verification of Party members, the Securitate's job was to remove those "enemy elements" who might have been swept in during the early years—in other words, to scrutinize the Party itself in great detail. From a membership of 1,060,000 in February 1948, almost a third were purged by May 1950; from 1948 to 1952 no new Party members were accepted; by 1955 the membership was 595,363 (Tănase 1998: 50). Tănase observes that the very process of carrying out the verification campaign was what consolidated the Securitate as an organization (54; see also Oprea 2002).

The Securitate's precise status in the government is somewhat anomalous, as some uncertainty surrounds its top chain of command and reporting status.[28] Although it was created within the Interior Ministry, its generals seem not to have reported there; thus, the Prime Minister—supposedly the superior of all ministers of state—never controlled this ministry or its component Securitate. Furthering the Securitate's relative autonomy from the government was that its top leaders were all agents of the KGB—and were directly supervised by councilors from the Soviet Ministry of State Security. Soviet advisors were also attached to each directorate to oversee the training of recruits (Deletant 1998: 88–92). Of all the structures in Romania's political apparatus, the repressive forces were the ones most closely tied to the Soviet Union (Tănase 1998: 60).[29] They spied on Party members without constraint until, in 1954 and 1957, the Romanian Politburo began limiting what the Securitate could do with respect to Party members.[30] (As Dej put it, "[Securitate] agents don't have the right to question the actions of people holding high positions in the life of the state and members of the Party leadership" [Anisescu 2002: 45]). The limitations increased the Party's control over the Securitate, further reinforced when Soviet troops were withdrawn from Romania in 1958 (Oprea 2002: 19).

The significance of the Securitate—and thus of Soviet shaping of it—both for transforming Romania's political institutions and for implementing collectivization cannot be overstated. Its repressive apparatus was the principal weapon of political change during the early period, when the Party-state had not yet been fully institutionalized and did not control economic life. The exercise of coercion would prove essential to forming the collective farms: whenever coercion was relaxed, the collectivization drive stagnated until repression reap-

[28] Tănase (1998: 60) argues that at first it operated autonomously, subject to no political control (other than that of the Soviet Union). Oprea, on the other hand, suggests that both the Securitate and its parent ministry had an abnormal status: by decision of the Politburo, from at least 1952 on, the Interior Minister reported directly to the General Secretary (Gheorghiu-Dej), while another member of the Politburo (Chişinevski) directly supervised the Securitate (2002: 19–20).

[29] The Securitate named the heads of the MAI (Ministry of the Interior) and analyzed its activities (Oprea 2002: 22).

[30] This included ruling that Party First Secretaries in the regions and Party Secretaries in the districts should know who the Securitate agents were within their regions (see Anisescu 2002: 41–50; Oprea 2002: 29).

peared.[31] Precisely because of the Securitate's role at the most localized level of the political hierarchy, its archive, when suitably read, provides particularly valuable evidence about Party strategy and the responses of villagers to it.[32]

ORGANIZING THE PARTY-STATE

The term "Party-state" usually refers to a sui generis political formation in communist societies, based on parallel and interwoven hierarchical bureaucratic structures of administration, management, and control.[33] The Party was the ideologically mobilizing organization that established the values and procedures, ostensibly deriving from Marxism-Leninism, that the branches of the state bureaucracy would manage; it also exercised surveillance and control over how state bureaucrats—not to mention other Party members—carried out their work. Each half had its function: the Party's was to provide political and ideological direction, the state's to provide technical and economic administration. Jowitt, with his characteristic flair, referred to the result as "charismatic impersonalism" (1992). Although the two sets of bureaucracies interpenetrated, not only might the interests of each diverge from the other but both were also internally splintered into rival factions.[34] This was certainly true in Romania, as we will indicate further in chapter 2.

With fraternal oversight assured, the Romanian government began the process of creating a Party-state with dual interlinked structures, in the Soviet image. There was, on the one hand, the revolutionary Party organization with its hierarchy of positions and organizations (Party secretaries, Party cells, and so on), and, on the other hand, the administrative chain of command and associated organizations (government ministries, legislative and executive bodies, etc.), which we will refer to as the "state" structures. Each set of positions

[31] This dynamic was present throughout the system. See Kligman 1998.

[32] The Securitate archive became selectively available to researchers in 1995 as the Archive of the Romanian Information Service (ASRI); by 2000 with the creation of the National Council for Study of the Securitate Archives (CNSAS), the ASRI was closed and rules for access through the CNSAS were modified. Both of us applied for research access in 2002 and received permission. Access does not, of course, mean that one will be given the files one requests, and it is difficult to request files because the organizational categories of the archive are not public: one must intuit them, or else apply for the files of individuals by name. We are grateful to the director (at the time, Dr. Gheorghe Onişoru) and board of CNSAS for granting us permission to use this archive, as well as to Dr. Florica Dobre and her assistants for helping us obtain files.

[33] Although the proliferation of state and Party institutions and segments renders inadvisable our use of the reifying noun "Party-state," we nonetheless follow that simplifying convention.

[34] Kotkin summarizes the resulting politics, for Magnitogorsk: "The everyday functioning of the dual apparats brought forth suspicions, grudges, webs of alliances—in short, everything from petty squabbling to bureaucratic warfare, which, although mostly invisible, was quite real and was compounded by the parallelism" (1995: 297).

and structures ran from the national level in Bucharest down to the level of communes and villages and (for the Party) workplaces. They were articulated in several ways, all shared with the Soviet Union and other People's Democracies. First, the state administrative apparatus was always subordinate to the Party apparatus at any given level. This preeminence of the Party was enshrined in the constitution, and it made the state apparatus largely an instrument for achieving the Party's policies (Dobre 2004: 7). Moreover, all the most important positions in both structures were occupied by specially vetted Party members, based on two lists (one with the major Party and state positions, and one with approved potential occupants) that together formed the "nomenclatura."[35] The Bolsheviks had taken over this practice from the tsarist regime and passed it along to their East European clients (Ionescu-Gură 2005: 236n42). Occupants of all these positions were subject to surveillance by the Soviet-controlled Securitate.

We will not provide an exhaustive account of Romania's political organization, but some idea of it is necessary to discussing both how collectivization was accomplished and the RCP's relation to Soviet precedent, for the Party's organization followed that of the Soviet Union very closely. At its head was the First or General Secretary (different labels prevailed at different times), the most powerful person in the country. Romania had only two significant incumbents of this position: Gheorghe Gheorghiu-Dej (1945–65) and Nicolae Ceauşescu (1965–89). The Party's principal executive body was its Central Committee (CC), whose numbers increased steadily over time (from 57 in 1948 to 466 in 1989); at the height of the collectivization campaign (1957–62) there were 97 to 110 people in the CC. The CC had three and then two executive bodies: the Political Bureau or Politburo, containing between 7 and 18 members; the Organizational Bureau (or Orgburo, 1950–54), with 11 to 17 members; and the Secretariat, consisting of 4 or 5 people, the most powerful figures in the country (see Dobre 2004: 12). These bodies, and not the CC as a whole, were the effective decision makers.[36] The Central Committee further contained a variety of sections by branch of activity, such as the Agrarian Section, the Agitation and Propaganda Section, the Cultural and Scientific Section, the External Affairs Section, etc.

As in the Soviet case, the Party hierarchy was constituted on a territorial principle based on workplaces. At the level below Bucharest were the regional Party organizations, each headed by a First Secretary and represented by a political bureau. The districts also had their Party organizations, headed by a Party Secretary, as did the communes. Attached to the lower-level Party orga-

[35] A detailed listing of the uppermost reaches of the Romanian Communist Party can be found in Crişan 2004.

[36] With Ceauşescu's ascent in 1965, this arrangement was reorganized (see Dobre 2004: 11–13).

nizations were sections such as the Organizational, Economic, Agrarian, and Educational. At the bottom of the Party hierarchy were the "base organizations" (*organizațiile de bază*), or Party cells, the fundamental political units of every village, commune, institution, and workplace. A Party secretary headed each one, alongside general assemblies that elected executive bureaus or committees. The chain of command thus went from the First/General Secretary of the Romanian Communist Party in Bucharest through the First Secretaries of the regions, down to the Party secretaries of the districts and communes, ending with the Party secretaries of workplace cells. In addition to their secretaries, each of these units had a variety of cadres referred to as instructors, agitators, and activists, who carried out specialized tasks.[37]

Operating alongside these Party structures was the state administrative hierarchy. At the top, its principal organs were the presidency and prime ministership, the Grand National Assembly (the supreme organ of state power and sole legislative body of the country), the Council of Ministers (the chief instrument of state administration), and various state committees.[38] At each of the lower administrative levels (the regions or counties, districts, and communes) were "People's Councils" (*sfaturi populare*), whose deputies elected an executive committee headed by a president (later renamed mayor). Each People's Council had its administrative secretary, not to be confused with the Party secretary (although such a person was a Party member), and each could form its own sections by branches of activity—Agriculture, Finance, Cadres, and so on—corresponding to those of higher state bodies.[39] Other sorts of entities within

[37] These tasks were arrayed in multiple forms of "work" (*muncă*), such as "cultural work," "explanation work," "visual work," and "political work." Beyond this hierarchy of positions were certain specialized organizations attached to the Party, such as the Union of Communist Youth (organized similarly to the larger Party) and professional organizations within the Party, such as those for university students and faculty. There were also a variety of so-called mass organizations, formally separated from the Party but integrally connected to its activities. These included the trade unions, the Union of Democratic Women, and Nationalities Councils.

[38] The organizational structure of the state can be found in the constitutions of 1948, 1952, and 1965. For the first two (of interest to us in this book), see Republica Populară Română, "Constituția Republicii Populare Române," *Monitorul Oficial*, part 1, no. 87, and Republica Populară Română, "Constituție a Republicii Populare Române," *Buletin Oficial al Marii Adunări Naționale a Republicii Populare Române*, no. 1, 27 September 1952. See Republica Populară Română 1952, art. 43, for a list of the committees and art. 50, for a list of government ministries, twenty-eight in number as of 1952.

[39] To show the complexity of the district administration, here is the list of sections for its People's Council for the Orăștie district in 1950, with the number of cadres employed in each: section on cadres (four people), secretariat (eight), juridical section (thirteen), communal economy and local industry (thirty) with bureaus for planning, accounting, and financial control, etc.; commercial section (five) with subsections; sections on agriculture (seventeen), education (three), culture (two), work and social welfare (five), sanitation (seven); a committee for physical education and sport (two); and the canteen of the district council (four). The source lists the names of everyone in these positions, their job titles, salaries, and salary categorizations (DJAN HD, Fond Sfat Raion Orăștie, file 4/1950, n.p.).

the state structure—for example, the State Committee for Collections of Agricultural Produce, the State Planning Committee, or the State Committee for Provisioning—would be represented at lower levels through activists, instructors, collectors, etc., whom the region or district sent into every village. At the bottom-most levels of the Party and state bureaucracies, where collectivization ultimately occurred—the villages—there were several political positions and organizations: the local Party cell with its secretary and executive bureau, one or two delegates to the People's Council in the commune under which the village was subsumed, and a Party organizer responsible for the work of setting up the collective farm, with—in the better-organized villages—an initiating committee. Once formed, the collective farm would have its president, council, audit committee, technicians (agronomists, veterinarians), and work brigade leaders.

To implement collectivization required creating an enormous bureaucratic apparatus, extending from one end of the country to the other. Given the dual structures of the Party-state, this apparatus was also dual, creating much duplication of effort and problems of coordination, not to mention huge cost. Party, state, and security organs of various kinds at each level were to submit weekly and monthly reports concerning various aspects of the progress of collectivization; the result was extensive documentation (albeit disorganized and of sometimes questionable validity) overwhelming to both bureaucrats and hapless postsocialist researchers. Staffing these bureaucratic positions was initially not easy, given the Party's small numbers and the low levels of education and ideological preparation of many who joined in the first few years. The remarkable degree of bureaucratic hypertrophy (characteristic to some extent of the interwar Romanian state as well) was an essential feature of socialist systems in general and of the collectivization process in particular.

Crosscutting the proliferating hierarchies and positions were informal relations of patronage and intersegmental alliances that formed a complex system of clientelistic networks. The various groupings were in frequent competition, as were the major segments of the Party and state bureaucracies. For example, as in the Soviet Union, the military and heavy industry tended to be the most powerful sectors of the economic bureaucracy, light industry after that, and agriculture at the bottom, but officials in each of these branches strove to accumulate resources for themselves at the expense of the other branches and segments. The result was a perpetually shifting field of political forces, in which individuals and cliques vied for favor, undercutting their rivals through denunciations and purges, in transient alliances always responsive to the possibility of changes higher up in Bucharest or Moscow. Ideally speaking, this set of powerful networks and the long-standing habits of personalism underlying them should have given way as the Party organization was gradually institutionalized, but if anything, under socialism these networks proliferated further. They were not written into the blueprint, but the Party-state could not have functioned without them.

* * *

So much for the blueprint. Setting it into motion in Romania generated a number of problems, aggravated of course by the Party's fundamental weakness. Some of the problems came from the manner of its growth. "Going from one thousand to one million members in only four years would produce difficulties in *any* organization. Its coherence and functioning decline. Such growth makes the party uncontrollable, a chaos of parallel structures, or personal fiefs, with imprecise boundaries between party and society" (Tănase 1998: 48–49). Throughout the 1950s it was in a process of formation and consolidation (see Jowitt 1971) through which it would *become* the Party, as cadres attempted their work—that is, it would be constituted through its members' actions. Just as the job of verifying Party members formed the Securitate and the work of collectivizing formed the Soviet OGPU/NKVD/KGB (Viola 1996: 234), the same was true of the Romanian Communist Party: the tasks of requisitioning food and collectivizing were crucial to its consolidation. In the meantime, however, centralization and the absence of infrastructure (e.g., inadequate transportation systems for centralized redistribution, poor means of communication across the country, etc.) generated enormous problems in realizing the Party's objectives.

Special complications emerged from the relation between Party and state structures—that is, from the Party-state form of the blueprint—which proved exceedingly difficult to institutionalize. The necessity for the dual structure arose from the same source in both the Soviet and Romanian cases: a lack of sufficient cadres, which required both the Bolsheviks and the Romanian communists to retain numerous specialists from various professional bodies (military, educational, civil service, etc.) from the previous regime. Lenin posed the problem thus: "We now have a vast army of governmental employees, but we lack sufficiently educated forces to exercise real control over them. . . . [A]t the top, where we exercise political power, the machine functions somehow; but down below, where these state officials are in control, they often function in such a way as to counteract our measures."[40] According to Kotkin, the best way to ensure their loyalty was to surround them, in certain institutions, with

> party members who worked in these bodies. . . . By "shadowing" the gamut of institutions, the party sought to verify [*kontrolirovat*] that their operation conformed to what was defined as the "interests of the working class," determined by the party leadership. Thus was born a structural division between expertise and "'proper" ideology, with the latter becoming the duty of the party and the justification for its

[40] Cited in Fainsod 1953: 330.

> prominent post-revolutionary role. . . . Party "'verification" . . . institutionalized a permanent dualism in the Soviet political system, which appropriately came to be called a party-state. (Kotkin 1995: 292, 293)

Well after the suspect specialists had been replaced, the system continued to operate as a check on the conduct of lower ranking Party and state officials. We see, then, that surveillance was one of the very first practices to be institutionalized. This makes it even clearer why the Soviet blueprint entailed gaining immediate control over the secret police, as described above.

The consequences of adopting this dual model in Romania are evident in the minutes of meetings among the top Party leadership in the Party Secretariat, Politburo, and Orgburo, which show constant organizational difficulties. Some of these concerned the relations between the representatives of Party and state in addressing specific problems, especially the collection of food quotas. The minutes reveal complaints, for instance, that the state authorities were too passive in the face of uncollected food requisitions and that the Party shouldn't simply leave collecting them to the state administrative apparatus but must itself become involved, as in the Soviet Union. Perhaps local state organs were captive to class enemies: the Party would have to become more active in combating this, or the problem with collections would be its own fault.[41] The underlying point was that Party leaders wanted to increase interpenetration between the state and the developing collective farm sector, but Party members lower down did not want to implicate themselves or join the collectives.[42]

There was also concern about the poor coordination of higher with lower-level authorities. In a 1951 meeting of the Secretariat, participants deplored the refusal of some (state) officials in local People's Councils to extract the required quotas from their peasants. "The law is clear but it is not respected," observed Finance Minister Luca, adding that if local organs did not respect the Party's laws, they undermined the authority of the state. Those present agreed that local state functionaries who were resisting collections should be arrested as enemies of the state, tried, and dealt with mercilessly.[43] In another such example that year, the same issues emerged. The People's Councils were protecting wealthy peasants rather than extracting quotas from them, but then local-level Party members were no better: in one area, 70 percent of Party members had not given their requisition quotas, and peasants were saying that therefore they wouldn't give either. Thus, the Party's moral authority was as vulnerable as the state's.[44] That local officials in either the Party or the state bureaucracies or both

[41] ANIC, Fond 1, file 178/1950, 24, 27-32, unidentified date and forum (RLA).

[42] Constantin Iordachi, personal communication.

[43] ANIC, Fond 1, file 3/1951, 6–10 (RLA). Opposition to Party and governmental decisions applied to all domains, not only to collections: for example, any Party member who acted against the currency reform would be sanctioned, perhaps excluded from the Party, and tried. See DJAN MM, Fond Comitetul Raional PMR Vişeu, file 33/1952/V, 91.

[44] ANIC, Fond 1, file 55/1951, 21 (RLA).

were mishandling food requisitions was the subject of repeated complaint in CC meetings.[45] Leaders remarked that in some areas, the local officials weren't aware of what was happening and that the Party needed better organization. Gheorghiu-Dej offered a concise summary: "We have to create cadres who will do what we want them to do."[46]

Further problems came from Party members in the villages, who often colluded with the "class enemy" instead of assisting local officials. For instance, in one area when quotas went unfulfilled and rich peasants insisted they had nothing left to give, their surpluses were found hidden with other peasants, including Party members (Dobeş et al. 2004: 42). More significantly, village Party members often refused to join the collectives—a matter repeated often in central documents—or, at best, tried to join with only part of their land; their co-villagers used this as grounds for not joining. In Maramureş region, when officials investigated why the pace of collectivization was so slow, they found that of 5,114 Party members in agriculture, fully 2,756 had not joined any form of socialist enterprise (45). One peasant complained to the Central Committee and the Ministry of Agriculture, "Not even Party members are willing to join the collective farm because all the drunkards, freeloaders, and speculators have joined it" (26). We will revisit the behavior of local officials in chapter 3.

The problems were not only with the relation of Party and state or center and locality but also with coordination across the vast field of endeavor being organized by this sprawling set of bureaucratic institutions. In one of the 1951 meetings described above, for instance, the representative from Hunedoara region declared, "Our biggest problem is the lack of coordination between the State Committee for Collections and the various state apparatuses."[47] In other forums, Central Committee members worried about the poor coordination of government ministries and the inability to deal with local specificities,[48] noted that a visit by Politburo member Constantinescu to Hungary had revealed the Hungarians' vastly superior organization for collecting meat compared with the Romanian Ministry of Agriculture,[49] and showed themselves endlessly concerned with who was to blame for things that were going poorly. In a set of exchanges among Cabinet members, participants observed that the Ministry of Light Industry was actually doing the job of wool collections although the State

[45] These officials told peasants they need not go to the collection stations and held back on collecting for fear that they wouldn't be reelected; functionaries of the People's Councils were not delivering the quotas they collected or opposed collections outright; new cadres in Craiova turned out to be "bandits, fascists, and chiaburs" (i.e., *kulaks*, "rural bourgeoisie"). See, among others, ANIC, Fond 1, file 205/1950, 117–123; file 178/1950, 21–32; file 3/1951, 1–22; file 99/1951; file 3/1952, 1–16; file 6/1952, 1–22 (RLA).

[46] ANIC, Fond 1, file 3/1952, 6; file 4/1952, 50 (RLA).

[47] ANIC, Fond 1, file 55/1951, 24 (RLA).

[48] ANIC, Fond 1, file 2/1951, 17, 51 (RLA).

[49] ANIC, Fond 1, file 4/1952, 40–41 (RLA).

Committee for Collections was responsible for it, and they tried to track down one million missing sheep from Sibiu region that seemed to be "scattered all over the country," agreeing with one another that there must be better organization and improved accounting for sheep and wool.[50] In reading such comments we must always bear in mind the competitions and rivalries among bureaucrats and their segments—at all levels—that could lead to criticism and casting blame. But even with this caution, the Party seems to have faced formidable organizational problems, exacerbated by the country's basic infrastructural limitations.

While the Party was getting on its organizational feet, however, the dual state structure also offered some advantages. Among them was what we have just seen: each set of bodies could avoid responsibility for repression or unpopular decisions by casting blame onto the other, or onto lower levels, a very efficient tactic for evading accountability all around. Blaming was also a form of "othering," central to the politics of difference that fueled intra- and interclass warfare (see chapters 4, 6, and 8). A second advantage concerns the very possibility of collectivization—that is, how a Party that was initially so weak could manage the task of collectivizing at all. To make this point requires a brief digression concerning relations between the Romanian state and the peasantry prior to the communist takeover.

Precommunist Romanian governments controlled the peasantry through two complementary systems.[51] The first was the administrative apparatus, modeled on the highly centralized French arrangement. Elections for local office notwithstanding, state-appointed county prefects had considerable power over local affairs, through their control of the police and the local mayors, who exercised absolute control over their domains. The state's control of the peasants through the network of prefects, sub-prefects, and mayors enabled it to extract taxes, manage election results, and impose conformity with the party in power. The second element of the peasantry's subjection was their patron-client bonds with large landowners, upon whom they depended for access to land.[52] These patron-client relations persisted until the land reform that followed World War I, which eliminated the large landowners as a social and political force. A communist land reform in 1945 (see Şandru 2005) further reduced the basis for patron-client relations, thereby removing an important form of social control over the peasantry. Party leaders sought to counteract this effect by reorganiz-

[50] ANIC, Fond 1, file 1/1952, 83–84 (RLA). The hiding of all forms of property was a significant problem, of which this is one example.

[51] We are indebted to Constantin Iordachi for the ideas in this and the following paragraph.

[52] This system of patron-client relations in villages was less prevalent in Transylvania than elsewhere, owing to the different ecologies and histories of Romania's different regions. Antedating the communists, this system was different from the one that developed in the Party after World War II, referred to above.

ing and strengthening the administrative apparatus in the countryside and drawing functionaries and local officials into the Party, with its disciplinary mechanisms. In addition, they fortified the apparatus of repression (police, army, and Securitate) for use against the peasants.

These solutions did not adequately compensate for the loss of the earlier forms of social control, however. The still-nascent Party-state was better equipped to destroy existing forms than to put new ones in their place. Iordachi, commenting on this weakness, asks how the communists nonetheless managed to collectivize. His answer helps us to discover another advantage of the dual Party-state structure: it enabled a weak Party to control the local administration,

> which was very extensive and rested on a long tradition of bureaucratic control over local communities. In other words, when collectivization began, the Party was weak but the state was strong. This is how we can explain why a Party that was so young, without cadres and without experience, managed to transform the rural world fundamentally.[53]

That is, a weak Party organization was able to graft itself onto the preexisting strong state structure to gain control over the peasantry.[54] This situation is distinct from pre-Soviet Russia, for example, where state control over the countryside was fairly weak and the peasantry had not yet been "captured" (see Hughes 1996), and from Poland and East Germany, where state organizations had disintegrated at the end of World War II to a much greater degree than in Romania.[55]

The Party's use of the state apparatus presumed two things: that there be some continuity between precommunist and communist-era administrative practices, and that this continuity not be so great as to disrupt the communists' agenda. Continuity was limited by numerous reforms of the territorial-administrative system during the Party's first two decades, replacing the old system with one borrowed from the Soviet Union that was to improve economic rationality and administrative efficiency. The reforms gradually reduced the number of administrative units while increasing their size and therefore the degree of political centralization (see Helin 1967). The largest units went from being counties to regions, and their number went from fifty-eight counties in 1944 to sixteen regions in 1956, with not only the regional boundaries but those of constituent districts and even communes being repeatedly modified.[56] We need

[53] Constantin Iordachi, personal communication.

[54] Pamela Ballinger (personal communication) points to similarities between communist policy and that of Italy's fascists, who also created a dual party-state structure, with the intention of gradually sucking the life out of the state structure to the party's advantage.

[55] Lynne Viola, personal communication, and King 1980: 39.

[56] While the first reorganization was being put into place, the new entities were governed by

scarcely add that these continual modifications of the administrative boundaries disrupted the hierarchies of reporting and made it very difficult to compare figures from one time period to another.

Nonetheless, the authorities took care to maintain some degree of continuity with precommunist practices. For example, during the 1950 reorganization, Party directives sought to ensure that settlements which lost their status as communes would transfer their archives carefully to their new administrative seat. On September 15, 1950, the Provisional Committee of Hunedoara region sent down to the Provisional Committees of the districts some instructions for how to turn over the archives of the former administrative units. The instructions read, "The preservation of these archives presents great importance, for on the one hand the documents in question are necessary to ensure continuity in administrative work . . . and on the other hand any possibility of withdrawing or degrading the dossiers found in the present archives must be forestalled."[57] The fruits of this concern with administrative continuity, given Iordachi's argument above, included maintaining the advantages of the centralized precommunist state for a weak Party parasitic upon it.

Other means by which some of these same practices persisted into the communist period included personnel policies. Early top-level discussion kept pointing to a major difficulty: where would they get the people to staff this huge dual apparatus? Representatives of the old bourgeois order were ideologically suspect, but the social groups the communists were now raising up were the ones least likely to have completed more than elementary-school education. As is clear from both the untutored signatures on Party documents of the early years and frequent reference to the matter in the reports of Party meetings at every level, illiteracy and substandard education were rife among lower-level cadres and officials (see chapter 3). Some administrative officials from the old regime could be brought into the new one because in the "bourgeois" period, those in government employment were not allowed to be members of political parties. Once the communists took over, however, these officials could save their jobs by joining the Party, since they had no history of belonging to one of the now-banned political formations of before. Party leaders intentionally sought out some of those who had been active in prewar social and political life and whose complicity therefore made them vulnerable; becoming Party supporters would help to wipe out the stain of their previous membership in the bourgeois judiciary, army, educational institutions, or now-stigmatized politi-

"provisional committees" at each level (village, commune, district, and county/region), and it was these committees that laid the initial groundwork for collectivization. In 1968—that is, after collectivization was complete—the precommunist division into counties was restored but they now numbered forty; the district level disappeared, and communes became the next administrative level below counties. This division is still in existence as of 2011.

[57] DJAN HD, Fond Sfat Raion Orăştie, file 1/1950, n.p. (15 September 1950).

cal parties.[58] The drawback of such converts, of course, was—as Lenin had warned decades earlier—that the Party could not be wholly certain of their loyalty; hence, its obsession with whether or not "enemy elements" were "infiltrated" (*strecurați*) in the Party apparatus.[59] The advantage, however, was the maintenance of certain forms of bureaucratic regularity and continuity.

We have been exploring some specifics of Romania's political organization that gave particular content to the imposed Soviet form of the Party-state. These particularities underlay early Soviet encouragement of departures from the Soviet blueprint (see this chapter's third epigraph). Indeed, Soviet researchers have uncovered evidence that early in the game, Stalin genuinely envisioned multiple national paths to socialism, recognizing that not everyone had to follow the Soviet model. He is reported to have told Czechoslovak premier Klement Gottwald in 1946, "Our path was short, rapid, and cost much blood and sacrifice. If you can avoid this—avoid it" (Volokitina et al. 2002: 37). Later, however, after the United States announced the Marshall Plan, he changed his mind, pressing for the rapid sovietization of Eastern Europe (Ionescu-Gură 2005: 24). In the early 1950s the essentials of the Soviet model were laid down, including the concentration of absolute political and economic power, the one-party state, the ideological monopoly of Marxist-Leninist ideology, a centralized economic system, and so forth (25). As we have already observed, the presence of the Soviet councilors, the Red Army, and a KGB-controlled Securitate were the chief mechanisms by which the Soviet model became imprinted on Romania. The task of Romania's leaders thereafter would be to build up the Party's infrastructure, through major tasks such as collectivization.

Collectivizations Compared

Collectivization was the single most far-reaching reform the communists would introduce, and in Romania, the plan for it conformed closely to the Soviet blueprint. Romania's leaders appear to have been divided initially over the wisdom of collectivizing but fell into line after a 1948 Cominform conference, at which the Soviet Union forced the East European representatives to vote for full collectivization.[60] As we will show at the end of this chapter, the results

[58] Our thanks to Dorin Dobrincu and Constantin Iordachi for these observations. See also Grama 2009: chapter 2.

[59] Similar problems assailed other East European countries where the Communist Party had been very small, such as Poland. See, for example, Grzymała-Busse 2001.

[60] Dobrincu (personal communication) contends that conversations in which some of them state their doubts about collectivizing reflected not their true feelings but their strategy of trying not to scare the population about their intentions until they had secured better control over the countryside.

varied greatly from one East European country to another; in the Romanian case, Stalin-style collectivization was the order of the day not only up to the time of Stalin's death but well past it. In this section we discuss how collectivization was accomplished in the Soviet Union—that is, we ask what, exactly, *was* the process by which the model was created that was then urged upon East European contexts wholly different from the Soviet one. We begin with an account of why people thought it a good idea.

In the abstract, there are a number of rationales for collectivizing agriculture. Frederic Pryor, for example, summarizes some of Stalin's arguments, such as reducing inequality and petty-capitalist accumulation in the countryside, fully integrating the economy for better planning, increasing production through economies of scale and more effective agricultural modernization, and civilizing a "barbarous" rural population whom Marx, Lenin, and Stalin all viewed with contempt as "a source of spiritual pollution for the rest of society" (Pryor 1992: 46–51). Yet other reasons include the fragmentation of peasant holdings, which could be more rationally cultivated through field consolidation (this was particularly important for Romania). Joan Sokolovsky (1990) offers three more comprehensive reasons: collectivization would be a means of (1) advancing socialist ideology in villages, through promoting class warfare; (2) securing control over the food supply for rapid industrialization in circumstances of low capital accumulation; and (3) state-building, by extending the Party's control over the peasantry—that "sack of potatoes" Marx decried as incapable of revolutionary consciousness.[61] These three rationales are not alternatives but point usefully to different aspects of the process (see also Jowitt 1978). Finally, we have the cultural arguments preferred by Viola (1996)—that collectivization was a means of altering the peasantry's cultural system, comparable to the "civilizing mission" of western European colonialism. Although we agree that this was a signal effect, we place greater stress on the economic and political arguments.

To discover the "rationale" for collectivization in Romania, of course, one need go no farther than Moscow. Independent of Soviet imperial interests, there was practically no internal constituency for the policy, and Party leaders saw reason for caution (Cătănuş and Roske 2000: 14). This is not to say that Romania had none of the conditions of Soviet agriculture. Both had largely peasant-based economies with over three-fourths of the population employed in agriculture, which was underdeveloped in both, having comparatively low yields and little complex technological investment. In both, agricultural land

[61] One important effect was the destruction of rural institutions, but the most persuasive Soviet historiography argues that Stalin did not have that idea in mind at the outset (e.g., Lewin 1968; Getty and Naumov 1999); this makes it inappropriate to include among our "rationales" for collectivizing. We argue that the destruction of rural institutions was basic to how the Romanian Communist Party constituted its authority (see also Jowitt 1978).

was divided into small strips, although in the Russian case the persistence of periodic land reallotment eased the problem somewhat. In Romania, however, a 1921 land reform had aggravated the fragmentation, delivering nearly four million hectares in small plots into the hands of poorer peasants lacking other means of production for cultivating them. A program to consolidate these strips and work them in large blocks with machine power (i.e., collectivization) might develop the agricultural sector in both countries more rapidly than alternative policies would—even though doing so entailed far-reaching changes in ownership. Therefore, to describe Soviet collectivization should give us some insights into Romania's experience. We begin by asking about the conditions that led Stalin's Central Committee to decide to collectivize in the Soviet Union and then briefly outline the process through which that was accomplished.

Collectivization in the Soviet Union

Initially, Stalin was opposed to collectivizing agriculture; indeed, as late as 1925 he was thinking instead of *giving* land to the peasantry (Pryor 1992: 46).[62] Although the reasons for his change of heart are still uncertain, most specialists appear to agree that it was precipitated by a grain procurement crisis, beginning in 1927 and worsening through 1929.[63] That crisis, in turn, was partly the effect of the Party's having prepared no new program to replace Lenin's market-oriented New Economic Policy, which the leadership was now abandoning. The failure to create grain reserves from good harvests earlier in the decade contributed further to the crisis, as did low state prices for agricultural produce (see below)—a policy motivated by the plan for rapid industrialization, which would require cheap food. The crisis, then, was as much the effect of deficient central planning as of scarce grain.

When Soviet Party leaders began to realize in 1927 that food supplies for the cities were dwindling, their first move was to intensify the collection of foodstuff requisitions, known as quotas (which had been introduced during World War I under the tsar and maintained throughout the civil war). Peasants reacted by hoarding their grain or hiding it from the authorities. Given the discrepancy between what the state paid for quotas and the price of food on the open market, other peasant reactions were to divert their resources to higher-paid livestock or moonshine, or to pay the fine for not turning over their grain and then sell it on the market at a tidy profit. But the Party leadership did not

[62] We include here only the Soviet Union and Eastern Europe (where the Soviets were directly involved), not collectivization in Asia or elsewhere, which would take us well beyond our purposes in this book.

[63] This section is largely based on the work of Davies (1980), Lewin (1968, 1985), and Viola (1987, 1996, 2000).

want to pay higher food prices: extorting grain directly from the peasants would enable planners to transfer agricultural surpluses into industrial development more effectively. In a January 1928 speech, Stalin observed that the proper solution to the crisis would be to create more collective and state farms and, eventually, to socialize agriculture altogether (Davies 1980: 109). The issue was not merely to control the food supply for the Party's purposes but to export grain, so as to repay the sizable loans taken out for purchasing equipment from western countries. A persistent shortage of grain would therefore jeopardize the industrialization program, planned urban expansion, and the country's international financial credibility.

With this, the collectivization of twenty-five million rural households began to gather steam alongside the increasingly stringent requisitions. The two policies worked hand in hand, for saddling peasant households with enormous quotas was one way to drive them into joining collectives. Another was to terrify people by beating, humiliating, and at length deporting the village elites and others labeled *kulaks* (the "rural bourgeoisie" and wealthy peasants), sent to the North, where they died by the tens of thousands (see Fitzpatrick 1994b, Viola 2007). Stalin decreed this policy of "liquidating" village kulaks (or "dekulakization") in December 1929. All three policies together—quotas, collectivization, and dekulakization—aimed to give the center full control over both the peasantry and the food supply, facilitating industrial development by holding down urban food costs. In the process, the Party and Security apparatuses were to be consolidated and the state strengthened, as the independent village institutions of the peasantry were shattered.

Collectivization proceeded at breakneck speed into early 1930, producing chaos and determined peasant opposition. The chaos had several sources, on which we elaborate below: (1) the insistence on haste, (2) weak bureaucratic planning, (3) unprepared cadres, and (4) vague instructions from the center, which resulted in massive abuses of authority as local officials strove to outdo one another in forming collectives. An obsession with speed marked the entire process. This is understandable, given the Politburo's view that if the Party could not capture in kolkhozes the productive capacity of the middle peasants, who produced the bulk of the country's grain, then by 1931 the entire industrialization program would collapse. But the costs of speed were astronomical, in part because cadres basically did not know what they were doing. "It is clear that when they launched this winter offensive, the leadership had no idea of the scale on which their mass collectivization drive was to take place. They were not thinking in terms of engulfing fifteen million households in the kolkhozes" (Lewin 1968: 519).[64] A further sense of urgency came from the fact that wealthy peasants were trying to escape the label "kulak" by selling their land and inven-

[64] The figure of fifteen million may refer only to Russia; the figure generally used for the number of peasant households in the Soviet Union is twenty-five million.

tory and then moving to cities; both they and other peasants had begun selling or even killing their livestock, to avoid having to turn them over to the kolkhoz "for free"—a pattern we later find in Eastern Europe as well.[65] These slaughters show both the further need for haste and the problems it had created: if the tempo had been more leisurely, forming collectives could have kept pace with the manufacture of tractors and other equipment to work the farms, but collectives were formed with such speed that they would have to be worked with peasants' draft animals and implements instead (hence, animal slaughtering was a serious problem).

As the pace accelerated in late 1929, projections of when it would be done became ever more fantastic. Stalin was convinced that collectivization could happen *in a few months*, "if only a sufficiently powerful and compelling means could be devised for driving the mass of the peasantry to join the kolkhozes. This he found in dekulakization" (Lewin 1968: 519). The very fertile Central Black Earth region had 8 percent of its households in kolkhozes in October 1929 and 82 percent of them four months later (514). In the USSR as a whole, following the January 1930 laws about dekulakization the numbers of peasants in collectives reportedly went from eight to fifteen million in a single month (Davies 1980: 252)! Chaos resulting from the excessive speed led to an interruption in March 1930; millions of peasants withdrew from collectives and the work had to be started again.

An effect of speed was poor planning, not to mention organizational problems and bureaucratic infighting. "In its feverish haste," Lewin writes, "the Politburo delegated responsibility to so many organizations that there was soon a veritable administrative tangle, the results of which were harmful in the extreme" (1985: 111). Viola, too, describes the administrative transformation in the countryside in early 1930, the height of collectivization mania: "Lacking the constraints of legality, precision, an orderly hierarchy, and an orderly world, plans tended to unravel downward around an ever-widening regional spiral once they had left Moscow" (1987: 101). In place of a routine bureaucratic structure were newly instituted Party instructors and "plenipotentiaries" (dignitaries with special powers to override all local decisions). These people

> raced from institution to institution, from village to village, to enumerate, implement, and enforce policy. Policy assumed the aspect of administrative procedure, all of its separate and theoretically distinct aspects combined into one. In this way each

[65] Conquest gives the following figures: 43 percent of cattle, 65 percent of all sheep, and 47 percent of all horses. People killed their livestock because the quotas left nothing to feed them; or they sold them so they would gain some money instead of giving the animals away for free; or because they wanted to keep the collectives from taking the animals (1986: 153, 179). Sometimes people would set their horses free rather than kill them. Many of the animals taken into collectives died from poor care. One result was that there was more grain available, since livestock were not eating it. A consequence of these slaughters, however, was that the collectives began with a more meager inventory, preventing them from a successful start.

> level of the party and government hierarchy instituted a plenipotentiary blitzkrieg upon the next successive regional level or sometimes even over the head of the regional level immediately subordinate and directly on to the district or village level. (Viola 1987: 77)

Inevitable effects of the disorganization were contradictory orders, turf battles, and intersectoral rivalry, as well as a huge proliferation of administrative bodies duplicating each other's work. "The confusion grew steadily worse at the lower levels of the administration" (Lewin 1968: 424–25). Reading through this literature one can only assent to Lewin's observation concerning the frenzied pace of October 1929 through February 1930, applicable to other collectivizing states as well:

> The State caused an upheaval in the countryside without having prepared its administrative organs to take the strain. This is why collectivization was carried out not by the normal machinery of village administration, but by *ad hoc* bodies hastily mobilized for the purpose. . . . [T]he cost of these policies in terms of losses suffered was enormous; seldom was any government to wreak such havoc in its own country. (1968: 515)

Third, reinforcing bureaucratic disorganization was the poor preparation of cadres. Again, Lewin: "During the previous year, nothing had been done to prepare the Party cadres for the important tasks that lay ahead of them, and all of a sudden they were being called upon to act as pioneers in a revolution which they did not understand and which was not of their choosing" (1968: 434–35). The mostly urban Party activists tended to regard villagers with incomprehension and disdain, while the few who were from rural areas were ill-trained; in the 1920s, only 4 percent of them had any secondary education (Viola 1987: 21). "All too often, the Party cells proved to be totally incompetent" (Lewin 1968: 126). There was a persistent shortage of the specialists whose work was supposed to create brilliantly successful farms that would attract ever more peasants. Although Russia had plenty of agricultural specialists who had worked to reform peasant agriculture before the revolution, the Party deemed them unreliable and dismissed them; with them went the entire network of rural institutions they had built up to organize the peasantry in support of government programs—which, coincidentally, had been the government's main effective presence in the villages (Yaney 1971: 9–12, 32–35). In these circumstances, collectivization entailed the center's unleashing a quarter million urban communists and police as agents of the authorities, "sent out from towns to cajole or bully 25 million peasant households into transforming their way of life, [with instructions] that a million of these households were to be treated as implacable enemies" (Davies 1980: 205). These militants had de facto power to do anything they could organize. Some took grain, some formed collectives, but there was no systematic control over them.

Problems with cadres appear throughout the literature on Soviet collectivization, as in that from Eastern Europe. As we have already seen for Romania, many rural Party members and officials refused to hand over the quotas assigned them, even at the risk of losing their Party membership. Entire Komsomol cells refused to participate in extracting grain (Manning 2001: 25). Officials and Party members alike declined to join the collectives. Where local Party cells were dominated by peasants, the people responsible for collecting taxes might instead ally with them. Penner reports for the Don region,

> In Atamansk county, at the most critical moment of the auditing season, the entire inspection committee, members of which included the village soviet chairman and the local cell secretary, went away on vacation. . . . In other cases, members of the village soviet, farmers themselves by occupation, deliberately underestimated their own sown acreage, warned their neighbors of an upcoming audit, or were the initiators in a village-wide tax evasion scheme. . . . A considerable number of farmers resigned from office early precisely because they did not agree with Soviet tax practices, while others stayed in office, but hindered the tax-collecting process at every turn. (Penner 1995: 260, 267)

In Riazan, according to a secret police report, members of the local soviet spoke out against collectivization, were sympathetic to the class enemy, gave kulaks breaks and extensions on their quotas, supported their own kulak relatives, and took bribes for lowering quotas (McDonald 2002: 104). They could be very explicit: "These are our people and if we apply the control figures [for grain quotas] in their entirety, then the peasants will tear us to pieces" (105). Examples such as these could be multiplied a thousandfold for every Soviet bloc country. They remind us that much of collectivization entailed a vigorous struggle in which the Party leadership strove to replace resistant local officials with others better suited to the task.

There was no shortage, however, of cadres who abused their authority in the opposite direction, using violence to overfulfill their targets in hopes of building their careers or perhaps settling personal grievances. Reports of such "excesses" are legion, as they are in Eastern Europe as well. On December 27, 1929, when Stalin decreed that kulaks should be liquidated, he offered only vague directives as to how.

> In the absence of any instructions which might have curbed their excesses, the local activists, wherever they were so inclined, set about the process of dekulakization in a manner that was chaotic, brutal and cruel. There was . . . a strong tendency among the activists to fall upon the enemy with the utmost ferocity, in order to have done with him as quickly as possible. (Lewin 1968: 487–88)

Unsurprisingly, the peasants resisted. They wrote petitions and appeals. They protested their quotas by withholding grain, they slaughtered livestock to keep the kolkhoz from getting them, they set fire to piles of grain to keep it out of the collectors' hands, they burned down the houses of activists—or even their own, to prevent their possessions from being confiscated. After their kulak neighbors were deported, three thousand peasants went to church wearing black mourning armbands; they refused to follow further orders to destroy kulak property. In meetings to persuade people to join the kolkhoz, women would shout "Christ has risen!," sing loudly to drown out the agitators, arrange to have someone disrupt the meeting by rushing in partway through and shouting "Fire!" or make a hubbub to prevent a vote, literally silencing the Party's agents. We find these forms of resistance repeated in every country undergoing collectivization.[66]

Active forms of peasant unrest increased from a reported 933 in 1927 to 27,586 in 1930, involving over two million people (Manning 2001: 33; Viola 1996: 4), and the resistance was often violent. Everywhere, peasants murdered cadres, lynched them, beat them up; local officials fled in panic to avoid being slaughtered by angry women. Rampaging peasants set upon one activist, bludgeoned him to death, gouged out his eyes, and disemboweled him.[67] Indeed, Viola (1996: 69, 130) argues that the violence of the resistance itself brought on more violent repression, the two feeding off each other. The pace of collectivization intensified as the rebellions did, until finally in March 1930 the Party was forced to retreat, signaled by Stalin's famous speech "Dizzy with Success." A massive wave of departures from already-formed kolkhozes then followed. In September the process was resumed more slowly; by the end of 1934, 90 percent of the land was in collective farms (Conquest 1986: 182). Overall, the rhythm was uneven: fairly slow collectivization up to 1928, a gradually more rapid increase to the frenzied pace of January and February 1930, a retreat, then a more moderated resumption in summer 1930. Comparable oscillations marked East European collectivizations also, albeit on a different time scale.

In his speech, Stalin asked how such excesses could be occurring and blamed the violence on the zeal of local officials "dizzy with success"—thereby signaling an effort to centralize control over the process and over the use of force (Getty and Naumov 1999: 114–18). Instruments for accomplishing that included the 1929 recruitment of urban proletarians known as the "25,000ers," politically active urban cadre workers and factory activists who were sent to the countryside to help with collectivization and then to remain as local officials and managers of the collectives (see Viola 1987). At issue, then, was the balance of initiative between the Party center in Moscow and lower-level authorities. We will revisit this question later, for it is important in Romanian collectivization as well: how much of the brutality of the process came from the center's inability to control subordinates, and to what extent did it tacitly encourage them? There

[66] This was true of every collectivization experience, including those in Asia. See, for instance, Lee and Yang 2007, for China; MacLean 2007: 42–46, on Vietnam.

[67] These examples come from Conquest 1986: 159; Fitzpatrick 1994b: 51; Manning 2001: 36; McDonald 2002: 89; Viola 1996: 59, 89, 146–49.

is evidence that the center was trying to rein in its subordinates, calling for discipline and issuing decrees such as one in March 1930 that threatened to fire any cadre who did not struggle against excesses (Viola 1987: 129). The Central Committee cabled a number of regions criticizing their leaders for running ahead and ignoring the center's plan—one regional boss had requested that his target for deported kulaks be raised from five thousand to fifteen thousand (Viola 2000: 16). The secret police, concerned that the dekulakization process was getting out of hand, ordered its officers to stick to the numbers of arrests assigned to them, not to exceed those, and to stop the competitions for ever-bigger numbers of arrests; "out-of-control" regions were condemned (Viola 2000: 21).

Historians of Soviet collectivization agree that lower administrative levels presented the central authorities with plans far exceeding what was expected and that Moscow lost control of repression to regional and local Party committees.[68] Yet Penner reports the testimony of plenipotentiaries being told by a superior, "gather another 1,000 poods or every last one of you will be arrested and sentenced," and of one official who announced, "Bring in 500 poods of grain each. It would be better to hang all of you, than to risk having one of us be sentenced" (Penner 1995: 354). From what level in the hierarchy did such initiatives emanate? Was there a clear break between Moscow and the "local officials" Stalin charged with mayhem in "Dizzy with Success" (which set the tone for blaming the excesses on local cadres and deflecting it from the center)? Did some high authorities officially condemn excesses while informally encouraging them? That interpretation gains traction if, as Conquest maintains, "the errors were universal" (1986: 162). What is certain is that collectivization had unleashed a vicious struggle for control across all sectors and levels of the apparatus, and that Moscow had lost the reins. The result was a campaign of unparalleled brutality, in which millions of people died. Although East European collectivizations too included repression and violence, they were on nothing like the Soviet scale, at least partly because Eastern Europe's communist leaders explicitly strove to avoid that (see, e.g., Stillman 1958: 69).

Viola concludes her study of the "25,000ers" thus:

> Although centrally instituted and endorsed, collectivization became, to a great extent, a series of ad hoc policy responses to the unbridled initiatives of regional and district rural party and government organs. Collectivization and collective farming were shaped less by Stalin and the central authorities than by the undisciplined and irresponsible activity of rural officials, the experimentation of collective farm leaders left to fend for themselves, and the realities of a backward countryside and a traditional peasantry which defied Bolshevik fortress storming. The center never managed to exert its control over the countryside as it had intended in the schema of revolution from above. (Viola 1987: 215–16)

[68] For Example, Davies 1980: 133; Getty and Naumov 1999: 523; Viola 1987: 216.

While this shift of emphasis from a top-down to a bottom-up vision of the process was highly salutary in its time and remains valuable, we would place the emphasis a bit differently, at least for some of the East European cases: collectivization was an essential means through which the Party-state centralized its hierarchy, consolidated the power of the leadership, and created itself for the future. If the Party was not in control throughout much of the process, it was much more so by the end of it—in Romania, certainly.[69]

Here, then, is the Soviet blueprint for collectivization: not an appealing precedent. It was a blueprint not just for a certain structure, policy, and implementation but for a plethora of problems as well, amply manifest in the collectivization process in Romania. Nearly all phases of the Soviet case are relevant to what would happen in Eastern Europe, often through negative example. We find the same structuring of the process, the uneven rhythm, the improvisations, the center's loss of control as cadres outstrip their mandate and exercise violence, the same desire to control the food supply, the same ill-prepared cadres, and the same internecine struggles for power within the Party-state. We also find striking similarities in the forms of peasant resistance: attacking and beating up activists; awaiting the "persuasion" teams with pitchforks, scythes, hoes, pistols, and axes; writing petitions and contestations; withholding their requisition quotas and killing or selling their draft animals; defending the kulaks whom the Party sought to stigmatize and deport; disrupting the meetings at which activists sought to persuade them to join; and so on.

In particular, we note the frequency of rebellious acts led by peasant women rather than men.[70] Whereas men perpetrated most hidden acts of terror, women specialized in public protests. They were particularly agitated by the collectivization of livestock, biting the hands of the men who came to take away their cows for fear their children would have no milk. During large disturbances, women would repossess the collectivized cattle and redistribute them to the original owners (McDonald 2002: 99). In the forefront of resistance to quotas, it was they who wielded pitchforks and scythes to obstruct the removal of grain or seeds from their villages, striving to protect the food supply. They defended those who were being dekulakized and organized against deportations, accompanying deportees several kilometers beyond the village while cursing the communists. In meetings they would band together to defeat official proposals

[69] Viola herself says something similar in her study of the role of the OGPU/NKVD in dekulakization, a process it began to manage even before the Politburo's authorization: "What this essentially meant was that Stalin and the Politburo had handed over control of a key operation with momentous political and economic implications to the OGPU, thereby allowing the OGPU to take the first step toward the institutional aggrandizement that would turn it into a state within a state by 1937" (2000: 37).

[70] See Viola 1986. Except where otherwise noted, the majority of these examples are from Viola 1996: chapter 6. In Romania, women were also at the forefront of revolts; see chapter 2. Women all over the world have led revolts to protest food prices or other issues that affect the reproduction of the household.

by creating a ruckus over which the activists could not be heard. Riots took on a common battle formation: men stood off to the side but were present to defend the women if necessary; women would come to the fore using their children as shields, in the firm—and mostly accurate—belief that the police would not touch them. We find similar gendering of protest in our Romanian data (see chapter 2), as does Andrew Port (2007) for eastern Germany; we assume it was more widespread.[71]

It is clear that peasant men and women were manipulating Soviet leaders' stereotypes, according to which women—whom they intended to emancipate through gender equality—were passive, irrational beings, incapable of agency or political consciousness and thus incapable of political protest (Viola 1996: 203). The authorities saw women's riots as merely evidence of hysteria or of their susceptibility to kulak influence. Viola cites a secret police report that says, "It was the condescending relations of the punitive organs to women . . . that enable[d] the strengthening of opinion about the invulnerability of women" (1996: 198). Furthermore, peasants manipulated not only stereotypes but Soviet ideology itself: men being pressed to join a collective would hide behind their wives, saying they wanted to join but their wives wouldn't let them, and since now there was equality of the sexes they had to treat their wives' opinions with respect (Viola 1987: 106). Indeed, many women showed up at meetings to drag their husbands off or threatened to divorce them if they joined; there were reports of real marital strife over the question.

As we often find among peasants cross-culturally, men bear responsibility for reproducing the community and their family's place in it, while women bear special responsibility for reproducing the household and feeding their children. When Soviet women rioted and chastised their husbands for considering the kolkhoz, they were not simply profiting from Soviet stereotypes. They were trying to ensure food for their families, engaging in a rearguard action to keep their households alive against the juggernaut that was crushing entire communities into pieces. Perhaps we see similar gendered responses to collectivization across the socialist bloc because of the centrality of family reproduction in all these places—a fact that communist parties came to appreciate, manipulating kinship relations and threatening family members so as to consolidate their power in the countryside.

One additional similarity across cases is the military language through which collectivization—along with so many other aspects of Party rule—was conducted. The story of Soviet collectivization and of Party rule more generally is shot through with military imagery, a feature integral to the East European cases as well. Throughout the communist period and especially in the collectiv-

[71] Polish journalists have written about women's resistance to collectivization there. See "Kołchoz we wsi Witosa," *Dziennik Polski*, August 13, 2009 (no author); Stanisław Podemski, "Wojny chłopskie," *Gazeta Wyborcza*, May 17, 2008; Alicja Zielińska, "Kołchoz? Nasze baby się zbuntowały!" *Kurier Poranny*, May 2, 2008. We thank Elżbieta Matynia for these references.

ization campaigns, military language was rampant: war, aliens, infiltration, fronts, enemies, sabotage, offensives, insurgents, killing, mobilization, battles, campaigns, and—the signature slogan of collectivization—class war. Where did it come from?

An argument of a general kind comes from Jowitt, who says that the Party as a form of bureaucratic charisma requires a combat environment (1992: 126). More concretely, however, it seems likely that Soviet leaders invented this language during the civil war in 1918–21, when the country was little more than an armed camp; thereafter it infused the language of East European communisms as they imitated the Soviet model. The Party's first response to the grain crisis in 1927–28 was to reinstate immediately the system of requisitions that had saved the Bolsheviks during the civil war; the situation now was defined as a "war for grain," and predictably, it called for a massive recruitment of volunteers to make up for the lack of rural cadres: the "25,000ers" mentioned above. This recruitment effort fed upon war metaphors. Memories and imagery from the heroic civil war inspired over 70,000 workers to volunteer, motivated by the certainty that the nation was at war and collectivization was necessary to its survival. Of these, 27,519 were selected, many of whom had served in the Red Army (Viola 1987: 43–44).

A return to the methods of the civil war was easy, for cadres and bureaucrats already had the habits ingrained from the earlier period (Lewin 1968: 482). Moreover, Trotsky observed in *The Revolution Betrayed* that demobilizing five million Russian soldiers proved crucial to forming the bureaucracy, as military commanders took leading posts and introduced everywhere the regime that had brought success in the civil war (cited in Lewin 1968: 483). Davies writes of discussions in the November 1929 Party plenum, as a gradual consensus emerged that the kulaks' economic power must be destroyed; Stalin and other top leaders presented the problem as an all-out war, referred to those charged with resolving it as an "army" with a "staff," and spoke of the class struggle as "just like at the front" (1980: 173). According to Maurice Hindus, a student told him in 1930, "This was war, and is war. The *koolack* had to be gotten out of the way as completely as an enemy at the front. He is the enemy at the front. He is the enemy of the *kolkhoz*" (cited in Davies 1980: 173). Indeed, some cadres found the job to be worse than war: one Party activist recalled, "Each one of us would have preferred to be back at the front again" (Penner 1995: 42). The imagery produced its own reality: according to Viola, the effects of the 1930 rebellion included further fueling the militarization of society, enhancing the atmosphere of enemies all around. The countryside became a siege state, "an enormous staging ground for the amassing and training of legions of troops loyal to the state's apparatus of repression" (1987: 179). Another effect of using military metaphors through talk of "battles," "offenses," and "shoot-outs with kulaks" was that they mobilized an ongoing feeling of urgency and excitement, which dovetailed nicely with the leaders' insistence on the need for haste

(36). Moreover, the sense of urgency strengthened Party unity: "The atmosphere of the Civil War was . . . in effect recreated. This was not merely useful against the peasantry. It also gave all the benefits of an emergency to the feelings of the Party activists. Moderation was, or was to be, crushed or swept away on a wave of partisan emotion" (Conquest 1986: 111).

Thus, circumstances peculiar to the Bolsheviks' revolutionary experience of civil war shaped the military language and permanent siege mentality through which collectivization would be pursued throughout Eastern Europe, and elsewhere as well. With this, the Party's entire language was coded as male—appropriately enough, for the highly patriarchal order it was constructing, but in flagrant contradiction with the expressed goal of gender equality.

* * *

Paul Gregory writes, "Collectivization was an institutional mechanism to control grain collections. If peasants had been willing to sell to the state at its [very low] prices, collectivization would not have been necessary, as a June 1929 statement by Mikoian attested" (2004: 39). This is true, but as Jowitt (1978) indicated decades ago, it was far more than that. To a Soviet leadership still unsure of its control over society and particularly over its vast peasant masses, heavily indebted to some western countries and boycotted by others, with rapid industrialization seeming its only hope of survival yet lacking the resources to achieve it—in these circumstances, destroying the peasants' way of life was a route both to control over grain and to heightened stability and power. Even if, as seems likely, Stalin had no clear plan for collectivization at first, he was a master at recognizing the lessons in unexpected turns of events and profiting from them. In addition, the process molded the emergent Party-state, providing grounds for strengthening the security police (so central to the later purges), for shaping broader police practices (through social policies leading to mass migration, banditry, homeless children in the cities, etc.), for replacing rural officialdom with more committed Party cadres, and for permanently alienating the labor force in the countryside. Collectivization played a central role in the formation of Stalin's Soviet Union. It would have these same effects in Eastern Europe as well.

Collectivization in Eastern Europe

The collectivization of agriculture in Eastern Europe took a number of forms, most of which followed the Soviet experience, though with significant differences among them. Soviet collectivization was distinctive from all the others, however, in a number of respects. First, when Stalin began to collectivize agriculture, there was no model of any kind for how to accomplish this enormous task—pushing twenty-five million peasant households into collective forms of production. By 1928, when the operation was underway, the Bolsheviks had barely established control over the Soviet Union; in 1930, collectivization was still an empty concept (Fitzpatrick 1994b: 7). All the East European cases, by contrast, did have a model: that of the Soviet Union, which was eager to export it. They too lacked organizational capacity, but not a sense of what the result should look like or how to get there.

A second difference derives from this: the Soviet Union collectivized on its own, with a sense of mission to develop itself differently from the West (Kotkin 1995: 12). East Europeans, by contrast, had it largely forced on them. Not that there was no communist support in Eastern Europe: there was, especially in Czechoslovakia (not just in industrial centers but in the countryside) and in Bulgaria as well. In Yugoslavia and Albania, communists led successful resistance movements against the Nazis and came to power on their own as national liberators.[72] With the possible exception of these latter two, however, it is doubtful that communists would have taken power anywhere without Soviet backing; in most East European countries, communist ideas had minimal traction. In consequence, far fewer of Eastern Europe's cadres were committed and enthusiastic, able to persuade peasants into collectives from their own conviction. If Stalin's Politburo brought collectivization upon the Soviet Union, then what brought it to the satellites was the Red Army. The fact that most East Europeans saw collective farming as an alien imposition aroused hostility to it from the outset.

Third, there was a fundamental difference in the relation of peasants to land in the Soviet Union (particularly Russia), compared with that in Eastern Europe. In 1927, 95.5 percent of Russian peasant households lived in villages with communal forms of land tenure (Lewin 1968: 85),[73] whereas in Eastern Europe such communities were exceedingly rare. Instead, households owned land, sharecropped it, or worked for those who owned it. The difference was significant, for it meant that Soviet activists could often collectivize entire communities via a single vote of the village council (see Fitzpatrick 1994b: 44), without having to persuade peasants in small groups or one at a time—a very labor-intensive activity for communist parties not well endowed with cadres. This difference may have contributed to the Soviets' ability to complete collectivization in an enormous country in much less time than was required in far smaller East European ones.[74]

[72] Tito's communist partisans won over many Yugoslavs during World War II, but in that case Tito's umbrella also brought together many people who were not communists.

[73] According to Lewin, the Stolypin reforms introduced early in the twentieth century had made inroads into these communal villages (*mirs*), which fell from containing over 90 percent of the peasantry to below 50 percent; by the 1920s, however, many communities had reverted to communal tenure (1968: 85).

[74] Lynne Viola (personal communication) doubts that the *mir* had much of an effect on the speed of collectivization, attributing it to the blitz of plenipotentiaries and other outsiders. We beg to differ, based on what we have learned about "persuasion work" in villages lacking communal tenure.

Fourth, collectivization in the multinational Soviet Union had a stronger component of denationalization than occurred in Eastern Europe (see, e.g., Gribincea 1996: 130; Lévesque 2006: 1; Martin 2001: 320–25; Swain 2003). Part of this was intentional, part was simply an effect of expropriating and deporting national elites in areas like Ukraine and, later, Moldova and the Baltic states, an action that struck at the heart of potential national movements. Part was the result of Stalin's fear that in the impending war, minorities would form a fifth column against the Soviet state (Shearer 2001: 530–32). More than in Eastern Europe, Soviet collectivization involved mass deportations of minority peoples; resistance to it was stronger in the non-Russian areas (Martin 2001: 294) and was often couched as a fight for national existence. This is not to say that there was nothing comparable in Eastern Europe. In several countries, for example, Germans were targeted for discriminatory treatment, as ineluctably "bourgeois" and as representatives of the fascist wartime enemy. In Romania, beginning in 1946 Germans were deported for war reparations labor in the Soviet Union, and those who returned to Romania thereafter might subsequently be deported again *within* the country. Nonetheless, this link between nationality and collectivization policy was less marked than in the Soviet experience.

A final difference between the Soviet and the East European cases was that the latter did not face grain crises as catastrophic as the former. There were indeed serious food shortages and famines, and there were war reparations that had to be paid to the Soviets in foodstuffs, but two things mitigated the food problem. First, according to Mosely, World War II bequeathed to these countries the systems the Nazis had put in place for requisitioning food from peasant households; those systems would initially help to supply the necessary grain. "The satellite countries, unlike Russia of 1929, ha[d] an existing administrative alternative to collectivization" (Mosely 1958: 62). This did not mean the grain would flow automatically, but at least the infrastructure was there. A second mitigating factor applies to only some East European countries: Czechoslovakia, East Germany, Poland, and to some extent Hungary. They had higher industrial capacity than did the Soviet Union, and correspondingly, the "primitive accumulation" plan that underlay Soviet collectivization was less urgent for them. It remained a factor, however, in the Balkan countries.

By 1948 if not earlier, communist parties had fully taken power in each East European state. Sometime between 1945 and 1948, most had carried out land reforms of varying magnitude. Per capita, the most land was redistributed in Hungary (where two-thirds of the peasants had been landless) and Poland, then Albania, then Romania and Czechoslovakia, then Yugoslavia, and last Bulgaria. Where a great deal of land was redistributed, the communists initially gained some popularity—a clear objective of the reform—though recipients would later have to give it away.

In 1948, at Soviet urging, the Cominform expelled Yugoslavia on the grounds that Tito was too independent, was ignoring class struggle in the countryside, and was not drawing the appropriate lessons from the Soviet experience but instead trying to build socialism with private property. The participants affirmed the wisdom of collectivization and the leaders of the remaining countries fell into line. For the most part, they followed a similar trajectory at the outset: the initial drive began in 1948–49, interrupted by a period of retreat after Stalin's death in 1953; the process was then resumed around 1955, sometimes with interruptions (e.g., the Hungarian revolution of 1956) and often using less coercive tactics; by 1962 if not earlier it was brought to conclusion in Albania, Bulgaria, Czechoslovakia, East Germany, Hungary, and Romania.[75] Poland and Yugoslavia began to collectivize but did not pursue the second stage, remaining with large percentages of privately owned land. The process was fastest and most violent in Bulgaria, which closely followed the Soviet procedure and finished by 1958, and slowest in Romania, which completed it in 1962.[76]

On the whole, Eastern Europe proved harder to collectivize than had the Soviet Union. This is partly because most leaders tried to hold down the pace so as to avoid the excesses of Soviet violence,[77] and partly because peasants in Eastern Europe had a longer history of private landowning and were harder to pry loose; they had invested much more in their farms than had Russian peasants. And as Stillman puts it, "The apathy of the Eastern European mass parties and the absence of any genuinely national revolutionary élan . . . made it impossible (or unwise) to mount more than a calculated war of attrition against the peasants" (1958: 69). Moreover, the marked change in climate after Stalin's death, including Khrushchev's rapprochement with Tito in 1955, meant that from then on, greater divergence was permitted as each country adapted collectivization to its own peculiarities. (The quashing of the Hungarian revolution in 1956 showed, however, that there were limits to departures from the Soviet example.)

As a consequence, their paths had differed considerably by the 1960s. The countries fell into three groups: (1) Poland and Yugoslavia, as mentioned; (2) Albania, Bulgaria, and Romania (as well as the Baltic republics, taken into the Soviet Union with the war), which all achieved more or less full collectivization on the Soviet model; and (3) Czechoslovakia, East Germany, and Hungary,

[75] By this time, more cadres had been trained than in the earlier round, enabling districts to overwhelm villages with activists (Ross 2000: 113). Most of the countries introduced alternative forms of cooperation less radical than fully collectivizing (on the model of the Soviet TOZ) but eventually turned these into collective farms by fiat.

[76] The process was officially declared complete in 1962, although many peasant households were still not in collectives by then.

[77] According to Migev (cited in Szalontai 2003: 429), Stalin "advised the Bulgarian leaders not to . . . copy blindly the Soviet experience of the 30s and to artificially heighten the tension in the country." We thank Balázs Szalontai for this reference.

which ended with modified forms of collectives, as well as greater possibilities for investing in agriculture owing to their greater industrial development compared with the others (Enyedi 1967: 362). It is probably no coincidence that the countries most resembling the Soviet Union and least endowed with industry collectivized fully, the better to pursue industrialization with forced savings and a proletarianized rural labor force. The diverging trajectories arose from each country's specificities on a number of variables, such as the Communist Party's size, its organization and support in the countryside, existing levels of industrialization, the balance of forces between peasantry and regime, and (related to this) the extent to which the government had made itself independent of Moscow. Ironically, because Soviet collectives owed much to traditional peasant practices, what Eastern Europe received was as much Russian (or Ukrainian) as it was Soviet, requiring ever-greater efforts at accommodation where rural economies departed more from Russian forms. We will not offer a full discussion of each country but merely note some of the differences.[78]

In Hungary, initial attempts to collectivize turned villages into battlegrounds, but both in 1953 and with the 1956 uprising the campaign was interrupted and peasants withdrew from the collectives *en masse*. After the uprising was put down, the new Party leadership was wholly dependent on the Soviets for its existence; it was completely compromised in the eyes of the peasantry—won over in 1945 by the large land distribution—who now saw it for the Soviet puppet it was. In pursuing collectivization nonetheless, the Party leadership had to make a number of concessions, which included retaining some reforms passed during the uprising, making expertise readily available to the collectives and their workers, paying rent for land brought into collectives, downplaying ideology in favor of results, and in general being willing to pay some of the costs of developing agriculture rather than simply squeezing it dry for industry (Adair 2001: 144). The Hungarian leadership departed early from Stalin's policy of liquidating the kulaks, who were instead invited into the collectives in hopes that their high status would attract their fellows to join. These divergences plus experiments with various forms of contracting and a robust second economy made Hungary's collectivized agriculture the most successful in the bloc (see Swain 1985). In this case, as István Rév argued in his famous paper "The Advantages of Being Atomized" (1987), the peasants forced the regime to a draw.

Poland offers a useful contrast.[79] Here, as in Hungary, the regime was completely dependent on the Soviet Union at the outset—which was unfortunate, given Poles' Russophobe inclinations—and the Party was very poorly organized in rural areas, where there were few Party members. Its first leader, Gomułka, attempted to keep a certain distance from the Soviets and was purged for it in 1948, but not before he had made plain his view that although collec-

[78] For information on these trajectories, see Creed 1998; Hann 1980; Kideckel 1993; and especially Pryor 1992.

[79] This summary is drawn from Crampton 1994 and Sokolovsky 1990.

tivization might be strategically correct, in Poland it would have to wait, for no Polish government could last without support from the peasantry. Given the amount of wartime devastation, the process was begun slowly and not pushed very far. Brutality was at its lowest in Polish collectivization, with the Party disciplining cadres who violated its proclamations against the use of force. In 1956 Gomułka returned to power and reasserted his drive for increased independence from the Soviet Union, renouncing collectivization (it comprised 23 percent of the land as of 1956). While the other bloc countries launched their second wave, then, most of Poland's collectives fell apart; the leadership preferred private agriculture as both a better source of food for the country's sizable working class and, therefore, a more certain route to regime stability. Instead of collectivizing, the government would put resources into agriculture and build up the state farm sector—Gomułka's "collectivization without peasants." In Sokolovsky's judgment, what kept Poland free of collectives was the government's desire for greater independence and its consequent need for a solid base among its peasant and working classes (1990: 84).[80] The outcome in Yugoslavia was similar, and for broadly similar reasons.[81]

East Germany offers yet another variant.[82] There, the leadership—like Hungary's and Poland's—was highly dependent on the Soviet Union but had initially declared that it would not collectivize. In the context of an agrarian crisis in 1952, however, that decision was revisited. Progress was slow at first, owing to the Party's weak control over its rural cadres, who were dubious of the benefits of collectivizing and were as likely to dissuade farmers from joining as to convince them. Resistance was very stiff, with nasty reprisals against cadres. After the relaxation in 1953, when masses of collectivists withdrew from their farms, a milder campaign was continued, but in 1958 a second assault began with extreme force. By this time the Party had trained many more cadres, and—much as in the Soviet Union—it blitzed the countryside with urban activists. Whereas previous persuasion brigades had three to five members, they now had forty to fifty agitators from the police, mass organizations, and factories; decrees sent out as many as half of all local functionaries "and required worker brigades to live in the villages in order to assure a steady barrage of exhortation" (Port 2007: 221). The intensity was such that, Ross reports, in one district there was one agitator for every four farmers (2000: 116). With this ratio, the country was fully collectivized in two years. Here the rural population

[80] There are numerous explanations for why Poland was allowed to continue without collectivizing its agriculture. Among them are that the Polish Communist Party never fully consolidated its position in the countryside; that the Party needed to cement its relations with workers in the new lands and would not risk the food supply; that with the largest peasantry in the bloc and one of the smallest communist parties, enforcing collectivization would require resources beyond what the government could muster; and that changes in Poland's boundaries made it advisable to give rural inhabitants in the new territories a stake in the land.

[81] See Woodward 1995 for a discussion of collectivization in Yugoslavia.

[82] This summary is informed by Ross 2000 and Port 2007.

gained no leverage over the Party, as in Hungary. Nor did Party leaders need rural supporters, as in Poland, given that over 40 percent of the labor force worked in industry and that the East German leaders (unlike the Polish) had no plan to increase autonomy from the Soviets.[83]

Romania had some elements of these cases but in its own peculiar mix. Like Poland, at the end of World War II it had a minuscule Communist Party poorly organized in rural areas, shared a border with the Soviet Union, and also had a history of Russophobia. Its communist elite was completely dependent on the Soviet Union, like Poland's and Hungary's, but initially had few plans for greater independence, which meant less reliance on peasant support (hence less peasant leverage against collectivization) than was true in Poland. Unlike Poland or East Germany, its level of industrialization was low: in 1950, 74 percent of the population was employed in agriculture and only 12 percent in industry. Making slower progress than Bulgaria against heavy peasant opposition, the pace of its campaign resembled Czechoslovakia's, abating between 1953 and 1955, then gradually picking up speed after 1956. Between 1958 and 1962 a concerted assault—driven in part by a deal in which Soviet troops left Romania in exchange for evidence of loyalty—brought most of the peasantry into collective farms. At no point had the peasants found themselves with any leverage against the Party, as had Hungarian peasants. Therefore, the leadership made no concessions in collectivization policy (no reforms, constant propaganda, and no funds to develop agriculture, which was instead sacrificed to industrialization). The country's collective farms remained among the least successful in the bloc.

These variations aside, the stories of collectivization in Eastern Europe contain many similarities to the Soviet one: land reforms, communist parties that were not well organized in the countryside, problems with securing reliable cadres who would actually join the collectives themselves, a fair amount of chaos and improvisation, lower-level officials often running ahead of or ignoring directives from the center, an active police presence, the pursuit of "class struggle" in the villages and a brutal assault on village social structures, the use of force to secure "voluntary" membership in collectives, and widespread, sometimes-violent resistance from the villagers subjected to it. In many, one result was a strengthened, more centralized Party-state. In all, the beginnings of this process were overseen by resident Soviet advisors to the Central Committees.

In one crucial respect, however, no East European country emulated Soviet practice: all utilized coercion, the so-called kulaks were persecuted, hounded, and humiliated, and their class basis was destroyed, but they were not "liquidated" as in the Soviet Union (that is, they were not executed or deported to anything like the same degree). This single departure from Soviet policy may account for not only the slower pace of collectivizing in Eastern Europe—recall

[83] This figure (for 1950) is diminished by the Soviet removal of a number of East German industries as war reparations.

that dekulakization was what compelled so many Soviet peasants into collectives so fast—but also a lower level of violence. There was indeed repression and people died, but not on the Soviet scale. A Maramureş peasant summarized the contrast succinctly: "Collectivization in Romania didn't use as much force as in Russia. In Russia, when it started, they executed the old people, the owners. Here, no; they just sent them off to work and then they died later."[84]

This does not mean that Eastern Europe had no gulags: each one did, for political prisoners and other important "enemies"—Romania's infamous Danube Canal and prison system for "reeducation," Czechoslovakia's Jachymov uranium mines, and so on. Yet although in many places kulaks might be deported for a period of time to frighten villagers into submission and zealous cadres in one or another area may have persecuted kulaks with excessive force, for the most part comparable mass expulsions and countless deaths of kulaks from cold and starvation did not occur. Instead, communist parties struggled over what to do with them—send them away or allow them into the collectives, which they might sabotage from within—but in the end kulaks joined collective farms. In many communities, that was the point at which large numbers of villagers who had resisted joining gave in and did so. In this sense, the class struggle in the countryside and the battle over collectivization were paradoxically won not by the communists but by resilient village hierarchies.

[84] D. V., Kligman interview.

Chapter 2

The Village Community and the Politics of Collectivization, 1945–62

> In constructing socialism, the goal followed by the members united in the collective farm is, through well-organized work done together and using shared means of production, to assure our victory over the *chiaburs*, exploiters and enemies of the working people, to do away forever with the darkness and backwardness of small individual farms, and to obtain instead the most production possible.
> —*Annual Report, GAC "Scânteia," Ieud, 1952*[1]

> When the CC representatives leave Bucharest for the regions, then even the most remote houses in the most remote village should know that they will be collecting quotas, and not even the smallest fly will get away with not giving absolutely everything it is supposed to give.
> —*Romania's collectivization czar, Ana Pauker, 1952*[2]

In her pioneering work on Soviet collectivization, Lynne Viola conceives of it as an important means of modernization, including economic development, state-building, colonization of the peasantry, geographic expansion and border defense, and political centralization. Here she joins James Scott (1998), who places the entire Soviet experiment in a "high modernist" mode as a variant of an Enlightenment project, offering an alternative to the modern state and modern industrial forms. For the particulars of these kinds of processes, both owe a debt to Charles Tilly, whose work on state-making gave paramount importance to the problem of controlling the food supply (e.g., Tilly 1975). The story of Romania's collectivization is the story of how the Romanian Communist Party, with its Soviet advisors, managed to gain near-total control over the food supply and place it in the service of industrial development, in a manner rather different from those that Tilly and others have described for Western Europe.

Providing an overview of that process is the task of the present chapter. We begin, however, with an outline of social organization in Romanian villages prior to the Second World War, for villages were the targets of the collectivization process and the loci at which activists intervened most directly in peasants' lives during the campaign. After describing the place of kinship and social in-

[1] See DJAN MM, Fond Comitetul Raional PCR Vişeu, file 42/1952/v. V, 50. This report is signed by the Secretary of the Party cell, Ieud.

[2] Ana Pauker, meeting with representatives of the CC and the government on problems with collections. ANIC, Fond C.C. al P.C.R.–Cancelarie, file 3 /1952, 11 (RLA).

equality in villages and their accompanying notions of personhood and identity, we summarize the main features of Romanian collectivization, which we then dissect in subsequent chapters.

Village Social Organization before World War II

Defining "In" and "Out"

Unlike Soviet Russia, with its communal villages wherein revolution and civil war had left the state with a relatively weak presence, in Romania (organized on the French model) the presence of the state in the countryside was strong, and collectivization would strengthen it further. Although the primary administrative unit in Romania, as in France, was the commune, the primary units of inclusion and exclusion were villages, which had firm boundaries. In lowland areas (where collectivization was concentrated), they acquired this quality with the decomposition of feudalism, abolished variously between 1848 and 1864 in different parts of what became Romania. During feudal times the unit of belonging had been the feudal estate, bounded not by villages but by the lord's domains, for serfs could be moved at will from one village to another in which the lord needed more labor. The end of serfdom gave rise to settlements with both relatively stable (impropriated) peasants and more-mobile laborers seeking work on large estates or land to sharecrop. A modicum of fixity in village places came from taxation and inheritance of land (more significant in Transylvania) and from relations of patronage with large landowners (more significant in the rest of the country). Further enhancing rootedness-in-place was a major land reform legislated in 1921.

Kinship connections provided additional fixity: among village toponyms in Romania we find a number based on names that can be thought of as clan or lineage designations. For instance, the suffix -eşti (as in Bucureşti) localizes the people of an ancestor (Bucur) in a kin referent that is also territorial. (There are many other kinds of place names, but the ones indicating localizations of kin groups are particularly suggestive.) As compared with the more diversified lowland villages, kinship-based inclusion and solidarity were particularly high in upland regions where the feudal economy did not penetrate, such as in the kin-based communal villages whose formation and workings were brilliantly analyzed by Romanian historical sociologist Henri Stahl (1958–65, 1980). In both lowland and upland villages prior to World War II, defending land resources against an influx of competitors pressed toward relative village endogamy and a localist resistance to "outsiders" (*străini*). Villages were not fully endogamous (partly a function of their size) but tended in that direction.

Socialism would uproot and redivide space, as collectivization effectively broke apart the tight village communities that defined "in" and "out" for countless people (see also Viola et al. 2005). Breaking open communities meant destroying networks of relationships that rooted people in villages, and taking away their land uprooted them further. Outsiders of many kinds came in. The new state and collective farms often violated village boundaries, for villages might contain more than one collective, or part of a collective, or a collective plus part or all of a state farm. Party cadres violated village boundaries too: they were nomadic, with policies designed to keep them from rooting (see chapter 3). But most important, what defined "in" would become *class or Party membership*, not villages. Fomenting class warfare—framed expressly as a matter of "in" and "out"—was central to this. Villages contained enemies that must be driven out: in the Soviet Union they were physically expelled, but in Romania they were primarily persecuted, humiliated, stigmatized, and finally integrated into collective farms. Thus, with socialism, ways of determining "in" and "out" ceased to be based mainly on territory except for the largest entity, the socialist bloc, ringed by an iron curtain.

Kinship and Hierarchy

To appreciate the techniques by which collectivization took place requires an idea of the social organization of Romanian villages before the communists came to power. This varied somewhat by region and economic/ecological adaptations (predominantly grain farming, mixed grain and animal husbandry, predominantly fishing or animal herding, mining, etc.). Certain principles, however, were widespread: kinship as the main organizing idiom for cooperation and social reproduction, households as the basic units for production and consumption, and land- (or herd-) based status hierarchies as the chief form of inequality.[3] We will concentrate our brief summary on these elements.

Households generally consisted of patrilocal stem or nuclear families and might contain people beyond immediate kin (servants, more-distant relatives, neighbors). Relations among them were organized by kinship, understood as a practical, performative kind of embedded social relationship that involved more than just bloodlines or marriage relations. It meant specific behaviors and expectations, such as cooperating for agricultural work and life-cycle rituals, helping out with money or other favors, caring for the elderly (who might not be one's parents) in exchange for inheriting their land, and so forth. Reckoned bilaterally, kinship provided a person with a broad and flexible range of possible "relatives," and a patrilateral bias shaped loose kin groupings known as *neamuri*,[4] extended family lines we will call lineages. A well-developed kinship institution was ritual godparenthood, which linked families of unequal means

[3] See Jowitt 1978: 21. On village social organization, see Kligman and Verdery 2006, from which we have also drawn.

[4] Sing. *neam* (pronounced n^{e}AHM; the superscript *e* indicates an on-glide). *Neam* can also be

through marital and baptismal sponsorship. The junior couple (*fini*) provided labor, deference, and perhaps votes for village office while the senior couple (*naşi*) who sponsored them would mediate disputes and provide loans, protection, and favors. Their relationship was affectively very rich.

These were not egalitarian villages. At the pinnacle of the rural hierarchy, especially in southern and eastern Romania,[5] were the large landlords (*boieri*), owning hundreds if not thousands of hectares. They served as godparents and patrons for many of the poor peasants, who were wholly dependent on them for access to land in exchange for labor on the estates (see, e.g., Eidelberg 1974; Lăţea 2009). This interdependence is critical to understanding both the vulnerability of the poor peasantry once the large estates were liquidated and also their revolts in the late 1940s (sometimes successful) against the deportation of their landlords (see Iordachi 2003: 18, for Dobrogea, and Dobrincu 2002, for Bihor and Arad). A second set of people whom villagers placed above themselves were the village "intellectual elite," usually consisting of the priest, teacher(s), and notary. Often these people had little or no land, but the symbolic capital contained in education outweighed the criteria by which the peasants ranked themselves. Higher education conferred high status and was something the most ambitious peasants aspired to: educating one or more of their children was a prime mobility strategy.

Below these kinds of people was the hierarchical universe of the peasantry itself. Distinguishing households and lineages from one another were differences in social standing, based on both material wealth and symbolic and social capital. An important idiom for status was *visibility*: some families or households were more "visible" (*văzuţi*) than others. For those accorded greater and lesser status honor we find a variety of terms. A high-status peasant or shepherd was not just *văzut* but known as *gazdă* (a property owner and household head), *bogat*/*bogătan*/*bogătaş* (rich), or *gospodar* (a good manager). Beneath the highest-status peasants were "middle" peasants (*oameni de mijloc* or *mijlocaşi*), and, at the bottom, the "poor" (*săraci*), "needy" (*lipsiţi*), "landless" (*fără pământ*), and so on. These categories had moral entailments. In the rural status ideology, being prosperous was considered a sign of virtue and hard work: villagers often attributed such qualities to the well-to-do even if they were lacking. Being poor indicated lack of character, laziness, or bad habits such as drinking (rather than, say, simple bad luck). Such qualities were thought to be inherited.

Despite the designations of "wealthy" and "middle," the amounts of land in question were generally very modest. Table 2.1 gives the distribution of land for

---

used to refer simply to one's relatives, with no implication of a membership grouping. A *neam mare* or great (large) family had status rather than size connotations, as did a small family.

[5] In the interwar period such landlords were somewhat less prevalent in Transylvania, where the agrarian reform of 1921 had been more stringently applied so as to undermine the largely Hungarian landed elite.

Table 2.1
Distribution of Agricultural Land by Farm Size, Romania, 1930

Size Class (Ha)	*% of All Farms*	*% of Cultivated Land*
0–5	75.0	35.8
0–1	18.6	2.1
1–3	33.5	14.4
3–5	22.9	19.3
5–10	17.1	24.2
10–20	5.5	13.3
20–50	1.7	7.9
50–100	.4	4.2
>100	.4	14.6

Source: Roberts 1951: 370, table xix.

Romania as a whole in 1930, showing that three-fourths of all farms contained under five hectares. Most of these farms produced primarily for subsistence, marketing only what was necessary for taxes and other cash needs—except for those who marketed so as to buy more land. With 92 percent of all farms being 10 hectares or smaller, it is clear that most prosperous villagers were far from being serious exploiters of labor.[6] (This did not stop the communists, however, from finding "exploiters" among them, as chapter 6 will show.) The struggle to obtain land was a constant of peasant life and a major theme in literature, including the famous novels *Ion* (*John*) by Liviu Rebreanu and *Crima pentru pământ* (*Crime for Land*) by Dinu Săraru.

Land ownership was the principal basis for prosperity and status, but also important was the number of animals one worked with, or (for shepherds) the size of one's herds. Although we write primarily of land, our discussion of status differences applies to ownership of animals as well. The amount of land and animals required for "wealthy" status differed by community and region, but a crucial ingredient was having enough land to be able to control one's own labor process and not have to work for others (see below). Evidently, these were the values of households of means, but they had wide currency, and the poor often strove to realize them.

In many areas, landholding and kinship were intertwined, vestiges of more extensively developed kin institutions from previous centuries described by Stahl. A series of Romanian words referring to land and kin share a single root, *moş-*. A midwife is a *moaşă* (also an old woman), a *moş* is an old man, grandfather, or elder, and *strămoşi* are ancestors. *Moşia* is an estate, a holding; *moşteni* is to inherit; an heir is a *moştenitor*. Thus, one root enters into talking about

[6] Stan (2001: 96), drawing from Roberts (1951), points out that in 1941, family members accounted for 83 percent of exploited labor; a "combination of family labor and salaried [workers]" accounted for 15 percent, and "salaried workers" only accounted for but 1.5 percent.

ancestors, land, inheritances, and birth, as well as their reproduction, connecting material patrimony to a kinship unit. (Note that this ideology sees landless people as having no history and no kin.)[7] Although land commodification attenuated these connections beginning in the late nineteenth century, vestiges of them persisted even into the postsocialist period.[8] The kinship shadow of landholdings made "giving away" one's land in collectivization more than a simply individual matter: an aim of that process was to get land out of the hands of peasants, but those hands were not individual, for land was embedded in kin groups, households, and networks that were reproduced over time. To obtain it, cadres would have to disrupt those connections.

In communities of cultivators, landowning determined a number of aspects of a household's trajectory. First, together with kinship it determined local political office: the mayor (elected by the villagers) was usually from one of the wealthier as well as larger families and had numerous kin (including ritual kin), who provided him with a "clan" basis for mobilizing votes. Local power was concentrated in him (and, in some parts of the country, in councils of village elders). Second, the amount of a household's land in relation to its offspring affected how the children could marry and, thus, the cross-generational reproduction of family status. Daughters generally received some land as dowry, if possible, and sons divided the remaining inheritance. For all but the landless, land transfer (actual or willed) was the condition of marriage. It was possible to marry well without much land, but difficult. Therefore, parents exercised great power over their children, especially in the better-off households. Because the senior generation withheld a portion of their land until they died, land also served as a form of pension. Control over land was how the household head controlled the behavior of his children and ensured care in his old age. This is vividly seen in the following comment one respondent attributed to his ailing father-in-law on the day he joined the collective:

> My father-in-law said to me, "Sign up, we have no more choice. Since I can't work, if somebody wants to give me some bread, fine, and if not, I'll die." Because he lived from the land. "So, from now on if you want to give me something to eat, that's good, and if not, don't! I don't have anything anymore. I don't have a right to anything."[9]

[7] The centrality of kinship to people's self-conceptions informs the view we sometimes heard that activists and Securitate officers were people "without mother or father," indicating their supposed immunity to the kinds of obligations and sentiments that governed normal human beings.

[8] Vultur found something like them in Domaşnea: A respondent replied thus to the question of how things were going after he got his land back, "I'm fine! We have our estate back [*avem iar moşie*]!" nicely illustrating the person-possession links (2003a: 78). Verdery's work on decollectivization in Vlaicu in the 1990s also elicited this kin-land ideology, such as one woman's reply to a question about her lengthy lawsuit to recover land: "I have this land from my ancestors [*de la moşi-strămoşi*]! How could I let [X] keep the field I got from my ancestors?" Many villagers justified their claim to land by saying, "Because it's my inheritance! It's from my ancestors!"

[9] 72, Verdery interview.

Elderly people without children would either adopt a child from a large family or make an arrangement with someone to care for them in old age in return for inheriting their land.

Third, landowning conditioned the control of labor, which is particularly important for what happened during collectivization. Wealthier peasants generally had too much land to work with family labor alone; at peak periods they drew upon their neighbors, kin, and ritual kin. Indeed, a prosperous peasant was socially defined by not working alone but by having the resources that enabled him to mobilize others—by having *wealth in people*. Hiring extra day labor or having servants was one common way of doing so; ritual kinship was another. A couple with many ritual kin might call a "work party" at which their *fini* and perhaps other families would come and help with the harvest, after which all would be treated to food and drink. This kind of "big man" arrangement is common to many societies throughout the world. One did not have to be rich to have others working with one, however, for families associated with each other to make the job of plowing or harvesting or herding go more quickly and easily. These simple labor exchanges might involve neighbors or kin, whether close or distant; they signified that a family had land or other means of production, could organize the work of themselves and others for it, and therefore were people of good moral character. In these kinds of communities, that was what counted.[10]

An additional source of labor was from mountainous areas in Romania, whence people would come each year to lowland villages to help with the harvest. Sometimes they formed regular friendships with particular families and would return year after year. A few might decide to move down permanently to escape poor conditions at home; but even though they continued to supply labor, they were less warmly received. In long-settled Romanian communities,[11] there was a sharp distinction between "locals" or "natives" (variously referred to as *localnici*, *băştinaşi*) and "outsiders" (known as *străini*, *venituri/venetici*, etc.). "Outsiders" were of several kinds. Most obviously, they were people who came into the community for one or another reason and then left (tax collectors, folklorists, politicians seeking votes, itinerant merchants, etc.). Then there were those who had married into the community, though once they had lived there for a few decades, they might come to be considered almost locals. Seasonal workers were a third kind, and those who moved in permanently for work a fourth. In the primarily land-based rural economy, locals generally regarded outsiders—including those who married in—with suspicion (see Kligman 1988: 22), an attitude in keeping with the strong territorial and social boundaries characterizing most agricultural communities.

[10] See Kligman 1988: chapter 1 and Verdery 1983: chapters 5–6.

[11] This is as opposed to those settled partially or wholly by colonization in more recent times, such as Rovine, Mircea, Sântana, Tomnatic, and Jurilovca, in our sample.

In a world governed by dense social interconnections, a fundamental practice was hospitality. It drew together kin, neighbors, friends, and even outsiders in preparing as well as enjoying food and drink, gossiping, telling stories, knitting or weaving, and otherwise passing time. Romanian peasants are wonderfully hospitable and find many reasons to socialize. We mention hospitality because it was essential not only to our research but also to the persuasion work of Party activists who tried to draw peasants into the collectives. Peasants often tried to treat persuaders as guests—even those who forced their way in or demanded to be so treated—thereby affecting the process dynamically.

Status Ideals: "Persons" in Precommunist Romania

Understanding collectivization requires knowing something about the relation between village status hierarchies and ideas and practices concerning the *person*—what it meant to be proper social beings.[12] Because such ideas are often connected with property, we might expect abolishing private property to affect villagers' sense of personhood and identity. Indeed, being deprived of land dealt a mortal blow to personhood for those aspiring to the dominant landowning ideal—and offered those who had fallen short of it a chance to reset that ideal. This was part of the communist program to create a new kind of subject, the "new man" (see Kligman 1998). Without recognizing how status was connected with ideals of the person, one cannot grasp how thoroughly destabilizing class war was to much of the peasantry.

We do not assume there is only one person-ideal in a given social order; there may be several interlinked ideals jostling together, reflecting different social positions or modalities of livelihood. One set may be more or less hegemonic at a given time, or accepted by a significant part of the population but not by others (such as the poor). Moreover, personhood is performative and is always a "work in progress," being continually revised as contexts and person-ideals change. Notions of person suited to the world of private property might gradually morph into something else as property is lost.[13] Finally, we do not assume that the person is the unified autonomous individual, a construct long privileged in western ideology (and opened to scrutiny with postmodernism). Person-ideals may be characterized precisely *not* by their autonomy from others but by their social embeddedness. Unlike "individuals," which have an indi-

[12] The literature of anthropology is full of writings on the notion of person (e.g., Carrithers 1985; Geertz 1973; Harris 1989; Mauss 1954; Strathern 1988), referring to culturally specific, normative ideas about what makes a proper or good human being in a community: how such people are thought to behave, their personal attributes, their material and social properties.

[13] Whether or not this amounts to a thoroughgoing and permanent change is a matter of theoretical debate. Iván Szelényi (1988), for instance, argued that the ideals of the rural bourgeoisie were reproduced throughout the communist period.

visible core and clear boundaries separating them from others, "embedded persons" are defined by their connectedness (see Dunn 2004; Strathern 1988). We find this notion appropriate for our material.

Romanian has a phrase that expresses what we mean by personhood: *a fi om* (pl., *oameni*), to be a person. Implicitly it means to be a *male* person, privileged in a patriarchal order—*om*, like the English "man," being used in both a generic and a gendered fashion. Our discussion uses the generic sense but we are mindful of the gendered meaning as well. Prior to World War II in most of the agricultural communities we worked in, we believe there was a hegemonic ideology of personhood centered on the well-to-do farmer. This ideology had three essential elements: social embeddedness, independent possession, and strong character, of which industriousness was a central virtue.[14] The ideal person was deeply embedded in social relations with kin, neighbors, and others, and he had possessions, in significant amounts of the most valued goods; with these, he had a claim to status. Preferably, such persons controlled their own labor process (rather than working for someone else, or working for themselves on someone else's land): they were "masters" (*stăpâni*) of themselves and the land they worked. Finally, they had characteristic moral traits—were hardworking and industrious (*harnici, vrednici, muncitori*), had dignity (*demnitate*), did not attract ridicule (*batjocură*), and were decent (*cumsecade*) and hospitable (*ospitalieri*).[15] The principal qualities of such persons were interconnected: native conceptions tied together lineage, land, and person through the idea of work, which requires agency and initiative—but not necessarily independence and autonomy, for land and labor were both embedded in relationships. Although much of the data for our ideas of personhood comes from interviews in the 1970s and afterward, we find in literary and other ethnographic sources evidence that similar ideas prevailed before the communist period as well.

Central to precommunist notions of the person was deep entanglement in social relations: first those of family and kinship, then those of neighborliness and friendship, and finally those of community. The person was quintessentially a social being, constituted by these relations. Sometimes the idea was expressed as a kind of possession: people would often say that they "have" others (e.g., *are pe cineva*, "she or he has someone"). "Having someone" could refer to a valuable connection to someone higher up—such as to the university profes-

[14] Our sources for this picture are our interviews, literary works (such as Rebreanu's celebrated novel *Ion* and Preda's *Moromeții*), material in the archives, and our previous fieldwork. In our interviews, we tried to get at this dimension by asking respondents to tell us what kinds of people their parents were, in the knowledge that when speaking of the dead, they were likely to mobilize idealized images. Indeed, they consistently told us that their parents had been "very hardworking" (*harnici, vrednici*).

[15] This complex of qualities characterized male household heads in particular; they also applied to women, though, along with other characteristics such as modesty, kindness, nurturance, and so on.

sor who would judge your child's entry exam, or to the activist who would set your quotas—but it could also mean having dependents or clients, in a patron-client system. Generally, it meant having people who could help you out: it might be said of an elderly childless person or someone with no local kin, for example, *n-are pe nimeni*, "he has no one."[16] If someone had many connections and dependents, he had wealth in people, an essential attribute of the high-status person. Anyone having a large family was wealthy in people, as were successful politicians who secured allies and clients, as Caroline Humphrey showed so well in *Karl Marx Collective* (1983). Scholars often refer to this kind of wealth as "social capital," though as an attribute of the person, we prefer to call it *network embeddedness*. For Romanian villagers, then, individual autonomy was not an absolute value; one wanted rather to be a social being, dependent upon or having many others, especially kin. That was how persons could be self-directing social actors.

In addition to being embedded in networks, the ideal person in Romanian rural conceptions *had things*. The most important things to have, as we indicated above, depended in part on local ecology: transhumant shepherds had sheep or cattle; fishing populations had boats and nets; landowning peasants had land; and peasants working the land of others had work animals and carts. In short, they had means of production, and their social status depended on the amounts they controlled. Although land was paramount, having animals and equipment was important too. According to Lățea, for example, in Dobrosloveni (as elsewhere in southern Romania), where many villagers had no land and worked for very large landowners well into the twentieth century, what defined the person—what made someone *om*—was the cart and oxen (*carul cu boi*) with which he worked the land he sharecropped. To be deprived of them was to jeopardize both livelihood and identity (Lățea 2003: 20).

Animals were a possession of a special kind. Some of our respondents' most vivid memories concerned the loss of their draft animals, whom they had considered almost like family members. At collectivization, some even had their pictures taken with their animals before turning them over. For this reason, losing them was akin to losing a relative, as the following reflection from Reviga poignantly expresses: "After I entered, they slaughtered my horse of nine years. He was like our son, we had him from when he was a colt!" (Chelcea 2003b: 38). One respondent held out against joining the GAC so she would not have to give up her horses: "I felt worse about this than about losing my land!" she said, and began to weep.[17] In Jurilovca, the activists "moved things around from place to place so that people wouldn't be upset to see their old stuff. My mother-in-law

[16] "Having people" was an essential quality in all socialist countries. See, for example, Kenedi 1981; Wedel 1986.

[17] 24, Verdery interview. The weeping had a contemporary aspect, since she had recently decided (in 2002) to give up her cow, after a lifetime of always having cattle.

would have fits when she saw her horse and wagon used by the GAC. She had a very nice horse. . . . Eventually they took the horse and the wagon to another village and exchanged them" (Iordachi 2009: 129). And a Vlaicean told Verdery how his mother had suffered from the loss of their animals, whose neighing and mooing had defined her daily ambience: "The old lady practically went crazy, 'cause she didn't hear that noise any more."[18] The animals apparently shared the sentiment: another respondent described how after collectivization, every day when the GAC cowherd took the cattle to pasture, her mother was tormented by the mooing of their former cow, which stopped at their gate and tried to come in.

This digression suggests that Romanian peasants did not have what a modern western sensibility would see as sharp boundaries separating humans, land, and animals, each of these a distinct kind of entity. Instead, each partook to some degree of the other—just as persons were co-constituted by their social relations rather than being individualized autonomous actors. It is not that people were incapable of thinking of objects as separate; people did talk of "having things," of "my family's land," and so on. Our point is rather to stretch the reader's notion of "owning" by softening the boundaries among persons and things (see also Anderson 1998; de Coppet 1985; Stephens 1986). For this kind of property relation, we find "possession" a better word than "ownership," because the meanings of this word bleed into one another, the possessor also being the possessed.[19] Given these interpenetrating conceptions, collectivizing land would render a kind of violence rather different from that for which land and livestock were already fully separate from the person.

The "possessive person" we have been describing was defined not simply by having things, of course, but by their quantity, on which social status was based. One's place on a scale of possessing was an integral part of self-identity. Essential to the self-image of a middle peasant family, for instance, was that because they were richer than some people and not as poor as others, they could expect deference from some and would give it to others, owing to differential possession. Poor peasants who accepted these values would be defined by the struggle to work and buy land. This said, however, it was very possible to be of modest means and still enjoy respect because of exemplary moral behavior, which epitomized what it meant to be human (*a fi om*). What counted was not always what one had but how one dealt with the fact of having less than others—for

[18] 7, Verdery interview.

[19] A. S. Byatt's novel *Possession* exemplified that superbly. The relationship did not exclude alienation, of course: as collectivization loomed, peasants sold not only land but also animals—or even slaughtered them, so as to hold onto some of their value rather than having to give them away "for nothing." How can we reconcile their attachments with this slaughter? As with all personal relationships, those with animals were instrumentalized; just as a person might be better dead than communist, a cow was better dead than part of a GAC, where it would become skin and bones.

instance, through exemplary honesty and dignity, which might win one the label *om bun*, a good person.[20]

Although land, animals, and other means of production were the main aspects of personhood based on possession, more personal items might figure significantly in the collectivization process, through the confiscation of personal goods from people who were unable to pay their quotas or taxes, for example. To have one's household possessions—clothing, furniture, blankets, the woven rugs and embroidered towels wives and daughters produced as signs of family wealth for display, use, and dowry, and so forth—confiscated and carted through the village for all to see was cause for deep humiliation, accompanied by emotional pain and trauma.[21] It signaled that the household head was impotent, unable to protect his family from the forces organized against them or to manage his affairs with the state advantageously.[22] Prior to World War II, those most likely to suffer such mortification had been poor peasants mired in debt (see, e.g., Preda 1955: 294); in the 1950s, by contrast, they were the most prosperous peasants, against whom exorbitant taxes were levied. The expropriation of land, livestock, and other possessions, then, was a fundamental blow to the person-ideal of possessing. It attacked the very meaning of "home," "family," and "person" for *every* peasant, but especially for wealthy ones, because these possessions were essential elements of being a *bun gospodar*, a good household manager—an image central to their identity. Indeed, possessing too much was made a burden, a source of torment, a handicap rather than a sign of honor; in the words of one respondent, "a man would lose his appetite for saying 'I have this and that.'" Also jeopardized were values closely associated with having land: working it and controlling one's labor.

If embeddedness and possession were two desirable attributes of personhood, another was industriousness. Crucial to earning respect and self-respect was that one be hardworking and exercise initiative. Also crucial was to work *for oneself* as much as possible, not for others—to control one's labor process. A respondent from Reviga put it thus: "People used to do what they pleased, as they had their own land and plow. They weren't used to taking orders. You could work today and feast tomorrow" (Chelcea 2009: 417). For this combination of hard work and initiative we use the term "self-directing." Peasants working their own land looked down on the sharecropper or wage-laborer, who did not control his own work process as a proprietor could. For the wealthiest peasants, controlling the labor process meant having other people work for them and directing those people's labor—a sign of the highest status. We find similar values in other ethnographic work in Eastern Europe. For instance, Martha

[20] Thanks to Puiu Lățea for this phrasing.

[21] See Kligman (1998: chapter 2), and Schneider (1980) on "trousseau as treasure."

[22] See, for example, ANIC, Fond C.C. al P.C.R.–Agrară, file 28/1952, 2.

Lampland describes the significance of work in the self-conception of precollective peasants in Hungary:

> One's relative independence in work, particularly for men, was important for one's sense of social respectability and honor. . . . [B]eing forced to work for others was demeaning and deprived one of initiative and integrity. . . . The more one controlled one's labor, the more prestige one enjoyed. Conversely, the less one was master of one's own labor, the less respect one was accorded. . . . The central concern of villagers was to be one's own master. (1995: 35, 41)

Here was a major obstacle to joining collective farms, in which someone else would completely determine the labor process of the members. As one respondent put it, "When you joined the collective you had to write a petition: please accept me into the CAP since I'm no longer able to manage my affairs. When they called me they were going to beat me, but I said I won't write this, that I 'can't manage.' How could I sign something like that?"[23] For a fictional example, here is how Mărin Preda's Party secretary (n.b.) explained to an activist why collectivization was a bad idea:

> The collective farm is good if you want to have it, but if you don't, no matter how terrific an idea it is it won't work, because people don't like others to order them around. How many haven't I talked with?! "I'd rather eat polenta with ashes than go where Mărin son of Garlic will order me around." (1967: 313).

Worst of all was to be ordered around by a poor man, a "nobody," like the Mărin of this example—or by "inferior" Roma. To lose control over one's work was tantamount to a loss of identity. We see in the metaphor of serfdom that some respondents used to describe their life as collectivists the same emphasis on self-directed labor and its denial, serfs representing to them the ultimate in lack of control over one's work conditions. (By contrast, during the 1990s respondents might express their satisfaction at repossessing their land like this: "Of course I'm doing well now, because I'm my own boss, I do whatever I want,"[24] and those who received no land expressed resentment at having to be the "serfs" of others [see Verdery 2003: 175–77]).

Ideas about work were so central to villagers' notions of person and self that they figured importantly in representations of other nationalities, especially Roma and Germans, seen respectively as lazier and more hardworking than Romanians. In 1951 a note to district authorities discussed problems resulting from a rich peasant who was telling people that if they signed into a GAC with Roma, "They'll work 'til their eyes pop out because Roma don't like to work."[25] Germans, by contrast, were a model of the work ethic in the communities

[23] H. V., Kligman interview.

[24] N. W., Vultur interview.

[25] DJAN HD, Fond Comitetul Regional PMR Hunedoara (henceforth CR PMR HD), file 103/1951, 252.

where they lived. A colonist settled in Sântana recalled how at first, Germans were the main GAC labor force, and they exerted an influence over other GAC members:

> The Germans worked like you wouldn't believe!! And they earned, it was clear they were earning a lot, these Germans, with their little kids and older ones, everybody. And our Romanians saw how much the Germans were earning. "Well, damn those Germans to hell! Are they better people than we are? [*Ei-s mai oameni ca noi?*] Can't we earn too?" And they too started working.[26]

The result was one of the few successful collective farms in our sample. Note the expression *Ei-s mai oameni ca noi*? which we could render "Are they better [more industrious] persons than we?" showing that work makes one *om*, a person. Similarly, a former CAP leader from the 1970s said, "Those who were poor made *oameni* of themselves after the collective was formed."[27] The poor, in other words, given a chance to work and improve themselves, became persons.

To be a person, then, in precommunist times was to be deeply embedded in social relations, to own things of value, and to work hard, controlling one's work process; this meant exercising agency and initiative, through autonomous self-direction. It did not, however, mean complete independence, given the high value placed on social embeddedness and working with others. Beyond this, the ideal person was a good household manager (*bun gospodar*, *om gazda*); he was a person of thrift and moderation (he was not a drunk or a womanizer), and especially a person with dignity. Many of these were, evidently, male values. The qualities appropriate to women were similar in some respects, though not wholly. They too had to be good household managers and know how to raise children; they had to know their place and be respectful of their husbands' wishes as well as of the family's honor by being modest, demonstrating propriety in social relations, and not gaining a reputation as gossips. And they too should be concerned with their dignity. (As we will see in chapter 6, the concern with dignity and with not being ridiculed underlay the treatment that cadres accorded wealthy peasants, who were humiliated without mercy as part of attacking their self-esteem and public image.) Nevertheless, the pillar of a family's *omenie* (humanness or personhood) was its male household head.

* * *

From this account of precommunist village organization and values we underscore six points. (1) In communities governed by hierarchy in which as many as one family in five might be virtually landless, conditions of life could be brutal

[26] V. B., Goina interview.

[27] V. S., Chelcea interview.

and oppressive for some even as others strove to be respectable persons. That is, in the collectivization drive the communists could legitimately hope to secure allies among the village poor. (2) For families with land, to "donate" that land to the collective farm would thoroughly endanger their accustomed life-strategies. The problems included, as Lățea puts it, "how are my children going to get married? How shall I manage to build a house for them? Who am I going to be, in relation to the other villagers? And, most importantly, how shall I survive now and later, when I am old?" (2009: 345). (3) Beyond this, "donating" one's animals could be like giving over a loved person, not a mere beast. (4) As a household head signed up, he was relinquishing much of his authority, for he would have no way of controlling his children and would no longer organize household labor: the collective would do that. To expect a man to sign up of his own accord was to ask him to annihilate his identity voluntarily. It is no wonder that persuasion work was so fraught and so often culminated in violence. (5) Aggravating it was the prejudice that made the villagers close ranks against outsiders, who included activists and other persuaders. (6) The main criterion for naming "rural exploiters," known as *chiaburs* (the rich peasants or kulaks of the Soviet experience)—namely, that they exploited the labor of others—would prove extremely difficult to apply in a context where people exchanged labor within a kinship idiom. Although some wealthy peasants did indeed pay wages at peak periods or keep servants, far more of the labor they mobilized was deeply embedded in social relationships with them. This fact is crucial to understanding why "fomenting class war" proved to be so difficult, as we show in chapter 6, for village inequalities resided in networks of kin-based status groups, not in "classes."

This, then, was the existing social structure that collectivization assaulted. It provided the main force fields within which social life was lived, based particularly on relations of kinship and unequal status. Within these force fields, the Party's techniques would disrupt the mechanisms that reproduced both the community and its households, as well as the networks and cultural systems linking them all together. Turning kinship relations to new Party purposes and expropriating land and animals would cripple the reproduction of households. Class war would disrupt the status hierarchy and prevent the reproduction of elite status in the village, undermining notions of person and senses of striving based on those ideals. New concepts of relatedness, inequality, and gender roles would sustain these actions. We turn now to an overview of how this village organization was overturned.

Preparing Collectivization: Land Reform and Quotas

Although it did not become certain until 1948 that Romania would indeed pursue full collectivization in the Soviet manner, as early as 1945 Party leaders began implementing a number of agrarian policies that would later prove essential precursors to collectivizing. These included the selective deportation of Romania's ethnic German citizens in 1945, an agrarian reform legislated in that same year, and food requisitions that began in 1946. Accompanying these measures was the elaboration of a set of social categories to be used in applying the regime's agrarian policies differentially to the rural populace. In our discussion of the policies and the politics through which collectivization was accomplished, we emphasize the continual debates, revisions, and oscillations in the measures applied. Because such an agenda could easily form its own large book, we keep our discussion fairly streamlined, inevitably leaving out many fascinating and significant details.[28] Our emphasis is primarily on the implementation of policies made at the top; in chapters 4–6 we will say more about the constant negotiations and contestations from below that accompanied it.

The regime's agrarian policy varied across space and time. Spatially, areas of high agricultural productivity or having strategic importance (including in ideological terms) tended to be targeted for collectivizing earlier than mountainous areas or those without strategic significance. Temporally, the Party was obliged to engage in what Goina (2009) labels "flexible accommodation," responding to exigencies caused by both external events (such as Soviet demands or the 1956 Hungarian uprising) and internal ones (such as peasant resistance and infrastructural constraints). In brief, here are the main developments. Between 1949 and 1953, 10 percent of the land in Romania was collectivized (Dobeş et al. 2004); the process began slowly in 1949, then intensified in 1950, relaxed in 1951, and intensified again in 1952. A period of relative stagnation ensued between 1953 and the end of 1955, following Stalin's death. During that respite, cadres placed emphasized on consolidating existing collectives rather than forming new ones. A new and less radical form of cooperation, known as an "association" (*întovărăşire*), also appeared during these years and soon outpaced the formation of full collectives. At the Second Party Congress, December 23–28, 1955, the leadership decided to resume collectivization. Progress abated briefly after the Hungarian uprising in 1956, but in late 1957 the "final assault" was launched. By this time, the balance of forces between the Party-state and the peasantry had shifted decisively against the latter, and in 1962 the Party leadership declared collectivization complete.

Alongside the Party's history of devotion to the Soviet Union, already indicated in chapter 1, we note an additional feature of the RCP's leadership during this period that affected these fluctuations: pervasive factionalism, which char-

[28] Among the things we leave out, regrettably, is an account of the legislation around collectivization; we refer readers to a summary of the main events in Iordachi and Dobrincu 2009: 485–91, as well as to Iancu et al. 2000. This chapter is especially indebted to the papers by Levy (2009) and Oprea (2009), as well as to the following works: Bălan 2000; Dobeş et al. 2004; Iancu et al. 2000; Jowitt 1971; Levy 2001 and archive notes Levy provided us; Montias 1967; Roske 2005; Şandru 2005; and Tănase 1998.

acterized the Party both before it achieved power and afterward. According to Tismăneanu (2003), three centers of power within the Party constantly vied for supremacy, producing chronic instability. It was only gradually eliminated, as General Secretary Gheorghe Gheorghiu-Dej consolidated his position by eliminating the "fiefdoms" of his main competitors, as of about 1961 (Jowitt 1971: 195).[29] The Party leaders most often mentioned in this book because they were central in setting collectivization policy represented two of these three factions (the third was insignificant in the collectivization debates). One faction included Gheorghe Gheorghiu-Dej (the General Secretary), Alexandru Moghioroş, and Iosif Chişinevschi,[30] and the second contained their most regular opponents: Ana Pauker, Vasile Luca, and Teohari Georgescu.[31] We will refer to these as the Dej and Pauker factions. Pauker headed two critical commissions—the Agrarian Commission, formed in 1949 for the sole purpose of creating collective farms, and the Agrarian Section of the Central Committee, which replaced the Agrarian Commission in January 1950.[32] Crucial in Dej's consolidation of power as General Secretary was his purge of the Pauker faction, in

[29] Romanian historiography has generally seen only two factions, referred to as the "national" and "Muscovite" factions. This has accompanied a nationalist move to attribute all the "bad" aspects of collectivization to the communists trained in the Soviet Union (heavily Jewish and Hungarian), while the "good" communists were Romanian patriots. A number of scholars have debunked this tendentious interpretation, among them Deletant (1999) and Tismăneanu (2003).

[30] Gheorghe Gheorghiu-Dej (a Romanian from Moldavia) joined the Communist Party in 1932, rose in the hierarchy and became the Party's General/First Secretary from 1945 to 1965. Alexandru Moghioroş (a Hungarian Jew from Transylvania), active in the Party as of 1929, held a number of high positions including membership in the Politburo and Central Committee; he was also vice president of the Council of Ministers. Iosif Chişinevschi (a Jew from Bessarabia) became a communist in 1928 and headed Romania's Agitprop department; he was a member of the Politburo and the Secretariat of the Central Committee until purged by Dej in 1957. For notes 30 and 31, see also Tismăneanu 2003: 120–127; Dobre 2004.

[31] Ana Pauker (a Romanian Jew from Moldavia) joined the Socialist Party in 1916 and the Communist Party in 1919, spent much of the Party's "illegal" period in Moscow, and returned with the Red Army in 1944, serving as de facto General Secretary until (and even after) Dej's selection. Becoming a powerful member of the Politburo, the Secretariat, and the Central Committee, she was named Foreign Minister in 1947 and Secretary for Agriculture in 1948, from which post she inaugurated the collectivization campaign. She was purged by Dej in 1952 with her two main allies, Vasile Luca and Teohari Georgescu. Georgescu (a Romanian from Moldavia, falsely rendered Jewish by the Romanian right after 1989) joined the Party in 1929; he too became a member of the Politburo, Secretariat, and Central Committee, and he served as Minister of the Interior from 1945 to 1952, when he was purged. Vasile Luca (a Hungarian from Transylvania) became active in the Party in 1919 and held a number of high positions like his two allies, as well as being Minister of Finance (1947–52) until his downfall.

[32] The positions of these two factions resembled those of Preobrazhensky and Bukharin, respectively, in Soviet debates about economic development. Preobrazhensky argued that agriculture should be plundered as a source of primitive accumulation for building industry, Bukharin that agriculture should be developed so it could serve as a market for industrial products. The former course meant impoverishing the peasants, the latter enriching them. In both Romania and the Soviet Union, the former policy won out.

1952.[33] With this, in Câmpeanu's words, "anti-Soviet Stalinism won out over pro-Soviet Stalinism" (n.d.: 32).

Factional disputes within the RCP were regularly trumped by the "advice" of the Soviet councilors discussed in chapter 1. Between 1944, when the RCP was first brought into coalition governments, and 1947, when it consolidated its supremacy by ousting Romania's king, Party leaders argued over the wisdom of attempting to collectivize a peasantry they viewed as more tenacious proprietors than those in pre-Soviet Russia. Although some, especially Dej, promoted the policy from the outset,[34] others believed that collectivizing would make it harder for the Party to build up its rural base, better strengthened by an agrarian reform and by postponing it (see Levy 2001: 96–100). Moreover, some of the leaders knew very well that it was an extraordinarily difficult task. Pauker had attended the Lenin School in Moscow; in March 1930 she had been sent to the Volga to help in "correcting the mistakes" of collectivization there (47). She had had more opportunity than any of her colleagues to see the problems attendant upon the Soviet version of the policy. As Levy demonstrates, she consistently fought for a gradualist strategy once the Soviets insisted that Romania collectivize, effectively ending the debates.[35] We will expand upon this matter below.

Legislating Agrarian Reform

In March 1945 the communists embarked upon an agrarian reform (already part of their program from the previous year), which expropriated land from people holding more than fifty hectares and redistributed it among the poor and landless.[36] Designed to create allies among a peasantry whom information about Soviet collective farms had made deeply skeptical of the new government's intentions, the reform was the regime's first significant effort to build a relationship with the poor and middle peasantry. Indeed, it did help to reduce

[33] Pauker and her allies were labeled the "Muscovite [that is, foreign] faction" and accused of both right and left deviations. These alliances were not always fixed but often shifted according to the issue. For example, Pauker and Luca were initially allied on not liquidating the rural bourgeoisie, but his position later changed (Levy 2001: 120–23).

[34] In a March 10, 1948, meeting of the Ministerial Commission, Dej stated emphatically that collectivization would proceed, regardless of proposals to the contrary, and that he would "strangle the chiabur who spread false rumors [about collectives] for disturbing the public order" (ANIC, Fond C.C. al P.C.R.–Cancelarie, file 5/1948, 2, [RLA]).

[35] Levy's argument in this connection is worth underscoring, in view of the decades of vilification heaped upon Pauker by her successor, Gheorghiu-Dej, who blamed her and her "faction" for all the abuses committed in the collectivization campaign up to the time she was purged in 1952. The Party archives Levy consulted after 1989 definitively give the lie to any notion that she was behind the excesses of the policy.

[36] See Decretul-Lege nr. 187/1945, text in Iancu et al. 2000: 1–5.

suspicion of a party long seen as lacking national roots (Tismăneanu 2003: 90). The reform, purportedly aimed at achieving social justice, also aimed to steal the thunder of Romania's other political parties, with their varying plans for land reform, and to build the communists some political capital for the elections to be held in 1946.

Even prior to legislating the reform, the Party had acceded to the Soviet demand that able-bodied Germans, as representatives of the defeated power, be deported from Romania to the Soviet Union for war-reparations labor. In January 1945, some seventy thousand Romanian citizens of German ethnicity, about 13 percent of all Romania's Germans, were sent to the Soviet Union (Poledna 2001: 82; also Bălan 2000: 38–40).[37] The agrarian reform law confiscated the land of 154,500 German families without compensation (Poledna 2001: 99), creating a reserve for impropriating poor peasants and war veterans. Although Germans comprised only 4 percent of the country's population, the confiscated land totaled 24 percent of all land to be redistributed (Brus 1986: 586), which shows their much greater wealth, collectively speaking, compared with ethnic Romanians. The first act of collectivization, then, would prove to be the deportation of Germans and the confiscation of their land (perhaps in retribution for their role in the war, as occurred with national minorities in other countries in the area).[38]

The reform began with the communists' inciting peasants to preempt alternative land reform programs by occupying the estates of the large landowners, even before the Party had taken over the government and before the procedures of the reform were legislated in March 1945. The reform law expropriated 1,443,911 hectares from 143,219 owners, distributing 1,057,674 hectares to 796,129 peasants whose holdings were below 5 hectares and reserving 387,565 hectares as state property (Şandru 2005: 190–91). Some of that reserve would form the basis of state farms, while other parts went to establishing experimental agricultural stations and providing small plots for factory workers. State lands were greatly augmented in 1948 by expropriating another 940,000 hectares from among the remaining landowners, war prisoners, "enemies of the people," and institutions such as churches and schools (Montias 1967: 89n5). The reform also expropriated all the agricultural machinery on the affected

[37] See Poledna (2001: 75–81) for his explanation of the reasons for this Soviet demand. Romania's population of German ethnicity was 745,421, in 1930; in 1941 the figure was 542,325, and in 1956, 384,708 (177, 187, 191). Bălan (2000: 39–40) reviews statistical differences based on sources, noting those of the Ministry of the Interior as the most credible.

[38] We note an even earlier expropriation: of land belonging to Jews. Deletant (2006: 107) gives a figure of 52,500 hectares seized from Jews by 1942, with amounts between that figure and 42,000 hectares in other sources. The problem with assessing the impact of these expropriations on collectivization is that it is unknown how much of this land might have been returned before that process began. The amounts were in any case small in relation to the total land expropriated—according to Brus (1986: 590–91), about 2 to 3 percent. Thanks to Yossi Harpaz for raising this question.

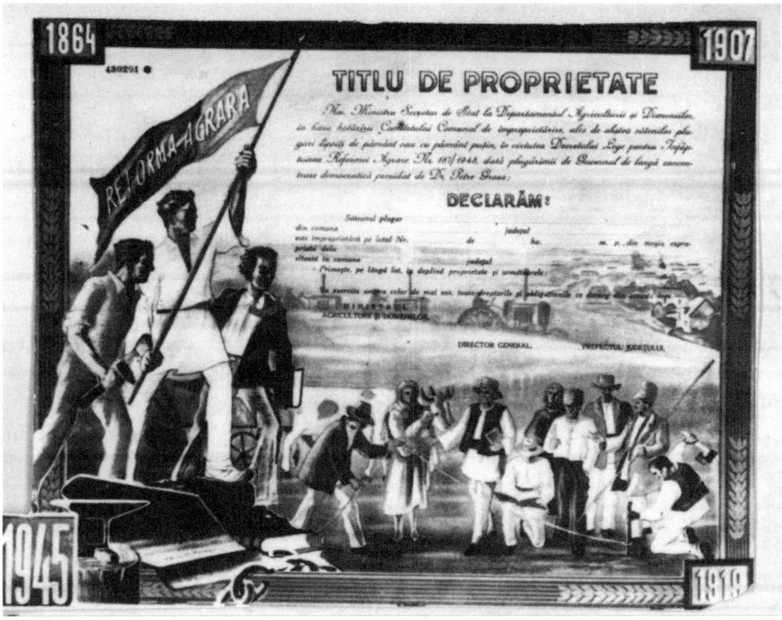

Figure 2.1. Land title issued to poor and middle peasants after the 1945 reform. Courtesy of *Fototeca online a comunismului românesc*, photograph #W027, *cota* 19/1945.

holdings, thereby creating inventory for state farms. That the 1945 land reform was not of even greater proportions was due to the magnitude of an earlier reform legislated in 1921, following World War I—among the most radical in Europe at the time.[39]

The 1945 land reform did not affect all areas of the country equally. The average holding distributed countrywide was 1.3 hectares; in Transylvania and the Banat—the areas with by far the greatest number of expropriated owners—the average holding distributed was 1.7 and 2.4 hectares, respectively, exceeded only by Dobrogea, with 2.9 hectares. In all other areas, the distributed parcels were about a hectare or less.[40] These discrepancies are important for our project, since the initial windfall had indeed made the Party some allies in villages,

[39] This earlier reform had expropriated over six million hectares—more than a third of Romania's agricultural surface—distributing 3.9 million of them (the remaining 2.1 million hectares consisted of communal pastures and forests, plus some land reserved for general needs; see Roberts 1951: 367). For more on the reform, see Mitrany 1930. Also radical in their effects were land reforms in the Baltic states.

[40] Calculated from figures in Stănescu 1957: 48. It was not as if there were insufficient land to have given out more: land set aside for the state ranged from 4 percent of the total expropriated to 38 percent. Given the locations, those largest figures are probably for forestland.

but those supporters would vary by region and even by settlement, according to just how much of a difference the reform had made.

Added to the 1921 reform, the one in 1945 further leveled the property structure while increasing the problematic fragmentation of parcels, already characteristic of interwar Romanian agriculture. Moreover, farms below five hectares now came to dominate Romanian agriculture (Iancu et al. 2000: xiii). The aim of the reform had been to liquidate the great estates, not to consolidate small and medium properties (Şandru 2005)—evident in the fact that necessary means of production were not made available for working the newly acquired plots. As such, the reform undermined agricultural productivity without offering an alternative solution. It thus contributed greatly to a crisis in agriculture, which created serious challenges for the Romanian economy, for the communists could never hope to develop heavy industry in the Stalinist mold with the dwarf farms that now predominated. In 1948, however, when the Soviet Union insisted on collectivization throughout the bloc, the issue became moot. But the peasants who had received land in the reform would prove difficult to pry loose from their newly acquired possessions.

Food Requisitions and Quotas

The agrarian reform presented the new government with an extremely important problem—the provision of foodstuffs for urban residents—that would generate innumerable debates among the leadership.[41] By eradicating the rural stratum that most reliably produced a marketable surplus and by greatly increasing the number of households oriented to subsistence, the reform jeopardized the urban food supply (Levy 2001: 97). This effect compounded the wartime devastation of Romania's productive potential (which did not recover 1938 levels until the late 1940s).[42] In addition, the terms of the armistice saddled Romania with heavy war reparations to the Soviet Union—the heaviest of any East European country—part of them in grain. The reparations absorbed a large portion of Romanian produce and were estimated, when added to wartime spoliation by the Red Army, to have been worth as much as $2 billion (Montias 1967: 17).[43] Both aggravating and aggravated by these claims on the

[41] This section owes a great deal to the project report of Octavian Roske (2003) and his published paper (2005).

[42] In agriculture, gross output figures for crops did not recover 1938 levels until 1953 (Ronnås 1984: 134).

[43] Different figures appear for this total; we use those of Montias, nonetheless recognizing that it is almost impossible to quantify the value of wartime losses alongside the more certain figures for reparations. By the terms of the armistice, Romania was to pay the Soviets $300 million in goods over six years, from 1944 until 1952. Half would be in petroleum products, the other half in ships, timber, and grain. Moreover, Romania had to pay damages to Ukraine, Bessarabia, and Bukovina in grain (one million tons), three hundred thousand head of livestock, and sixty thousand tons of

food supply were the effects of serious drought and famine in 1946–47, so severe—especially in the north and northeast—that some Party leaders began to think collectivization might be needed to solve food shortages, as had happened in the Soviet Union (Levy 2001: 97). Transports of food from Maramureş, for example, so diminished the local food supply that peasants were starving, a scenario similar to that in the Soviet Union earlier.[44] An unanticipated benefit of famine (from the Party's point of view), however, would have been the weakening of village social relationships, owing to extensive emigration from stricken areas and the abatement of patterns of hospitality that sustained social networks. Thus, famine was a prelude to the damage the Party would later inflict by its collectivization techniques.[45]

In 1946, urban food needs, reparations, drought, and famine led the government to institute Law 68/1946, reimposing food requisitions (known as "quotas" [*cote*]). These had been a staple of the wartime economy since at least 1939, as an extension of Romania's agricultural exports to Germany (see Şandru 2005: 42–53).[46] The requisitions would prove integral to collectivization once that task was launched; in addition, they expanded the relationship with the peasantry that the land reform had begun, but now in a negative direction. The repressive measures taken against peasants who failed to hand over their quotas could be extreme—for instance, in addition to crippling fines, up to twelve years in prison for not giving the amounts specified, or five to fifteen years' hard labor for hiding one's produce, with confiscation of all one's wealth (Roske 2005: 126). If a wealthy peasant agitated against them, according to an instruction sent to the Securitate in 1950, "he can be shot on the spot, so everyone who might dare to withhold their quotas can see they would suffer the same fate" (Roske 2003: 46). These measures were very effective in reducing opposition to the quotas.

Over the next several years, repeated decrees perfected the system, which involved assigning each household a quota for each of several grains and vege-

other foodstuffs, all worth $508 million. The commodities were to be delivered at 1938 prices, well below those of 1945. The Soviet Union later extended the term for paying these from six years to eight, and halved the balance in 1948. (Data from Montias 1967: 17–18n40–41.) Added to these figures, however, were funds reflecting the value of Soviet goods and currency brought into Romania for war purposes prior to the armistice signed between the two countries in 1944. Duţu claims that this total was about 500 million rubles (at the time, about $2.5 billion at the official exchange rate) and that the amount represented one-fifth of the entire Romanian budget for the fiscal year 1944–45 (1994: 902).

[44] DJAN MM, Fond 53, file 123/1946–1947, 1, 5; file 150/1947, 40.

[45] Famine accompanied the onset of collectivization in many other countries as well, such as parts of China and North Vietnam (see MacLean 2005).

[46] Those requisitions, in turn, drew upon the *Kriegsrohstoffabteilung* developed by Germany for collecting and allocating raw materials in World War I and elaborated by socialist economists Ludwig von Mises and Otto Neurath (see Tribe 1995; thanks to Thomas Fleischman for this information).

tables, meat, dairy products, and wool.[47] As noted in chapter 1, the Soviet leadership had imposed similar quotas on its peasants from 1929 into the 1930s, in response to grain procurements crises. The Romanian system was based on the Soviet one. Initially, households were assigned fixed amounts according to the productivity of the soil (divided into six categories of average production). By 1950 each district was placed in one of five categories reflecting the overall fertility of the soil in that district. Fixed quotas for each category were then established for the amounts of land each household owned, the percentages increasing with the size and quality of the holding (see Iancu et al. 2000: 127–40). The law assigned quotas not only to individuals but also (at a lower rate) to collective farms.

As an example, table 2.2 gives the quota figures for 1950, showing the total assessments in kilograms per hectare for all agricultural products combined (wheat, barley, oats, corn, sunflower seeds, peas, beans, and lentils). Separate quotas were established for onions, potatoes, hay, clover, wool, and other specialized products. (See figure 2.2.) At first the state paid for goods taken as quotas at a fixed state price, but by 1950 they had become an obligatory tax in kind.[48] If a household could not give its assigned quotas, the arrears would be compounded with huge fines ranging between 3 percent of the total value of the quotas for a ten-day delay to 20 percent for over a month's delay, added on to the subsequent year's quotas (Iancu et al. 2000: 139). The collection of laws and decrees from this period in Iancu et al. (2000) makes clear that the subject of collections was the most frequent topic of regulation throughout the first decade of the new regime.

To summarize more briefly, here are figures showing the percentage of all farms, by size-class, and the percentage of all quotas that each size-class gave. They show that although wealthy peasants gave disproportionately large amounts relative to their numbers, it was middle peasants who actually gave the bulk of all quotas.

Whereas at the outset the quotas aimed simply to respond to famine and shortages from natural causes, increasing rates of urbanization fueled those shortages and cut further into peasant harvests. Between 1948 and 1966, the urban population grew at a rate of 2.5 percent annually.[49] In addition, as of 1949 the quotas began to take on increasingly repressive qualities, becoming a cen-

[47] Leaders argued as to whether the quotas should be assigned on the basis of actual production per hectare or, rather, the surface area adjusted for soil fertility. The latter solution prevailed, in the hope of stimulating peasants to produce more, whereas requisitioning a fixed amount of the actual harvest would discourage them from intensifying their labors. These debates can be found in stenograms of the meetings of the Party leadership. Our thanks to Jon Fox for excerpting the content of these documents, supplied by Robert Levy.

[48] See Hotărârea Consiliul de Miniştri, nr. 571/1950.

[49] Ronnås 1984: 200, 203. According to Ronnås, the rural population increased in all but four counties due to high birthrates, offsetting urban population growth. By 1966, one-third of Romania's population lived in urban areas.

Table 2.2
Quotas Assessed in 1950 (totals for all agricultural products), by Zones of Soil Fertility

Farm size (Hectares)	*Zone I (Kg/Ha)*	*Zone II (Kg/Ha)*	*Zone III (Kg/Ha)*	*Zone IV (Kg/Ha)*	*Zone V (Kg/Ha)*
0–0.50	—	—	—	—	—
0.51–1	70	50	30	—	—
1.1–2	110	80	50	20	10
2.1–3	150	120	80	35	25
3.1–4	200	160	120	50	40
4.1–5	250	200	160	70	55
5.1–6	300	250	200	100	75
6.1–7	350	300	250	130	95
7.1–8	410	350	300	165	120
8.1–9	470	400	350	210	150
9.1–10	530	450	400	260	180
10.1–12	590	510	450	320	220
12.1–15	655	570	500	380	280
15.1–20	720	640	560	430	320
20.1–25	775	690	600	480	375
25.1–30	820	730	640	530	405
30.1–35	850	755	670	570	420
35.1–40	875	775	690	600	430
Over 40	890	800	710	620	435

Source: Iancu, Țârău, and Trașca 2000: 129.

tral weapon in "class war" (see chapter 6). Quotas tended to increase over time both in quantity and in the range of goods covered, reflecting a persistent crisis in the food-supply system as collectivization got underway. According to Roske, a household that in 1949 gave 70 kilograms of corn per hectare for two cultivated hectares would have to give 180 kilograms for the same surface in 1951, as well as 20 kilograms of beans per hectare. A wealthy peasant who in 1952 had quotas assessed on six different products would be assessed on ten products two years later, at a higher rate.[50] In 1953 a new decree increased the

[50] Onions were in and peas out, and beef, pork, milk, and wool were added—even for people who had no cows or sheep (see Roske 2005: 119–120). Central planning did not consistently respect the provision of quotas based on local land conditions, leading to negotiations between local, regional, and central authorities. For example, the Vișeu regional Party noted on February 2, 1951, that those who proposed the quota levels did so from their office, not knowing the terrain, that they "did not take either the land conditions or people's possibilities into consideration . . . and that they had to clarify the region's situation so that in the future, the quotas would not present such serious difficulties." (See DJAN MM, Fond Comitetul Raional Vișeu–Economică-Agrară, file 8/1951, 59.) Regarding cultivation plans received from the Ministry of Agriculture, the Provisional Committee for Maramureș, together with the citizens of several villages, directed their concerns to the Central Committee, asking that they be allowed to grow more oats and wheat rather than the barley as-

Figure 2.2. Weighing wool for quotas. Courtesy of Artexpo Foundation.

quotas on wealthy peasants by 30 percent. In addition to the burden in kind generated by quotas, a steeply progressive agricultural tax was imposed beginning in 1949;[51] like the quotas, it too aimed at "limiting the economic power of the wealthy peasants and curbing the exploitation of the masses of working peasants, by obliging the wealthy to turn over to the state a significant part of their household incomes, created from exploiting the village poor."[52] In addition, local People's Councils could add a further 20 to 50 percent on incomes of wealthy peasants owning over 10 hectares (Turnock 1986: 181).[53]

The quotas were at their heaviest from 1950 to 1953, during which time the amounts taken from peasant households were unprecedented. A middle peasant from the Odorhei region put it in modest terms: "I agreed that the peasants should give produce for society, since we too get produce and other things we need from society. But what they expected of us then was very exaggerated."[54] The common expression we heard was, "They came and took *everything*." Here

signed them, which did not grow well in their northern area (DJAN MM, Fond Comitetul Județean PMR, file 89/1950, 31).

[51] See *Buletin Oficial* nr. 45/14 July 1949.

[52] The quotation is from Vasile Luca, from his speech explaining the new law on agricultural taxation (Luca 1949: 8; cited in Roske 2003: 20).

[53] The taxation rate was set at 7 percent on incomes of 12,000 to 15,000 lei, increasing to 37 percent on 400,000 lei. Initially these taxes were set without respect to disability or the number of children in a household; they were later revised to take this into account (Iancu et al. 2000: 280–85).

[54] 10, Oláh interview.

Table 2.3
Quota Contributions by Size of Holding, 1951

Size of Holding (Hectares)	*% of All Farms*	*% of All Quotas Given*
.5–3 (poor peasants)	52	9
4–10 (middle peasants)	35	59
11–20 (wealthy and chiaburs [kulaks]—see below)	2.4	24
> 20 (chiaburs)	.5	8

Source: Spulber 1958: 156. *Note*: An additional 10.1% of rural households were exempt from obligation. These figures may be low because at least some of the wealthy peasants were in hiding or otherwise unable to provide their quotas.

is a more extended account from Slobozia, in the southeast, not far from Bucharest:

> They assigned you amounts you could never fulfill. They took everything you produced all summer. "Do you have anything more to give?" Well, I've given it. They confiscated everything. They took my clothes, my sewing machine. Corn, the biggest lamb, my best suit of clothes, my fur-lined coat. I hid the lamb in the house, and it kept looking at itself in the mirror. Everything they took they auctioned at the market in Slobozia. When they came to get the quotas, they slept here; you fed them. They'd say, "You still owe more!" When they came, they'd say, "Kill that hen over there. Get out some wine." People who had things hid them with their poorer relatives; they helped us out. I had a hole in the ground to keep them from taking all our grain. It held about 4,500–5,000 kg of wheat. You had to work at night so your neighbors wouldn't rat on you. (Chelcea 2003b: 27)

As this person makes clear, peasants tried to evade their quotas. The job of collecting them was so unpleasant that collectors might collude with the peasants to reduce their obligations. Cadres themselves sometimes disagreed with the policy and worked to ameliorate it. For example, a Securitate officer reporting in 1951 on the "popular mood" mentions great agitation around the quotas, adding "They *are* too high," and he reports taking a high-level official from the region out to a village so he will see how bad the problem is and reduce the burden.[55] An activist from Tîrgu Secuiesc complained in 1956, "We have mistakes in the system of collections because the number of family members is not being taken into consideration, and I proposed that this be taken into consideration."[56] Problems with quota collections even made it into novels: the second volume of Marin Preda's celebrated *Moromeții*, for example, has a scene in which peasants refuse en masse to deliver their quotas; they tell each other

[55] ACNSAS, FD, file 5, 17.
[56] ANIC, Fond C.C. al P.C.R.–Organizatorică, file 43/1956, 72.

that if everyone refuses, then the authorities can't do anything about it; ultimately their opposition forces cadres to reduce the assigned quotas, giving peasants a major victory.[57]

As early as 1952 but increasingly often as of 1955, the officials substituted enforced contracts for obligatory quotas. The Party was supposed to pay for the goods, but meetings of the Central Committee show that often this did not occur, for top leaders would ask what was happening to the money sent down to pay peasants for contracted produce. Then in January 1957 (probably in response to the October 1956 uprising in Hungary), decree 728/1957 abolished the quotas[58]—as occurred in other countries of the bloc around the same time—for all products but meat and wool, and the system of contracts was strengthened. At this point the collectivization campaign was stepped up; by the time it was completed in 1962, collective and state farms had taken over from quotas the responsibility of provisioning the cities.

Although during our interviews many of our Romanian respondents conflated the quotas with collectivization itself, these two integrally connected policies are separable. Quotas preceded and were essential to collectivization. What unites the two is that both helped to consolidate the Party's control over the food supply and over the peasantry as a social group, just as Stalin had done in the Soviet Union (see Lewin 1968). This control, in turn, was crucial to the policy of forced industrialization followed by the Soviet and Romanian communists. Although both quotas and collectivization served similar functions, albeit in different ways that deserve to be noted independently, the quota system filled certain needs that were unique to it.

Quotas had six main functions: (1) to force agricultural surpluses into accumulations for industrial development (following Preobrazhensky's theory of primitive accumulation); (2) to provide food for urban workers at low prices; (3) to contribute war-reparations payments to the Soviet Union; (4) to push peasants into joining collectives; (5) to stimulate them to produce more goods on their private farms; and (6) to foment class war among different strata of the peasantry. The first two of these were common to both quotas and collectivization, with quotas fulfilling them between 1946 and 1957 and the collectives gradually assuming them thereafter, as more peasants signed up. The third function, contributing to war reparations, is self-evident: as long as Romania was required to pay reparations to the Soviets in foodstuffs, requisitions were a prime means of obtaining them. The fourth function, likewise, is obvious: as quotas increased on individual households but were reduced for those joining collectives, they became a motive for joining. Already in 1951, the quotas assessed were so high that some peasants sought to join collectives simply to get out of their quotas. The Party was aware of this and opposed it. As Gheorghiu-

[57] Preda 1967: 258–61, 288.

[58] The decree was published only in 1957, though it was issued in 1956.

Dej objected at the CC Plenum of February 29–March 1, 1952: "You don't find, either in the classics of Marxism-Leninism or anywhere in history, an example of a class self-destructing."[59]

To explain the fifth and sixth functions—the fifth specific to quotas, the sixth characteristic of both quotas and collectivization—will require us to clarify the Party's view of rural social organization. Villages were held to contain five social groups: landlords, owning more than fifty hectares of land; wealthy peasants, owning roughly ten to fifty hectares; middle peasants, with five to ten hectares; poor peasants, one to five hectares; and landless agricultural proletarians holding under one hectare.[60] Since the land reform had eliminated the first group through expropriation, as well as most of the last group by giving them the former's property, there were really three classes in the countryside: wealthy, middle, and poor peasants. Among the wealthy (and a few middle) peasants were some whom the Party had labeled *chiabur* (pronounced kya BOOR). We discuss their importance to the story of collectivization in chapter 6 but will briefly explain the term here. These were the people known in the Soviet Union as "kulaks," a term sometimes used by Romanians as well, especially the political elite. Although usually translated as "wealthy peasants," it is best understood to mean the rural bourgeoisie, who might include innkeepers or traders with relatively little land who had the capacity to exploit others. The root of the word chiabur is the Turkish *kibar*, meaning "good farmer," "rich," or "noble."[61] Not all wealthy peasants were chiaburs, nor were all chiaburs wealthy peasants, but the two categories did overlap considerably.

The idea behind the Soviet concept of "kulak" lay in the theory of class war central to Leninism. Labeling people kulaks/chiaburs would render visible a rural class defined by exploitation, and this would constitute the basis of fomenting class war in the countryside—critical in collectivization strategy. As exploiters, they were the rural enemies of socialism. Identifying specific members of exploiting and exploited classes would facilitate turning the latter against the former. It was fairly easy to define who was a poor peasant: one who owned small amounts of land and had to hire out his labor. Chiaburs, however, were not so easy. Sometimes cadres spoke primarily in terms of amounts of land held, sometimes in terms of other criteria. In (Marxist-Leninist) theory, they were recognizable by virtue of certain characteristics, and indeed, lists of chia-

[59] ANIC, Fond C.C. al P.C.R.–Cancelarie, file 13/1952, 117. Cited in Levy 2002: 101.

[60] See Şandru 2005: 55. These amounts were not fixed; discussions within the Party leadership might use different figures at different times, particularly in determining what constituted a "chiabur."

[61] Sometimes the word chiabur is inflected in the feminine as well: chiabură, chiaburoaică. For the ease of the reader, we will use the plural "chiaburs." The Turkish root also refers to someone from a good, cultured family. Its connotations paralleled the status-based meaning of prosperous peasants (see chapter 6), while the Party's usage of chiabur transformed it to mark the class distinction between exploiter and nonexploiter. The term had not been known in most villages until the communists introduced it.

burs in Romanian archives look precisely like that—names are followed by inventories (the amount of land and agricultural equipment held, the number of family members who work the land, any servants or day laborers, etc.), with a summary justification based on this list. For example: "I. S. 3 family members, head is 65 years old. Possesses 6.83 ha of land/hayfields. Was merchant in the past. Sharecropped his land out. Presently works it with day-laborers."[62] Such clear-cut descriptions notwithstanding, it proved very complex to identify actual chiaburs—as was true of kulaks in the Soviet Union as well.

Almost as hard to define were the middle peasants. The boundary separating them from chiaburs was very permeable, and here lay a problem. In the Party's view, it was the "nature" of middle peasants to hesitate or "waver" (*a şovăi*) in their support of collectivization and to become the allies of the richer peasants rather than of the poorer ones, as the Party wished. But middle peasants were critical to the success of collectivizing, since they would provide a larger fund of land—and the motivation to work it productively—than could be achieved by bringing in the poor and landless. Moreover, in both the Soviet Union and Romania it was they who held the bulk of the country's grain (Lewin 1968: 77). Therefore, middle peasants were the ones who had most to be disciplined, and labeling chiaburs helped to do that.[63] In a sense, it was they who were the real target of that process: the label "chiabur" would frighten middle peasants away from accumulating capital lest they too be so labeled. Owing to their importance, then, it was essential that cadres not misclassify them as chiaburs; various means were available for reclassifying them "properly," should a mistake occur.

How did all this relate to food requisitions? To begin with, quotas and agricultural taxes were assigned as a function of one's social category and the amount of land one held, with exponential increments across categories (see table 2.2). Officials would then exert tremendous pressure on all groups to turn over their quotas in a timely way, with large fines if they did not. Even poor and middle peasants found them onerous, but for chiaburs they were often crippling. This strategy, mirroring that of the Soviet Union in the 1930s, differed from it in one important respect, mentioned above: whereas Soviet practice was ultimately to *liquidate* the kulaks, in Romania the chiaburs were to be merely "*limited*" (*îngrădit*), prevented from reproducing their class position. Romania would not repeat the Soviet experience of the expulsion and starvation of millions of wealthy peasants.

The reason—and here we return to the problem created by the agrarian re-

[62] ARO, Fond Sfat Popular al Regiunii Stalin, file "Despre chiaburi din raza raionului Odorhei 1951." Nr. Inventor 38, 42. Courtesy of Sándor Oláh.

[63] Lewin observes (1968: 417) that the regime's use of the kulak's fate to threaten the rest of the peasants was very effective, precisely because many peasants could not tell the difference between themselves and those being persecuted.

form—was that the chiaburs' agricultural production was essential to the Party's plans. They were the only group in the villages who regularly produced the marketable surpluses essential to building up industry and an urban working class. At a 1949 meeting of the Secretariat, Luca observed, "We can't liquidate the chiaburs before we can supply bread and we can't promote class war before we consolidate the decisive alliance of the poor and middle peasants."[64] Moghioroş expressed a similar opinion in 1950: "It's not for the love of chiaburs that we avoid liquidating them, but we are not economically prepared. The chiabur still has an important role concerning commodity production. . . . It follows that liquidating them prematurely [would be] a strong blow against ourselves."[65] To compel them to provide more of the necessary commodities, chiaburs were assessed quotas designed both to extort their entire surplus from them, so as to prevent them from expanding their operations (here is the meaning of "limiting" them), and also to force them to produce even more than they were already accustomed to doing, so they might have something left over for their families to eat after the collectors had finished. A smart chiabur, the reasoning went, would try to improve his farming to keep up with his quotas; the state would be the beneficiary. The reasoning made sense, since the very low productivity of Romanian agriculture left much room for improvement. Even middle peasants had to work hard to fulfill their quotas; quotas might move them also to greater diligence so as to increase their harvests.

The final connection between quotas and the "class" categories had to do with the Party's strategy in the countryside, which was to base itself on the poor and landless peasants; seek to build an alliance involving them, the working class, and the middle peasants; and create class war between that bloc of actors and the chiaburs. Quotas played an important part in this strategy. The huge sanctions for delay or nonfulfillment would most often be imposed upon the wealthy peasants. Party cadres expected that because it was chiaburs who had to give the most, they were the ones most likely to sabotage the process—to hide some of their grain and then complain that they could not pay up because their harvest had been small, to use their superior resources to bribe the quota collectors or to devise stratagems for stealing back some of their produce, to call upon poorer villagers to store some of their excess grain and later return it, etc. Here the quotas would serve our sixth function: fomenting class war in the villages, for it was expected that poorer peasants—the Party's allies—would denounce these acts of sabotage and help bring the guilty to justice.

Ana Pauker pointed out, however, the difficulties with this expectation and the importance of proceeding nonetheless: "The poor peasant doesn't want just to show us where the chiabur's grain is hidden, he asks us not to let the chiabur

[64] ANIC, Fond C.C. al P.C.R.–Cancelarie, file 15/1949, 8 (RLA).

[65] ANIC, Fond C.C. al P.C.R.–Cancelarie, file 56/1950. Quoted in Ionescu-Gură 2005: 506.

find out *he* was the one who told us. If the majority of peasants see that the communists know how to expose the chiabur, then even the poor will see that they're stronger than the chiaburs."[66] As we will show more fully in chapter 6, the policy of promoting class war in the villages was a centerpiece of the entire period from 1948 to 1962. The chiabur, the quintessential "class enemy," would be hounded, vilified, humiliated, and economically driven to the brink of ruin. But—and this is key—the practical side of persecuting chiaburs was that they could be pushed further than the others to provide food for the industrial drive upon which Romania's communists were determined to embark, and harassing them would keep the middle peasantry in line.

Nevertheless, finding the right balance between marginalizing chiaburs and still being able to use them was an enduring problem. If chiaburs were jailed, the Party would not benefit from their production, as Ana Pauker observed in a high-level meeting: "Three hundred kulaks arrested. But will they be planting seeds in the spring?"[67] In 1952 it was decided to expel chiaburs who had joined collectives but to compensate them with land and other assistance, since it was "unjust [*nejust*] not to return their land, because to do so would mean . . . depriving the state of the quotas and taxes that this large number of chiaburs is supposed to give."[68] In 1954, in its ongoing assessment of the lists of chiaburs, the Party leadership decided to permit them to give their land to poor peasants and remove themselves from the lists; large numbers took advantage of this opportunity, with the consequence that food collections fell—in Constanța region, from 2,411 chiabur households with quotas totaling 12,504 tons of grain in 1954, the numbers dropped in 1955 to 167 chiabur households with quotas of only 417 tons (Oprea 2009: 54). As a result, Party leaders decided to reverse the policy, insisting that chiaburs repossess the land they had given away and plant crops on it for their quotas (54). A remarkable example of this same problem—that getting rid of chiaburs meant a decline in the food supply—comes from a 1952 Politburo decision that instead of jailing peasants who had not given their quotas, their sentences were suspended so they could produce food before serving their time, since it was the middle of the harvest season. This dilemma—that penalties for inadequate procurement would further reduce procurements—led Party leaders to consider sending chiaburs home from jail as an act of clemency, so they could produce their quotas![69] Indeed, Kligman has both interviews and corroborating archival data concerning chiaburs who were temporarily released from jail (with a bribe on the wife's part) to plant or harvest

66 ANIC, Fond C.C. al P.C.R–Cancelarie, file 6/1952, 19–21 (RLA).

67 Ibid., 11 (RLA). This was her response to Ceaușescu in a meeting of CC members and the Council of Ministers. He responded that they must be forced to.

68 ANIC, Fond C.C. al P.C.R. (source unspecified), July 15, 1952, 5, and file 754/1952 on chiaburs infiltrated into GACs.

69 ANIC, Fond C.C. al P.C.R.–Cancelarie, file 107/1952, 9–10 (RLA).

their quotas and then sent back to finish their sentences.[70] Thus, the logic of procuring food was at odds with the logic of enforcing its procurement.

Determining exactly how to organize the quota system occupied a great deal of the time of the top leadership, and discussions in their closed meetings reveal considerable confusion as to what they were doing and how it should be done. The matter was exceedingly complex, for it was closely related to pricing policy in agriculture—an issue of major disagreement. One position, represented by Gheorghiu-Dej closely following Stalin, was to starve agriculture of investment and force its surpluses into developing industry, using quotas and collectivization as the means. The opposing position (most often represented by Pauker and Luca) was rather to develop the two together, industry serving agriculture with goods to absorb peasants' earnings; collectivization should wait until industry had developed sufficiently to perform these tasks. The former position argued for keeping agricultural prices low and the terms of trade negative, while the latter position argued for higher agricultural prices so that the peasantry would be able to serve as an internal market. As Pauker put it in a meeting of the Politburo in 1947, "[Y]ou don't gain anything, worker, when you buy things from the peasant with prices that are nothing. Then he won't be able to buy goods and you'll end up unemployed" (quoted in Levy 2001: 92–93). But this Bukharinist view did not prevail.[71]

What was at stake was nothing less than the growth or retardation of capitalist agriculture and what the Party's role in these processes should be. To promote the Pauker line was to argue for high agricultural prices, which would encourage peasants to accumulate capital and buy industrial goods toward making their agriculture more productive. The scenario would work only if prices were relatively free, not fixed, as the opposing faction wished. Dej expressed his displeasure with this policy: "We want to achieve a socialist accumulation at the expense of the capitalist elements in the countryside: to siphon it off from [them] and put it in the industrial sector" (quoted in Levy 2001: 95). He preferred to suppress the market and fix prices, so the peasant would sell "at the price we want and not the one he wants. . . . Let the peasant chase after [industrial goods] with his tongue hanging out. It's not good if he makes money so easily" (95). When even the quotas did not produce enough foodstuffs, a parallel debate arose, as to whether peasants should be allowed to sell produce on the market once they had given their quotas and taxes, and if so, whether the state should control the price of those goods or let it float, at the risk of creating capitalism in the countryside.

This debate had serious implications for food requisitions. When prices went up, peasants took their grain to market rather than fulfilling their quota

[70] B. S., Kligman interview.

[71] See note 32 above.

obligations. When prices fell, they hoarded their goods, claiming that they had nothing, until prices rose. The first scenario delivered agricultural commodities to urban centers, but at prices the workers could not afford; the second caused shortages. To feed urban workers cheaply, the easiest solution was to seize agricultural commodities by force—precisely what the quotas were designed to do. Pauker herself gave the most succinct rationale: "Until we succeed in improving agricultural productivity, collections are what give the state the possibility to acquire quantities of produce."[72] The policy decided upon, then, would be the Stalinist one: to push heavy industrial development at the expense of consumer industries, depriving peasants of any incentive to market their goods, and that in turn would require force to get food out of their hands into the cities.

Central Party meetings were full of discussions about the difficulties of collecting the quotas, of unfulfilled plans for requisitions, and of what to do about them. Leaders commented favorably on a solution that worked well in some locations and should be used more widely: cadres had organized teams of peasants who *had* paid their quotas to go house to house, ferreting out the hidden produce of their fellow villagers.[73] The minutes of meetings show a constant preoccupation with the numbers, along with worries that peasants who claim they have nothing to give are fooling—or corrupting—local cadres. In a discussion concerning the police, it was reported that "lower levels are collaborating with the chiaburs. Last evening I found a case in Roseti, where the policeman boards with a chiabur. When a comrade from the Financial Section went to sequester the chiabur's possessions, the policeman's wife said they were *her* things and in fact they were the chiabur's."[74] In addition, a comment from Pauker:

> We have to fulfill the plan because in the first place we need grain, and in the second place so peasants can learn once and for all that they can't get out of this obligation. . . . Next year we'll do better, but then too we'll have problems with peasants who won't want to give and will devise new methods to deceive us. But first we have to impede their finding new methods and then make [the peasant] realize that we're not stupider than he is and that we're determined to find him out.[75]

In response to all these concerns, harsher penalties were meted out, as warnings to others; thousands of peasants were put on trial and sent to labor colonies or prison for not giving over their quotas (see Bălan 2000).

[72] ANIC, Fond C.C. al P.C.R.–Cancelarie, file 6/1952 (RLA).

[73] Moghioroș in a meeting of representatives of the CC of the P.M.R. and the Council of Ministers, ANIC, Fond C.C. al P.C.R.–Cancelarie, file 6/1952 (RLA).

[74] ANIC, Fond 1, file 99/1951, 7–8 (RLA).

[75] ANIC, Fond C.C. al P.C.R.–Cancelarie, file 6/1952, 2 (RLA). We note that in many of these discussions, speakers emphasize not wanting the peasants to make a mockery of the Party. By the same token, a central theme of our village respondents was that the Party had made a mockery of them.

The top leaders were also concerned with the actions of lower-level cadres—and justifiably so, for local officials charged with collecting quotas hated the job and often would not enforce the law, for fear of alienating the peasantry or suffering local repercussions. Instead, they lobbied higher-ups to have the quotas reduced. Even Party members and civil servants did not give their assigned quotas; reasonably enough, peasants complained that if not even those people would give them, how could everyone else be expected to do so?[76] Teohari Georgescu emphasized,

> If it was a matter only of kulaks, it would be an easy problem to solve, but you have here lawbreakers who are also in the state apparatus. What measures can we have the police take against middle or poor peasants when even the president of the People's Council or his deputies oppose handing over quotas? 99% of the functionaries haven't given their quota. . . . The apparatus that is supposed to apply [the law] are the ones who don't respect it and give nothing."[77]

Party leaders worried that the Party's moral authority was being compromised by the state's inability to enforce quota collections and blamed themselves for inadequate work with lower-level cadres.[78] What with natural disasters, hidden produce, sympathetic local officials, Party members who undermined the state's authority, and a variety of other subterfuges, it is no surprise that the plans for requisitions generally went underfulfilled. We can see this in numerous documents that list "amounts planned" against "amounts received," frequently with huge gaps between the two sets of figures.[79]

Brutality and abuses often marked the increasingly stringent legislation and the activities of collectors. Our respondents uniformly remembered the time of quotas as the time when "they took everything. We had nothing left to eat." The wealthier peasants in particular, they recalled, had such high requisitions that they had to buy products on the market to give as quotas. (We note, however, that this sometimes constituted a form of resistance that our respondents did not know about or had forgotten: wealthy peasants would sell their own goods on the black market at a good price but then buy the equivalent at the state price, to give as their quotas.) Anyone who claimed not to have enough to cover his quotas might have his harvest confiscated, along with valuables from his house and courtyard. Members of the Securitate and police accompanied collectors at harvest time, plainly revealing the coercion necessary to gathering foodstuffs from

[76] One member of the Agrarian Commission noted in February 1951 that of 306 secretaries of local Party organizations across the country, only 109 had handed over the quotas for 1950; 86 handed over partial quotas, etc. (ANIC, Fond C.C. al P.C.R.-Cancelarie, file 10/1951, 3 [RLA]).

[77] ANIC, Fond 1, file 3/1951, 8–9 (RLA).

[78] See, for example, the notes from a meeting of the Central Committee with the presidents of regional people's councils, ANIC, Fond 1, file 55/1951 (RLA).

[79] For a random example, see ACNSAS, FD, file 7/v. 1, 24–30, in which the percent realized relative to the plan ranges from 99 percent down to 24 percent. (Courtesy of Smaranda Vultur.)

the peasantry. Their reports are revealing of the leadership's concern for sabotage by both peasants and cadres alike. Here is an example.

Report Sent by the General Directorate of State Security in Bacău to The General Directorate of State Security Concerning Collections.

11 August 1952

In response to your order no. 254/234419 of August 8, 1952 concerning the collection of agricultural products, we report:

On our beat, threshing began almost at the end of July [and] the collection operations have proceeded satisfactorily. Thus, at present, of a planned total of 12,289.69 tons of wheat, 344.80 tons have been collected, representing 28% [sic]; of a planned 430.17 tons of rye, 224.5 tons were realized; of a planned 302.25 tons of oats, 22 tons were realized, representing 1.0%; of a planned 220.10 tons of barley, 111 tons were realized, representing 50.2%; of a planned 478.46 tons of peas, 14 tons were realized, representing 2.93%. . . .

Difficulties owing to enemy elements that tried to help the peasantry not to give their quotas . . . were noted as follows [names and locations of nine chiaburs and one middle peasant], all of whom had enemy manifestations that caused problems for the operations of collection. Measures were taken against the above-mentioned by collecting evidence and in keeping with your orders they were handed over to labor colonies and referred to Justice.

As enemy elements infiltrated into the apparatus of collections our attention was called to . . . the Director of the Regional Receiving Center, S. Gh., who was referred to the regional RWP for removal from his post for being dishonest, a drunkard, a womanizer, making no effort at work and not checking up on his subordinates.

The mood of the poor and middle peasantry is satisfactory, inasmuch as there is a good harvest and they have enough to give their quotas, there have been no cases up to now of dissatisfaction.

[signatures][80]

As we saw early in this section, peasants did not necessarily comply with their assigned quotas. Other reports as well as our interviews show them hiding grain, land, or sheep; bribing collectors where possible or colluding with them to recover some of their produce; selling it before the collectors came and then claiming to have nothing to give; weighting wool and grain quotas with sand; slaughtering animals or sending them to relatives' herds in other villages; and so on. And, especially after 1949, as quotas became a political weapon rather than being merely a response to famine, peasants responded with uprisings, which were brutally put down.[81]

[80] ASRI, Fond D, file 9404/14, 78–79. (See Roske 2003: 62–64.)

[81] See multiple examples in Roske 2003; Robert Levy archive, UCLA; volumes of the journals *Analele Sighet* and *Arhivele Totalitarismului*; Iordachi and Dobrincu 2009.

In summary, quotas were the first of the Party's two major policies for compelling a recalcitrant peasantry to produce more foodstuffs, thereby contributing to the payment of war reparations, ensuring an urban food supply, generating surplus to be transferred into industrial development, and encouraging peasants to join collectives. In addition, quotas helped to promote friction between groups in the countryside, to prevent wealthy peasants from accumulating capital, and in that way to obstruct the development of capitalism in rural areas. Quotas were considered a necessity precisely owing to the underdevelopment of capitalism in agriculture. (At the same time, by compelling peasants to sell or buy goods for quotas they could not fulfill, the quota system increased commodification and the circulation of money.) Moreover, because the agrarian reform had eliminated many market-oriented farms, in no way could surpluses be generated other than by forcing peasants to produce—and in particular, forcing the group that produced the most to produce even more.

Initially aimed at securing food, the quotas increasingly became a weapon in the class war and an essential component of collectivization. In all these guises they generated resistance on the part of peasants and violence on the part of cadres charged with collecting them. After they were ended in 1957, food procurement had to rely on contracts. Lest the peasants see the shift as a sign of Party weakness, however, the authorities rearrested "enemies" who had already been released from prison prior to 1956, as a precautionary measure.

Collectivization

Despite some of the leaders' doubts about the wisdom of full collectivization, the Soviet Union's determination to push for it prevailed when the Cominform conference voted for it in 1948. This led Romania's communists to initiate collective farms; the decision was announced at a Plenary session of the Central Committee, March 3–5, 1949. The decision would end the economic and political independence of the large majority of Romania's population, 77 percent of whom lived in villages at the time. It would involve by far the most massive exercise of force against the peasantry in Romania's modern history. To the extent that the peasantry represented—as many Romanians believed—the repository of the national identity, that too would be placed in question (Negrici 2003: 8). Notwithstanding significant differences between Romanian and Soviet rural life, the model employed would be the Soviet one, with some variations (such as the matter of liquidating the kulaks, mentioned above, and the fact that Romania had relatively less agricultural machinery when the drive began).

This is not to say that the Party spoke with one voice on the matter. Notes on the meetings of the Central Committee, Politburo, and other top leadership forums contain much evidence of divergent views of the kind we have already discussed concerning quotas, the terms of trade between agriculture and industry, and so on.[82] For instance, there was frequent debate about the pace of collectivizing: should it be gradual or forced? Proponents of the former view—that of the Pauker faction—feared that speed would permanently alienate the peasants, compromising both the food supply and Romania's economic development, while proponents of the latter view argued that gradualism would reinforce the autonomy of peasants and constrain the Party's freedom of maneuver. Until Pauker was forced out, one or the other view held sway, producing frequent changes in policy that made the process far from linear. There were also arguments about whether chiaburs were to be permitted to enter the collectives or should rather be left out, or even expelled from their villages, as they had been in the Soviet Union. Moreover, leaders disagreed as to the very status of the class category "chiabur": was it immutable—once a class enemy, always a class enemy? Could people shed their chiabur status? Was there such a thing as a "former chiabur"? It was important to know this, as long as Party policy was to prevent chiaburs from joining collectives, which, it was feared, they would sabotage.

Another source of dispute concerned whose initiative should undergird the formation of collectives: the peasants' or the Party's? If peasant initiative were to be the basis for forming a collective, then the Party would not have the leading role; better the Party should *create* peasant initiative through propaganda work. The correct line was formulated at a 1950 CC meeting as follows: "[T]he socialist transformation of agriculture does not happen by itself, for that task falls to the party and the proletariat. The initiative to move towards socialism does not belong to the peasants" (quoted in Levy 2001: 103). Yet another argument concerned which of the possible forms of cooperation should be emphasized (in addition to the state farms, already being created from confiscated land): should there be only one, the Soviet artel or kolkhoz, or should other forms of associating for agricultural work or the marketing of produce be encouraged?[83] Initial emphasis was placed on the Soviet-type kolkhoz; the mid-1950s brought other organizational forms but these were later phased out, leaving only a single form as the campaign drew to a close.

In discussing how collectivization proceeded, we must distinguish between state and collective farms, for both the process of their formation and their functioning were very different (see Verdery 2003: 52–55).[84] The basis for creat-

[82] For further discussion of intra-Party debates, see Levy 2001 and Tismăneanu 2003. These debates contributed crucially to Pauker's downfall.

[83] See Stănescu 1957: chapter 2 for discussion of the various possibilities.

[84] A state farm, modeled on the Soviet sovkhoz, was at first called a State Agricultural Farm (*Gospodărie Agricolă de Stat* [GAS]), and later a State Agricultural Enterprise (*Întreprindere Agricolă de Stat* [IAS]). A collective farm, modeled on the Soviet kolkhoz, was known at first as a Collective Agricultural Farm (*Gospodărie Agricolă Colectivă* [GAC]) and later as an Agricultural Production Cooperative (*Cooperativă Agricolă de Producție* [CAP]). The most common form of simpler associations was called an *întovărășire*, modeled on the Soviet TOZ and using the Slavic

ing state farms (initially known as GASs) was laid as early as the 1945 agrarian reform, when the state began to acquire land by confiscating and nationalizing the property of "enemies of the people" and of large landlords. GASs were generally begun on large blocks of expropriated land; their labor was paid a fixed wage; the land in them was state property, belonging to "the whole people"; they received significantly higher levels of investment than collective farms; and they worked with their own machinery. By contrast, collective farms (initially known as GACs), consisted of tiny parcels of land that were not confiscated but "voluntarily donated" by villagers to form a common fund, of which not "the whole people" but the farm's members jointly were the proprietors. Pay in GACs was not a fixed wage but a combination of cash and goods in kind, remunerating the number of labor days each member family contributed.[85] Except for some extensive investments at the beginning of the collectivization campaign, GACs received much lower levels of investment than did GASs and did not have their own machinery—they were served by state machinery parks known as SMTs (later SMAs).[86] Throughout the communist period, land was moved back and forth between collective and state farms. The process we discuss in this book largely concerns the formation of collectives: how Party cadres compelled households to "donate" their land and to become an underpaid and undervalued labor force.

As initially established by the Party and following Leninist principle, a GAC should be created through the "free consent" of people signing their land over to common ownership and management. The leaders saw the principle of free consent as crucial to establishing the legitimacy of the Party and the legality of its actions, even if only by a façade; free consent was to demonstrate support for the regime performatively. Thus, throughout Romania's collectivization campaign, leaders frequently asked whether or not the principle of free consent was being trampled (as it often was).[87] Perhaps anticipating that consent might be less than forthcoming, cadres began the campaign by targeting peasants who had firearms from the abundant supplies left over after the war. In some areas these were being used in the anticommunist resistance; the authorities feared their further use against collectivization. The Securitate had various means of

---

root meaning "comrade" (*tovarăș*). See Miller 2009 for discussion of the various legal forms and their differences through time.

[85] See Kideckel 1993 for a description of variations in the way collective farmers were paid.

[86] *Stațiune de Mașini și Tractoare* and *Stațiune de Mașini Agricole*.

[87] The abuses suffered by peasants whose "free consent" had to be obtained are detailed in the many memoirs and scholarly works that have appeared since 1989, too voluminous to cite here. In responding to complaints by peasants from Hunedoara region about abuse, Dej skillfully responded: "Only those who are convinced that the collective is better than an individual small farm must enter. Slowly, slowly, others will be convinced and will come of their own good will, not forced. A collective cannot be made with force. . . . Coercive methods are foreign to us and badly harm our Party." See ANIC, Fond C.C. al P.C. R.–Cancelarie, file 23/1951, 5 (quoted in Anghelache 1999: 615).

Figure 2.3. A model State Farm. One of the slogans reads "Long live the Romanian Workers' Party, the vanguard of the working class!" Courtesy of Artexpo Foundation.

finding out who had weapons and would then go to demand them. In many villages, Securitate officers came in and took away a number of those suspected of having weapons, beat them severely, and threatened them with jail to make them give up their arms. Alternatively, they would be told that if they gave up their weapons at once and joined the collective, they would suffer no further reprisals. Often enough, the police themselves would bring a weapon into the house of some recalcitrant peasant, "find" it, and arrest the person in consequence.[88] In this way, potentially dangerous villagers were rendered harmless.

Following the March 1949 Plenary, the CC invited each county to propose a small number of localities that might become the first GACs. They were to select these localities carefully, so as to meet certain conditions, such as a minimum number of members and enough high-quality land to yield a minimum total size that would generate good results. Of the first 60 proposals offered in 1949, the CC approved only 21; of the 1,350 proposals received by early 1950, it approved only 120 (Levy 2001: 102). The goal was to establish model GACs and GASs whose performance would be far superior to the results of individual farming, and by these means to attract additional peasants into joining them or forming new GACs of their own (see Goina 2009). As it happened, those signing into the first GACs tended to come disproportionately from the poor and

[88] For example, Iordachi (2003: 25) reports widespread use of this technique in two districts of Constanța region and one in Bucharest region. See also OSA RFE Item No. 2569/1958, "Constanța, Difficulties of Peasant Life," 8.

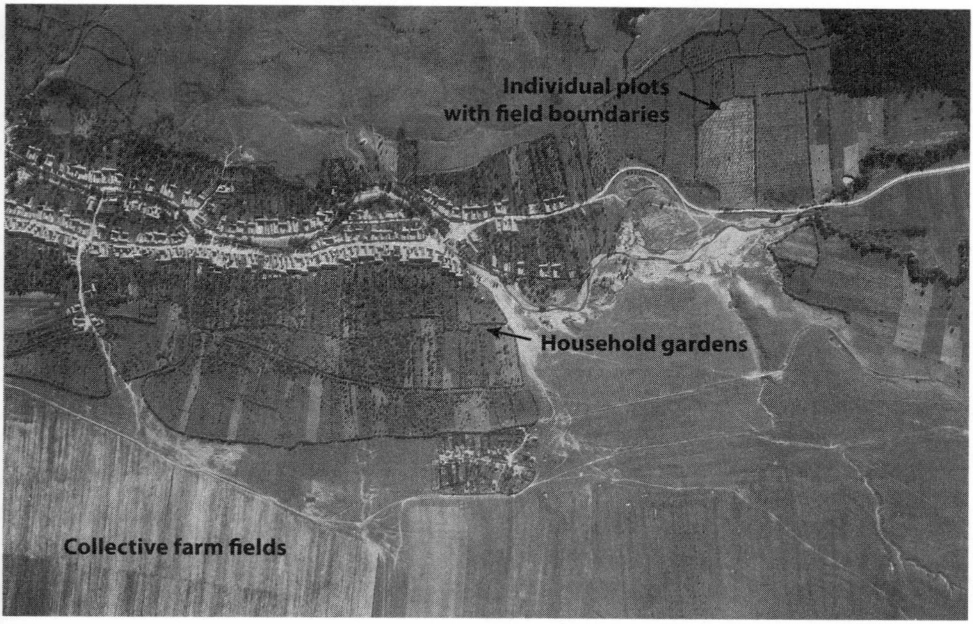

Figure 2.4. Romos village after collectivization (completed 1962). Note the contrast between the large unbounded fields of the collective, lower left, formed by plowing over villagers' land parcels (traces of which are faintly visible), and the boundaries around individual plots at top right, as well as around household gardens. Courtesy of I.C.F.C.O.T., Siebenbürgen-Institut, Gundelsheim, Germany.

landless peasantry, who had little to lose and the most to gain if the GACs were a success. Because they were unable to bring in much land, the state supplied additional land from GASs or other sources to bring the surface area of a new GAC up to one to two hundred hectares.

The quality of the soil and the concentration of state investments made productivity on the early GACs (in our sample, Sântana and Pechea) much superior to that of individual farms, but power politics within the Party leadership soon altered the course of the experiment. Beginning in the summer of 1950, the first of a long series of policy reversals forced an increase in the pace of forming GACs as the center ceded control over the process to local authorities, following Pauker's departure from the Agrarian Section for medical reasons in June. Her replacement, Moghioroş, hewing closely to Soviet advice as Pauker had not, began pushing for the formation of one thousand new GACs. He assigned each region a fixed target and encouraged local cadres to surpass it. The violent summer that ensued in the countryside was the work of these cadres, as they set about the task with considerable license. Counties began trying to outdo one another in "socialist competitions" to see which could form more of them; "free consent" went out the window at the local level, and although the center still upheld the consent principle, reports of coercion became commonplace. So did violent resistance, as peasants revolted against the attempt to force them in (see Bălan 2000; Iordachi and Dobrincu 2009; Mungiu-Pippidi 2010). Central Party officials, recognizing that they had ceded too much control to local cadres, instituted another reversal of policy that brought these uprisings and the formation of GACs to a halt, restoring central authority over the collectivization process. In 1951 no new ones were created beyond those already approved the previous year, and peasants who had been forced to join collectives were allowed to leave them. Reasons for the reversal included problems with the food supply and the return of Pauker to her job. Tănase (1998: 141) suggests a more systemic reason:

> After two years of generalized assault on the peasants and individual property, the elite—in comparison with the other [East European] communist elites—registered the least progress. They were forced to interrupt the collectivization campaign in 1951. 80% of the arable surface remained in the private sector. The main cause of this first major defeat of the Romanian communist elite was the relation of forces between that elite and the peasantry, a relation favorable to the peasants.[89]

For the remainder of 1951 (and later as well), more emphasis was placed on strengthening existing GACs than on forming new ones. This entailed further field consolidation and exchanges of land between members of the GACs and those who had refused to join—exchanges that usually resulted in centrally located land of high quality going to the GACs, while the owners received marginal land of low quality in return. These exchanges were supposed to be registered, with the signatures of those whose land was effectively confiscated by these means, but such registration often did not take place.[90] Another modification of strategy at this time was that the Party began to introduce a less stringent form of cooperation, called "associations" (*întovărăşiri*, also TOZs), which allowed peasants to keep their land and implements but required them to cultivate in common.[91] Peasants were familiar with such forms from the prewar cooperative movement and joined them more readily than the GACs. Finally, in addition to these changes, Pauker decreed stiff penalties for any cadre who forced peasants into GACs, including trial and expulsion from the Party. She expressed her views succinctly in a meeting of the Central Committee's Agrar-

[89] This followed the Soviet pattern that we see in Viola's work (1996).

[90] Decree 151/1950 specified that the exchanges were "obligatory for all owners whose lands are subject to consolidation" (Cătănus and Roske 2007: 163; see Verdery 1994: 1090–93 for more details). Field consolidations were never popular with peasants and caused considerable resistance.

[91] As some peasants aptly put it, the TOZ was the collective's fiancée! (See Dobrincu 2009: 288.) Tănase observes that TOZs represented a compromise between the elites and the peasantry—the former "unable to impose Soviet-style collectivization, and the peasant class unable to hold onto what it had obtained through the agrarian reforms of 1921 and 1945" (1998: 164).

ian Section in 1951: "Only someone irresponsible, only an adventurer, only a person cut off from the masses and from our party . . . can think that it is possible to establish collective farms with people who are forced, and that such collective farms can possibly be viable" (Levy 2001: 109). With this attitude at the helm, it is not surprising that by 1952, Romania had the smallest percentage of land in collectives of any bloc country (111).[92] Equally unsurprising is that Romania's leaders were frequently finding it difficult to shoehorn Romania into the Soviet model.[93]

The proponents of speed once again took over in 1952, leading to more GACs, more violations of free consent, more peasant uprisings, and more reprisals. The increase probably owed something to further intervention by the Soviets, connected with their role in creating a currency reform in that year, at which time they complained that food requisitions were not proceeding fast enough and progress was too slow (Levy 2001: 116). Quotas were increased, and peasants streamed into collectives to avoid them. Following Pauker's purge later that year, the violence and coercion intensified; the center gave back to local officials the authority that Pauker had centralized for forming collectives, and abuses increased in consequence. As Levy (2001: 129) puts it, "The familiar dynamic of the periphery's leading the center soon took over." A new offensive against chiaburs occasioned further violence, with mass arrests and trials of over one hundred thousand middle peasants exposed or "unmasked" as chiaburs. Cadres shaved the heads of chiabur women who failed to hand over their grain, kept chiaburs standing all night long or put them up in trees, staged mass public trials in which they were vilified and humiliated, and assigned them lengthy prison sentences. In the six months after Pauker's departure, there were eight thousand trials of chiaburs (132).

Stalin's death in March 1953 precipitated yet another reversal. Taxes and some quotas were reduced, and paid contracts began to appear alongside the quotas. Between 1953 and 1956—a period of relative relaxation—far more peasants entered the TOZ associations than the collectives. We see this in table 2.4, which shows the progress of collectivizing up to the point at which collectives and associations were merged. The table reveals that when peasants had the option of the less radical form, they preferred it. Because increases in the urban population were outstripping the ability of GACs to supply it with food, during 1955 the market was liberalized and Securitate pressure on villagers re-

[92] According to Roske (2000: 31), land collectivized by this date represented: 3 percent in Romania; 3.5 percent in Poland (where collectivization was later abandoned); 8.1 percent in Hungary; 19 percent in Czechoslovakia; 51 percent in Bulgaria.

[93] See, for example, discussions during the Party meetings of February 14, 1952 (ANIC, C.C. al P.C.R.–Cancelarie 2/1952, 253) and May 22, 1952 (forums unidentified, 296). At the former, Luca observed that the situation is different from the Soviet Union because Romania has millions of individual farms that have to be prevented from accumulating capital; at the latter, it was noted that the Soviet model is not well applied in Romania because the SMTs work in a disorganized way and plow the lands of all categories of peasants to make their plan.

duced; both policies were also related to Romania's being accepted into the United Nations (Oprea 2009: 54).

This respite came to an end at the Party's Second Congress, in December 1955, which, despite the destalinization occurring elsewhere in the bloc, decided to make collectivization a top priority in the second Five-Year Plan. Quotas were increased again, markets were closed, and ever more peasants joined the associations to avoid their quotas. Armies of activists, including twenty-five hundred from the Central Committee itself, headed for the countryside to intensify propaganda. Oprea argues, however, that although the leadership had acknowledged the necessity of increasing the pace of collectivization, there had been no planning for the logistics:

> [N]o strategy for action had been formulated, nor were the institutions charged with coordinating the work at all ready. Efforts to reorganize and mobilize the bureaucracy and rejuvenate the activist network that had previously managed the collectivizing operations were not accompanied by a clear plan. The officials and activists knew what they had to do, namely, increase the number of new GACs and TOZs. However, without the repression used in the first three years of collectivization, they did not know how to do it. (2009: 59)

Their model, he suggests, would soon emerge from the so-called Galați experiment, an attempt to step up the pace in one eastern region. The experiment, whose methods proved so successful that they would be imitated all across the country, involved convincing Party members already living in villages—over ten thousand in number—to join the collectives where they lived, something many of them had not wanted to do. They would then press for collectivization from "inside" their communities (see chapter 3). Moreover, the majority of territorial instructors (what we later call "outside" cadres) now moved with their families into the villages whose members they were trying to seduce. This was seen as a crucial improvement over the earlier method of sending "teams from the Center," who would work over the heads of local Party organizations and undermine their authority.[94] The territorial instructors worked with an arsenal of films, posters, expositions of superior produce from GACs, and so on. Moreover, the instructors and propagandists thus sent out were much better adapted to their sites. They organized themselves according to groups of houses, which they assaulted with methods of persuasion not always based on "free consent" (see Oprea 2009: 61). That GAC members rarely showed up for work was conveniently ignored as the Party leadership, at a meeting in June 1956, proclaimed this model the one for achieving full collectivization.

[94] In this way, peasants were deprived of the ability to delay joining the collectives by holding out for "someone bigger" who might reverse the decisions of communal or district collectivizers. Márton explains how during the mass withdrawals from GACs in the Mureş region in 1950–51, delegates from the Central Committee had gone out to some villages to calm things down; thereafter, peasants refused to speak with anyone from a lower hierarchical level, saying that "they were too small" compared with the CC representatives (2005: 52).

Data sent from the regions to the capital revealed the large numbers of actors whom the "Galați method" mobilized and sent to villages for the task. For example, the Baia Mare region would later report to the Central Committee that to complete its campaign in March 1962 it had required 369 activists, 131 students from the Party school, 2,126 other activists, 422 engineers and technicians used in political work, plus local agitators totaling 19,714 people, and an additional 3,561 employees of local People's Councils. In all, it took over 26,000 people to complete collectivization in that region (Dobeş et al. 2004: 55), the total rural population of which was around 500,000 at the time. That means about one activist for every four households.[95]

The events in Hungary in October 1956 again slowed the campaign, however, as Romania's leaders sought to regroup in hopes of forestalling similar movements. In predominantly Hungarian parts of multiethnic Transylvania, some GACs were abandoned and reconstituted only with difficulty; even in Romanian villages peasants were heard encouraging fellow villagers to support a similar counterrevolution.[96] A forester in Stalin region observed that "if in Hungary they won their liberty, in three or four days we will win our Romanian legionary liberty too."[97] To quell their concern, Party leaders took additional precautionary measures that included rearresting political prisoners who had already been released. They also made important concessions, the most notable of which was eliminating the system of obligatory quotas, now fully replaced by paid contracts. The relaxation was brief, however. A blitz in the region of Constanța similar to that in Galați involved mobilizing 30,000 activists (for a population of 635,950); excluding urbanites, already-collectivized peasants, children, and the elderly, we get a total of one activist for every three peasants (Tismăneanu et al. 2007: 246–47). They succeeded in fully collectivizing Constanța region by October 1957, making it the first in the country and a model to the other regions (see Iordachi 2009). Among the causes of this success were that properties there, settled by colonists prior to World War I, were the largest of any in Romania, but the productivity of its soil was poor; the

[95] The 1966 census (the nearest date to the one for the 26,000 cadres) gave 498,882 rural residents for Maramureş. (Although GACs were also formed in towns, the majority of the collectivization effort was in the villages; hence, to estimate the density of activists we use the rural population only.) If we use an average of 5 people per household—on the low side for Maramureş—we get 99,776 households, or 3.8 households per activist. If we use a larger number per household, the number of households per activist is even lower.

[96] For example, the 1957 archives for Hunedoara region contain a lengthy file on the penal investigation of the breakup in 1956 of GACs in Jeledinți, a largely Hungarian village, and two other partly or wholly Romanian villages near it (DJAN HD, Fond CR PMR [Agrarian section], file 2431/1957). Securitate investigations from 1956 and 1957 also show villagers being reported on for having encouraged others to follow the example of the Hungarians (see, e.g., ACNSAS, FI, files 3936/2 and 13933, and FP, file 1362).

[97] ANIC, Fond C.C. al P.C.R.–Organizatorică, file 43/1956, 17. The same file mentions student movements in 1956 in various university towns; on these movements, see also Tismăneanu et al. 2007: 681–93.

Figure 2.5. Peasants using a mechanized thresher (1952). Courtesy of *Fototeca online a comunismului românesc*, photograph #W078, *cota* 5/1952.

state's extensive investments in mechanization attracted many peasants for whom the new collectives would provide a better living than if they continued to farm on their own (Iordachi 2009; Şandru 2005: 45). (See figure 2.5.)

As of 1957, then, the campaign to collectivize was once again in full swing, with techniques imitated from region to region and phalanxes of activists moving across the landscape from one just-completed area to another. They sought to form both GACs and TOZ associations that would later be converted to GACs. The tactics employed, which we will discuss at greater length in chapters 4–6, included false promises, threats, and outright violence. As the pressure increased, so did peasant revolts, which were reported for a large number of communities. They were put down brutally: hundreds of peasants were shot (one hundred in one village alone, Vulturu, in Focşani district, where several more revolts occurred as well); others received prison sentences of as much as twenty to twenty-five years, similar to the sentences meted out in the late 1940s to those who had revolted then. One of the most dramatic revolts occurred in 1957 in Vadu Roşca, in the Galaţi region, which Politburo member Nicolae Ceauşescu was charged with repressing (Bălan 2000: 285; Stoica 2009: 423–24), another in Nucşoara, Argeş region (Mungiu-Pippidi 2010; Liiceanu 2003), and numerous others of considerable amplitude elsewhere in the country, through 1962 and even after.[98] Only rarely did the rebels register successes, such as when those in Focşani were allowed to withdraw with their land and implements

[98] For additional examples, see, for example, Cătănuş and Roske 2004; Roske 1992. Bălan notes that revolts on the scale of those in 1949–50 were not registered again until 1958, after which they continued to erupt through 1962 (2000: 284–88). Reliable data on the numbers killed in such revolts do not exist.

from the collective into which they had been forced without their "free consent" (Stoica 2009).

In autumn 1958, the Party announced its plan to push collectivization to conclusion by 1962, three years ahead of the initial plan. The balance of forces was now very different from that of earlier years. Owing to price trends unfavorable to agriculture, villages that had once been fairly independent of the center had been made more dependent on it by supplementing agricultural incomes with industrial and seasonal work. The center, for its part, was less dependent on the peasants than it had been, for it now enjoyed the benefits of an alternative resource: industrial development. As Tănase puts it, "In 1958 when the elite launched its second generalized assault on the peasantry so as to complete collectivization in the next few years, the peasantry was weakened. The CC Plenary of 26–28 November 1958 gave the signal for this new campaign to bring the peasants under control, ending in 1962 with their defeat" (1998: 143). As with the previous attempts to speed up the pace, authority to form GACs was decentralized: only the approval of the regional People's Councils, not the Council of Ministers in Bucharest, was required to ratify the formation of a new GAC (Dobeş et al. 2004: 49). This facilitated turning the TOZ associations into collectives: local cadres would arrange to have TOZ members "vote" for the change in unannounced meetings attended only by trusted confederates; the next day, peasants who thought they were still proprietors of their fields and inventory would discover that they now had to "donate" these to the new GAC (Şandru 2005: 57).

Among the additional weapons of the final assault were increasingly heavy penalties for "threats to public order" and other offenses, of which a network of informers for the Securitate kept Party cadres well apprised. There were also multiple means of intimidation. Among them were forms grounded in kinship relations: industrial workers based in villages would be sent home to persuade their families to join, lest the worker lose his job; families would be threatened with expulsion of their children from school; teachers would humiliate the children of those who hadn't joined by making them stand and mocking them, so they would then plead with their parents to sign up; and so on. This time, however, there were more incentives of other kinds. Activists would promise money or gifts to peasants for joining—or special deals, such as that they did not have to bring all their animals or land, or could take the harvest from their land in the first year, or could remove a hectare from the GAC for their daughter's marriage. Many such conditions appear on the backs of the petitions of entry (see chapter 5).[99] (These promises were illegal, and the conditions on entry petitions were later nullified.)

Decree 115, issued in 1959, prohibited all forms of land rental or wage labor in agriculture, compelling peasants to leave these arrangements for collectives.

[99] For a fascinating discussion of these conditions, see Lăţea 2009.

By the end of 1959, 71 percent of Romania's arable land and 73 percent of its peasant households were in socialist organizations (Şandru 2005: 58). The campaign was briefly relaxed for part of 1960, then resumed in December of that year at the cost of still more peasant revolts. Teams of twenty to thirty activists put constant pressure on peasants who had not yet signed up, ignoring the principle of "free consent" in their determination to complete the drive in 1962.

> In addition to Party cadres, the teams included employees of various state enterprises and offices (accountants, tax collectors, tractor drivers, medical personnel, etc.), unprepared and unfamiliar with farming, former Iron Guard members, even non-Party members, and dubious elements who engaged in provocations, all of them unprepared, with no experience in agriculture. (Oprea 2009: 72)

When Romania's top communists went to the Soviet Union for advice in September 1961, they returned with an even tougher line (73).

By early 1962, regional and district Party organizations were sending out teams of activists with instructions not to return home until they had signed people into GACs. "In Ruginoasa, in Paşcani district, for example, whose peasants were the last in the region of Iaşi to enter the collective farm, these delegates stayed almost two months, following villagers who had hidden themselves so as to avoid signing up and using violence against those they found, to compel them to join the association" (Şandru 2005: 59). In some areas the activists stayed far longer. Relentlessly blazing their way to full collectivization despite ongoing peasant uprisings, the Romanian communists triumphantly declared the campaign completed, at the Central Committee's Plenary of April 23–25, 1962—the last East European country to do so. (See figures 2.6 and 2.7.) Officially, only 3.5 percent of arable land remained in private ownership, though in fact there were still many families who had not yet signed up.[100] But rebellions continued on into 1963 and 1964, as peasants sought to withdraw from collectives they were not finding satisfactory.[101] Table 2.4 shows the trajectory of collectivization nationwide through 1962, according to official figures; it indicates the peasants' preference for associations over collectives, when the former option was available, and shows the effects of the "final assault" that began in 1957.

The end result was a varied landscape wholly different from that of the 1930s. It included three very different property regimes (individual private farms, state farms belonging to "the whole people," and collectives belonging jointly to their members) as well as other forms of joint and state ownership with respect to resources such as forests, pastures, and minerals. Over time, the system of

[100] In addition, the local Party authorities mirrored peasant tactics in "hiding" data so that collectivization could be declared complete. For instance, in two districts of Maramureş, mountainous regions were simply dropped from the official reports so that percent of land collectivized neared 100 percent (see Dobeş et al 2004: 59).

[101] See Vultur 2003a, on the community of Domaşnea.

Figure 2.6. The Extraordinary Session of the Grand National Assembly at which Gheorghiu-Dej declared the completion of collectivization, April 1962. Courtesy of MNIR/ www.comunismulinromania.ro.

contracts would draw individual farms tightly into the planned economy, thereby compromising their nature as private property. A division of labor would encompass all these forms, generating a single system, with ongoing experimentation in the balance among them.

Discussion

This brief summary of the course of Romania's collectivization shows that the process was not a linear one but contained frequent reversals and modifications. The shape of the campaign was constrained by both disagreements among the leadership and unrelenting resistance from the peasantry, as well as by practical problems such as the food requirements of the growing urban population.[102] Aside from the sinuous course of the campaign, we underscore six other features of it: the process whereby private property was decomposed; a dialectic of centralization and decentralization; difficulties with organization; the Party's apparent concern with legality; differentiation by region; and the use of violence, along with extensive popular resistance and rebellions, particularly by women (as in the Soviet case). Since some of these points will reappear in subsequent chapters, we do not treat them at equal length here.

[102] Here, the RCP benefited from being slow to collectivize, for the experience of other East European countries had already shown that collectivization tended to reduce food supplies (Tănase 1998: 77).

Figure 2.7. Peasants in festive garb happily read *Scînteia*'s report of the Extraordinary Session concerning the completion of collectivization. Courtesy of MNIR/www.comunismulinromania.ro.

The Process of Decomposing Ownership

The policies reviewed in this chapter help us to understand the dismantling of one property regime and the installation of another. Following Salameh (1997),[103] we begin with the three basic rights of private ownership in Roman law: rights to use a particular good (*usus*), including the right to obtain and use the necessary inputs and to control the production process; the right to take its fruits or revenues (*fructus*); and the right to alienate it (*abusus*) through transfer, sale, inheritance, and so on. In the precommunist era these rights were bundled in particular ways; under socialism, they would come to be bundled differently. "The Party-state" would hold the principal rights and would allocate further rights to exercise them downward to state officials running state enterprises, to cooperatives/collectives, and to individuals. Whereas the precommunist bundling involved rights of "ownership," under socialism the relevant property rights were, rather, of administration (see Verdery 2003: chapter 1). For "the Party-state" to hold these rights, however, required prying them from

[103] Salameh's analysis for Poland is based on her work on the transition from socialism in Poland, but we find it more generally useful for thinking about the property transformation.

Table 2.4
Evolution of Farm Types, 1950–62

	Percentage of Land In[a]			
Year	*Collective Farms*[b]	*Associations (TOZs)*	*State Farms*	*Individual Private Farms*
1950	2.8	—	5.9	88.0
1951	2.9	—	6.7	86.4
1952	7.0	2.0	6.9	80.0
1953	7.7	2.5	7.0	75.3
1954	7.9	3.3	7.2	75.1
1955	8.2	4.0	7.2	74.1
1956	9.7	7.8	7.9	69.2
1957	14.5	20.2	9.3	52.0
1958	17.5	24.3	10.4	44.7
1959	27.3	30.3	12.9	26.0
1960	41.8	25.3	13.7	15.7
1961	53.5	13.9	15.9	13.1
1962	77.4	1.5	13.9	3.5

Source: Ronnås 1984: 56, using official figures.
[a]Figures do not total 100% because other forms of state ownership have been left out.
[b]Includes amounts in use-plots of farm members.

the hands of other possible holders of property rights by becoming a sort of co-owner while transforming the kinds of rights involved.[104]

The process began with the 1945 land reform and accompanying expropriations, which proved to everyone that the Party had the power to eradicate ownership for some and to create it for others of its choosing. That is, before even a single family had joined a collective, the reform showed the rural population that the Party monopolized control over the very conditions in which property rights might be guaranteed, assigned, exercised, and annulled: they were no longer held to be inviolable.[105] Then came the quotas, which took on a crucial role in the process of decomposing private ownership. With quotas the Party made inroads into *fructus* by claiming a share of the output and determining its "price," to the Party's advantage. Quotas also infringed on *usus* by affecting production profiles (one had to produce the specific goods for which quotas were assigned); in this way the Party asserted a co-claim to peasant control over the goals of production. Moreover, it limited *abusus* by

[104] For further discussion of socialist property formation, see Miller 2009.

[105] One could argue that the process began even before the communists took power, for the requisitions system had taken shape before and during the war for exports to feed Germany's war effort.

preventing wealthy peasants from selling their land so as to reduce their quotas. Therefore, even before they launched collectivization, Party leaders had begun to erode private ownership in favor of state-driven administrative rights.

As full collectivization was introduced and peasants were refusing to join—or were joining and then withdrawing from collective farms—Party cadres introduced the new TOZ associations, with their several variants. Each involved somewhat greater socialization of the means and processes of production short of fully giving away ownership rights to land and implements. The associations occupied a very significant place: they continued the gradual reconfiguration of rights—as elements of the "ownership bundle" were first disaggregated, then attenuated, then partly reassigned—but in a less visible form than direct collectivization. Through this form, peasants could grow accustomed to their loss bit by bit.

Full collectivization only deepened these tendencies, with the Party further insinuating itself as co-owner. Increasing quotas continued to erode *usus* and *fructus* until they nearly vanished (the usufruct plot from the collective farm being their last remnant). In theory the members of a collective jointly owned the land and jointly decided upon its use, but in fact all decisions were taken by an unelected leadership following a plan determined from the top, not by local GAC assemblies. As for the right of *abusus*, it evaporated with a single stroke of a pen as peasants joined the collective, their last act of alienating their land. In a considerable number of cases, even that assertion of agency was denied them: many who joined the intermediate TOZ form would discover, following a vote to which they had not been invited, that they were now members of a GAC.

We could continue this analysis by examining how people's access to production inputs became increasingly precarious—especially for chiaburs—just as their taxes were rising, but the point is clear: the Party's procedure was to take apart what owning meant and put more and more pressure on each aspect until cultivation became so unbearable that villagers would renounce ownership "of their own free consent." At that point, the goods in question would enter into new socialist property forms. The pressures entailed both placing constraints on inputs, production, revenues, and alienation, as discussed above, and on attacking the kinship and social relations that sustained both the labor process and village life, as we will show in chapters 5 and 6. Inasmuch as the idea of "property" includes the social relations in which items of value are embedded, and these in turn implicate notions of the "person," we see here the basis not only of forming the widely ramifying networks characteristic of socialism at all levels (see Verdery 2003: chapter 1) but also of producing persons of a completely new type: "new men," whom we will revisit in chapter 8.

A Dialectic of Centralization and Decentralization

Concerning Soviet collectivization, James Hughes writes, "Policies were not always vertically channeled 'from above' in pure totalitarian fashion but often emerged from a complex bureaucratic interaction between the centre, regional and local tiers of government" (1996: 207; see also Easter 2000). This perspective applies equally to Romania. Throughout the collectivization drive, primary responsibility oscillated between central and more localized actors. In 1949, no GAC could be formed without the approval of the Agrarian Section and the Central Committee; during the first speedup in June 1950 the center gave county committees this task; by early 1951 the center had reassumed its supervision, only to cede it again in 1952 (see Levy 2001: 105). On the whole, when the pace of collectivization increased, responsibility tended to devolve to lower levels, because that way approval could be researched and granted more quickly. When affairs at the local level got out of hand or the center resumed the supervisory role, this inevitably slowed things down, which was partly a way of retaining control over the local cadres. In addition, abuses were more likely to be committed when leaders in Bucharest decentralized the process, for competition and careerism among lower-level cadres then took over, as each sought visibility for creating the most collectives. Sometimes it was precisely to contain such abuses that centralization was reasserted.

One effect of this dialectic was that local cadres never knew how long they would have the initiative. That in turn may have contributed to their abusing their power when they had it, giving free rein both to their own sense of how the process should be run and to their interpersonal grievances. Another effect may be that because policy kept changing and local cadres were sometimes overruled by higher levels, the authority of those locals may have been compromised in the eyes of the peasants they were seeking to persuade. It was this, after all, that constituted the chief innovation of the successful "Galați experiment" of 1956: removing the teams of outsiders who operated over the heads of local officials. Yet those outsiders were sometimes necessary to keep the locals from getting out of hand, as we will discuss in chapter 3.

The dialectic of centralization and decentralization is not easy to track, for it cannot be simply read from Party documents. Even as the top Party leaders made decisions affecting the locus of initiative (as with the June 1950 decision that local officials should have final say in setting up GACs), they also exculpated themselves by insisting that if things were not going well, it was the fault of lower-level cadres. Stalin had established the precedent in his "Dizzy with Success" speech, and Dej proved an apt pupil. For example, he blamed riots in Galați on the regional leadership: "What happened was an 'adventure.' We have nothing to do with this adventure because the regional Party Committee bypassed the Central Committee" (quoted in Oprea 2009: 70). Oprea reports that after violent rioting in several areas in winter 1961, the authorities managed to reestablish order, "blaming local Party activists as usual" (2009: 72).

Difficulties with Planning and Organization

Stenograms of Politburo, Secretariat, and Central Committee meetings are eloquent on this point, as some of our examples have already indicated. Marius Oprea's analysis of organizational problems in collectivization from 1953–62 is especially revealing; we quote him at some length.

> Less than a week after its restructuring [in 1956], the Ministry of Agriculture seemed taken by surprise by the most recent political decisions and its new prominence in relaunching the campaign, a role for which it proved to be not at all ready. Ministry inspectors were criticized for their lack of involvement in collectivization and GAC activities. Eugen Alexe, of the Agriculture Department of the Central Committee, revealed that "it is true that they were not concerned with the problems of the cooperative units. The management occupied with this work in the Ministry had declared that the problems of the collectives were the business of the government and the Party, more than of the Ministry." He was asked to repeat his statement, as if the other participants had not heard right. He did so with anecdotes from his field trips when GAC chairmen drew his attention to the lack of interest of the Ministry officials: "they merely follow the actions taken by the Party and the government: they record deeds or actions, but it is rare that they initiate any." . . . Alexandru Drăghici jumped in promptly, accusing the Ministry officials of "accustoming themselves to dumping the collectivization burden on the Party's shoulders." The Ministry of the Interior explained the "demobilization" that caused the agricultural plan to fail as resulting from a lack of accountability, combined with "many hostile elements within the Ministry of Agriculture, elements with dubious pasts." (Oprea 2009: 57–58)

Furthermore, Oprea quotes an activist from the Central Committee's Agrarian Section who criticized the Ministry of Agriculture as follows: "We hold this meeting following the Party Congress. The spirit of the Congress, the fight for the socialist transformation of agriculture[,] must be reflected in every act we take. The Ministry leadership must think of this not as only the duty of the Party branches but as its own duty too" (58). For this campaign, he said, "all forces must be used to organize GACs and TOZs. People going [to the villages] from the Party and from the state need instruction in this problem so they can carry out political work and persuade the peasantry. . . . Every living thing in the Ministry of Agriculture must be in the field" (58). These passages illustrate the problems not only with the organization of the Ministry of Agriculture itself, but also between the organs of the Party and the state, as we discussed in chapter 1. Although the passages concern meetings and problems from one specific year (1956), our experience of the broader corpus of the Party archives indicates the generalizability of these same issues.

The Party's Apparent Concern with Legality

Closely related to the difficulties of controlling cadres was the Party's seeming desire that all measures taken conform with the laws and decrees that had been passed and directives given. Documents from the earlier years of collectivization frequently show a concern with legality. In a 1951 meeting of the Secretariat, for example, Luca insisted that it would be better not to make laws than to fail to respect them, which would lead to "the death of any state." Chişinevski added, "Non-observance of the law is more dangerous than anything else. . . . A People's Council that breaks any law, decision or order of the state should no longer be functioning."[106] Another example comes from a lengthy CC meeting on problems of collections in 1952, in which one member reported that activists had gone house to house searching for hidden grain, to which another replied, "You entered the house of poor and middle peasants. But based on what law did you have the authority to do such searches? There are the constitution [and] laws of this country that prohibit such a thing."[107] It is hard to believe that the many comments of this sort, made in closed Party meetings, were mere window dressing. Rather, central authorities seem genuinely disturbed about abuses of the law—particularly Pauker, concerning violations of the rule of free consent.

What might we say about this concern for legality? Shearer, discussing the similar concern with legality in the 1930s Soviet Union, argues against those who see in it a shift toward political moderation and universal principles; instead, "[i]t signaled the legal politicization of 'ordinary' crime" (1998: 143), a sign of the regime's inability to control Soviet society. While the same situation characterized Romanian society as well, an alternative possibility is that references to the law indicate intra-Party struggles, where "the law" could be an instrument against one's rivals.[108] Dej, for instance, often accused others of having disobeyed the law as grounds for punishing or excluding them, especially in the early years. He generally began by asserting the Party's supreme authority, asking, "Who authorized these methods?" In a 1950 meeting of the Secretariat, he remonstrated, "What methods were used? Torture, revolvers, etc. All of these methods used everywhere, where do they come from? Maybe you [employees

[106] ANIC, Fond C.C. al P.C.R., file 3/1951, 6, 10 (RLA). Luca continued: when laws are not respected, "the state cannot fulfill its function of protecting society and disintegrates" (6).

[107] ANIC, Fond C.C. al P.C.R.–Cancelarie, file 6/1952, 16 (RLA). Yet another instance comes from a Politburo meeting in 1952 at which Dej noted, in questioning the general prosecutor and the Justice Minister, "We are building socialism, not prisons," and asked, "Have things proceeded correctly? Has the law been respected? Is it necessary to have such a large number in prison?" (ANIC, Fond C.C. al P.C.R.–Cancelarie, file 107/1952, 7 [RLA]).

[108] We thank Dorin Dobrincu and Constantin Iordachi for this suggestion.

of the Agrarian Section] suggested them? . . . I haven't read a single instruction saying 'seize [the chiaburs], try them, dechiaburize them, confiscate their land.'"[109] Perhaps leaders' use of the law served primarily to establish the rules of the game, for each Party leader changed the Constitution and, with it, the legislative framework.

Similar rivalries at lower levels might inform the following example. In Bistra commune (Turda region), the local Securitate overstepped its authority in an action that left three chiaburs fatally shot. The General Directorate of the Securitate sent an officer to investigate the circumstances. Not satisfied with the local bureau's account, he found that with the assistance of the Regional Bureau in Cluj, it had fabricated information to mask its own misconduct. Concluding that the Regional Bureau had "proven its lax discipline before superior organs, had attempted to lead them astray, and had failed to ask for the approvals required in such circumstances," he proposed disciplinary actions against the Regional Bureau and underscored that its irregular behavior was "foreign to our institution and can lead to even graver situations, alienating villagers from the Securitate and creating an atmosphere of terror in the bosom of the population" (Cătănuş and Roske 2004: 223–28).

Whatever the explanation for the emphasis on legality, it provided an instrument others could use differently. First, peasants made good use of it: for instance, in cases in which their land had been exchanged, they petitioned higher-level authorities to provide the requisite legal documents. The large number of such requests stating they had never gotten either documents or actual land reassignment suggests the heedlessness of officials in completing the exchanges; as a result, peasants tried to *force* them to be concerned with legal property forms.[110] Second, some officials may have used it to support a sincere desire to build up communist morality, while others—particularly those in the state administration, perhaps carried over from the bourgeois era—could use it to rein in the collectivization process against the tendencies of overzealous cadres. Archival evidence in support of this possibility comes from the village of Vlaicu during the 1950s. A peasant, C. I., appeared frequently in the surveillance files of the Securitate. On March 7, 1959, he was arrested for "plotting against the social order" and jailed. In his penal file are statements from three villagers, claiming that he had told people the Americans would be coming soon (see chapter 7), made statements against collectivization, and praised the rebels in Hungary's 1956 uprising. The examining officer, however, requested permission to extend the original warrant of arrest (n.b.) so as to get new witnesses; according to his later report, the previous witnesses had withdrawn their testimony, saying they never imagined it would lead to C. I.'s arrest and admitting

[109] From the stenogram of the meeting, available in Cătănuş and Roske 2000: 184. (Source: ANIC, Fond C.C. al P.C.R.–Cancelarie, file 59/1950, 7–8.)

[110] See, for example, the petitions in DJAN HD, Fond Sfatul Popular al Raionului Orăştie, file 139/1959.

they had made everything up, to get even with him for personal reasons. The officer closes the file and declares that for lack of evidence, C. I. is freed and the goods sequestered from him are returned; the state will pay court costs.[111] This file is not unique among the Securitate files we consulted, in its apparent respect for evidence and legal procedure.

Differentiation across Space

Owing in part, no doubt, to how labor-intensive it was to persuade peasants to relinquish their land by their own "free consent," there was tremendous spatial variation in the work of collectivizing the countryside. Many indicators plotted across space would reveal this variation; we choose to illustrate it with differences in the degree of collectivization over time.[112] Table 2.5 shows the unevenness of collectivization across Romania's regions, indicating that of all land susceptible to being collectivized, the amount actually in GACs as of 1958 (just before the final push) ranged from 90 percent in Constanța region down to 3 percent in Suceava region. We also see that even at the end of the campaign, not all the arable land in every region had been collectivized—in Hunedoara Region, the lowest, only 74 percent of the arable land was in collective and state farms.[113] The table allows us to imagine the possible mobility of some of the activists overseeing the campaign: the waves of those who had produced high rates for Dobrogea, Galați, and the Banat (all high grain-producing regions) up to 1958 would be available for assaults on other regions between 1958 and 1960, and for still others up to 1962.

Although we cannot explain all of these variations, we can offer a few suggestions. The very first regions to be completed—Constanța and Galați—were both areas of high agricultural productivity, with strategic locations near the Soviet border and surrounding the Danube River delta. It is known that the Soviet advisors pushed the idea of an early collectivization of the Constanța region, which contained Romania's largest port city, downstream from its largest iron and steel complex in Galați and crucial to the Romanian economy.[114] Occupied by a significant Soviet military force (nine thousand soldiers), the area was critical to strengthening Soviet control of the Lower Danube and the

[111] ACNSAS, FP, file 1360/v. 3, 8bis, 8bis v., 10–12.

[112] Other possibilities include suggestive data from a Securitate document giving arrests by region and social category for 1951–52 (see ASRI, Fond D, dos. nr. 7778, vol. 27, f.1–10). It reveals great variation in the numbers arrested as well as in the social groups that predominated in the arrests. The unreliability of categorization by class, however, makes us reluctant to accept the figures as showing anything more than precisely that.

[113] The figures themselves may not be accurate but we believe they reflect relative rates of collectivizing.

[114] The region also contained the infamous Danube–Black Sea Canal, which served in the 1950s as Romania's gulag.

Table 2.5
Percentage of Arable Land Collectivized in Each Region, 1958, 1960, 1962

Region	*1958*	*1960*	*1962*
Argeş	4	36	91
Bacău	*3*	*12*	*95*
Banat	**42**	**76**	89
Braşov	**22**	38	94
Bucureşti	16	**95**	**100**
Cluj	*8*	*37*	*87*
Constanţa	**90**	**97**	**100**
Crişana	*8*	*29*	*89*
Galaţi	**52**	**72**	97
Hunedoara	*7*	*33*	*74*
Iaşi	8	38	**100**
Maramureş	*9*	*35*	*87*
Maghiar Autonomous Region	12	33	93
Oltenia	7	33	94
Ploieşti	7	19	94
Suceava	3	14	**96**
Total for Romania	**20**	**50**	**94**

Source: Montias 1967: 94, from Romanian statistics (we have rounded off his figures). Notes: These figures exclude land in state units. The top four in each year are in boldface; figures for mountainous regions in italics.

Balkans (Iordachi 2009). Among other areas completed fairly early was the area around Bucharest, which would facilitate controlling the food supply of the capital, Romania's largest city by far. Similarly strategic is the Banat region, not only one of the country's most fertile areas but also located on Romania's border with unreliable Hungary and "Titoist" Yugoslavia. Moreover, many Germans had been deported from that area, their large holdings confiscated and available for setting up farms (see Iancu and Ţârău 2000: 162; Vultur 1997, 2009a).

Mountainous regions tended to be collectivized late, for several reasons. First, they were more difficult to pacify—many uprisings occurred there—and often successfully resisted collectivization for many years, as villagers hid in the forests and resisted the authorities. Thus, when Gheorghiu-Dej complained in April 1958 about laggard regions such as Maramureş, Hunedoara, Bacău, and Cluj, one reason may have been partisan opposition in difficult terrain (Dobeş et al. 2004: 47; Kligman 2009). Second, because hilly and mountainous areas were harder to mechanize and had poorer soils, they were unlikely to make successful GACs. Therefore, in the early days the formation of GACs in such areas was not usually approved, for they would provide only negative models. Moreover, collectivizing them would not contribute much to the total food supply, and as long as that was an urgent concern, more-productive areas would come first. These reasons may help to explain why Transylvania (the hilliest part of the country) presented few requests for creating collectives, as Pauker noted in a February 4, 1952, meeting of Central Committee members. Montias suggests that areas with sizable Hungarian minorities might have been slower than other areas (see 1967: 92–93), perhaps an effect of the 1956 events in Hungary, although these regions also tended to be more mountainous. For some of the mountainous counties, the final figures reflect the leadership's decision to remove mountainous surface areas from calculations of collectivizable land, thus raising the percentages—and the "completion" rates—by reducing the denominator for computing (see note 100 above). This knowledge makes the figures for 1962 especially questionable.

Violence and Resistance

Citing Hannah Arendt's views on the relation between the use of terror and the presence of a large surplus population, Tănase (1998: 25) suggests that because Romania disposed of large population reserves in rural areas, the Party could exercise terror on those populations without jeopardizing labor power for urban industries. To gain full control of the food supply, the regime could use repression even at the cost of rural bodies. Although Romania's collectivization came nowhere near the level of violence and destruction caused by the same process in the Soviet Union (with its even vaster human reserves), recourse to violence remains nonetheless a fundamental feature of it.[115] Whenever violence was reduced, the pace of GAC formation slackened, yet where violence was limited, there was greater acceptance of joining (see Goina 2009; Bodó 2009). Only at the very outset, in 1949, were collectives created without it. Its forms ranged from threats and fines to beatings, arrests, public trials, deportations, imprisonment, and murder. We will return to this topic in chapters 3 and 4, briefly summarizing here what has emerged from our account so far.

Notable in these reports is that women were particularly likely to be the instigators of rebellions, as we noted in chapter 1, concerning Soviet resistance to collectivization.One report of such an uprising had it that "[t]he most ferocious in this battle were the women."[116] In the village Micfalău, in Trei Scaune county, a rebellion that lasted five days was led by a widow with eight children.[117] In Gruia, Ilfov county, "A group of women pounced on a mechanic, dragging him

[115] Among multiple sources concerning the use of violence are Cătănuș and Roske 2000 and 2004; Cesereanu 2006; Ionescu-Gură 2005; Iordachi and Dobrincu 2009; Levy 2001; Roske 2001; Tismăneanu et al. 2007.

[116] "Peasants' uprising in 1957." OSA RFE Item no. 5181/59. (Information courtesy of Oana Mateescu.)

[117] See ANIC, Fond C.C. al P.C.R.–Cancelarie, file 59/1950, 57 (RLA).

down from a tractor, beating him up and ripping off his clothes. Among the women were Party members. The threshing operations were halted."[118] There were scenes of women and children throwing themselves in front of tractors to make them stop (Dobeş et al. 2004: 69). And women were the leaders of the last peasant revolt in the village of Mărceşti in the Dâmboviţa region, which resulted in over 150 arrests.[119] When women ceased to rebel they might nonetheless express their sentiments about joining the collective by showing up for the signing in full black mourning dress.[120] Documents from the CC expressly state that women are the main enemies of collectivization (see Kligman 2009).

The more violence was used, the more resistance it met. In settlement after settlement, teams of activists coming to persuade the peasants encountered their targets waiting with pitchforks, scythes, hatchets, and guns. To be an activist at that time was a potentially deadly occupation: peasants often beat them up, threatened their families, damaged their property, or even killed them, including the presidents of newly formed GACs.[121] Leaders were well aware of the risk: to preempt riots at meetings for founding GACs, for instance, Gheorghiu-Dej cautioned that supporters of collectivization must be in the majority: "When we go to a meeting, we have to be absolutely sure that all the peasants are favorable to us and that we won't leave the meeting beaten up. It would be a major political failure. If there are only 10–20 of us, we may be at a disadvantage, but if we are in the majority, there is nothing they can do to us" (Oprea 2009: 70).

It is important to emphasize the extent of this resistance, given the reputation of Romanians as passive victims of communism's excesses. In 1949–50,

> [l]ong sieges were laid against entire regions, and with the help of some "partisan groups" the peasants fought pitched battles against the forces of the government. The regions Dolj, Argeş, Bihor, Bucharest, Timişoara, Vlaşca, Hunedoara, and the part of Western Transylvania populated by Moţi were the scenes of such events. (Ionescu 1964: 200; see also Kligman 2009)[122]

[118] See ASRI, Fond D, file 4640: 162–163 (RLA). The rebellion escalated upon the arrival of three Party activists from the PMR Ilfov. "When they entered the village, bells began ringing, and within a short time over three hundred men and women surrounded the activists' car, and the activists were dragged from the car, severely beaten, and confined in two peasant houses. At the same time, approximately one thousand people surrounded the Provisional Committee headquarters, blockading the functionaries and militia men inside the building. . . . As a result of this situation, two platoons were displaced to the village."

[119] See Bălan 2000: 287. We might note that in the Polish-Ukraine borderland, where women were also in the forefront of violence, Kate Brown reports that this was especially likely in areas with Baptists and other Protestant sects, which were gender-egalitarian and had women preachers (2004: 106).

[120] Ibid.; also Dumitrescu 1960. (Source courtesy of Oana Mateescu.)

[121] For example, in Biharia, in the Bihor region, several comrades were gravely beaten. In Uileacul de Munte, also in this region, the secretary of the Party cell was attacked (ASRI, Fond D, file 4638, 74).

[122] Revolts in the early years were as much against the imposition of communism as against

In general, peasants who opposed the regime with force ended up in prison, or dead, but they could be imprisoned for much less, such as for merely refusing to join their "voluntarily constituted" GACs. They could be jailed for swearing at the GAC president, or for failing to follow orders to plow under the stubble of their newly harvested fields in some unmeetable time frame, or for urging others to withdraw from the collectives, or for spreading rumors that the regime would soon collapse because the Americans were coming. Data from the Ministry of the Interior indicate that 34,738 peasants were arrested during 1951–52, resulting in 439 public trials.[123] A much larger figure comes from a report by Nicolae Ceauşescu at a 1961 Plenary, which claimed that in summer 1950 and the second half of 1952 alone, 89,000 peasants had been arrested.[124] Neither set of figures is reliable, but at least they indicate a threshold above which the actual numbers arrested lie.[125] Although in the fourteen settlements covered by our project serious uprising and repression figured in only one village (Vadu Roşca; see Stoica 2009), in several of our study areas smaller-scale actions occurred, and the documentary record makes clear the great amplitude of such actions. We ask readers to keep the extent of this violent opposition in mind, for in subsequent chapters we do not draw particular attention to it, focusing instead on resistance of other kinds.

Peasant unrest was substantial enough to require the police and Securitate to mobilize sizable numbers to combat it, as is suggested by some figures from a Securitate report concerning widespread revolts in Bihor and Arad in 1949. They occupied the twelve villages that had risen up and arrested scores of peasants, executing a number of them.[126] Assuming contamination from Tito's "rebel" Yugoslavia, they organized preemptive deportations from the frontier zone, targeting 40,320 persons for removal.[127] Deportees were sent temporarily

quotas or collectivization. (See also Bălan 2000: 258–93.) In the "final assault," however, revolts were distinctly against collectivization, for the Party was well entrenched by the late '50s and the quotas had been stopped.

[123] ASRI, Fond D, file 7778/27, 1–10. The figures by social stratum are chiaburs 22,008 (63 percent), middle peasants 7,226 (21 percent), poor peasants 5,504 (16 percent) (see also ACNSAS, FD, file 53, 21).

[124] Fifty-five thousand (62 percent) of them were allegedly chiaburs (ANIC, Fond C.C. al P.C.R.–Cancelarie, file 53/1961/I, 222, cited in Cătănuş and Roske 2000: 31–32. See also Levy 2001: 142).

[125] Although we would like to offer an estimate of the number of peasant revolts during the years of collectivization (including revolts against quotas and against the communists in general), it is impossible to come up with a plausible statistic. Certain zones have been more heavily studied than others, particularly where revolts happened on a larger scale and brought out the forces of repression en masse to quell them (e.g., Argeş, Bihor, Vrancea, etc.). It will take many more years of research in the Party and Securitate archives before we begin to have a more complete picture. Also see note 98.

[126] See Bălan 2000: 281–82; Cătănuş and Roske 2004; Dobrincu 2002, 2002–03; Roske 2003: 129ff.

[127] See Deletant (1999: 142–45), from which this information is drawn. The action began in 1951 and required 2,656 railway cars and 6,211 trucks to transport those evacuated. Deletant notes that the Securitate classified deportees in the following groups: foreign citizens, Bessarabians, Macedo-

to labor camps, to the Bărăgan steppes, or to the dreaded Danube–Black Sea Canal (see Bălan 2000; Deletant 1999; Vultur 1997, 2009a).[128] For this task, 315 police and 65 Securitate agents were assembled in every settlement, organized in teams, each assigned to one or two residences whose inhabitants they would deport.[129] The same source also gives the kinds of penalties meted out for not paying quotas or for other infractions connected with collectivization: arrest, public trials, prison, internment in work colonies, obligatory domicile at a workplace, and so on.

The frequency of arrests and forms of brutality waxed and waned as the collectivization drive was intensified and relaxed. With the final assault, beginning in late 1958, the number of arrests and sentences to labor colonies and prisons increased vertiginously, as the regime equated any action hostile to collectivizing with attempts to undermine the political system. Harsh penalties were meted out for offenses like instigating peasants against joining the collectives or to withdraw from them, threatening the functionaries charged with implementing collectivization, writing petitions for anyone who wanted to withdraw from a GAC, criticizing GACs, or participating in actions against them (Roske 2003: 104–29).

To summarize, without force Romanian collectivization would have been impossible. Yet, as in the Soviet Union, its use entered into a vicious circle: the role of force confirmed the regime's inability to draw peasants into collectives but was also a reason for this inability. Force also entered into a schismogenic process (Bateson 1936), in which resistance bred more force, and force more resistance. We concur, then, with Viola's assessment of Soviet collectivization: peasants' unwavering refusal compelled the regime into ever more violent behaviors (1996: 69, 130). These revealed its fundamental weakness. Also concerning Soviet collectivization, Kate Brown writes, "Stalinist violence in the thirties exposes an ineffectual state desperately trying to maintain power by last-ditch efforts—threats, coercion, and violence" (2004: 53). The sad paradox, if James Scott (1985) is right, is that the overall effect of peasant revolts is to increase the state's centralization and repressive capacity. Therefore, we might say that the Romanian peasantry's valiant opposition to the Soviet model helped to create the very state capacity that would finally bring them under its yoke.

---

nians, persons who collaborated with the German army, Germans, "Titoists," people with relatives abroad, people who assisted anti-Communist resistance, "enemies" of the socialist order, kulaks and innkeepers, former landowners and industrialists, and convicted criminals. For more on deportation, see Bălan 2000: 132–74; Vultur 2003a.

[128] On official propaganda about the Canal, see Ilie 2001. Although touted as "one of the greatest achievements of socialism," most associated it with terror and death. See also Bălan 2000: 132–74.

[129] ASRI, Fond D, file 4638, 35–42.

Conclusion

In this chapter we have described the village social organization that collectives were to displace and the process of Romania's collectivization, from the 1945 land reform through the final celebrations in April 1962. At the beginning of the process, some peasants had no land at all, but most had at least a hectare (the result of the 1921 and 1945 land reforms), most worked it with family labor (perhaps supplementing work on their parcel with work for larger landowners), and most did so largely for subsistence, with some marketing on the side. Both they and their fellow villagers considered them good and worthy people if they worked very hard and controlled their own labor process, not having to work for others. By the end, nearly all Romanian villagers owned no land at all; the small piece they worked for themselves was accorded to them only conditionally, not in permanent ownership; they were able to market very little if anything; and hard work in the collective gained them less admiration than did slacking off and stealing from the collective for their families.

As we made clear in chapter 1, Soviet influence lay at the heart of this process. The policy was imposed despite the hesitation of some of Romania's leaders, and the Soviet models of the kolkhoz and sovkhoz predominated by the time the campaign was finished. The degree of Soviet involvement was virtually unparalleled in any other East European country. This fact is surely relevant to the similarities between Romanian and Soviet collectivization, as well as to the country's difference from the course taken by Yugoslavia, Poland, and Hungary—all more fractious Soviet allies during the 1950s. The situation would gradually change, as first Gheorghiu-Dej and then Nicolae Ceauşescu asserted greater independence, culminating in Ceauşescu's condemnation of the Soviet invasion of Czechoslovakia in 1968. But by the time that occurred, collectives were well and solidly entrenched in the Romanian countryside. Along with them, however, came the permanent rebellion of the Romanian peasantry, which quickly learned to give the collectives their most minimal effort. In this sense, we can agree with Ionescu's opinion (1964: 300), "Rumania has proved no exception to the rule that agriculture has been communism's greatest failure."

Chapter 3

Creating Party Cadres

> May God help us to raise up as many cadres as possible.
> —*Ana Pauker*[1]

> The secretary of the People's Council in Romos does not measure up to the politics and tasks of Popular Democracy in our country, he has close relatives who are chiaburs and supports the indignities they perpetrate and purposely tries to attract the new president into them.
> —*From an informative note by Orăştie district Party officials*[2]

> I was working at the mill one day, and this fellow Nestor came from the train station, entered, and greeted me; said he wanted to talk with the miller: "Look, I'm from Bucharest, from the Central Committee. I've come as the agricultural agent." "To give us guidance," I replied. "We actually need someone like that around here." Then he saw a rope of onions hanging up. "Hey!" he says, "is that what you do with this?" So he didn't know that you make onions into a rope.
> —*Former miller, from Aurel Vlaicu*

In the previous two chapters we have outlined the creation of the communist Party-state in Romania and the methods by which it gained control over the food supply, inspired by the Soviet blueprint. We have indicated that because the Romanian Communist Party was not a fully formed entity when it began implementing these policies, collectivization itself would serve as a generative process for many of its subsequent practices. Most organizations do not come into being full-blown and then acquire tasks and personnel: they take shape as part of those tasks and of the behavior of their personnel, coevolving both with the policies being implemented and with the formation of the cadres who do the work. Thus, the Party did not spring into life and then collectivize: instead, the action of collectivizing simultaneously helped to create the Party-state that accomplished it.

This process of creation began with the people most central to the entire program: the Party and Securitate cadres. Forming these cadres—a process fraught with difficulties, as this chapter will show—was crucial to forming the Party itself. It was they who had the task of bringing the imported engineering project to life; they were the ones entrusted with the power to construct a new social order and also to construct the very forms of power that would sustain it.

[1] ANIC, Fond C.C. al P.C.R.–Agrară, file 60/1949, 37.
[2] DJAN HD, Fond CR PMR, file 888/1953, 67.

They were to serve as the "vanguard," as the Party's pedagogues and moral exemplars. The fate of the Soviet blueprint was in their hands. Who were they, and how did they proceed?

Although our project data are not extensive, in this chapter we hope to provide a novel viewpoint on the collectivization process—that of mid- and lower-level cadres, as opposed to the top Party leadership discussed in most histories of the Party (e.g., Jowitt 1971; King 1980; Tănase 1998; Tismăneanu 2003). To do this is neither fashionable nor easy, for Party cadres have been so demonized in the popular imagination (often justifiably) that it is difficult to recuperate them as human beings; works by Jochen Hellbeck (2006) and Andreas Glaeser (2010) are among the very few attempts. In Romanian scholarship, aside from a book of documents concerning Securitate cadres (Oprea 2002) and another of interviews with former activists (Rostás and Momoc 2007),[3] the vast literature on communism's victims has made little room for the victimizers. To understand better how the regime worked and how it departed from the blueprint, however, we should try to see the world through the eyes of its cadres—perhaps discovering in the process, as Getty and Naumov suggest (1999: 16), that alongside their sometimes bestial comportment toward the peasants, they were very frightened. What was their life like? What was their relation to the regime they served? How did their behavior shape the specific form the Romanian Party took?

One motive for inquiring into the life of cadres concerns the matter of the new regime's legitimacy. Although legitimacy is generally considered in terms of the masses' "consensual" relation to their rulers, we find it important in this case (where the Soviet Union guaranteed the rulers' position) to examine instead rulers' relations to their cadres and cadres' relations to one another. Because the Romanian Communist Party came to power with very inadequate and ideologically uncommitted personnel, it faced its first major legitimacy test among its own cadres. If they were not behind the transformative agenda, they would not reliably implement it. This encourages us to ask how Party leaders sought to form new cadres, establish relationships among them, and develop modes of surveillance and discipline over them, to be sure they were indeed promoting the agendas of their leaders, including those in the Soviet Union. Our discussion also joins with Ken Jowitt's Weber-inspired discussion of "neotraditionalism" (1992). Jowitt suggests that over time, the Soviet regime of "charismatic impersonalism" was routinized in the direction of traditional authority, in a process he calls "regime corruption." Central to the resulting charismatic neotraditionalism was "the party's inability to sustain cadre impersonalism," as cadres were increasingly transformed into "traditional-type patrons and 'big men'" (126–27). Although we avoid Jowitt's term "corruption," we find his argument a useful way of organizing some of our material concerning the

[3] For some work on cadres in the Soviet Union, see Siegelbaum and Sokolov 2004; Hooper 2006.

cadres' development of personal networks, which transformed the "impersonalism" that was supposed to mark Leninist parties. We seek to show some of the roots of the resulting personalism, so characteristic of Soviet-type communist parties, in the cadres' efforts to protect themselves from the Soviet-inspired technologies of rule exercised upon them.

We add to this Weberian mix some scholarship indebted to Foucault, for whom a central problem is the relation between power and subjection, with power emanating from multiple sites rather than being concentrated "at the top." For the installation of communist power, the very first subjects who had to be formed were the Party's own cadres, who would then institute the new system of power and subjection more widely. In the end, it proved impossible for Romania's Party leaders to control lower-level cadres, and this, in turn, created a particular relation between state and subjects, as well as particular behavioral habits. In exploring these themes, we explore not just what the exercise of power repressed but what it produced. We suggest that the resistance to becoming obedient subjects, which became a hallmark of socialism, was commonplace among its cadres as they evaded, reinterpreted, or overexecuted their orders, just as it was among the peasantry. Our image is of a regime that attempted to permeate all realms of life but at the same time structured resistance to it among its very own: much as in Michael Mann's *Dark Side of Democracy*, we find a "dark side of socialism" that brought its own people to oppose its utopian ideals. Although we do not have enough material to make a convincing argument to this effect, we hope at least to be provocative.

What Was a Cadre?

What exactly do we mean by "cadres"? Lewin states that in the Soviet case, "everyone other than rank-and-file members was a 'cadre'—in other words worked in an apparatus where each person held a precise post in a hierarchy of disciplined functionaries" (2005: 38). In this chapter we will use the term in a broad sense, to indicate anyone directly employed by the Party-state in an official capacity, whose work entailed serving the apparatuses of Party, state, or Securitate at any level of the political hierarchy. We note that the term "cadre" is rarely used by villagers in our interviews—they speak more readily of "activists," or else "they," "their people," etc. "Cadre" and "activist" appear regularly, though, in the speech and writing of those we call cadres.

Our broad usage glosses over a number of distinctions we ought to make but do not, for lack of space. Some analysts (and some of our respondents as well) would want us to distinguish between "Party" and "state" employees; where we think it important, we use the word "functionaries" to refer to the latter. That identity is unstable, however, since people in state employment were often dragooned into doing the work of Party activists or could move over into Party leadership positions. As state employees, they were required to do whatever the Party asked of them, for they had no independent source of income (see Oláh 2003: 57); they would move in and out of "activist" status as called upon. That is, these and related terms refer not to individuals but to roles and functions that people could assume and change. In addition, we might distinguish between cadres out in the field and those doing office work (a parallel distinction to the previous one), or between those high up in the Party-state—the nomenclatura—and lower-level district, commune, and village cadres.

What kinds of people did collectivization require at the ground level? In our documents we find many: Party secretaries and administrative secretaries, at national, regional, district, and communal levels as well as workplaces; members of collectivization commissions and of regional, district, and commune Executive Committees or Politburos; various kinds of technicians (cadastral, veterinary, agronomical, etc.); presidents and vice presidents of regional and district People's Councils; presidents, brigade leaders, and leadership councils of collective farms; directors of state farms; mayors; village deputies; village delegates to the commune, delegates to threshing machines, and collectors of peasants' food quotas; members of Provisional Committees and Initiating Committees; and so on. Among the many kinds of Party workers were "activists," a general term referring to people employed by the Party for political tasks or removed for a period of time from regular jobs in factories, mines, agriculture, or socialist institutions; agitators, who were to whip up enthusiasm among peasants for joining the Party, giving their quotas, or joining the collectives; multiple kinds of instructors, who provided education or explanation, offered advice, sent local information upward, and made suggestions; and propagandists, who created films, posters, slogans, and other vehicles for popularizing the collectives. We find people who have to draw up work plans and action plans; to write reports, minutes of meetings, informational notes; to disseminate propaganda and talk persuasively with peasants. In brief, collectivization required a sizable and well-trained apparatus of cadres—what Horváth and Szakolczai call a "standing army" of them (1992: 80).

This, however, was precisely what the newly communized Romania lacked. As we explained in chapter 1, the Romanian Worker's Party in 1944 had approximately one thousand members, mainly urban, though its numbers rose rapidly once the Party gained a foothold in the government in 1945. By June 1946 it had almost three-quarters of a million members, and by February 1948 over one million (King 1980: 64).[4] But the rapid influx caused Party leaders constant worry that "class enemies" might infiltrate the Party and subvert it from within. Following the "verification campaign" of 1948–50 that reduced it to just under six hundred thousand, it had an *actif* (corps of active cadres) of

[4] In Poland, by contrast, there were twenty thousand members in 1944 and one and a half million in 1948, a seventy-five-fold increase, as compared with Romania's thousandfold increase (Stoica 2006: table 1).

about one hundred thousand, a significant portion of whom would be thrown into the work of collectivizing. The verification campaign established very early an atmosphere of backstabbing and a scramble for influence that would continue throughout the Party's existence.

Who were these cadres? When they started out, many were illiterate; large numbers of them had little commitment to the ideals and practices of Soviet-style communism, having joined the Party to promote or protect themselves rather than from conviction. [5] They were members of families, neighbors, participants in localized status systems; many were embedded in villages like the ones they were now assailing. They came encrusted with habits, needs, loyalties to kin, and perhaps resentments against others more respected in their communities. As supposed exemplars of "new socialist persons," they had to negotiate among Party directives, local social relations, and situations of great flux—a flux their actions were instrumental in perpetuating. Their job would be to turn life upside down for the country's twelve million villagers. How were they to become the sorts of people who could do that?

In the following sections we look at how these cadres were shaped and how they survived their grueling assignment. What were the Party's pedagogies for training them, paralleling the pedagogies they themselves were to use on the peasantry? (We will discuss this in part 2.) What work did they accomplish? What problems did they encounter? To ask about the formation of cadres enables us to examine how the Party constructed its authority among those who would exercise it. The task was to be difficult, for when we read Party documents, we find that the bulk of cadres were completely unequipped to handle the gigantic project they were expected to complete. Yet they would be required to sit through countless interminable meetings, to write lengthy and frequent reports, and to travel constantly (sometimes returning home only months later) with the charge of "persuading" people to do something many of them did not really understand or believe in.

Our discussion is somewhat limited in time, space, and social location. If the formation of cadres is our theme, the period from 1949 (when collectivization was launched) to the mid-1950s is particularly crucial. Most of the archival material we present comes from this period. It includes the initial attempt in 1949 to create model GACs that would "naturally" attract other peasants, through the sudden push to create many new GACs by force during 1950 and then the effort in 1951 to clean up the mess thereby created; there followed a

[5] Tănase (1998: 46–47) observes that the new Party members included opportunists of all stripes, agricultural workers, members of dissatisfied national minorities, prisoners of war returned from the Soviet Union, and former members of the Iron Guard and other fascist parties, especially if compromised. In addition, there were people from higher social groups, such as generals and officers, some Orthodox bishops, heads of the interwar secret police, writers, journalists, university professors, entrepreneurs, bankers, and large industrialists—all wanting to buy a place in the new order as they had in the previous one. This mix made for a very heterogeneous communist elite.

second period of intensive mobilization and then the relaxation that began with Stalin's death in 1953. Our data are uneven across space: our most extensive documentation is for the Orăştie district of Hunedoara region, as well as the Odorhei district in Stalin region (later the Hungarian Autonomous Region), Dobrosloveni commune in Craiova region, and the districts of Sighet, Vişeu, and Rodna in Baia Mare, Maramureş, and Rodna regions. We will bring in material from the other villages that formed part of our project but will concentrate on these, which bias our discussion toward Transylvania.[6] Concerning social location, we see the district and commune levels as key sites for investigating cadre formation: not only were there more of them at these more numerous lower levels, but they were the ones engaged most fully in the day-to-day job of creating collectives and making those function. We will bring in some commentary from the archives of the Party Central Committee and other central organs, but far more of our data come from the lower-middle reaches of the apparatus.

We start by discussing the bureaucracy that contained most of these cadres, whose reports and instructions followed circuits that gave the whole apparatus some coherence. Then we ask what qualifications cadres had and what sorts of work they were expected to do, leading us to discuss the shortage of cadre labor throughout the early collectivization process. Next we describe the problems caused by early recruitment patterns and the exercise of surveillance over cadres that was designed to ferret out and exclude the unsuitable; we focus on their personal peccadilloes, their work habits, their social relationships, and their abuse of power. In this respect, the present chapter inverts chapter 6: there the emphasis will be on discovering and isolating the "class enemy" who was *outside* the Party, whereas here we concentrate on finding the enemy *within* it.

The Party-State Bureaucracy

The organizational scheme of Romania's Party, state, and Securitate bureaucratic segments followed that of the Soviet Union, including the nomenclatura system central to ensuring that Party and state were intertwined. The nomenclatura lists included the most important positions in the political hierarchy, held by the most powerful cadres in Party, state, and security apparatuses nationally, regionally, and in the districts, as well as heads of major state enterprises, unions, and the Communist Youth (UTM). To provide a sense of the composition of this most powerful body of cadres at the regional level, where the daily tasks of collectivizing were organized, we present table 3.1. It characterizes nomenclatura positions for the Central Committee and regional as well

[6] From what we know of the other regions of the country, there should not be significant variations in these processes.

as district and municipal Party committees in 1957, broken down by occupation, parents' occupation, nationality, age, length of time in the Party, education, and sex.[7] The table reveals a corps that is slightly understaffed (by its own standards), 78 percent working class, 92 percent of worker or peasant origin, 80 percent Romanian, and overwhelmingly (90 percent) male. About one-fifth of them have no Party schooling, and just under two-thirds have four to seven years of education, the largest single educational category. Most have spent only one to two years in their positions, suggesting the speed at which cadre ranks expanded. From this table we also learn how political positions in this part of the bureaucracy were labeled and categorized. Missing, however, is a very important figure that appears in other tables: the age of cadres. A document like this one from Hunedoara in 1959 shows that in the regional apparatus, 13 percent were between twenty-six and thirty years of age, fully 64 percent between thirty-one and forty, and 23 percent over forty years of age. The relative youth of cadres as compared with the peasant population they were collectivizing doubtless affected the success of the campaign.[8]

Besides accomplishing the crucial tasks of collectivization, the bureaucracy asserted the Party's discipline and control over its cadres and state functionaries, instilled proletarian morality, policed misconduct, and socialized cadres and other Party members into what it meant to be a good communist. Persons employed in this huge bureaucracy generated interminable reports, assigned blame, "unmasked" enemy elements, and applied the self-criticism mechanisms through which Party discipline was maintained and policies thereby carried out. The illiteracy of cadres and their unfamiliarity with communist principles being substantial problems at the outset, the bureaucracy's tasks included programs of schooling, alongside other activities we also see as pedagogical, such as the discipline of regular reporting, attendance at Party meetings,[9] and public application of various sanctions, which included reprimand, censure with a warning, or—the highest sanction—expulsion from the Party, CC, or other significant body.

Over time, the apparatus increased in size. In the early years, food requisitions were a principal task; when promoting class warfare gained prominence, more cadres were needed for that work, which expanded as the numbers grew and as the verification of chiaburs intensified. The more ambitious the plans for forming new GACs, the more cadres would be required for persuasion and organizing; as GACs formed, more cadres would be needed to staff them and keep them functioning, alongside the continued persuasion and organizing work. Binding the bureaucratic apparatus together were lengthy trails of paper,

[7] We note that the Securitate and police are not included in this list.

[8] DJAN HD, Fond CC PMR, file 39/1959, 8–12. There is no reason to think that Hunedoara had a particularly youthful apparatus, compared with other regions.

[9] See Horváth and Szakolczai (1992) for a discussion of the socializing effects of Party meetings.

Table 3.1
Composition of Cadres Active in Political Work in the Aparat of the Party Central Committee and in Regional, District, and Municipal Party Committees as of April 1, 1957

		A. Central Committee Apparatus	*B. Lower-Level Party Committees*	*Total*	
				No.	*%*
1. No. of cadres	a. Needed	432	9406	9,838	100
	b. Actual	415	9000[a]	9,415	96
2. Occupation	a. Workers	240	7,107	7,347	78
	b. Working peasants	0	504	504	5
	c. Intellectuals	102	433	88	.9
	d. Functionaries	64	886	45	.5
	e. Small trades	0	70	70	.7
3. Parents' occupation	a. Workers	193	4,196	4,389	47
	b. Working Peasants	111	4,117	4,228	45
	c. Intellectuals	0	0	0	0
	d. Functionaries	48	348	396	4
	e. Trade/commerce	50	291	341	4
4. Nationality	a. Romanians	303	7,274	7,577	80
	b. Hungarians	35	1,228	1,263	13
	c. Jews	52	248	300	3
	d. Russians/ Ukrainians	9	138	147	2
	e. Germans	2	26	28	.3
	f. Serbs	2	34	36	.4
5. Year joined Party	a. ≤ 1944	38	137	175	2
	b. 1945–1946	257	5,177	5, 434	58
	c. 1947–1948	96	2,551	2,647	28
	d. ≥ 1953	16	1,091	2,007	21
	e. Candidate members and Communist Youth	0	42	42	.4
7. Time in present position	a. 6–10 yrs.		538		[6]
	b. 3–5 yrs.	"Satisfactory"	1,926		[2]
	c. 1–2 yrs.		2,590		[2]
	d. < 1 yr.		3,946		[4]
8. State schooling	a. 4–7 Primary Grades	78	5,852	5,930	63
	b. 4 grades of industrial apprenticeship	89	1,671	1,760	19
	c. 1–4 yrs. middle school	55	591	646	7

Table 3.1 (*continued*)

		A. Central Committee Apparatus	*B. Lower-Level Party Committees*	*Total*	
				No.	*%*
	d. 5–10 yrs. middle school	68	548	616	7
	e. Higher education	111	338	339	4
9. Party schooling	a. Higher Party school	98	500	598	6
	b. 1 yr.	85	2,736	2,821	30
	c. 3–6 months	46	3,823	3,869	41
	d. Marx/Lenin night school	78	349	427	5
	e. No Party schooling	100	1,592	1,692	18
10. Sex[b]	a. Males	[364]	[8,118]	8,482	90
	b. Females	[51]	[882]	933	10

Source: Ionescu-Gură 2006: 369-375, from ANIC, Fond C.C. al P.C.R.–Cancelarie, file 63/1957, 18-22. *Note:* Because figures in the source table are only partial, totals in columns A and B do not always equal the totals in row 1-b.

[a]Of these, only 4,129, or 46%, had been confirmed in their posts.

[b]The source does not give numbers, only percentages, from which we have calculated the numbers using 415 and 9,000 for the two columns.

described in our introduction. Each level of the hierarchy was required to make regular reports to levels above it, on a variety of topics such as the amounts of produce gathered through collections, the progress of the agricultural campaigns for sowing and harvesting, problems encountered in the collectivization drive, and so on. Upper levels in the hierarchy sent down instructions, decrees, requests for information; every section in both the administrative and the Party organizations documented its work with reports; Party cells at every level developed work plans for their employees and wrote minutes of every meeting. Alongside writing all the reports was answering citizen petitions (to be discussed in chapter 4).

In our view, this paper trail was essential to creating the corporate agency of the new bureaucratic apparatus.[10] Bureaucracies are heavily materialized social collectivities; files are their most concrete realization, building up corporate agency through the documented participation of a variety of actors. Although the documents in a file have individual authors, those authors are not always

[10] Our argument here parallels that of Hull (2003), but as our wording makes clear, we have not followed him wholly onto the terrain of actor-network theory. (Thanks to Puiu Lățea for this clarification.) See also Stoler (2009: 28), who suggests that colonial archives were technologies that reproduced their states, and Trouillot (1995).

clearly indicated; the documents' ritualized form and circulation collectivize them. Reinforcing this feature is a writing style that effaces authorship, even when the signatory is given, by devices such as the widespread use of subjunctive or passive constructions and of plural rather than singular pronouns, as file producers regularly refer to the Party as "we" or "our organs."[11] Matthew Hull, whose ideas we borrow here, proposes that graphic artifacts are not simply instruments of an existing social organization: rather, they serve to precipitate that organization, by forming networks and groups through the trajectory of their circulation (2003: 291).

Thus, the extensive bureaucratic documentation we find in the Party archives contributed to consolidating the Party's capacity to rule. We can see a similar functionality in the extraordinary duplication of effort that emerges from these archives, with their multiple reports from different people about the same events in slightly different or even identical words—how many GACs have been formed, with what inventory and what repairs, and so on.[12] From these we see a "graphomaniacal" bureaucracy in the process of constituting itself as a corporate agent. Graphomania further bound together the people who produced and read those reports.[13] Perhaps the seemingly wasteful duplication of effort betrays a pedagogical practice: the point was not (just) to get specific information but to train many people in a process of producing it. Or perhaps we see merely the hyperproductionist mentality of central planning.

The discussion so far raises two important questions. First, all this graphomania presupposed a literate base of cadres, but we already know that initially, this did not exist. How was this created? Second, given the remarkable duplication of effort, could there be enough cadres to manage it all? These questions lead us to consider more carefully the qualifications of Party cadres and the persistent shortage in their numbers.

"You're Going Away an Ox and You'll Come Back a Cow": Personnel Policies and the Qualifications of Cadres

The Party's personnel policies contained some serious contradictions between ideological orthodoxy and empirical consequences. Concerning ethnonational identity, the ideology held that groups should be represented more or less proportionately, yet minorities such as Jews and Hungarians tended to be overrepresented. In a 1952 list of 546 middle and upper-middle positions in the CC, for instance, half of all heads and adjuncts of sections and 40 percent of all heads of

[11] See introduction, note 42, on "wooden language."

[12] For example, DJAN HD, Fond CR PMR, file 2429/1957.

[13] Scholars of the Soviet Union, too, have commented upon the graphic artifacts in Soviet-type bureaucracies, which are famous not just for the anonymity of their records but for their multiple control agencies and consequent duplication of effort.

sectors, adjuncts, and instructors were ethnic minorities (Ionescu-Gură 2005: 234)—this in a country 86 percent Romanian, lending credence to the popular belief that communism was imposed by "others."[14] One of our (Romanian) respondents recalled the many Hungarians in political positions in the Orăştie district administration of the 1950s: the chief prosecutor, the head of police, the district First and Second Party Secretaries, and the wife of a third. "There was a point when we'd go to gatherings of Party officials and hear only Hungarian spoken—in both the district and the region."[15] This kind of experience did not sit well with Romanians, who would be less likely to respond positively to these minority cadres than to their own kind. The same was even more true of Roma, who figure prominently as cadres in the recollections of interviewees and sometimes in the documents as well (see Kristó 1999: 91).[16] The stigma attached to Roma identity was such that most Romanians would not find them persuasive or willingly regard them as political superiors. For similar reasons, women were less likely to be successful cadres than men and were very underrepresented, despite the Party's professed goal of increasing gender equality.

Roma were frequent recruits owing to another policy: cadres should have "healthy" social origins—that is, proletarian or poor-to-middle peasant backgrounds. Indeed, documents show that those at the commune and district levels were often from modest peasant families or were miners, railway workers, or other forms of skilled and unskilled labor. Villagers who entered the Party's service also tended to come from marginal groups: not just Roma but other poor and landless peasants, or people who had married or moved (rather than been born) into the community—a significant social liability, in village status terms, as we indicated in chapter 2. As of 1951, for instance, forty-two of fifty-three deputies and employees in Poiana village were listed as "poor peasants."[17] A shepherd from that village recalled in an interview, "these folks who could barely read. Why, here's how the People's Council was then, the president a Gypsy woman from Cernavodă. . . . She knew only one thing: 'Long live Ana Pauker, our beloved leader who gave rights to all the women of the world!' And what a mess she made."[18]

[14] This was especially true in Transylvania, owing to experiences of discrimination during the interwar period. The peace treaties following World War I resulted in "Greater Romania," a country whose territory and population were doubled by acquisition of regions with majority Romanian populations from neighboring states. Politicians of this new Romania worked hard to unify a disparate set of provinces into a "unitary national state," inevitably stepping on the toes of non-Romanian groups. The main group who did *not* figure prominently among Party cadres were the Germans, whom Romania's Communists—following Stalin's lead—regarded as irrevocably bourgeois class enemies.

[15] A.D.T., Verdery interview.

[16] It is possible that these representations reflect respondents' sense of the ultimate indignity of the reversals being suffered rather than actual Roma employment by the Party.

[17] Stewart and Stan (2009: 256), from the Archive of the Local Council in Poiana Sibiului commune, file 46/1951.

[18] A. Ţ., Stan interview for M. Stewart.

There were two problems with this policy. One was that, as we just suggested, having cadres who were stigmatized in local communities—as the people with "healthy origins" mostly were—would compromise their effectiveness in the field. Stewart and Stan argue that recruiting such people created a structural weakness of the newly created communist organs.

> The great difficulty the new regime had was that those labeled *chiaburi* had enjoyed a prestigious status within the community, and were regarded as good householders. The rhetoric of exploitation was often counter-productive in a milieu where people considered wealth to be the result of hard work, and of appropriate, even exemplary behavior in one's own household and in the community. (2009: 256)

Therefore, in local status terms, people with "unhealthy" origins would have had much more success with their fellows than would the "healthy" ones. We return to this matter in chapter 6. The second problem was that people with healthy origins were the least likely to have adequate skills.[19] They were illiterate or had little formal schooling, they could barely write, much less master the genre rules for the multiple kinds of reports their superiors demanded, and they had little or no experience with managing an office or an organization. Those in collective farms required mathematical skills too, as we learned from a Ieud respondent explaining who could become a brigade leader: "Only people who knew mathematics, and how to write a person's name. He would know Romanian and math pretty well, that was it. But it couldn't be just anyone. A person who didn't drink, because if he drank then he would take liquor from people in exchange for putting more workdays down for them and stealing workdays from someone else."[20] Evidently numeracy had its drawbacks, in the wrong hands.

The archives—from the topmost level on down—as well as our interviews are full of references to cadres' lack of qualifications. In a 1951 meeting of the Secretariat, for instance, numerous participants detailed the shortcomings of policy for hiring new cadres in Teleorman region, which displayed a "total lack of vigilance" and was bringing "enemy elements" into the Party's work.[21] Concerning managerial experience, in 1955 the president and Party secretary of the collective farm in Lueta resigned from their positions, claiming that they had been trained as tradesmen and wanted to return to their jobs: "Being originally

[19] Similar problems also beset the installation of the Communist Party in other contexts. For instance, MacLean writes of Vietnam that following the removal of over one hundred thousand cadres during the verification and purge of Party members between 1945 and 1951, the Party promoted new "purer" cadres who were mainly illiterate and had no administrative experience. "These profoundly unqualified individuals collectively formed the first generation of 'peasant bureaucrats'" (MacLean 2005: 85–86).

[20] Kligman interviewed a former brigade leader from Ieud who described the complexity of calculating the basis for members' pay, clearly requiring good mathematical skills (P. V., Kligman interview).

[21] ANIC, Fond C.C. al P.C.R.–Cancelarie, file 118/1951, 1–24, here 6.

from the city [the president] doesn't really understand administrative work" and "[the secretary] didn't really have experience in resolving these new tasks." From other archives of Odorhei district we find that "[t]he first sign of the installation of new cadres in the local state and Party structures was an abrupt decline in the qualitative level of practices of preparing papers and documents. This is apparent in both the spelling and the style of expression" (Oláh 2003: 53). In Maramureş the Party cell of the first GAC consisted of four members, only two of whom were literate.[22] Regional authorities noted this problem in a 1950 note to the higher-ups in Bucharest: "We have problems with the minutes of the village Party cell because we have a few secretaries who can barely write their names and the other comrades in the bureau are not much better. They do the best they can, only we can understand very little from their minutes."[23]

Confirming this impression of an initially ill-prepared leadership are the recollections of our interviewees, such as, "He was a Party member but he couldn't even read the name of his village on the welcome sign at the entrance!" (Stoica 2009: 429). A functionary in the Orăştie People's Council described his First Party Secretary, a former miner: "Imagine! This man knew absolutely nothing about administration . . . and he didn't try to learn, either. When he held meetings—he called me 'Guruţa' [Little Mouth]—'Hey, Guruţa! Come over here.' And I'd tell him absolutely everything he should say, how to say it, how to conduct the meeting, *everything*!"[24] A poor peasant from Ieud observed colorfully of an activist: "Let me tell you, people who were poorly trained, with those seven grades they didn't do when they were kids. And then, with the communists, he had to learn too much material all at once and he went crazy. His mind caught on fire!"[25] One former chiabur remarked that a Party activist co-villager had tried to convince him and others to join the Party, allegedly so it would not have to resort to "uneducated people" (Kligman 2009: 177). Finally, the following excerpt from a German villager from Vlaicu shows wonderfully the compromises the Party would have to make at first if it wanted skilled officials. This man explained how after the war, Romanian military authorities hunted down and sent to the coal mines all Romania's Germans like himself who had fought in Hitler's army when the two countries were allied; he had hidden but had eventually been found.

> When I was summoned before the military commission, a captain stood up—his name was Ivan. . . . He says, "Colonel, ask this fellow what schooling he has, or look at his handwriting." I was shaking. "Hey, Ivan, what do you have in mind?" he says.

[22] See DJAN MM, Fond Comitetul Raional PCR Vişeu, file 33/1952, 31. The GAC in Ieud was created in March 1950. In nearby Săliştea, there were also four members, two of whom were illiterate, a typical ratio in the region.

[23] DJAN MM, Fond Comitetul Judeţean PMR, file 89/1950, 77.

[24] C. D., Verdery interview.

[25] P. V., Kligman interview

> "I ask you, do you want to take someone with a fourth-grade education to keep the records here in the territorial center in Deva?" "Well, Ivan, you're right," he says, "come on, write something." I ask him, "What should I write?" "What's your trade?" And then I wrote down, "I was a shopkeeper." And Ivan takes it and shows it to him. "See, Colonel? Take a look at that handwriting. What more could you want!" "Fine, Ivan," he says, "leave him here at the center."[26]

Thus, owing to his unusually beautiful script, this irretrievably "bourgeois" enemy of the people was brought into the Party's service.[27]

In many of their recollections we should suspect that our respondents are distancing themselves from the cadres they speak of, especially if they themselves are people with higher education. Nonetheless, official statistics confirm the point. In 1944 Romania's rural illiteracy rate was estimated to be 49 percent; by 1948, following the introduction of a campaign to fight illiteracy, the overall rate for the total population was said to be 23.1 percent;[28] but those with little or no schooling were likely to be the poorer people who were preferred as cadres. Thus, it is fair to say that cadres of the Romanian Communist Party had a serious educational deficit (see also table 3.1). Their knowledge of agriculture in particular was often rudimentary, if not absent altogether. And owing to the haphazard manner of their recruitment, their ideological commitment was often shaky as well, as illustrated by a former activist's comment, "I wasn't a communist, I was a Party member. That's what I used to tell my friends."[29] A crucial consequence of this lack of preparation and ideological commitment was that they were ill equipped to carry out the work of persuasion essential to collectivizing without resort to force, as we will show in chapter 5.

Some of our sources suggested that the Party cultivated uneducated people deliberately, not just to invert the status order but to ensure the relative obedience and loyalty of those it promoted. A former guard at the infamous Sighet prison where so many of Romania's intelligentsia perished in the 1950s noted, "The regime involved uneducated people because those with more knowledge would have resisted."[30] A high school graduate from Timişoara echoed the sentiment, observing that an uneducated person (whom he likens to an animal) could be directed "to see only the class enemy . . . like a horse that, once trained to the harness, goes where it's supposed to even without one" (Vultur 2003a: 44).[31] These views notwithstanding, there is no doubt that the Party was con-

[26] 258, Verdery interview.

[27] It turned out that a girlfriend of this German (K. F.) had a friend whose boyfriend was from a neighboring village and worked in the Secret Service in Deva; he was a friend of Captain Ivan and had told him to keep K. F. around. K. F. not only had superb handwriting but was a whiz at numbers and an extraordinarily intelligent fellow, a real catch for an office in need of good assistants.

[28] See Tismăneanu et al. 2007: 296 and Diac 2004: 22. No rural rate for 1948 is included.

[29] 197, Verdery interview.

[30] P. S., Kligman interview.

[31] See also Tănase (2005: 142), who states, "Moscow prioritized the promotion of Party leaders

cerned with raising the educational level not only of the population as a whole—and this was one of its genuine achievements[32]—but especially of its cadres, even if at only basic levels. For example, in Pechea commune, where one of the very first model collectives was inaugurated in August 1949, four of its members were immediately sent to Bucharest to complete a short course (forty-five days) specializing in cereal production; after they returned they took on various leadership positions in the GAC (Şandru 2003: 9). Similarly, in Sântana (another model GAC), as one of our respondents recalled:

> In fall 1953 they called about four of us to the office. "Sântana commune is almost completely collectivized . . . and we need cadres. You should go do a five-month course for brigade leaders, in Arad." . . . They put us up, room and board, everything; the conditions couldn't have been better. And we had teachers on every subject: agriculture, animal husbandry, mechanization, political economy, . . . geography, Romanian, all kinds of topics.[33]

There was a variety of courses for activists to attend, lasting from a few weeks to three years.[34] Short courses were especially likely to attract would-be cadres from villages and communes, most of whom could not withdraw their labor from their households for longer periods. A lengthy report from Orăştie district in 1953 noted that all of the presidents and secretaries had completed twelve-day courses but some refused to go to the longer three- or six-month courses.[35] Sometimes people recruited as agitators would not go even to very short training: as the campaign to form new GACs heated up in Romos commune (Hunedoara) and a permanent brigade of district cadres moved there, creating a group of twenty-one agitators from the local population to help them recruit GAC members, the Party secretary would give weekly instruction about the work, but only 55 percent of the agitators showed up.[36]

Even people who attended such training courses might find them wanting. An inspector from the Agitprop section of the Baia Mare regional Party committee was very critical of the Party schools he visited: problems were not analyzed, no conclusions were drawn, lessons were merely mechanical description. Some of them were full of errors and confusion. The reasons he noted were that the Party committee and propaganda sections were not checking up on them, some people were skipping class but were protected by highly placed comrades,

---

from peripheral areas. This was a tactic aimed at keeping the Party under control, with leaders who were non-representative, isolated, marginal from ethnic and social perspectives, and with inferior educations."

[32] By 1956 literacy was reported to have reached 90 percent, though it was lowest in rural areas and among women.

[33] M. M., Goina interview.

[34] On Party schools and political education for Party and candidate members, see Năstase and Olaru 2002.

[35] DJAN HD, Fond CR PMR, file 1953/888, 148.

[36] DJAN HD, Fond CR PMR, file 103/1951, 288–89.

and some instructors neglected to cover basic communist teachings and were very poorly prepared.[37] As late as 1955 a report from the Central Committee noted, concerning regional and district committees in Constanța:

> A permanent preoccupation with good instruction of the Party apparatus does not exist. Often the instruction is done superficially, in a few minutes, and in some cases the activists are sent into the field with no instruction at all. Rarely are activists given background material on the problems they will be treating in the field, and there is no verification of the extent to which they are competent to guide and control the organs of the Party organizations about the respective problem, and upon their return the manner in which they have fulfilled their assignments is not analyzed. Activists prepared in this way for work in the field cannot always give qualified and comprehensive help to Party organizations.[38]

A former collective farm president recalled his attendance at Party schools, beginning with his being sent off to school in 1960 before he became president. He went again in the mid-1980s when he was proposed for a higher position. Asked what he learned there, he mentioned ideas about socialism and capitalism, using the word "comrade," how to write reports—"You had to begin with certain opening phrases, like 'owing to the lovely achievements of our Party'"—and other formulaic expressions such as "we have the honor [*avem onoarea*] to report," "we have the honor to request," and so on. He also learned to type, something that would make his reporting infinitely more readable to its recipients and cut down their work time. Following this interview, his wife added slyly that when he went to Party school she had been very upset because she had a full house with lots of work and he would be gone six months. She had remonstrated, "You're going away an ox and you'll come back a cow!" When he returned with top grades on his report card, he remarked, "See? I didn't go away an ox, and I'm not coming back a cow."[39]

Attendance at Party schools was one of several ways in which cadres could be trained. Another very important one was through writing autobiographical sketches for their files, which not only formed a "rite of consecration" but taught prospective activists the categories in terms of which they were to think (see Cîrstocea 2002: 52). Other means of training were by constant instruction through memos from higher levels to lower ones, detailing how they were to fill out a report or resolve an issue and following up with visits from higher levels;[40]

[37] DJAN MM, Fond Comitetul Regional PMR Baia Mare, Secția Propagandă și Agitație, file 38/1956, 83.

[38] Fond C.C. al P.C.R.–Cancelarie, file 130/1955, 9.

[39] 186, Verdery interview. His wife's words were "Tu pleci bou și te întorci vacă!" Asked what she had meant by this, he replied that it had at least two meanings: (1) You go away a dolt (*bou* means both ox and blockhead) and come back even stupider, and (2) you go away potent and when you come back everyone will screw you.

[40] See, for example, Arhiva Primăriei Șibot (jud. Alba), file I/1/1953, 4. This is a questionnaire sent from the district with instructions for how to write minutes of meetings—what information

the standardization of reporting forms; tutoring by instructors sent from the region or district; and participating in work together with other cadres. In 1950, the Orgburo sent down to the counties an instruction entitled "How Minutes of Meetings Should Be Prepared," with exactly the rubrics that should be included, negative examples, and general advice on the form—they should be short and concise, cover only essential issues, and give the decisions reached along with the persons assigned for implementation, etc.[41] We provide a second example in chapter 6, a lengthy admonition that cadres in Odorhei district received from the region in summer 1953, chiding them for not responding in a timely fashion to the task of verifying whether those labeled chiaburs were in fact middle or even poor peasants. The document continues with very specific directives for how these cadres must handle a request for such verification: a commission having certain officials as its members must write a report that gives the following pieces of information (a lengthy list of items) and attaches particular proofs, with copies to go to the commune, district, and regional offices.[42] A final example of top-down instruction comes from a Securitate major who had received a lengthy report on an interrogation, written by a Captain C. He wrote at the end, "And after all this I expected to read your proposals, comrade C., but I see you don't know how to assess this material. What is your opinion???" At the top of the first page he put a note to the district authorities saying, "Within ten days make some concrete proposals, and don't send us any more material from which the district's position is not clear. [If] the district is apolitical, [it] can't assess the situation so as to make proposals."[43]

Yet another form of pedagogy for cadres was to standardize the reporting forms, either by centrally directed instruction or by providing blank forms to be filled out.[44] In requiring the completion of standardized templates in place of poorly (often hand-) written reports of widely varying content, the Party was

should be in them, in what order—and a note that a delegate from the district would make sure they held weekly meetings and would verify the minutes. "Deviations from the above instructions will no longer be tolerated. Failure to respect the above indications will be considered as neglect or negligence on the job and will be punished as such."

41 ANIC, Fond C.C. al P.C.R.–Secția Organelor Conducătoare de Partid, Sindicale și de UTM, file 90/1950, 41–43. Also see ANIC, Fond C.C. al P.C.R.–Secția Organizatorică, file 36/1954/3-10v for instructions on how files on nomenclatura cadres were to be organized, and so on.

42 See ARO, Fond Sfatul Popular al Regiunii Stalin, Dosar despre chiaburi din raza Raionului Odorhei, Nr. Inventar 38, July 31, 1953, 68–69. Courtesy of Sándor Oláh. The document stated twice, "For no reason whatsoever is the district's decision to be communicated to the petitioner or the commune until you receive the result of the definitive decision of the Regional Commission for the Verification of Chiaburs," indicating possible problems of collaboration between cadres and chiaburs.

43 ACNSAS, FI, file 3936/v. 2, 6, 14.

44 Scott (1998) argues that the modern state requires legibility to manage its population, which cadres capable of producing legible reports enable. Standardizing and shortening them is one way to achieve this, as MacLean shows for Vietnam (2005: 200–9; see also Caplan and Torpey 2001). See also note 19.

training its cadres in what they should observe and what was unimportant. A number of our Romanian collaborators observed in their documents a gradual formalization across time, as reports lost their specificity and came to be written in a uniform, ritualized style from which local information was increasingly absent. Cadres responded to set rubrics or filled out questionnaires, rather than noting what seemed significant to them in their locality. At the same time, statistics and percentages became ever more frequent, abstracting local realities into forms more easily transmitted—and more easily falsified. These practices would seem to have shortened the time necessary both to read and to write reports, thus permitting cadres to turn more quickly to their other tasks. Scholars of Soviet and Vietnamese collectivization have observed a similar progression from varied and idiosyncratic reporting to increasingly standardized templates there as well.[45]

Thus we see one of the chief contradictions in the recruiting of cadres: although the "revolution" required people who were educated and knew how to organize and manage, the Party's ideology required using the poor and oppressed—the people least likely to have schooling or managerial experience—who were to enjoy virtually no authority in their local communities because of their lowly origins. At the same time, the well-to-do and state employees (who were educated and had local authority) and fascists (who knew how to organize) were to be persecuted. For want of better raw material, the Party did have to make use of such people, thus raising the specter of class struggle and ideological contamination within the apparatus. That, in turn, required internal surveillance, which—in the context of cadre verifications and expulsions—sharpened the fierce competition among them. Particularly after the purge of the seemingly untouchable Ana Pauker in 1952, they could never know whose head would roll next. We return to the questions of surveillance and competition below.

A Shortage of Good Cadres

Our discussion of the need to educate cadres takes us to the larger problem of whether there were enough to go around. From early stenograms of Central Committee, Secretariat, and Politburo meetings we see clearly the center's preoccupation with this issue, and numerous communications from below exhibit it also. In table 3.1, the very first line shows a concern for the gap between the actual number and the number needed, with a shortfall of 4 percent. At a 1950 meeting, Ana Pauker observed that to create socialist agricultural forms would require great effort, owing to the lack of cadres. She asked another participant whether they could get 350 people for a particular task, and he replied, "We do

[45] Viola, personal communication; MacLean 2005.

indeed have a lack of cadres," noting his plan to send some workers to school for this purpose.[46] From our interviews, an agronomist from Săpânța who had worked in the State Planning Commission on collectivization in the early 1950s observed, concerning technical agricultural specialists, "There were few. . . . They had four primary grades and then four grades of middle school in agriculture. And the regime made use of these imperfect cadres to begin collectivization."[47] This same respondent implied that the initial strategy of setting up a small number of model collectives (rather than pushing a broader campaign) resulted in part from a lack of cadres qualified to run such farms. Further underscoring the dearth of technical cadres is the story of a woman from one of Romania's wealthiest and most influential aristocratic families, the Sturzas. Against her parents' wishes, she pursued an education in agronomy, in part so she could manage the family estate (thousands of hectares), but after the estate was confiscated, she—the archetypal class enemy—was sent out to a village to help create a collective farm.[48]

From documents we learn that the Party relied heavily on agitators who were not Party members—clear evidence of both a recruitment problem and ideologically uncommitted activists. Although most of our examples here come from the Hunedoara regional archives, the forms used were required of all regions, and there is nothing to suggest that Hunedoara was atypical. For example, an April 1951 monthly report on the number of agitators for Orăștie district by kind of unit (state enterprise, state or collective farm, institution, village, commune, etc.) showed that in almost all categories there were more agitators who were *not* Party members than who *were* (see table 3.2). These "agitators" were often peasants from already-formed GACs being sent to tell other villagers about their success. An earlier report indicates that the problem was one not just of numbers of agitators but of their diligence: two right-hand columns show the "number of agitators who work" (79 percent) and "number who work less" (12 percent).[49]

Further problems are indicated in a document complaining that the Party cell failed to recruit agitators from among the peasants who *agreed* with collectivization and had joined, so they could serve as an example to those among whom they were agitating.[50] Additional use of "surrogates" comes from a surprising entry in an Orgburo report of the Securitate dated March 14, 1949, which states, "The number of policemen was insufficient to accompany all the commissions. To cope with these situations, recourse was had to diverse expe-

[46] ANIC, Fond C.C. al P.C.R.–Cancelarie, file 38/1950, 16–17, 32–33. Document courtesy of O. Roske.

[47] D. H., Kligman interview.

[48] Personal friend of the authors, born 1916.

[49] DJAN HD, Fond CR PMR, file 200/1951, 60.

[50] DJAN HD, Fond CR PMR, file 20/1952, 82.

Table 3.2
Party and Non-Party Members among Agitators, Orăştie District, 1951

	Concerning the situation of agitators			
	Number of agitators in the district			*Number with Party/agitation training*
	Party members	*Non-Party members*	*Total*	
In enterprises	219	146	365	331
In institutions	82	105	187	108
In machinery parks	5	20	25	25
In state farms	2	16	18	18
In collectives	17	51	68	60
In villages	352	396	746	364
In neighborhoods	35	10	45	35
Totals:	712	742	1454	941 (65%)

Source: DJAN HD, Fond CR PMR, file 200/1951, 69.

dients (in Sălaj county, one hundred poor peasants were dressed in military clothing and used as such)."[51]

The crisis of cadres perdured.[52] A report from the Agrarian Section of the CC in 1953 observed that the section was working badly because it was understaffed, with cadres being brought in not according to their expertise but catch-as-catch-can.[53] A 1956 report from the Hunedoara region showed how long it would take for each district to reach the Party leaders' goal of 65 percent collectivization by 1960, if the present rhythm were sustained; the figures ranged from 27 years to 152 years.[54] The number of collectivizable households per activist ranged from 75 to 181, for a total number of 1,016 activists—compare this with the 26,000–30,000 cadres (1 for every 3–4 households) that were needed to complete the task in Maramureş and Constanţa (chapter 2).[55] Two years later another report gave the numbers of cadres in villages; one heading reads, "How many of the total number of active cadres are not Party members": 20,594, of which 11,182 (54 percent) were in agriculture.[56]

One obvious effect of these shortages was that a significant amount of work might go undone or be performed inadequately. In documents from the district

[51] ASRI, Fond D, file 9916, page number illegible.

[52] On cadre shortage and Soviet collectivization, see, for instance, Viola 1987: 14, 150.

[53] ANIC, Fond C.C. al P.C.R.–Agrară, file 70/1953, 170.

[54] This brings to mind the 1980s joke, "We will make the five-year plan in four and a half years even if it takes us a decade."

[55] DJAN HD, Fond CR MR, file 2106/1956, 29–30.

[56] DJAN HD, Fond CR PMR, file 83/1958, 128.

or regional archives such as the following from Hunedoara, we find a sense of great urgency alongside massive delays, as work is needed that is not being finished. One report concerns the lapses of the agricultural agent, comrade R., in Turdaş (Hunedoara), "who is in relations with chiaburs and sharecrops their land. . . . [but] until now not a single measure has been taken on the part of the bureau of the Party Committee because too much work has piled up."[57] A peasant from Dâncu Mare village wrote to his district Agrarian Section in 1954 to complain that cadres were manipulating the amount of land he was supposed to have and he could not keep up with the taxes assessed on him. To this complaint—and similar ones as well—the district replied, "As soon as we have time we will send a technician to measure your entire surface area. Until then we will keep your petition in our files."[58] The reasons for "not having time" were amply apparent: the district had 105 villages and a population of 13,752 peasant households, many of which might be wanting a cadastral technician to come and measure their land, but the People's Council had only two such technicians. A similar sense of work overload comes from a file labeled "Reports and Situations on the Resolution of Letters from working people."[59] There we find reports about the importance of answering citizens' letters, with statistics on the number of letters received, whether they were sent down from the Central Committee or came directly from within the region, how many had been resolved, how many of those were resolved within the required time limits, and so on. One from 1953 shows that of a total of 1,404 letters received to date, only 596 (42 percent) had been resolved. The secretary responsible for resolving them was admonished for not having gone out into the field to investigate the situations the letters revealed (with a thousand or more such letters each year, one can see why). She was demoted.[60]

The effects of cadre shortage could also be much more substantial than incomplete office work, as we see from reports of how the government coped with emergencies such as mass withdrawals of peasants who had joined GACs (see chapter 2). László Márton (2005: 55–56) describes at length the response to massive departures from GACs that spread across the entire Mureş region in 1951. Dividing the problem collectives into three categories according to the seriousness of the situation, regional leaders sent one activist and one Party organizer into those with the least severe problems and three activists into those that were somewhat worse. To the most severe cases (eighteen in number) they sent a member of the bureau of the district Party Committee, who would have to go every other day and stay for a day or two if necessary, as well

[57] DJAN HD, Fond CR PMR, file 93/1951, 116.

[58] DJAN HD, Fond Sfat Popular al Raionului Orăştie, file 134/1954, 405.

[59] DJAN HD, Fond CR PMR, file 16/1959. The file is dated 1959 but contains documents from 1952–53 as well.

[60] DJAN HD, Fond CR PMR, file 16/1959, 8–11, 12–15, 20.

as ten well-prepared agitators from among the best activists and functionaries of the People's Councils, who would go into neighboring settlements as well. In effect, the entire apparatus of the Party, the People's Councils, and district and regional activists was mobilized, even including members of the Central Committee and the Minister of Agriculture; the regional Party bureau held meetings every two days.[61] Márton concludes, "[T]he resistance in autumn 1950–1951, by requiring the concentration of a large number of activists, saved many localities from collectivization, even if only briefly" (66). Another such incident involved the villages of Jeledinți, Mărtinești, and Turmaș (Hunedoara), where nearly everyone withdrew from the collective farms in early 1957 and retrieved their inventory, even selling off some of their animals. The regional administration took "sixty good agitators from factories" and instructed them on how to resolve the problem.[62] These events, the report concludes, "obstructed the rhythm of the socialist transformation of agriculture because so many Party and state activists had to be concentrated in these communes who could otherwise have worked effectively for society."[63]

"The Village Was Suffocated by Cadres": Kinds of Cadres and Their Work

A variety of things contributed to the shortage of cadres, including the multiple kinds of them that were required and the tremendous amount of work they were supposed to cover.[64] At the bottom-most level alone—the commune and village—positions proliferated. In Dobrosloveni during the 1950s, for instance, there were collectors, delegates to the threshing machine, persons responsible for the threshing ground (*arie*), delegates for the transport of food requisitions, members of the inventory commission, members of the commissions for supervising material subject to taxation, for fixing agricultural incomes, for updating the Agricultural Register, or for verifying the truthfulness of wine and spirits declarations. There were members in the day or night service of the communal guard, caretakers at the artificial insemination station, zoopastoral administrators, directors, conference leaders, and chauffeurs for the Culture House; caretakers for reproduction, field guards, watchmen at fixed and mobile control points and at the exits of villages and communes, volunteer firemen, and others (Lățea 2009: 334–35).[65] For the decade of the 1950s in that commu-

[61] Such trips by members of the highest body were not unusual. For instance, during a revolt in Vadu Roșca (see chapter 2), CC member and future First Secretary Ceaușescu himself went to put it down.

[62] DJAN HD, Fond CR PMR, file 2431/1957, 103.

[63] DJAN HD, Fond CR PMR, file 2426/1957, 44.

[64] In the original, the title of this section is "satul gîfîia de instructori" (Lățea 2003: 73).

[65] DJAN Olt, Fond "Prefectura Romanați," file 97/1941, Fișa comunei Dobrosloveni, Romanați,

nity, Lățea identified at least eighty positions (not including guards and volunteer firemen, which would have meant almost the whole village). Not all of these qualify as "cadres," but they show something of the range of jobs to be done. The labels referred less to fixed occupational identities than to the tasks a person was charged with at the moment—and those, in turn, varied by settlement.[66]

The most significant thing to note about lists like these is the number of people who were being drawn into Party service and who "at least for one summer, had to obey or pretend they obeyed the official rules, to assume responsibilities and often to act against their own principles and against their close friends or relatives" (335). Thus, people were increasingly drawn into complicity with the Party by becoming its employees. That, in turn, may reflect Party leaders' response to their initially weak base: to build up Party cadres by implicating people in actions that would then make it difficult for them to resist, as networks of others who knew too much about what they were doing gradually tightened around them.

Clearly, with so many kinds of positions, the pool of available talent would have to be large. The kinds of work they did reinforce that conclusion, for cadres were expected to accomplish widely varying tasks. Organizing their work was a central activity of regional and district Party committees, which developed detailed "work plans" for various groups or individuals. The plans would state who was going where to do what, on which date. Individual cadres also wrote up their own work plans, as well as activity reports once the work was done. Sometimes the tasks are specified in minute detail. In summer 1953 the People's Councils in Sânpaul and Lueta communes, alongside their other tasks for organizing the threshing of grain, received the following instructions from the district: "On the threshing ground, in each of the four corners the nastiest dogs in the village must be tied with a long chain. Inform the chiaburs that after nightfall they have no business in the fields, nor at their neighbors" (Oláh 2003: 54).[67]

Other kinds of work that cadres performed included a category we will discuss at length in chapter 5, persuasion work (*muncă de lămurire*). They were charged with persuading people to become Party members, to come out for spring planting or harvesting in summer and fall, to give their quotas, and to join the collectives and the associations—and if they later withdrew, to join

pe 1941; Arhiva Primăriei Dobrosloveni, file 5/1944, Decizii ale Primăriei Comunei Dobrosloveni 1942–1944; Arhiva Primăriei Dobrosloveni, Registru decizii 1944–1962.

[66] For example, the two villages of Corund and Armășeni (Odorhei district) differed in that in one, teachers as well as employees of the People's Council and local consumer coop—in other words, state employees—performed the work of activists, whereas in the other these people were given only minor tasks not tied to forming the collective, a job done largely by organizers from outside (Bodó 2003: 59–60).

[67] ARO, file 56/1953, 83.

again. Toward this end, they organized and attended countless meetings and seminars among themselves, with lower-level functionaries, and with citizens to exhort, inform, or instruct on everything from socialist morality to the extirpation of Colorado bugs. They analyzed and discussed new laws, decrees, orders, instructions, and decisions communicated from above, clarifying these for themselves and then for ordinary citizens. They provided educational courses, especially in adult literacy, and urged other cadres to attend Party schools. They led reading circles in villages, organized village general assemblies, arranged for films, performances, and discussions in villages and towns, posted wall gazettes, and mobilized the Communist Youth or Women's organizations in villages and communes. Every activist wrote frequent, often lengthy reports and read the reports of his subordinates—tasks assisted by the spread of typewriters to replace the near-illegible scrawls common in the early 1950s. They dealt with petitions and contestations (most concerning chiabur status or quotas), a particularly time-consuming job: for instance, between May 1, 1952, and May 15, 1953, the total number of them in Hunedoara region was 24,807![68] All these tasks comprise a small fraction of the kinds of work that appear in Party documents.

To accomplish them, cadres traveled continually: instructors, activists, and Party secretaries went from the regional capitals to the districts to resolve problems there, district cadres traveled into communes and villages to "persuade," verify contestations, and mobilize peasants for one or another in the endless series of campaigns, and commune officials traveled to other communes and to villages to help with persuasion and to monitor progress. They went out every Sunday for persuasion work, since peasants were at home then. Even Central Committee members would travel for these purposes, especially when there was trouble. To consolidate fields for collective farms, cadastral technicians and others would travel widely, overseeing and documenting the exchange of parcels between GAC members and villagers who did not wish to join. Stoica observes that according to his respondents, the top (regional) level included largely activists from other regions. "The low number of trustworthy Party activists at the national level in the 1950s may explain this pattern, for the shortage of activists made it necessary to rotate them among various localities and counties throughout the country"—with yet more travel (Stoica 2009: 430). A consequence of these circuits, if we follow Benedict Anderson's insights (1983), would be to give cadres a sense of belonging to a larger unit and broader endeavor.

The problem with all this travel was the inadequate infrastructure for it: the Romanian transportation network linked all parts of the country with Bucharest but in the countryside, it could be very difficult to get from peripheral communes or districts to the district or regional centers. As one former activist put

[68] DJAN HD, Fond CR PMR, file 1082/1953, 145.

it in describing his job, "I spent a lot of time on the run, whole days in a row in train stations trying to get where I was supposed to go."[69] Moreover, after hours spent on trains and buses, they might have to hitch a ride with a passing oxcart for a bone-shattering trip across dirt paths. The difficulty of traveling such distances may be one reason why cadres sent out into the field sometimes preferred not to go. Another reason was that there were no accommodations for them: a report on cadres' work in remote Vrancea, Moldavia, for instance, noted that the construction of housing for activists and technicians was essential because "[m]any of them sleep on tables in public buildings, always separated from their families. For this reason many of the technicians refuse to go to this area."[70] These kinds of infrastructural difficulties worsened the labor shortage, for if it took one person the better part of a day or more to go to his assigned village and back, he could not do any other tasks.[71]

The work of cadres could be dangerous: angry villagers often beat them up, sometimes fatally. One day in 1950 the president and a few workers from the GAC in Ieud went to get wood, returning late at night. At the edge of the village they were attacked by four chiaburs and a poor peasant; the president was so gravely beaten up that he could not speak.[72] A report from 1951 indicates that Party members and especially the poorer activists in Hunedoara region were going around in constant fear, being continually set upon.[73] A former activist from Vlaicu described his attempt to take the horses and cart of a newly signed-up chiabur in the late 1950s: "He wanted to stick a pitchfork in me. I saw him pick it up, I shouted at him to put it down, and he did." This followed his tale of being unable to find people to go take the same items from another chiabur, well known for his violent temper. Because violence against cadres occurred throughout the country, to become one meant putting one's life at risk. Even without fear of violence, the work was very stressful. As the widow of one district functionary said, when the verification of chiaburs was in full swing and people were coming to their house day and night, "Finally he'd say 'Stop!! I can't take it anymore!!' He suffered a *lot* in this work."[74]

The amount of work was absolutely overwhelming, and overwork was a seri-

[69] 197, Verdery interview.

[70] ANIC, Fond C.C. al P.C.R.–Agrară, file 70/1953, 157.

[71] Moreover, the weekly reports cadres had to write were often so sensitive that we doubt they were sent through the mail; more likely, a lower-level unit sent these documents by courier, over miserable roads or with prolonged train rides. In the archives we find numerous and often lengthy telegrams sent, for example, by the Securitate in the countryside to Bucharest, again indicating problems with mail service. Some of the Party's business was conducted by telephone (at the head of certain documents appears the notation "Telephone note"), but if the quality of telephone service we encountered in the early 1970s is any indication, telephones in the 1950s were a very unsatisfactory instrument for conducting Party business.

[72] DJAN MM, Fond Comitetul Județean Maramures, file 95/1950, 11.

[73] DJAN HD, Fond CR PMR, file 305/1951, 26–27.

[74] A.D.T., Verdery interview.

ous problem, aggravated by the ever-increasing demands of the bureaucracy. In 1951 the CC Section on the Party's Leading Bodies issued a twenty-eight-page report titled "Bureaucratic Methods and Superficiality in Party Work," which condemned the ballooning demands of the bureaucracy that made life impossible for its officials.[75] "An avalanche of questionnaires and written or telephoned instructions" asking for statistics on virtually everything, right away, had led to superficial work because there was too much to do; disorganization was snowballing. The introduction of these forms of information gathering "has formed, from the Sections of the Central Committee down to the district committee, . . . an uninterrupted chain of comrades who have to feed this bureaucracy." The report gave multiple examples of requests for information that had kept cadres up all night telephoning other cadres for data—ultimately producing information overload.[76] In more local terms, the Party secretary in Ieud, for instance, proposed that he "be replaced from the post of secretary of the Party cell for the reason that . . . I have excessive production obligations where I have to work nights as well and I can't do everything, if I deal seriously with one thing then I get behind in another and things can't continue like this."[77]

The work was not only excessive, it was tremendously variable. Cadres could never anticipate what might be coming next, for at any moment Bucharest might issue a new decree and command them to implement it immediately regardless of other things they might be doing. In addition, each of them checked up on the activity of everyone else, purveying information that might lead colleagues to receive warnings, censure, firings, arrest, and the worst punishment available: exclusion from the Party. It was an extremely stressful life, requiring constant vigilance.

Given the danger, the stress, the overwork, why would anyone want to become a cadre? There were several possible motives. Some hoped for social advancement or for recognition they had long been denied, others for good regular incomes, yet others to be in the thick of things where they could exercise initiative, rather than letting initiative go to others less capable. A former chiabur from Ieud reported in his memoir a discussion between Ieud's most recalcitrant Uniate priest and a Party activist (originally from a chiabur family of Ieud), during which the latter allegedly said: "I would like smart and earnest people to join the Party, so that we won't need to bring in Gypsies or uneducated [stupid] people, although in the end, the Party needs to be formed with whatever people it can be. It isn't that I don't appreciate Gypsies, as they too are people like us but they aren't yet cultured and . . . they weren't raised to lead and

[75] ANIC, Fond C.C. al P.C.R.–Secția Organelor Conducătoare de Partid, Sindicale și de UTM, Sectorul Documentării de Partid, file 26/1951, 2–32.

[76] Martin reports that Soviet leaders found this a serious problem. Molotov complained in 1926 that there was simply too much information. "The Central Committee secretaries hardly read it, it takes too much time" (Martin n.d.: 64–65).

[77] Fond Comitetul Raional PCR (PMR) Vișeu–Organizația de bază, Ieud, file 157/1956/v, 68.

there will be hell to pay if they are leaders."[78] Some could not manage (or were afraid) to say no when Party activists put the squeeze on them. Some became cadres to help their families who were being persecuted as chiaburs or for other reasons; others wanted to overcome black marks in their past, such as membership in fascist groups. A considerable number of people who became cadres hoped to preserve some semblance of their social standing within the new rules of the game. Finally, some were committed to communist ideals and welcomed the opportunity to bring those to life.[79]

Cadre Hunger and the Nature of the Communist System

Why, we might ask, was there so much work? This question leads us to consider the nature of the system that generated it, a matter addressed by scholars such as Jowitt in his work on "revolutionary breakthrough" in Romania (1971) and "neotraditionalism" in communist systems more generally (1983), Gross in his on the "spoiler state" in Poland (1988), Hungarian sociologists Horváth and Szakolczai in their fascinating study of midlevel cadres (1992), and Stark and Bruszt on networks in postcommunist Hungary (1998). They and others have pointed to the essentially mobilizational character of Bolshevik-type regimes, which recognized the importance of colonizing routine elements of behavior and attempted to penetrate daily life more fully than any modern regime hitherto. Party activists saw themselves as realizing the Party's historical mission: to fulfill human happiness by satisfying all social needs, a view that made politics ubiquitous (see Rév 1987). Underlying these regimes was the idea that

> power was related to the source of life and movement, but that it was a dangerous, evil force that must be constantly supervised and regulated—and the resurrection of the Greek concept of power as *arkhé*, as initiative, as opposed to the idea that power is simply rule or position. The consequence was that bolshevism tried to influence and supervise all decisions, all movements, all initiatives. . . . It tried at once to destroy and then to replace, stimulate and instigate all activities. (Horváth and Szakolczai 1992: 216)

Hence the constant emphasis on campaigns, on enforced participation in activities, on continual celebration, as well as the concern with people's "mood"—all designed to keep everyone mobilized, stimulated, pointing toward the fu-

[78] B. S., "Cum s-o colectivizat Ieud," no date or page number. Similarly, a man who achieved a high position in the Orăştie administration had doubts about even joining the Party, but his superior at the factory said to him, "We should join the Party because all these idiots, all these Gypsies, and so on, are doing it. Do you want *them* to run the country?" (A.D.T., Verdery interview).

[79] The interviews in Rostás and Momoc 2007 make this clear. Several of them state forthrightly their belief in Communist ideology, even in interviews done in 2004–5, when such an admission would not be popular.

ture. These authors summarize the system's rationality as (1) the Party must be everywhere for things to work as planned, (2) all possible resources should be withdrawn from other hands to be concentrated under the Party's control, (3) the Party must civilize the entire population by instilling its values through education (79–80).

Good vanguardists that they were, Party cadres assumed that people would not work of their own volition, that some sort of supervision was necessary, and that cadres could do it better than anyone else. This infantilizing attitude, however, had the effect of creating ever more work over time until the need to intervene in everything had become completely embedded in their outlook (see Horváth and Szakolczai 1992: 50–58). In short, the communists implemented a modernization strategy that created a huge bureaucratic edifice and then used it to micromanage daily life, with no sense of the limits to its intrusions. Although this conception took time to become fully developed and was unlikely to have exacerbated cadre shortage during the 1950s, perceiving it as a tendency helps us to understand the Party's voracious appetite for cadres.

We have been arguing that the RCP suffered from a labor shortage, which we might expect would benefit the cadres, giving them a certain amount of structural leverage (see, e.g., Burawoy 1985). Furthermore, it should have reduced competition among them, for there would be more than enough posts to go around. A structural situation of labor shortage does not mean, however, that actors perceive it as such. Instead, cadres saw their situations as precarious, and the reason is the verifications, denunciations, and surveillance that accompanied Party leaders' obsession with finding the "enemy within." *Anyone* could be unmasked as an internal enemy, even the most powerful leaders, as happened in 1948 (with Lucreţiu Pătrăşcanu) and 1952 (with Secretariat members Pauker, Georgescu, and Luca). This leads us to explore further the nature of surveillance and discipline over cadres.

Discipline and Punish

> All the rogues had become communists. I. L. [a Party member since 1945] wore the green shirt, he was a legionary. He meddled in things wherever he saw there was a bone to gnaw on. [Then there was] one of the more civilized gypsies, D. C., his mother was Romanian and his father a fiddler. He went from one to the other, from the legionaries to the communists. There were other legionaries too, they held meetings. . . . And M. M. [an official in the People's Council] was a legionary and a communist and of every other color.
>
> *—Chelcea 2003b: 20, concerning cadres in Reviga*

The hunger for cadres led the Party to take some consequential recruitment steps. In chapter 1 we mentioned the fascist Iron Guard (or Legion), a well-organized movement from the interwar years that was banned in 1940, following an attempted coup. Its very existence, however, posed potential problems for the communists, whose territorial representation and organizational skills were both inferior to the legionaries'. In 1945 Ana Pauker expressly invited them into the Party, with the approval of other leaders and of Moscow. King explains this in terms of the Party's urgent need for a core of disciplined cadres who would follow instructions and take initiative in consolidating the Party's power position.

> [T]he Iron Guardists not only possessed certain skills and attributes the communists needed, they were also extremely anxious to prove their loyalty to the new rulers, and were thus more willing to carry out party instructions faithfully. . . . [They] provided a more reliable base than the members recruited from among the working class and the peasantry on the basis of ideological commitments and socioeconomic considerations. (1980: 66)

Evidence available more recently nuances the picture. Pauker herself explained the decision in 1953 as a tactic to undermine the opposition and prevent peasants and workers from being lured to the right. She claimed that the Party made a deal according to which legionary leaders would tell their adherents, "The road to rehabilitation is open if you participate actively in the struggle against yesterday's leaders and their politics, and against the other reactionaries and their politics."[80]

Later recognizing this as a mistake, Party leaders attempted to purge some of their erstwhile allies (primarily the former leaders); the 1948–52 verification campaign was aimed partly at them.[81] That they had indeed been numerous and significant, however, contributed to the constant search for "hostile elements" in the Party apparatus. A key practice in all communist systems was to find and purge the "enemies within"; for Romania, among the chief enemies were the legionaries, together with chiaburs. Accusing someone of being a legionary, or attributing acts of sabotage or resistance to them, became a central idiom for demonizing and casting blame, an activity that Party leaders engaged in constantly. The following is a typical example: "In some places, enemy elements without doubt infiltrated the lower-level Party cadres, for the frankly fascist hooligan methods that were used can only come from enemies, which also pushed onto this path honest elements from the Party apparatus who have shaky training."[82] In emphasizing the real basis of concerns about fascists we do not mean to suggest that such statements were always an accurate representation—the impetus to blame was systemic, and it could make symbolic use of

[80] See the summary in Ionescu-Gură 2005: 211–12.

[81] Despite the verification of Party members in 1948–50, almost 12 percent of those retained in the Party had legionary or otherwise "reactionary" backgrounds (Ionescu-Gură 2005: 214).

[82] ANIC, Fond C.C. al P.C.R.–Cancelarie, file 59/1950, 78 (RLA).

anyone (see chapter 4). Nonetheless, real experience gave some symbols, like fascist cadres, especially rich resonance.

The Enemy Within

Tismăneanu observes, "Detecting enemies 'within our ranks' was even more important than detecting obvious class enemies, because the former were much more difficult to unmask. . . . True Stalinists distinguished themselves by detecting the invisible traitor who claimed to be 'one of ours' but in reality subverted the party's grand achievements" (2003: 95). To ensure this, Party organizations would maintain a continual struggle to cleanse the Party's ranks of enemy elements. Periodically the Party would turn against its own—the show trials of the Soviet 1930s and East European 1950s are the most extreme instances—expelling them from their posts or from the Party itself, or even murdering them. Other methods included denunciations, interrogations, verification campaigns, and the Soviets' famous "criticism and self-criticism" sessions, also used in Eastern Europe, at which cadres could offer each other guidance or unmask class enemies among them.

Details on show trials suggest to us that the exercise of purging was a kind of ritual sacrifice. In Soviet practice, according to Hellbeck, sacrifice emerged from the Party's conception of itself as surrounded by and riddled with enemies, a fear that went back to the early revolution; periodic purges would maintain its "purity" (2006: 34). He and other scholars of Stalinism such as Getty and Naumov (1999) hint at the ritual aspect, as when Hellbeck observes that the regime "practiced ritual expulsion scenarios, graphically severing individuals from the collective body" (2006: 361). What leads us to label these purges ritual sacrifice is their scripted character, with most victims clearly understanding that they had a specific role to play: for the good of the Party, they were to accede to the charges against them, confess their errors publicly, and embrace their fates. That is, there was an accepted ritual form of behavior for persons placed in this role, even though not everyone targeted for purging played the role expected of them.[83] Bukharin, for example, infuriated his colleagues when he refused "to serve the party and ritual by playing the prescribed role . . . thereby contesting the entire ritual space" (Getty and Naumov 1999: 406, 407). Getty and Naumov describe these rituals astutely, observing that moments of ritual sacrifice (our term, not theirs) often served to transform the meanings of symbols, filling them with new content.[84] After such rituals, "enemy" would

[83] Hellbeck says, of the writer of his Soviet revolutionary's diary (2006: 337), "He had emerged from the nine-month purgatory as a better and purer person" and is grateful to Stalin for having tested him, as well as to the NKVD for their work of purification, through which he sees that his life has acquired historical meaning. After he was rehabilitated he still supported the purge campaign.

[84] See also our appendix 2.

mean something different from what it had meant before, and new patterns of alliance would have emerged. Show trials were practiced upon especially visible Party cadres, but purging on a lesser scale remained a signal feature of the life of cadres, through perpetual surveillance and the fear that accompanied it.

In the literature on life under Communist Party rule, much is written about surveillance of the general population, but in our view, at least as important was the surveillance the apparatus exercised over itself.[85] Constant scrutiny kept cadres in a state of continual ferment, contributing to the anxiety-producing climate in which cadres operated, as well as to their struggles to outdo rivals for better posts by showing excessive zeal in their work. They were monitored and denounced by ordinary citizens, by other cadres, and by the Securitate, sometimes resulting in the loss of their posts. The motives could be other activists' concern to have a good working collective, a desire that the Party not be compromised by its cadres' bad behavior, or nasty personal vendettas—just as we will discuss for the denunciations of "class war," in chapters 4 and 6. Like education and verification, surveillance and discipline were a form of pedagogy. Here we encounter yet another contradiction in Party policy: it desperately needed good cadres, but it was always getting rid of them.

Objects of Surveillance

The Romanian Party had reason to monitor its cadres closely, not only because of the early pact with the legionaries but because it initially had to recruit a fair number of cadres from the prior administration (see chapter 1) who were likely to have bourgeois pasts, thus allowing "dangerous enemy elements" to infiltrate the apparatus.[86] From these strategic compromises emerged the unrelenting search for "unreliable" cadres that we see across the full spectrum of the polity. For example, in the secret files of the Dobrosloveni People's Council is a 1954 document from the district headquarters asking for data on who has or has not given their quotas (as we point out below, many had not). It specifically requests numbers "by category, such as Party members, members of the Communist Youth, district and communal deputies, the women's delegate, union members, to include functionaries by branch or by district." From this it is clear that the majority of those holding power locally were closely watched by the next higher level (Lățea 2003: 28–29). Documents in the files for the State Com-

[85] Igal Halfin (2007) has written about the "communist hermeneutics" through which cadres and CP members could be distinguished as revolutionaries or impostors. The preponderance of verbal practices leads him to observe that the Bolsheviks saw words as a window into a person's entire moral disposition. Crucial to this are cadre autobiographies—a form we unfortunately do not have space to elaborate upon.

[86] The same problem of having to hire holdovers because of a shortage of cadres appears in China and Vietnam as well (see Shue 1988; MacLean 2005). This pattern is also found in many other socialist countries and in many other revolutionary situations.

mission on Quotas regularly listed—separately from other people—how many Party members had turned over their required amounts. A Securitate report on an uprising in Bihor recommended close supervision of cadres and "the verification and elimination from the state apparatus of all the enemy elements who have placed themselves in the service of the class enemy, participating in counterrevolutionary chiabur actions" (Roske 2003: 142).[87] This sort of surveillance, which saturates the documents we consulted, created a highly unstable environment in which everyone felt constantly watched, was ready to denounce and unmask not just chiaburs but other comrades, and kept careful track of whose star was rising or falling.

How was one to know a "bad" cadre or Party member? What kinds of "deviations" raised suspicions about a cadre's "true" nature? As we see not only in stenograms of Secretariat and Politburo meetings but in innumerable reports from regional and district Party Committees, there were multiple causes for concern. We group the complaints lodged against cadres into four overlapping types: (1) moral lapses and character flaws unsuitable in a Party leader, (2) bad work habits and failure to perform their jobs as directed, (3) the problem of "personalism," and (4) abusing their power position and perverting the Party line. Any one of these could be interpreted as revealing a cadre's true nature as a "chiabur," "legionary," or "bourgeois," which became synonymous with "enemy." We will provide some examples of each.[88]

MORAL LAPSES AND CHARACTER FLAWS

> Lenin said that whoever relaxes his vigilance serves the bourgeoisie, for the class enemy searches out the weaknesses of Party members and makes use of them, as is the case with Comrade D. S., First Secretary of O. district, who hired as his secretary a person unqualified for the job and took her many times to the district Party headquarters, where he had sexual relations. [I]n this way he compromised the Party, never mind that he also went on drinking sprees and in this way he could no longer have the authority that a district First Secretary must have. Not surprisingly, he didn't implement the decisions of the Party, and his failings led to inactivity by the whole district apparatus. . . . [We] criticize the instructors from the Region, who saw these cadres go from error to error and did nothing.
> —*From minutes of a regional Party Committee meeting*[89]

The Communist Party, as the vanguard of a utopian future, proclaimed itself the repository of the highest moral, ethical, and behavioral standards. Although expected of every Party member, such standards were first and foremost re-

[87] ASRI, Fond D, file 4638, 90.

[88] The archival and interview material on this matter is vast, and we have reluctantly sacrificed much fascinating detail, summarizing issues more often than we exemplify them.

[89] DJAN HD, Fond CR PMR, file 442/1952, 1–2. Words dropped from the quotation are not indicated here.

quired of cadres, who were supposed to provide examples for others to emulate.[90] They were to be the new "saints" in a culture that venerated saints as models for action. Their behavior was to reflect their inner faith as communists, but this faith could be corrupted; therefore, cadres were highly attentive to behavioral signs of contamination in their comrades that might affect everyone's work and jeopardize the Party's goals. There was plenty of material, for the archives are full of evidence that many of those serving as leaders at various levels had not absorbed the principles of socialist ethics and morality, for all their origins in the upright worker and peasant classes. Their failings could begin with basic personality traits: "he's a good fellow but needs help," "he promises but doesn't follow through," "he's easily influenced by chiaburs," "he doesn't take any initiative," "he's too flabby," "she's indecisive," "he's not a good organizer," and so on.[91] Then there were flaws such as openness to bribes. Although these traits were significant failings, three areas were of special concern for policing morality: sexual behavior, theft, and drinking.[92] All three, notably, are forms of reciprocity (either positive or negative), that is, direct exchange. Perhaps a regime deriving its legitimacy from redistribution (a vertical form) was particularly disturbed by horizontal exchanges it did not mediate.[93]

Of the many possible corrupting influences, sexual license was seen as particularly endangering to new "saints," for cadres were to model ideal family relations, being monogamous and refraining from divorce. As we see in the example immediately above, comrades would criticize one another for sexual peccadilloes, and ordinary citizens (especially women) might denounce cadres for making passes or demanding sexual favors.[94] Interviewees too recall Party activists as womanizers. This behavior could cause them problems with villagers where they worked. In Vlaicu, for example, activist C. F. was badly beaten up after a dance, because he had paid too much attention to someone else's girlfriend.[95] Another predictable effect of cadres' sexual relations with villagers was that the women consenting to them might receive favors that compromised the Party's goals. In Vadu Roşca, the beautiful daughter of the village's only

[90] Kharkhordin (1995) understands this as part of a deeper transformation in the nature of the self, which accompanied the communization of Soviet society. Whereas pre-Soviet Russians had been largely left alone to practice their religious rituals and not quizzed about the content of their beliefs, beliefs came to be of great interest to the new Soviet power. "A true inner faith was posited as the essence of a New Soviet individual who—like a lay saint—was supposed to know the discursive content of communist doctrine by heart and consistently demonstrate saintliness in every action" (1995: 212). Thus, the Party's goal was to transform subjectivity by creating new believers and policing their behavior so it conformed with their new belief.

[91] See, for example, DJAN HD, Fond CR PMR, file 305/1951, and other files concerning documentation of cadres.

[92] Because so many of these "sins" appear so widely, we cite few sources.

[93] We owe this observation to Puiu Lăţea.

[94] For example, DJAN MM, Fond Comitetul Raional PMR Sighet, file 51/1952/S. 38; DJAN HD, Fond CR PMR, file 333/1951, n.p.

[95] ACNSAS, FI, file 3936/v. 1, 10ff, and Verdery interviews.

chiabur slept with one of the quota collectors, who advised her father how to escape his chiabur status (Stoica 2009: 434). In a twist on more familiar tales of Party members in positions of authority taking sexual advantage of women, a member of the Vişeu district agit-prop section was criticized for demanding that his wife return home from Party school when he realized that, as an activist, she would not have time to clean the house. He recognized his error and vowed to correct his behavior and thinking.[96] These possibilities were precisely why it was considered so important for cadres to stick to the straight and narrow if they were to do their jobs properly.[97] "Their personal life thus became a kind of identity card for Party members" (Oprea 2002: 51).

The theft of collective (or individuals') property by cadres was another behavior that appeared regularly in interviews and Party documents—throughout the entire communist period, in fact. Although most references to the theft of goods from collective farms focus on the peasantry, documents as well as interviews show that cadres at all levels of the hierarchy engaged in it as well, from lowly brigade leaders to the top nomenclatura.

> The former accountant at the district People's Council in Odorhei committed a series of infractions, such as: while he was accompanying the quota transport he pocketed various sums of money he had received for cereals, 133 lei representing the salary of the controller at the thresher, 145 lei from the sale of wood.... He stole a jug of brandy belonging to the People's Council. And he received money from various citizens on the understanding that he would intervene on their behalf.[98]

A peasant from Săpânţa explained how brigade leaders stole from the collective: "With a pen, they stole shamelessly. Instead of writing down three hundred hours, they wrote one hundred, leaving two hundred extra."[99] Activists fomenting class war would confiscate and appropriate objects from the houses of chiaburs: "They would break down the gate, go over to the fence, rip off the door, and take a cart they'd seen from the road, then load it up with clothes."[100] "I had about $3,000–$4,000 and about 2,000 gold francs, these were the last things they took because everything else was taken earlier. It was easy for them to take what was accumulated over 250 years, tens of generations—it was gone

[96] Fond Comitetul Raional PMR Vişeu, Procese verbale de la Şedinţele Biroului Raional, file 1/1950/v. V, 24.

[97] Attitudes about women were a particularly fraught area of proletarian morality in a patriarchal culture. For instance, the directors of the tractor station and many drivers created an unhealthy situation in the Constanţa region through their sexual relations with various women. (See ASRI, Fond D, file 4054/1950, 168). Or, in Maramureş, comrade president propositioned a female comrade who had been sent to the village, suggesting she spend the night in his room (see Dobeş et al. 2004: 38).

[98] ARO, file Cercetarea cauzelor şi măsurilor luată (*sic*) pe anul 1956, n.p. Nr. Inventar 133–40. Courtesy of Sándor Oláh. (The accountant spent three months in jail.)

[99] Fürtös and Bârlea 2009: 336.

[100] B. L., Stan interview for M. Stewart.

in twenty-four hours."[101] Collective farm officials would either take home or give to their political superiors products or animals from the collectives they were running. Peasants working in transport for the collectives told us of being asked by their bosses to take cartloads of corn and potatoes to one or another Party leader. Such breaches of not only the new communist morality but also the older village-based one further alienated peasants from the whole enterprise, convincing them that collectivization was in effect one immense theft in which they would be the losers. These thefts also contributed, by their powerful example, to decades of peasant counterstealing from the collectives.

The moral lapse that appeared most often in our interviews and documents, however, was excessive drinking. Concern with it is evident in reports from the Central Committee on down through regional, district, and commune Party committees, as well as GAC councils; villagers' predominant image of cadres also paints them as drunks and lowlifes. Discussions in Central Committee meetings point to serious problems with drunken cadres, who should be dismissed.[102] In addition to the two drinker-cadres presented in the quotation at the head of this section, here are three more.[103] A report from Maramureş county in 1948 notes that the financial administration is very weak, "because all the agents and tax collectors in our county are drunks." When the Vişeu Party First Secretary questioned a comrade and his colleague about their repeated drinking, they said they drank "because they don't like Party work and want to be sent home."[104] Multiple notes from Sânnicolau Mare district (Arad) describe cases of theft, fraud, and drunkenness by cadres in Tomnatic village (Vultur 2003a: 47). As for peasants' recollections of cadres, Hungarian villagers, recalling their pasts, wrote to a newspaper in 1996–97: "A policeman and a drunk member of the People's Council [kicked at the door, yelling]"; "Father and other kulaks were often summoned to the People's Council at night, where drunk activists would shout at them"; and "Many of them came from the lower class of the village: they were slackers avoiding work, alcoholics, and illiterates" (Kristó 1999: 10, 58, 64). After peasants in Reviga found that the Party Secretary liked to drink, they gave him brandy so he would help them out (Chelcea 2009: 407).

[101] N. W., Vultur interview.

[102] For example, ANIC, Fond 1, file 55/1951, 31 (RLA).

[103] We have countless amusing anecdotes concerning cadres' drinking but will limit ourselves to one more. A Maramureş activist who was unable to control himself continually went to the village tavern, where he drank himself into a stupor. After one such binge, he went to the Party headquarters and lay down on a bench, but, nauseated, he fell on the floor, where he was found the next morning. When questioned by the First Secretary about his drinking, he responded that he would not stop. After he sobered up, he failed to engage in self-criticism, instead going back to the tavern. For his unabashed insolence, he was formally reprimanded, all active Party members voting to give him a formal warning and relieve him of any further Party work. (DJAN MM, Fond 10 Comitetul Raional PMR Vişeu, file 2/1950, 9)

[104] DJAN MM, Fond Comitetul Județean PMR Sighet, file 43/1948, 68–69.

In Vadu Roşca, interviewees remembered the quota collector as "a pimp, a pauper, and a drunk" (Stoica 2009: 433).

In assessing these kinds of evidence, we must bear in mind that cadres often competed with one another to move upward in the hierarchy, and accusing other comrades of drunkenness could place a black mark in a competitor's file. Among our village respondents, it was perhaps *the* symbol of moral turpitude and a likely trope for recalling the evils of the communist period. Nonetheless, the frequency of complaints about drinking, especially in the documents, makes us believe that it was indeed a problem. Why did cadres drink, and why were Party officials so worried about it?

Several possible reasons could lead a cadre to the bottle. It is not as if Party activists had no need of a stiff drink: as we have already observed, their lives were extremely stressful, for every day they faced angry peasants who hated what they were doing, might gang up on them, and might even try to kill them. An activist from Timişoara region was so afraid of being beaten up by chiaburs that he tried to hang himself.[105] Cadres in Ukraine were chastised for drinking liquor "for bravery" during collectivization there (Brown 2004: 103); Romanian cadres had similar reasons. Some drank because they liked to, others (particularly those with local ties) drank because they disliked what they were being asked to do to their neighbors, kin, and friends: for many, being compelled to exercise force went against their character and created veritable crises of conscience.[106] An additional reason for drinking might be that cadres needed sociality, and by the norms of village life, drinking was a prime means for that. Even the cadre who needed a stiff drink would almost certainly be drinking with others. (We return to this point later in the chapter.) Some drank because villagers always offered it, presumably to soften them up. This is so utterly in keeping with peasant norms and strategies that Jean Băileşteanu's novel *Drum în tăcere* (*Quiet Travel*) makes note of it, in a long discussion of persuasion work.

> Pitrache and Piliuță went alone through the village to persuade people, but in vain. People absolutely did not want it. They reported the situation to the district, and after a while even comrade Gae began to take things more slowly. He told them one day to get at least 20 or 30 families so they could complete the experimental farm. A couple of times they partied a bit at the home of some open-handed families who, for fear of the collective, would pull out a jug of wine with the thought that in this way they could get in good with the commission and make it leave them alone. (1987: 201)

Why did higher authorities care so much about the drinking? First, as we have said, drinking as a character flaw indicated a person who might not be a reliable Party worker, so his habits had to be followed closely. Second, as some

[105] ANIC, Fond C.C. al P.C.R.–Agrară, file 40/1950, 189.

[106] Ivo Banac (personal communication) reports that Yugoslav cadres charged with collectivization had devastating crises of conscience as they were ordered to execute people who refused to join; this contributed to the policy's reversal in 1948.

of our examples show, a man with a weakness for drink would be open to bribes with alcohol that might affect his duties: collectors might take less than the full quota, activists might abandon persuasion and recruit fewer collectivists, functionaries might help chiaburs escape into the middle peasantry, secretaries might give a worker extra work points, and so on. In short, drunks were corruptible, and the Party was right to worry about that. We return to these matters below.

BAD WORK HABITS AND FAILURE TO PERFORM JOBS AS DIRECTED

> We're behind in collections, because the commune collector is not working hard enough and has no plan. He is doing nothing about chiaburs in arrears. . . . And also because some comrade deputies have not given *their own* quotas, so for this they could not do persuasion work.
> —*From a report on collections in Darabani, 1957*[107]

> [They threw you out] for things like going to the movies instead of doing your work, or getting drunk . . . and it got around very fast—the information system functioned very well. . . . There was a lot of envy among us.
> —*Interview with former activist, in Rostás and Momoc 2007: 36, 40*

A second set of "deviations" that raised questions about a cadre's "true" nature was that they did their jobs poorly, arousing suspicion that perhaps they wanted the Party to fail. On the evidence of numerous documents, it is clear that many cadres had highly defective habits of work.[108] They did not prepare their work or have a plan; they used dictatorial methods; they went out and told others to agitate, then took off, and no one kept track of their work; they held open meetings with whole villages instead of doing persuasion work house to house or person to person as directed; they went to their offices for a couple of hours and then went home to plow their land; they never went out into the field to verify situations they were to resolve; they would drive by in their cars but never get out to analyze what was happening; they failed to answer letters or resolve contestations within the prescribed time limit, and therefore peasants contesting their quotas would deliver nothing while awaiting resolution; they kept inadequate records of their actions. Many of these posed particular problems be-

[107] DJAN BT, Fond Sfat Pop. Com. Darabani, file 8/1956 (sic), 220–22. (The date is 1957 on the document.)

[108] Visits from Soviet advisors could prove embarrassing for this reason: for instance, the head of the Propaganda and Agitation department of the CC, Leonte Răutu, told of a Soviet comrade who had visited a GAC near Bucharest, where he found the president of the "colhoz" playing chess with the accountant and a policeman. When he asked, "Have you nothing to do?" they said no, all the work was done. So he took them out to the fields and asked why they weren't gathering up snow and putting it on the land for better irrigation. Răutu's comment was that the Party organization was not sufficiently agitating for the use of advanced methods. (ANIC, Fond C.C. al P.C.R.–Propagandă şi Agitaţie, file 3/1950, 110)

cause, as the Baia Mare regional Party Committee wrote to its subordinates, "To work superficially means to lead the top organs of the Party into error" and thereby compromise the regime.[109]

Closely related to these poor work habits was simply not doing the job one was given, or actively sabotaging it. This was a frequent concern of Party leaders, as well as of officials in regions, districts, and communes. At the top of their lists were that functionaries saw forming GACs as a burden and waited to be pushed or forced to participate, and that lower cadres were refusing to collect quotas, join GACs in their villages, or give quotas themselves. They would neglect the oxen they had confiscated from chiaburs, so the animals became very thin and provoked derision from "reactionary forces" instead of attracting peasants to sign up.[110] They showed no interest in the entire spring planting or summer harvesting campaigns; they procured seed too late to sow it; they failed to foment class war; they had incorrect attitudes toward national minorities (a 1953 report took note of cadres' hostile behavior toward Romania's German minority in the regions of Timişoara, Arad, Stalin, Cluj, Hunedoara, Baia Mare, and the Hungarian Autonomous Region, whom they expropriated incorrectly and whose houses they had ruined);[111] and many more.

Simply making cadres show up proved to be a challenge. (They, in turn, had difficulty making collectivists show up to work, as we shall see.) For example, D. D., a Vlaicu villager from a poor family, was persuaded to become a Party cadre, sent to Party School for a month, and then returned to his district as an activist. His job was to go to his assigned villages and try to persuade people to join the collective, but he disliked the work. He recalled saying to his Party superiors, "I can't urge people to join when I know we haven't got enough tractors and other things to make the collective work properly," but they would reply, "You have to do it." He hated it so much, he claimed, that instead of going off to do as instructed, he would hide in his hayloft and write reports according to the template, saying he'd been where he was supposed to go. Finally discovered, he was moved to an office job in town.[112]

Sometimes it was very difficult to show up, especially if travel were required. Shepherd populations were especially problematic, for they would often claim, when asked how many sheep they had, that they were watching someone else's animals with their own. To assign quotas or verify the status of a shepherd, then, would require checking two or more shepherds at the same time, which was impossible, given the shortage of cadres and the difficulty of travel. It took a full day on bad roads just to reach the village, where one was unlikely to find household heads, since most of them spent only a few nights per year there; they were usually found in hill shelters that took even longer to reach (Stewart

[109] DJAN MM, Fond Comitetul Regional PMR Baia Mare, file 65/1949, 51.
[110] DJAN HD, Fond CR PMR, file 93/1951, 147.
[111] ANIC, Fond C.C. al P.C.R.–Agrară, file 79/1953, 165–167.
[112] 197, Verdery interview.

and Stan 2009: 262–63). A respondent from Poiana, discussing whether inspectors verified the numbers that shepherds declared, said, "If they actually went to count them, yes. But who was going to leave the People's Council to go and count? You had to go up to the shelters for two months and stay with them until every group came through the shelter, but you were supposed to be down in the People's Council doing your work."[113] Even under less extreme circumstances than these, cadres sent long distances far from their families would leave without doing their jobs, producing reactions such as one sent from the Hungarian Autonomous Region Party Committee to its district People's Councils in January 1953:

> We have determined that members of the district and commune executive committees are leaving the district territory or the commune where they work, without good reason. To prevent these absences we give the following instructions:
>
> Members of the district executive committees are not permitted to leave the territory of the district except with the prior approval of the Executive Committee of the People's Council of the region.
>
> Members of the communal executive committees are not permitted to leave the territory of the communes where they work except with the prior approval of the Executive Committee of the People's Council of the region. (Oláh 2003: 50)

Therefore, when some cadres didn't do their assigned work, the reason might be that it was essentially impossible. The dismal state of transport contributed to some of the absences: respondents in Reviga, for instance, claimed that because the settlement was fifteen kilometers from the nearest railway, there were no higher-level cadres interested in traveling there for persuasion (Chelcea 2003b: 2). With such cadres to rely on, the Party's programs would never bear fruit. Whether they simply were not up to their jobs or were actively resisting their orders (like those who refused to join their GACs), they were obstructing progress and would have to be discovered and sanctioned.

Surveillance over cadres would turn up such deficient habits, but it might also entrap people who were doing a conscientious job. An activist who had held numerous important jobs in the mining center of Petroşani explained to an interviewer how he came to be sanctioned for completing a predecessor's project to build a stadium for the miners' recreation. Because he expanded its size, the originally planned construction with wood was inadequate, so he built it with metal. An anonymous denunciation earned him an official reprimand, because "it wasn't allowed to use metal for nonproductive purposes. . . . I thought I was doing a good thing for miners, [but] the denouncer did it out of revenge, out of malice." He observed that anyone could go to the Securitate and say, "'See my boss, the head engineer? Make mince-meat of him'—because he wanted your job." But if you asked the Securist to show you the denunciation,

[113] B. L., Stan interview for M. Stewart.

he wouldn't, so you never really knew where you stood (see Rostás and Momoc 2007: 49–51, 56–59). This case perfectly fits Rév's observation that because the Party could not blame itself or the system, it had to have ways of continually generating responsible parties and deviations, which could then be purged. Consequently, cadres did not know how to meet the demands on them without being made deviationists in the next campaign. The result was a climate of constant fear (Rév 1987: 340). Therefore, even as cadres inflicted fear on others, they lived with it themselves.

THE PROBLEM OF "PERSONALISM" AND THE SOCIAL LIFE OF CADRES

> Comrade Secretary is also the President of the GAC [and] spends a lot of time on personal matters, drinking, and maintaining close ties with one of his brothers, who was a political prisoner[,] and with other enemy elements in the commune. . . . He does favors only for some of his relatives or his friends from the GAC leadership.[114]
>
> —*From an informative note on work by the local Party cell to consolidate the GAC*

The idea of "bureaucracy" as we have inherited it from Max Weber presupposes the replacement of personal connections with impersonal, procedural, rule-governed administration. This kind of bureaucracy did not exist in the Soviet-bloc countries (if, indeed, it has existed in "the West"). Instead, we have one of the system's most characteristic traits: its reliance on personal networks. That was not, of course, part of Bolshevik thought, in which "strong personal feelings appeared as 'unsocialist' feelings" (Alexopoulos 2008: 95). Rather, it was an effect of how the system developed, from Jowitt's "charismatic impersonalism" to neotraditionalism.

As we indicated in chapter 2, precommunist Romania was a society steeped in personalism, with social relationships an important form of wealth. This characteristic was if anything strengthened under socialism. The official policy was both to manipulate and to destroy preexisting social relations and then develop new ones based on loyalty to the Party. In short, the Party aimed to reconfigure social relations altogether. Toward this end, surveillance and chastisement were aimed at policing the social relations cadres had with those they were acting upon. From now on, a cadre's family would be other cadres, fellow comrades, not their families from the "bourgeois" era. But because they were so frequently moved from place to place, activists would find it difficult to solidify their relations with other activists, especially in the competitive climate already described. They might make friends whom they would see on occasion at Party meetings,[115] but this was hardly enough to sustain the soul. Especially for Romanian cadres, a nationality whose self-image includes being among the most

[114] DJAN MM, Fond Comitetul Raional PMR Vişeu, file D33/1952/v. V, 31.

[115] As described to Verdery by a former activist from Orăştie (C. D.).

hospitable people in the world, the Party's strictures on social life set up a constant tension between doing their jobs and being domesticated into social relations that might compromise their effectiveness. For companionship they socialized among themselves, but also with those they were collectivizing. This, too, was a matter for surveillance.

The first kind of entanglement the Party targeted was kinship and family relations, which were both instrumentalized and attacked, in a manner Alexopoulos has described for Stalin's time (2008). Romanian cadres embarking on persuasion work were often ordered to start with their kin and families, as we will show in chapter 5. Party leaders waged a constant battle with cadres who tried to protect their families, such as an activist in Teleorman who admitted to having gotten his family members good jobs in place of the working-class people initially assigned there,[116] or others who helped relatives cover up their abuses and incompetence (Ionescu-Gură 2005: 272). Cause for special concern was cadres with chiabur kin. A member of the Party Committee of Hunedoara region was called to task because having missed a meeting, he was unaware that his wife should have been classified as a chiabur. He was criticized for lax attendance at meetings, but more importantly, other comrades questioned his ability to put Party rules into practice in the countryside if he could not even discern that his own wife was a chiabur. They went on to discuss another member who, by contrast, had divorced his wife three days after he learned that she came from a chiabur family.[117] Another example comes from M. H., who held a position in the People's Council and whose father was classified a chiabur:

> Wherever there were the most difficult cases, that's where the district president would send S. H. and me, because he knew that we resolved things in people's favor. . . . (*During the time you worked there, did you have reason to help people even when it wasn't strictly according to the correct line?*) Yes, because I always thought about my father, who lost all his land. He lost his entire fortune. And after I started working there, . . . I managed to get his land back for him.[118]

Thus, M. H.'s family origin led him not only to favor his chiabur kin but to regard other chiaburs with sympathy. To ferret out such class enemies infiltrated into the apparatus was a vital function of surveillance over cadres.

A second kind of dangerous personalism was fraternization with the locals and even siding with them. Party policy considered those who allied themselves with rich peasants "enemies" (although as Rév points out, without such alliances a cadre might get no results at all [1987: 339]). Giving peasants advice to help them weather collectivization (to the detriment of the newly created farms) was one possible outcome of these relationships. One respondent, describing the scene when his family was overrun with activists and finally de-

[116] ANIC, Fond C.C. al P.C.R.–Cancelarie, file 118/1951, 6.
[117] DJAN HD, Fond 16, file 442/1952, 26.
[118] M. H., Verdery interview.

cided to sign up, said, "There were a lot of them, including Haţegan [whom he knew]. And Haţegan told me quietly, 'Sell one of your horses! Sell it!'"[119] Others described having been advised to sell their high-quality cattle and buy cheaper ones to give the GAC, keeping the surplus money for themselves.

Having one's quotas reduced was another possible outcome. In our interviews we asked how people got by, during the time of quotas, and specifically if it was possible to get a break by making friends with the collectors or the delegates to the threshing machines, as higher authorities believed. The answers varied. Often collectors were from other settlements, not their own; thresher delegates might be locals, but another delegate from the district was likely to be present. A former village delegate from Reviga denied the possibility of collusion, saying he was afraid to favor anyone because it might get him into trouble. Although nearly all respondents from Reviga agreed that such collusion was not possible, two said they had succeeded in obtaining some breaks and even bargained with the collectors (Chelcea 2003b: 26–27). In Vlaicu, a former delegate to the threshing machine presented himself as having helped the villagers take back some of their produce from collections. After threshing, he would go home to eat, leaving the sacks of grain out in the field, and take his time, knowing they would come back to remove sacks from the pile; then he would pretend not to notice. "I kept two booklets, and I'd show one to V. K., the district prosecutor who came to check on us, but it wouldn't be the real one. V.K. would ask, 'Hey, are you lying to me?' 'No, Comrade Prosecutor, I'm not lying.'"[120]

An especially serious infraction was to fraternize with chiaburs, and the archives contain many instances of it, such as the one that opens this section. Presidents of newly established collectives, policemen, Party secretaries, collectors, and others were repeatedly criticized for partying all night with chiaburs and other reactionaries. Cadres might indeed have had reason to party with chiaburs (still the elite, in villagers' eyes) so as to show that they could keep elite company. For chiaburs, the stakes were very high, and it made good sense to entertain Party activists in their houses for a promise of help with their burdens. This was precisely why Party dictates forbade such contact. I. Ş., from Vlaicu, who was the son of one chiabur and the nephew of another, explained that his family had been declassified (removed from chiabur status) with the help of two friends he had made: two Hungarian miners who came as commune mayor and vice mayor to carry out collectivization. They were from very simple backgrounds and had eaten nothing but black bread all their lives; he would give them white flour, and they became friends. "The Party told them, 'Don't eat with people like chiaburs!' But where were they going to get something to eat? from the poor?!? Poor people didn't have food, but *we* did. They came around looking for people to haul stuff, we did it and would offer them food, drink. Then came the problem of chiabur status. As soon as they found

[119] 72, Verdery interview.

[120] 186, Verdery interview.

out our situation, they got my uncle out and my father too."[121] In a second example, a man from Romoşel (Hunedoara) was given a high office in the district but demoted when his misbehavior came to light: instead of doing his previous political assignment as regional Party instructor, he had drunk often with a chiabur, whom he removed from chiabur status, instead putting in someone else whom he disliked. The report went on,

> In this village it will be hard to set things right because the reactionaries are well regarded by the elements whom we put in leadership positions[;] instead of unmasking they go and get loaded with them, and we wonder why work is going so poorly in all the organizations in the village, and [someone] said that they shouldn't do harm to chiaburs, perhaps tomorrow or the day after the wheel will turn and then we [cadres] will be in real trouble.[122]

Particularly interesting here is the activist's assessment of the regime's stability and his strategies in case it should fall.

To continue this discussion of "personalism" we must make a distinction that was widespread in our interviews, between two kinds of cadres. We call them "inside" and "outside" cadres, according to whether or not they resided in the settlement in which they were doing their work or had been sent in from the district or region.[123] Even this way of putting it oversimplifies, as we see from the following interview fragment from Dobrosloveni. The respondent has just recalled asking a policeman from outside the village where he's from:

> He said, "I'm from Zănoaga"
> —"Well! I have a sister married in Zănoaga!"
> "What's her name?"
> —"Her name's . . ."
> "Aha! Well, why didn't you say so, man! I would have left you some extra [food]. You'll be dying of hunger! Here's what we'll do. If you have someone you can trust, look, this neighbor here, you take some there. I'll send the guard away to lunch, I'll tell him I'll cover for him here."
> And he sent that guy Braică to eat and so we took 10 small bushels of corn to this neighbor. That was all. . . . He says "If you'd said something earlier, you could've taken more!"

In this case, simply because the respondent had a sister in the policeman's home village, the "outsider" helps the respondent to keep some corn by sending away Braică, the "inside" cadre. The incident shows us that "insider" and "outsider" are not spatial concepts but refer to personal relations, known versus unknown, "Us" as opposed to "Them."[124]

[121] 59, Verdery interview.
[122] DJAN HD, Fond CR PMR, file 93/1951, 144.
[123] See Bodó 2003 and Stoica 2009 for useful discussions of inside and outside cadres.
[124] Thanks to Puiu Lăţea for the point and the example from his field notes.

We first raised this distinction between inside and outside cadres in discussing the "Galați experiment" of 1956 (chapter 2) and will discuss it again in connection with "persuasion work" (chapter 5). Here our concern is with the implications of this difference for cadres' social relationships. The ratio between insiders and outsiders was partly a matter of effective strategy: persuasion teams seemed to work best with a mix of them. It was also a function of community-level possibilities for recruitment into the Party: if there were no usable locals, then cadres would have to be sent in from outside. There was great variation among villages in this regard: for example, in Sântana, locals held the important positions and were very successful at it (Goina 2003), but in Darabani, people from outside the locality—some from quite far away—held all the major posts: a few were from other communes in the district, but others hailed from the Banat, Bucharest, Iași, and three from across the Soviet border (Dobrincu 2003a: 68).

Inside cadres were more likely to be deeply embedded in social relationships with locals, whereas outside cadres had fewer such connections. The most obvious entanglement was the kinship and friendship relations we have already discussed, which affected a cadre's behavior. So did one's broader status as a community member. An activist from Poiana, when the local head of the police asked her to help identify exploiters and take away their property, described why she refused:

> The policeman wanted to take me with him, . . . but I didn't want to go. I didn't need their sons to beat me up afterwards. "What's on your mind?" I told him: "You, mister, are going to be in this village for one year or two. Or maybe five. Then, you move away. That's how it works with your job. But I'm here to stay. I'm not going anywhere.". . . I told the policeman: "You won't have me open people's doors and break into their homes. No way! I'm not insane! How could I take things from their homes? You take their things. It's your job!" (Stewart and Stan 2009: 259)

Insiders had to figure out how to keep living in their communities while engaging in a task most of their fellow villagers detested. Their embeddedness made them especially vulnerable to surveillance through denunciation, as in the case of the activist D. D. mentioned above. When summoned to account for his poor performance, he was told there were many denunciations from his village. He seemed to know who had written them, noting, "They were my friends. But I had become an important person and they didn't like it. They reported me because they saw how far I'd gotten, that I'm an important person, and they wanted to bring me down. Being a Party member: you were somebody! So they'd sabotage you."[125]

Inside identities constrained in other ways, as we see in Lățea's discussion of the nuances of local social relations involving cadres. Activists who were pri-

[125] 197, Verdery interview.

marily locals were susceptible to being drawn into village norms of polite behavior. Once, the mayor of Dobrosloveni came to persuade a certain I. B., who decided to use hospitality to constrain the mayor's zeal, reminding him that he was a local first and mayor only second:

> "Hey B., what are you doing, aren't you going to join the collective?"
>
> —"What the hell, you came to my house to bullshit me? You came here to drink a glass of wine!"
>
> There were three guys, together with the secretary. I slaughtered a chicken, my wife put it on the grill. . . . We talked and talked all kind of things. . . . We put the wine on the table, we ate the food, and then:
>
> "What do you say? Sign up now, or else they'll kick me out of the mayor's office!"
>
> —"So what, let them do it! I'm not going to join the collective. . . . I won't! Pay attention to what I'm saying: today I'm not signing up! But remember: without me, the collective won't be set up in this village! Without me, there'll be no collective!"
>
> "Sign up now!"
>
> —"I won't!" (Lățea 2009: 340)

Especially interesting here is not just I. B.'s use of hospitality to postpone persuasion, seeking to redefine the encounter as a social one, but also the mayor's signaling both the constraints on his authority—he was watched and controlled from higher up the chain—and his attempt to gain I. B.'s compliance by enlisting I. B. in preserving his job; he too needed to maintain his family like everyone else.[126] After 1957, as the drive to collectivize Dobrosloveni heated up, more activists came in from outside the locality, "about whom it was thought that they would be harder to co-opt into the local canons of reciprocity" (36).

That may have been true, but it did not mean outside cadres stood completely outside local relationships; villagers might try to make friends with them, perhaps lubricated by hospitality and bribes, and to benefit thereby—like I. Ș. above, with his white flour. Outside cadres generally did not stay long enough on any one trip to form deeper relations with villagers, but that might change if they came repeatedly or stayed longer, as happened when an area had been targeted for a final push. Especially in recalcitrant or isolated areas such as Maramureș and Vrancea, activists might stay for as long as two years, in which case creating relationships with locals was inevitable.

For all these reasons, the Party had very explicit policies for managing cadres. In general, and especially in the early days, cadres were assigned to locations other than their native places. District officials followed new cadres closely, expecting them not to become too familiar with locals lest such personal relations prove an obstacle to efficient Party work: activists would fail to do persuasion, would not be "combative," and might help fellow villagers (Oláh

[126] In the same vein, a GAC leader in Dobrosloveni replied to someone's complaint, "Hey, Auntie T., do you want them to throw us out? They press down on us and so we press down on people! If I speak up [for you] and they throw me out, I'm left out in the cold!" (Lățea 2003: 29).

2003: 48). To be effective, a good cadre was expected to break his normal social ties and not try to be popular with those whose lives he was disrupting. In a 1953 meeting of the executive committee in Lueta, the district delegate criticized the president with these words: "We ask comrade president to change his behavior and to give his attention first of all to the Party's directives, to implement them rather than trying to gain the people's sympathy. . . . His task is to guide the commune politically, not to seek people's trust. He must do his duty in accordance with the interests of the working class" (49).[127] Equally important was to move them often (see, e.g., Nelson 1980). One activist explained that once he became an instructor with the Communist Youth, he was moved around a lot, "because they didn't keep you long, maybe three months, and then they'd change you" (Rostás and Momoc 2007: 34). Respondents saw this policy as designed to keep activists from becoming friendly with villagers or colluding with other local officials to protect their families and friends, or even to resist collectivizing.[128] A Maramureş activist described the policy of rotation thus:

> I was taken to Bucharest and took part in some meetings. So: orders came down from Moscow that there must be a change. . . . It was said categorically: move all cadres throughout the entire country—and that was the reason why mass collectivization succeeded—they took notaries from the whole country, who weren't in favor of collectivization; they were people with some education . . . so they understood the dynamic of what was happening, and they dislocated every one of them. The same thing happened in the agricultural sector, for example, they transferred me from here and they transferred my colleague from Dej here in my place.[129]

Thus, the aim of the political elite was to create an apparatus of cadres fairly immune to appeals from the surrounding society—an apparatus of eunuchs, in effect (Oláh 2003: 50; see also Stoica [2009: 431–33] for the Vrancea area). Working against this were villagers, desperate to smoothe their paths by domesticating one or another cadre through bribes, ritual kinship, offers of drink, and other devices.

The policy of rotating cadres had a number of negative effects, including weakened morale owing to the constant uprootings and diminished efficiency in some aspects of their work. The Maramureş activist quoted above observed, "Now, you know that when you go to a new place of work, you need a period of accommodation, to study the program of activity, what you have to do and how. . . . It's not such an easy thing."[130] His comment points up the artificial scarcity of good cadres that Party policy engendered. Paradoxically, rotating cadres from place to place made them rely *more* heavily on local villagers for

[127] DJAN HA, Fond 164, file 5/1952, 115.

[128] See MacLean 2005: 89 for discussion of this same matter in Vietnam. This practice is not specific to communist regimes; the State Department rotates career diplomats for similar reasons.

[129] H. D., Kligman interview.

[130] H. D., Kligman interview.

knowledge they lacked and inadvertently embroiled them in local conflicts they understood too little to avoid.[131] It also exposed them to loneliness, which might make them vulnerable to the wiles of villagers and earn them a reprimand for fraternizing and drinking too much.

We noted above that drinking was the moral failing that appeared most often in our sources and we offered some possible explanations for it. Now we want to suggest that it was a vital means by which cadres, sent in from outside or rotated frequently from one place to another, could create social ties and thereby reduce the strains and isolation of their work. Expected to give their all to the Party, they too were human and needed to socialize. Previously their main connections had been with their kin and neighbors, from whom their Party work might now estrange them. For companionship and relaxation, they would have to create new relationships, both with villagers and more significantly with other cadres. Drinking was the main way to connect with villagers, who had no established rules for relating to people like them but for whom alcohol, long a part of maintaining social relations, was a readily available solution. But for all the reasons we have already explored, fraternizing with villagers had its pitfalls. The problem was that despite the Party's isolating policies, cadres were not—and could not be—sprung free of local social relations, without which they could not accomplish their jobs. This posed a serious difficulty: how could the Party develop a separate stratum with authority and efficiency if cadres were getting drunk with their targets in the collectivization drive? Although it was far preferable for them to rely on other cadres, activists assigned to villages did not necessarily know one another beforehand. Moreover, in a very uncertain environment saturated with surveillance and competitiveness, they needed to watch their backs at all times. They also had to develop allies who would help them do so, and drinking was a prime means.[132]

Thus we come to the matter of relations not between cadres and villagers but among cadres themselves. Our evidence on this matter is thin but nonetheless suggestive, and drinking is central to it. We begin with Băileşteanu's *Drum în tăcere*, where practically no encounter occurs among cadres, activists, and villagers without "a brandy" or "a bottle of wine"; the reader finds such encounters about every five pages. Further testimony comes from a village innkeeper, explaining how he knew collectivization was coming:

> How could I not, because they [activists] always came to the pub where I worked. They would be there all night, blabbering away. I'd drink with them, with the Party instructors. They stayed over here at the priest's house, that's where the instructors had their headquarters. Well, they would go there at night and drink. At 1:00 a.m.

[131] On similar practices in certain religious movements, see, for example, Mack (2008) on early Methodism.

[132] An unanswered question is who was benefiting from the sale of all this liquor.

they'd wake me up to go and get them drinks. You had to get up . . . but I got along with them well enough.[133]

And an official of the Vlaicu collective farm recalled his relationship with one of the district inspectors:

He was an impressive guy. He'd come here and say to me, "I've come to help you, but first, let's go to the bar and drink some rum." I'd say, "I can't, this is a regular workday." . . . But he insisted. "You're coming with me!" So I'd go and drink a double shot of rum with him. Then he'd say, "You have work to do, I'll go off and come back this evening, to see how you're doing." They weren't such bad people, only a few of them.[134]

This, of course, meant that the inspector was not doing adequate supervision, but the remark is illuminating for what it suggests about how alliances were formed.

As Kideckel learned in his work in the Jiu Valley, alcohol is considered essential to male bonding and camaraderie, as well as to establishing one's masculinity (2008: 201). That it should serve these functions among (mostly male) cadres makes sense (see also Glaeser 2010: 288, for East Germany). Thus, the pattern of alliances through drink was distinctly gendered, for the few women cadres were subject to different sexual and social expectations from men. Although drinking is culturally permitted for Romanian women, their mixing with groups of tipsy men would not be. Women cadres too were expected to comport themselves chastely and modestly, but from our documents and interviews, we learn that they did not all do so. Moreover, villagers often asserted that female cadres slept their way to the top (an option not open to men). Whether true or not, this sensitizes us to the fact that women activists had little access to the collegial bonding we have described. Perhaps some did indeed sleep their way to the top, but a reason would have been that their exclusion from the rituals of men narrowed their possibilities for forming networks for protection, so they had to find alternatives.[135] In villages, marriage alienated women from their natal families; they were similarly estranged from the larger family of the Party by male bonding among their colleagues.

Additional information about social patterns among cadres comes from two men, C. D. and M. H., who had been well-placed officials in the Orăştie district administration (that is, representatives of the "state" rather than the "Party"). The conversation with M. H., an agronomist, began as he was speaking of the two wonderful friends who had protected and helped him when he had a nervous breakdown in the late 1950s.[136] Both had been his colleagues in the Peo-

[133] 154, Verdery interview.

[134] 186, Verdery interview.

[135] For similar ideas about women sleeping with their bosses, see Fitzpatrick 2005: 252.

[136] The cause was his having lost a possible promotion, stabbed in the back by another cadre who knew his unhealthy class origin.

ple's Council, and they had all become intimates, addressing one another in the familiar, serving as each other's ritual kin, and socializing regularly together. This continued after each of them left his position for other work. On another occasion, M. H.'s wife described at length the parties they had, as well as the connections made for them with successive Securitate directors.

> People didn't know each other at first, but we got to be friends. We always felt comfortable with the Securitate officers, knowing that they had our back. How nice those parties were! We'd go to the spa, and food and drink would appear—we could stay there for days and never have to pay anything. That was really important, because at first we were very poor compared with the rest of them. I remember P. M. [the district Securitate head] was talking one day about furniture and I said we didn't have any. He asked if I liked his, and the next thing I knew, furniture was being delivered to my house.

A second respondent, C. D., suggests that there were divisions among cadres in their patterns of socializing. Asked to identify his most important friends, he named mostly others in the state administration (like himself) and some professionals (a doctor, a school principal). Then he observed,

> There was a conception then that Party activists did not get together very much with those from the administration. (*Why was this?*) I don't know. That was their conception. (*"Their conception"—people's own, or the Party's?*) Also the Party's. It was the guideline. They [the activists] had certain gatherings to which they didn't [invite us]. And we too took trips with our own employees. To the river, the forest . . . every now and then, to relax. And they, the Party and the Securitate, did theirs together.[137]

He went on to describe his excellent relations with the president and vice president of the regional administration—again, state functionaries—who covered his back when necessary. In both cases he had met them through his job and a friendship developed. He presented his relation with the president, D. R., as particularly close, starting with their very first meeting, when D. R. came to inspect his work and they talked for hours about all manner of things, administrative and otherwise. Thereafter, he said, D. R. would come to town and go not to the president or the mayor but to him. Later he described how D. R. had supported him in a struggle with the First and Second Party Secretaries of the district and prevented them from getting rid of him; on another occasion, he had gotten into a terrible scrape, and D. R. had telephoned someone high up to get him off the hook.

We have included these details to show a process that was all-important: the creation of networks linking members of the apparatus to one another, and possibly the development of new hierarchies and status groups among cadres—that is, among the very people who were destroying older status groups in the

[137] C. D., Verdery interview.

villages.[138] These networks and status groups were not ordered from above: they were the result of cadres' attempts to make livable lives for themselves within the strictures imposed on them and within their ideas of their proper station. Networks could help a man keep his job against enemies jealous of his abilities (as with both C. D. and M. H.); they could provide useful information not otherwise available, assist in procuring materials, get one out of a scrape with a well-placed phone call. Not having good networks made one vulnerable. In Reviga, a newly arrived mayor from a nearby village was known to beat people, including a woman from whom he wanted information. But "he was tempered by the levels immediately above and below him, for gradually what he was doing was discovered. For instance, after C. T. was beaten the vice-mayor found out, and he said to the mayor, 'You are not allowed to trample this point of proletarian morality.' Along with this there was another person who could criticize the mayor: the district representative, who was friends with the vice-mayor" (Chelcea 2003b: 21). Here, an abusive mayor was reined in because others had networks that were more powerful.

The new status groups gave cadres some people they could socialize with in place of the now-dangerous friends they may have had before and the kin who were likely to get in the way of their doing good work. It was relations like these that gave life to the new regime. These reports are useful in suggesting how cadres developed support among themselves to mitigate the competitive, demanding, and atomizing environment they worked in. Cadres drank together because Party work demanded social ties, yet was so organized as to make these difficult. Like other people, cadres were social persons, not just propaganda machines; for Romanians, an essential ingredient of personhood is socializing together. When several of them finished their day's work, drinking together gave them the experience of bonding that made them feel like human beings. Their jobs had placed their old networks for socializing under threat, so they had to create new ones. Drinking, then, was vital to both a cadre's career and his sense of well-being.

Nonetheless, it did not relax the mind entirely, as we see from M. H., the chiabur's son described above. For this man—a great drinker, marvelous raconteur, and life of the party, beloved by other cadres throughout the region—living with his unhealthy social origins caused him endless anxiety. He observed that he never sought advancement, "because I was always afraid they would look into my past." Then he described receiving a prestigious job offer, but his boss, who hated to be outshone, wrote him a bad reference, reminding M. H. that he knew his social origin. The offer was withdrawn, and M. H. had a nervous breakdown. For some cadres, the surveillance the Party maintained over its own had a heavy cost.

[138] Although we have no way of knowing how widespread this distinction between Party and state cadres was in their daily lives, the mere possibility adds an unexpected nuance to the workings of the dual "Party-state," its hierarchies supposedly bound together by crosscutting connections.

The patterns of socialization we have explored underlay the network-embeddedness and clientelism that were hallmarks of Romanian communist society, preserving links among cadres even after the system collapsed in 1989. These patterns inserted personalism right into the heart of a system that strove to eliminate it, banishing Weber's impersonal proceduralism from the bureaucracy and defining it instead as a "mobile network of personal links" (Horváth and Szakolczai 1992: 199): "The apparatus was not just an organisation aiming to provide bureaucratic supervision to the vast network of membership, but itself embodied the duality of a strict, hierarchically organised bureaucracy and a mobile, personalised network" (202–3). This too was part of the Soviet blueprint—not a formal part, but how it worked out—and was found everywhere from Moscow to Berlin and Sofia, suggesting that certain structural features of the intended design (notably the dual Party-state structure with heavy surveillance over and rotation of cadres) produced the same internal contradictions, the same fault lines, and the same kinds of solutions, throughout.

ABUSING THEIR POWER POSITION AND PERVERTING THE PARTY LINE

There is one final area of "deviation" connected with surveillance over cadres, alongside the moral breaches, bad work habits, and personalism we have been discussing: abuses of one's position of power. A particularly serious problem throughout the collectivization drive was that while some lower-level cadres were not doing their jobs, others were going well beyond what they were asked to do, or abusing their positions for both personal gain and political maneuvering room. The worst form of "excessive zeal" entailed using force: to extract quotas, to neutralize chiaburs, and above all to compel peasants into the collectives. Such actions contravened the Party's Leninist instruction about "free consent," an instruction sent repeatedly from Bucharest to the regions and districts, such as the warning that those who practiced such methods, regardless of their position, would be severely sanctioned.[139] In stenograms of Politburo and Secretariat meetings in 1950–51 (Arhivele Naționale ale României 2004) we see top Party leaders repeatedly raising the matter of abuses by cadres. As Interior Minister Georgescu observed at a 1950 meeting with regional Party leaders,

> Tens and tens of letters of complaint come to the Central Committee Chancery every day, from citizens all over the country, publicizing abuses. These letters prove that people have faith in our Party, but they also show that our comrades who have

[139] For instance, the following appears in the district archive in Vișeu, Maramureș: "Any kind of method of constraint or of economic or administrative pressure to induce working peasants to enter the GAC will be decisively combated. Anyone who consciously or unconsciously practices such methods, regardless of his position, will be severely sanctioned; if he is a Party member, up to expulsion from the Party, and whether a Party member or not, on a case by case basis, state authorities may institute legal proceedings" (DJAN MM, Fond Sfatul Raional Vișeu, Secția Agricolă, file 13/1953, 117).

> the job of secretary and responsible positions in the state apparatus are not doing their duty, because abuses were going on right in front of them. . . . When hundreds of thousands of people were drawn into responsible positions in the state apparatus and the Party, it might have happened that some are elements whose past inclines them to commit such illegalities. But the problem is even more serious when comrades with responsibility in the Party organization directly or indirectly support these illegalities.[140]

Some protested that the Party "does not teach us to form GAC's with a club" and that if the directives of the government were distorted, honest people would not want leadership positions in villages because they would be attacked.[141]

Many activists ignored the instructions to avoid force, particularly in the periods when the collectivization drive was in full swing (summer-fall 1950, 1952–53, spring-summer 1956, 1957–62). The first wave of abuses began with Ana Pauker's departure for Moscow in 1950, when Alexandru Moghioroş, her temporary replacement, decided to speed up the formation of GACs and the peasants rebelled. With Pauker's return in early 1951 the abuses and rebellions subsided, but with her ouster in 1952 they continued in waves right through 1962, when the campaign was declared complete—and even after it, as in settlements such as Domaşnea, where intimidation and resistance continued for another three to four years (Vultur 2003a: 57, 83–90). As we indicated in the previous chapter, documentary and oral history evidence of coercion is ample: beatings, torture, public humiliation, exemplary deportations and killing, etc., all in hopes of frightening the peasants into signing up. We will present more examples in chapters 4–6, where we discuss violence as one of the many forms of pedagogy the Party used upon the peasantry. Here, however, our concern is with the relations between lower-level cadres deploying violence and the central authorities. What role did higher Party officials play in encouraging this violence or at least turning a blind eye to it? The answer to this question is murky. Two things are undeniable: first, lower-level officials (as well as the Securitate) did exercise physical violence on a mass scale—sometimes in reaction to the peasants' violent resistance, as we suggested in chapter 2—and second, these excesses show the complicated and contradictory nature of relations among the Party, its cadres, and the rest of society.

For one thing, Party leader Gheorghiu-Dej repeatedly expressed indignation at the extreme use of force—the deportations, shootings, and torture—which he viewed as a deviation from the Party line. He demanded to know who had ordered methods such as these, which were not "the leadership's methods." Sometimes, as in a lengthy meeting of the Central Committee Secretariat in October 1950 when coercion and resistance reached new heights, he insisted on this question over and over: "Then who gave directions to use those kinds of

[140] ANIC, Fond C.C. al P.C.R.–Cancelarie, file 56/1950, 9. Document courtesy of O. Roske.

[141] ANIC, Fond C.C. al P.C.R.–Cancelarie, file 56/1950, 14. Document courtesy of O. Roske.

methods?" "Didn't you participate in the meeting when it was emphasized . . . that in no case whatsoever should coercive methods be used, only persuasive ones?" "You want to make collectives by pressuring people?"[142] Berating Party comrades who had not followed the rules, he blamed violence on Pauker ("only comrade Ana Pauker intimidated peasants," he asserted at the November 1958 Plenary [Oprea 2009: 70]).

Robert Levy, on the other hand, argues that in all likelihood Dej himself had ordered the coercion, for he took no measures other than verbal ones against those who had perpetrated the abuses and even promoted them to better jobs. It was Pauker who insisted upon sanctions for abusive behavior, and once she was purged in 1952, the same methods reappeared. Again, during the final push after 1956 Dej lambasted local officials in 1961 for coercing the peasants, but he then did nothing to temper their actions. Despite pious statements about "free consent," his actions were scarcely neutral. By giving local officials the prerogative of approving the formation of new collectives while handing them strict mandates on the numbers they had to achieve, he made force all but inevitable while freeing himself of the responsibility for it (2001: 111).

On the basis of our documents and interviews, we would like to nuance this argument, which strikes us as placing too much emphasis on decisions made in Bucharest. That view "from the top" suggests a coherence we suspect was absent: Party leaders acted without fully understanding the system they had created. Because we believe the Party at that time was not sufficiently consolidated to direct the process fully, we prefer a more dialogical picture involving interaction between the center and lower-level officials.[143] Party leaders often blamed lower-level cadres during their discussions—just as Stalin did in a similar conjuncture (see chapter 1). Some of the latter even confessed to it (which doesn't mean, of course, that they were guilty). In the October 1950 meeting, two officials from Trei Scaune county, comrades Toth (sic) and Nagy, were being harangued about the widespread use of coercive methods in their district. They had decided to form three collectives in that period and had done so with great difficulty, Toth said, but then Nagy had come back from Bucharest with instructions to make many more.

> We said to each other, "What do you think, we make a plan to do three GACs, when Odorhei is doing twenty-four, Ciuc twenty, Târgu Mureş thirty." . . . Then we too made a plan and alongside our three we put another fifteen. From here on we lost our heads. . . . We made the mistake of inaugurating fifteen collectives in July. It was too many, we couldn't manage it all, we couldn't keep chiaburs from infiltrating or prevent the use of force. . . . But without these kinds of measures we couldn't have made a single collective in Trei Scaune.[144]

[142] From a meeting on October 11, 1950, after the first speedup had precipitated huge peasant uprisings. See Arhivele Naţionale ale României 2004: 339–72; also see chapter 2.

[143] See Kligman 1998 for a similar argument about Ceauşescu's reproductive policies.

[144] Arhivele Naţionale ale României 2004: 355, 361.

In this exchange Toth invokes the famed "socialist competitions" (*întreceri socialiste*; see chapter 4) that had regional and district cadres struggling to outdo each other in the competitive environment we described above. Omitting the name of whoever gave Nagy his instructions to increase the numbers, he distributed blame among the leaders of all those other districts who were competing to form ever more collectives and had in effect shamed him into joining them. The abuses were therefore a collective product of systemic contradictions.

Although the center (under Soviet pressure) clearly ordered the application of force, there is good evidence that the response exceeded central intention and that the center had difficulty reining it in. As we suggested in chapter 2, policy across the entire period oscillated between centralization and decentralization: when Party leaders wanted to control the process, they tried to centralize it, inevitably slowing the pace. When they wanted to increase the pace, they had to decentralize; this, in turn, led to their losing control and to local abuses of power, as cadres competed to sign up more villagers.[145] Following the first major decentralization in that same year, an opponent of the policy (Georgescu) remarked, "I'm concerned that the [local] Party secretaries, wanting to fulfill the plan, go and coerce people. That's why things have to be led [from here]" (cited in Levy 2001: 125).[146] Comrade Pauker framed the problem succinctly at the June 6 Orgburo meeting in spring 1950:

> This spring our organizing methods went through several changes. While last year the center of gravity of organizing the first collective farms was the CC apparatus and the Agriculture Ministry, this spring the Party and state organs in the counties were more actively involved. This led to positive results and should be utilized further in our work; that is, *without the leadership of the CC losing control of the process* (our emphasis).[147]

Levy writes that after the leadership informed county secretaries in 1950 that they could confiscate the property of one or two of the most hostile chiaburs in each village: "Confiscations of kulak property soon commenced throughout the country, but they quickly surpassed the central authorities' established parameters" (2001: 121–22). As for cadres at lower levels, Iordachi describes the "shock troops" organized by the People's Council of Jurilovca commune that were composed of poor and landless peasants: "Because collectivization depended in the first place on their use of intimidating force, these shock troops were given weapons, which they used against those who resisted. In time, these troops, which were intended to ensure collectivization and the defense of the commune, got out of control, organizing thefts and abuses amply described by

[145] A file in the Organizational Section of the CC in 1950 documented multiple difficulties with collectivizing and indicated repeatedly that a major reason was a lack of effective oversight (ANIC, Fond C.C. al P.C.R.–Organizatorică, file 124/1950, passim).

[146] Viola describes a similar result for Soviet collectivization (1996: 27–28).

[147] ANIC, Fond C.C. al P.C.R.–Cancelarie, file 41/1950, 30 (RLA).

my respondents" (Iordachi 2003: 44). Finally, Stoica explains the bloody uprising in Vadu Roşca in 1957 partly by the excessive zeal of regional and district authorities and the teams sent into the neighboring settlements. They had followed the lead of the First Party secretary of Galaţi region, who had achieved "remarkable success" in collectivizing Dobrogea through using extremely violent methods (Stoica 2009: 444). It therefore seems appropriate to conclude, as does Márton in his discussion of the mass withdrawals from GACs in the Mureş region in 1950–51, "Power is not in control" (2005: 66).

It is easy to see, however, that central directives might readily be misinterpreted. As we mentioned in chapter 2, the definition of chiabur was far from clear, and the measures to be taken against them were also up for grabs. Pauker's comment, "Severe punitive measures should be taken against those who manifest enemy attitudes against collective farms,"[148] leaves plenty of room for discretion as to how forceful those measures might be. Similarly, when Moghioroş commented at a meeting in June 1950 that they had decided to aim for a thousand new collectives that year and said, "We have to tell the Party organs that we will probably have to act with greater firmness and at a faster pace, in the work of preparing the creation of collective farms," attentive subordinates who knew his mind might assume this meant using force.[149] Moreover, as Oprea reports, Dej "put enormous pressure on district leaders by constantly asking them to speed up the pace of collectivization, and to invite him to ceremonies marking its completion in their districts" (2009: 70). District cadres would not need a direct order, under these circumstances, to start beating up peasants.

In all likelihood, there was a process of reciprocal learning going on at all levels of the hierarchy. The center would give an order, lower-level cadres would try to figure out how to implement it, preferably in ways that might also build their careers, and sometimes go beyond its intent in the process. Then peasants would resist, and those cadres would perhaps be sanctioned and have to accommodate, creating solutions the Party leadership would then have to take into account in the next round of decisions.[150] In brief, Party leaders engaged in "flexible accommodation" (see chapter 2) with lower-level cadres. For example, the report from the October 1950 meeting of the Secretariat, already mentioned, presents an image of cadres from below constantly outstripping orders, developing their own ideas, and having to be restrained by a center that admit-

[148] Ibid., 34 (RLA).

[149] Ibid., 25 (RLA).

[150] MacLean suggests precisely this dynamic in his analysis of lower-level cadres in Vietnam during the 1950s: more moderate policies at the center produced increased abusiveness in the countryside, leading the center to attempt to curb the violence that ensued. Then, responding to central directives that were impossible for local conditions, lower-level cadres devised solutions that effectively convinced higher authorities to retreat on collective-farm agriculture (2005: 146–48).

ted to not having given adequate guidelines.[151] At one point the leaders discussed the criteria for setting up new GACs, which they had initially set at a minimum of thirty families who brought a mean surface area of three hectares each. But at the local level, cadres launching some GACs had been unable to persuade more than nine to ten families, most having very little land. Because this precluded their becoming successful models for others to emulate, the center had reinforced the original idea, requiring a minimum of thirty-five families and a total surface area not of three hectares each but of thirty-five times the village mean. The result had been an increase in violations of "free consent," which was now causing the center to reconsider its plan. One participant observed, "I think that here, in fixing the number at thirty-five, lies part of the root of pressuring peasants to force them to enter the collectives. It was hard to convince thirty-five families in a short time, so pressure began on the poor and middle peasants to join up," using "all kinds of bestialities" so as to attain or surpass this figure.[152]

The final part of the report put it as a struggle between district- and county-level authorities: "At the beginning of summer, many county committees were working directly at the local level to establish collectives, going around the district committees. When it was underscored that district committees must be instructed to do this, some county committees relaxed their control over the work below, and after that we had the majority of the aberrations."[153] This and other discussions at the highest level insisted on blaming the problems with collectivization in 1950 on a combination of inadequate planning and action at the top with persistent violations of orders by lower-level cadres, whose careerism they saw as the primary problem. Building one's career was indeed a serious motive for such people to exceed directives, in hopes of making a good impression. Whenever Party leaders picked up the pace, they made it clear that they wanted results and that the ends justified the means. Activists in settlements, communes, districts, and regions vied with one another to produce the most new GACs; those with the best results were promoted, regardless of the methods used. Leaders complained that if they issued a specific plan, cadres soon acted as if fulfilling the plan were more important than keeping to the Party line or using correct methods. "In chasing after fulfilling the plan all manner of grave aberrations were committed."[154] Clearly the center was unable to control the process at least some of the time, and that gave license to those at lower levels. That everyone wanted to blame everyone else illustrates both an arrangement in which accountability was not clearly sited and a center not yet fully in control. The situation would change later in the decade, as Gheorghiu-

[151] ANIC, Fond C.C. al P.C.R.–Cancelarie, file 59/1950, 74–81. Document courtesy of O. Roske.

[152] Ibid., 13–18, 76–81, here 14–15, 79.

[153] Ibid., 80.

[154] Ibid.

Dej firmly consolidated his rule as Stalin's most faithful postmortem disciple and pushed full collectivization regardless of the means.

Insecure institutionalization of rule as a general explanation for the violence cadres displayed still leaves room for additional ways of understanding it. Perhaps the shortage of cadres made higher levels reluctant to sanction violators across the board, lest there be even fewer activists for all the work. Doubtless the Soviet Union, through its control of the Securitate, stirred things up periodically to force the issue when the leaders were disagreeing. Perhaps the fragile commitment of some cadres to the project hampered their effective verbal persuasion and led them toward using force, especially if they had career ambitions; this then aroused peasant resistance, which in turn required more force, in an escalating spiral. Debates over the best options and constant reversals of policy (not to mention purges and sanctions) created a wholly uncertain environment in which ambitious cadres had to choose between a wait-and-see attitude and short-term calculations involving force. Perhaps those choosing the latter were those with black marks in their files that they hoped to overcome by demonstrations of revolutionary fervor—people from social categories disfavored by the Party, cadres already criticized for poor performance, or former legionaries. In one case, the local Party organization in Pechea had criticized an activist for his lax work; he was later one of the two most savage in beating Pechea's peasants (Şandru 2003: 19). In a second, the Constanța regional Party leadership was criticized for the performance of a team of activists who, in terrorizing chiaburs well beyond Party guidelines, "start with a legionary method, if you verify you'll find legionaries among them" (Iordachi 2003: 20).[155]

Rather than expand upon these possibilities, we wish to explore the cultural representations and social relations in which activists were embedded. First, concerning representations: as chapters 4 and 6 will show, Party propaganda depicted chiaburs (special targets of violence) not only as exploiters, terrorists, and traitors but also as pigs, snakes, vermin, and demons—that is, they were not human. Moreover, as in the Soviet case, the majority of the cadres setting up collectives were industrial workers and other urbanites for whom the peasantry was a lower form of life, a kind of beast, subhuman. Viola suggests that in Soviet collectivization, these images enabled activists to cast aside scruples about attacking them and to behave with unrestrained cruelty: because both kulak and peasant were less than human, brutality toward them was appropriate (1996: 35–38). We find this perspective apt for Romanian collectivization as well.

A second argument about abusive behavior returns to our discussion of the social relations among cadres. Behind some of the excesses, we suspect, were rituals of male competition and male bonding—an underappreciated aspect of

[155] There is no reason to think that legionaries actually *were* among them, but the accusation shows how hard a former legionary would have to work to overcome this stigma.

Party-building, already alluded to in our discussion of drinking. Just as male violence against women is a product not (only) of the male-female relationship but of competition among men (Collier and Rosaldo 1981; Pateman 1988; Smuts 1992), so the exercise of violence against the peasantry may have served as a vehicle for cadres either to outdo one another in making their careers, or to form bonds by participating together in the violence.[156] This possibility, suggested also by Schnell for the Soviet Union (2009: 3), is the greater given that in Romanian villages even before collectivization, physical violence among men, particularly younger ones, was a normal way of sorting out enmities and alliances. Village events like dances and meetings routinely involved fights. Most Party cadres were younger men: in 1952, 80 percent of cadres in relatively senior positions Party-wide were under forty, with 43 percent between thirty and forty (Ionescu-Gură 2005: 234), and those at lower levels, more likely to be involved in collectivizing, would tend to be on the younger side.[157] These same men had probably also fought in World War II. For these reasons, we find it even more likely that they might fall into local patterns of aggressive male relations.

A final point about violence comes from studies of the biological effects of anxiety and stress, which show that high levels of these are often associated with violent behavior.[158] If the lives of cadres were as stressful and anxiety-filled as we have suggested, then here is another contributor to the violence of those times. To this we could add particular biographies, in which members of national minorities or the formerly poorest villagers, for example, took advantage of the chance to wreak vengeance against earlier forms of discrimination.

From all these possibilities we find violence basic to producing the identity of cadres in the field. What might be the psychological effects of its exercise? Concerning this we ourselves have no data but we wish to quote Bukharin on the issue, for the Soviet Union. He was of the opinion that the tragedy of collectivization lay less in the terrible sufferings of the peasantry than in the "deep changes in the psychological outlook of those communists who participated in this campaign and, instead of going mad, became professional bureaucrats for whom terror was henceforth a normal method of administration . . . indicating a real dehumanization of the people working in the Soviet apparatus. 'They are no longer human beings'" (see Nikolaevsky 1965: 18–19).[159] Conquest (1986:

[156] We thank Carol Worthman for suggesting this idea.

[157] Recall the definition of the sample for this statistic as given earlier in the chapter.

[158] See, for example, Sapolsky's (2004) highly regarded compendium of findings around stress, social subordination, and their effects. Our thanks to Carol Worthman for this reference.

[159] The passage is from Nikolaevsky's report from a series of interviews conducted with Bukharin in 1936; the internal quote contains Bukharin's words. The parallels between Bukharin's fate and that of Romania's Ana Pauker, who sought a gradualist solution to collectivizing, are worth noting. See chapter 2

343) also reports a Party official who stated, "Those of the Communists who had been directly immersed in the horrors of collectivization were thereafter marked men. We carried the scars" (see Kravchenko 1946: 107). Collectivization was formative for cadres also, and for many it was a very bad experience.

Conclusion

In this chapter we have sought to show the complexity of the world of the cadres upon whose shoulders collectivization rested. Their situation was rife with contradictions. Surveillance exercised over them was at least as pervasive as that over the rest of society. The relative shortage of trained cadres facilitated abusing their power over peasants with relative impunity, yet they perceived their situation as precarious, which precipitated constant preemptive action by overexecuting their orders. Against the much-touted solidarity of the Party were policies isolating cadres from each other and from those they were to collectivize. Expected to give their all to the Party, they too were human and needed sociality. More significant, in a very uncertain environment, they needed to watch their backs at all times and to develop alliances with others who might help them do so. All these effects came from the way power was institutionalized. Thus were formed the so-called careerism, insubordination, network-embeddedness, and clientelism that came to define Romanian communist society and that compromised the Party's intended "bureaucratic impersonalism."

At the root of this outcome were its small initial size and the magnitude of the task of collectivizing a primarily agrarian country. As a result, Party leaders drew in as many people as they could find, including many whose pasts made them totally unsuitable for the work. Concerns over what these people might in fact be doing—concerns, that is, that early membership policy had empowered "the enemy," who would have to be purged—generated verifications of members and cadres, as well as permanent surveillance, especially by the Securitate. Because that organization at first responded directly to the Soviet Union, Soviet distrust of the Romanian Party may have heightened the level of surveillance cadres experienced. The Soviet role, in turn, contributed to the relative weakness of the Romanian Party and to the inconsistency of its collectivization policies through time, for in any factional struggle, invoking the Soviet example could tip the balance and kill policies better suited to the Romanian situation.

Aggravating the center's weakness was the vanguardist conception that escalated tasks beyond the ability of cadres to do all the work. At the same time, surveillance and inconsistent policy created an environment in which cadres never knew what to expect, fostering competition and rivalry for career success. Therefore, the Party leadership repeatedly lost control of what was going on in the countryside and was unable to curb the abuses of cadres lower down, which, in turn, increased peasant resistance and necessitated ever more force. The violence of collectivization emerges, then, less as an aberration than as the product of sociocultural shaping and of deep problems with how the Soviet blueprint came to be implemented. These included unmeetable targets with inadequate resources, a new political form (the Party-state) that did not fully control its own means of repression, administrative incompetents facing massive projects of social engineering, and an ideal of consent from subjects, many of whom abhorred what was happening. Unlike Russian peasants in their communal villages, these well-rooted smallholders clung desperately to land if they had it. Consent would have to be forced on them. Instead of a gradual and integrated process of moving from one form of society to another, Romanian society in the Soviet orbit was being completely rearticulated, a process in which violence was inevitable.

What can we conclude about the role of cadres in shaping the new Party-state? First, their adaptive construction of the horizontal and clientelistic networks that cushioned them against political surprises helped to turn the apparatus into a feeding ground for competitive fiefdoms and shifting alliances (see Verdery 1995). These organisms, the offspring of Jowitt's charismatic neotraditionalism, ate away at the resources mobilized in society until they sapped any coherent purpose Party leaders might still have marshaled. Meanwhile, the networks held incompetent cadres in place, diminishing the effectiveness of persuasion-by-example and undercutting any interest the peasants might have had in the collective farms. The strength and resilience of these networks enabled them to persist well past the Party's collapse after 1989 and to generate competitive displays of "corruption."

Second, cadres willing to violate the "free consent" rule so as to force peasants into collectives continued in the habit of treating the "masses" with disdain. Their unmoderated behavior compromised the Party's authority in villagers' eyes. Moreover, the Party's certainty that only a vanguard could properly accomplish its work stifled initiative throughout society, as "democratic centralism" proved to be far more centralist than democratic. Cadres constructed the Party's authority in a patriarchal mode, meanwhile striving to move upward so as to expand the zone in which their own initiative could be exercised. In this way they obstructed the emergence of the state-subject relation posited by communist ideas, one that would mobilize and stimulate people to bring about the radiant future.

Finally, a salient feature of Romanian communism was that no matter what techniques were used, the ideology never fully took hold. The "new socialist man" was not formed; the governmentality proper to the radiant future failed to develop. This was true not only of the masses of Romanians who were not Party members but of many Party cadres as well. The circumstances in which they worked, and the contradictory demands placed on them, put a premium on survival strategies that sacrificed ideological goals to expediency and to creating protective webs of social relationships. For the most part, these were people interested in an opportunity to exercise initiative and power, for whom Party membership was no more than a means to that end. Deep commitment to the utopian ideology was not a requirement.

Therefore, the answer to a problem we posed at the outset—how the legitimacy of Communist Party rule was established for the Party's own cadres—is that for many, it never was. In a sense, the entire issue of "legitimacy" is, as Benedict Anderson (1990) has eloquently argued for Java, a red herring in this case, for it rests on the ethnocentric assumption that power should have something to do with consent. Backed by the Soviet army and the entire apparatus of the Soviet Union, "consent"—other than the crucial consent of Soviet leaders—was scarcely at issue in the Romanian Party's survival. It was quite possible to forge an apparatus resting on no more than joint enjoyment of the power to rule, "concerned more with public awe than public legitimacy" (Jowitt 1992: 136). In these circumstances, it is no surprise that in their efforts to persuade peasants into collectives (chapter 5), cadres failed to instill communist convictions, for many of them had no such convictions themselves; force would be their recourse. To the extent that adherence to the Soviet blueprint entailed new forms of subjection, we might say, then, that resistance to communist subjection began with the Party's cadres.

Part II

PEDAGOGIES OF POWER: TECHNOLOGIES OF RURAL TRANSFORMATION

The preceding three chapters have set the stage for the peasantry's experience of collectivization in daily life. Through this massive social engineering project, the young regime would put its transformative goals into motion, creating socialism in and through practice. The magnitude of the task cannot be overstated, for the Romanian Communist Party, guided by its Soviet mentors, would have to "sell" collectivization to the Romanian populace—no small feat. But as a revolutionary Party in the Soviet mold, the leaders believed they held the keys to a better, socialist future and had the specialized knowledge and means to achieve this goal. It thus fell to them to enlighten the Romanians.

In the next three chapters, we explore how Party leaders both established organizational and cultural instruments and also sought to impose their agenda through these. In doing so, we face the challenge of conveying what it was like for Romanians of all stripes to confront and live through the most thoroughgoing restructuring of their lives. How did they respond to this chaotic moment? How did they seek to catch the future as it was presented to them in terms of a confusing new set of possibilities and constraints? What kinds of mutual learning took place as cadres experimented with ways of getting Party members to fall into line and peasants to join collectives? Most especially, how did peasants go from resisting the collectives tooth and nail to accepting their inevitability, giving up after years of struggle?

Answering this question is a major task of these three chapters. We describe a variety of techniques whereby the communist authorities sought to make collectivization seem inevitable—techniques involving assaults on village social relationships together with instructional practices such as propaganda and learning by example, each designed to educate the populace and convince it of the Party's wisdom. We organize these techniques into two broad groupings, which we call "pedagogies" and "organizational breakthrough." "Pedagogies" stemmed from the Party's vanguard attitude toward enlightening people about how to realize socialism's promise. To educate and convince the "masses," Party activists employed a set of representational and participatory instruments that communicated the Party's vision while simultaneously educating and disciplining. "Organizational breakthrough" refers to reconfiguring village organization, a social parallel to Jowitt's notion of "revolutionary breakthrough," by which he meant "the decisive alteration or destruction of values, structures, and behaviors which are perceived by a revolutionary elite as comprising or contributing to the actual power or potential existence of alternative centers of power" (1971: 7). Although that definition concerns primarily the reorganization of the national polity, the concept is relevant to local social relationships, as Jowitt's own treatment of collectivization confirms (1978). This is so because power is not merely organized "at the top" but courses through relationships of many kinds, including those that bound villagers to one another in specific ways in their daily lives.

The notion of "pedagogies" is fairly straightforward, but we might explain more fully what we mean by "organizational breakthrough." Creating socialist agriculture changed relationships in the countryside fundamentally. It ripped apart one kind of social organization—tightly bounded and territorially structured household-based communities arrayed in status hierarchies, described in chapter 2—and replaced it with two kinds of formal organization: state and collective farms, informed by a particular ideology of class equality. As we explained earlier, the villages of before had been organized around personal relations of kinship and status; political positions were few, mostly selected by the villagers. There was considerable variation among villages in the extent of their internal solidarity and homogeneity.

By contrast, both collective and state farms had a hierarchy of formal positions for which people could be recruited from within the village or without, mayors being imposed from above, not elected. The work force of state farms might come from any of the surrounding villages or even farther afield; their directors could come from anywhere. State farm boundaries were not fixed but flexible: they spilled across village borders, and pieces of land could be readily transferred to some other entity. The organization of collective farms was intermediate between that of precommunist villages and state farms in these respects. Except for the early years, when collective farm chairmen might be brought in from outside, they were generally locals, as were most of the nonspecialist personnel (accountants, brigade leaders, working members, etc.). In theory, work in collectives was organized by teams and brigades recruited independently of other social relationships, and it was performed by and paid to individual farm members; in practice, however, it was organized and remunerated by household. The boundaries of collective farms were somewhat less fixed than villages, for pieces could be moved into other enterprises and farm boundaries were not necessarily coterminous with villages, since a farm could contain more than one village and a village more than one farm.

To move from the customary village community to this new kind of formal organization would require enormous changes in people's lives. It required breaking up various solidarities that interfered with creating and operating the collective and state farms, accustoming people to new work and payment norms, weakening village boundaries, and disrupting the connection of households to parcels of land and to one another. It also required disrupting the community status order so as to replace it with class, for otherwise "class struggle" would be an empty concept rather than a tool for abolishing exploitation. These are the kinds of changes we mean by "organizational breakthrough": creating a breach in familial relationships and subverting the recruitment of the village elite, as preludes to bureaucratizing rural society. That is a wholly different matter from the internal colonization of the peasantry that Viola (1996) sees in collectivization.[1]

In this largely agrarian country, the primary, most encompassing, and most enduring technology of both pedagogy and organizational breakthrough was collectivization itself. Serving that broader end were a variety of less encompassing techniques through which the Party sought to persuade or discipline villagers to participate in its goals (by sowing their fields well, bringing in a good harvest, giving their quotas in full and on time, joining the Associations or the GACs, denouncing their neighbors and kin who opposed Party policies, persecuting chiaburs, and so on). The various techniques might be distinct or might overlap with one another. For example, quotas were their own distinct policy, but they also overlapped with collectivization, often serving as the tipping point between people's joining and not. Because pedagogies and organizational breakthrough interpenetrated, we cannot divide them cleanly into different chapters. Nonetheless, we organize these three chapters in a movement emphasizing the pedagogies first (chapters 4–5) and then the instruments of breakthrough (chapters 5–6). The exercise of these techniques across the decade at length brought 95 percent of Romania's agricultural land into collective farms, but not entirely on the Party's terms.

Our goals in part 2 are twofold. First, we show the practices whose implementation created the Party-state, endowed it with authority, and shaped political subjectivities. What sort of government was communism inaugurating, and what sort of relationships were being inaugurated between the Party and "the people"? How did it teach its subjects to relate to it, and what were their reactions? Second, we suggest that despite the exercise of massive force and its undeniable effects on social relations and practices in the countryside, the tenacity of peasant social organization severely constrained the Party's projects and caused it to modify its plans. Cadres' efforts to break through village organization succeeded only through recourse to many of the community's own organizing principles; this, in turn, would compromise the intended formal-organizational result.

[1] In disagreeing with Viola's argument, we recognize that of course collectivization *was* partly internal colonization, as Stalin himself made clear in arguing that the peasantry could be "used" like a colony since the USSR did not have access to "real" colonies (see Viola 2007: 15). But collectivization was also something else: taking one kind of unit—a village—and replacing it with a series of formal organizations, structured according to functions and roles very different from those of a village, which was definitely *not* a formal organization. The bureaucratization of rural society is different from its internal colonization (see also Jowitt 1978).

Chapter 4

Pedagogies Of Knowledge Production and Contestation

> The events in Arad and Bihor counties show us that the chiaburs' counterrevolutionary actions depend heavily on legionaries, Manists, leftovers of the historical parties, army defectors, certain village priests, especially Catholics and some Baptist leaders. . . . Moreover, chiabur actions show that the class enemy counts on assistance from the imperialist powers and from the support of the traitor Tito—all confirmed through their promoting rumors that the Americans are coming to help and their shouting slogans that laud Tito.
> —*From Securitate report on peasant uprisings, 1949–50*[1]

> It is no secret, our peasants are still very backward culturally and do not know how to work the land scientifically. . . . Hence, it is important not to engage in abstractions, but to disseminate progressive methods for cultivating land, raising animals.
> —*Propaganda Minister Leonte Răutu*[2]

> The immense educational force of propaganda and agitation must be directed toward combating capitalist influences on people's consciousness, against mystical views, prejudices, and superstitions, and against the bourgeois and petty-bourgeois outlook on issues of morality, attitudes toward work, toward public property, toward one's obligations to the state.[3]
> —*From a Central Committee report at the Second Party Congress*

Because communist power arrived in Romania from without, not through an internally generated revolutionary process, the Party faced a population minimally predisposed to its ideas. It would have to build a revolutionary society and raise people's consciousness simultaneously, transforming the class structure while enlightening them about proper forms of expression and the new conceptual categories in which they were expected to think. The notion that the Party had to educate the masses—Lenin's notion of the "vanguard Party"—came straight from Soviet experience, as did many of the means of doing so.[4] We refer to these means as pedagogies. They constituted a massive

[1] ACNSAS, FD, file 4638, 68.

[2] ANIC, Fond C.C. al P.C.R.–Propagandă și Agitație, file 3/1950, 112.

[3] *Raport de activitate al C.C. al P.M.R. la Congresul al II-lea al partidului*. București: Editura de Stat pentru Literatură Politică, 1956, 145.

[4] Holquist argues that Soviet vanguardism was part of a larger shift in forms of governance, as the gathering and purveying of information became critical affairs of state. "Propaganda" thus con-

arsenal for the production of new kinds of truth and knowledge, much of it wholly antithetical to the truth of the world as the peasants had known it. Involving new words, new categories, and a new language, they also involved new ways of disposing and disciplining people's bodies.

The principal pedagogies we discuss are these: (1) *propaganda* tools such as Party newspapers, wall gazettes, the arts (e.g., literature, theater, music, films); (2) *socialist contests* (*întreceri socialiste*), which posed competitive challenges between individual workers, brigades, collective farms, entire villages, and which also stimulated production; (3) *modeling by example*, or *mimesis*, accomplished in a variety of ways such as by taking peasants to the Soviet Union or to successful "model" GACs in Romania (so they would be convinced to join in their own villages), as well as by exemplary disciplinary techniques such as public humiliations, deportations, arrests, and executions designed to frighten people into submission; (4) *denunciations and unmaskings*, whether public or private, meant to expose enemies of communism and to engage "new socialist persons" in the Party's repressive repertoire; (5) *writing letters and petitions*, an important way in which peasants learned the new language and categories of socialism and were socialized into the regime's practices; and (6) a number of techniques referred to by the expression "*explanatory (or enlightenment) work*" (*muncă de lămurire*), which we will translate here as *persuasion*, nevertheless keeping in mind that all techniques were persuasive in form and scope. This arsenal of techniques was used not only for collectivizing but also more broadly throughout the process of communist transformation. We cover the first five in this chapter and the last one in chapter 5.

Some of these tools invited more active engagement on the part of individuals than did others, mirrored in the order in which we present them. For instance, propaganda did not necessarily require people to do anything other than acknowledge its messages—if that. Mimesis provided both positive models for emulation (successful socialist farms and behavior fitting for new socialist persons) and also negative examples to be avoided (such as beaten bodies). With denunciations, unmaskings, and petitions, by contrast, citizens actively participated in lending authority to the socialist norms and values they were learning, as they used the Party's terms to make their claims. These different forms entailed varying degrees of consent, whether coerced or not, and, in the process, often made them complicit with the Party's repressive mechanisms. But as we will see at the end of this chapter, the Party's pedagogical techniques also engendered alternative ones, which we call counterpedagogies.

Effective education, however, first required language competency and communication skills. Besides introducing a mass campaign to eradicate wide-

---

textualized becomes a modern form with analogues in other, non-Soviet, cases. "The propaganda state—or more accurately, the Enlightenment state—was not solely a Bolshevik ideal" (1997: 435).

spread illiteracy, the new socialist order being formed introduced a new language with which the "new socialist person" would think and speak. In emphasizing this new language, we join with Kotkin (1995) and others (e.g., Halfin 2007; Hellbeck 2006; Yurchak 2006) in attending to the nexus of language and power in understanding socialist transformation. "Speaking Bolshevik" was a skill required far beyond the land of its invention. This new language redefined social organization, creating a new category system to classify persons and everyday practices. The Party sought to shape "socialist" identities against other categories of identification whose customary interrelations in the old bourgeois order it disrupted and transformed, in the interest of attributing new meanings and social locations to them (see Brubaker et al. 2006; Gal and Kligman 2000: 24; Yurchak 2006). The emerging system of categories simultaneously elaborated a socialist moral universe of positively and negatively valued attributes and actions. We refer to this new system and its deployment in everyday life as a "politics of difference." Party policies actively instrumentalized difference where it existed and created it where it did not.

In the remainder of the chapter we review key features of the new "socialist" language (see also the introduction) and then turn to the first five pedagogical techniques mentioned above, concluding with a cursory discussion of counterpedagogies. We remind readers that all this was happening in the context of a wider destruction of village values, as cadres assaulted kinship norms and other features of village social organization as well as religious belief (placing constraints on worship and outlawing certain faiths). In response to the imposition of these techniques, people at all levels of society strove to negotiate their lives in accordance with the new policies: to participate in and perpetuate them, to evade them, to postpone collectivization as long as possible, and on the part of cadres, to implement them—sometimes abusing their limits, sometimes failing to implement them at all. Different policies targeted different groups, however, and reactions differed greatly from one peasant household or village to another. Nonetheless, our project data show striking commonalities along the spectrum of local variation. We draw on material from many of our project sites to illustrate.

Since the lines separating the Party's techniques of rule were often blurred, and since implementing each of them conjoined seamlessly the reactions of the cadres doing the work with those of the peasants on the receiving end, it is difficult to organize a narrative around these themes. Instead, we tack back and forth among specific methods used to draw people in, some of the effects of these methods, and reactions on the part of those they targeted. We begin with the new language and categories of action that Party leaders introduced and then move to ways in which they drew the populace into making use of these instruments of transformation—that is, we show how a set of abstract categories was turned into lived objects of discourse and practice, as peasants appropriated the new language for their own ends.

Language and the Politics of Difference

> The power of imposing a vision of divisions, that is, the power of making visible and explicit social divisions that are implicit, is the political power *par excellence*: it is the power to make groups, to manipulate the objective structure of society.
> —*Bourdieu 1990: 138*

The new language that the Party introduced both reflected and shaped ideological tenets and goals. Creating an egalitarian society required the collective participation of the population qua "people" (*popor*) or "masses" (*mase*). To achieve equality among workers in a workers' state, status hierarchies had to be leveled, individual interests subordinated to those of the collectivity, and loyalties to kin and community transferred to the regime. To these ends, Party activists were intentionally engaged in developing and inculcating a new vocabulary that would simultaneously enable and oblige people to speak and to "be" differently—even if these concerted efforts to manage meaning did not necessarily yield the desired reception. Party cadres' actions were performative, as we have argued for practices of the bureaucracy: they acted in the name of the very socialist order they were in the process of creating.[5] Endless repetition of socialist forms and modes of speech and action normalized them in everyday practice. Saying and doing, through what became the ritualized reiteration of Party reports, meetings, publications, forms of address, and methods of persuasion and control, enacted the new socialist order into being.[6]

The language invoked to express Party goals and mobilize the masses emphasized celebration, construction, and transformation, on the one hand, and perpetual struggle and combat, on the other. The former heralded the new order, the latter the demise of the old. The Party, its luminaries, and its institutions were lauded for their enlightened leadership with toasts wishing them longevity (e.g., "Long live Stalin!" [*Trăiască Stalin!*]; "Long live the Party!" [*Trăiască partidul!*]; "Long live the GAC 'New Life!'" [*Traiăscă GAC 'Viață nouă!'*]). (See figure 4.1.) Dramatic change required active, mobilizational, often militant language (see also chapter 1). Typical stock phrases, of which we can present but a small sampling, included an emphasis on the *construction* (or building, creation, formation) of socialism, of the collective farm, of the new person; or socialist *transformation* of property, of agriculture, of society.[7] Against the bourgeois past, the masses were commanded to be always on their guard, to fight against enemies or for socialist democracy or peace.[8] Their efforts were harnessed into campaigns, whether to vote, eradicate illiteracy, or harvest wheat.

[5] Brubaker and Cooper (2004: 15), discussing identification and categorization, note the modern state's "power to name, to identify, to categorize, to state what is what and who is who."

[6] On the ritualization of politics in Romania, see, for example, Kligman 1998. See also Horváth and Szakolczai 1992; Yurchak 2006.

[7] In Romanian, *construirea/crearea/formarea socialismului, a Gospodăriei Agricole Colective, a omului nou; transformarea socialistă a proprietății, a agriculturii, a societății.*

[8] *A lupta împotriva dușmanilor, pentru democrație socialistă, pentru pace.* Other words rein-

Figure 4.1. Long live Stalin, initiator of the first GACs! Courtesy of Artexpo Foundation.

But who comprised this new society, who would build it and fight for it? Here, the Party created categories of people who would become "new socialist persons," liberated from those who had formerly oppressed them.[9] To level social differences, people were to address each other as "comrade" (*tovarăş*), an unmarked category distinct from the forms of address that previously had marked individual status differences, such as Mrs., Mr., Dr., etc. Comrades were (in theory) equals, just as they were workers whose labor would collectively contribute to constructing socialism.[10] Not surprisingly, the new classification system broadly categorized people by the kinds of labor they performed:

forced the revolutionary efforts required to achieve success: war, combat, sabotage, infiltration, fronts. See also chapter 1.

[9] The concept of the "new socialist person" (Russian *novyi sovetskii chelovek*, Romanian *omul nou*)—often rendered as "new socialist man"—occurred in all Soviet-type systems. The word *om* in Romanian, like *homme* in French and *man* in English, denotes not just the male of the species but the species itself, humanity, or a human being. To play up that meaning without gendered overtones we prefer "person."

[10] An older peasant recalled his difficulty in addressing his platoon commander as comrade: "I saluted him, 'Long life, Sir, Lieutenant!' Then, everyone was a comrade, you couldn't talk about gentlemen [*domni*]. 'Sirs are in jail . . . Here, we're all comrades.'" (P. V., Kligman interview). As to equality, some comrades were more equal than others (e.g., the Party elite), just as some were more valued than others (e.g., poor rather than wealthy peasant workers). Exposing the ongoing patriarchal basis of socialist society, comrades remained gendered: *tovarăş* and *tovarăşă*.

for example, peasants became peasant-workers, housewives, activists.[11] Their profiles were further nuanced by a set of moral and ethical standards that extolled Party ideals and virtues, and, as we will see, castigated those not living up to them.

The new classification system created categories of difference—and a vocabulary to characterize them—that (re)cast relationships among individuals, society, and the Party-state. The recognition of difference is a first and fundamental step in creating a new social order; categories of difference simultaneously label or name a subject or an object and evaluate it, approving or disapproving of it relative to the "self," be that self individual or collective. The new system distinguished those categories of people valued by the Communist Party from those who were not, relentlessly scapegoating the latter through linguistic and practical forms of othering.[12] The definitional contours of categories of difference or otherness—like the symbols and identities they represented—were flexible, elastic, and variable; they could be applied instrumentally to anyone at any time, thereby making everyone vulnerable.[13] Their boundaries could expand, harden, or shift. In short, they were intrinsically situational and contextual. Categories of difference both labeled and valorized (either positively or negatively) a variety of groups, actors, and behaviors, and attributed symbolic weight to their instrumentally variable meanings (see Getty and Naumov 1999: 22.)[14]

Enemies of the People

> Never trust priests and merchants, even when they're buried six feet under!
> —*Gheorghe Gheorgiu-Dej*[15]

"Enemies" (*duşmani*) in diverse guises—many of whom are listed in the opening epigraph—formed the most encompassing category of difference or otherness. We have already seen something of the use of "enemies" in disciplining cadres. All enemies could be classified as "enemy elements" (*elemente duşmănoase*), alternatively called "subversive elements" (*elemente subversive*).[16]

[11] See Cîrstocea 2002: 47.

[12] Stan (2001: 107) notes that categories of difference created the means by which the regime would implement what she calls its "discriminatory politics."

[13] To paraphrase Gal and Kligman on national identities, we note that the socialist category system "always has within it the logical potential for further splintering, further segmentation, the formation of more . . . categories that oppose the ones already constituted" (2000: 24). On complicating categories, see also Boris and Janssens (1999).

[14] Getty and Naumov (1999: xiii) view these labels as symbolic codes that function as tropes and metaphors: "Labels—really tropes—like *Trotskyist* were filled and refilled with content by different people at different times and used to ascribe meanings to various operations and events."

[15] ANIC, file 30/1958, 100–103. Cited in Oprea 2009: 70. (No fond given.)

[16] See Colas (2002) on Lenin's list of enemies and Szalontai (2005: 168) on Kim Il Sung and the "complicated situation" of enemies in North Korea.

First and foremost among them were *class enemies* (*duşmani de clasă*), whose pernicious, exploitative pursuits the Party would vigilantly combat through class war (see chapter 6).[17] Class enemies counted among their ranks wealthy peasants, those who owned means of production, and other members of the bourgeoisie (e.g., bankers, shop owners). Individuals were instrumentally and repeatedly threatened that they would be classified as an "enemy" if they resisted the Party's will, incurring both social and legal consequences.[18] Delineating class positions and raising class consciousness about them were fundamental to realizing socialism's ideological goal of creating a classless society. Unlike other categories of identification such as religion or nationality, class could be invoked and manipulated at will in the service of promoting social conflict. But as Sheila Fitzpatrick (2005: 29) observed for the nascent Soviet Union, "Bolsheviks . . . found themselves obliged to invent the classes that their Marxist theoretical commitments told them must exist."[19] So too in Romania: the road to class equality would paradoxically be constructed through the production of classes and class stratification.[20] As we discussed in chapter 2, following the 1945 land reform the resultant class spectrum consisted of three categories: poor (*sărac*), middle (*mijlocaş*), and wealthy (*chiabur*) peasants. Party initiatives in virtually all domains of activity differentiated villagers according to these class assignments, privileging the poor, cultivating class alliances between the poor and middle peasants, and punishing the wealthy. Although the goal was to drive a wedge between chiaburs and others, chapter 6 will show that this goal was not fully achieved.

Although the class enemy loomed largest, the Party identified a host of political parties and movements, religious faiths, and other subversives who opposed its rule. Each was considered an "enemy of the people" or an "enemy of the Communist Party and the government," each akin to traitors.[21] Prominent among those explicitly categorized as *political enemies* (*politici*) (keeping in mind that all opposition was by definition political) were (1) legionaries, members of the Romanian fascist movement; (2) members of the historical parties

[17] Semelin (2003: 197) importantly draws attention to the enemy as suspect, as someone who has "a secret and a dangerous side which masks his immediate appearance." That is, the enemy is not what he represents himself to be, and, in consequence, vigilance is necessary, as is the enemy's elimination.

[18] Those who refused to join the GAC were threatened with being named an enemy or chiabur (ANIC, Fond C.C. al P.C.R.–Cancelarie, file 59/1950, 35, 74 [RLA]). The juridical system by which enemies were accused and classified was as varied as it was convoluted. For an example of these categories, see Dobrincu 2004: xxviii–xxix.

[19] She goes on to note: "This provides a striking confirmation of Bourdieu's proposition that classes in the real world are at least partly a product of the Marxist theory that purports to describe them" (29).

[20] See Lefort (1986) on the paradoxes of modernity; also see Yurchak's use of "Lefort's Paradox" in his discussion of late socialism in the Soviet Union (2006: 10).

[21] See DJAN MM, Fond PCM-M (Partidul Comunist Muncitoresc-Maramureş), file 15/1946, 51–52.

such as the National Peasant Party, the National Liberal Party, and the Social Democratic Party;[22] and (3) army deserters and anticommunist partisans, sometimes affiliated with the historical parties. "Politicals" of diverse stripes were often associated with "gangs" (*bande*) whose armed anticommunist resistance earned them additional labels applied interchangeably and indiscriminately, such as "bandits," terrorists, *partizani*, and "Titoists" (after Yugoslavia's leader, Marshall Tito, who broke with the Soviet Union).[23] Last but not least among the various political enemies were those in the Party leadership itself who became victims of intra-Party power struggles; they were cast as "deviationists" (accused of deviations from both the "left" and "right").

Religious enemies constituted another important group of "others," marked by their difference. The RCP understood the central role of religion and faith in village life and the enormous authority priests, in particular, enjoyed. Even though socialism promoted secularism, religion was not formally or fully destroyed in Romania but, rather, minimized in the public sphere and manipulated in the service of the Party. The 1948 law on religions asserted the state's control over religious life, reducing the previously recognized denominations from sixty to fourteen and charging the Ministry of Cults with the responsibility of acquiring information about and keeping surveillance over the activities of all faiths.[24] Those that submitted to Party control were tolerated to greater or lesser degrees (and with greater and lesser degrees of surveillance and persecution). Most notable among them was the Orthodox Church, which was considered (by law also) the national religion of Romania.[25] Those religions whose allegiance could not be assured, however, posed threats to the Party's authority. In consequence, the Greek Catholic Church (also known as the Uniate or Eastern Catholic Church), widespread in Transylvania, was outlawed in 1948.[26] The

[22] In 1947, the Peasant and Liberal parties were dissolved, their leaders and hundreds of others arrested; the Social Democrats were merged with the Communist Party.

[23] See ACNSAS, FD, file 5, 302. This list is representative, not exhaustive. Anticommunist partisan fighters hid in Romania's foothills and mountains and engaged in armed resistance across the country. See, among others, Dobre 2003; Voicu-Arnăuțoiu 1997; Liiceanu 2003; and Cătănuș and Roske 2004: 41.

[24] See DJAN MM, file 1/1951. The Ministry of Cults was the body through which the State scrutinized religious activities in Romania. Numerous reports were sent to it, including: "[The] analysis of the problem of some activists' celebrating Christmas shows the problem of mysticism in the light of dialectical materialism, the role of priests, their actions, and the attitude we must adopt about these problems." See DJAN MM, Fond Comitetul Raional PMR Sighet, file 48/1952/5, 19. Any recognized denomination that did not acquiesce in Party policies could have its recognition revoked. See also Deletant 1999: 88–114; Tismăneanu et al. 2007: 258–88.

[25] On the relationship between "the nation" and "religion," see Gillet 2001. While the Orthodox Church is viewed as the national church of Romania, denominational diversity has always existed there. On the repression of religion in Romania, see Caravia et al. 1998; Dobrincu 2004, on the Dej period. On the persecution of Orthodox priests, see Bossy 1955; Păiușan and Ciuceanu 2001.

[26] Greek Catholicism was the product of the Counter-Reformation, especially the Habsburg imperial expansion eastward in the sixteenth and seventeenth centuries. The Uniate church was

Party confiscated its properties and arrested those priests, nuns, and monks unwilling to convert to the Orthodox Church as enemies of the state who "fought for the cause of Christ and toward that end, fought for the overthrow of the regime."[27]

Although not persecuted to the same degree as Uniates, members of other religious confessions including Roman Catholics and various Protestants were also incessantly scrutinized and called to task, their activities increasingly constrained. Because of the many Hungarians in Romania who were Roman Catholics, the Party trod carefully around the Roman Catholic Church so as not to be accused of discriminating against the Hungarian nationality; instead, it set unquestionably tight limits on Roman Catholicism.[28] It classified other denominations under the broad canopy of "religious sects," derogatorily labeled *pocăiți* (penitents), that included Neo-Protestants, among which were Baptists, Evangelicals, Pentecostals, and Seventh-Day Adventists, as well as illegal groups such as Jehovah's Witnesses and Reform Adventists.[29] As to the Jews, after World War II Romania's Jewish population was greatly reduced; a majority of the more than 110,000 Jews in Transylvania had perished in concentration camps, and the remaining Jewish population of approximately 375,000 looked toward Israel and emigration (see below).[30] Other denominations such as the Armenian Church and Moslems were also persecuted because of their difference.

In addition to institutionalized religions, the Party's list of potential enemies included those who believed in what may be viewed as popular religious practices (see Kligman 1981, 1988). Activists and agitators went to villages armed with brochures and speeches designed to combat the "mysticism" and rumors that together undermined the Party's efforts to enlighten the population. As we

---

created to draw followers from Orthodoxy by introducing certain doctrinal aspects of Roman Catholic dogma approved by the Council of Ferrara–Florence (e.g., recognition of the Pope as leader of the Church, the Filioque clause, the existence of Purgatory, and the use of unleavened bread in Holy Communion), while largely retaining the Orthodox ritual. The Communists argued that abolishing Greek Catholicism would restore Orthodoxy to its proper preimperial status. See Vasile 2003a, 2003b. We thank Cristian Vasile for clarification of doctrinal differences.

[27] ACNSAS, FP, file 84/v. 4, 45. On the Greek Catholic Church, see Vasile 2003a, 2003b; also the articles in *Anul 1948—Instituționalizarea Comunismului* (*Analele Sighet* 6), 1998.

[28] See, for example, Bossy 1955; Bozgan 2000; and *Procesul unui grup de spioni* 1952.

[29] For a discussion of Evangelicals, Neo-Protestants, and others under communism, see Dobrincu 2003b, 2004b; Pope 1992.

[30] On estimates of the Jewish population, see Rotman 2004: 26–32; Braham 1994; and Ioanid 2000. The Jews of southern Transylvania, Banat, and the Regat were discriminated against but generally fared better than those of northern Transylvania. Even so, Romanian forces participated in the murder of the Jews in Bukovina, Bessarabia, Transnistria, and Moldavia. Of the estimated 410,000 Jews who perished during the Antonescu regime, 240,000 of them did so under Romania's watch. We thank Dorin Dobrincu for a summary of these figures. We add that Jews who applied for emigration were immediately suspected of being Zionists and untrustworthy, with links to foreign capitalist interests.

will see in chapter 6, activists accused chiaburs of purveying false information and manipulating mysticism, as the following suggests: "The class enemy uses mysticism, different religious sects and servants of the monasteries, successfully influencing some peasants with backward ideas not to support collective agriculture."[31] But it was not only class enemies who caused problems for the Party in this realm. Much to the leaders' consternation, some Party members continued to go to church (Orthodox or otherwise) on religious holidays, suggesting that their loyalty to the Party's atheist line was questionable.[32]

Another category of difference thought to harbor enemies—*nationality* or *ethnic difference*—was largely determined by context: in ethnically homogeneous settlements it was insignificant, but in mixed ones it might become a tool for activists to use in fomenting conflict, or for villagers to use in resolving problems created by Party policies. To illustrate, collectivists were not excused from work on religious holidays. In Sântana, on Orthodox Christmas or Easter, German members covered for the Romanians, who did the same for the Germans on their holidays (see also chapter 7).[33] For our purposes, we note that Soviet nationalities' policy, based on the organizing tenet "national in form, socialist in content," served as a blueprint for Romania's policies toward its co-inhabiting nationalities. These policies were designed to recognize national cultures but quell nationalist aspirations, which were potentially destabilizing where territorial legitimacy was contested (as in Transylvania).[34]

In Romania, each region of the country had a different ethnonational composition, as well as different kinds of intergroup conflict. For example, the main groups in Transylvania were Romanians, Hungarians, Germans, and Serbs, whereas in southeastern Romania they were Romanians, Bulgarians, Russians, and Turks. Real or suspected Hungarian designs on Transylvania have been a perennial if variable Romanian concern in that region. Among the many other groups not already mentioned were Roma (Gypsies, who were never considered a national or ethnic group), Ukrainians or Ruthenians, Lipoveni (Russian Old Believers), and Macedo-Romanians. Overall, according to the 1956 census the main groups were Romanians (85.7 percent), Hungarians (9.1 percent), Germans (2.2 percent), Jews (.8 percent), and Roma (.6 percent), but any given settlement had its specific composition.

The fortunes of the Hungarians and Germans were tied to the outcome of World War II. In the early years, Hungarians (along with Jews) were dispropor-

[31] ANIC, Fond C.C. al P.C.R.–Cancelarie, file 62/1956, 19.

[32] DJAN MM, Fond Comitetul Raional Vişeu, file 297/1960/v, 33.

[33] G. A., Goina interview.

[34] On Soviet nationality policy, see Martin 2001; Slezkine 1994. On Romania's nationality policies, see Brubaker et al. 2006: chapters 1–2. In general, groups classified as nationalities could maintain their cultural institutions and practices, study in their mother tongue, use it in certain public forums, and so on, although what was permissible changed over time; the politicization of cultural identities was always prohibited.

tionately represented in the Party. Stalinist nationalities policy helped temper the expression of nationalist tensions, although they were not completely absent. After the war, Germans were a disgraced population, punished for the atrocities of World War II through mass deportations (both within and beyond Romania's borders) and the expropriation of their land, houses, machinery, etc. Indeed, nationality was situationally invoked to legitimate the transformation of property and property relations in Romania more generally.[35] In the case of Romania's German "enemies," their expropriated properties were used by collective or state farms; houses and land were assigned to poor villagers or to colonists recently (re)settled in communities being collectivized and developed (who would later prove easier to collectivize than were villagers of long standing). Otherness articulated through class, political affiliation, nationality, and religion provided rich fodder for the construction of enemies, whose status could be further solidified by the attribution of individual behaviors seen as antithetical to the Party's moral and ethical standards. As we indicated in chapter 3, drunkenness, womanizing, disrespect for the law, laziness, and the like functioned as categories of behavioral difference that signified poor character, loose morals, and lax ethics.[36] Such breaches of "proletarian morality" were especially reprehensible among Party members, who were denounced, humiliated, demoted, and even expelled, in consequence.

We emphasize, however, that categories of difference were not always made salient. In homogeneous contexts, religious and national/ethnic differences were not "marked" (that is, made significant). For example, in Party documents from densely settled Hungarian areas (e.g., Covasna), nationality did not typically figure in reports, whereas it did in areas of mixed populations. Similarly, in Orthodox Christian communities, religion was unmarked; however, where different confessions existed in the same village, or where the Greek-Catholic Church was dominant, that difference could make someone into an enemy.

Nor were various categories of difference mutually exclusive; instead, they often formed a litany of "enemy elements." Class enemies could simultaneously be categorized according to putative religious and political views or be labeled bandits or terrorists, their moral-ethical behavior condemned.[37] To illustrate, in Maramureş, many Uniate priests refused to switch to the Orthodox Church and instead went underground, often hiding out for periods of time with other "enemies" on the run. According to the Securitate, terrorist groups—as they

[35] See the articles by Bodó, Iordachi, Lăţea, Oláh, Ţârău, Verdery, and Vultur in Iordachi and Dobrincu 2009.

[36] A long list of adjectives described an individual's moral and ethical limitations, including, for example, insincere (*nesincer*), venomous (*mărşav*), hoodlum (*derbedeu*), fanatic (*habotnic*). Communist and precommunist morality were pitted against each other, depending on one's class position. Chiaburs defined communists in the very terms the latter used against them. See Lăţea 2009.

[37] Although political and religious affiliations could correctly represent the person in question, they could also be assigned arbitrarily to create a dense web of enemies.

were labeled—had both a political leader (usually a Legionary or a Manist) and a spiritual one, invariably a Uniate priest.[38] After his arrest, one priest from Ieud was characterized in his penal file as "a mortal enemy of socialism who is a danger to society . . . he is also a drunkard, a womanizer, surly, and immoral in every respect."[39] But such a profile might be contradicted (in part or in full) in another report in the same file about the same person: this Uniate priest also happened to be the regional Vice President of Maniu's Peasant Party and was elsewhere in his file classified as someone filled with vices, calm (rather than surly), ready at any moment to fight with other enemies to overcome the working classes (49).[40] The point of these categories of difference was not consistency. Rather, "enemies" had to be created, identified, classified and then treated as such in an ongoing performative process (see chapter 6).[41]

The politicization of difference meant that enemies were best isolated from their families and communities, where many of them were highly regarded. In addition to the hundreds of thousands sent to Romanian prisons or deported to labor camps and the infamous Danube Canal, still others were forcibly resettled in villages and regions other than their places of origin. Or, to avoid incarceration, many enemies of the state spent years hiding in the mountains, whence they would engage in anticommunist acts of resistance. They were able to visit their families only infrequently, under cover of darkness when it seemed safer to do so. Such social dislocations served several purposes: they removed people from their everyday networks, thereby weakening those networks, while increasing their or their family's vulnerability to the Party's actions.

The politics of difference and the language in which it was embodied—literally and figuratively—shaped new modes of representation, action, and understanding in everyday life. It also provides the keys to making sense of the pedagogical techniques explored below by which cadres promoted the Party's interests and ordinary people negotiated theirs. We begin with the modes and instruments of representation through which the new categories were propagated and made familiar.

Propaganda Tools

> The kolkhoz peasantry has come a long and glorious way. . . . Kolkhoz agriculture is the most mechanized and electricity-powered in the world. From the application of

[38] The dual leadership structure paralleled the dual Party-state structure (see ACNSAS, FP, file 84/v. 11, 86). Some groups did engage in armed resistance and attacks against the regime, but many in the mountains were hiding to evade incarceration for opposing the regime.

[39] ACNSAS, FP, file 84/v. 9, 293.

[40] Ibid.

[41] The scripted quality of trials becomes evident in reading the voluminous documentation produced during them. The accused and all witnesses end up corroborating each other's stories, often agreed to under the pressure of torture.

> modern techniques and advanced agro-biological science, Soviet kolkhoz agriculture gives the most plentiful harvests in the world.[42]

One of the principal pedagogical tools used by all communist regimes (as well as by governments of many other types) was "propaganda," which aimed both to legitimate the regime and to educate the masses in new ideas of truth.[43] Propaganda was rich and diverse in oral, written, and visual means, and, taken as an ensemble, constituted what Bonnell (1997) referred to as an "iconography of power." The Party assumed the immanent truth of its positions and agenda, as well as its obligation to enlighten those it ruled.[44] State institutions and Party representatives, from the Central Committee to village Party cells, were charged with the massive vanguard mobilizational task of disseminating Party ideology through diverse communicative means, for which the Propaganda and Agitation Section of the Central Committee played a vital role (in and out of the classroom) in directing—and subordinating—all activities.[45] To raise the "political and cultural level of the masses," the Party trained and sent agitators and propagandists across the country to spread its wisdom and mobilized multiple media—several of which we discuss below—to extol the virtues of collectivized agriculture. A variety of educational methods and forums enlightened peasants on a wide range of topics from the necessity of class war to planting techniques and the life of "kolhozniks."[46] Armed with newly gained knowledge about the superiority of modern socialist agriculture over capitalist exploitation, peasants would be emboldened—and empowered—to promote class war, and this would at length issue in collectivization.

To educate the masses and spread the Party's message, cadres and propagandists had to be instructed in Marxist-Leninist ideology and socialist agricultural methods. Agitation and cultural work were considered crucial "weapons in class war."[47] Hence, in courses for agitators, for example, "particular attention [was to] be paid to the forms that class war takes and to the means and methods

[42] Gheorghe Apostol, in ANIC, Fond C.C. al P.C.R.–Secția Propagandă și Agitație, file 5/1953, 54.

[43] On propaganda, see Kenez 1985; Bonnell 1997; Negrici 1997, 2005; Dobrincu 2009: 286–88. See also Dobrenko and Naiman 2003 on art, ideology, and space in the Soviet Union. Negrici (2005) discusses the main stages of socialist propaganda production in Romania.

[44] The mission of the Party has been likened to that of the Catholic Church or fundamentalist movements. See Lane 1981. Ideologues and theologians draw on similar practices that include unquestioning devotion, ritualization, and confession (self-criticism being one such form; see Kharkhordin 1999). See also Kligman 1988: chapter 5; Jowitt 1978, on the Communist Party as a charismatic organization. Gentile developed this further, addressing the sacralization of politics in totalitarian-revolutionary movements (Gentile as cited in Iordachi 2004: 22–24n81).

[45] *Îndrumare* (direction) was a key word in the new vocabulary. As Vasile (2007: 54) noted, the "new culture . . . was inseparable from the 'direction' that came from the top of the Party." See his article for a succinct discussion of the Propaganda and Agitation Section.

[46] ANIC, Fond C.C. al P.C.R.–Agrară, file 54/1950, 3. "Colhoz" is the Romanian spelling of the Russian kolkhoz; we use the latter except when directly quoting a Romanian source.

[47] ANIC, Fond C.C. al P.C.R.–Propagandă și Agitație, file 3/1950, 113.

Figure 4.2. Promoting literacy. The old woman asks the worker: "Comrade, will you read me what is written in the Five Year Plan?" "Many things, including that soon you yourself will be able to read whatever you want." (From the magazine *Urzica*, May 1, 1952.) Courtesy of MNAC.

for discovering enemy machinations."[48] But, as we mentioned in chapter 3, from the outset Party leaders had to contend with the problems posed by illiteracy; combating it was considered an "important element in the cultural revolution."[49] As in other key mobilizational campaigns, the Soviet Union served as a shining model: Lenin had signed a decree in 1919 ordering those

[48] ANIC, Fond C.C. al P.C.R.–Agrară, file 48/ 1950, 45.

[49] See Tismăneanu et al. 2007: 295.

between eight and fifty years of age to learn to read and write. On December 16, 1945, Romania's then–Minister of Education, Ştefan Voitec, following in the Soviets' footsteps, gave a speech, "To Eradicate Illiteracy," that signaled the beginning of the campaign.[50] (See figure 4.2.)[51]

The most urgent task, of course, was to educate cadres themselves, as we have discussed in chapter 3, for many local Party representatives and leaders did not know how to read and write. Since literacy was a basic skill without which cadres would be unable to produce the endless reports that the massive bureaucratic apparatus being constructed required of them, combating illiteracy among them was a pressing issue.[52] Persons holding positions in the Party and GAC, in addition to being able to prepare extensive written information, were supposed to stay well informed about and indoctrinated into socialist developments through their daily reading of *Scînteia*, the national Party newspaper, and ongoing reading of Party-produced brochures on a variety of topics.[53] For instance, they learned from "'A Guide for the Party Activist' about political and cultural activities in the period of agricultural work" that this brochure "must form the basis of the work of village Party cells in persuading peasant workers."[54]

Just as local leaders needed the basic skills of reading and writing to keep up with Party developments and reports, so did the population at large. Many peasants were similarly handicapped: Party leaders received reports that fully 80 percent and even 90 percent of collective farm members were illiterate.[55] Party officials recognized that knowledge was power and that, if illiterate, even peasants from "healthy origins" could fall victim to the deceiving ways of the exploiting class.[56] Although propaganda often was audio-visual in form, a great deal of it was written. Peasants who could not read and write would not only miss its messages, but also be at the mercy of others in preparing and signing petitions and contestations. (See figures 4.3–4.5.)

Multiple forms of socialist propaganda adorned the environment, some of which countered the limitations that illiteracy posed for spreading the Party line. Especially in the early days, every settlement had loudspeakers that blared out information, communist songs, and slogans. In state institutions of all kinds (e.g., ministries, schools, hospitals, clinics, bus stations) and in diverse locations

[50] See Diac 2004: 18. This speech was then published in the journal *Şcoala Nouă*.

[51] Thanks to Nicoleta Zăvoianu for calling our attention to this and other cartoons.

[52] See DJAN MM, Comitetul Raional al PMR Vişeu, Fond 10, file 15/1951, 27.

[53] They were expected to read the paper between 6:00 and 7:00 a.m. before going to work. See DJAN MM, Fond 10, nr. 15, 8 (Organizaţie de Bază, 26 iulie 1951).

[54] ANIC, Fond C.C. al P.C.R.–Agrară, file 48/1950, 45.

[55] ANIC, Fond 1, file 58/1951, 5 and file 219/1951, 93, regarding illiterate teachers (RLA). Also see Moraru et al. 2004: 512. According to communist estimates in 1944, illiteracy stood at 49 percent in rural areas (Tismăneanu et al. 2007: 477). Other factors hindered the eradication of illiteracy, such as parental fear that "in school, children would be changed by atheistic propaganda, . . . preconceived ideas that girls don't need education," and so on (296).

[56] See ACNSAS, FP, file 160/1952/v. 2, 519.

Figure 4.3. Bread for the people! The caption reads: "Reaping on time, all the people will have bread, our homes will prosper, the Patria will flourish!" Poster by Nicolae Popescu. Courtesy of MNAC.

Figure 4.4. Peasants and workers building socialism. (From the newspaper *Scînteia satelor*, January 1, 1949.) Courtesy of MNAC.

(e.g., a town or village), socialist slogans such as "Workers of the world unite!" and "The collective farm—the path to abundance and well-being for agricultural workers!" were plastered on walls and signs and chanted at public meetings. Socialist symbols brightened the landscape with hammers and sickles, flags, and the pictures of the Party's cherished leaders, representatives of socialist "divine" power and knowledge.[57] All institutions, toponyms, and street signs served as conduits for socialist edification—down to their very names, which reflected communist symbols, leaders, and important historical dates. Thus, collective

[57] Not everyone was impressed by icons of the leaders displayed over the gated entrance to a state farm. As a class of veterinary students approached the farm on a monthly day trip to it, one of them, on seeing the portraits of the seven principal members of the CC (Ana Pauker had not yet been purged), whispered to another, so the joke goes: "Six oxen and one cow destroyed the whole country!" See HU OSA file 300-1-2:30. (The Radio Free Europe files are archived at the Open Society Archive in Budapest. We thank Pavol Salamon for his assistance.)

Figure 4.5. The sign reads: "Giving our quotas, we fulfill our duty to the Patria!" (From the newspaper *Scînteia satelor*, August 14, 1949.) Courtesy of MNAC.

farms bore names such as "The Spark," "Victory," "The Red Star," "Progress," "23 August," "Stalin," etc.[58]

In addition to teaching the basics, cultural centers and schools purveyed rationalism, ever vigilant in their exhortations against mysticism and superstition (in seminars such as "Science and Superstititions"), their preaching of atheism (even as the Orthodox Church maneuvered to maintain itself in the good graces of the Party),[59] and their inculcation of communist doctrine, supplemented by practical experience. For example, to learn about socialist agriculture, each school class usually had its own small plot of land where students learned to cultivate and harvest what they had collectively planted.

School and community libraries were also important repositories of communist propaganda, charged with fostering knowledge about collectivization and socialist agriculture. Included among their holdings were titles such as "About the Statute of the GACs" (with a Romanian print run of 300,000) and

[58] See Iancu et al. 2000; xxiv; Dobeş et al. 2004: 40; Cătănuş and Roske 2005: 324–26; and pertinent case studies in Iordachi and Dobrincu 2009.

[59] Party cadres devised various schemes to prevent people from celebrating religious holidays, requiring adults to go to work on such days, children to attend school, etc. In Odorheiu Secuiesc, the educational section of the People's District Council received orders to organize sport competitions to take place on April 9, 10, and 11, 1955, coincidentally the dates of Catholic Easter. See Oláh 2003: 36.

"This is How We Create a Better Life" (180,000 copies).[60] At a meeting in December 1957 of the Executive Committee in Lueta, a delegate from the Odorhei district asked how the library contributed to transforming socialist agriculture, to which the librarian responded, "by reviewing books with agricultural themes and organizing reading circles that focus on books about socialist agriculture and its superiority over small household production."[61] Socialist literature, to which we return briefly below, enhanced libraries' holdings, with authors such as Marin Preda and Mihail Sadoveanu offering fictional works about the wonders of socialist agriculture.[62] The library of the GAC "Victoria" located in Lenauheim, Timişoara region, boasted of having a diverse collection of more than 3,000 books and brochures, including works on agriculture, ideology, technical matters, arts and literature. Villagers were said to have enjoyed reading Soviet and Romanian writers, with particular interest in literature that appeared after August 23, 1944 (liberation day).[63] They also read magazines such as *The Village Woman* (*Săteanca*) and *Woman* (*Femeia*), both targeted to elevate women's cultural and political knowledge. Libraries organized lectures on practical subjects, often linked to the seasons.[64] Manuals discussing scientific approaches to agricultural practices were available for reading, and "agro-zootechnical circles" were formed to discuss them and related concerns. In 1961, some 150 books about the country's leading GACs were published in 900,000 copies (Oprea 2009: 74). (See figure 4.6)

Newspapers, Wall Gazettes, Radio

The Party's message was materialized in a variety of forms. Among the multiple media at the Party's disposal, *Scînteia* (*The Spark*)—officially the organ of the Central Committee—was the leading newspaper.[65] Comrade Ana Pauker, in a

[60] ANIC, Fond C.C. al P.C.R.-Agrară, file 40/1950, 117.

[61] Oláh 2003: 37. During the final push to complete collectivization in 1962, in the Vişeu district some 30,000 citizens participated in 1,846 reading circles, where they listened to agitators reading from Gheorghiu-Dej's address to the Collective Farmers' Conference and other materials. See DJAN MM, Fond Comitetul Raional Vişeu, file 42/1962, 16–20.

[62] Dumitriu's *Nopţile din iunie* (1950), Preda's *Desfăşurarea* (1952) and *Moromeţii* vol. 2 (1955), Sadoveanu's *Mitrea Cocor* (1949) and *Aventură în Lunca Dunării* (1954), and Stancu's *Desculţ* (1968) figure among the literary works dedicated to socialist agriculture. See Negrici 1995, 2002, 2005, on socialist literature and poetry.

[63] See Martin et al. 1959: 193. This book, published under the aegis of the Propaganda and Press Section of the Ministry of Agriculture and Forestry, is a superb example of celebrating the achievements of socialist agriculture. We thank Călin Goina for providing it.

[64] Cultural work was loosely linked to the seasonal labor cycle. Artistic brigades performed in different locales, depending on the time of year. Winter, when people had more free time, was especially suited to cultural-educational work. See Oláh 2003: 35.

[65] See Moraru et al. 2004: 485.

Figure 4.6. Agrotechnical circle, Jobel commune, Timişoara region (1950). Courtesy of *Fototeca online a comunismului românesc*, photograph #W070, cota 2/1950.

meeting on January 26, 1951, of the Central Committee's Politburo devoted primarily to the work of *Scînteia*, commented:

> The general line of *Scînteia* is politically correct and has an internationalist character, that of a paper representing a Party constructing socialism, a paper that has correspondents from the masses, who take up all domains of [socialist] construction, of culture, education, and Party activities [*viaţă de partid*].[66]

Despite its good work, the Party paper had its shortcomings, which required criticism and improvement. Pauker pointed out, for example, that for *Scînteia* to carry out its mission, it had to have a relationship with the masses. "You have received 57,000 letters, and published only 3 percent of them," a number that had to be increased.[67] Moghioroş noted that the paper had not adequately treated the state agricultural sector and urged that the "transformation of socialist agriculture" be under the direction of the paper's leadership rather than the Agrarian Section of the paper's staff.

To help create a relationship with the masses, every community was to affix *Scînteia*, *Scînteia Satului* (*The Village Spark*), and articles from local papers on poster boards or in window cases.[68] Regional and local papers supplemented *Scînteia* in enlightening the peasantry about socialist agriculture, making it

[66] Ibid., 480.
[67] Ibid.
[68] ANIC, Fond C.C. al P.C.R.–Agrară, file 48/1950, 46.

more comprehensible through localization. Not surprisingly, their titles also invoked the symbols and promises of the construction of socialism, among them *The Red Flame* (from Arad), *For Socialism* (Baia Mare), *Forward* (Craiova), *The Red Flag* (Bacău), *The Road to Socialism* (Deva), and *The Hammer and Sickle* (Piteşti). They covered a wide range of topics, from information on modern agricultural methods to ongoing articles under rubrics such as "Who Benefits More?"[69] and "Questions and Answers" about GACs.[70] To assess their effectiveness in conveying the national, regional, and especially local Parties' decisions, plans, and achievements, the editors of these papers in the provinces were convened several times a year. At such meetings, they were briefed by *Scînteia*'s editor-in-chief on "the current state of class war and the role of the press," and by the deputy editor on "the role of the local press in fulfilling the state plan."[71]

Needless to say, the editors of local papers were criticized for various deficiencies pertaining to the coverage of issues or their failure to proofread copy before it went to print, resulting in embarrassing mistakes. Craiova's *Forward*, for instance, paid too much attention to economic concerns (such as the GACs) at the expense of political ones and virtually ignored local village problems. That said, most provincial papers were chastised for not devoting enough attention to popularizing the collectives, especially among middle peasants and women, the latter of whom were allegedly "under the influence of religious sects and chiaburs."[72] Other weaknesses applied to the production process. In the paper *Vörös Zászló* (*Red Flag*), typographical errors discovered only after an article had been published led to an investigation into sabotage. In "Our Working Women against Chauvinism," a change of words—"socialism" replaced "nationalism," and "chauvinism" replaced "socialism"—altered the revolutionary gist of the article.[73] Such slipups, intentional or not, happened more frequently in some locales, suggesting that the respective propaganda sections were not vigilant enough in their work. They were reminded that, ultimately, they answered for their papers' content and mistakes.[74]

One of the major functions of all Party newspapers was promoting the new communist morality, recognizing the achievements of "good" productive citizens and exposing the deeds of "bad" ones, all the while trumpeting socialist goals and successes and denouncing actions that sabotaged them. Propaganda complemented the public unmaskings and denunciations so essential to demon-

[69] ANIC, Fond C.C. al P.C.R.–Cancelarie, file 62/1954, 16.

[70] ANIC, Fond C.C. al P.C.R.–Agrară, file 48/1950, 48.

[71] ANIC, Fond C.C. al P.C.R.–Propagandă şi Agitaţie, file 1/1950, 125.

[72] Ibid., 126.

[73] For example, "The PMR has shown the path that must be taken to liquidate nationalism through persuasion work" became "The PMR has shown the path . . . to liquidate the remains of socialism" (Ibid., 14).

[74] ANIC, Fond C.C. al P.C.R.–Propagandă şi Agitaţie, file 3/1950, 118.

Figure 4.7. Chiaburs fleeing socialist production. The caption reads: "The larger our harvest, the smaller they [chiaburs] become!" (From the magazine *Urzica*, June 20, 1950). Courtesy of MNAC.

izing class enemies and criticizing comrades whose conduct was unacceptable, which we discuss in more detail below. Chişinevschi, at a meeting of the Central Committee's Political Bureau, emphasized, "The class enemy's actions must be exposed concretely, documented, [and] verified. This must become a line of activity of every communist gazette."[75] While *Scînteia* took the lead, local Party papers were expected to be actively engaged in spreading the word about social-

[75] Moraru et al. 2004: 491.

Figure 4.8. Listening to *Scînteia* being read aloud. Note the wall poster to the left praising the leading brigade. The slogan in the background reads, "Let us constantly engage in socialist competition." Courtesy of Artexpo Foundation.

ism's forward march and exposing those intent on undermining its advances. Headlines announced, on the one hand, "All villages in Maramureş will have telephones!" "New achievements of the community provisional committees!" "New collective farms have been founded in the country!" and, on the other, "Out with enemy elements, so harmful to production!" "Strike the class enemy without mercy!" "Out with chiaburs and opportunists in the cooperatives!"[76] Some articles were more tempered, reviewing both successes and weaknesses in collective farm work.[77] (See figures 4.7 and 4.8.)

Successes and sabotage were additionally publicized in "wall newspapers"

[76] These headlines are representative of headlines around the country and are reproduced with the original spellings. See "Toate satele din Maramureş vor avea telefon," *Graiul Maramureşului*, January 29, 1949: 1; "Afară cu elementele duşmănoase, dăunătoare producţiei!" *Graiul Maramureşului*, April 16, 1949: 6; "Loviţi fără cruţare în duşmanul de clasă!" *Graiul Maramureşului*, May 1, 1949: 6; "Afară cu chiaburi şi afaceriştii din cooperative!" *Graiul Maramureşului*, September 25, 1949: 5; "Noui realizări ale Comitetelor Provizorii Comunale," *Graiul Maramureşului*, September 4, 1949; "Alte Gospodării Agricole Colective au luat fiinţă în ţara," *Graiul Maramureşului*, September 4, 1949.

[77] See "Succese şi lipsuri în munca gospodăriei agricole de stat Bârsana," *Graiul Maramureşului*, August 21, 1949: 5.

or gazettes (*gazete de perete*) displayed in town and village centers, and in all socialist agricultural institutions (e.g., SMTs, GACs, GASs);[78] their content also included practical information and promoted Party policies such as five-year plans, planting and harvesting drives, and so on.[79] The Agrarian Section ordered that the gazette "For an Improved Harvest" be put to good use "in all villages to popularize Soviet colhozes, to create GACs and to unmask and isolate chiaburs."[80] Like newspaper articles, wall gazettes applauded the achievements of "good" citizens (e.g., surpassing planned work norms) and shamed "bad" ones, as indicated in the following "Activity Report": "Wall newspapers . . . play an important role. Look at the example of the wall gazette in Cuhea where the editorial committee takes care to change articles weekly, exposing abusers, writing about the organization of work for threshing, harvesting."[81] Wall gazettes also posted caricatures of enemies of the people, especially chiaburs.

Radio was another significant propaganda vehicle used widely and effectively to reach the masses. Taking cues from the Soviet Union, the Party and government took steps to expand the number of stations, installing them in factories and towns. While many functioned well, some suffered from programming and technical difficulties attributed to oversight failures. Those held responsible came under increased scrutiny and were expected to implement the recommendations designed to improve operations.[82] Radio programs were varied, broadcasting Party speeches and congresses, "how to" lessons, propaganda about collective farming, as well as local and national folk music.[83] While the CC's Propaganda and Agitation Section viewed radio as a "wonderful medium" to disseminate the Party's ideals, platforms, and plans, western radio stations such as the Voice of America (VoA) were regarded as bastions of enemy activity, spreading false claims and rumors about the evils of communism. Mood reports and penal files are filled with assertions that X listened to VoA (and later, Radio Free Europe, BBC, etc.), an act contrary to the interests of the state;[84] such claims were not unfounded, as the following representative comment from one of Dobrincu's respondents indicates: "I listened to the BBC, Voice of America . . . although I didn't tell anyone; if I had, I don't think I would be here today!"[85] In a climate of suspicion, all manner of rumors circulated,

[78] See Fond ANIC, Fond C.C. al P.C.R.–Organizatorică, file 26/1951, 6.

[79] Reports called "Dări de Seamă" regularly reported on such matters. See DJAN MM, Fond 10, file 15/1951, 27, 29, for the Party cell in Ieud, among others. See also DJAN MM, Fond 10, file 6, 81–132, on propaganda, and Kligman interview with B. S.

[80] See ANIC, Fond C.C. al P.C.R.-Agrară, file 48/1950, 46.

[81] See DJAN MM, Fond 274, file 14/1950, 40 (Sfatul Popular Raional Vişeu).

[82] See ANIC, Fond C.C. al P.C.R.–Propagandă şi Agitaţie, file 2/1950, 8.

[83] Oprea 2009: 74.

[84] See ACNSAS, FD, file 5, 200. On the role of Radio Free Europe in Romania, see the documentary *Cold Waves*.

[85] M.V.I., Dobrincu interview.

such as, "Soon, they will confiscate all radios except those of Party members and trustworthy persons."[86]

Cultural Tools

Culture figured large in propaganda's diverse arsenal. Cultural institutions were customarily paired with educational ones, underscoring culture's pedagogic and ideological roles. Constituted and transmitted through literature, the arts (e.g., music, art, theater), and film, Culture with a capital C was vetted by Party cadres. These various representational forms were designed to help convince peasants why the destruction of their familiar way of life was desirable and, crucially, that it would result in a better, "radiant" future. However, neither cultural forms nor the cadres tasked with persuasion work did much to help their audiences envision what collectives and life in them would be like. Literary works, for example, focused more on transforming consciousness about broad social themes such as the fight against the class enemy or the inner struggle to join the GAC. Romanian literary critic Eugen Negrici, who has written extensively about the literature of propaganda, suggests that it shared parallels with medieval religious literature in its form, albeit in a secular version, both being geared toward "educating" and "idealizing" (2005: 154). He characterizes its linguistic features and observes that this literature was initially written in a politico-military rather than persuasive style, emphasizing social conflicts and the demonic chiaburs. After 1952, however, antichiabur texts virtually disappeared (158),[87] replaced by the "wavering" peasant who is eventually "enlightened" into joining the GAC, thus becoming a model for emulation. Even so, his epiphany resulted not from a clear vision of the collective, but rather from tearing himself from the malefic influence of wealthy relatives, or from resolving internal conflicts (typically helped by an understanding activist or Party secretary) that had prevented his realizing his potential (159–60).

Such works tended to be complex, and given the level of illiteracy among the peasantry, had to be read aloud through the ubiquitous public address systems—not the most effective way to "read" a novel.[88] Understandably, as Negrici remarked, literary propaganda did not play "a major role in convincing peasants about the GACs' advantages" (2005: 156); in his view, the more likely audience was a fairly narrow urban one of functionaries, teachers, and Communist Youth, to which we would add pupils who were introduced to the

[86] ACNSAS, FD, file 5, 248.

[87] In Party reports, statistics by class position also became less frequent.

[88] The length of novels made them less suitable for public readings, whether over loudspeakers or in gatherings at people's houses. People came to listen to radio and later television at the houses of those who had them, much like girls who gathered at someone's house to embroider and weave their trousseaus.

works of socialist realist authors in their classes. According to Diac, teachers were given instructions on what fragments to emphasize—for instance, among the key themes for Sadoveanu's *Mitrea Cocor* was "the peasant worker's taking over of the land . . . his belief in the future, his decision to fight on behalf of peasant workers' coming together in the GACs, following the example of the Soviet colhozes, thus creating a fulfilling and happy life" (Diac 2004: 60). In the first five years (1948–53), propagandistic poetry held broader sway than other literature (Negrici 2003: 10), with verses about class war such as A. E. Baconsky's:

A night passes, then a day
The war between the classes sharpens
And chiaburs show themselves to be
Ever greater enemy elements.[89]

Socialist agriculture and class war were also the subject of plays, with young actors from the State Theater in Botoşani, for example, traveling to nearby villages to perform them (Dobrincu 2003a: 49). According to Goina (personal communication), peasants in Sântana's artistic brigade wrote their own plays advocating collectivization and performed them in neighboring villages. The group's organizer emphasized that their performances were appreciated because in contrast to the wooden language of Party propaganda pieces, the performers spoke the same regional dialect and understood what issues resonated with the life experiences of locals. As the end of the collectivization campaign drew nearer and work to create GACs intensified, the Maramureş regional Party reported that 239 amateur artistic groups "gave 449 performances, attended by some 51,500 people."[90]

Visual arts also represented the advantages of socialist agriculture and, like radio, did not require literacy. The definition of visual arts was broad, encompassing varied forms to maximize their use for propaganda purposes. A Work Plan issued by the Party District Committee in Vişeu specified the activities that had to be undertaken to fulfill the Central Committee's order regarding the preparation and execution of the spring planting campaign, including the following point: "In every village, measures will be taken such that visual agitation will be well prepared. There should be [Party and political] slogans dealing with [the spring] planting and the currency reform on all GAC entrance gates and slogans placed aslant at the People's Council, cooperatives, and other institutions, and at the entrances and exits of villages also."[91] Socialist realist paintings were another visual form used in the service of ideology. Reading the Party daily *Scînteia* was the focus of various paintings, such as Elisabeta Ghidali's of cadres reading it and Lidia Agricola's of peasants being read to in the fields.[92]

[89] Negrici 2005: 156.

[90] DJAN MM, Fond Comitetul Regional PCR Maramureş, file 42/1962, 19.

[91] DJAN MM, Fond Comitetul Raional PCR Vişeu, file 33/1952/v. V, 5.

[92] This painting depicted an activity that teachers were ordered to carry out: to read the newspa-

The most novel visual medium, however, was film, especially when shown in villages where peasants were treated to what seemed fantastic: people "living" on a screen.[93] According to some older peasants interviewed in Dobrosloveni, the first they learned of collectives was through the propaganda films with titles like "The GAC Red October" that were shown in the village center, projected against a building wall. Many of these films had been made in the Soviet Union and showed large groups of people working and singing together, great quantities of agricultural machinery, immense herds of cattle, and uniform fields unbroken by property borders. Virtually the whole village came to see how things were supposed to be in Russian kolkhozes. They watched "with mouths wide open" in astonishment, as if the herds of cows and sheep were from "the other world" (see Lățea 2003: 64). Romanian films supplemented those produced in the Soviet Union, providing documentaries that extolled the virtues of Romanian collectives as well as screen adaptations of various socialist realist novels, such as the above-mentioned *Mitrea Cocor*, published in 1949 with its film premier in 1950 (see Diac 2004: 59).

That said, how the peasantry understood what they saw remains uncertain. Were those images to be believed? The peasants interviewed by Lățea (2003: 64) were not convinced. One respondent wondered how such an illusion could have been created: "Where could they get so many people?" The experience surpassed her sense of what was possible. Although it seemed to represent some *other* world—Paradise—it purported to be about *this* world. She could not imagine such a place, with such mobs of people and animals, so much equipment, working in such mysterious ways that defied elementary notions of social time and space (67–68). How could there be that many cows, all equally fat? How could there be so much grain to divide up? In short, the films were all very well, but they were not persuasive as images of reality, much less a reality that viewers could expect for themselves. Cadres, as we will see in the next chapter, would have to come up with other imaginative means. But the evidence shows that they themselves were equally in the dark: frequent reports of Party members refusing to join the GACs indicate that activists could not generate images that persuaded even village communists, much less others.

Be that as it may, seeing a film was a festive occasion, accompanied by slogans and songs such as "Working together in the fields / Brings us prosperity" (Stoica 2003). Oprea (2009: 74) notes that 140 film caravans showed movies in villages across the country during the "Village Film Festival," held between December 1, 1961, and February 28, 1962, the end of the collectivization drive.[94] In Maramureș alone, 31,555 people viewed "314 films associated with collective agriculture, such as the documentary 'Maramureș, a blossoming region' and

per in a loud voice to a group taking a work pause. See also Bodó 2009: 358. For additional socialist realist paintings, see, for example, Constantinescu-Iași 1954.

[93] See Lățea 2003: 64.

[94] In 1961, some 1.3 million people were estimated to have viewed films about collective farms.

the artistic film 'Thirst'" in 1962.[95] After the screenings, agitators often held discussions about topics related to the films.[96]

In addition to these varied media, an entire new folklore was created to celebrate socialist advances.[97] Collectivization was a favorite theme, geared toward a still largely illiterate rural population. Procollectivization songs such as the "Song about the Life of the GAC Ieud's Collectivists" and "My Dowry" were performed at public meetings, published in *Scînteia*, etc. These two songs drew upon familiar folk poetic conventions, integrating into their verses new topics such as the benefits of joining the collectives, of working together to lead in meeting production norms, and of unmarried girls having dowries from the fruits of their labor (instead of inheritance), enabling them to marry:[98]

Song about the Life of the Ieud GAC Collectivists

Spring is coming and the whole country is blossoming,
The plains are blooming too, and so is our Collective.
Let's work, brother, if you want us to have crops,
Come on, comrades, faster, so Ieud can be in the lead:
And let's neutralize the chiaburs, and we will live well.
Where the plow used to cut, now it's the tractor that plows.
The chiaburs who are still around are ever angrier
When they see the tractor running and the colhozniks singing,
They sit around and talk among themselves,
What to do but poison myself!
Things aren't like last year anymore,
For a bit of tobacco
I have to plow on the hillside.
The collective is working again, getting ready for spring.
More serious preparations, the five-year plan lies ahead,
We carry out the five-year plan and create our future.
Work in the collective is good,
You don't see sheep with thorns anymore
Nor chiaburs as neighbors.
I have a comrade by my side who fights and works
I help him in a comradely way
This is our proud freedom; all of you unite, brothers,
Let's go to the Collective, to strive for Peace,
Because the Party leads us.

95 See DJAN MM, Fond Comitetul Regional Maramureş, file D42/1962, 19. In addition, forty-three films were presented to a total audience of 4,300 courtesy of eleven film caravans.

96 DJAN MM, Fond Comitetul Judeţean Maramureş PMR, file 91/1950: 42. Film journals included summaries of the collectivization campaign's progress, how many GACs were created, and so on. ANIC, Fond C.C. al P.C.R.–Agrară, 40/1950, 117.

97 On the new folklore, see Bărbulescu 1952; Dobrincu 2003a; Kligman 2009; Stere 2002, 2003.

98 See DJAN MM, Fond 10, file 8/1951, 57; also Suliţeanu 1952.

To improve ourselves, it called on us to go to school,
So the capitalists can see how the collectivists work.
They work happily, to get out of poverty,
They work enthusiastically, to create socialism.
He who made the colhoz, may his life be blessed
Because people live well, and I live an easier life
I never want to die.
I like being alive and working in the Collective
I work wholeheartedly and my labor is paid.
Work, bread, and life, that's what the Party teaches us.
We fight for peace too.

My Dowry

Green leaf, little leaf,
Come to me, my loved one.
If you want me as your wife
Join our collective!
Come to my house any time
My beloved, if you love me!
Come and have a look around
See my dowry, from days working
I worked the whole summer
And gathered four cartfuls of produce
I now have a stack of produce,
I'm the best in the collective.
I wanted to have at home,
A big and beautiful dowry,
Come now, my beloved, to our village
I'm ready to get married.[99]

Other poetic creations focused on quotas:

We, who've been plowing
We hurry to submit our quota,
Helping our village.
From our small quota
And our bit of grain
We, from the fields
We send them help
To those in the factories
In the factories and the mines
Come on, brothers, let's go threshing
To fulfill our quota to the state.

[99] Collected by G. Tănăsescu in Mitoc, Săveni district. In *Zori Noi*, nr. 4.429, March 4 1962, 2.

Whoever is a democrat
An honest farmer.

. . . .

Lovingly giving to the state
Giving the best wheat
For the state to use.[100]

Adult choruses, children's folklore groups, and artistic brigades all performed songs and dances praising life under socialism.[101]

Celebration was collectively institutionalized in the marking of socialist holidays and socialism's extraordinary achievements (see Binns 1979–80; Lane 1981), including the inauguration of new GACs (see figures 4.9–4.10). For occasions like these, virtually the entire propaganda toolkit was deployed, with nothing left to chance in the planning.[102] Slogans, speeches, songs, artistic groups of diverse kinds, marching bands and masses of mobilized socialist workers created a festive atmosphere. In addition, conferences addressing issues associated with the holiday in question lent scientific weight to the day. For May 1 celebrations, the Romanian and Soviet national anthems were sung, with a rendition of the "Internationale" bringing the formal speeches to a close.[103] The end of the collectivization drive, announced by Gheorghiu-Dej at an extraordinary session of the Grand National Assembly on April 27, 1962, was cause for pride and elation. The trains that transported the celebrants to Bucharest for this momentous occasion were outfitted with Romania's three-colored flag with its socialist insignia as well as red flags, garlands of greens, and victory slogans such as: "Blessed PMR, the proven leader of the people, inspiration for and organizer of all our victories!" "Long life to and strengthening of the alliance between the working class and collective peasants, the strong foundation of the popular democratic regime!"[104] Befitting this great success, propaganda ruled the day as Gheorghiu-Dej proudly declared to those assembled:

> Creatively applying Lenin's cooperative plan to our country's conditions, learning from the Communist Party of the Soviet Union's vast experience in constructing socialism in the villages, [our] Party has overseen the unfolding of a long and patient effort to convince the working peasants to unite their small households into large socialist collectives. . . . We who are present in this hall will remember with well-

[100] Ion Tomşa and Bizău, peasants, Poienile Glodului, Maramureş region, in *Graiul Maramureşului*, September 25, 1949: 3.

[101] See Martin et al. 1959. Later, under the rule of Nicolae Ceauşescu, cultural production and participation became the means and ends of the national festival "The Singing of Romania" (Cîntarea României). See Giurchescu 1987; Kligman 1981.

[102] See ANIC, Fond C.C. al P.C.R.–Propagandă şi Agitaţie, file 2/1950, 20–27.

[103] DJAN MM, Fond Comitetul Raional Vişeu, PCR file 33/1952, 128.

[104] ANIC, Fond C.C. al P.C.R.–Cancelarie, file 51/1962, 1–2.

Figure 4.9. Inauguration of a GAC in Ilfov county, 1949. Courtesy of MNIR/www.comunismulinromania.ro.

deserved pride that we took part in the work of this high forum . . . consecrated to this victory. (cited in Dobrincu and Iordachi 2005: 471)

Socialist Competitions

With these examples of rituals and conferences we move beyond enunciative propaganda forms to those that engaged the population in action and interaction. One such form that, like propaganda, figured in all aspects of transformation at virtually every level of the Party-state hierarchy save the very top was socialist competitions (*întreceri socialiste*). On the one hand, these competitions involved massive numbers of citizens directly in constructing socialism and celebrating the achievements that propaganda touted, and, on the other, they stimulated progress and production, introducing a socialist alternative to "market" competitive stimulus. In addition to spurring participants on to meet or surpass production norms, the competitions also taught them to work in teams and cooperate to fulfill norms and obligations to the state. Report after report underscored that "special attention must be accorded socialist competitions."[105] The Confederation of Teachers' Unions was charged in the late 1940s with organiz-

[105] ANIC, Fond C.C. al P.C.R.–Propagandă şi Agitaţie, file 2/1950, 79.

Figure 4.10. Two years since the founding of the GAC "Lenin's Path." Ana Pauker's portrait, with signs reading "Long live the great leader I.V. Stalin," "The workers' collective of State Farm 'Leonte Filipescu' brings a comradely greeting to the GAC 'Lenin's Path,'" "Long live the farms that build socialism in the R.P.R.," and "Long live the Romanian Workers' Party." Also note portraits of Stalin and Marx. Courtesy of MNIR/www.comunismulinromania.ro.

ing contests between schools and unions to "stimulate the development of literacy courses" (Diac 2004: 22). In the 1950s, GACs intensified their calls to others to participate in competitions to increase production and "assure that collectivists would receive plentiful yields" (115).

Competitions were organized among regions, GACs, brigades, teams within brigades, households, and individual members.[106] Socialist realist poems lauded the spirit that incited participants to break production norms, pushing ever onward, as in Eugen Jebeleanu's "In Sahia's village":

> Four youngsters are pricking up their ears
> To listen to a fifth boy:
> Hey, I nearly went mad!

[106] In the 1950s there were competitions among enterprises producing equipment for the oil industry (ANIC, Fond C.C. al P.C.R .–Propagandă și Agitație, file 2/1950, 79); in the 1980s, among hospitals to increase the number of births, lower infant mortality, and so on (see Kligman 1998). See DJAN HD, Fond CR PMR, file 20/1952, 127–28, which reports that there were 15 competitions among communes, 23 among villages, and 863 among households in what appears to be a three-month period, though it is not specified.

Just as I had fallen asleep
Istrate barged in. The school says
"Silver Flare" completed his quota
Not once, but four times over!
It was like someone put hot embers on me.
Hey, I'm telling you, I'll be damned if
From now until dawn,
I don't get ahead of him with my work.
You'll be reading about it, amazed again,
It'll be right up here, on the board of honor.
I'll have the norms piled higher! (from Negrici 2003: 122)

In 1956, the GAC "Victory" in Lenauheim invited all collectives from the Timişoara region—most of which responded—to participate in a number of competitions with varied goals such as surpassing production plans by 15 percent, keeping accurate and up-to-date records, helping new farms reach the level of leading ones, and so on (Martin et al. 1959: 184). Later, in 1959, the same GAC competed with all other collectives in the district to become its model GAC. Toward that end, they had to meet criteria such as "realizing an average production per hectare of at least 2,300 kg of wheat, 4,200 kg of corn, 40,000 kg of sugar beets, 2,400 kg of sunflowers and 8,000 of hemp stalks; . . . increasing milk production to at least 2,700 liters per cow, 45 liters of milk and 2.8 kg of wool for each ewe and 130 eggs for each hen, etc." (185). Every member of the collective participated in these competitions, the results of which were determined by a commission comprised of the GAC president, an agronomist, zootechnologist, bookkeeper, and a top-ranking worker (185–86).

Collectivists, GACs, and regions all across Romania were officially recognized for their yeoman efforts. In 1958, the "Victory" collective was awarded the flag for being the leading GAC in the country in the cultivation of industrial plants, for which it also received a truck, "The Red Flag" (185–86). Individuals received medals and certificates recognizing them as "heroes of socialist labor" for their steadfast contributions. (See figure 4.11.) In honor of the successful conclusion of the collectivization campaign in 1962, for example, the State Council of the People's Republic of Romania conferred on Comrade X a certificate for his active participation in collectivizing agriculture. One respondent said he received a very nice medal for having been the best worker who transported the most goods between the town of Arad and Sântana commune.[107] Part of completing the collectivization drive entailed increasing the number of GACs in the country as well as the number of members in new and existing

[107] V. B., Goina interview. For several years, he was sent by the People's Council a number of times per week or daily, depending on his orders. This work was "voluntary," but with a hefty fine if he didn't go. In the end, he got a medal for his dedication to building socialism.

Republica Populară Română

Brevet

Consiliul de Stat

prin Decretul nr. 296/1962

conferă

1962

Medalia

„În cinstea încheierii colectivizării agriculturii"

Tov. ....

pentru participare activă, la munca de colectivizare a agriculturii şi de întărire organizatorică şi economică a gospodăriilor agricole colective.

Preşedintele Consiliului de Stat

Figure 4.11. Certificate for "active participation in collectivization work." Courtesy of Ion Băban.

collectives.[108] Socialist competitions were announced in the service of each of these goals. As with other pedagogies, these contests also led to abuses, when eager cadres resorted to "unfair methods" to get peasants to join in increased numbers and in record time. What was especially significant about them for our purposes, however, was that they helped to create socialism as an inhabited ideology by engaging people very actively in its terms, regardless of their convictions.

Mimesis

> The flourishing of collectivized agriculture in the USSR shows us what socialism means for agriculture. Soviet agriculture . . . is the most productive in the world.
> —*Cătănuş and Roske 2000: 19*

[108] ANIC, Fond C.C. al P.C.R.–Agrară, file 28/1952, 2.

Learning by example, or mimesis, was another staple of propaganda and important pedagogical tool that drew people directly into the Party's categories, often in embodied ways. This technique had deep roots in a Christian tradition that communism adopted: the *Imitatio Dei*, or selection of a personal hero to imitate in daily life (Kharkhordin 1999: 356–59); its use was broadened to include not just individual heroes for emulation but collectivities. The supreme referent was the Soviet Union, its leaders all-knowing and its collectivization experience ever exemplary. Comrades studied the lives of Lenin and Stalin and those of Romanian leaders to gain inspiration from what was represented as a secularized form of sainthood.[109] If people were not moved by these texts alone, more dramatic inspirational methods were applied. In one instance, "[p]eople were arrested and placed before the portrait of Stalin and told to bow down and beg him to make them see the importance of the collective farm." They were given a half hour to be inspired and then ask to sign up for the GAC. If such inspiration failed them, they were beaten and then, further humbled, were again placed before Stalin's image.[110] (See figure 4.12.)

As we discussed in Chapter 1, the Soviet Union's historical experience with collectivization served as the template for Romania's "chosen" path toward modernized socialist agriculture. Higher levels sent instructions down the hierarchy to the lowest rungs, reminding subordinates of the vast Soviet experience in whatever problem was at hand; the subordinates invoked that experience in their speeches.[111] To take fuller advantage of Soviet wisdom, Romanian comrades were carefully selected for *schimburi de experiență*, exchange visits to the Soviet Union, where they could see "representative" Soviet kolkhozes with their own eyes. Soviet Comrade Bobovnicov, in a discussion with members of the Agrarian Section of the CC, advised his Romanian colleagues to make the maximum use of those who visited the Soviet Union: "A person has two memories, a mental memory and a visual one. When he can see something, and have it in his visual memory, it makes a very strong impression. . . . So having peasant workers visit collectives is the best method for organizing [more of] them."[112] Romania's Minister of Propaganda, Leonte Răutu, concurred on the importance of "seeing is believing." He noted that peasants want to wait and see how things turn out before they commit to joining a collective, especially hesitant middle peasants who "don't make decisions quickly, they want to see. So it is really our responsibility to make collectives that are model farms whose ex-

[109] In this respect, the use of such exemplary biographies continued the earlier use both of the lives of Orthodox saints and of heroic historical figures. See Marino 1951; Verdery 1996: chapter 3; Kantorowicz 1957; Brown 1981.

[110] ANIC, Fond 1, file 75/1952, 244 (RLA).

[111] Arhiva Primăriei Șibot (jud. Alba), file I/1/1951, 20–27; file I/1/1952, passim.

[112] ANIC, Fond C.C. al P.C.R.–Agrară, file 138/1952, 47. He went on to say that delegates who didn't then tell their compatriots about the wonders they had seen and participate in organizing GACs in Romania were highly suspect and most likely enemies.

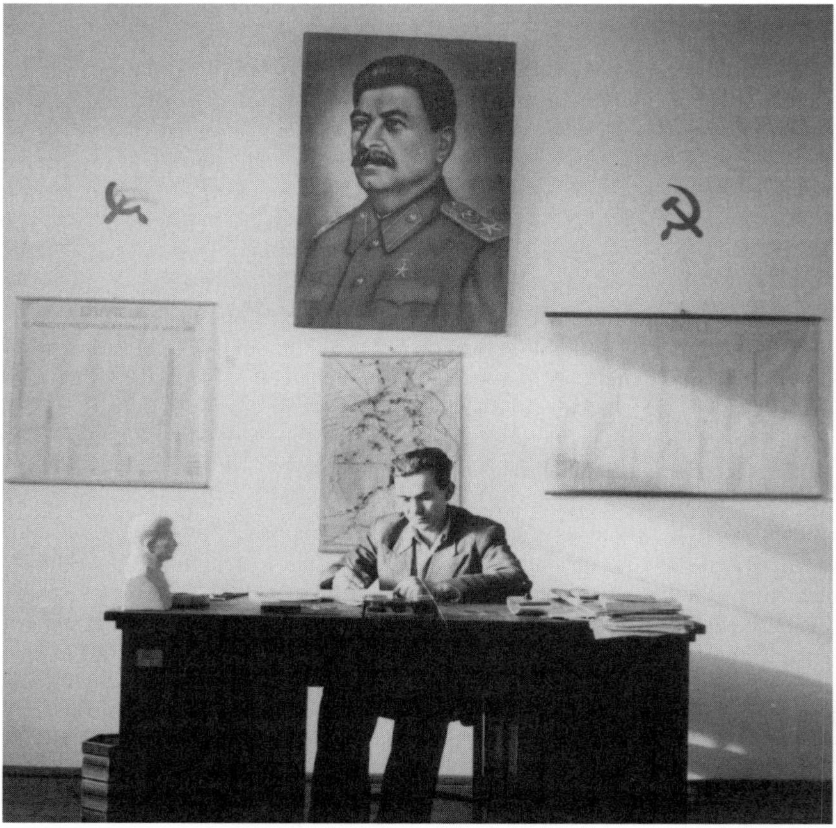

Figure 4.12. Inspired by Stalin. Courtesy of Artexpo Foundation.

ample will speak most loudly. Peasants should come from different parts of the region to see for themselves."[113]

Gheorghe Goina, the mayor of Sântana, was among the early delegates sent to the Soviet Union in 1949. After his return, he inaugurated one of the first such model GACs, "New Life," in 1950, which by all accounts functioned quite well, in part due to his leadership (see Goina 2009 and below). Over the course of a decade, many delegations from around the country—more than 220 delegates from collectives in other regions—and from abroad (e.g., from the USSR, Poland, Hungary, the GDR, China, France, and the United States) visited the GAC "New Life." Moreover, "all of these delegations were clearly impressed by the new life that our collective farmers live" (Martin et al. 1959: 198). They were "convinced personally and [saw] the achievements of the GAC, which once and

[113] ANIC, Fond C.C. al P.C.R.–Propagandă și Agitație, file 3/1950, 116.

for all put to rest the rumors spread by chiaburs."[114] Delegations from the GAC "New Life" also benefited from the visits they made elsewhere in the country and abroad.

As the above suggests, exchanges of experience were reciprocal, with delegations of Romanians visiting the Soviet Union and Soviet delegations visiting Romania. A group of 12 Romanian activists who went to the Soviet Union visited "6 colhozes, 1 state farm, 2 research institutes, and 2 food industry enterprises during a seventeen-day trip."[115] Their fourteen-page report provided information on production and the means used to increase it, such as large-scale mechanization; the great strides made in improving the kolkhozniks' lifestyles, both culturally and materially; and the dual emphasis on popularizing successes and positive work experiences and criticizing shortcomings, using some of the pedagogical tools we have already discussed such as wall gazettes and newspapers to do so. The report also called attention to ongoing revisions in Party organization and structure to improve performance, underscoring the role of relative local autonomy: "Each Party organization has full control over its administrative activities. . . . The village Party council (*sovietul sătesc*) . . . not only is responsible for all social-cultural and construction-related activities . . . but has the right to direct and take decisions on any domain of activity pertaining to the GAC" (14).

As to delegations of Soviets visiting Romania, one group of specialists comprised of kolkhoz and state farm members, S.M.T. specialists, and representatives from the Soviet Ministry of Agriculture spent a month in Romania, during which they went to "15 regions, 35 GACs, 24 state farms, 15 S.M.T.s, and 7 experimental stations."[116] They attended 102 meetings in which a total of 38,500 people participated.[117] The resulting twenty-eight page report was mixed with praise and constructive criticism. In making suggestions, the Soviets typically foregrounded their own vaster experience, noting, for example, that they pay special attention to educating cadres and do so more intensely—and efficiently—in the winter months when agricultural work does not require much time (13), or that their experience underscores the importance of the brigade system. They applauded the many workers across Romania who were dedicated to producing better yields, yet they were troubled that these experiences were not transmitted to others elsewhere so that such practices could be integrated (15). The report concluded with ritualized formulaic toasts: "Long live Romanian-Soviet friendship!" "Long live the CC with its leader, Gheorghe Gheorghiu-Dej!" "Long live the leader of the workers of the world—Comrade Stalin!" (15).

How Romanian peasants viewed their experiences in the Soviet Union varied. An allegedly impressed one remarked, for instance, "I went to see how a

[114] See DJAN MM, Fond Comitetul Județean PMR Maramureș, file 91/1950, page unclear.

[115] ANIC, Fond C.C. al P.C.R.–Agrară, file 8/1959, 1.

[116] ANIC, Fond C.C. al P.C.R.–Agrară, 29/1951, 1.

[117] Ibid.

poor peasant lives in the Soviet Union. I wandered through many villages and stayed in the homes of many collective members. In the Soviet Union, there are no poor peasants; they're all well off. Their houses are clean and tasteful."[118] But not all peasants shared the positive views gained from such carefully arranged visits (and the data at our disposal are decidedly more negative). Romanian prisoners of war returning from the Soviet Union related tales of the collective farmers' hard lives, noting that "in Bessarabia, those in the collective were dying of hunger and begged from the others who weren't, who gave them [food] out of pity,"[119] and also cautioning that "we're all going to end up eating with a common ladle like the Russians" (Goina 2003: 18). Or as another retorted, "Mind your own business, I've had it with the collective; I saw six and a half years of a collective, with the Russians! I need another collective? Me?!"[120] A woman in Bârsana, Maramureş, a village not far from the Soviet border, declared in front of Party officials that peasants starved in collectives, and asked why—if it was so great in the USSR—they didn't just open the borders, or at least let them get close enough so they could look across and see for themselves.[121]

Reinforcing these negative images were memories of the behavior of Russians during the war, graphically described by our respondents: "It was terrible, terrible, what those Russians did to us! A bunch of rough and dirty men in baggy pants . . . they'd eat you alive! Girls, poor things, would flee, women would hide . . . we'd hide them in lofts . . . [the Russians,] after them, like wolves!"[122] This respondent went on to say that given Russians' character, the idea of the kolkhoz was appropriate for them, since they were numerous, poor, "nonpeople." Comparable folklore of Russian soldiers as unwashed and smelly, drunken, rapacious, and bestial is common throughout Romania, and their wartime presence is remembered as like a state of siege. This association was hardly auspicious for the soon-to-be-founded collective farms. To counter such negative press about kolkhozes, activists shifted their focus to *collectives*, about which peasants knew rather little—despite the intense propaganda efforts.[123] According to one of Lațea's respondents, cadres began to avoid mention of the word "colhoz," such that a propagandist was alleged to have said, "We'll arrest whoever says that a colhoz is being formed! We want to make a better and happier life!" (2003: 68).

[118] See Dobeş et al. 2004: 34.

[119] ACNSAS, FD, file 4054, 187.

[120] D. S., Dobrincu interview.

[121] See DJAN MM, Fond Comitetul Raional PMR Sighet, file 22/1951/v. 10. The atmosphere regarding the creation of a GAC in this community was described as "unhealthy."

[122] D. T., Lățea interview.

[123] The women's organization was among those charged with proselytizing among women about Soviet colhozes and women's lives in them, and also about collectives in Romania (ANIC, Fond C.C. al P.C.R.–Agrară 54/1950, 5.)

For those who could not experience the mimetic effects of visits to the Soviet Union, documentary films of successful Romanian collectives or visits to them provided a substitute. In Pechea, among the earliest-collectivized villages (in 1949), the very first documentary film was made to extol the virtues of a Romanian collective farm (Şandru 2003: 16). In 1952, a group of eight to ten members of Rimetea's Party cell visited the GAC "Victory of Socialism" created in 1950 in Iara, Turda district, where they were persuaded that GAC members "have everything and lack nothing" and that the "rumors hawked by chiaburs were simply outrageous lies" (Țărău 2003: 37). Peasants from uncollectivized villages might be brought to witness advance distributions of produce from successful GACs (see figure 4.13). Supplementing these films and visits were testimonials from happy collective farmers, who waxed eloquent about the advantages of having joined—like this one from the GAC "6 March" in the Sebeş district, Hunedoara region: "Because of my work for the GAC, I have built a house, bought a sewing machine, gas stove, washing machine, a bicycle, and in the course of a regional contest, I was awarded prizes of a radio and watch" (Oprea 2003: 53). Such positive assessments were highlighted in glowing articles in national and local papers recounting "What I Saw at the Collective Farm"[124] and the benefits of being a collectivist, such as: "You who are in associations and independent peasants! Follow the road the Party has set with conviction, the road of abundance and happiness—the collective farm! Each one of you, compare your incomes with those of the collectivists! You have more than enough examples! Your brothers, collectivists, await you with open arms" (Dobrincu 2003a: 50). In some cases, experience mirrored the propaganda claims. A peasant in his eighties, from Comlăuş, commented about the early years (but not the later ones):

> People got interested by the fact that at first, they began to pay well in the collective. . . . When a peasant saw that [a collective member] came home with thirty sacks of grain, some barley and who knows what else . . . [he began to think], 'Man, it's good in the collective, I'll go too, I won't be a servant anymore for the rich peasant, or for the German, I'll work from 8 to 5, look how much grain I got, oats.' (Goina 2003: 1)

Others expressed their gratitude to the Party for making their lives so much better. The President of a GAC in the Argeş region declared, "Today, our collective members live better, they dress and eat better. For all that we've done, and all that we will realize from now on for our new life, we thank the Party, which has steered us toward this abundance, from the bottom of our hearts!" (Oprea 2003: 53).

Even so, such achievements and the material riches and hope for the future that model GACs represented did not spark an enthusiastic rush to form new

[124] See Şova Gheorghe, "Ce am văzut la gospodăria colectivă." *Graiul Maramureşului* July 2, 1950: 3. Similar articles were published throughout the country.

Figure 4.13. Advance produce distribution at the GAC "Roma," Botoșani, overseen by portraits of Marx, Engels, Lenin, and Stalin, with the Romanian Party leadership below them. Note the slogan at the top: "Workers of the World, Unite!" Courtesy of MNIR/ www.comunismulinromania.ro.

ones. Instead, authorities found that peasants were more impressed with (and repelled by) unsuccessful collectives: they understood mimesis, but the examples they chose were the "wrong" ones. They were quick to compare the collectives' poorer harvests with the better ones among noncollectivized households, or note that the collectives were behind schedule in planting or harvesting, and the like. Here is the Orăştie district Party secretary in September 1951, writing his superiors about the GAC at Şibot (just completing its first season):

> People are commenting that the existing GACs have a lot of deficiencies that cause difficulties in creating new collectives, as with Şibot where collectivists are dissatisfied with the tiny advance they received and the majority of the collectivists pose the problem that they worked all summer and were unable to earn enough grain and winter is coming and they didn't receive any money at all and they're going barefoot. . . . They say they have to go work for wages at private farmers so they can get enough money for clothing . . . so only 15–20 out of 50 are coming to work in the GAC so we're behind in our tasks.[125]

In spite of the incessant propaganda and living examples, then, many remained unpersuaded and doubted that hard work would be the source of their

[125] DJAN HD, Fond CR PMR, file 103/1951: 252.

promised success. (Already in the early 1950s, peasants understood that bribes could help negotiate one's class status, assigned quotas, etc.) Undeterred by setbacks, however, Party activists and the propaganda machine forged ahead with plans to finalize collectivization throughout the country. In 1957, based on the "Galați experiment" described in chapter 2, Party leaders publicly declared Dobrogea the first fully collectivized region of Romania, and "the region with the highest rural standard of living." Following upon this "achievement," Iordachi observes (2009: 105), "every other region was supposed to follow this example and to see the province *as modeling its own future*," which sparked an imitative campaign in other regions that contributed to Gheorghiu-Dej's declaring collectivization complete three years ahead of plan. Accompanying this success was an imitative campaign in the intensification of violence.

And as was true of other pedagogical techniques, learning by example had its dark, repressive side. For those who refused to join the collectives or turn in their quotas, or who instigated subversive acts against the regime, or who generally caused trouble through their recalcitrant behavior, the regime endorsed making public examples of them. Such examples constituted what we might call negative mimesis. Targeted public humiliation of enemies was designed to teach others that the Party knew best and that resisting its wishes was ultimately futile. Thus, in January 1951, at a meeting of the Party's Secretariat, Moghioroș argued:

> Among those kulaks who have refused to give or have struck a collector, who broke the law, hid produce or divided it among relatives or poor peasants, or who have tried to fool the state or collections apparatus, we will select a couple of the leaders or the worst cases in every village, and try them. We will gather the villagers at the trial. . . . These methods must be applied in [all] regions. . . . We have to sentence [a few] to serve as examples for all.[126]

This Party-sanctioned approach to disciplining the population was both successful over the long run and counterproductive. While learning by seeing what happened to others was largely effective, the brutality of the methods simultaneously alienated peasants, making the ever-glorified propaganda less and less credible. Those who refused to join the collectives suffered diverse forms of abuse. Beatings were common. Dobrincu's interviews, for example, are filled with people's recollections of seeing the effects of physical brutality. One man recounted having been beaten over the course of three days because he refused to join the collective. He was sent home on the fourth to confer with his wife about his recalcitrance. When she saw him black and blue from head to toe, she pleaded, "My man, let's sign up . . . rather than have you die [from more beat-

[126] ANIC, Fond C.C. al P.C.R.–Cancelarie, file 3/1951, in Moraru et al. 2004: 456. Pauker commented in 1952: "It's important not only that three hundred kulaks are under arrest; it's especially important that they were not able to deceive us, and that the poor and particularly the middle peasants see that the kulak is not what he used to be" (ANIC, Fond C.C. al P.C.R.–Cancelarie, file 6/1952, 20 [RLA]).

ings], let's join the collective."[127] In many areas of the country, people were routinely deported from their villages, "disappeared" for having engaged in antiregime activities or for being suspected or accused of disloyalty to the Party.[128] The tens of thousands deported for precautionary reasons all provided negative mimesis.

"Enlightenment" through examples took even more dramatic embodied forms than public humiliation, savage beatings, and harsh forced labor regimes (the latter two of which could result in death). When deemed necessary, enemies were killed, their murders meant to teach an unequivocal lesson to those who doubted the Party's determination (or its ruthlessness).[129] We reiterate that the intention of such punishments was, in good measure, pedagogical: to intimidate people, to strike fear into them. Such physical and psychological warfare made uncertainty an everyday mode of being. Yet, as we will see in later chapters, while intimidation often ended in public compliance and an unwanted dependency on the Party, it did not produce loyalty, respect for, or agreement with the Party's abuses of power.

Denunciations and Unmaskings

Among the most insidious pedagogical tools were denunciations (*denunțuri*) and unmaskings or exposures (*demascări*). Each constituted an attempt to undermine or destroy an individual's authority and dignity, with respect both to political rivals and to traditional social hierarchies, by recasting the "truth" about that person. Although these forms are often seen as aspects of repressive totalitarian power, we examine them in terms of what their exercise produced. The Party actively taught citizens to employ them and, in so doing, to participate in the repressive apparatus of the state, becoming complicit with it. That is, these instruments did not just make the Party's categories familiar: they invited people to live inside the categories and act in accordance with them. The forms were pedagogical in two senses, then: in educating people in the language and ideological tenets of the regime, they at the same time engaged people in a new relationship between the state and its citizens, subtly making them its accomplices in the exercise of power.

Denunciations and unmaskings shared certain features but differed in their organization and general pedagogical effects. What were these techniques? How did they operate? We begin with denunciations, citing Fitzpatrick and Gellately's definition:

[127] C.S.C., Dobrincu interview.

[128] On deportation, see chapter 2.

[129] To this list of horrors must be added the perverse "reeducation" programs that occurred at Romania's most infamous prisons such as Pitești. See Bălan 2000 and the various memoirs written about these experiences. For a preliminary list of them, see Bălan 2000: 202–3; Dobrincu 2008.

> Denunciations may be defined as spontaneous communications from individual citizens to the state (or to another authority such as a church) containing accusations of wrongdoing by other citizens or officials and implicitly or explicitly calling for punishment. Typically, denunciations are written and delivered privately to an addressee rather than published. They are likely to invoke state (or church) values and to disclaim any personal interest on the part of the writer, citing duty to the state (or to the public good) as the reason for offering information to authorities. (Fitzpatrick and Gellately 1996: 747)

Denunciations functioned in similar fashion in Romania: they happened in private, secret exchanges—written or oral—usually between an individual and a Securitate agent or higher-ranking member of the Party. Much like informers, denouncers provided information about someone's enemy activities or suspect behavior, performing their roles clandestinely; their identities were not publicly known (although others might suspect them of such activity).[130] Referring to the denunciation of a village mayor for having been a legionary, one older respondent explained, "You put the information into an envelope addressed to the district Securitate and mailed it. You didn't need to use your name, only an address. Secretly."[131] A poor person might denounce his neighbor, as happened to A. L. from Vlaicu, who had been labeled a chiabur. The neighbor, whom others characterized as being from a family of drunkards, denounced A. L. for not having plowed all of his fields overnight, as ordered.[132] Because A. L.'s wife was the neighbor's godmother, the denunciation was especially heinous. Personal enmities based on any number of reasons could readily bring one person to denounce another (Gross [1982: 375] notes that "private enmity was the primary motivation"). Or a peasant who was caught hiding grain might then rat on where his neighbors were hiding theirs,[133] lest they get away with tricking the Party-state. (In this way, he fulfilled the folk wisdom of the old Romanian saying, "Death to my neighbor's goat.") For good measure, Decree 64/1951 included material incentives for poor and middle peasants to denounce chiaburs for not fulfilling their quotas, offering them "25 percent of the confiscated produce" (Roske 2005: 123).

Whatever the motivation for denouncing others, the effect was to erode social trust between relatives, neighbors, and friends, while increasing informers' intimate relationship with and dependency on the state.[134] Gross argues forcefully that

[130] Informers, however, tended to have a "regular, often paid relationship with the police", who actively cultivated them (Fitzpatrick and Gellately 1996: 747). Informers often submitted information using an agreed-upon pseudonym, although not all reports were signed.

[131] P. V., Kligman interview. The mayor was removed from office.

[132] 151, Verdery interview.

[133] ANIC, Fond C.C. al P.C.R.–Cancelarie, file 6/1952, 10 (RLA).

[134] Ioanid (1999: author's note, n.p.) poignantly observes that prisoners sometimes broke down and "denounced their comrades, which didn't exclude them from the long list of victims of the

> the principal mechanism which accounts for the penetration of the state into the private domain has been the practice of denunciation. An act of effective denunciation (i.e., one followed by reprisals against the denounced) can be seen, paradoxically, both as a service *rendered to* the state (providing the state with sought-after information) and as a service *rendered by* the state (providing an individual citizen with prompt settlement of some private dispute in his favour). (1982: 375)

By inviting citizens to settle scores or promote their advancement with this instrument—by not just accepting denunciations but fomenting them—activists drew them into a web from which they became the Party's prey. To drive that point home further, Fitzpatrick and Gellately (1996: 757) assert that the most "totalitarian" form of denunciation was that by children who denounced their parents, recognizing "a higher duty to the state" instead. The frequency of such intrafamilial betrayals is unknown, but they "figured prominently in Soviet and Nazi propaganda" as well as that of the fraternal countries (757; see also Hooper 2006). The incitement to denounce or unmask, like the recruitment of informers more generally, shows us how the Party-state invested itself in local networks of social relations so as to transform people's knowledge of one another.

Unmaskings or exposures were related to yet different from denunciations, in that they were public, ritualized spectacles that operated simultaneously as propaganda, legal-political consolidation, and public intimidation.[135] A host of Party declarations underscored the significance of exposing enemies, whoever they were: "One of the most important goals of the masses must be the unmasking of chiaburs," "One of the principal responsibilities of the Party press concerning . . . the class enemy is exposing all of these thieves' tricks. . . . [T]he local press must pursue a campaign to show middle peasants that they too are exploited by chiaburs, that their path is the GAC. . . . [C]hiaburs' rumors and propaganda from the religious sects must be exposed."[136] Chiaburs were to be unmasked "by all means," an admonition reiterated and elaborated two years later in a work plan issued by a district Party committee: "Where the class enemy exists, the Party cell will unmask him at meetings, public gatherings, on wall posters, and through caricatures."[137]

Like the devil in Christian lore, enemies presented themselves in a variety of forms and worked hard to remake their identities in keeping with the times.

communist dictatorship." On prisoners and "ratting" or "squealing," see also Fitzpatrick and Gellately 1996: 765–66.

135 These "exposure ceremonies" were introduced more systematically in 1958, after the Soviet Army left Romania (see Tănase 1998: 158, 2003: 180) and, like arrests and trials (whether public or closed show trials), played an important role as "disciplinary" pedagogies. For a seminal work, see Fitzpatrick 2005.

136 DJAN MM, Fond Comitetul Regional PMR Baia Mare, file 65/1949, 286; and ANIC, Fond C.C. al P.C.R.–Propagandă și Agitație, file 1/1950, 61.

137 ANIC, Fond C.C. al P.C.R.–Agrară, file 54/1950, 3, and DJAN MM, Fond Comitetul Raional PMR Vișeu, Maramureș, file 33/1952/v. V, 91.

But an enemy was an enemy, regardless of an impostor's makeover. On this point, Fitzpatrick incisively observed, "The impostor is one who has assumed or claimed an identity to which he or she is not entitled. In a revolutionary situation, it is extremely important to unmask the impostors who are falsely claiming revolutionary identity" (2005: 4). No one was invulnerable to being exposed, regardless of rank within the Party. To make certain that everyone understood the full import of enemy activities, on July 20, 1953, the GAC's Party cell in Ieud, Maramureş, discussed among other items the unmasking of Beria in the Soviet Union, which had been addressed in an article in *Scînteia* on July 11, 1953.[138] In July 1952, the Executive Committee of the Şibot commune People's Council (Hunedoara) replayed the unmasking of the Pauker "gang" by unmasking its own vice president as a chiabur and exploiter of working people. The example shows beautifully how show trials rippled pedagogically down the political hierarchy. According to the minutes, a comrade brought things to a head by saying that

> many achievements in building socialism have been hindered by representatives of the rightist deviation of V. Luca, A. Pauker, and Th. Georgescu, against whom measures were taken by the CC of the Party. The rightist deviation was also observed at the regional and district levels. He cited some cases from the financial section of our district. Just as in the district, there was also a representative of the rightist deviation in the People's Council at Şibot, I. Bonţa—the president's deputy. He applied quotas unfairly favoring the chiaburs and the wealthy. . . . Last year he sabotaged the threshing campaign.[139]

During the proceedings, his brother too denounced him for supporting chiaburs and stealing village property. Similar unmaskings must have unfolded all over the country in those months.

Unmaskings, or "public rituals of repudiation" (Hooper 2006: 63), typically occurred during community meetings organized by the Party and were held in public venues such as community centers or performance halls. These "people's courts," as one of Ieud's peasant chroniclers called them, were announced ahead of time with the date and time that X would be tried in the village cultural center.[140] In 1952, over three thousand chiaburs who had entered into collective farms were unmasked and thrown out (Ionescu-Gură 2000: 291). Following the Party directives mentioned above, such public spectacles were also reported in newspaper articles and wall gazettes. For example, a headline in a local paper revealed that "Chiaburs from the Iza Area are Exposed and Tried," for having hidden quantities of grain owed the state and for sowing fields with poor seed.[141]

138 DJAN MM, Comitetul Raional PMR Vişeu, Maramureş, Fond 10, file 71/1953, 6.

139 Archive of Şibot commune (jud. Alba), file I/4/1952, 148–66.

140 Pleş-Chindriş, n.d.

141 See Chindriş, *Graiul Maramureşului*, April 16, 1950: 3. On unmaskings, see Fitzpatrick 2005; Tănase 2003: 167–80. People could reveal themselves unwittingly (not to be conflated with self-

Unmaskings created ritualized public demonstrations of "loyalty" to the regime as those exposed were heckled and humiliated by the assembled crowd. At the same time, the public process by which someone was unmasked enabled the Party to show socialist justice in action, regardless of the publicly known secret that such unmaskings were dramatic examples of intimidation.

While unmaskings and denunciations were closely related, unmaskings tended to result from either denunciations or information provided by paid informers. Workers might denounce a "comrade" who had fleeced them and the state of funds. The thief's activities were then researched and, if there was cause, exposed as an example to others of like mind that they should realize "the working class does not sleep," its vigilance is constant.[142] For good measure, the Securitate tracked data on the number of "threats, exposures, arrests . . . ," which included the number of unmaskings that followed from denunciations; this information was circulated within the secret police every trimester.[143]

Writing to and Meeting with Party Officials

Another pedagogical strategy to engage citizens directly in the Party-state's creation of "new socialist persons" was to solicit letters and petitions from them or hold meetings with them. Party leaders encouraged these practices, requesting the assistance of individuals in convincing their kin and neighbors to join the collectives, or to express their patriotism and loyalty to the Party by calling attention to the misdeeds of cadres or others that had given rise to their grievances. Whether through a formal letter or a petition or a meeting with Party leaders, communicating with them entailed becoming fluent in the new language reviewed at the beginning of this chapter, thus refashioning themselves. Moreover, writing letters or petitions and meeting officially with leaders were performative acts that transformed individuals' relationships with the Party-state, further shoring up its paternalist character.[144]

For example, in the interest of convincing people to join collectives, a Party directive ordered regional and local Party organizations to intensify their efforts to have factory workers and urban residents write letters to their relatives

---

criticism, which individuals did knowingly if not necessarily proudly). For example, one mayor who was not eager to push collectivization in his village was accused by a group of agitators that he had "unmasked [him]self. You're against collectivization!" He was threatened with prison, and so on. See Stoica 2003: 20.

[142] See "Să ştie toţi tâlharii de teapă inginerului Decei Ovidiu că nu dorme clasă muncitoare." DJAN MM, Fond Comitetul Raional Vişeu, file 2/1950, 3.

[143] See, for example, ACNSAS, FD, file 53/v. 25, 1, 16–19. Such reports were issued by the State Security Council, Section "C."

[144] On denunciations and letter writing, see Fitzpatrick and Gellately 1997. Fitzpatrick outlines three frameworks for analyzing letters: state paternalism, citizen relations, and cultural analysis (1–10). We additionally include meetings with leaders in this genre of Party-citizen exchanges.

and friends in villages;[145] they could also send them postcards with scenes of life and work in the collectives, which were being printed expressly for that purpose.[146] Local Party cells were to organize and assist GAC members in sending letters to peasants in other villages, urging them to create collective farms.[147] In addition, Party members with standing in the hierarchy often wrote letters to their village kin, attempting to enlighten them. In one such epistle, two brothers (one a general and the other a museum director) responded at length to troubled letters they had received from their brother in the village. They tried to make him understand that if he and members of his extended family—all of whom were viewed as enemies of one kind or another—mended their ways, and that if "you behave well and demonstrate your sincere devotion to the regime and to the interests of the working class, then certainly you will be reinstated in your former position or to a more important one." They reminded him that as head of the family, it was his responsibility "to set the tone and, if necessary, impose it." After two-and-a-half pages, single-spaced, in which they spelled out Party principles, they signed off by wishing the family well and embracing their brother "with fraternal best wishes." A postscript declared that "the letter is not secret, anyone is welcome to read it," a hint that they may have written it to demonstrate their own fidelity to the Party despite their extended family's antiregime ways.[148]

Letters of Complaint and Meetings

Party leaders not only directed the writing of such letters but also invited letters from the citizenry. Newspapers featured regular letters to the editor; other letters were addressed to the higher-ups, including Gheorghiu-Dej himself or members of the Central Committee, seeking fair resolution to some complaint.[149] These letters were akin to denunciations, in that they often complained to the authorities about breaches of Party doctrine by cadres, relatives, or friends and could also result in punitive consequences. They differed, however, in taking an officially solicited form rather than being a secret communiqué to the Securitate. While such letters enabled the writers to call upon the Party's wisdom and justice and to establish a relationship with the paternalist Party-state by showing themselves as proper socialist citizens, these letters, like denunciations, simultaneously entwined their authors in the exercise of the state's

[145] ANIC, Fond C.C. al P.C.R.–Agrară, file 54/1950, 3.

[146] ANIC, Fond C.C. al P.C.R.–Agrară, file 48/1950, 49.

[147] ANIC, Fond C.C. al P.C.R.–Agrară, file 54/1950, 3.

[148] ACNSAS, FP, file 248/v. 2, 23–24.

[149] In responding to these complaints, the Party "discovered many unjust matters that were then corrected and resolved many contestations, the contents of which were largely fair" (ANIC, Fond C.C. al P.C.R.–Agrară, file 70/1953, 31).

repressive mechanisms. Or, as Alexopoulos wrote regarding Soviet petitions of the disenfranchised, "denunciatory speech in petitions for the reinstatement of rights illustrates how victims can become victimizers" (1999: 652). Her insightful observation applies equally well to letters that contain accusatory speech.

Letters to Party leaders began with formulaic introductions addressed to "beloved Comrade Gheorghiu-Dej," for example, followed by declarations about Marxist-Leninist teachings, which situated the ensuing complaint within the acceptable genre.[150] In many cases, that meant unmasking enemies and activities that violated the good intentions of the Party. As we discuss in chapters 3 and 5, the letters might expose cadres for behaving improperly in some way, thereby contributing to the destruction of the collective and Party unity. Other, more vigilant colleagues or everyday citizens could call such deviations to the attention of Party officials higher up. To illustrate, three Party members wrote to Gheorghiu-Dej complaining about the conduct of various leaders of the GAC "Lenin's Flag" in Bujoru commune, Galați region, as well as of other Party officials in the district. Among their complaints was the GAC president's hoodlum-like behavior: not only had he brought two barrels of wine from another community—ostensibly for the holiday celebrating the coming of spring—but he had sold it to collectivists at an exorbitant price, turning the collective into a bar; in addition, he stole a mirror from the other community, which was found in his house, and two cart wheels from a poor peasant there.[151] The comrades who wrote to the Party defending its (and undoubtedly their) interests couched their claims in the new language and signed off with a series of slogans: "We fight for peace!" "We fight for Lenin's and Stalin's great cause!" "Long live the Romanian Workers' Party!" (We do not know the final disposition.)

Grievances could also be expressed in face-to-face meetings with Party leaders, including those at the very top of the hierarchy, during which one or more supplicants sought satisfaction and counsel. The Party leaders who were present listened to the complaint or litany, posed questions that also tested the doctrinal mettle of those seeking their sage advice, and offered recommendations to resolve the problem. When appropriate, one or more Central Committee members might go to the locale where the problem arose to make certain that it was taken care of, whether in favor of those making the appeal or of the local leaders about whom the complaint was made.

To illustrate, we summarize key exchanges during a meeting that three peasants from the village of Cistei (Hunedoara), held on May 15, 1951, with Gheorghiu-Dej and Moghioroș.[152] The encounter allowed the two leaders to

[150] On letters in the Soviet Union, see, for example, Davies 1997.

[151] ANIC, Fond C.C. al P.C.R.–Agrară, file 6/1951, 2–3.

[152] Moraru et al. 2004: 546–50. Because there is less written about such meetings, we focus on its content at length rather than on letters of complaint. We revisit complaints through formal petitions next.

demonstrate the Party's willingness to listen and propose a solution, all the while underscoring the Party line and what it meant to be a proper socialist citizen. After Comrade Gheorghiu-Dej asked what brought them to the capital, Mihai Ciortea, the apparent leader, responded in the name of 28 families with a complaint about how the GAC in their village was being formed: activists had threatened with deportation to the Canal everyone who did not sign up in twenty-four hours. For good measure, they had shown what happened to those who resisted, beating up six villagers, after which 180 out of 192 families signed up. Next, eight peasants were labeled chiaburs, even though none of them had more than ten hectares of land. Gheorghiu-Dej, sensing they may not have understood what a chiabur was, questioned them in detail, to which they gave the proper criteria (exploiting labor, owning means of production) but added that chiaburs were devious, etc.

As the meeting unfolded, Moghioroş inquired whether the village Party cell had taken up these problems: they had not, for no one had the courage to bring up complaints after those initial threats; people were too afraid to say anything. Ciortea commented that they were frightened about what would happen when they went back, to which Moghioroş responded, "Anyone has the right to come to the Central Committee." Therein lay the crux of the matter: unable to have an impartial review in the village, these peasants acted on their rights as good socialist citizens, yet they feared retribution at home for going over the heads of the local Party officials who might themselves "pay" for having allegedly abused Party principles of conduct.

The discussion now turned to whether they were GAC members of their own free will (to which we return below). Ciortea revealed that despite the pressure on him to join, his wife had said she would divorce him if he did so. Caught in the middle, he ended up beating her. Gheorghiu-Dej criticized him, saying that force is counterproductive and that "you aren't allowed to beat her." This paved the way for a sermon on Party tenets, as Ciortea next claimed that the District Committee advised him to leave his wife, which would make her come around. Gheorghiu-Dej responded that they had given him poor advice: he, Ciortea, was at fault: "As a Party member, you shouldn't use beatings, but be patient, act nicely, gently, let her convince herself, learn; let her understand that you are interested in what is best for her." When Ciortea acknowledged that his wife had read an article by Ana Pauker saying peasants should join the collectives voluntarily, Gheorghiu-Dej elaborated, "With force you can't create a collective. If you strike fear into people, you can't convince them . . . and peasants don't forget. Such methods are foreign to us and hurt our Party." Going on at great length, he regretted that what happened in Cistei was not unique, that many peasants didn't initially want to join, but setting examples of the benefits of collective agriculture would eventually convince them. The meeting concluded with Gheorghiu-Dej reiterating the importance of free will in joining the GACs and suggested that a Central Committee member go to Cistei, a job for which Moghioroş volunteered.[153] Meetings such as this one, like the letters addressed to Party authorities, were customary practices, although we do not know their frequency. Their pedagogical effects, however, are clear: drawing citizens directly—and instrumentally on both sides—into the Party's vocabulary and its political and cultural practices.

Petitions

Among the most widespread pedagogical practices was the writing of petitions, especially to join the collectives "of one's own free will."[154] Long a significant genre among Russian peasants (see Burbank 2004), the petition (*cerere*) had also been a consecrated form of communication among people in different hierarchical locations throughout the Romanian lands since at least the eighteenth century. It was especially well developed in the border areas of the Habsburg empire (the inner slopes of the eastern and southern Carpathians).[155] Peasant petitioners might be asking for something outright, or they might be complaining about or contesting something, implicitly asking for redress. Particularly frequent during the Habsburg period were complaints to the Emperor about the behavior of lower-level imperial officials, such as the petitions that preceded a massive peasant uprising in 1784 (see Prodan 1979).

The genre of the petition entered into the communist period (albeit with some modifications) often encouraged by the authorities.[156] Analyzing a form specific to the Soviet Union, Alexopoulos (1997) discusses the writer's self-presentational style, which involved an account of suffering and hardship framed in the Party's rhetoric of social justice and fairness; such "ritual la-

[153] Moraru et al. 2004: 548, for quotes. Again, we do not know what ensued; our interest is in the occurrence of such meetings.

[154] There is often a fine line between letters of complaint and petitions; however, there are categorical distinctions: letters of complaint were less formal and do not fall under specific rubrics, such as joining the collective, changing one's class status, petitioning for the return of land, etc.

[155] Dumitru Şandru, personal communication. Historians Sachelarie and Stoicescu (1988: 96), writing about feudal institutions in the Romanian Principalities, explain that anyone believing himself unjustly treated could submit a petition, which set in motion a formal procedure in the realm of manorial justice. This form was well established before the eighteenth century; by the mid-nineteenth century, peasants could use it to address the prince directly. For relations with local authorities in the villages, however, the main forms of address were oral until reforms of the mid-eighteenth century sought to generalize written procedures there as well. (Thanks to Dorin Dobrincu for this reference.) Two persons were especially important in mediating relations with authorities: the teacher and the priest; in Transylvania, in addition to these two was the village notary. Any of those persons might write petitions for illiterate peasants.

[156] According to the law on taxes, for instance, citizens had the right to forward petitions contesting decisions they felt unjust, thereby demonstrating the law's "democratic character." See, for example, DJAN MM, Fond Regional PMR Baia Mare, file 65/1949, 106.

ments," as she calls them, were meant to appeal to the paternalist benevolence of those to whom they were addressed. Her ideas about what makes the lament form compelling are broadly applicable to other kinds of petitions, whether written or presented in face-to-face meetings: "The kind of audience which a lament presupposes is one with agency; only the reader of the petition can reverse the writer's cycle of misfortune" (1997: 129). Petitions as a form acknowledge where power lies, while seeking to manipulate it; they are especially suited to contexts in which the center of power is understood as an ordering principle, with part of its high status consisting of acting for the powerless (see Humphrey 2002: 28–29).

Petition writing involved ordinary citizens both in learning the appropriate language and in binding levels of the bureaucracy through the circuits of paper discussed in chapter 3, as each petition precipitated correspondence from the level that received it and from the levels tasked with disposing of it. Citizens could be very persistent, multiplying the circuits of paper with repeated efforts to solve their problems. Often, petitions violated the proper administrative hierarchy—being sent, for instance, directly to the Central Committee or Gheorghiu-Dej himself (or sometimes both; see below). District files contain orders from their regional headquarters to take care of problems that had been inappropriately addressed too high up; sometimes the regions gave a deadline for the case to be resolved, and the district files might then include a memo to the region on the disposition of the case. In corresponding about their petitions, then, citizens would gradually learn the hierarchical responsibilities of the bureaucracy that subjected them. Knowing and using the proper legal form affected the petitioner's fate. In one example, sixty contestations were rejected for not having been correctly prepared or signed, and illiterate persons were excluded from consideration because they could not legally make a claim without a signature.[157]

Petitions were utilized all across the social spectrum. Regional officials petitioned the Central Committee for permission to establish one or another GAC, or for changes in policies that they feared would lead to uprisings. In 1947, the Director of the Economic Bureau, Maramureş, petitioned the Department of State Provisioning to request ten trainloads of maize: "So that starvation does not paralyze the life of the entire region and provoke massacres, mass revolts and population exodus, a distribution of grain is urgently needed."[158] People of all kinds wrote petitions to become Party members. As for peasants, they petitioned to join the collective, to withdraw from the collective, to request colonization on new lands, to have their quotas reduced, to donate their land to the state so they could escape their quotas, to contest their designation as chiaburs (see chapter 6) or their expropriation in the agrarian reform, to try to recover

[157] ACNSAS, FD, file 5, 17.

[158] DJAN MM, Fond 53, file 123/1946, 5.

good land that had been exchanged for bad, to dispute other policies such as their deportation or the confiscation of their house and property, and for myriad other reasons. In one unusual instance, Vultur reports that Romanian citizens of German ethnicity in the Banat, anticipating their expropriation in the 1945 agrarian reform, petitioned to be recognized as French, a claim they based on the "French" origin of their ancestors colonized in the eighteenth century, which would exempt them from expropriation as Germans (Vultur 2003: 7–8; see chapter 7). In the remainder of this section, we focus our discussion on the petitions to create and to join the collectives, then evaluate this basic pedagogical form that taught people an etiquette of address and exchange between themselves and the state.

Following the Soviet model, it was the Party leadership's insistence on Lenin's "principle of free consent" as the basis for forming collectives that dictated the use of petitions both to establish a GAC and also to join one. These formal documents simultaneously provided legal cover and a paper trail for the Party's actions while legitimating them. Here is one that exhibits the concrete effects of mimesis, described above:

REPORT

Concerning the work of constituting the GAC "New Life" in Dobrosloveni

Comrades:

The working peasants of Dobrosloveni and Potopin villages visiting the Agricultural Collective Farm in Reşca village that was formed last year were able to realize the superiority of that GAC compared with agricultural associations and, through large-scale mass political work, the working peasants under the leadership of communists from Dobrosloveni and Potopin villages have decided in a fairly short time to request to create an agricultural collective farm.

The basis of this decision is the example of the Agricultural Collective Farm August 23 in Reşca village, which even though it was recently formed succeeded in giving per workday: fifteen kg wheat and corn and five lei in cash, onions five hundred grams, sugar and other, for example the family of Ţucmeanu D-tru with three work-hands gave five hundred workdays and received eight thousand kg wheat and corn, twenty-five hundred lei cash, and other products.[159]

Those who joined a collective had to provide a record of having signed up voluntarily, concretized in a common wording: "of my own accord and uncoerced by anyone" (*de bunăvoie şi nesilit de nimeni*). (As one of our respondents put it,

[159] Arhiva Primăriei Dobrosloveni, file GAC Dobrosloveni, nr. 5/1961, Poz. 148, Documentele de constituire a GAC Viaţa Nouă din Dobrosloveni şi satul Potopini [*sic*] pe anul 1961.

"The same as what you say when you're married."[160]) There were a number of set formulas for such entry petitions, whose content was generally standardized, but which might also vary considerably from case to case. They might be handwritten, or they might be a mimeographed form letter with blanks filled in—the latter were particularly common in the second wave of collectivization in the late 1950s. One of Goina's respondents recalled that in trying to get him to join the collective, activists told him, "Look, you have to sign this petition, I've got it ready so you don't have to write it yourself!"[161]

Most entry petitions were fairly brief. They consisted of a request to join (we found a number of different wordings for this), the amount of land being donated, the numbers of animals and implements, and the number of laborers or "work hands" that the household would contribute; some might include additional information (e.g., requests to harvest the already-sown crop, health problems that might keep someone from working in the GAC). The style of these petitions reflects the relationship being constructed between the petitioner and the Party: many begin with an exhortation, begging the Party to "be so kind" as to welcome them. Moreover, most of them ended with one or another ritualized slogan (with which readers are by now quite familiar), such as "Long live the struggle for peace!" "Long live the Romanian Communist Party!" "Long live the Romanian People's Republic!" "We fight for the fatherland!"

For many, the matter of consent—"of one's own free will"—was a matter of interpretation.[162] Rather than joining of their own free will (*de bunăvoie*), our respondents clarified—engaging in a bit of wordplay—that they joined of necessity (*de nevoie*). Across the country, peasants consistently reported having been forced to consent. Several examples from Darabani are representative of the brutality experienced, especially by men: "No, not jailed, beaten! Beaten with a club until you gave in. Enough! I joined the collective! And worked for it for twenty-eight years";[163] "[they beat people] so they'd join the collective . . . they joined out of fear . . . they called you to the town hall, beat you, locked you in, and you joined out of fear! Not out of free will . . . that's how it was."[164] They beat old people, even a few women, and poisoned the beloved dog of someone who refused to join. Fellow villagers witnessed their compatriots returning home, bloodied, and joined rather than suffer the consequences. In this way, people were literally beaten down until they "crossed over" (to the collective's side) and "consented" to sign the petitions placed in front of them. On paper,

[160] *Așa cum se zice la căsătorie.* 59, Verdery interview.

[161] V. B., Goina interview.

[162] As noted in chapter 2, the Party also debated whether peasants entering on their own initiative undermined the initiative of the Party (ANIC, Fond C.C. al P.C.R.–Cancelarie, file 11/1950: 11 [RLA]).

[163] M.I.D., Dobrincu interview.

[164] V.A.R., Dobrincu interview.

however, the forced aspect of their consent was effaced as they "begged" to be accepted.

What did these petitions look like? Their form varied widely; it might list the implements to be given, provide considerable detail about the location of the fields being donated, or simply state the amount of land. Here are two examples, one for the GAC in Dobrosloveni and one from Darabani.

> 1) Comrade President,
> The undersigned N. D. from the village of Dobrosloveni, Caracal District, Craiova Region, request to join the Collective Agricultural Farm in Dobrosloveni, bringing a surface area of 7.54 hectares arable land, currently part of the "Second Congress of the RWP" Association in the village of Dobrosloveni, Caracal District, of which 3 hectares are sown with wheat.
> My inventory:
> One cart
> One plow
> One harrow
> Two oxen
> Working hands: I have five
> Husband [signature]
> Wife [fingerprint and signature]
> December 23, 1969
> Long live the fight for peace![165]
>
> 2) Comrade President
> The undersigned Andruş V. Mihai from the village of Darabani requests to join the Darabani Collective Agricultural Farm with an area of 2.5 hectares arable land.
> Inventory, 1 horse, one colt, nothing else. I ask that the general assembly approve that I work with my own equipment (that is, my cart and two horses.)
> Also, I ask that I harvest this year's wheat crop. I have [forty prajini] of wheat sown on Podiş field.
> . . . I am joining the collective with two working hands.
> Husband Andruş Mihai
> Wife Andruş Elena
> Comrade President of the Darabani Agricultural Farm[166]

(Note the conditions attached to the second petition, which we will discuss in chapter 5.) Some of the petitions could become very personal: after requesting to join the GAC, one Ştefan Marie writes,

[165] Arhiva Primăriei Dobrosloveni, file 5/1961, Inv. Nr. 5/961, Poz. Nr. 154/4. Documentele de constituire a GAC Viaţa Nouă din Dobrosloveni şi satul Potopini pe anul 1961.

[166] Arhiva CAP Darabani, file Cereri de înscriere în GAC Darabani, satul Suseni, n.p.

> I'm ill and have problems with my kidneys since 1957. I'm thirty-four years old and even now I'm not feeling well. I also mention that my husband has agreed for me to join the collective farm. He's now working for the railway in Sighet. I ask nothing for my husband from the leadership of the collective, only that you ensure that I can have the job where I am now. And for you to ensure that I have a vegetable garden, in conformity with the statute.[167]

Peasants who signed these petitions took them with deadly seriousness, suggesting a belief that something written on a piece of paper had a special kind of force. When they revolted against what was being done to them, they might occupy the commune People's Council where the petitions were held and burn them or demand they be given back (see, e.g., Stoica 2009: 423). Indeed, in Nămoloasa, Galați, peasants demanded that their petitions be destroyed because they had been forced to join, violating the much-propagandized principle of "free consent" (Oprea 2009: 69). And when Nicolae Ceaușescu was sent out to pacify resistant peasants in Nănești in 1958, he acceded to their demands to hand the petitions back to their signers, since they had been obtained by force (Stoica 2009: 433; see also Roske 2003: 109–19).

Although the petition forms for any given GAC might be fairly standard, there were minor differences from one place to another, indicating that local authorities had some flexibility in what they expected peasants to sign or that different people who wrote the petitions for the signers were making use of general rather than specific models for them. Many contained the critical clause reflecting "free consent" (missing from those above): "The undersigned requests to sign into the GAC willingly and uncoerced by anyone" or "of my own accord." Sometimes these were embellished, as in this one from Nănești: "The present petition is made by the undersigned on his own initiative and unsolicited by anyone and springing from the desire to participate actively in the socialization of agriculture in our nation, the Romanian People's Republic. Long live the fight for peace!" (Stoica 2003: 11–12). Sometimes the petitions gave further kinds of reasons for joining—for example, in Darabani, they included the phrase, "I ask that it be recorded that I willingly give over this parcel because I can no longer work it" (Dobrincu 2003a: 11).

The writing and signing of petitions took place in the presence of the organizers of the collective or of the cadres sent to sign people up. They might occur in public places where others could see, or they might happen in people's homes, though neighbors would of course be aware of what might be happening. Discrepancies between the signatures and the writing on the petitions make it clear that most signers did not write their own, a supposition confirmed by the fact that many petitions from a given village were written in the same hand (see, e.g., Dobrincu 2003a: 46; Lățea 2003: 46; recall our discussion

[167] DJAN MM, Fond CAP Iza, Sighet, file 1/1962: 55.

of illiteracy at the beginning of the chapter).[168] Likewise, a respondent from the Reviga GAC leadership disclosed that he himself had written out the petitions for thirty-two people (Chelcea 2003b: 31), and a woman of poor-peasant origin from Vlaicu recalled the two functionaries at the newly forming GAC who had helped people write petitions.[169] Another from Ieud who had joined the Party and been taught to write remarked that she had written out many entry petitions for people, but confessed that although she could *copy* a model, she could not in fact *read* what was written in it! (Kligman 2009: 177). Petitions might be written beforehand and given to people to sign, or they might be written in the presence of the signers; occasionally the signers themselves might write them on the spot, possibly with advice from the officials present.

It is this advice, the prescribed models, and the formalized, ritualized language of so many petitions that make us see them as a pedagogical technique. Most Romanian villagers did not want to join GACs, and they would never have given their free consent if not pushed into it one way or another. So in creating the templates for people to sign, or in tutoring them as to what should be in the document, the Party was reinforcing the categories of thought that it had created. It was also urging people to think in terms of developing literacy, especially if they lacked it and had to find people to write for them. In their petitions, they would state their conviction of the superiority of socialist agriculture, their acknowledgment of poverty and exploitation in reference to their village, their adherence to "peace" and to the concept of "fight" or "struggle" (*luptă*); they would refer to their country by a new name (the Romanian People's Republic) and invoke the newly ascendant party (the Romanian Workers Party).

Importantly, the petition form was also compelling complicity in the collectivization project, a crucial technique for compromising people's independence and initiative. Like other pedagogical tools, it was teaching them to be obedient subjects, to join "willingly and uncoerced" regardless of their inner dispositions, even at the cost of misrepresenting themselves. (In this manner, the petition form also compelled duplicitous practices. See Kligman 1998.) For some, it was understood as an intentional effort to humiliate them as social persons. For instance, chiaburs might be expected to state, "I ask you to accept me . . . because I'm no longer capable of managing my own affairs." To sign such an admission was to compromise utterly their image of themselves as men and to lie about their circumstances (Kligman 2009: 179). Moreover, as mentioned above, the petitions customarily required villagers to *ask to be received* into the GACs, placing them in a dependent posture—would you be so kind as to let us join—instead of, for instance, saying, "I choose to give my lands and inventory to the collective farm." The implication of this act of asking—as supplicants—

[168] Similarly, signatures in the voluminous penal files Kligman consulted differ from the handwriting of the statements provided.

[169] 56, Verdery interview.

was that if they were accepted (and not everyone was), they would be grateful. Dobrincu observes, "We cannot help noticing the cynicism of the authorities, who obliged those being dispossessed of part of their property to feign gratitude" (2003a: 11).

The same process of learning the categories of the Party informs other kinds of petitions as well as those to join the collectives. People regularly contested having been designated chiaburs and petitioned to have their status reclassified. Although we review such reclassification petitions (as we call them) in greater depth in chapter 6, here we discuss how these petitions reveal in even more detail the kinds of things peasants had to learn to enter into dialogue with the Party. The following extract from Dobrosloveni illustrates our point:

> 1. Whereas the undersigned has not exploited agricultural labor, the work having been done by myself and my family, I gave on time and as required by the Decision of the Council of Ministers the quotas assigned me, and I am fully paid up on my taxes and duties to the state, I ask you to research my affirmations as just and true.
>
> Also, I wish to mention that, contrary to the interpretations made by certain comrades, I was and am a simple tradesman. Free and uncoerced by anyone, I placed myself at the service of the Party and the Republic. . . . When the needs of the county required that my press for making bricks be put in operation to cover the needs of the Republic, I gave it of my own free will and uncoerced by anyone, on the basis of my knowledge and of the obligations of the [Five-Year] Plan set out by the county. Since 1945 I am engaged in the workforce [*în câmpul muncii*], in the interest of the commune.[170]

From this and other petitions like it we see people who have learned to use (or whose tutors have recommended to them) certain stock words and phrases—"own free will and uncoerced by anyone," "workforce," "attached to the poor," "comrade," "middle peasant," "exploiters," and "chiabur"—and to appeal to principles of equity and social justice, obligations to the good of the people, simple and honest work, the Plan. They especially play on the Party's sense of fairness, insist on their own humble origins or miserable state, make clear why what might appear to be exploitation on their part is precisely the opposite, and, where necessary, seek to render themselves politically bland. Whereas some of these points resonated with precommunist values (the virtues of hard work, the appeal to justice), most were new, particularly the concept of exploitation, which the petitions spell out to mean having a servant, employing hired labor, having means of production for profit, and so on. These new terms had to be rehearsed, brought into villagers' lexicon, instilled in people's cognition. The petitions were a way of doing that.

Sometimes we can even see the process whereby this learning occurred. A set

170 DJAN Olt, Fond Sfatul Popular al comunei Dobrosloveni, file 1786/1952, petition 1, 27 October 1952. The petition was not successful, the district People's Council instructing the commune to "inform the residents verbally" that they have remained in the category of chiabur.

of petitions from Vlaicu contains four different attempts by a villager we will call B. P., who was contesting his designation as a chiabur.[171] The documents justifying his chiabur status read, "Had his own store and rented the village tavern until 1948. Also had servants. Possesses 7.31 hectares land. Uses wage labor."[172] The principal problem with B. P. was his relationship to the tavern: by selling liquor to peasants—by engaging in commerce, an activity the communists condemned—he was exploiting them for his own profit. B. P. filed his first (very brief) contestation as early as 1950, and in 1954 he did three more, the final one lengthy and replete with documentation. The first of them (filed February 26, 1954) made the following points: he's a war invalid with 80 percent disability, aged sixty-four; he has only 7.67 hectares of land, which he works with his family; he never did any kind of politics, "being handicapped"; he has only two cows, which he uses to work his land; he has never been convicted of any crime. He claims to have been made a chiabur because since he was an invalid, the commune leased him the communal tavern—"the permit belonged to the commune and was not my property. The commune fixed the prices and the commune took the income." Therefore, he can't be seen as an exploiter. On June 18, 1954, the district reported to the region thus: "He was not removed from the category of chiaburs for the following reasons: He possesses 7.20 [*sic*] hectares. There are two persons in his family, he had a servant until 1950, he uses more than thirty days' wage labor per year, he had a tavern and a store until 1950."[173]

Two days later, B. P. refiled his contestation with the People's Council, making most of the same arguments but specifying that in fact he has 6.35 hectares, not 7.46, the rest belonging to his son and registered as such since 1925. He also adds, "All those who have had commune taverns have been removed from chiabur status." On July 2, B. P. submitted a third petition, to the district this time, and annexed to it (1) a copy of his 1924 medical examination by the Ministry of War stating the extent of his war disability, and (2) a statement from the commune People's Council noting that he holds the tavern "in conformity with dispositions at the time, that war invalids should be asked to take over commune taverns" and confirming that the notary, not B. P., set the prices. The commune officials added that in 1940 the invalid B. P. had tried to get out of running the tavern because he couldn't manage it adequately but the commune forced him to take it back; he closed it again in 1944 but was again forced to open it, and in 1947 he closed it definitively. The district sent its agent to research the case and on July 30, 1954, it declared him removed from the category of chiabur.

It took B. P. four tries, but by responding in ever-greater detail to the charge that he was an exploiter and substituting for it his handicapped status, of which

[171] DJAN HD, Fond Sfat Popular Raion Orăştie, file 9/1950, n.p.; file 7/1954 (n.p.).

[172] DJAN HD, Fond Sfat Popular Raion Orăştie, file 37/1952 (n.p.).

[173] It is unclear why the amounts of land in the petitions differ, but owing to the multiple sources used to determine a person's landholdings, this was not uncommon.

he gave proof, he managed to become a middle peasant (or at least a "former chiabur"). By this time he knew very well what constituted "exploitation"; he had either made contact with the Ministry of Defense or turned his attic upside down to find the proof of his handicap; he had gone to the next administrative level with his case, thus learning the appropriate hierarchy for dealing with authority; and he had convinced the authorities that far from being an exploiter, he was always trying to flee from the job that made him take his fellow villagers' money, even if it was only to benefit the commune and not himself.

From comparing the handwriting on petitions like B. P.'s with the signatures, it is clear that as with the entry petitions into the GAC, few of them were written by the petitioner. Who helped people write this kind of document, as well as others in which villagers voiced a complaint of some kind rather than a desire to join the collective? Aside from the fact that some of the petitions were typed, which possibly indicates the assistance of some kind of functionary, we have little evidence except for some hints in our interviews. We quote at length from one such interview, in which G.D.B. from Darabani describes how someone he believes was a local functionary wrote a petition for a wealthy peasant, Florea, who had refused to join the collective. A Party member had illegally plowed up two hectares of Florea's land and taken the grain for himself. Florea (who was illiterate) was complaining to others about this treatment:

> One of the guys listening to him said, "Hey, write a petition to the Ministry of Agriculture!" But he couldn't write. So he asked where he should do it, because he can't write. And the guy said, "Mister, I'll do it for you, but don't you tell on me, not to anyone. I'll do it for you." So he did it, and the fellow went to the Ministry of Agriculture, and they grabbed him to make him tell them who wrote the petition for him. Who did it for him? The fellow thought carefully and hesitated, didn't tell them that this guy had written his petition. They said they'd put him in jail. "Listen, if you don't tell us we'll put you in jail!" "Well, you can put me in jail, you can do that, but listen who wrote it for me, I'll tell you who: I was coming to the market here moaning and complaining to everyone on the street about my troubles, and a man on the street wrote it for me. I don't know the person who wrote my petition. I didn't do it because I can't write, but this guy did it for me, because I had a problem. . . . And so I wrote to you. If I'd known what kind of justice I'd get from you, I'd never have written you!" And they sentenced him to three months in jail. . . . And when he got back home from jail, that guy gave him some two sacks of wheat because he didn't tell on him.[174]

Here we see Party officials alarmed at the tutoring an illiterate "class enemy" was receiving—tutoring that must have been well informed, judging by the reaction. The authorities wanted to find out who was helping peasants understand the system so well that they could work against it, in its own terms. The writer, meanwhile, was willing to do the job but wanted to remain anony-

[174] G.D.B., Dobrincu interview.

mous—and the authorities' response shows why. The kinds of people most likely to be able to write this kind of petition were petty functionaries or people like teachers and priests who had learned the system well enough to operate in it (and perhaps needed to make some pocket money).[175]

Another pedagogical aspect of these kinds of petitions is that they taught villagers something about the Party's administrative hierarchy. Where should they direct their petition for maximum advantage? This was a question about which most petitioners would have rather little information and might need the advice of others. In the contestation of B. P., discussed above, he tried to deal with at least three administrative levels, writing to the district, the commune, and the region, which forwarded his petition back to the district with a summary indicating how to read its contents. Some petitioners had their own ideas about where to write—recall that there were numerous petitions to the Central Committee, for example, and even directly to Gheorghiu-Dej.

In one unusual case, we have an idea of who might have directed a petitioner to a particular hierarchical level. B. E., from Vlaicu, was deported from the village together with her daughter and granddaughter in 1952.[176] In October of that year, she sent a petition to the Ministry of Internal Affairs complaining about being deported and asking to go home; she signed it "B. E., worker" (although technically speaking she was a "peasant"). She affirmed that they were not chiaburs and not exploiters of the working class, but "the most typical proletarian workers," "always attached to the cause of the proletariat"; she asked that their case be investigated and overturned "so we can go home to our land that is waiting for us to work it, so we can give our dear Republic the quotas and taxes it deserves and contribute our labor to fulfilling the First Five-Year Plan, to the construction of socialism in our patria." Between January and September of 1954 she sent at least three more petitions with similar content, one addressed to the Central Committee, another to the Ministry of Internal Affairs, and the third to Gheorghiu-Dej himself. The petitions aroused activity at several of these destinations. Of particular interest is a note sent from the Securitate of the district up to the region stating that she had been deported because her son, trained as a lawyer, had been active in the fascist Legionary movement, and she should not be sent home. The reason: "We presume he has contact with his mother even now, because the handwriting in ink on her petition is his handwriting." That same hand had directed her petition up to the Ministry of Internal Affairs, office of deported persons—as well as framing her petition in terms central to the Party's self-representation.

Petitions might have pedagogical effects beyond teaching people the categories necessary to talk with the Party and the locations for addressing it: they taught the police what people were thinking, and the consequent repression

[175] Dobrincu notes that just such a person wrote petitions in Darabani in the 1980s, charging five to ten lei for the work (Dobrincu, personal communication).

[176] The file with this case is found in ACNSAS, FP, file 15162, n.p.

taught peasants the bounds of complaint. On the basis of documents Vultur consulted for the Banat, she finds that the Securitate paid very close attention to any petitions or contestations, whether to prevent a situation from getting out of hand or to ascertain what "negative aspects" they revealed that might require taking "measures" (Vultur 2003a: 62). In November of 1962, dissatisfaction with the distribution of the harvest led seventeen villagers from Domaşnea to head for Bucharest "to complain about their petitions to leave the GAC and the fact that they had been investigated by the Securitate, [which asked them] from whom they had received the model for petitioning to withdraw from the GAC, from where they had sent it, and what was the content of their complaint to Bucharest" (Vultur 2003a: 86–87).[177]

Thus, petitions were a complex pedagogical device, one that cadres required of people in compelling their "voluntary adherence" to collectives or invited them to submit in contesting chiabur status; one that peasants themselves employed (as they had for two or more centuries) to contest the Party's actions—petitioning to withdraw from collectives, to complain about cadres' behavior, to seek justice; and one that the apparatus of surveillance used to discern the population's mood. In requiring peasants to petition to join the collectives, Party cadres adopted a preexisting form for communicating with the authorities and sought to turn it to new purposes, but the long tradition underlying them continued, sometimes to opposite effect.

Persuasion and Resistance

The rural population did not widely share the Party's embrace of socialist agriculture. Here we briefly take up what we call counterpedagogies—that is, pedagogical tools which countered the Party's claims on knowledge and offered an alternative framework for making sense of everyday life. Persons othered by the regime themselves engaged in an inverse process of othering, thereby asserting their own legitimacy. Thus, they deployed a politics of difference reciprocally.[178] Peasants, especially chiaburs, used a related repertoire of discursive and physical actions "through rumors, discrediting the GAC and voluntary associations, and, when these were not effective, through more open actions like threats or direct opposition to measures taken by the Party and government" (Vultur 2003a: 59–60). This politics of difference drew on the Party's own language and categories, discussed in the beginning of this chapter, and constituted a dynamic, interactive relationship between "them" and "us," the positive and negative connotations of which varied according to the speaker's or actor's position.

[177] Goina (2003: 26–33) discusses in detail the epidemic of petitions to leave the GAC in Sântana.

[178] Bonnell (1997: 205–6) notes a similar process during the Civil War in Russia in which the Bolsheviks and Whites battled each other through propaganda as well.

Both sides were trying to persuade peasants—one to support the regime, the other to defy it. For the former, their aims were revolutionary, for the latter, resistance; their *modi operandi* reflected their locations within the political hierarchy.

The battle lines between the regime and those who opposed it endured throughout the years of the collectivization campaign and class war. Peasants might be called to the village cultural center to attend films, reading circles, speeches, and unmaskings, or cadres might seek to persuade them in their houses; when cadres came to persuade, peasants hid or fled; propaganda lauded agricultural successes, which chiaburs contested through rumors or by persuading fellow peasants to engage in work stoppages. While the regime constructed a set of enemies who allegedly or actually engaged in oppositional or subversive activities aimed at undermining or overthrowing it, those enemies, in turn, disseminated their own antiregime propaganda, if more discreetly. Because such activity was outlawed, their options were fairly limited. We heard from many of our respondents about "weapons of the weak," which included a variety of counterpedagogies expressed through rumors, popular and critical poetry, jokes,[179] hidden histories in the form of memoirs, and the like. In our discussion here, we concentrate on rumors and slogans, briefly addressing popular poetry in chapter 6.[180] We emphasize that not all counterpedagogies can be considered forms of resistance: until 1989, a number of them (e.g., memoirs, critical poetry) were, at most, known to a very small and trusted circle of family members and friends, serving instead as means for people to unburden themselves in a private mode of "truth" production. Difference of opinion could be uttered in public only at great risk, although documents attest that "reactionary" youth shouted antiregime and anticollective rhymed couplets at Sunday village dances.[181] Written materials, to the extent that they circulated beyond a restricted group, were posted (a seeming variant of the wall gazettes) or delivered under cover of darkness.[182]

"Political enemies" in the broadest sense were the driving force behind the spread of antiregime propaganda and activity. The Securitate Bureau of the Sibiu region reported to Bucharest that "due to the propaganda promoted by the religious sector and their activities, poor and middle peasants have little faith in the regime."[183] An instructor who worked in the documentation section of the Sighet PMR sent a report about the national problem and enemy activi-

[179] See note 57 for one example.

[180] A link to a sample of poems can be found on the website www.press.princeton.edu/titles/9615.html, along with project Final Reports.

[181] ASRI, Fond 10, file 2/1950/Maramureş, 5.

[182] Manifestoes were posted in the middle of the night, such as one addressed to "[f]ellow peasants and intellectuals, sons of the mountains: Christ has risen," which goes on to urge them to fight against communism (see ACNSAS, FP 35094, file 1, 38). Political and religious books also circulated underground.

[183] See ACNSAS, FD, file 7/v. 5, 153.

ties in that city to the Regional PMR committee (Maramureş), asserting that, "Chiaburs are the motor of the rumor mill and intrigues between people in the collective."[184] "The class enemy makes use of the populace's lack of [class] consciousness and floats different rumors to frighten people."[185] For years the slogan "the Americans are coming!" fueled both anticommunist resistance and the Securitate's obsession with and fear of it.[186] Yet, at the same time, we underscore that the slogans and rumors that "enemies of the people" allegedly circulated mirrored formulaically the very categories the Party promulgated. Moreover, they are the same or similar all over the country, revealing a remarkable consistency (which makes one suspect that some of them, at least, were planted). Our material is culled not only from interviews, but from the Securitate's pulse-taking "mood reports"; from responses to questionnaires by local Party cells about enemy actions, the spreading of anticooperative rumors, or rumors in general;[187] and from unmaskings contained in newspaper articles, wall gazettes, and penal files, all of which were documented by or known to the Securitate. It is widely held that the secret police throughout the socialist era floated rumors to test the waters, to determine whether or not they could maintain control over a situation. In view of these sources and the danger associated with popular propaganda, some of the material we discuss below must be read with a degree of circumspection.[188]

Antiregime rumors, often in the form of fantastic stories, tended to address consistent themes. Because most of the ones we cite are representative of rumors circulating elsewhere in the country, we do not present multiple versions. Many were about the Soviet Union and life in collectives there (see also above): "The Bolsheviks aren't capable of leading and people will die of hunger in the collectives."[189] Salvationist rumors, of which the Americans' coming was the most widespread, offered false hope that communism was a temporary evil that would be defeated by the forces of good. This basic rumor about the Americans was augmented by claims that they had "developed a new tear gas bomb that left you numb."[190] These kinds of rumors could even survive American defeats: a Securitate mood report from 1950 stated, "There is much commentary, espe-

[184] ASRI, Fond D, file 4054, 196.

[185] DJAN MM, Fond Comitetul Judeţean PMR Sighet, file 89/1950, 93.

[186] Penal files are filled with accusations against peasants who allegedly circulated such rumors, many of whom probably did. They were said to be hiding in the hills waiting to join forces with the Americans. Photos of the accused often showed them with rifles slung across their chests with which—fighting together with the Americans—they would defeat the Soviet Union. (See, for example, ACNSAS, FP, file 84.)

[187] See, for example, ASRI, Fond D, file 4054.

[188] We also see remarkable consistency in the counterpedagogies at work in other communist regimes, whether in the Soviet bloc, China, or Vietnam.

[189] ASRI, Fond D, file 4054, 187 from the Constanţa region; Cătănus and Roske 2004: 43, Bârlad.

[190] ASRI, Fond D, file 4054, 219. "The Americans are coming" constitutes a secularized form of the salvationist and messianic beliefs widespread in rural Romania during the interwar years.

cially by reactionary elements, on the defeat of the Americans by the Korean People's Army in Korea. . . . People say the Americans let themselves be beaten on purpose so the Soviet Union will underestimate them and then lose in the coming war."[191] Closely associated were stories that "the war will begin and the communists won't be able to take more grain" (Cătănuş and Roske 2004: 43), meaning that obligatory quotas would cease. Some even intimated that "in a few days, the Yugoslav partisans who are in the nearby forests" would come to liberate them, a wish that Tito, the defiant Yugoslav leader whose fighters were already in Romania hiding in the woods, would save them from the Soviet yoke.[192]

Related to salvationist rumors were tales of divine intervention and retribution: "A man, upon seeing that his wife had replaced the icons of Mary and Jesus with a portrait of Stalin, ordered her to take it down because Stalin wouldn't come to her aid when she was in need. Not long thereafter, she became sick: both of her arms were paralyzed and she couldn't eat by herself. Her husband refused to help her; instead, he told her, 'Now, call upon Stalin to help you!'" (Oláh 2003: 31). Another woman who was a Party member took all of the prayer books from her house and threw them away in the outhouse, which happened to be located at the edge of a hill. The outhouse, with the blasphemous woman inside, toppled over (39). In Vlaicu, one I. S., who had married into a village family of modest means and become a big communist, not to mention dutiful police informer, public derider of chiaburs, and tormentor of his animals, received his due:

> One night a bunch of cadres came to his house and were socializing together. At one point, he went out to relieve himself in the barn, where he kept some stallions. Time passed and the others began wondering why he hadn't come back. They went out to the barn and found him dead: the stallions had killed him! Probably he beat them and they struck back. Some say that he wasn't completely dead, for when they were burying him, several people including his wife said they heard him moving around in his coffin. But they buried him anyway.[193]

In a society in which public sources of information were centrally controlled, rumors increasingly acquired popular legitimacy as alternative sources of truth production. Chiaburs, for example, spread all kinds of rumors about GACs in general and what would happen to those who joined. A widow kept telling oth-

[191] ACNSAS, FD, file 5, 242.

[192] ASRI, Fond D, file 4638, August 20, 1950, report, page unclear; Cătănus and Roske 2004: 43, see also chapter 2, note 54.

[193] 151, Verdery interview. Such attributions of divine justice also have an afterlife in the postsocialist period. Local Party officials and Securitate who had abused their fellow villagers suffered for their deeds, felled by debilitating conditions or death. "God didn't let them off the hook" (Vultur 2003a: 68). Those who survived long years of imprisonment, torture, and the like all volunteered (to Kligman) that their former abusers had died well before them, the hand of God at work.

ers "it would be better to cut off your fingers than join the GAC," and two men, one of whom was said to be a former legionary, warned that those "who join the collectives will die of hunger."[194] In the Caraş district, peasants dissatisfied with the inadequate state provisioning circulated a rumor that in Timişoara, "certain individuals cut several children into pieces and sold them to the population in place of meat" (the rumor was noted in Timişoara itself).[195] Some chiaburs told their fellow villagers that "it wasn't good that they'd formed a collective because . . . the communists are like scabies that cannot be gotten rid of easily."[196] A local Party report claimed that a chiabur prophesied that "the sky will darken and it will rain fire." (Commenting on the susceptible mentality of the peasants, the Securitate report continued, "The result of this . . . they've bought candles.")[197] Others cautioned that they would be sent to Siberia. A village midwife "who received a salary from the state" told a poor peasant woman suffering from an eye problem "who had joined the collective that if she did not withdraw from it, she would go blind!"[198] And a dissatisfied GAC member cursed those who duped her into joining, telling everyone that, as retribution, "their eyes were going to dry up."[199] She also said that "the Soviets are laughing at us because we formed a collective when they've dismantled theirs!"[200]

Yet others threatened that when the Party collapsed—like other parties, it wouldn't last long—they would strangle the communists, or take out their eyes and tongues, etc.[201] The events of 1956 in Hungary raised hopes and rumors about the imminent overthrow of communism in Romania: "what happened in Hungary will happen here in Romania in a week at most" (Stalin region), "if they don't put an end to these quotas, then what happened in Hungary will happen here" (Piteşti region). In the Reghin district of the Magyar Autonomous Region a Romanian exclaimed, "I'm the only chiabur left on the list and I paid the taxes of an exploiter, but the events in Hungary have turned the tables on Hungary's communists, and they will turn here as well. The Hungarians proved that nationalism counts more than anything, proving that they are Hungarians first and then communists." He added that the "Hungarian flag with the hammer and sickle was replaced with the [Romanian] tricolor."[202] Slogans formed

194 DJAN MM, Fond Comitetul Regional PCR Maramureş, file 42/1962, 20.

195 ACNSAS, FD, file 5, 298.

196 ASRI, Fond D, file 4054, 226.

197 See Arhiva Primăriei Ieud, "Raport despre mersul schimbului de teren în c. Ieud, în vederea formării GACului PMR, j. Maramureş," 25.II.1950.

198 See ACNSAS, FP, file 248/v. 2, 9.

199 ASRI, Fond D, file 4054, 187.

200 Ibid., 49

201 ASRI, Fond D, file 4054, 219. It is interesting that eyesight is so often mentioned as a form of affliction against those who failed to see what communist enlightenment was. Presumably removing tongues was punishment for all of the lies they spread.

202 For the rumors about Hungary, see ANIC, Fond C.C. al P.C.R.–Organizatorică, file 43/1956, 17, 19, 72.

part of the arsenal of popular propaganda, mirroring its Party analogue. These too were formulaic in character, with the same or similar slogans reported across the country. Standard slogans included "Down with the communists!" and "Down with the Jews and Communists!" which were more likely pronounced during antiregime revolts than in everyday encounters. Political slogans such as the ubiquitous "the Americans are coming" additionally praised enemy leaders such as King Michael and Iuliu Maniu (head of the Peasant Party): "Long live the King and Maniu, the parents of all Romanians!" "Whoever has blood coursing through his veins should vote for Maniu!"[203] Religious slogans exhorted "Long life to the Pope!" There were also slogans pertaining to obligatory quotas and the collectives: "We won't give one grain of wheat!"[204]

Aside from turning to opposite effect the slogan form that cadres used in their propaganda work, peasants might register their reactions in yet another consecrated propaganda form: folk poetry. Here is a fragment from a poem entitled "Persuasion Work," from Ieud (Pleş-Chindriş 2009: 126–27):

Why are you still waiting, comrade?
Willy-nilly, you won't escape
Don't you know that the entire country
Wants collectivization?
To achieve happiness
Just sign your name
Do it the earlier the better
Right now, even. Why are you waiting?
. . . .
You'll see how good it is
To work in the collective
When from your own concerns
You will escape for good.
I fell into the illusion
And believed everybody
Those who do propaganda
And say that bad is good.
And so by signing my name
I've gone from being master to servant
With a fixed wage
Seven lei for a day's work.
. . . .
Those who sit in the shade all summer
Like dogs at the sheepfold

[203] ACNSAS, FP, file 84/v. 4, 45.

[204] This slogan was a basic one, which was often further elaborated, "because it will be commercialized by Jews" (Roske 2004: 43, from Bihor).

> Those who don't do a thing
> Except to call you and order you about,
> They took my horses and cart
> They took my plough and my harrow
> And everything I had in my house
> And put a hoe in my hand.
> . . . .
> Let's divide the rewards of our work
> Among those who waste their time
> Long live the lazy!
> That's how it is all over the land.

Antiregime propaganda in these counterpedagogical genres circulated largely in restricted circles, clandestinely, anonymously, or in the heat of the moment during peasant revolts.[205] Perhaps most importantly for our purposes, we note that these counterpedagogies served the interests of the secret police in legitimating their claims about enemies, that is, in persuading others—Party officials and sympathizers, judges, and colleagues—that the regime's enemies employed diverse and pernicious means to work against it. In this way, as we suggested in chapter 2 concerning the dialectic of violence and resistance, we see a process of reciprocal learning in which the Party's tools of persuasion are appropriated and sometimes turned against it, causing an intensification of its methods.

Conclusion

In this chapter we have described a variety of methods by which the Party's leaders and cadres sought to transform consciousness and gain adherence to its collectivization project, through propagating a new regime of truth. Guided by the Soviet example, they recategorized the social world, reinstituting and politicizing forms of difference—religion, nationality, political orientations, and so forth. They created a mobilizing language aimed at specific goals and deployed it in multiple media: films, wall gazettes, art forms. Then they devised a number of ways of putting this language into people's mouths, beating it into them when necessary. Through teaching peasants to denounce and unmask enemies and to communicate with the benevolent paternalist Party in its own terms, these techniques inculcated new rules for producing truth and for understanding the

[205] Political propaganda in support of Maniu and others circulated before the fateful election that the communists "won," but public expression was curtailed after these leaders and prominent intellectuals were imprisoned. Some who had anonymously threatened the two GAC presidents that "their houses would be blown up with dynamite" or who instigated others to engage in violent acts received sentences of ten years of hard labor. See Roske 2003: 116.

world. That the techniques also provoked counterstatements is less important than that the counterstatements adopted the Party's language.

There were, of course, other forms of reaction to the pedagogies of collectivization, which we have emphasized in earlier chapters: violent uprisings, attacks on cadres, overt acts of sabotage, and so on. In choosing to focus here on the less spectacular forms of resistance, we do not wish to suggest an absence of violent opposition but rather to highlight forms less often reported—forms that had the paradoxical effect of both opposing the Party's intentions and enabling its categories to take firmer root, as peasants used them toward their own ends. These counterpedagogies were the more pervasive means by which peasants responded to the symbolic violence that Party officials employed to build a case for collective agriculture, alongside the more-often-noted beatings and coercion. To dismiss this pedagogical dialogue as insignificant leads to an impoverished understanding of the complex process whereby peasants at length signed over their land and the Party created its practices of power.

Whether created and deployed by Party agitators and others, or created and spread by enemies, all these pedagogies served as potent tools of persuasion. They were joined with one more, perhaps the most potent among them: the one-on-one persuasion work with which collectivization cadres were charged, to which we now turn. Armed with the pedagogical arsenal discussed thus far, they set off on the daunting task of convincing peasants that socialist agriculture held the keys to a better and brighter future. The pedagogical tools at their disposal were meant to enlighten peasants, to enable them to understand what was expected of them in creating the new social order. But when enlightenment fell upon deaf ears, the Janus-faced aspect of persuasion work kicked in. Cadres added physical violence to the repertoire of pedagogies, making certain that their lessons were well embodied and would not soon be forgotten.

Chapter 5

Pedagogies of Persuasion

> How can you think that these people, who are ready to kill each other over a piece of land, people who cry more over losing some cattle than over losing a child, how can you think that these people can suddenly put their cattle and land together, that they can part with their cows and land?
> —*Ana Pauker, 1951 meeting of the Agrarian Section of the CC*[1]

> Around the end of July 1950, it was a Sunday, comrade Moraru Ion, the party secretary from Aiud, came and called us all to a meeting. They told us that those who join the collective get 3 hectares of land, 50-*ari* garden plots, and can keep a cow for milk, 10 sheep, and other things. Then comrade Moraru said: "You listened to what I had to say, but know that, whether you want it or not, there will be a collective! If I have to bang your head against the walls, we'll have a collective!" We thought about what this collective could be because it hadn't been explained to us. We went home and on Monday went to work as usual. On Monday evening a car came and they picked up two chiaburs, two poor peasants, and a middle peasant, and took them away. . . . and they came back on Tuesday. They were horribly beaten up and Varadi Ion's head was bleeding.
> —*Susana Ciortea, peasant, describing persuasion work to Pauker and Gheorghiu-Dej, 1951*[2]

> You had no choice but to join. Voluntarily! Of necessity voluntarily! [*Obligat voluntar!*][3]

As THE PREVIOUS chapter has shown, the Romanian Communist Party had many means of drawing the peasantry into its communicative forms and rituals and from there into collective farms, as well as into a new state-subject relation.[4] Now we will concentrate on another set of techniques for creating such relations: "persuasion work" (*muncă de lămurire*), one of the most fundamental categories of the work of a political activist during the collectivization campaign. Persuasion work was another element of a new regime of truth or knowledge production, as is evident from the meanings of its root term: *lămurire*, which can be translated as "explanation," "clarification" or "clearing up," or, most broadly, "enlightenment." We refer to it as "persuasion," because the knowledge

[1] Cited in Levy 2001: 108, 109.

[2] Moraru et al. 2004: 542.

[3] Unnamed German respondent, Goina interview (2003: 40).

[4] Sections of this chapter (along with parts of chapters 3 and 4) were published as an article in *East European Politics and Societies* 25 (2), 2011, and appear in this book with permission.

it propagated was mobilizational; it aimed to enlighten peasants about the benefits of the new order, to spread the Party's ideas in the villages, and to alter consciousness. Pedagogical intent was its essence. Persuasion work began with "plans of action" developed in Party meetings at each level—region, district, commune—and applied to people at every level as well. Higher-level cadres would do persuasion work with lower-level ones: to enlighten them was at least as important as enlightening the peasantry, if they were to do their job. Persuasion was used toward a number of different goals—making peasants hand over their quotas, pay taxes, bring in bigger harvests, and so on—but for the villagers, it came to mean especially the attempt to get them into the associations (TOZs) or collective farms, and that is how we will treat it here.

Ostensibly, the object of persuasion work was a person's will, owing to Party leaders' insistence that peasants must join collectives only by their "free consent" (*liber consimțământ*). A peasant from Ieud put his finger squarely on the problem: as he was being pressed to sign up, he reportedly asked, "I still want to know just one thing: Is it mandatory to request joining the collective? Clearly, it's obvious that if it's a request, it's not mandatory, and if it's mandatory, it's not a request."[5] The basic paradox was that Party cadres wanted subjects who seemed to consent, but they had to *produce* those subjects. The various means included physical violence; we should not see this as an aberration, however, but as reflecting that central contradiction.

In seeking to produce consent, persuasion involved an apparent incitement to speech, drawing the peasants into dialogue with cadres during which they would learn to inhabit the Party's categories (see chapter 4). This point is important. We believe it is deceptive, in thinking about the effects of persuasion work, to emphasize a changed state of belief—what we would usually understand as "persuasion." Perhaps except for the initial round of collectives (formed in 1949 and early 1950), persuasion rarely convinced peasants of the superiority of collective agriculture. Nor, it seems, did many cadres care about that, for what they ultimately sought was the *performance* of consent, a behavioral matter rather than a matter of inner conviction (see also Yurchak 2006; Wood 2005). Peasants had to sign up, whether they believed in socialized agriculture or not; once they did so, they were considered persuaded. Their participation in the encounter, however, did persuade them in a significant way: into the terms of discourse for living with the Party and the practices that exhibited their "persuasion." Had cadres been better trained and more adept at communicating the virtues of collectives, this performative dimension might have been less pronounced.[6]

[5] P.C.G., Kligman interview.

[6] That is, in emphasizing the performative, we are motivated not primarily by the fashionableness of this notion in contemporary theory but by its suitability to our specific case. If Holquist is correct, here we see an important respect in which Romanian communism was "premodern": he argues that modern governmentality concerned itself precisely with inner states of belief, not just with achieving behavioral submission (1997: 436).

Persuasion was ongoing, always in process, never finished. People might be persuaded to join the collective, but then some event would convince them to withdraw from it and they would have to be persuaded all over again. Moreover, persuasion came in a wide range of forms and involved widely different kinds of actors. Its prototype was talk—indeed, in the words of one respondent, the main selection criterion was that a person be a smooth talker (Stoica 2009: 432). Some of our respondents could recall activists who did observe the stricture of free consent and who sought to convince them by explaining how life in the collective would be better for everyone. Others mentioned the negotiated quality of some of the interactions, as agitators not only offered arguments for joining but also made promises, gave gifts (watches were a favorite), and accorded favors. But if these tactics failed, cadres might move on to increasingly explicit threats and force including arrest, deportation, incarceration, and physical violence. Although activists of the time might not have called the latter actions part of "persuasion," we do so, following the usage of many of our interviewees, who commented sarcastically on the idea of "free consent."

Unlike many of the technologies discussed in chapter 4, which engaged people collectively (propaganda, invitations to imitate or to unmask), persuasion work brought peasants into more direct, sustained, and individualized contact with cadres seeking to collectivize them; it was carefully targeted at particular kinds of people. But it was still quintessentially social, in two senses. First, it made use of social distinctions meaningful within villages, such as kinship, gender, or degrees of wealth; and second, it was propagated through social links, as people talked with neighbors or looked out the window to see whom activists were accosting in the street. In this sense, persuasion work was both a pedagogy and an instrument of organizational breakthrough. More than most of the techniques discussed in the preceding chapter, and like the practice of fomenting class war to be discussed in the next, persuasion work made direct use of the prewar village social organization we presented in chapter 2. The two basic principles of that organization were kinship and differential status, based especially on landholding; together these determined relations among households and the control of labor. Kinship and landholding were intertwined in ideas about blood, birth, land, and inheritance, as well as in generational transmission of land. These notions also underpinned local ideologies distinguishing "locals" from "outsiders," a distinction that was important in persuasion work.

Persuasion work built upon the forms we have already described—new cultural categories, a politics of difference, propaganda, and mimesis, especially the use of positive and negative mimetic examples. Because villagers had always kept track of who was where, neighbors knew whom cadres were visiting, and word spread. When someone was beaten, he was an example to all those who saw him stumble home bruised and limping. Unmasking and other forms of public humiliation, too, were simultaneously forms of persuasion work. Thus, this chapter is intimately tied with the previous one. We begin by asking what peasants understood a collective farm to be, then present some of their recollections of the persuasion process. The bulk of the chapter considers different aspects of persuasion work and its dynamics over time and space, including the forms of resistance peasants mounted against a process whose success by no means seemed to them inevitable, at first. Throughout, we identify a tension between an idea of informed consent and a performative emphasis for which inner states were irrelevant: truth was in the performance, not in conviction. The reason was at least partly that many cadres did not really understand what they were supposed to be creating.

What Was a "Collective Farm"?

Cadres were dispatched to persuade peasants to join the collectives, yet local idioms and organizational forms did not offer them much to work with.[7] Unlike the Russian communal village (the *mir*; see Fitzpatrick 1994b), for instance, or the extended family among Macedonian peasants that provided a plausible local idiom for collectivization (the *zadruga*; see K. Brown 2003), Romanian peasants had little positive experience with collective forms. Coming from the social world we described in chapter 2, what did they think a "collective farm" was? How did they envision it, and how would it work? How would it solve their life problems? Through persuasion work, cadres were supposed to give them an image of a collective farm and of how people would live and work in it. Obstructing their task, however, were a number of negative images, including those from villagers who lived near the Soviet border or who had spent part of World War II on the Soviet front or as prisoners of war.[8] "Collective farms enjoyed a bad reputation because of prisoners of war, who adamantly denounced the difficult life of Soviet peasants in *kolhozes* [sic]" (Stoica 2009: 443). Doubtless aggravating these negative images, as we have already indicated, were unfavorable stereotypes of Russians.[9] If collectivization was a kind of technology transfer, one of its chief impediments was that unlike other circumstances in which a technology or its bearers are admired, in this case both were held in contempt.

[7] We owe a debt to Puiu Lățea, who first raised this question and provided many of the ideas and examples in this section.

[8] Additionally, men who had been prisoners in Russia in World War I had learned some Russian and could communicate with the Soviet soldiers who came through during World War II.

[9] Imagery of this kind is nonetheless tamer than that reported among Russian peasants, who understood collectivization as the apocalypse: "In the collective farm . . . invalids and the elderly will be killed, there won't be any husbands or wives, [all] will sleep under a one-hundred-meter blanket. . . . Children will be taken from their parents, there will be wholesale incest." "Some said the collective farm signaled the reign of the Antichrist on earth" (Viola 1996: 59, 45). See also Fitzpatrick (1994b) and Davies (1980).

Romanian villagers had an advantage over peasants in the 1930s Soviet Union, where the kolkhoz was invented: at least some Romanians had heard of it before they had to join one. Judging by the recollections of our respondents, what they knew was definitely not positive. One aspect is worth specific mention: images related to food. According to one respondent, retreating German soldiers at the war's end "shouted through their megaphones, 'Brother Romanians! You've seen how it is in the USSR, in the *kolkhoz*! They'll feed you in a canteen!'" (Stoica 2009: 438). This idea was widespread: "Yes, I'd heard about the kolkhoz. I heard people would have to take a little ladle and a bowl to go and get their soup."[10] "Everybody at the *kolhoz* ate from a big, single pot" (Stoica 2009: 439):

> That's what people said, that we'd get to eating from a ladle, like the Russians. There were people in Russia who didn't have houses, they didn't have anything, you know, and everyone lived there and ate there . . . and people said we were going to do the same, go out there and eat together [at the collective]. Nobody had a house, in Russia, that's what people said. . . . People who had been to Russia, they were the ones who said that. (Goina 2003: 18)[11]

Canteen, big pot, people without their own houses—peasants thought of the collective as an undifferentiated mass, and this diminished their interest in it. Imagery that involved eating in common had significant implications for the destruction of village customs regarding hospitality: if no one had food at home, people would no longer be able to create their own work groups or socialize with their kin—that is, they could no longer live within social units of their own making.[12] They would have nothing left for currying favor with high-status people or cadres who might protect them, nor for the obligatory feasting on the many saints' days that had marked their work time. Compromised sociality meant compromised community of the kind they had known. As chapter 6 will show, that was precisely an effect of class war, which compromised rural hospitality patterns and community reproduction.

Another image—that of *grămadă*, a mass, heap, or pile—resonated with that of "eating from a big, single pot" and similarly fueled peasants' reticence to embrace the benefits that collective farms would supposedly bring them. A number of examples drawn from different regions of Romania show the variety of ways the image appears in our respondents' reflections about the collectives

[10] 108, Verdery interview.

[11] S. A., Goina interview. It is worth noting that in 2002, when the interview took place, this illiterate peasant woman thought that this was how things still were in Russia—that people had no food and ate at the collective from a common ladle. Ceaușescu's systematization plan, launched in the mid-1970s with reports of common kitchens and toilets, may have affected people's memories on this matter.

[12] Other words expressed the same idea: eating "*la gamelă*" (at the canteen), "*la șaică*" (with a ladle)," "*la cazan*" (from a cauldron). "Old people told us that we would end up like in Russia, like in Russia. From a cauldron."

Figure 5.1. Weeding carrots "la grămadă" in the GAS "G. Coşbuc," Mediaş. Courtesy of MNIR/www.comunismulinromania.ro.

and collective practice: (1) "Every house had two oxen and, if they could, a cow as well. . . . But when collectivization came, they gathered up everything, they made a pile [*grămadă*] there. . . . Oxen, carts, cows, everything." (2) (*How much time passed before the animals were taken away?*): "Not right when we joined because they had nowhere to keep them, until they made the stables and so on. Where could they gather them all in a heap [*grămadă*]?" (3) "They wouldn't let people thresh wheat at home as we used to, they gathered it out in [the pasture] all *la grămadă*." (4) "They plowed up all the land *grămadă*, there was just one big furrow, there were no more boundaries." (5) "[People] said, 'The colhoz is coming and then we'll all work *la grămadă*.'" (6) "The brigadier was a good fellow. He measured after we reaped, since we all worked *la grămadă* . . . by teams." (See figure 5.1.)

Like eating from one big pot, *grămadă* evokes an image of the collective as crowded, jumbled together, and disorderly. It contradicts the ideas of rules, order, proportion. Furthermore, its elements are undifferentiated. Unlike what people had considered normal social relations, forms of eating, work groups, animals, piles of wheat, pieces of land, and so on—which were differentiated by family status and social relationships—items in the collective were indistinguishable from one another. In a *grămadă*, one person's cow or horse, or piece of land, or pile of wheat, or labor power was treated no differently from another's. The new social order of the collective was no order at all.

How was the Party leadership to combat such images, rumors, and ideas and to create a representation of something the peasants would want to join? We have already discussed some of the techniques used, including propaganda, various artistic forms (film, plays), and visits by groups of peasants to model Soviet and Romanian collective farms, as well as visits by peasants from successful collectives to other settlements. In this way, peasants were pressed into the work of persuasion alongside cadres: "They took us to Orăşeni so we could tell the general assembly there what our life is like in the collective. We had to show what harvest we had, how we worked the land, what we earned for our workdays."[13] But these examples proved unpersuasive, compared with the negative instances, which were sometimes so unappealing that members would leave those GACs to go and work on the Danube–Black Sea Canal, Romania's gulag, where political prisoners were sent![14] This was part of what made the GAC implausible and therefore (many believed) unlikely to last. Cadres' problem in creating an attractive imaginary was aggravated by a widespread sense that the collective was ephemeral—partly because it violated all social norms, as we have been suggesting, and partly from the persistent hope that the Americans would come to the rescue. Here is an example:

> You know what kinds of rumors there were in those days. We had a bit of land [two hectares], let's say, my father raised animals here, we had a plow, we had a horse, we had everything we needed. So then, how was I to leave and let all this go to waste, and go work in a factory. . . . And what if the Americans came and we'd get our land back and I wouldn't have any animals to work the land with. . . . That's how they'd confound us. . . . We were so confused we didn't know what to do! (Ţârău 2003: 19)

With this kind of thinking, cadres seeking to enlighten the peasantry would have needed true inspiration to create interest in collective farms.

The evidence suggests, however, that they themselves were equally in the dark: frequent reports of Party members refusing to join the GACs indicate that activists could not generate images that persuaded even village communists, much less others. To begin with, they were not performing their jobs, a frequent complaint in Central Committee and Politburo meetings.[15] In Darabani, "[i]nstitutions and firms with the task of assigning employees every day to go to the commune's villages . . . for the work of collectivizing did not send these people," and "employees, Party members, and other GAC members residing in the villages did not involve themselves in the work of persuasion" (Dobrincu 2003a: 43). Second, many cadres did not believe in what they were doing or know enough about it. As late as 1957, the president of the Executive Committee of the People's Council in Lueta reported his frustration with the Committee and other council members:

> We called a meeting of the organizing committee and discussed urgent issues. We concluded that even on the organizing committee there are representatives who are still not convinced of the superiority of socialist agriculture, and who still have not joined the socialist sector and, moreover, who have not made their petitions to join. These comrades have no moral standing to conduct persuasion work with anyone else. Even on the executive committee there are people who own land and keep clear

[13] 3, Oláh interview.

[14] ACNSAS, FD, file 5, 277 (for 1950).

[15] For example, ANIC, Fond 1, file 55/1951, 9–11 (RLA).

> of the collective farm, like Orban Gyorgy [sic] for instance, who says he completely supports the strengthening of the socialist sector but he's not going to join just yet. Miklos [sic] Anna, the vice-president, has also been staying away. The executive committee cannot rely on such people. (Oláh 2003: 37)

The same complaints recur elsewhere:

> Agitators from the communes and villages were trained to work for the creation of GACs and Associations . . . [yet] the new presidents and secretaries of the commune councils . . . don't know [the relevant decrees] or the model statute of GACs, and they often cannot answer questions that peasants put to them, making a lot of political mistakes. We have to give them special lessons about how to create GACs.[16]

A high-ranking activist, participating in a 1954 meeting with Moghioroş, reported on a persuasion session he had attended: "A Party meeting was held and people raised the problem of not understanding what is meant by work in common. We had to demonstrate it on the blackboard in front of everyone. It wasn't understood, and wasn't understood even by the Party activists."[17]

When Romanian peasants asked cadres what a collective farm meant, in practical terms, then, it often seemed no one could tell them very precisely. Comparisons with the Soviet experience show the same thing: the great majority of the activists invading Soviet villages had no knowledge of agriculture and sought to persuade the peasants on the basis of theory, making rash promises. They had no answers to the peasants' practical questions about how the work would be organized, thus increasing the peasants' suspicions (Lewin 1968: 418, 431). With dynamic leadership like this, it is scarcely surprising that in our interviews, respondents were hard pressed to recall specific arguments about how the collective would work. Although they could remember tactics such as being told "You have no choice! You have to join!" or "We'll throw you out of your job and your children out of school," the more positive arguments—the ones that would enable them to envision their lives as collectivists concretely—came less easily. For example, here are some of the characteristic responses to our question, "What arguments did they make?": "They told us how good it would be, how you'd work all over and boundaries would disappear, everything would be a single field and the harvest would be good and the collectivists would be really well paid. That kind of thing."[18] "It'll be fine, we'll give you whatever your heart desires."[19] "Look, it'll be better in the collective, you won't have to work as hard."[20] "This is the Party's policy! It will be better, there'll be machinery, you'll

[16] Report by the Orăştie district Agrarian Section, DJAN HD, Fond CR PMR, file 20/1952, 82, 84.

[17] ANIC, Fond C.C. al P.C.R.–Cancelarie, file 14/1954, 2, 4 (RLA).

[18] 217, Verdery interview.

[19] M. T., Lăţea interview. Quoted in Lăţea 2003: 68–69.

[20] P. N., Budrală interview for M. Stewart.

work like in the factory eight hours a day, no more getting up at 3:00 a.m."[21] And most tellingly, "Join the collective, 'cuz it'll be sort of . . . 'cuz it's good, 'cuz communist doctrine . . . 'cuz passing from one phase to another is hard."[22]

These were not compelling arguments for joining, nor did they provide a clear image of what life in a collective would be. They utterly failed to address questions basic to any peasant household's existence: Without land and animals, what will happen to the elderly? To our daughters' dowries? How will people get married if there's no land? How will we know who is an honorable man? Such questions preoccupied primarily the middle and wealthy peasants, for whom land was inextricable from the reproduction of status through marriage and social relations, and it was the lack of answers to such questions that kept all but the poor from lining up to join. Evidently, cadres were not being well enough prepared to endow the collectivization effort with vision. (Indeed, a visiting Soviet delegation in 1951 made precisely this point: "Wherever we went, we found work with cadres poorly organized, and agricultural specialists are not yet sufficiently mobilized to instruct cadres properly.")[23]

Because poorly trained cadres were unable to produce a satisfactory collective imaginary, the persuasion process was to be prolonged and ritualized, with numerous breaches of the rules of etiquette and increasing resort to force, as we shall see. If activists could not help peasants to imagine the collective and join it willingly, then they would immobilize or constrain peasants' bodies until people were finally worn down, gave up, and joined. Cadres' failure to present a compelling vision—a consequence of their inadequate numbers and weak preparation—was what transformed persuasion from being a matter of conviction to a performative matter. Let us explore the experience of persuasion in greater detail.

Remembering Persuasion

Our project's archival data and several hundred interviews contain innumerable comments about persuasion in response to our questions about how collectivization took place, indicating that persuasion was an indelible feature of the process. We begin with a lengthy interview conducted in 1960 with a refugee from the Constanța region—that is, this interview, unlike ours, was done at the time of collectivization—followed by the recollection of a state functionary

[21] 186, Verdery interview. This respondent was at the time a candidate member for the Party and might have had a better idea than most as to what the activists were saying.

[22] S. A., Lățea interview.

[23] ANIC, Fond C.C. al P.C.R.–Agrară, file 29/1951, 13–14. A year later, the Ministry of State Farms requested the extension of a Soviet advisor's stay, since this Ministry "is a new apparatus and could not create superior technical cadres specializing in the problem of State Agricultural Farms" (ANIC, Fond C.C. al P.C.R.–Agrară, file 10/1952, 6).

about doing persuasion work. We then present a number of other examples that give a sense of how our village respondents retrospectively represent persuasion—often with humor—after which we will systematize some of its most important features. (We do not indicate ellipses or respondents' repetitions.)[24]

First, extracts from a report of the 1960 interview:

> Dobruja (the Constanța region) was the area where the RWP acquired much experience in the collectivization drive, enabling them to adopt and introduce a number of refinements to the older methods.
>
> The general agitator, who before had been a youngster of the fanatic type, was replaced by a middle age activist, more tactful. His first task was no longer that of directly "persuading" the peasants to join or set up a collective farm, but that of winning over one or two leading peasants in the village. The second move was a ceremony organized by the administration cultural center of the district (not the Party one) on a Sunday. To this ceremony were invited all the local peasants, as well as a number of already collectivized peasants from neighboring villages. The latter continually boasted about the blessings of collective farming, etc.
>
> The third move was the arrival of the tax-collector. He started assessing all individual property, and then served the bills to the apprehensive peasants. Taxes on land are payable in advance in money, as well as in kind, in particular milk and meat. Having served the bills on the peasants, the tax-collector would leave the village, announcing that he would be back in a couple of weeks to collect the money. He would also warn the peasants that those who failed to pay would have their property, including their homes, sold at auction.
>
> The peasants would find that their taxes would be well above what their land was worth. With little hope they would file a contestation with the nearest district Fiscal Center. There they would be advised by non-Party employees (most of whom would have relatives in the neighboring villages) that they should become collectivized, this being the only way and the best way of their being absolved of their debts to the state.
>
> When finally doubt begins to find its way into the peasants' mind, the time has come for the village informer to announce to the center that "the village is ripe." This would be the sign for five or six truckfulls of collectivized peasants to visit the village. They are invited to the People's Council together with the local peasants. There they watch one or two leading peasants (those who had been won over in the first phase of the campaign) sign before the notary public to the sound of bands and applause of the visiting collectivists. This gesture is imitated by a series of relatives (godfather and mothers, etc.) and by all those other peasants who wish to do so or have to do so (because of the taxes). In case some form of resistance is encountered (this comes particularly from the wives) the collectivization committee has the freedom to leave in the peasant's private ownership one or two hectares of land (with which the Communists deal later on when the time is "ripe" again, or even before that time).

[24] See also Băileşteanu (1987: 192–273), whose novel contains a great deal of information on persuasion work in the Dolj region. (Thanks to Puiu Lățea for this reference.)

Generally, whenever the collectivization drive encounters serious resistance, the security troops are called in. Nowadays they no longer shoot to kill, but, nevertheless, leave behind them some wounded, and never leave the village without at least a handful of prisoners. If this type of action proves necessary, the peasants are "appeased" by being given a scapegoat. A Party agitator and/or one or two members of the collectivization committee are arrested. Sometimes Party representatives from the nearest organization tell the peasants that those "beasts" will be expelled from the Party and severely punished for having used terror while the Party and comrade Gheorghiu-Dej had recommended respect for the peasants' "free will." However, the drive and the same methods for achieving collectivization go on nonetheless, relentlessly.

"A very intensive work of 'enlightenment' was carried on by the Communists," says source. "They visited every house and insisted on its members signing the application for joining the kolkhoz. My hostess and their daughter asked my advice on what to do, I advised them strongly to give in because there was no way of avoiding the end of this problem. Finally they consented to sign. But what impressed me much," said source, "was that the woman put on black clothes and a black scarf, and signed the application in that attire, of a mourner. She considered that day a day of mourning."

When this "peaceful campaign of persuasion" was considered at an end but no satisfactory results, the regime went over to the last phase of "persuasion." The village was "literally invaded" by about 300 Party activists, Party members, workers and functionaries from the enterprises of the Focşani, Tecuci, Galaţi neighboring towns accompanied by a fully armed detachment of militia summoned from the Focşani town. They set up quarters in the various official buildings, and organized themselves as if some special tasks had to be carried out.[25]

Next, a recollection by a state functionary drawn into persuasion work:

In the period when associations were being re-formed to make way for collectives, I went with a team to a village where people had set fire to their harvested crops. A Party official locked everyone in a room all day trying to get them to join. After a while [one of our team] said, "You're burning down your own food, you won't have anything to eat." A fellow said, "Sir, I keep asking myself why the Americans aren't coming to free us from the Russians." Here's the reply: "Let me tell you a story about a ram and a fox. One long cold winter a fox was very hungry. Right at the edge of the forest it sees a huge, fine ram with immense testicles, munching on the grass. As the ram walks back and forth, its balls swing magnificently from side to side. The fox says to itself, 'I'll just wait here, and soon those balls will fall off and then I'll have a great feast.' It waited and waited, and finally it died of hunger. Good people, don't burn your crops or the same thing will happen to you, because the Americans are not going to come."[26]

[25] Dumitrescu 1960: passim (original in English).

[26] M. H. and K. L., Verdery interview (1999).

Finally, the words of some of our village respondents:

They divided us into sectors, and they came to everyone and the verdict was "either you join the collective or I'll throw your child out of university." A case was the cousin of the teacher, A. D. She was a student in agronomy and they threw her out. Another method was with jobs. They sent them home from work and said, "I won't give you back your job until you bring an affidavit that you've joined the CAP." Another method was, since there were a lot who'd been arrested as "politicals" and been in prison, to tell them, "What's the idea, are you resisting the state? Do you want to go back to jail?" The Securitate was here, a lot of people resisted and they would come in the evening with a [black] car, take them to Orşova and hold them for a day, then send them back the next night. I don't know if they beat them but they drove them around. And this was how they started the CAP, with these methods. One they'd catch for being a political, another for having kids in school, another because he wanted to send his child to high school and they wouldn't take him. Many joined then to let their children stay in school.[27]

They called my husband too, but he was away looking for work. He'd gone to the gold mines. He'd left me home alone. . . . And that's how all this happened to me. He was away, he didn't have to worry about it, and they pressured me to go and sign up. And they called me in, and I didn't sign. Then they came one night. Two people; they knocked and kicked the door. They knew my husband wasn't at home, and they kicked the door 'til I thought it would break. But I didn't say a word, they could do whatever they wanted outside, but I was thinking they still didn't have the right to knock down someone's door in the middle of the night. So I didn't say anything, and they left. They came back in the morning, they came back again. Well, what was the leadership thinking, that these men could come at night and I would open the door? We were just a few who hadn't joined, and we kept thinking this and that, but eventually they signed us all up. It was like this, the men wouldn't do it, but the women signed up.[28]

So, in 1949, they started collectivization; they would go door to door, trying to persuade you. The guy would blabber on about advantages, how much money you'd make, and who knows what else they'd go on about. And some people would slam the door in their faces, some would curse at them, throw them out, others would listen to what they had to say and so on. There was one [activist], poor guy, a Hungarian from Arad, he was a musician. He knew all this agriculture stuff so well that he couldn't tell a potato plant from alfalfa! (Goina 2009: 382)

There was one fellow, Botez, a professor at the local high school who had fled here from Bessarabia. He spoke nicely and was a decent guy; they made him do it, he didn't want to. Coming from Bessarabia, he knew what a collective was! If people

[27] P. C., Vultur interview.

[28] SA01, Ţârău interview.

refused, he wouldn't insist. Well, in the evenings three or four activists would gather to persuade people. Botez had a nervous tic that looked as if he were shaking his head "No." One of them would be making arguments about why people should sign up, and he'd shake his head, so people would dig in their heels even more. Finally they had to remove him from the team.[29]

In Pechea, one fellow hid himself in the oven to avoid the team that had come to visit him, but his foot stuck out just a bit. "Sign up!" ordered one of the guys in the team. "No!" And the guy put ink on his toe and so he signed up "of his own free will." He didn't even have to get out of the oven.[30]

They'd come into the house! One guy, Didă, an uncle of mine, he hid under the bed! They used to say, "We're not leaving, bring us something to eat, to drink, and . . . we're gonna sit here all winter, if you don't join!" This guy, when he saw them—swoosh!—under the bed. They were waiting for him to come, and he was breathing, breathing in, breathing out and . . . they heard something, he had to cough. When they heard him: "Hey, get out of there!" they pulled him out by the legs, like a pig you drag to the slaughter. . . . Hauled by the bridle, like an ox, to the slaughterhouse![31]

Those who supposedly joined willingly, they did so because they were lazy, but those who worked hard to acquire their land, one little patch at a time, were heartbroken when they signed that petition. Yes, I have to, so I don't get beaten anymore. Because at the time there was no one in the leadership who could think straight. "Hey, let's talk to people, let's tell them nicely!" No, as everyone knows, they put a bunch of thugs in charge, I can call them that. Thugs! Thugs, exactly that! Yes. But that's how it was.[32]

We see in these extracts many of the signature traits of persuasion work: entering without invitation; trying to strike bargains; coming back day after day, night after night, many times per day; coming in excessive numbers—not just four or five but ten, twelve, even three hundred; staying for hours and keeping people from their work; threatening their children's future; outlasting peasants' efforts to hide; eating and drinking well beyond the bounds of propriety—and, worse, *telling* the host to offer hospitality ("He's not here? Fine, give us something to eat and drink, and we'll wait for him"); treating the peasants with disdain; driving them around at night in the infamous "black car"; insisting, insisting, and insisting, to wear them down; and so on. The continuum of "persuasion" ran from dialogue among family members through complex negotiations and economic compulsion to arrest, beatings, and imprisonment, occasionally even death. As we will see, the reactions of the peasantry were similarly varied: from efforts to domesticate the activists with food and drink, to putting them off with

[29] G. Z., Verdery interview.

[30] 15, Stoica interview; see Stoica 2009: 442.

[31] S. A., Lățea interview.

[32] V.D.A., Dobrincu interview.

excuses, to flight, to signing up and then later withdrawing, to violent revolt using pitchforks and scythes, sometimes killing an activist or GAC official. Persuasion was a two-way street: in response to cadres' persuasive efforts, peasants sought with guile and increasingly desperate invention to persuade cadres to leave them alone. Each response in turn shaped the next encounter.

Thus, it is impossible to describe the techniques of persuasion except as interactive: cadres invade, peasants flee, cadres intensify their coercion; they exert pressure on kin, peasants manipulate kinship too; and so on. Persuasion work created a highly dynamic landscape and was an intensely dialogic process. Almost as with show trials, cadres were trying to teach the peasantry a script: they had to learn to say the right thing—"I join of my own free will." In this sense, persuasion work was a lengthy set of rehearsals for the performance of signing up. We will expand upon its techniques by focusing on the following: (1) problems with creating the authority of persuaders, (2) reciprocal manipulations of kinship and gender, (3) disruptions of the accustomed spatial and temporal organization of village life, (4) bargaining and negotiations, and (5) more overt forms of coercion. For each, we show how cadres' practices threw the peasants off guard by disturbing one or another norm of accustomed behavior, and how they responded within their own familiar idioms. We begin with who the persuaders were and how they were organized.

The Work of Persuasion

The people who carried out persuasion work were of many kinds and came in many possible configurations. The activists might be Party cadres or members of the police or Securitate forces. They might be state functionaries of People's Councils, or teachers, school principals, and village notaries, as well as doctors, engineers, and even priests, brought into the process because they had authority with the peasants (Şandru 2003: 16); they might be students and, especially, factory workers and agitators from industrial centers near the villages being collectivized. They might be peasants from already-established GACs, brought to other villages to tell of the success of their farms. They were not necessarily Party members. As the second wave of collectivization drew to a close between 1958–62, even chiaburs or others having strong influence with villagers but no Party connections might be used to go out and tell people not to wait any longer.

Persuasion was usually conducted in teams (*echipe*). A team of persuaders might mix together various kinds of people, and it might be as small as two or three, or as large as thirty, forty, or even more. There might be only one team working in a village, or there might be many. They might come and stay for only a day or two, or they might set up residence for several months, often determined by the degree of resistance encountered. Here are some examples of persuasion teams from the work of our project participants. In Reviga commune, an older peasant recalled that initially a team of agitators consisted of seven to eight locals who always spoke politely with him, but later people from outside the village came and dealt with him aggressively (Chelcea 2003b: 34). A member of a persuasion team in the Banat region described how the Party Secretary had organized the work in several commissions, each responsible for a sector containing a number of houses. There were about twenty such commissions, with four or five people; they received lessons in how to carry out the persuasion work and in the particulars of agriculture (Vultur 2003a: 72). In Darabani, peasants recalled that many outsiders came into the commune's villages in the final period in March 1962; they came from neighboring communes in the district up to thirty-five kilometers away, from the cities of Iaşi and Suceava, from other districts and regions, and even from Bucharest (Dobrincu 2003a: 47).[33] By contrast, in Ieud, in 1950, the first outside team met violent resistance upon entering the village, after which outsiders were fortified by regional security forces and locals. Later, in Vadu Roşca, where a major peasant revolt occurred in 1957, the composition of the teams changed from being strictly outsiders before the revolt to incorporating peasants and workers from local areas where collectivization had already been successfully concluded—among them a worker from town, a tradesman from a nearby village, two local people of various professions, and an activist from the district (Stoica 2009: 431–32). The former mayor of a neighboring village remarked, "These guys were supposedly backing me up, but I couldn't stand them. . . . Two hundred of them would enter the village and go from one end to the other" (431). We see that persuasion was flexibly organized; so were the tactics it employed.

Creating Persuasive Authority: Inside and Outside Cadres

As is clear from the above (and as we explained in chapters 2 and 3), both the Party and the villagers made an important distinction between inside and outside cadres, referring to whether or not they were implicated in social relations with villagers where they were assigned to work. Cadres born in a village were clearly insiders, as were those who had worked and lived there for some time; but even a seeming "outsider" might become "inside" through familiarity with someone in the community. Initially, most persuasion cadres came from outside a given settlement—activists sent from the district or region or even, sometimes, from the Central Committee itself.[34] Over time, the tendency was to bring in fewer people from the national and regional capitals, and more from the districts, communes, and villages, in larger teams, who stayed for longer periods. The celebrated "Galaţi experiment," which provided the model for collectivization everywhere else (see chapter 2), required all Party members living in villages to join their collectives and take on the work of enlarging them.

[33] For Bucharest, he mentions the case of Captain Florian Lehu, who had been employed by the Securitate for a decade.

[34] See also chapter 3, note 61.

Meanwhile, most of the territorial instructors from outside now settled in their target villages with their families, and the numbers of people sent in were greatly increased.

As we showed in chapter 3, Party policy was to try to prevent cadres from forming relationships in the villages they were to collectivize, lest this compromise their effectiveness. Cadres were generally not assigned to their own villages but some distance away, and they were regularly rotated.[35] In Jurilovca the activists sent in from nearby villages were changed every three or four days, at most every week (Iordachi 2003: 44). But collectivization required inside knowledge and connections of the sort only insiders could have; this was especially true with persuasion work. Maintaining a balance between inside and outside cadres was very tricky. Although persuaders from outside might work effectively because they were fairly immune to the pressure of village ties, precisely this fact may have made it easier for them to exercise brutality and thus alienate villagers. Moreover, if they were urbanites they might know nothing about agriculture—like the one sent into Sântana who "couldn't tell a potato plant from alfalfa" (Goina 2009: 382). Their lack of knowledge completely undermined their authority as spokesmen for a new kind of agriculture. Locals, on the other hand, were likely to have better arguments for fellow villagers, whom they knew well, and they could manipulate local friendships, kinship, and enmities that outsiders could not know about; but they were also more readily drawn into social relations and local status conceptions that made their work harder and their loyalties suspect. Being an activist could strain one's kinship relations. A local teacher in Năneşti warned his aunt and uncle in advance when his team was coming to them; they would reply, "Mind your own business and don't come around here with those guys! Remember, we brought you up!" (Stoica 2009: 432). He continued, "I had to be careful what I said when I was with the team. It was a kind of duplicity [on my part] but I had to, because the activists would be going back to Galaţi, yet I had to stay here in the village with everyone. And they would have burned my house down!" (432).[36]

This sort of concern may help to explain why in Armăşeni, for example, when the persuasion team would enter a household, the first to enter were always the group's local members, whose role was to make contact; after that they withdrew, and persuasion was then the job of the external organizer or the local GAC leadership (Bodó 2003: 10–11). Likewise, the propaganda campaign of 1957 in Pechea benefited from no help at all on the part of the commune's Party members but was done by outsiders from higher up (Şandru 2003: 16–17). And in Reviga, persuaders were brought from other communes because if locals came around to persuade, people would have become venge-

[35] This did not apply to local cadres who came to villages as colonists, that is, resettled from elsewhere.

[36] Lăţea 2009 found similar wording in his work as well. Such examples, which are widespread, remind us that locals, whether cadres or people called upon to help them, were caught between village and Party and were scrutinized by both.

ful and "would have caught one of those stupid thugs and beaten them up. In this way, we sent our nincompoops to other villages and they sent theirs to us" (Chelcea 2009: 411).

Owing to the various pressures on these actors, we are cautious about accepting at face value our respondents' frequent claim that it was the outsiders who committed most of the abuses in forcing people to join—a claim with which local participants would naturally protect themselves. For instance, the president of the Jurilovca GAC blamed the higher Party organs for abuses, saying that the activists sent in from outside made all the important decisions. His strategy for attracting people was to create distance between himself and the work: "You said to them: 'I didn't come for myself, to take your horses, to take your cart. I came to . . . I'm sent by the state. We have to collectivize! It's written all over the place collectivization, collectivization, collectivization, so what more can we expect?'"[37] This enabled him to save face locally, repudiating responsibility by blaming outsiders.

Nevertheless, the role of the outsiders was decisive in a crucial way, which Bodó suggests on the basis of her work in two villages in Odorhei district:

> Their systematic, regular physical presence (more than their actual work) represented a powerful regularizing force for the villagers. By their physical presence these outside organizers demonstrated a "superior" power that "you couldn't oppose." Certainly their actions and words strengthened and increased this sentiment, but in general their physical presence was enough. Other research in this region demonstrates that in the vision of the locals the (incontestable!) legitimacy of these essential changes is given by the presence of people from outside, who actually embody the change. A local, "interior" person cannot legitimate them adequately. (2003: 61)

This valuable insight brings us to the crux of the matter of inside and outside cadres: it was a question not just of who could work more effectively but of how to establish a sense of the state's authority, such that peasants would see collectivization as inevitable and decide to join. That authority came from the superior power of outsiders augmented by the frequent presence, on the one hand, of the police or Securitate and, on the other hand, of professionals such as teachers or agronomists bringing higher learning into the mix. This helps us to understand the nature of the emerging form of power, which constituted itself as both inside and outside the local community but succeeded mainly by virtue of its exteriority—by being seen as "them" to the peasants' "us." A classic fractal distinction, "us-them" worked all the way up: from the dialogue of villagers and activists to the relations of lower- and higher-level cadres to those between Romania and Moscow, there was always a "them" who perpetrated this fearsome experiment upon "us."[38] But their interpenetration was confusing and threw

[37] M. T., Iordachi interview.

[38] Gal and Kligman (2000) use the notion of fractal distinctions to similar effect in discussing gender and politics under socialism.

villagers off balance. Is the village schoolteacher who comes into our kitchen with those guys from the capital one of us or one of them? Can I trust him to help me with the life dilemmas collectivization is creating?

A second critical characteristic of persuaders, related to the inside-outside distinction and equally disturbing to peasants, further underpinned this exteriorization of the locus of authority: the relative social status of collectivizers and collectivized. Bodó writes of the locals in Corund who had entered Party service and occupied an intermediary role, inferior in rank to the activists but superior to most peasants. "People saw them as good-for-nothing second-raters, who had risen to power from 'the dregs' of the village. Working alongside the leadership, they achieved a new position not because of their own merit, but through the support of outside authorities" (2009: 361). For middle and prosperous peasants, lifetimes of understanding both self and world in terms of a certain status hierarchy were jeopardized by a new order that raised up a village's poor and marginal families over its "good" ones (see chapter 8). A more chaotic and distressing possibility was hard to imagine. Another instance comes from a Jurilovcan drawn into persuasion work:

> These pushy types would come in, and they'd take some of us people from the village—I was a state employee—to go with them and say who lived where and to represent the village in their presence.
>
> (*Did you talk [with villagers] as well?*)
>
> Noooo!!! *The others* did it!!! How would *I* know what to say? What did I know! Did I have the courage to talk with people? "OK, buddy, I'll sit and listen to you!" What? Didn't people know who I was? *I* should be persuading someone with land, when I, my parents, didn't have any, and no ancestor of ours had any connection with land? I should be the one to say, "Hey, join the collective," stuff like that? How could I know if it would work or not? And besides, I was just a kid.[39]

This respondent highlights the fundamental dilemma in using the formerly poor as cadres (as well as his unwillingness to be associated with the activity of persuading). As we explained in chapter 3, the ideology behind Party personnel policies favored recruiting the poor and disadvantaged, yet they lacked the skills and the authority necessary to their work. Cadres were generally younger than their targets, a severe liability in villages where authority was seen as rooted in age and experience. Moreover, Romanian villages were saturated with differential status; the people most essential to the collectives' success were the middle and well-to-do peasants, who would bring land into the GACs, but they had only disdain for the poorer villagers recruited as Party cadres. Coming from humble backgrounds, like this man, they lacked the clout to persuade their "betters."

Precisely this situation, we suspect, contributed to making external legitimation by "outside cadres" so essential: the entire edifice of persuasion would have

[39] V. Z., Iordachi interview.

collapsed if it had rested solely on village recruits into persuasion work. Yet as we indicated above, outsiders were by definition suspect; they were most likely to be esteemed if they had superior education, but as chapter 3 has shown, this was seldom the case, initially. Considerations of this kind surely informed the Party's efforts to increase the educational level of its cadres, and to bring into persuasion work the educated local elite, even if they were not Party members and might possibly be class enemies. In all communities, schoolteachers as well as other intellectuals were pressed into service. Their prestige seems to have protected them, in the eyes of villagers, who might treat them with understanding. Here is a village schoolteacher, drawn into persuasion work: "I would go into a house, I'd greet them, they'd offer me a chair, I'd sit down, and I didn't even have to state why I was there. They would tell me, 'Don't say a word, sir, we know why they sent you, so we could talk a bit, and if we're asked we'll say you were here and you said what you were supposed to'" (Bodó 2003: 60). This does not mean that being brought into persuasion work was not costly for them. A former high school principal said, "We teachers who were drawn into this work didn't feel good about it—yet we couldn't show that or we'd suffer consequences. . . . I went to Băcăinţi to help get people into the TOZ. I was sitting behind the First Secretary for agriculture, and he saw me: 'Hey, why are you so upset? You don't like it, do you; I know you don't like it.'"[40]

The same man offered an intellectual's (rather self-serving) view of why the Party would nonetheless want to use people like him in the persuasion process:

> When they started making collectives, the majority were without schooling, bad people—even now people still talk about them. They did nothing but harm until collectives were made properly and they were thrown out. They abused their power, forced things, beat and deported people. . . . Things changed only when the teachers came in and tried a different kind of persuasion work. . . . We quit throwing people's children out of school, using ignorant folk and "administrative measures" like labeling people chiaburs, increasing their quotas, and so on. All that hadn't gotten many members. After we started, we got the best people in, the best farmers and the most influential. Then people would follow their example and say, "I'll sign up because so-and-so is there."

This comment suggests that peasants responded to the actions of those they held in high regard, whether teachers or chiaburs—a point we will revisit in chapter 7.

Manipulating Kinship and Gender

In the minds of many of our respondents, the most disturbing purveyors of persuasion were people's own children, who were threatened with expulsion

[40] M. H., Verdery interview (1999). Untaped interview, reconstructed from notes.

from school or jobs or were subjected to humiliating treatment and told to persuade their parents to join. An activist in the Odorhei district described his approach to the youth population: "We worked a lot with the village youth, seeing them as means to persuade their parents. We worked hard to defame the old order and praise the new one in the eyes of this youth having great receptivity, no past, and no history. We stuffed their brains, but with little success" (Oláh 2009: 235). Mao Zedong's appreciation of this same point was a hallmark of China's Cultural Revolution. The tactic reflected the Party's aim to transform families into new socialist ones, which required destroying traditional ideas about kinship while using them opportunistically (see Kligman 1998). Playing people off against each other was a standard strategy of the Party and the Securitate, which understood well the meaning of family and the affective bonds among its extended members.

There were endless possibilities for manipulating kin relations, placing people in untenable emotional binds. The following scenario occurred between two chiabur brothers, one of whom the Securitate sent from the nearby town where he and his family lived to pay a visit to his natal village and persuade his brother to join the collective:

> You know, they told me I too will lose my job if you don't join the collective, as will you [the brother in the village commuted weekly to a job in that same town]. Do what you think is best, but I came to tell you that you may also end up in prison and me without a job. You and I each have children. . . . And if you enter, you won't be alone since after you, everyone else will follow and you won't be on your own. . . . And if you do this, I probably won't lose my job and will help you out with your kids when they go to high school, they'll live with us [in town]. I'll help you too as much as I can.[41]

This incident shows one of the most common tactics for using kinship to compel villagers into collectives: sending people employed in factories or towns back home to persuade their kin into joining the GAC, usually under threat of losing their jobs.

Another was to enlist children to entreat their parents to join, on pain of being disciplined while doing their military service or expelled from school. Children's education had long been key to rural strategies for household reproduction and upward mobility, occasioning tremendous sacrifice that would pay off once the child secured regular employment and could help the family in turn. Therefore, threats to deprive family members of these possibilities were very serious. "You, why don't you want to join? Well, your son will vanish from high school. If you don't join, he's out!" His mother responded, "OK, I'll join; who knows what will happen. It's better to leave my child there to make a future

[41] B. S. and B. G., Kligman interviews. In the end, the brother in the village did join the GAC, having few attractive alternatives.

for himself."[42] Another elderly peasant recalled: "Even in the Army there was politics. When they saw you were sending a postcard to your parents, a sergeant would grab you and ask, 'Hey you, what did you write? Tell your father to join the collective farm,' because otherwise we didn't. I'd add a note, 'Dad, I had to. Do what you think is right.'"[43] In a more dramatic case, a peasant woman who was arrested in 1958 and held without food for forty-eight hours for not signing up related how her own mother brought her child to the local council building where she was being held. He stood at the door and begged her: "Come on, mama! Sign up! They're swearing at us again and cursing us, and they even beat us" (Vultur 2003a: 70). Some respondents said that they joined on the strength of their children's pleas alone.

Thus, when threatened that a child would not be allowed to acquire an education or that spouses or siblings would lose their job, or any number of variants on these themes, most people sooner or later acquiesced to the Party's demands. All these threats and techniques went to the heart of both kin attachments and household reproduction strategies, chipping away at village social organization. Party leaders themselves were well aware that this was abusive, as we see from the charges lodged against Party Secretary Tóth Géza (mentioned in chapter 3), who among other abusive behavior "also used sending home from school students whose parents refused to join the GAC, with the disposition that they would not be allowed back until their parents joined."[44]

Cadres employed kinship in other ways, presuming its vitality even while sapping that vitality with their actions. They might trick someone by telling him his kin had already joined, so he might as well join also; they would tell his relatives the same thing. One state functionary active in collectivization, asked whether kinship figured in his strategies, replied: "If we were looking for someone to be [GAC] president or other cadre, we'd look for one who had lots of kin and *fini* [godchildren] in the village, so they were likely to be wealthier. We'd come and say to him, 'Help us collectivize, explain it to your relatives, your *fini*.' We wanted him to have as many relatives as possible in the village, to be an influential person there."[45] Sometimes family members would avoid those they suspected of being used in this way, or make trouble for them. The president of the Jurilovca GAC recalled that because the activists forced him to take his persuasion work to his kin first, he suffered numerous quarrels with his family (Iordachi 2003: 45). For a society in which cooperation among kin was a fundamental value, turning kin against one another in this way was profoundly disturbing.

Nonetheless, manipulating kinship was a game that two could play, and peasants proved very skillful at it. To reduce their quotas, households consist-

42 M. D., Lățea interview.

43 P. V., Kligman interview.

44 ANIC, Fond C.C. al P.C.R.–Agrară, file 50/1950, 4.

45 M. H., Verdery interview.

ing of a junior and a senior couple might divide, if they had two houses—a tactic that could be crucial for chiaburs hoping to avoid persecution.[46] (It also forced the persuaders to work on two households instead of one.) Oláh invokes this practice as the reason for a sudden increase in the number of households in Odorhei district (2009: 242). Because cadres were supposed to get the signatures of all adult family members, or at least minimally the household head, peasants played on who signed up. In early 1957, peasants in three villages in Mărtineşti commune (Hunedoara) broke up their collective farms. The report on this event commented (first observing that to reconstitute the GACs had required "work with collectivists who are kin"): "[T]he entry petitions to the collectives were not signed by the father, mother, father-in-law, or mother-in-law but only by their sons and sons-in-law and their wives. These deviations are used by enemy elements who say that the land belongs to the elderly, who don't want to stay in the farm because they are not members [and they are the ones who own the land]."[47] The report attributed this clever strategy—signing up only the younger generation, who had not yet received their inheritance, which meant that the collective was deprived of the land it thought it had—to legionary and fascist enemies of the state.

Further playing on who ought to be the ones to sign, wives would say that they could not sign up in their husbands' absence; husbands would say that their wives would not let them join, or that the land belonged to their wives, who were the only ones who could sign it over; or that it belonged to their mothers or their parents, who wouldn't give permission to sign it away. Wives regularly refused to sign petitions to enter the GACs in their husbands' absences, invoking traditional patriarchal norms as justification. One man recalled his mother's response to the initial team of activists that came to persuade him in the first wave of collectivization: "Go to hell! I am not giving my house and everything I have to the state; they're ours, mine, I inherited this from my parents." They attempted to sweeten the deal by saying that her son would be given a good position, as he deserved, but to no avail. He then told of going to the regional authorities and informing them that they had to erase his name from the collective: "There's nothing I can do about my mother. You have to erase my name so it doesn't figure in the register. I can't order her since she rules." But the second time around, in the '60s, "there was no choice since I had gone to work in the mines."[48] (He could keep his job in the state sector only if he joined the GAC.) Many a wife reacted much the same as this man's old mother in her late seventies, as did many a man who refused to enter to avoid family frictions and heated conflicts. Thus, villagers passed the persuaders around their kinship networks to delay the act of joining.[49] We

[46] V. D., Vultur interview.

[47] DJAN HD, Fond CR PMR, file 2426/1957, 46.

[48] I. S., Kligman interview.

[49] Another example of the counter-uses of kinship comes from Domaşnea, where the most im-

find an especially illuminating instance in a 1951 meeting some peasants from Şoimuş held with Pauker and Gheorghiu-Dej. Objecting to the means used to form their collective (see second epigraph of this chapter), the women asked for their land back:

> They should at least give us our land back and keep our husbands' land [in the GAC]; but they said it was the head of the family who was responsible, not us women. The land is ours, though, and isn't even registered in our husbands' names. . . . The men joined out of fear. They should give us back our land, not the men's, because they signed us up without asking us. If they don't give us our land back, we'll leave our husbands and go away to earn our living somewhere else.[50]

Officials were aware that "[t]he women are telling their husbands that they'll kill them, or they'll divorce them, if they enter the collective farm" (Levy 2009: 29). One man withdrew from the GAC because after he had joined it, "my wife left me three days ago and it is better for me to leave the GAC than lose my wife."[51] A report from one village during the first round of creating collectives stated:

> For our part, we made a mistake not to closely examine the wives of those who were signing up. Thus, the wife of a certain peasant, Petre Pârvu, when she heard that her husband had joined the collective farm, wouldn't let him back in the house. We summoned her to talk to us. She's a very difficult woman to convince, and in the end we were unable to convince her. One comrade, the person responsible for organizing at the Party's district office, also said that his wife doesn't want to join the collective. Generally, working with the women was very difficult. (Levy 2009: 30–31)

Rarely in our material do we find women like the wife of a former middle peasant who recalled in his eighties that his "old lady" had hammered away at him: "You fool, go and sign up! You good-for-nothing . . . we'll be the poorest people in the village otherwise. Don't you see that they take everything from us, while we give everything we have and they still find more to take, and we are left the poorest?!" (Goina 2003: 43).

As is evident, gender roles entered into these manipulations. From a traditional cultural perspective, women were not expected to make decisions on behalf of their households, whose heads were considered to be the men. Party propaganda, by contrast, emphasized gender equality, and sometimes the message sank in. Some women took pride in submitting petitions to join the GAC; another petitioned her GAC to readmit her husband, adding, "Perhaps, com-

---

portant kin groups divided themselves into those who fled into the mountains and those who joined the Party or the Securitate so as to protect their kin. In this way, those who had fled managed to avoid capture until very late in the game. Thus, powerful families could hold off the state by developing group strategies (Vultur, personal communication).

[50] Moraru et al. 2004: 543–44.

[51] See DJAN HD, Fond A672, file 93/1951, 177.

rades, you will condemn us women for getting mixed up in writing petitions, but we women have acquired this right, no longer subjugated as we were under the reactionary bourgeois regime" (Márton 2005: 37). Cadres themselves, however, often manifested "bourgeois" attitudes. For instance, a 1951 report noted, "In general, the women are the ones who protest against collectivization by any means [and] of course their husbands have put them up to it"—as if women had no reason to object on their own.[52]

On the other hand, cadres were fully prepared to violate customary norms about proper respect for women, whom they might take to the village council in the middle of the night to make them sign entry petitions in their husbands' stead, as we saw above. Such encounters could involve physical violence contrary to village norms, which regarded beating a woman as culturally acceptable between husband and wife but not between a wife and some "stranger." The following tragedy was, sadly, not an isolated case: "That was in '49 . . . they took Mama to the town hall to turn over our wheat. 'I won't give it,' she said. 'Let my husband do it, he's the head of the household,' and so they beat her, and she was six months pregnant. My mother died . . . and we four children were left motherless."[53] Such behavior flew in the face of villagers' assumption that the authorities would not use brutality against women (Márton 2005: 37).

Even while supposedly encouraging gender equality, Party officials found it very difficult to persuade women to join the collectives. Ana Pauker, discussing gender matters in a talk delivered at the Higher Party (Zhdanov) School, chastised Party members for contributing to women's reticence:

> [A]nd as happened in Teleorman, a comrade who found herself pregnant—a young woman whose man had left for the army without having married her first—and who didn't tell the comrade secretary that she was pregnant, when she started showing . . . she was excluded first from her job and then from the Party. What man would have been excluded for such a reason? . . . And with this way of viewing things, no wonder it is hard to attract women to [our] work.[54]

Indeed, as we noted in chapter 2, women were as resistant to collectivization as men or even more so, often leading revolts, doubtful that collectivization would enable them to feed their families (Vultur 2003a: 60; Levy 2009: 29–31). Some men claimed that in certain villages, the staunch opposition of "women with many children" ultimately made the formation of GACs there impossible.[55] Thus, we see that in attempting to manipulate kinship and gender, Party cadres were far from having the upper hand, even though their actions were deeply destabilizing. We examine further instances of this strategy in chapter 6.

[52] DJAN HD, Fond CR PMR, file 305/1951, 22.

[53] B. P., Kligman interview. See also Kristó 1999.

[54] ANIC, C.C. al P.C.R.–Agrară, file 60/1949, 22.

[55] C. G., Kligman interview.

Persuasion and Rural Spatial-Temporal Relations

If kinship became one of the prime force fields of persuasion work in ways destabilizing to the peasantry, space and time became another. Cadres invaded spaces hitherto not seen as public; resignified the uses of existing public space, turning "culture halls" into sites of political work; sent peasants fleeing across wide spaces or immobilized them in their houses for long periods of time. They violated norms of etiquette by coming over and over, at the "wrong" times, preventing villagers from working when they normally would, and by demanding hospitality, reinforcing the gender difference between largely male cadres and the women left at home to greet them. As for the peasants, by refusing to join and fleeing into the woods they compelled cadres to travel back and forth repeatedly, immobilized them with food and drink, and wore them out with endless excuses and delays. These interactions produced a dynamic landscape whose rhythms differed fundamentally from those of customary village life.

Cadres carved out multiple spaces for their work, spaces that corresponded to collective ("public") or individual ("private") targeting.[56] One common procedure was to show films and hold meetings in the village hall, school, or other public locale, or even out in the open, convening either the village as a whole or groups of people—summoned street by street, for instance—and trying to persuade them as a group. Alternatively, activists went from house to house in small groups, persuading "from person to person" (*de la om la om*). (This practice, interestingly, had been a favorite of the fascist Iron Guard.)[57] Singly or in groups, activists would call on people at home, sitting in their kitchens or living rooms to talk with them about joining. A few neighbors might also be rounded up for such an occasion. A third method was to come in the middle of the night and lead a family member away to the village hall or People's Council, or perhaps put him into a van and jolt him around over the fields for a long time, convincing him he was being taken to some distant place.

One Party activist from the Odorhei district enlightened us as to how some cadres thought about the use of space:

> During the agitprop campaign for collectivization we would send the entire district People's Council's personnel into villages. The secretary in charge of agricultural matters, as well as the one for cadres and other experts, came to respond to people's problems. There, *we would rarely do our persuasion work inside peasants' homes, because peasants would talk disrespectfully to us if they saw us on their property.* We therefore would summon them to the buildings of the People's Council or, if the village had no People's Council, to the school, *because there we were in control.* We made

[56] See Gal and Kligman (2000: chapter 3) on resignifying public and private spaces.

[57] DJAN HD, Fond Chestura de Poliție Deva, file 72/1937, 19.

them sit in the classroom and listen to long boring lectures and discuss propaganda brochures. Party chairmen from factories and cadres were all at our disposal. (Oláh 2009: 235, emphasis added)

Preferences for "being in control" might dictate the procedure in one village, but other reasons might determine a different solution elsewhere. For example, two neighboring Hungarian villages in Odorhei district experienced opposite strategies:

> In Armăşeni, . . . the organizers from town formed groups that went to every household. A group would have 4–6 members, of whom only one or two were organizers coming from elsewhere, the rest being local leaders, teachers, and employees of local institutions. . . . In the other settlement, Corund, the organizers did not go house to house but called household heads to the People's Council for a specific date. They would usually call three or four persons at the same time and attempt to convince them. The work of convincing was done by the outside organizers in the presence of the local president. (Bodó 2003: 10–11)

When they went house to house, recruiters were vulnerable to the disappearance of household heads, who would flee to the woods or hide in false walls that they had built into their homes, but if peasants were called to the People's Council, they were somewhat less likely to flee and would keep their "appointment."

The two possible sites for meeting with the activists—public spaces and peasants' homes—had very different implications for both the work of cadres and the Party's relation to the peasantry. To begin with, a strategy of going house to house, as well as a strategy of visiting the same house repeatedly, required many more agitators than one that called people to a central location and lectured them in groups. But despite the power dynamics recalled by the activist who preferred meeting in a public place, approaching people in their homes permitted both a more nuanced set of arguments tailored to them and the possibility of overwhelming them with numerous persuaders. Such private visits were tense and traumatic for those who recalled them (e.g., Lăţea 2003: 36)—though not as traumatic as being beaten behind closed doors at the People's Council and sent home with bruises.

When activists entered into people's homes, they were setting up an entirely new relation between villagers and state power. This was especially true if cadres entered the dwelling by force. As one middle peasant from Vlaicu put it: "They came ten to fifteen times, maybe even twenty times. When they came to the gate we'd lock it so they'd think we weren't home. (*And they didn't force their way in?*) Well, they shouted a lot. And my mother-in-law would go to the gate and say, 'Gheorghe isn't home.' At first, they didn't force their way into the house. But in the end they did. They even jumped over the fence."[58] They might

[58] 72, Verdery interview.

Figure 5.2. Joining the GAC "of their own free will" (1949). Courtesy of *Fototeca online a comunismului românesc*, photograph #W063, *cota* 9/1949.

violate social norms in other ways. A woman from Reviga reported that the village norm was to stop at the gate when you visited someone, but cadres entered "directly into the house without shame" (Chelcea 2003b: 30)—an observation made by numerous other respondents. Such meetings in peasants' houses, Lățea suggests, were "modalities of insinuating the agents of an exterior power, in the most palpable and consequential way . . . into what was beginning to be constituted as a relatively particular form of private space" (2003: 36).

This is not to say that there had been no private space before, but persuasion work resignified in different terms the private and individual space of the peasant household as a kinship unit. When persuasion brought agents of what was becoming "the Party-state" into the space of the family, they were colonizing a private sphere. Because neighbors knew who was being visited in the night, who was being harassed, and so on, it transformed the meaning of the home as not a family's safe haven resting on status but a quasi-private space vulnerable to outsiders who defined it by class. For this reason, the signatures on petitions to join the GACs are not in and of themselves sociologically revealing, for they do not allow us to distinguish between those who signed up in public meetings/spaces and those who signed in private, or those whose signatures were obtained through coercion as opposed to less dramatic forms of persuasion. The distinction would be useful in thinking about the relation of "willing" and "forced" consent, for public signings were more ritualized, more performative. The sight of respected members of the community signing away their land in front of many of their fellows, in an "obligatorily voluntary" way, underpinned much of the regime's performative legitimacy.

Aside from manipulating the spatial placement of their persuasion work, activists manipulated the timing. Both our documents and our interviews note this repeatedly. Cadres might show up at any hour: respondents recalled their coming at the end of the day when people were returning home from work in the fields; on weekends all during the day; repeatedly, day after day or several times in the same day; in the dead of night, or in broad daylight.[59] They kept people from sleeping and wore them down with constant appearances. For example, in Darabani, teams reported specific instructions about their work: "Persuading working peasants and attracting them into the GAC will be done continuously and without any rest" (Dobrincu 2003a: 30). Minutes of a 1953 meeting of the Şibot People's Council specify: "Field trips will be done every day between 3:00 and 9:00 a.m. and 17:00 and 22:00."[60] (Functionaries in the room where Verdery was copying this observed, "That was to get people when they were groggy.") A respondent from Dobrosloveni recalled,

> He kept after you constantly, he'd come, sit around for an hour, come again: "What've you been doing, have you changed your mind?" He'd sit some more . . . anyway, he'd come three or four times a day. We'd hide, people would hide . . . "I'm not here!"
>
> (*Uncle L. told me they would lock the gate and go stay in the garden.*)
>
> Yes, men would run away from home so they wouldn't have to join and only women were left: "He's not home!" They'd come again the next day.[61]

From Turda district: "People didn't want to join, but they were called around-the-clock. Someone would [be called in] in the morning, again at noon, he wouldn't sign and would somehow manage to get home, but in the afternoon they'd call him again. And they called everyone until people at last realized that there was absolutely no way of avoiding it, that they had to sign up."[62] For cadres as for ethnographers, winter was a favored time, since the peasants had no work in the fields and were more likely to be at home, whereas in summer their work was crucial to the Party's plans. Likewise Sundays, when peasants hoped to rest and to visit with their kin: "Every Sunday sixty agitators will be sent out by the district who will explain the importance of TOZs"[63]—thus undermining both sociability and religious practice.

In brief, persuasion assaulted every temporal norm of peasant life. Times of rest became times of grueling persuasion; times of work were interrupted as well; times when peasants usually socialized together were disturbed, as households "entertained" activists instead. At night, men hid in their gardens or in the woods rather than sleeping in their beds at home. Cadres breached norms concerning not just the timing but the proper length or frequency of visits. When we think of how basic to human functioning are temporal routines (see,

[59] These kinds of temporal violations are a classic tactic, found in many authoritarian regimes, including Stalin's Soviet Union and Argentina.

[60] Arhiva Primăriei Şibot (jud. Alba), file I/11/1953, 33.

[61] M. T., Lăţea interview.

[62] BA01, Ţârău interview.

[63] DJAN HD, Fond CR PMR, Comitetul Raional PMR Orăştie, file 21/1951, 61.

e.g., Bourdieu 1977), we can begin to see how these constant infringements of accustomed temporalities could become a means whereby the balance of power gradually shifted. Not everyone experienced the full brunt of such infringements, of course: those who signed up willingly were spared them. It was the most recalcitrant who suffered the manipulations of rural spatial and temporal norms the most; as others gradually resigned themselves to joining, they repossessed some part of their routines.

Until that moment, however, peasants fought back in the same currency. Despite the overwhelming power advantages of the Party's representatives, the villagers had one very important resource: time. They were in no hurry to sign up, and they had multiple ways of putting off the activists who wanted them to. One way, already mentioned and reported in all our areas, was postponement through flight, especially by male household heads (a tactic already consecrated by those seeking to avoid their quotas). They would disappear from home, sometimes for months at a time, stalling the efforts of teams who were bent on obtaining the signatures of just those people. Depending on the village's location, they might be simply hiding in their barns or gardens, or fleeing into the forests or mountains nearby, or making extended visits to relatives in other places. We heard numerous accounts of men leaping their back fences as the persuaders came into view or dashing up alleys when they saw the cars at their gate, leaving their wives to handle the intruders. In Dobrosloveni, Lățea reports:

> Women would stay at home and refuse any dialogue with the members of the persuasion teams, hinting thus at the stereotype of masculine authority in the household: "When the teams came, men ran from home, so they wouldn't join the collective, and women stayed behind: 'He's not home! The men aren't here [*nu sunt aci oamenii*] and I'm not getting involved in this stuff!'"[64]

Note the wording in which the wife uses the generic word for human beings, *oamenii*, to mean "men."

The strategy could not be used indefinitely, given that persuasion teams could return daily, or hourly, unannounced, and might catch men off guard as they did so. One middle peasant from Vlaicu described how he had hidden for weeks, only to be caught in his back garden by cadres who exclaimed, "Hey, Iosif, where have you been?! What are you doing out here!?" "I'm taking a crap."[65] In the meantime, however, they had resorted to the less-than-desirable expedient of having his wife sign the petition for both of them. As time passed and people were not signing up, cadres began to consider women as "people."

Tactics to delay discussion about joining the collective could be extremely subtle.[66] People might manipulate norms of hospitality, as in the example of

[64] M. T., Lățea interview (see Lățea 2009: 338).

[65] 194, Verdery interview.

[66] We are indebted to Puiu Lățea (2003), whose work has shaped much of this section.

I. B., who turned his mayor's persuasion work into an occasion for eating and drinking (see chapter 3). Or they could find forms of expression that gave them breathing space, offering reasons that "ensued from the very formulation of the problem by those charged with persuasion, who couldn't help placing the collective in the future, even though this was a near, almost inevitable, future. If the establishment of the collective belonged to a future register, one's logical salvation was to claim that one could not sign up *now*" (Lățea 2009: 339). Here is an example from Dobrosloveni, in which the respondent imagines a dialogue with persuaders who were telling him and other villagers that sooner or later they would have to sign up.

> They began persuasion work around 1957–1958. And everybody said: "There's no rush, there's enough time for me to sign up!" And they would get away with it this evening! Tomorrow evening again, the day after tomorrow again. . . . Three years went by with this talking . . .
>
> "Hey, have you signed up for the collective?"
>
> —"I haven't!"
>
> "And what do you say? I'm gonna write your name here. . . . How do I write? How do you sign?"
>
> —"For the moment, you write nothing! For the moment, we wait awhile!"
>
> We waited until the autumn of 1960. (Lățea 2009: 339)

In another report from the same village we see several different delaying tactics, some of them already mentioned:

> They'd come to the gate: "Hey, Ioan, and so on. . . . How are you? How've you been, what've you been doing? Hey, listen here: you know why we've come?" They'd get right to the point. "Hey, do you want to join the collective? . . . Join the collective! Look, let's make one of those big collectives, that's why we came, come on, let's all join the collective, it's a good thing, and so on . . ."
>
> (*And what would you answer?*)
>
> Then I'd say: "Well, let me think about it a while longer," or "Let me ask my father, let's see what he says, if he'll let me do it or not," or "He'll come, he'll come and sign up himself," or "Look, I'll come in a day or two . . ." Things like that.
>
> (*And wouldn't they go to your father's place?*)
>
> Sure, they'd go to his place: "Hey, old Ilie, old Ilie!" "What is it, huh?" "Hey, you have to join the collective, apply to join the collective!" "Uh, what? Should I sign up, am I still good for the collective?" He was elderly, 60-something, almost 70 years old . . . "Let this young'un join, . . . if he wants to!"
>
> (*So these were the excuses . . .*)
>
> There were others too . . . there were . . . "Let others do it first!" Yes, that's how it was! (Lățea 2003: 41–42)

Here, then, was a whole repertoire of replies all having the goal of postponing entry into the collective. "Not yet," "not now," "I'll wait and see," " I'm still thinking about it," "there's still plenty of time," "why me and not someone else?" "I'll sign up when everyone else does," "Let me talk to my wife/parents first," and "I'll wait, since if I sign up now, people will set my house on fire!" (42–43).[67] With these tactics, the people of Dobrosloveni managed to hold off collectivization for three years.[68] Meanwhile, they waited—for the Americans to come, for their son to marry, for the harvest, for the Korean War to end so they could see who would win—until something finally convinced them that joining was inevitable.

Bargains and Negotiations

As is already clear from this language, villagers often treated joining the collective as a process of negotiation. The bargaining was motivated, on the one hand, by their concerns about reproducing their households—how will my children marry? how can I manage to provide houses for them?—and, on the other hand, by the delaying tactics we have mentioned, which compelled activists to negotiate in various ways, for their time was not infinite. They were being pressed by their superiors, by socialist competitions, and by rivalries with their fellows to speed up the process. And so they bargained. Some of the bargains were highly individualized. For example, in Sântana someone agreed to join when he was promised admission for his daughter into the Pedagogical High School that prepared teachers—a promise based on the coincidence that the wife of one persuader headed the admissions committee of that high school (Goina 2003: 60). While such promises were offered from the very outset of collectivization, they became ever more likely as the campaign was drawing to a close and some peasants still had not joined.[69] Here is another example from Sântana, as explained by one of the last people to join the GAC:

> There were another thirty-two people, they said, who were waiting for me to join, if I didn't, then they wouldn't either. . . . Well, we kept on talking, and they kept trying to persuade me, and then I said, "Comrade president, you see that I've built myself a little house, maybe even a bit on the big side. And the walls and roof are up, but nothing else. If I join the collective, now that they've lowered the pay for collectivists, I'll never be able to finish it. I'll make a laughing stock of myself." . . . "OK," he said, "Listen here. . . . Sign the petition tonight and do what I tell you. In a month you come to me with 3,000 lei. We'll go to the cashier and pay for a cubic meter of lum-

[67] Lățea notes that comparable responses were to be found all over the Olt region, and in Dolj as well (see Băileşteanu 1987: 199–200, 206, 212).

[68] It is likely that this area was not seen as strategically important, or, we suspect, more force would have been used to get people to join.

[69] Peasants were often promised wood for their stoves and other goods, or told that they would receive clothes, a house, land, and money, or would not have to pay taxes. See ANIC, Fond 1, file 75/1952, 245 (RLA).

ber." So I went with the money, he put in the order and gave me a receipt, and by New Year's, look, all these doors—eleven of them, with glass and all—they were all done![70]

Having procured for him some lumber the man would otherwise have found it impossible to get on his own, comrade president gives us an excellent example of why Sântana's model GAC was one of the most successful in the country.

A third example shows us a more widespread practice:

> They called my father, because the land was in his name. They called him three times. He didn't want to sign up, he was very dejected. The first time he claimed he hadn't consulted me, his son, and therefore couldn't sign up. The second time, his excuse was that I was away and he couldn't discuss this issue with me. I was in hiding so he could have a good excuse. Then they told us that we didn't have to sign over all our land and that we could keep some of it if we didn't tell anyone. They told my father to transfer some of the land into my name so I could sign up and then they would give us back a parcel of land. They were telling my father all these things to strengthen his resolve to join the GAC. My father did as he was told, we both signed up, but left out two parcels of land. (Bodó 2009: 361)[71]

(Unfortunately, in the property restitution after 1989, this family and others who had done the same were unable to claim back the two parcels, which were not registered anywhere.) The strategy of signing in with less than all one's land, mentioned previously, is one reason why looking at the totals brought into a newly forming GAC does not necessarily indicate the wealth of those who had joined.

Sometimes, as in this case, the bargain was made in secret, but sometimes it was written on the entry petitions people signed to join the collective. This was done by using a language that counterbalanced the formalism of bureaucratic speech with alternative formulations, such as "I mention that . . . ," "I reserve the right to . . . , " "I obligate myself to. . . ," as well as frequent use of subjunctive verbs (translated below with "may" or "be" as in "May the harvest remain . . ." or "I mention that I be given . . ."). These formulations paid homage to the Party's wooden language while attempting to assert an individual's agency. In the examples we amassed, the promises vary greatly, but the concern with social reproduction is evident in all. For instance:

(a) We ask that our son . . . who is presently in the army, be assured a site to build a house and that the building authorization be approved by the city People's Council.

[70] V. B., Goina interview.

[71] Hiding land and livestock is a peasant strategy with a long pedigree. See, among others, Rév 1987; Verdery 1994.

(b) My petition is valid on the condition that my daughters retain their jobs and my son continue in school.[72]

(c) [In case] my daughter marries someone who isn't a GAC member, I reserve the right to request one hectare from the surface that I possess.[73]

(d) I wish my cart and oxen to be left in my use, to make bricks for my daughter's house. One ox is to be left to me, so I can get a cow to support myself, since I am ill.

(e) I mention that my horses and cart are to be left in use until August 1, 1961, when I am obliged to bring them to the GAC.

(f) I mention that I will sell the oxen I have and I commit myself to buy 1 (one) ox for the GAC.

(g) I mention that I wish to have reserved for me the surface of 2.50 hectares from the surface indicated above for my subsistence as I don't have other sources of income until I can get a job. Once I get a job, I will deliver the rest of the land to the collective.

(h) I mention that I borrowed the sum of 3,200 lei from the Bank of Craiova in order to buy the two oxen I possess. If the GAC Dobrosloveni commits to paying off the debt I still have to the Bank the oxen will remain in the GAC and if not, the People's Council should allow me to sell the oxen and pay my debt to the Bank.

Specific mention of retaining the harvest sown on one's land prior to joining the GAC appears in many of these petitions—a circumstance the GAC statute allowed for, even though cadres often refused it. (In Domaşnea, the families insisting on this condition appealed the GAC's refusal in the regional capital, and won [Vultur 2003a: 83–84].) Lăţea believes that these clauses were not in fact conditions but, rather, signs of the peasants' skepticism toward local authorities; therefore, they sought to legalize their concerns by noting down the concessions cadres appeared ready to make to get them into GACs (2003: 49–50). Alternatively, peasant skepticism might have reflected the widespread belief that because the Americans would liberate them, communism would not last very long. Occasionally the cadres kept their part of the bargain, but generally they did not—indeed, from the Party leadership's point of view most of the bargains were illegal. (A handwritten addition to item (*a*) above reads, "I withdraw the mention made on my petition and I bring myself into line with the model statute of the GAC.") They would promise to give land back but not do so or urge people to omit items from the inventory they declared, giving the impression that those things would be left to them, but later verify the inventory and confiscate the items omitted.

One way around that outcome was to preempt it. While some peasants made their donation of animals or implements conditional, others proceeded to sell

[72] Items (a) and (b) are from DJAN MM, Fond CAP Iza, Sighet, file 1/1962, 32, 34.

[73] Items (c) through (h) are from Dobrosloveni (Lăţea 2009: 344), source Arhiva Primăriei Dobrosloveni, file 5/1961, Inv. nr. 5/961, Poz. nr. 154/4.

items they would otherwise be expected to donate—especially horses, oxen, and carts—depriving the GAC of these means of production and keeping the money for themselves.[74] In such uncertain times, this made good sense. Others hid their livestock elsewhere, sending them to relatives in other villages. It was not only peasants who did this but even Party members and leaders of local Party organizations: in Pechea, for example, local officials would sell their cattle before joining the GAC—but would then make others who had done the same pay the GAC the sale price (Şandru 2003: 23). By closely analyzing the contents of people's entry petitions, Lăţea concludes that between these preemptive sales and various forms of omitting inventory, almost half of those who decided to join the Dobrosloveni GAC withheld at least part of what they owned (2003: 54–58). It seems that one could perform joining the collective without going all the way.

Direct Coercion

Threats against kin and tricking with false promises shaded easily into more overt forms of coercion, the final aspect of persuasion we will touch upon. Because we have already given a number of examples of the use of force in chapters 2–4 and will provide more in chapter 6, our coverage here will be brief. We begin with two examples of so-called administrative measures. The first concerns comrade Tóth Géza, secretary of the Party executive committee of Trei-Scaune county, disciplined for deviations from the Party line, the second some unnamed tax collectors:

> With his [Tóth's] knowledge five peasants were arrested in Leţ commune for having plowed the land of the Provisional Committee. When at the insistence of their wives comrade Vereş Iuliu intervened to have them freed, Comrade Toth Gheza' [sic] replied that they would not be freed until everyone signed up. . . . He also personally put in front of comrade Farkaş, president of the Provisional Organizing Committee and also a Party member, to sign either an entry petition for the GAC or a declaration that he's against the GAC and the regime, [and] this comrade joined.[75]

> In Călăraşi (Bucharest region) and Marghita (Oradea region) tax and quota collection teams were formed, which sequestered peasants' belongings while "explaining" that, once they joined the collective, they would be exempt from paying taxes and would be given back their possessions and the amounts of money they had already paid; at the same time, taxes were systematically increased for those who refused to join. Thus, P. A., a middle peasant from Buduşălu commune–Oradea, had his taxes increased from 600 to 3,333 lei and his furniture confiscated until he applied to join

[74] The GACs were initially expected to draw their means of production from the animals, carts, and implements "donated" by member families. On the petitions to join the collective, one had to list one's "live" and "dead" inventory, as well as all one's parcels of land (see chapter 4).

[75] ANIC, Fond C.C. al P.C.R.–Agrară, file 50/1950, 3.

> the collective. Another middle peasant had all the things in his house confiscated. Collection agent Szabó paraded through the village five carts with [P. A.'s] clothes and furniture to intimidate the peasants who had not joined the GAC.[76]

Cadres used threats of all kinds as part of persuasion. We have already mentioned threats against family members; there were many other forms of threats as well, including threats to raise people's quotas or taxes, have them classified as chiaburs, deport them, or beat them up. From Reviga: "Among the methods used by the persuasion teams were frame-ups and blackmail. . . . For example, one respondent declared that when teams of roughnecks came from Miloseşti, they slipped onto his porch a coin from the time of King Michael. Then they said, 'Look! He's keeping the King in his house!' using this as another compulsion for him to sign up" (Chelcea 2003b: 32).[77] From Turda district: "They frightened us, exerted all kinds of pressure, threatened us that we'll no longer have any rights to anything, we won't be able to do anything whatsoever, that we'll never find work" (Ţârău 2003: 61). Another tactic reported all across the country, which we already noted, was to shove people blindfolded into vans or "black cars":

> They'd stick five to six in a police van and drive them around two to three hours. And they'd say to them, "Now we're in Timişoara [about 125 miles], what do you want to do? We have the entry petitions, they're ready to sign. Do you agree?" Later, "We're at the border, what are you going to do? Are you signing?" And finally they'd sign. But they weren't in Timişoara, they were still right here![78]

Sometimes they would be told they were being taken to jail, or to be shot. A fairly standard addendum to this practice was to toss the person out of the black car into a field in the middle of the night, leaving him to find his own way home.

More crudely still, "Then they'd come again in the evening, they'd take a few of them away, give them a good beating [*câte o mamă de bătaie*], because that's the only way they were able to win them over. Otherwise it wasn't possible" (Ţârău 2009: 215). Such beatings served as examples to others, demonstrating that they had little recourse but to comply (for which they would "beg" or request to be welcomed into the collective!). Stories of beatings to extract people's "free consent" are widespread—and notorious—in all research on this period. From our project, for example, one former chiabur from Reviga recollected:

> I was sitting by the gate. "Join the collective!" I began swearing at them. "I'm not joining!" 30–40 people would come; they'd put you in their midst and hit you. I ran, but they caught me. R., the district president, took me to the village hall. "Why won't you

[76] ANIC, Fond C.C. al P.C.R.–Agrară, file 28/1952, 1.

[77] A coin with the image of the king was a problem because the king was considered an archetypical enemy of the people.

[78] 130, Verdery interview.

> join?" "Because I have 5 acres of wheat. Let me harvest it and then I'll join." Down by the bridge they beat me. 7–10 people would surround you and keep beating you up. (Chelcea 2003b: 37–38)

Similarly, in Pechea (Galați region), a peasant reported:

> Every day two cars would come with activists and dogs from Galați, who took recalcitrant villagers from their homes in the dead of night and led them out to the fields, where they would beat them. [One] was taken forcibly from his bed without even letting him get dressed, so he was removed from his house wearing only his underwear and taken in a van to the edge of the village of Nămoloasa, about 20 km from Pechea, where he was savagely beaten and left unconscious, unable even to realize where he was. (Șandru 2003: 21)

To understand fully the effects of this, we must ask ourselves what would happen next: the man would either be found or come to his senses and start to walk home with his bloodstained underwear in tatters and his body covered with bruises, encountering on his way other villagers for whom he would serve as an example of what could happen if you crossed the authorities. For the inhabitants of small rural communities where everyone knew everyone and where such insults to dignity and well-being would immediately become widely known, we should not underestimate the impact of these exemplary beatings—along with the examples of families deported from almost every village, their disappearance serving as a warning to others, as well as the arrests, imprisonments, and exemplary executions (see chapter 4 on mimesis).

Many of the more coercive forms accompanied the inclusion of the police or Securitate in the recruitment process; others were the work of zealous cadres or other members of the persuasion teams. Sometimes the coercion was exercised at a remove—for instance, activists would tell the village police to come back with a certain number of entry petitions or they'd lose their jobs. In Focşani, villagers maintained that factory workers were paid in relation to the number of people they convinced to join the collective, which fact might explain some of their excessive zeal such as their beating people up (Stoica 2009: 431). This excessive enthusiasm could become a sore point between local authorities and those sent from the district or region. Attesting to just such friction, the first president of the GAC in Năneşti observed,

> The teams had no idea how to talk to the locals. The activists leaped on people and beat them, so they hid wherever they could; but the teams would hunt them down with the help of the police. Party activists [sent in from the region] did terrible things; they beat up the peasants with clubs. During a Party meeting at the Party county offices, I told my bosses: "I'll collectivize, but without Party activists who beat people up!" (432)

Violence of this kind put all the other forms of persuasion into a context that completely altered their meaning, making it unmistakably clear to peasants that their convictions were not the aim of persuasion: all that counted was their signing up, by any means possible. The violence placed everything else against a backdrop of fear. As Goina puts it, "All these actions caused the state authority no longer to be perceived as benign or distant, but as extremely present and feared. Apprehension, fright, although they do not appear explicitly in the majority of the discussions I recorded, constitute a substrate without which they cannot be understood" (Goina 2003: 40). Fear operated systemically, and it affected cadres as well as peasants. It was a good reason for people to keep quiet, producing a climate noted by many of our respondents in which normally garrulous villagers avoided speaking to one another as they had been accustomed to doing. In this way, persuasion filled the air with talk while silencing those to be persuaded. The fear of violence, the verbal abuse and compulsion, derisively mock the polite style of the petitions described in chapter 4—"We beg you to be so kind as to accept us into the GAC." Humiliations of this kind were standard fare in persuasion work.

The Dynamics of Persuasion over Time and Context

> Priest N. A. (in March 1962): "Come along, come, Vasile, let's go, from now on this is the way, this is the path! What other way is there? Neither left nor right, you can't go left or right. This is the way, this is the road of communism, so we all live like equals and no one is richer or poorer any more. We're all equal!"
>
> Activist D. T. (after March 1962): "Tomorrow morning the Securitate is at the gate! This is the way, this is the path! Stop trying to get around it, stop turning aside, this is the way! Absolutely no objections allowed!
>
> —*Dobrincu 2003a: 50*

The conduct of persuasion and the place of force in it varied widely across time and social context. In chapter 2 we discussed the two waves of collectivization, the first lasting from 1949 to 1953, the second from 1957 to 1962. With each change in central policy, strategies of persuasion changed over time, relaxing as pressure on cadres let up and then tightening again. Coercion was largely absent from the formation of the first GACs in 1949 and early 1950; the center selected applicants likely to be successful (such as, in our study, Pechea and Sântana), then established model collectives there with huge investments to attract members—who joined willingly, especially the poorer families—with incentives and verbal persuasion (see Goina 2003, 2009; Şandru 2003). As of the summer and fall of 1950, however, violence began to escalate; the effects were felt in many communities, such as Ieud, where a GAC was set up in that year using brutal methods. Nationwide, violence was reduced again in 1951, then returned until the relaxation of 1953–56.

That relaxation saw a new, temporally conditioned form of peasant resistance: withdrawal from already-constituted GACs. Peasants who had joined under some form of compulsion began taking advantage of a clause in GAC statutes that permitted them to leave: "according to article 16 of the GAC Model Statute, 50% of the inventory brought into the GAC by the members enters into its unitary fund and the rest will be returned to members who leave the GAC" (Goina 2003: 26). The numbers could be very large: in 1954, 229 of the 523 member families in Sântana left the GAC. Not all who petitioned to leave were allowed to: a certain B. I. was refused, until he appealed successfully to Bucharest (26). Withdrawals continued across the country thereafter, but as the deadline for completing collectivization neared, petitions to withdraw were likely to earn one an unfriendly interview with the Securitate. Withdrawals such as these, of course, multiplied the work of activists, who had to replenish GAC memberships they had thought complete.

The second major wave of the collectivization campaign (1957–62) more often began with threats of job loss or expulsion of children from school than physical violence; in addition, as the GACs late in the decade allowed in more chiaburs who then became "models" for others (see chapter 7), less force was required. In the villages that had risen up in Vrancea in 1957 and been subjected to violent repression, for instance, the next wave of persuasion was much milder: instead of assaulting the villagers with force, cadres spoke more courteously and offered logical economic arguments for joining the GAC (Stoica 2009: 432, 439). The patterns varied by social status, of course. Poor peasants were rarely targets of violence (unless they were believed to be in cahoots with chiaburs), whereas people labeled chiabur experienced heavy repression in waves up through 1956—the end of quotas—then a gradual letup, though a few households might once again experience violence as a prelude to the final push. Those who had experienced violence in the first wave were worn down by years of resistance and deprivation; they were more likely to become resigned to joining in the final phase.

As time passed, cadres were more likely to cut corners in various ways, including the promises and bargains we have mentioned. In Rimetea, activists gave up trying to find heads of households who had fled into the forests and would try to persuade any member of the household to sign up, accepting signatures from wives or younger household members (Țârău 2003: 52). We suspect that this was true elsewhere as well. It appears that the arguments gradually ceased to focus on the economic benefits and emphasized instead that people had no choice, these were the orders, collectivization would happen whether they liked it or not, and they should simply accept reality.[79] In

[79] The inevitability of socialism was a trope of persuasion work in whatever form. In the letter cited previously (chapters 3, 4), two Party-member brothers reminded their village sibling that they had repeatedly explained to him [as in persuasion work] how things would be and that indeed, that is how things unfolded because "we are in touch with reality, we constantly study and know the laws by which society must develop" (ACNSAS, FP, file 248/v. 2: 23).

Table 5.1
Joining the Collective in Darabani

	Collectivization Plan		*Actually Realized*	
Date	*Families*	*Hectares*	*Families*	*Hectares*
9 February 1962	2,790	6,991	768	1,643
16 March 1962	2,790	6,991	3,204	7,703

Source: Dobrincu 2003a: 44, 51.

later years the sheer numbers of cadres assaulting villagers and households greatly expanded, enabling more intensive persuasion work of all kinds, from discussion to coercion. As the campaign drew to a close, however, places that had remained resistant were likely to experience the full effects of violence and coercion—in our project, the settlements of Domaşnea and Darabani, in particular. In Darabani, violence reverberates in the information in table 5.1 about the final six weeks of forming the GAC, just before the national campaign for collectivization was declared complete. In five weeks, the number of families in the GAC increased fourfold and the amount of land even more so, actually exceeding the amounts planned. Two thousand petitions—two-thirds of the total—date from only two days: March 14 and 15 (Dobrincu 2003a: 46).

Conclusion

From the first violations of the rule of "free consent" in 1950, when Ana Pauker departed on medical leave, persuasion ceased to be about creating an inner state of belief—a conviction of the superiority of collective agriculture. It became largely performative: a series of rehearsals that would lead to a particular spectacle, in which peasants, mostly male heads of household, would pick up a writing implement (or take their thumb) and put a mark on a piece of paper, signing over the rights to their land. We have shown here some of the conditions enabling that spectacle: cadres' colonization of kinship relations, their disruptions of the standard temporal and spatial order, their calculated use of insiders and outsiders to draw upon and then disturb accustomed social relationships, their bargains and promises, their use of force. And if the emphasis came to be placed on performance, we suggest that this resulted in part from weaknesses in the numbers and preparation of the cadres charged with the task. The consequences for state-subject relations were vast: as Yurchak (2006) has argued, subjects performed allegiance to the regime while going about their own business, leaving ever open the possibility that they were "enemies" in disguise.

In following the Soviet blueprint, Romanian cadres used many of the Soviets' techniques to lure peasants into joining the collectives: various forms of propaganda, mimesis with positive and negative examples, denunciations and unmaskings, agitation and persuasion, and so on. The Soviets, too, had a category called "persuasion," which came into play in response to complaints of excessive violence.[80] But the weight placed on persuasion work as opposed to outright force was greater in Romania, for two reasons. First, Romania's Party leaders rejected the extremes of violence that had marked the Soviet experience, which Pauker in particular had seen firsthand. Second, the history of smallholding and the minimal importance of communal tenure in Romania made its villagers more tenacious than Soviet ones in defense of their land, and this required more individualized and nuanced strategies to pry it from their grip. Activists could not simply force village councils to vote for collectives. They had, rather, to insert the Party-state intimately into villagers' lives, disrupting their accustomed rhythms and social ties and, in the process, creating new state-subject relations. To do so, cadres were forced onto the peasants' terrain, having to make use of the existing instruments of social organization and the cultural meanings these held.

One image for thinking about this process comes from language. Party leaders adopted a set of categories from the Soviet experience (enemies, "politicals," class, chiaburs, and so on) and then developed ways of drawing the peasants into conversation with them, so these categories would become lived objects of discourse. Most of the techniques discussed in these two chapters are based on forms of dialogism (which is not to say that the parties to the dialogue were equal). Persuasion work required dialogue between cadres and those they were trying to convince, even if the dialogue might be supplemented with threats and physical violence. Petitions involved dialogue between those writing them and those helping with the proper form; especially in the case of reclassification petitions and other forms of complaint, they initiated extended dialogue both with the petitioner and—even more so—within the bureaucracy. As Mikhail Bakhtin would have told them, however, their conversations could not begin with a *tabula rasa* but used words already imbued with certain understandings, and these necessarily pulled the conversation off center, from a blueprint point of view. Nevertheless, the power differential meant that cadres could more reliably enforce their meanings through practices that compelled peasant participation.

Thus, the new communist government put into place a new economy of speech and silence. It emitted propaganda messages that were not intended for reply, while in other respects inciting people to speak. It encouraged not only statements of loyalty and adherence to the Party but also contestations, not only positive discourse (such as about the benefits of collectivizing) but also denunciations. In daily life, however, the effects of persuasion work were silencing—

[80] Viola, personal communication.

one of persuasion's many ironies. Villagers would avoid one another, sometimes not telling even their spouses what had happened to them. That long-standing form of social discipline, "the talk of the village" (*gura satului*), was driven underground, replaced by an external source of discipline in the form of the Securitate and police. There had been police in villages before, but they had been fully visible: now their agents became shadows, informers whose identity people might guess at but could not know for certain. In these circumstances, it was wise to shut up. The balance between two capacities—speech and vision—shifted in favor of the latter. Although people ceased to speak as much, they saw: whenever cadres showed up at someone's home, neighbors knew; likewise when someone staggered home from a beating. Villagers had always kept an eye on one another to enrich their sources of gossip, and the Party knew enough to take advantage of this.

A second image for these processes comes from biology. Persuasion worked like a virus: activists attached themselves to an existing cell—a household, a community—that had its own mechanisms of reproduction, invaded that cell, and gradually turned its mechanisms to the service of reproducing something very different. In the process, the particulars of the cell lost their specificity: even after cadres left, a new relationship with power had been put into place. For some, the relationship would prove enabling, for others less so, for still others deeply destructive; but for everyone, the Party-state had been inserted into villagers' networks at the level of everyday life. This image is apposite for "organizational breakthrough." In describing persuasion work, we have emphasized practices that broke through the cell wall, throwing peasants off guard and producing moments of disorientation that could affect their judgments. In the next chapter we continue this catalogue with the final technology Romania's communists brought to bear: the fomenting of class warfare, with its devastating consequences for village social organization.

Chapter 6

Fomenting Class War

> The history of all hitherto existing society is the history of class struggle.
> —*The Communist Manifesto*

> Guided by the U.S.S.R.'s extensive experience in collectivizing agriculture, we continue to apply with determination the politics of class in the countryside, supporting peasant workers, cementing their alliance with the working class, and fomenting uninterrupted war to undermine the wealthy peasants.[1]
> —*Romanian Party leader Gheorghiu-Dej*

> Collectivization is more than an effort to economically and politically undermine landlords and kulaks; it is more than an effort to industrialize. It is an attack on the social institutions and cultural orientations of peasant society. . . . The distinctiveness of Leninist strategy may lie in collectivization as a particular means of undermining the peasant extended household and village.[2]

> If a family is destroyed, you feel pity; but a whole community?[3]

In the previous two chapters, we set out the principal pedagogies through which the Party introduced its ways of thinking to the peasantry and drew them into employing its terms, while making use of village social organization to persuade peasants into the collectives. Now we complete the discussion of organizational breakthrough by explaining another key instrument for carrying out the mammoth restructuring the communists envisioned: fomenting class struggle or class war.[4] Carried out simultaneously with the other techniques discussed so far, it provided the framework for the politics of difference we discussed in chapter 4, resignifying familiar persons, practices, and everyday language in new ways; it was also the subject of much persuasion work. Class war was crucial to creating the "socialist body politic" and setting the stage for the campaign to create the "new socialist person" (formalized under Ceauşescu). Through the exposure, persecution, and elimination of "enemy el-

[1] Gheorghiu-Dej 1955: 261. This quote is a variant of one that served as a mantra for the Party. We repeat it to underscore its ritualized repetition over the years. We note that such words of wisdom were used in multiple contexts and by multiple speakers.

[2] Jowitt 1978: 59, 63.

[3] M. T., Iordachi interview.

[4] We have chosen to use the less familiar "class war" because "class struggle" is so widely used that readers have associations we would like to bypass, emphasizing instead the techniques employed to set rural status groups against each other.

ements" such as chiaburs, the body politic was to be purified and purged of "foreign" beings.

In fomenting class war, Romania's communists once again took their lead from the Soviet Union, whose "extensive experience in collectivizing agriculture" served as their guiding light and provided the basic script.[5] Its central ingredient in Romania's villages was the demonization of wealthy peasants in discourse and deed.[6] Class war was meant to provoke social conflict as well as create unprecedented opportunities for the formerly poor. But with this policy, the Soviet blueprint ran into serious difficulties (and not only in Romania). In chapter 2 we described the traditional social organization of Romanian villages, based on differential status and notions of status honor. This fact created a fundamental dilemma for the implementers of class war: because their peasantry did not think in terms of classes, how could they foment class war (see chapter 4)? Thus, in Romania as in the Soviet Union, cadres hoping to use class struggle to break apart village social organization and promote class equality would paradoxically have to create classes and class stratification from the forms of status inequality proper to these villagers.[7] How they tried to do that is the subject of the present chapter.

As we explained in chapter 2, peasant status values emphasized possession of land and animals enabling self-directed labor, social embeddedness and wealth in people, and moral values centered on character and hard work. Communist categories, by contrast, saw these as based on exploiting the labor of others. Since differential ownership of the means of production grounded both labor exploitation and status based on possession, confiscating the land of wealthy peasants would seem one way to address the problem. That, however, would disrupt the supply of food to the cities, and so it was done only selectively. The challenge was to keep the wealthy peasants producing while making them pariahs and isolating them from other peasants socially—that is, undercutting their status honor and their wealth in people—while recasting the moral universe of the village through new ideas about justice. As with the material already presented, these actions involved instituting a new regime of truth, new

[5] In a number of respects, the Soviet blueprint for class struggle developed from conditions different from Romania's. An important one was that the Bolsheviks created it against Russian aristocratic categories based on an estate system (*soslovie*), the target and substrate of the new class categories—and different from the prevalent form of social inequality in Romania. Another was that the main incentive for collectivizing in the Soviet Union was a grain crisis that the leaders saw as revealing the strength of the rural bourgeoisie; hence, class war was an offensive against capitalist elements in the countryside, and "liquidation of the kulaks" destroyed them. The terms of the equation differed in Romania.

[6] Stalin emphasized that in the war "against the kulaks, you must fight with economic measures and within the framework of Soviet law," a point that the Romanian leaders repeated incessantly. (See Stalin, cited in Roske 2003: 162.)

[7] See Lefort (1986) on the paradoxes of modernity; also see Yurchak's use of "Lefort's Paradox" in his discussion of late socialism in the Soviet Union (2006: 10).

answers to perennial questions such as what is justice? what is exploitation? and how should wealth be gotten and enjoyed?

We begin our discussion with a brief summary of what the concept of "chiabur" (rural exploiter) meant and how the Party understood the problem of class war. We then take up three sets of actions put in practice to foment it: first, the "neutralization" of the chiaburs through quotas and other exactions; second, efforts to compromise their status honor; and third, pushing the notion of "exploitation," which would undermine their wealth in people. As in chapter 4, we emphasize how peasants of different social groups were drawn into these actions—in particular, how chiaburs themselves were encouraged to think differently about their relations to others through the process of contesting their chiabur status. We conclude with some brief comments about how these various actions were received.

Launching Class War

> The kulak is not an alien in the village who is seen primarily as an economic exploiter, but he is a key figure in the corporate household and village system of social identification, organization, and power. Leninism errs in its understanding of his character and role, but it does so in a way that leads to strategies and policies that undermine the kulak, the peasant household, and the village community as defining institutions in a peasant-status society.
> —*Jowitt 1978: 58–59.*

The opening salvo in rural class war was the confiscation of the largest estates in 1945, an action that fundamentally disturbed the system of interwar agrarian relations.[8] The removal of their patrons left Romania's many poor or landless peasants without protection or means of existence and opened them to manipulation by the communists, with whom they had few options but to collaborate. By these confiscations, the Party-state took upon itself the task of patronizing this group as their protectors and promoting the thesis of an unconditional alliance between them and the Party. To fulfil this role, they would have to provide the poor with access to land: collectivization would accomplish that goal. At the same time, however, the communists wished to break apart the village social structure oppressing the poor and to upset any alliance they or the middle peasants might form with the wealthier ones. In short, they would have to decapitate the village elite. First, however, they would have to agree on what that was.

"Who Was the Romanian Chiabur?"

Those who were to bear the brunt of class war were the chiaburs, the rural bourgeoisie. But exactly what and who was a chiabur? The chiabur, introduced

[8] We thank Constantin Iordachi for insisting on the points in this paragraph.

in chapter 2, was a child of the Soviet kulak. Although in Soviet parlance as adopted by the Romanian communists "kulak" officially meant a peasant who exploited the labor of others,[9] to villagers it meant one who was wealthy and respected—a fundamentally misguided conception, in the view of Party leaders. Even cadres and other Party members shared this error, revealing the power of the chiabur's "deception." As Gheorghiu-Dej put it:

> The chiabur—the village bourgeois—is a type apart from others, who has formed his household working, sweating, exploiting and speculating. . . . They aren't much different from other peasants if you look at their clothing or the fact that they work. That is why, in the eyes of peasants, the chiabur is an industrious and respected person, "*buni gospodari*." . . . This mentality and way of seeing them as good household managers has penetrated even into the ranks of our Party. (Quoted in Cătănuş and Roske 2000: 16)

Seeking to reduce the evident confusion in defining what a chiabur was, the Party leadership sent down to officials in the regions a document entitled "Basic Indicators for Identifying Chiabur Households," instructing them on precisely how to do so.[10] The main criterion focused on a person's ability to exploit others (rather than on the extent of his landholdings), such as his using hired labor for more than thirty days a year, owning means of production that were exploited for income, and having any kind of commercial enterprise.

But things were nowhere near this cut-and-dried. In a 1966 paper, Moshe Lewin asked "Who Was the Soviet Kulak?" answering, in brief, "It is, in the first place, he who is declared to be such by the authorities" (Lewin 1985: 126). Other scholars have followed suit: for example, Viola writes, "In practice, kulak status always remained in the eye of the beholder" (1987: 35; see also Conquest 1986: 74). Likewise Romanian scholars: Cîrstocea, for example, writes, "Detailed analysis of the archive did not enlighten me . . . about exactly what was a chiabur. . . . The concept . . . precedes the object to which it refers" (2002: 47).

According to Getty and Naumov (1999: 21), terms like "kulak" and "Trotsky-

[9] Kulak did not always have this meaning. Literally, the word means "fist," and in tsarist times it referred to village extortionists and usurers, who were not necessarily prosperous peasants. After the Revolution, however, the term was broadened to mean the rural bourgeoisie (Lewin 1985: 121, 123). The attempt to define specific criteria by which to recognize kulaks foundered on the complexity of rural economic and social relations—for instance, if a fixed land area such as eight hectares were the criterion, then what about differences in soil quality between two farms? If it were using nonfamily labor, then how about various forms of hiding that relation, such as adoption, or bringing in the neighbors for a workday? How about if the employee were a poor childless widow who *had* no family labor? And so on.

[10] See ANIC, Fond C.C. al P.C.R–Agrară, file 29/1952, 2–8, which provides regional Party Committees' responses to questions about criteria for categorizing chiaburs, and ANIC, Fond C.C. al P.C.R.–Cancelarie, file 32/1952, 39–42 (cited in Ionescu-Gură 2000: 289). See also DJAN HD, Fond CR PMR, file 430/1952, 252–263. This document and others like it followed on the Plenary Session of the CC, February 29–March 1, 1952, at which the guidelines for identifying "chiaburs" were spelled out.

ist" were attributive, not definitional, so there is no point looking for criteria to define them. They were political categories, not social ones: labeling someone a "kulak" simply said that the person was considered to be against the regime. Rather than being specific real people, kulaks/chiaburs were symbols for opposition, for disaster, for why things were not going well.[11] Some of our respondents saw it this way too. Many suggested that there were two categories of chiaburs: real ones and made-up ones, and most of them were the latter type.[12] One person, when asked how many chiaburs there were in his village, replied, "Oh, everyone [the Party] didn't like" (Vultur 2003: 43). A schoolteacher, when asked about chiaburs, responded: "If you said anything, the truth, or said anything against [them], they made you a chiabur. . . . Anyone whose tongue was more biting, that was it, chiabur!"[13] A former GAC chairman in Jurilovca: "Chiaburs? Is this a joke? The party appointed some thugs to name people chiaburs. Those were the times. If they saw a man with six children to feed and six hectares of land and they thought he was making propaganda against people's signing up for the GAC, they pinned him down by calling him a chiabur" (Iordachi 2009: 125).

Although the large majority of peasants opposed collectivization, it was those labeled chiaburs who were made to *embody* that opposition and to suffer the punishment. Moreover, chiaburs could be used to explain problems even in villages where none lived at all (Lewin 1968: 494). In this sense they resemble the "Jew." Both were represented in ugly caricatures as fat, distasteful, and nonhuman (vermin, bloodsuckers, vampires, etc.). This helps to make sense of another feature of kulak/chiabur status: the Party saw it as inherited, as a matter of essence that did not disappear once a chiabur lost his wealth.[14] Fitzpatrick likens them to Untouchables, an ascribed status rather than a class (2000: 28). As with Untouchability, chiabur status was polluting; it made impure anyone who came into contact with it (kinspeople, spouses, children). Such impurity warranted expulsion, even extermination.

This is not to say that all people labeled chiabur were completely innocent: some of them might well be sabotaging the collective farm from within, spreading rumors that the Americans were coming, throwing sand into their threshers to gum up the works, and so on. They might well be influencing their kin and poor villagers to resist collectivization, as the Party believed. A few former chiaburs whom we interviewed spoke proudly of how they had opposed collectivization. On the whole, however, people named chiaburs were the hapless victims of an ideological obsession with finding in the countryside a class

[11] Having fluid definitions was in fact helpful, for different factions could agree more easily on members of a loosely defined category than of a rigorous one. Lampland (n.d.) notes that in Hungary as well, the criteria to determine kulak status were also unclear to those meant to apply them.

[12] See, for example, Iordachi 2003: 42.

[13] T. S., Kligman interview.

[14] See, for example, the letters in Kristó 1999.

structure that was in fact absent. Robert Conquest's conclusion from his work on Soviet collectivization is fitting: that the chiabur was the physical manifestation of an abstract class enemy.

> Thus, by a strange logic, a middle peasant could become a kulak by gaining property, but a kulak could not become a middle peasant by losing his. In fact the kulak had no escape. He was "essentially" a class enemy, a sub-human. Yet the naming of the kulak enemy satisfied the Marxist preconceptions of the Party activist. It presented a flesh-and-blood foe accursed by history; and such a target made for a far more satisfactory campaign than mere abstract organizational change. And it provided the means of destroying the leadership of the villagers, which might have greatly strengthened the resistance . . . which they offered to collectivization. (Conquest 1986: 120)

Vigilance Against the Class Enemy!

At a meeting of the Orgburo of the Central Committee on June 6, 1950, Gheorghiu-Dej stated the task of class war as follows:

> We have to arrive at actions against the chiaburs by interesting and mobilizing the poor and middle peasantry . . . so that we don't create sympathy for the chiaburs but rather that the working peasantry see him as an enemy. . . . [W]e have to restrict him, force him to work the land, and prevent him from donating his land so that he is not seen as a benefactor in their eyes. We have to work hard to get the people to hate him. That way it will be easy to rid the villages of him.[15]

To change peasants' "misunderstanding" of chiaburs, the Party would engage in a multifaceted assault on them, demonizing them through propaganda, attacking them verbally and physically in public and in their homes, arresting, incarcerating, and deporting them. A primary task was to expose them for what they were and keep them from infiltrating the Party to pervert its goals, for chiaburs, like all enemies, were thought to be continually engaged in sabotage. "Working peasants" and workers were enlisted in this project, warned to be ever vigilant, ready to unmask the chiaburs' duplicitous deeds. According to a rhyme circulating in Transylvania's Hungarian villages, "The worker's fist is an iron fist; it hits wherever necessary" (*Munkásököl, vasököl, oda üt, ahová köll*; Kristó 1999: 43). Everyone was to be trained in the spirit of "revolutionary vigilance."[16]

Indeed, Martha Lampland argues that we ought to pay as much attention to vigilance as to fear and terror. Cultivating a disposition toward vigilance, for which class war was a central means, enrolled everyone in the effort to rejuvenate society and taught them that the greatest danger was to lapse into a false

[15] ANIC, Fond C.C. al P.C.R.–Cancelarie, file 41/1950, 24–25 (RLA).

[16] DJAN MM, Fond Comitetul Raional Vişeu, file 33/1952/V, 20.

sense of calm.[17] Accompanying the exercise of vigilance would be practices of exposure: the denunciations and unmaskings discussed in chapter 4. The masses were expected to submit concrete evidence of the devious ways in which chiaburs tried to trick the system, whether by spreading rumors, hiding property, joining the Party or collective farms under false pretenses, not paying their taxes or quotas, or other means.[18] But for good measure, there were penalties in place for peasants who helped chiaburs withhold their products or were in any way complicitous in their schemes against the government.[19] Răutu, the Propaganda Minister, warned, "However many times the enemy tries to reaffirm his social legitimacy, . . . he must be exposed!" (cited in Tănase 2003: 167).

Making Chiabur Lists

The result of vigilance, denunciations, unmaskings, and so forth was lists of chiaburs, who would then be subjected to all manner of punishments. How did people get on these lists? In the early stages of planning collectives, local Party cells supplied basic information about the targeted villages' social composition—including the number of poor, middle, and wealthy peasants; the religious denominations and political affiliations; and other general demographic data—and their material assets. These data set a baseline for creating chiabur lists, which existed for virtually every commune. Initiated at the commune level, usually by the Party cell, the lists had several sources. Party members applying the vague criteria they had received named some people, though the classifications often seemed arbitrary, for as we saw in chapter 3, cadres might use personal discretion in putting people on the lists according to whom they

[17] Lampland n.d. She likens vigilance to divination (in the search for the presence of evil forces) and sabotage to witchcraft. Researchers have begun to explore the relationship between vigilance and cardiovascular reactivity. "Vigilance for threat" is defined in this work "as a chronic search for potential threats from other people or things in the environment." It is hypothesized that vigilance for potential threat may have "behavioral, emotional, and physiological consequences" (Gump and Matthews 1998; we thank Carol Worthman for bringing this to our attention).

[18] See DJAN MM, Fondul Comitetul Regional PMR Baia Mare, file 65/1949, 286. "Lack of vigilance" led to the "infiltration" of chiaburs into the GACs, as a result of which there was a general effort to expel them in 1952. Those chiaburs who joined the GACs initially usually did so to avoid the high costs to them and their families of not joining. However, as the brunt of class war in these early years, enemies could not be included except under exceptional circumstances.

An example of deception, of how people "hid" animals and why, comes from a lengthy interview by Kligman with P. V., in Ieud, Maramureş, who said: "You had three cows, but you only listed two. You kept the third so that when your quota amount arrived, you milked three cows to be able to cover the amount listed for two. Or, if you had fifty sheep, you listed only twenty-five. Your quota included amounts for wool and cheese, calculated after the number of sheep you had. From their milk, you made cheese. You didn't give the milk, but however many kilos of cheese they told you."

[19] See, for but one example, DJAN HD, Fond CR PMR, file 728/1952, 44.

liked or who had bribed them. For instance, a former head of the agricultural section of the Orăştie district offices reported:

> I had a chiabur, Ştefănie from Beriu. The secretary of the People's Council was in very bad relations with him, and Ştefănie told me why: the secretary asked him for a sow and he refused to give him one. So I was there right in that period when they were making people chiaburs, and the secretary denounced him. I talked to someone at the Party offices about getting him out, but the secretary of the People's Council in Beriu had it in for him. After we would [remove Ştefănie from the list], he'd put him right back on again.[20]

List makers also enjoyed the help of villagers eager to denounce their fellows, vendettas and personal rivalries being important sources of naming—a pattern familiar from China's Cultural Revolution and similar contexts as well.

Even though "what" a chiabur was gradually became clearer, owing to centrally distributed instructions, "who" remained somewhat arbitrary—at least, in the recollections of our respondents: "How they considered you, that's how it was." "Whoever they wanted to destroy, they did; whoever not, they didn't." "Oh, if you aren't a bit obedient, those guys would burn you on the spot! If you raised your head a little, they made you a 'political,' and there was nothing you could do, they'd call you to the Securitate."[21] "They," in these instances, generally referred to local cadres and their village allies.[22] The local is important to foreground here: in daily village life, labeling someone a chiabur was considered a local affair, for that was where class war was to be waged, making people vulnerable to the grudges and envy of their fellow villagers.

"Neutralizing" the Chiabur

From the moment people were labeled chiaburs, they became the primary scapegoats for the Party's problems in creating collectives.[23] They were blamed

[20] M. H., Verdery interview.

[21] The quotations are from Vultur 2003: 44; Kligman 2009: 170; Dobrincu 2003a: 66. One man who had relatives in America and, together with his wife, about fifteen hectares, was "made" into a chiabur, about which he commented ironically: "Yeah, chiabur like hell—with lice!" See Manoliu-Furnică 1997–98: 254.

[22] Stan (2001: 104–5) notes that in villages where chiaburs could not readily be determined based on signs of "capitalist" behavior (e.g., owning means of production, exploiting others), labeling enemies became yet more arbitrary; land possession was then used as a "reserve criterion" to make middle peasants into chiaburs, thereby disciplining middle peasants opposed to the regime.

[23] Chiabur status was complicated by its interaction with other "enemy" categories. Former Uniate priests, for example, may have had "chiabur" origins. Chiaburs who hid in the hills to avoid paying taxes or providing quotas were often conflated with politicals involved in more violent anti-regime activities, and so on. Regarding collectivization, chiaburs were the targeted class enemy par excellence. See Kligman and Verdery 2006; Iordachi and Dobrincu 2009.

for spreading rumors against collectivization, for urging fellow villagers to delay planting and harvesting, and for encouraging others to use violence against cadres. According to Party cadres, chiaburs took every opportunity to sabotage the Party's agenda of bettering the lives of the exploited. For such actions they had to be "neutralized" and punished, as much in economic (i.e., through expropriation of their property, high taxes, and obligatory quotas) as in social terms. This was necessary for the plan to destroy their class basis—that is, to decapitate the rural elite—and uplift those with healthier social origins.

The policy of "neutralization" (*îngrădire*) meant preventing the chiabur from reproducing his economic power for himself and forcing him to enhance that of the Party. Early in the process, this was accomplished in part by confiscating a wealthy peasant's possessions, to give collectivizers a larger material base, frighten other villagers, and provide a negative example. A key device for this was a 1948 law on "combating sabotage in agriculture," which stipulated the arrest and imprisonment of a number of peasants already or soon to be named chiaburs, with confiscation of all their wealth. Through this law hundreds of people were sentenced all over Romania. For instance, Leonida Teodor, of Ilia commune (Hunedoara), possessing 9 hectares of arable land, two cows, two calves, a mare, and three colts, was condemned to thirteen months in prison, a 20,000 lei fine, and the confiscation of all his movable and immovable wealth for the crime of "economic infraction": "In the present agricultural campaign he did not harvest 4.58 hectares of wheat by the July 3 deadline, leaving the grain to fall off because it was too ripe. The accused also had 2.88 hectares sown with clover, which he did not weed properly. The accused also did not participate in the campaign to eradicate the Colorado bug."[24] The chiabur and perhaps his family might even be deported or sent to labor camps. This way of handling chiaburs began late in 1950 with the sudden increase in the pace of collectivizing, and abuses were quick to accumulate.[25]

Quotas and Their Evasion

Aside from these confiscations, the principal means for neutralizing were the exorbitant quotas and taxes we discussed in chapter 2, which our interviewees

[24] Document courtesy of Aurel Răduțiu; although the source is not indicated, it likely comes from the Fond Tribunal Deva in the Hunedoara County archives.

[25] Soon thereafter, the Party leadership launched an investigation of these abuses and determined that of a total of 789 confiscations from the "rural bourgeoisie"—599 of them chiaburs—only 34 (4 percent) were wholly justified responses to grave infractions; 343 were justified sentences for which the confiscations were judged "unjust"; 131 were sentences that were themselves unjustified by any real infraction; and 112 had been done with no judicial process at all. Unfortunately for the chiaburs in question, most of the land confiscated had been given to new GACs and was not returned (ANIC, Fond C.C. al P.C.R.–Organizatorică, file 134/1950, 1–5). The document does not state the unit for the investigation (the whole country? a group of counties?) and is not dated, though it refers to confiscations made "from May 1, 1950, to the present."

said "left them with nothing at all to eat." These burdens, designed to break people down and force their "consent" to communist authority, were not only for chiaburs, of course, but they were graduated, favoring the poor and harshly penalizing chiaburs, in the interest of minimizing their influence in their communities.[26] The point was to assign chiaburs such heavy quotas, with such stiff penalties for noncompliance, that they would be forced to adopt measures to increase production. A former chiabur recalled that the amounts they were expected to deliver to the state were intentionally beyond any reasonable possibility, thereby placing them in violation of the law: "They imposed a very high quota. You received a small notebook in which every quantity—of meat, wheat, barley, corn—was listed. They knew that no one could possibly give that much, so then they could say you were engaged in sabotage, and they locked you up. There was no one we could ask why the amounts were so high."[27] The excessiveness of these quotas and taxes often gave rise to despair. As a daughter of chiaburs recollected about her parents: "After a year, they were so destroyed that they just didn't know what to do. Because they were Catholics and believed in God, they couldn't commit suicide—they couldn't do such a thing, but they were so done in. The enormous pain I saw on my parents' faces, how much they suffered, how much they cried, I will never forget . . . their suffering, it is indelible" (Bodó 2003: 24). Collecting the quotas might be accompanied by violence, sometimes fatal, especially where deliveries had been slight and recalcitrance high. Another common tactic applied to those with quota or tax arrears was to enter their homes by force and take as many belongings as would be needed to pay for the quotas owed. "If you couldn't pay, they took bread right off the table . . . and the clothes you were wearing, and whatever was best in your house, they took it and sold it at auction, you couldn't recover it," a former chiabură woefully recalled.[28] Besides these confiscations, delinquent chiaburs could be tried and sentenced to anything from a fine to several years in jail or in a work camp.

Chiaburs developed a number of ruses for evading their quotas—as did all peasants subject to them. They hid grain with their kin and claimed not to have anything left when the collectors came. Or they hid it at home: "My father tried to hide some stuff and he built a fake wall in the stable, and he hid wine and foodstuffs behind it. But we were caught. . . . As a result, I was expelled from school" (Stoica 2009: 434). They divided their households into smaller units, whose combined quotas were less than that of the undivided family.[29] They tried to tough it out, like A. S. from Romos (Hunedoara), who refused categorically to give his quota of meat and milk, saying "that he would give the collector

[26] Certain goods were also graduated in price. For example, to buy a wagon of wood cost chiaburs fifty lei; middle peasants, thirty; and poor, twenty (I. S., Kligman interview).

[27] D. V., Kligman interview. Regional officials did complain to central authorities that due to the soil conditions, middle peasants and chiaburs could not meet their obligatory quotas. See DJAN MM, Fond 10, nr. 8/1951, n.p.

[28] P. V., Kligman interview.

[29] This strategy worked because the quotas increased exponentially as land amounts increased.

his member, in place of milk, and his horse's member, in place of meat for the workers to eat."[30] A document from the Hunedoara regional collections office elaborated further on chiabur tactics, noting that "[their] most common methods are separating their wheat sheaves from those of others, not registering the full quantity threshed, removing produce from the convoy, giving their land in sharecropping, selling produce unthreshed directly from their fields."[31]

Some of the ruses—far too numerous to detail here—went beyond avoiding one's quotas to damaging the economy of GACs. For instance, one common chiabur practice was to harvest their crops, pay the fine for not giving their quotas, sell the crops in town for more money than the fine, and use the difference to pay more for hired labor than the state and collective farms could afford to pay as wages. Peasants might then prefer to work for the chiabur rather than joining the collective farm. Another ruse that could cost the Party large amounts of money in lost chiabur quotas was to bribe officials, as we showed in chapter 3. Particularly successful at this were shepherds, among whom chiaburs were usually designated on the grounds that they exploited labor. (One shepherd could not manage a large flock on his own, hence he hired people to help him, a practice that landed him and many others on the chiabur lists.) Because their form of livelihood had enabled them to accumulate sizable fortunes, especially in the interwar years (see Stewart and Stan 2009: 258), chiabur shepherds were able to bribe local and district officials to have their names removed from the chiabur lists.

> My brother-in-law, my sister's husband, he had been declared a *chiabur*. . . . It was in '52–'53–'54, something like that, and my brother-in-law went to see this guy, the vice-president. And he gave him 80,000 [lei].[32] We went to the vice-president's home one night. "Neighbor"—he was his neighbor, you see—"Here you are." And he gave him the 80,000. After the first meeting, he was off the list. . . . That's how they did it. Everyone would find a protector. . . . In time, they were all removed from the list. One by one, until there was no *chiabur* left. (Stewart and Stan 2009: 258)[33]

Finally, some chiaburs hoped to escape the high quotas and taxes assessed them by trying to join the GACs or by donating their land and other property to the state. Indeed, in various communes where Party organizers recognized that the collective did not possess enough land, they deliberately modified the number of chiaburs on their lists, reducing the total and enrolling into the col-

[30] DJAN HD, Fond CR PMR, file 888/1953, 68.

[31] DJAN HD, Fond CR PMR, file 728/1952, 44.

[32] At that time, the average salary was about 1,000 lei. Compared to this figure, the economic power of the shepherds is obvious.

[33] N. I., Stan interview for M. Stewart. While memory seems to have played a small trick on the former sheep owner then in his early eighties, nonetheless, 81 percent of the thirty-seven petitions submitted to the local committee for removal from chiabur status were indeed approved—an unusually high rate.

lectives those they removed. While other comrades opposed such clear violations of class war's ethos, they were overruled by the need for land and livestock (Márton 2005: 7).

In general, of course, the Party leadership had established that chiaburs were not welcome in the GACs. Attempts to donate their holdings were also unwelcome, even though most GACs had insufficient land. Thus, ideological tenets and material needs were at odds. According to government decree 308/1953, chiabur efforts to renounce their agricultural land "must be viewed as attempts to sabotage agricultural production and to avoid fulfilling [their] obligations to the state" (cited in Ionescu-Gură 2000: 295). As class enemies bent on disrupting the collectives, chiaburs who managed to join them were to be rooted out and expelled as part of the campaign to neutralize them, while continuing to exact the results of the labor they expended to meet their quotas. Aware of the contradictions inherent in class war that made it virtually impossible to integrate chiaburs into the GACs with their property, experience, and community standing, some cadres nonetheless sought reasons to facilitate their inclusion in the early years. In the letter we mentioned in chapter 4, from two brothers to their brother in the village (Ieud), they skillfully engaged the Party's concepts and categories to that end, noting straight off: "Truth be told, you are not a chiabur, but a middle peasant" who, as a result of various enmities, ended up being associated with chiaburs, "all of whom will, one by one, be distanced from the new order being born."[34] They urged that their brother and his extended family get on board, not only for their own good but for that of society. As we will see, these brothers understood that policy toward chiaburs would have to change.

Verification Practices

As is evident, quotas served as a site for evasion of the policies designed to neutralize chiaburs. The struggle to enforce them also participated in another set of policies concerning chiaburs: efforts to verify their status. In chapter 2 we described the verification of Party members, which led to a reduction in the Party's size. Verification as a practice was systemic, the counterpart to the obsession with blaming and purifying; it applied not only to Party members, cadres, the Securitate, etc., but to chiaburs as well. To control against local-level abuses and mistaken identities, central authorities verified the lists of chiaburs that were sent to them up the hierarchy of command, from the communes to the district, regional, and central committees charged with verification. Some of these verifications were prompted by chiaburs contesting their assigned category, a practice we will return to below; some came from ques-

[34] ACNSAS, FP, file 248/1950/v. 2, 23.

tions raised about the grounds for including particular persons, as a list worked its way up the hierarchy. Those names were then sent back so that local Party representatives could justify their inclusion and perhaps learn from their mistake, as we see in the following case about two chiaburs whose status was considered questionable:

> If the persons named were designated chiaburs based only on their wealth, then you have committed a grave abuse of the party line. . . . Those named, if they do not have means of exploitation, are poor or middle peasants, given that they have large families and live in a mountainous region where the land is poor. . . . In our work, we have to use all our force and the laws of proletarian dictatorship against the chiaburs, but not against poor or middle peasants under any circumstances.[35]

As a former member of the State Planning Commission of the Ministry of Agriculture pointed out, however, "Laws and instructions were written in a civilized form, very nice, but how they were applied was another matter. It isn't all the same what is written on paper and what happened."[36]

This inquiry nonetheless left room to classify a poor or middle peasant as an enemy, although not necessarily a chiabur (recalling their common conflation), if s/he "has a past hostile to the democratic regime, was the leader of one of the historic parties [Liberals, Peasantists], or of the Legionary-fascist party, was knowingly involved in anticommunist activities."[37] Not surprisingly, a person's past was widely invoked to justify his or her designation as a class enemy. As to the two in question, the response made clear that they had been rightly categorized: "D.I. is part of the exploiting class [exploiting labor more than 30 days in the year]; D.V. has 6 hectares of land of the best quality, a cow, 2 horses, 12 sheep, a thresher, a mill, a small timber mill operated by water [owning and exploiting means of production]."[38]

The Party's concern that people be properly assigned to the chiabur lists accompanied the incessant propaganda that promoted the alliance of working and middle peasants. Party leaders repeatedly emphasized that it was not enough for commune, district, or regional commissions merely to state that someone was "correctly assigned to chiabur status," but that the commissions had to provide appropriate supporting evidence (i.e., X exploited labor more than thirty days, etc.). While such information was generally formulaic in character, it was intended to militate against personalistic motives for including people on such lists.

Why was the Communist Party so concerned about verifying chiabur lists? To explain this, we must briefly review the complex determination of chiabur policy, outlined in chapter 2. On the one hand, the Party's entire strategy for

[35] See ACNSAS, FP, file 248/v. 2, 17, regarding Ieud, Maramureş.

[36] H. D., Kligman interview.

[37] ACNSAS, FP, file 248/v. 2, 17.

[38] Ibid., 22.

collectivizing rested on winning over the middle peasantry so they would join collectives, their land and farming abilities helping to create model farms; it was crucial not to alienate middle peasants by misclassifying them. But on the other hand, because persons labeled chiabur had to give quotas far heavier than those assigned to middle peasants, it was crucial to have enough chiaburs to provide needed food supplies and a source of accumulation for the industrialization drive. These two goals had to be held in a delicate balance: if chiaburs were too harshly persecuted they would be unable to produce the required food surplus, but if they were treated too leniently they would accumulate capital and corrupt other villagers as well as cadres. In the verification process the note "appropriate for neutralization" indicates this balance, referring to a process that forced chiaburs to produce as much as possible, after which their product was expropriated, providing the state with vital resources while "neutralizing" the chiaburs, now unable to consolidate their economic positions.[39] Therefore, it was crucial to the Party's political as well as economic goals that people labeled chiabur be verified. In consequence, the Party invited peasants to contest their classifications. We underline this point lest the contestations by chiaburs be seen only as a form of "resistance."[40]

In this light, we understand better the significance of the following report. In 1954 the Central Committee did one of its periodic revisions of the instructions concerning chiabur lists. One year later, the Constanţa regional Party noticed that an intense period of reclassification (i.e., removal from chiabur status) had followed. The First Party Secretary from there reported that committees had spent two months verifying the lists, but had (inexplicably) kept only those who exploited labor more than thirty days per year on them. This meant that chiaburs who had donated their land to the village council or who renounced exploiting others were reclassified, and the consequence was a dramatic reduction in the number of chiaburs and also in the obligatory quotas collected (see also chapter 2). Not surprisingly, the authorities in Bucharest ordered that the lists be revisited, restoring to the Party's control the lands that cadres had erroneously returned to reclassified former chiaburs, reimposing their quotas, and sanctioning those who had applied the 1954 revisions so egregiously.[41] We need no clearer example of the importance of chiaburs' production—an aspect of their neutralization—even if it came at the expense of proper classification.

Of similar import is a document from Odorhei district. In July 1953, the Regional Commission of the Autonomous Hungarian Region sent a confidential, angry letter to the Odorhei District Commission for the Verification of Chiaburs, harshly criticizing its sloppy work:

[39] We thank Constantin Iordachi for clarifying the meaning of *îngrădire*.

[40] In earlier publications (Verdery 2009), we ourselves made this mistake.

[41] ANIC, Fond C.C. al P.C.R.–Cancelarie, file 43/1955, 1–2. It is possible that the rechiaburizations in 1955 mark the beginning of a new intensification campaign and thus did not affect Constanţa only.

> In our region . . . many comrade activists and district and commune councils have committed a series of errors regarding the drawing up of the chiabur lists, including in some cases, working and middle peasants, thus pushing honest citizens into the ranks of enemies. The Party and Government as well as the entire working class does not need honest citizens declared enemies of the regime. Despite warnings issued to those comrades charged with this responsibility, the commune and district committees have not taken these problems seriously enough. . . . In most cases, the district committees do their verification work superficially, resulting in harm to many honest middle and even poor peasants, and in so doing, compromise our popular democratic regime. . . . District-level comrades fail to respond to the regional commissions in a timely manner, thereby impeding the completion of levies by the fisc and CSC, with damaging effects on the national economy. . . . It must be understood once and for all that this problem is important and the comrades who are in these committees do not have the right to play with the lives of honest citizens. . . . We warn you that you are required to respond within 15 days of receipt of any correspondence about chiaburs.[42]

This was not mere window dressing: as the paper trail shows, the demand for serious verification was real.

Minutes from a meeting of the Secretariat in 1955 on the problem of reclassifying chiaburs hint at the possibility of a conflict between local-level cadres, who needed land for GACs and therefore reclassified chiaburs in exchange for their land, and central authorities, who tried to reverse the process when quotas fell. It may even be that local-level cadres were inventing a new category, "former chiabur," and using it both to get their land and to enable the children of these chiaburs to go to school (that is, they were striking a deal in which the former chiabur would give land in exchange for a label that was somewhat less stigmatizing). Participants in the meeting raised questions about the practice, complaining that local People's Councils were giving out this label too easily. In short, lower cadres' local adaptations had serious consequences for the national economy.[43]

Verifications consisted of inquiries at the village level that, when conducted properly, sent cadres from the district to ask questions in the village, talk with witnesses, and come to a decision. The reports and accompanying tables offer a means to track the social construction of class categories, especially of chiaburs, over time. For example, a preparatory report for establishing the collective in Ieud, a village that a regional Party activist characterized as the "heart of reactionaries," claimed that the village had forty-four chiaburs in 1950, a total that

[42] We quote this at length (the original being a much longer document) because of the forceful language used to underscore the Party's authority (clearly not taken as seriously as desired). See DJAN HA, ARO, Sfatul Popular al Regiunii Stalin, file "Despre chiaburii din raza Raionului Odorhei," Nr. Inventar 38, July 31, 1953: 68–69. See Oláh 2009 for further discussion of chiabur verification in the Odorhei district.

[43] ANIC, Fond C.C. al P.C.R.-Cancelarie, file 43/1955, 4–6.

Part of Verification List from Odorhei District, 1951

Chiaburs remaining on the list:

L u t i ţ a Village

252. Hegyi Sigismund. 57 years old, 13.45 ha. Had servants until 1946; hires seasonal and day laborers.
253. Sala Balasz. 37 years, 7.77 ha. Has a tractor with thresher and hires seasonal and day laborers.
255. Zongor Laidslau. 54 years, 13.20 ha. Always hires seasonal and day laborers; bought 50% of his property.
257. Torok Adalbert. 51 years, 7.77 ha. Always uses salaried workers, is a speculator and doesn't like to work.

Chiaburs removed from the list:

259. Hegyi Pal. 63 years, 11.12 ha. Never had servants, worked his land with family members; was on the chiabur list due to a personal vendetta.
260. Zongor Dominic. 54 years, 4.76 ha. Never had employees or servants. His mountainous land is poor; on the chiabur list by mistake.

Figure 6.1. Verification of Chiaburs, Odorhei District, 1951.
Source: Arhiva Raionului Odorhei, Sfat Popular al Regiunii Stalin, Despre chiaburi din raza raionului Odorhei, 1951. Nr. inv. 38, 59. Courtesy of Sándor Oláh. (Spelling errors *sic.*)

remained constant in 1951. After each name, the report noted how much and what kind of land the person held (e.g., arable, forest, orchards, etc.), how many and what kind of animals he had, and what other "resources for exploiting" he possessed (such as a mill, a thresher, a still, a felting machine). An additional comment specified that the person did one or a combination of the following: exploited labor, did so for more than thirty days per year, profited from his mill, was perhaps already condemned for political activities; further remarks noted that he was not yet under the eye of the authorities, or that he was ill-intentioned toward the regime; and so on.[44] But in 1952, as happened across the country in response to directives from Bucharest, Ieud's original number of forty-four chiaburs suddenly swelled to one hundred.[45] Ten of them subsequently petitioned to be removed from the list, half of whom were "erased."[46] In figure 6.1 we see part of a page from a verification file in Odorhei district for 1951, showing numbers 259 and 260 removed from the lists because they did

[44] See Arhiva Primăriei Ieud, "Raport despre mersul schimbului de teren," and Kligman interview with B. S; for 1951, see DJAN MM, Fond 274, file 25.

[45] See Levy 2009 on central directives, and "Tabel Nominal, chiaburi din comuna Ieud," DJAN MM, Fond 274 (Sfatul Popular al Raionului Vişeu), file D17/1952.

[46] See DJAN MM, Fond 274, file D17/1951. Although one person removed from the list had thirteen hectares and did engage help in the summer, he claimed he did not do so for more than thirty days. Another who had sixteen hectares continued to exploit labor for more than sixty days per year.

not exploit labor (260 made it onto the chiabur list "by mistake" and 259 from a "personal vendetta").

Moving up the Party hierarchy, other tables supplied aggregate data, summarizing the number of chiaburs and the reasons for their inclusion on the lists for the region as a whole. A 1954 report for Vişeu district (Maramureş) indicated the total number of chiaburs—sixty-five, reduced from one hundred—and the number in each commune, with detailed information about each individual who had petitioned to be removed from the list. Although the district and regional verification committees did not agree on all of the petitions, after several meetings to discuss them the regional committee recommended removing thirty people from the list and keeping twenty-five.[47] Of the total erased, two were brothers who lived with their mother and did not themselves have any property; the cause for their initial inclusion was "personal dislike on the part of the former village council president." While the brothers were approved, their mother, a widow, remained a chiabur. Similar reports were supplied for all districts of the country.

Despite the appearance of clear criteria, however, decisions about who became a chiabur or who was reclassified often seemed arbitrary and contributed to the population's increasing sense of vulnerability. Some of the peasants whose economic power was characterized as "appropriate for neutralization" were kept on the list, while others who had owned means of production or exploited labor were taken off. Or, as one man recounted, his father possessed a still to produce plum brandy; he was listed as a chiabur and then erased three times. It seems that the village council expected the father to donate brandy to them. He, on the other hand, expected the village council to pay for what it consumed. Each time the father refused to indulge them, he was placed on the chiabur list. While it is unclear why he was ever removed from the list, after the third experience of being designated and undesignated a chiabur, he gave up and sold his still to the state (Stoica 2003: 44).[48]

These, then, were some of the moves in the Party's policies for fomenting class war by neutralizing the chiaburs, with the goal of both expanding their production (so as to pay their exorbitant quotas) and undercutting their ability to accumulate further wealth. As we have seen, the policy produced resistance by chiaburs that included a variety of tricks to hide their output as well as bribes

[47] See DJAN MM, Fond 274, file 14/1954. Note that this totals fifty-five, not sixty-five. It is difficult to arrive at anything other than relative numbers since they vary from document to document.

[48] It was also unclear why some of the very cadres who made up the chiabur lists were not themselves on the lists. One Transylvanian Hungarian observed about a list maker who "could have been much more a kulak than many of us [chiaburs]," that he "was selling porcelain Marias . . . but he penetrated the communists, and made all of his relatives kulaks to show that he wasn't friends with big landowners" (Kristó 1999: 165). This person eventually became a school principal. In that role, he denounced a female teacher for teaching religion in class although it was prohibited. The school inspectors came to sit in on her class and asked the children who made the world. One little child answered: "The good Lord, with the help of our Party and our Government" (166).

paid to quota collectors. It also entailed verifications, designed to prevent class war from targeting people the Party needed as its allies while still maintaining a steady supply of food to the cities. The policy of neutralizing the chiaburs departed significantly from Soviet policy, which instead emphasized *liquidating* them by killing or deporting them en masse, to prevent their sabotaging collectivization and to provide a labor force for thinly populated areas (see Viola 2007). Chapter 7 will show an important consequence of the alternative Romanian strategy of keeping most chiaburs at home.

Assaults on Status Honor

If attacks on their possessions and economic power constituted one pillar of policy against chiaburs, a second involved efforts to compromise their status honor. They were subjected to social, psychological, and physical harassment, humiliation, and torment, in punishment for the sins of their class. Some of these practices might be used on other kinds of recalcitrant peasants as well, but they were deployed against chiaburs with especial relish. Many of them entailed treating chiaburs as sources of pollution; only by eliminating them could the health of village society be restored. Chiaburs served as excellent pedagogical fodder, their mortification as varied as it was seemingly endless. Slogans were plastered on building walls, doors, fences, and shouted at Party meetings or by Party members as they marched through the village: "The collective is with us; chiaburs into the garbage!" (*Colectivu' cu noi, şi chiaburii la gunoi!*; Vultur 2003: 43); or in the Hungarian area of Transylvania: "Make soap from the kulaks!" (*Szappant a kulákokból*; Kristó 1999: 115), suggesting similarities to the fate of the Jews in Hitler's anti-Semitic campaign.[49] In that same area, chiaburs were required to hang signs on their doors saying "I am a kulak," reminiscent of the stars of David Jews had to wear during World War II. Drawing from this stock, peasants were also told that "the chiabur-exploiter sucks your blood from you! . . . You yourselves form part of his wealth!" These also inform some of the many cartoon images of chiaburs, which, as we have noted, present them as fat capitalists with big noses, bellies, and wallets.

Stigmatizing Chiaburs

Literature, as we saw in chapter 4, was a rich source of chiabur imagery. Particularly during 1948–52, when the campaign was at its most virulent, "[a]ll the

[49] This slogan was reported in a Hungarian village in Transylvania. It likens the fate of the chiaburs to that of the Jews during World War II. In chapter 4 we noted that peasants often appropriated official slogans for their own ends. Accordingly, we thank Constantin Iordachi for pointing out that peasants countered the first slogan with "*Un, doi, un doi, colectivul la gunoi!*" (One, two, one two, the collective into the garbage!).

Figure 6.2. Chasing a chiabur wolf in sheep's clothing, on which is written "Certificate of middle-peasant status." (From the magazine *Urzica*, June 30, 1952.) Courtesy of MNAC.

most terrifying facts imaginable . . . and all the sins of society were loaded onto the chiabur, who became the universal lightning rod justifying all the errors and all the political mistakes made anywhere. Chiaburs exhibit a crescendo of unbridled aggressiveness" (Negrici 2005: 146). They are represented in multiple animal images: "The parasite that feeds on human blood (bed-bugs), the ravenous beast (wolves, hyenas, crows), lying in wait for exhausted beings so as to engorge themselves with innocent blood (blood again, always blood), unearthly wild beasts dangerous through their sudden appearance (snakes, rats, polecats), rabid monsters attacking in packs to dismember frail living things" (158). And they will use any disguise, any means, including their own children, to infiltrate and sabotage. "Most of them pyromaniacs, they are regularly caught carrying bottles of kerosene near important sites" (157).

Then there are the poems and rhymes posted on wall gazettes, taught in schools, and shouted in slogans. A respondent from Vlaicu in her mid-1950s recalled that her father often repeated the rhymed caption from a cartoon of a local woman: "I'm Filip Ana / and I'm labeled a chiabur, / and for seven years, dear, / I've paid a servant."[50] An official in the Şibot commune (Alba) People's Council still remembered (in 2006) a rhyme he had had to recite every day in school during 1959–60:

Refrain: Let's make a collective
In our village too
May work be our joy
And our life blossom forever.
The great collective
Old Mardare joined
With Frunzina—his old wife
And he told the chiabur:
In vain you're trying to trick us
With lies and with stories
As many years as we have left
We will build our new life.

As this man indicates, chiabur imagery made an impression on children. The same point emerged from an interview with a woman from Aiud (Alba), discussing a chiabur in her village:

> I know he was a tall man, elderly, and in the eyes of a child, the chiabur seemed a bad man, a man, how can I put it . . . a loafer, a lawless man, a man without God, that's sort of how he was described to us.
>
> (*And where did you get this impression?*)
>
> At school.
>
> (*And did you believe it?*)
>
> Yes. Sure.
>
> (*When you saw someone who was labeled a chiabur . . .*)
>
> Somehow it terrified you, after the descriptions we'd had. That they're bad people, who exploit, who profit from others' work and pay no money or produce. . . . That's how I saw him from what I'd been told at school. And when we saw him so upset, we were even more frightened. With the other children, we'd snigger, "That's the chiabur, look, there's the chiabur!"[51]

[50] 206, Verdery interview.
[51] 213Z, Verdery interview.

As is by now evident, humiliation was a favored means to humble chiaburs into submission and make others see that they were losing or had lost their influence in daily life; this would make them the objects of a negative mimesis, an example *not* to follow. Here is a shaming strategy used on someone who couldn't pay his quotas:

> They put you down with a quota for sheep, this many pigs, this many cows, all these people who were considered chiaburs. And there was one man here and he didn't give away his cow, you know? He had a cow and didn't give it to them. And then they came, there was a big gate, an old gate, made of planks, and they wrote in big, big letters, with white paint, like this, on the gate: "Here lives the chiabur Şuvană Gheorghe. He didn't turn in his quotas. Shame on him!" . . . To show the people how shameful it was when a person didn't give his quotas.[52]

It was humiliating for chiaburs to have to borrow produce and money from others to pay their quotas, for in earlier times, it was they to whom others would come for a loan. In addition, when the GAC took their land, chiaburs did not usually receive parcels of equivalent quality in exchange; the land they received was at considerable distances from the village, making it all the more difficult to eke out whatever production they could from the poor soil. Adding insult to injury, chiaburs were ridiculed as they trudged through their villages to their distant plots, worn out from the social, economic, and spatial reversal of their fortunes.

Officials mocked village norms of comportment in other ways that denigrated chiaburs. The son of a chiabur recalled how the cadres violated norms of hospitality; he was ten at the time of this example:

> I was coming home, and [activist] Plopşoreanu and another guy says to me, "Tell your father to cook up something because we're coming over." They come in, sit down, eat, drink brandy, and get drunk. Then one takes a piece of paper, sticks it under my dad's nose: "Sign!" "I'm not signing!" They go back and forth like this until one of them curses him by his mother's cunt. My dad was a big man, with huge hands. He starts to get up and says, "Don't you dare insult me in front of my wife and son!!" I see there's an axe on the bed and I think, "Now dad will pick that up and I'll pull their seats out from under them and he'll hit them." It took both of them holding him down to prevent that. "Don't you dare insult me in front of my wife and son!!" He had dignity and a strong family feeling, and he wouldn't stand being humiliated in front of us.[53]

Further humiliation accompanied the confiscations of their belongings, to which we have referred above. Having their possessions carted through the village for all to see, as had once happened regularly with the poor whose belong-

[52] N. I., Stan interview for M. Stewart.

[53] 59, Verdery interview (2008).

ings were confiscated for debts, was deeply shameful. It did not, however, always lead to the expected result:

> Those who didn't pay their quotas, I remember . . . they [officials] would auction their things, they'd take things from their homes, clothes, furniture. . . . The town crier would beat the drum and announce, "on such and such a day, there is an auction for the quotas of so and so." . . . And I remember, some bed sheets, rugs and pillows and blankets and things like that, they were there at the crossroads, there by the fence. They put them on the ground, so people would come and buy and the money would pay for the quotas. But nobody would come to buy someone else's things. Eventually they gave them back to this person, and he went and borrowed money from two, three, five people, as much as he could, and he paid.[54]

A former chiabur wrote to his local newspaper in 1996 that being one is a stigma you felt on your skin and carried around, like a hidden thorn in your palm that is not felt if you don't touch anything, but if something touches it in that place, you will cry out in pain (cited in Kristó 1999: 94).

The humiliation they experienced was often visible on chiaburs' bodies. Rather than standing tall, they walked with their eyes and heads down (in this respect, emasculated, as men mirrored the "traditional" stance of women walking in public).[55] Called to the village council every night over a period of time, they bore the brunt of verbal, psychological, and physical abuse. While there, they were required to remain standing. An old man, unable to stay on his feet any longer, dared to sit down, for which the council president kicked him—a behavior previously unthinkable (see Kristó 1999: 143). Respect for the elderly was not part of the new communist ethics, if they were chiaburs. And it was not only cadres who engaged in petty humiliations like that, as Bodó reports for Corund/Korond:

> When the cashier at the local theater refused to sell tickets to a chiabur, he could have done it without abusing his position but he often cursed, publicly insulting and humiliating the chiabur. There are many reports of insults in interpersonal communication, cases that demonstrate clearly that low-status people knowingly insulted the good *gospodars* who had previously enjoyed a much higher status than their own. Ethnography shows that these "small" insults left a deep mark on those considered chiaburs. (Bodó 2003: 26–27)

Villagers observing all this sometimes wondered about its limits. For example, in Rimetea, some wanted clarification about how they were to treat chiaburs in their midst. What were they supposed to do and what were chiaburs permitted? They posed a series of telling questions that the local cell

[54] 206, Verdery interview (2006).

[55] A bowed head is a sign both of deference and dependency, as captured in the apt Romanian saying "*Capul plecat sabia nu-l taie*" (the sword does not cut off a bowed head).

forwarded to the Cadre Section of the People's Council of the Turda district for edification:

> Are chiaburs allowed to drink in restaurants or bars? Can they have a good time at dances or the theater together with middle and poor peasants? And their sons and daughters? For example, can the daughter of a chiabur married to a poor peasant participate in village parties? If one of them doesn't want to follow orders from the commune council, what measures can the people's council take against them, can they be sued? Or only frightened? (cited in Țârău 2003: 47)[56]

There were other forms in which chiabur stigma was embodied, for instance, heavy or demeaning manual labor. A chiabur son recalled:

> My father would go every morning, at 8:00–9:00 he had to be at the Local Council, along with others who had good horses, were good farmers—not the ones who had a couple of mangy nags. These were the people they would gather, there were some activists around here too. And anyone who wouldn't sign up would get a paper ordering them to transport ten cubic meters of stone. And when they'd done that they would have to call someone from the council to check and sign for it. And then they were asked if they'd changed their mind, would they join the collective or not, and if they hadn't, they would get another paper to carry another ten cubic meters of limestone from the Mereşti quarry to the Vlăhița plants. This was called "time to think, self-persuasion time." And if the guy had finished carrying the limestone, the leadership would ask again if he had changed his mind. If the answer was no, they would order him to carry another ten cubic meters of stone. And that's how it went for three months, almost the entire winter.[57]

Chiaburs would have to sweep the streets, clear the drainage ditches, push Party officials through the village in wheelbarrows, and engage in other forms of menial labor that violated their former honorable status. The embodiment of chiabur status also included physical violence—again, not restricted to chiaburs but inflicted on them especially. They were forced to drink boiling water and if they could not finish, it was poured over them.[58] They were knocked about, like this chiabur from Dobrosloveni:

> When I went to the Local Council to sign, I was taken inside and this guy, I. C., was behind the door. . . . As soon as I entered, I. C., that dog, slapped me so hard that my hat fell on the floor. . . ."What's wrong with you, why did you hit me?" "Who hit you? Nobody did." . . . The mayor poured a glass of brandy and pushed it towards me, to drink: "Take a glass of brandy, Alexandru!" I was afraid they would poison me: "I don't want to, Mr. Mayor, I don't drink brandy!" "Come on, Alexandru, you can't say no to a glass of brandy! Look, I'll take a sip first!" . . . Well, I drank that brandy, I signed up and I started to go, but he poured another glass, asking me to drink that

[56] See DJAN CJ, Fond Primăria Rimetea, file 1/1952, 182.

[57] 6, Oláh interview.

[58] ANIC, Fond C.C. al P.C.R.-Cancelarie, file 96/1952, 7 (RLA).

> one too. I think he wanted me to get tipsy, so I wouldn't tell others how things were, and I didn't drink anymore, I told them, "Well, have a good day, now I'm going," when, from behind the door, I. C. slapped me again, on the ear. I almost went deaf! I say: "I. C., I didn't think you were like that!" And the mayor says: "Come on, Alexandru, let it go, it's so you remember how you joined the collective!"[59] (Lățea 2009: 347)

And as we already observed, they were beaten, sometimes even mortally. In the village of Comlăuş (Arad), the son of a chiabur was killed when his head was repeatedly banged against the basement wall (Goina 2003: 40). Here is another typical description from a chiabur's son who was just a child at the time: "They took my father to Cugir and beat him to a pulp. He came back home, and my mother whispered to me, 'They beat your father very badly.' She told me to peek through the curtain when my father was taking a bath. I saw these huge bruises and welts, black, blue, and red."[60] To avoid such treatment, chiaburs from villages near forests or mountains joined others resisting the regime by hiding there (or even, for those in plains areas, by hiding in their own haylofts). Inevitably discovered, they suffered not only beatings but imprisonment. Accompanying all these experiences was a stern warning to the victims not to tell anyone what had happened to them, lest they suffer even worse. The virtue of silence was a lesson taught to and learned by many, further ingrained during the often long prison sentences customarily meted out to class enemies.[61]

All these experiences made being labeled a chiabur deeply traumatic and stigmatizing, a form of both physical and symbolic violence that victims and their children might internalize and live with for decades thereafter. In addition to our own illustrative material, McDonald reports (2009) a 2004 interview with a Russian woman who said that in 1995—over sixty years after collectivization—she had *for the first time* heard another woman say, "I was the daughter of a kulak," enabling the respondent herself to say the same thing, which she had never said aloud up to then.

Persecuting Kin

Chiaburs' status as social pollutants was represented as contagious, both in general and specifically along bloodlines: they could contaminate their friends, kin, or marriage partners. The Securitate kept detailed files of the first-degree relatives of those in hiding or already arrested, among whom were chiaburs.[62] To avoid infection by those with "unhealthy" origins, extended family mem-

[59] A. B., Lățea interview.

[60] 59, Verdery interview.

[61] We noted in the introduction (note 85) that prisoners, prior to their release, signed statements swearing that they would never reveal what they had experienced, heard, or seen. Few broke their oaths until well after communism fell, so effectively had they learned the value of silence.

[62] See, for example, ACNSAS, FI, file 2426/v. 5, 87–98, which is a table consisting of "first degree relatives of arrested elements associated with the [Popşa] case." (One of the Popşa brothers was shot

bers and friends often avoided public contact with those whom the regime stigmatized.[63] A neighbor mentioned that he got into trouble for attending the funeral of the chiabur who lived next door (Kristó 1999: 45). Many friends became former friends, afraid to be seen in a class enemy's entourage.[64] Or, if they wanted to maintain contact, they did so at night when they hoped no one would see them, for the shadows of enemy status (chiabur or otherwise) were long and wide.[65]

Although chiabur men, as heads of household, were the primary targets in assaults on status honor, cadres persecuted them by also persecuting their kin, especially their wives and children. A chiabur's daughter recalled how heartlessly the village mayor himself took on persuading her mother—a widow whose husband security forces had shot in the back in 1950—to join the GAC. He tormented her by offering to reveal where her husband's body was buried if she would agree to sign up: "'If you tell me about him, then I will join the collective.' And that's how they took everything, and our land was signed over to the GAC! Who knows all the dirty tricks they played on people!"[66] Like men, chiabur women might be taken to the village council in the middle of the night, in a blatant violation of gender norms, with the aim of forcing them to sign the petition (see also Thelen 2005: 39, 43; chapter 2). Cadres ordered the women to clean public toilets (outhouses) and windows, for example, without any clean-

---

in the house of a chiabur family in Ieud, resulting in the arrest of all but their two-year-old son; relatives were kept under constant surveillance while the family's members were incarcerated.)

[63] Tănase illustrates this point with respect to Belu (Herbert) Zilber's experience, quoting an announcement that appeared in the Party paper, *Scînteia*, that Zilber had been "excluded from the Party, guilty of having maintained relations with enemies of the working class." As a result, friends and fellow travelers all did what they could, Tănase continues from Zilber's writing, "not to be suspected of solidarity with someone excluded for mysterious reasons." After his exclusion, Zilber felt the full force of what it meant to be "hunted" as an outcast, noting that is when his "civil death" began (Tănase 2005: 162–63.)

[64] See also Stoica 2003. One former prisoner told him that upon his return from prison, he was as afraid of others as they were of him. Having nothing to eat, he was caught taking beans from the collective's property. The brigade leader, who happened to have been his godfather, forced him to throw the beans away, leaving him humiliated and still hungry.

[65] For those who were imprisoned as politicals, the stigma was in some ways more enduring. Even after rehabilitation, they were shunned for fear that the tides might unexpectedly change, as they had before. General amnesties such as that in 1964 (Decree 411) released politicals from prison. Even so, they and others rehabilitated by the regime did not necessarily return to their natal villages, instead moving to small towns where they were somewhat more anonymous. The fear of associating with former politicals indicated another version of the mentality of waiting to see what would happen, in this case, whether the person would be rearrested. After the 1956 revolution in Hungary, many former prisoners who had completed their sentences were rearrested as a precautionary measure. Some persons—family, friends—did try to help prisoners' families. One aged chiabur from Reviga tearfully recounted how he discreetly helped a chiabur woman whose husband was in jail, finding ways to give her some oats for the horse and grain for her family (Chelcea 2003b: 22).

[66] C. I., Kligman interview. The father was allegedly engaged in anticommunist activities and was shot in an action organized by the police and Securitate. See ACNSAS, FP, file 84/1950/v. 7, 335.

ing supplies. Supervisors of these activities spat on them as they worked. As public punishment for her not having handed over the grain quota, one woman's head was shaved.[67]

One way in which chiaburs tried to negotiate the stigma and humiliation of their "enemy" status was through strategic use of marriage. In Gyergyóújfalu, Transylvania, a butcher who was not a chiabur lent money to a chiabur widow and her daughter so that they could fulfill their mandatory quotas. To avoid his being put on the chiabur list, he and the widow did not marry (Kristó 1999: 26–27).[68] Still others divorced to lessen or avoid the stigma-through-association experienced by their loved ones. Hence, those with lengthy prison sentences might divorce so that their children could more easily attend school or their wives get a job to support the family minimally (although none of this was easily arranged).[69] In a twist on this strategy, Party officials generously offered people the option to divorce: for example, in Sântana, a woman was informed she could remain in the GAC on the condition that she divorce her husband (they seemed not to have been living together for the previous four months), who was excluded from it for owning a thresher (Goina 2003: 25–26). Not only people of chiabur origin but those married into chiabur families were vulnerable, as we showed in chapter 3, concerning two activists criticized because they did not denounce their chiabur in-laws or divorce their wives.[70] Thus, Party members sought to divorce their spouses once they found out about family pasts that had somehow been unknown to them. One's career aspirations could be readily compromised if it became known that a spouse had "unhealthy origins," making divorce a helpful option for career purposes. However, if there were children in the marriage, divorce created other problems. Sometimes people simply had to choose: spouse and children, or the larger "family" of the Party.[71]

A particularly painful treatment involving family ties was based on the notion that chiabur status and accompanying traits were inherited, so chiabur parentage was used against children (which might mean the children would

[67] See DJAN CJ, Fond Primăria Rimetea, file 1/1952, 182.

[68] By contrast, others married to avoid being put on the list. Vultur reports cases in the Banat region (southwestern Romania) of women of German origin who, in the postwar period, married recently settled Romanian colonists to avoid the stigma of being German, only to learn later that their husbands and their families would be deported to the Bărăgan (2003: 31).

[69] Divorce in such cases was often instrumental. After a prisoner was released, for example, he might remarry his former wife (B. G., Kligman interview; see also Dobeş 2003). Or a former spouse might not agree to a reconciliation of any kind, as happened to a priest from Ieud who had spent several years in hiding and then many more in Romania's prisons. To keep her job as a teacher, his wife was forced to file for divorce and did (I. S., Kligman interview).

[70] One might get away with such origins if one had a history of not associating with these in-laws. A substitute teacher in Odorhei district was given an excellent reference for his work, followed by "[h]is failing is that his father-in-law is a chiabur, with whom however he has no connection" (DJAN HA, ARO, Secţia Invăţământ, Acte confidenţiale, Inv. nr. 54, 1953).

[71] DJAN HD, Fond CR PMR, file 442/1952, 29.

come home as youthful "persuaders"). Humiliating and shaming the children of chiaburs was done routinely and, in general, effectively, for sometimes parents would decide to join in reaction to their children's misery, rationalizing the decision as a moral, ethical act. The daughter of a chiabur remembered that the local policeman used to taunt her with a whip, shouting as he hit her, "Chiabur pup!" (Chelcea 2003b: 23). Some commented that the "injuries to one's soul" (Kristó 1999: 60) were hard to forget, leaving a lasting imprint on the young and impressionable who were taunted and called names, excluded from participating in youth cultural programs, sports teams, and the like (Kristó 1999: 60–61, 100–2). With a mother's sorrow, one chiabura recounted:

> In those times, in the village store, there was a list of the chiaburs on the wall, and we weren't allowed to be served there. Once, they brought candies. I had three children . . . and they were present when the candies were to be given out. The store manager asked who they were and the others answered, "They're S's children." The manager then pulled them out of the line by their ears. All because their father was a chiabur. The kids came home crying. (Bodó 2003: 22)

Parents reported being unable to bear that in the classroom, their children were constantly ordered to stand, publicly humiliated in front of their classmates.[72] Yet, sometimes young people did show solidarity with the stigmatized children of chiaburs. In Sânpaul, for example, when officials excluded those children from enjoying holiday festivities at the cultural center, most of the other youth walked out too (Oláh 2009: 241).

Although still young, chiabur children were not spared the privations to which their parents were subjected. While they were not jailed, they too were often forced to perform hard labor, hauling wood for long distances and the like. Often, they were further discriminated against by not being permitted to attend school. Those who managed to attend never received the highest marks, regardless of their performance, and if chiabur children (or others with "unhealthy origins," such as the children of Uniate priests) were allowed to graduate from primary school, they might not be accepted into high schools, vocational schools, or university. It took enormous—and costly—efforts to gain admission. Some chiaburs who resisted joining the collectives had to have someone else "adopt" their children so they could be educated (Roske 2003: 76).

Whatever their age, many chiabur children experienced the hunger that the children of poor peasants had so long endured. For their parents, this was yet another painful reminder of being unable to care adequately for their families. Thus, when one chiabur (better classified a middle peasant), himself the father of six children, was told that the local Party representatives would have to take his cow because he could not pay his quotas, he retorted, "Go ahead, but take my children too because I don't have anything to feed them."[73] Another told of

[72] Vultur interview Cota S.V. D.I.X. 2001.

[73] I. S., Kligman interview.

a chiabura with nine children who had hidden a kilo of flour behind an icon, thinking that the mayor and his team would not look there as they searched her house. When they found it, the mayor—knowing that she would have nothing to feed the children—took evident pleasure in scattering the flour on the floor as he backed toward the exit.[74] A neighbor remembered a poignant story of a child who was the only one in his family not arrested following a Securitate action at their house that had left one "terrorist" dead. Two years old at the time, he was raised by another neighbor until his own mother was released a year and a half later. At home, she remained under surveillance: "One day, when the police came to check on her, they threw from the table onto the floor the *mămăligă* [cornmeal mush] she had made. Her little boy asked her, 'what will we eat?' to which the police responded hostilely, 'You'll eat the devil!' The little boy again turned to his mother, asking meekly, 'Umm—is the devil good to eat?'"[75]

For nonchiabur villagers, the psychological effect of viewing those of high status honor treated in this manner was undoubtedly potent; regardless of whether they welcomed or abhorred the various spectacles of chiaburs physically and socially ruined, the Party's authority and its willingness to wield its power brutally were increasingly unambiguous. Destroying chiaburs signified the destruction of a "life" model, challenging the hegemony of a particular cultural form and showing, literally, that such a way of life held no future prospects.

Teaching about Exploitation

These persecutions of chiaburs' friends and kin struck a devastating blow at one of the most important aspects of their former status: their ability to mobilize labor, through their control of wealth in people. As we showed in chapter 2, wealthy peasants had many kin and godchildren; as people of good character and patrons to those less fortunate than themselves, they could secure labor when they needed it. That was not how the Party construed such labor exchanges, however, or the moral character of wealthy peasants: instead, they were accused of having exploited the labor of others. With this we come to the crux of class war: teaching peasants the meaning of exploitation.

Importing Exploitation

Aside from their ownership of various means of production, a key means by which the Party intended to distinguish chiaburs from poor or middle peasants

[74] B. G., Kligman interview.

[75] D. M., Kligman interview. The police action was against the "Popşa group" operating in Maramureş. See note 62 above, and ACNSAS, FP, file 84, for voluminous details on them and other groups.

was the former's exploitation of salaried labor for thirty days or more per year. Recall that wealthy peasants had enough land to need the help of others in working it, whether through salaried or different reciprocated forms of labor. Cadres now defined such arrangements as exploitative. A former chiabur, in his mid-eighties, elaborated further:

> If a man had a lot of land that he couldn't work alone, then he hired poor peasants. Here there was class war when those who had been servants rose against the wealthier peasants. "Look, you, that chiabur, he exploited you!" They said that, so one would hate the other. The poor who had worked for wealthy peasants were the first to join the collective. They [cadres] told them: "Hey, we'll take their land and it will be yours, you'll work here just by the village and we'll send them to work up in the hills, far away."[76]

The lesson was difficult to instill. One former collector of quotas, then in his eighties, observed, "Peasant chiaburs worked along with their servants. They didn't hang around with their hands in their pockets, no." Another chiabur, a Hungarian from the Miercurea Ciuc area, made a similar point about chiaburs as class enemies: "I can see how a baron or a count is a class enemy of the working class, even though I don't agree with that either. But how is a hardworking wealthy peasant, who worked day and night to have something, a class enemy? I could never get that into my head" (Kristó 1999: 179–80). A man who had been a regional First Party Secretary in the early '50s also commented retrospectively on the political construction of exploited labor:

> There was a limit, from so many to so many days worked with the paid help of others. . . . It was an absurdity, not normal. No one considered anyone a chiabur in the way the Party intended. You can't define a man as being something out of the ordinary because he employed the help of who knows whom for thirty days or more. But they [Party leaders] needed to find a reason to label them as exploiters.[77]

The use of hired labor for more than thirty days per year was a key criterion, as were having commercial enterprises or exploiting means of production (such as threshers) for income. And a key practice for inculcating these criteria were the contestations filed by people labeled chiabur.

Chiabur Contestations

In verifying chiabur status, as described above, cadres often responded to a contestation, in which chiaburs acted upon the Party's invitation to reject as unjust their assignment to chiabur status and to request reclassification.[78] In

[76] I. S., Kligman interview.

[77] P. G., Kligman interview.

[78] Citizens were invited to contest perceived errors in other domains as well: "he has the right to

this way, the Party created a form of dialogue that signaled the "democratic" give and take of the regime, paternalistically concerned about its citizens' grievances. To avoid the dire consequences suffered by anyone labeled "class enemy," chiaburs regularly took advantage of this possibility (as well as of the possibility of challenging their quota assignments, which could be a separate action). Claimants presented all manner of reasons in their own defense, professing not to understand their mistaken identification as chiaburs. In making such claims, individuals were careful to invoke the Party's categories of appeal and exhibit their ideological enlightenment, testimony presumably to the effectiveness of the pedagogical techniques reviewed in the previous chapter—and possibly to assistance they received in formulating their petition. Witness the following typical cases:

> After I finished 6th grade, I went to work as a servant for Ion [*sic*] Vlaicu, where I stayed for 3 years and then went to the army and the war, after I came back from the war in 1921, and in 1922 I married the daughter of my former master Ioan Vlaicu.
>
> My parents were poor people, my father was a servant from a very young age and later guarded the village fields.
>
> From my parents I inherited 4 yokes of land and with my marriage I received another 6 from my wife . . . . I note that in my life I never did any kind of politics although from 1932 to 1938 I was mayor but it may be proved that in my behavior as mayor in those years I was always attached to the poor and was never in any way on the side of those who exploited others. . . . In 1949–50 I was declared chiabur and I don't know why, at first I thought that this is what must be because it's a correct measure adopted by the Party, but now I see that there must have been a mistake with me, because I don't feel I rightfully bear this name when I don't deserve it.
>
> In the spirit of these statements I ask the district committee of the Party in Orăştie to do a detailed investigation and if it finds my statements just, to take me out of chiabur status.[79]

This petitioner from Vlaicu judiciously called attention to his having been exploited as a child—he had a "healthy social origin"—and noted that he had not been involved in politics until he was elected mayor, but even then, he fought for the poor against the exploiting class. Trusting in the Party's wisdom, he had not initially contested his having been named a chiabur; however, confident of the Party's infinite justness, he had finally decided to seek the Party's reasoned consideration of his status.[80]

---

make a complaint to the Provisional Committee of the Plasa, the region, or even to the Ministry of Finance," which, in part, demonstrated "the democratic character of the tax law" (DJAN MM, Fond Comitetul Regional PMR Baia Mare, file 65/1949, 106). See Bowker and Starr (2000: 207, table 6.2) for contestations to racial classifications in another totalizing regime, apartheid South Africa. Thanks to Rogers Brubaker for the reference.

[79] DJAN HD, Fond Sfat Popular al Raionului Orăştie, file 7/1954, n.p.

[80] Despite the commune's recommendation on August 24, 1954, that he be reclassified, on Sep-

A second case shows even more learning about how to speak the Party's language:

> Comrade President,
>
> The undersigned M. G., residing in the village of Dobrosloveni, Caracal District, asks that you order an investigation of my material situation and of the decision to reclassify me from a middle peasant to a chiabur. In support of my petition, I declare that of the total land area registered to my name, a total of 8.85 hectares, only 5.5 hectares are arable land, the rest being unproductive land and a house lot.
>
> As I have not exploited any agricultural labor, all the work being done by myself and my family, I have turned in the mandatory quotas in time and in accordance with the government decree and I have paid all my fees and taxes to the state to date, I ask that you examine my statements as accurate and true.
>
> Also, I wish to mention that, contrary to the mistaken interpretations put forward by some comrades, I am and have always been a simple craftsman worker. Of my own free will and uncoerced, I have put myself in the service of the party and the republic. I owned only one brick-making press, which I had bought as scrap iron in 1942 and restored to working order. When the needs of the county required that the press be put in service of the needs of the republic, I gave it up voluntarily and uncoerced. . . . Since 1945 I have been working, in the interests of the commune.[81]

This person understood that he must not have too much land, so he diminished its surface; that he must not have a brick factory but only a "press"; that he has exploited no labor but his family's; and that he has been a model citizen in his relations to the Party and the republic, which he serves. Beyond this, significantly, he uses twice the standard expression for donating land to the collective: "of my own free will and uncoerced by anyone," even though it is not really appropriate here. Nonetheless, his contestation was rejected: "Communicate to resident M.G. . . . that the result of our investigations is that he remains definitively in the category of chiabur."[82]

Or take the case of another chiabur, who disputed the claims that he had a servant until 1949 and that he had not worked his eight hectares of land on his own. He maintained that the information was completely false, that he had not

tember 18 the district executive committee wrote that he would remain a chiabur. Interestingly, a month later his former wife—sister of Romania's most famous aviator—was informed that she would be made a chiabur (possibly in the wake of her ex-husband's contestation). She appealed to the regional executive committee, which wrote the district that it must "take urgent measures" to remove her and report who had so classified her. On November 25, the district president wrote that she was removed. In this case, it would seem, the family's prestige trumped other considerations. These documents confirm Verdery's interview with the aviator's niece that his brother had also been reclassified.

[81] DJAN Olt, Fond Sfatul Popular al Comunei Dobrosloveni, Raion Caracal, secția Secretariat, file 1786/1952, n.p.

[82] DJAN Olt, Fond Sfatul Popular al Raionului Caracal, secția Secretariat, file 1879/1952 (2 December).

had a servant since 1925, and that those who classified him as a chiabur did so out of spite. In 1948, he continued, a fellow villager, "comrade Petru I.," insisted that he take in his nephew from a large and poor family in a distant mining town: "He stayed for five months in which time I bought him clothes and shoes out of the goodness of my heart, and he left very satisfied with the help I had given him. This help that I gave to someone needy was seized upon by some of my enemies who affirmed that I had help in working my land, that is, a servant."[83] At the end of his petition, he presented a list of thirty-two villagers (many of them his ritual kin) who would vouch that he had not had servants or exploited anyone in many years (seven of the names were checked off, indicating considerable verification). His petition was successful and on April 30, 1954, he was removed from the list of chiaburs.

As we saw also in chapter 4, petitioners might choose to circumvent the commune or district levels, appealing directly to those higher up with the hope that the wise men of the Party would see through the interpersonal dynamics that landed the petitioner unjustly on the list. For example, in Odorhei, of 125 chiaburs contesting their status, 70 directed their petitions to the Regional rather than District Council while 22 sent theirs straight to the Central Committee. (Of the total number of petitions, 49 were approved for reclassification.) That chiaburs addressed their contestations directly to higher levels of the Party may reflect less a sense of confidence in the leaders' benevolence than the long-standing customs we mentioned in chapter 4, of petitioning the "good emperor" or king for redress of wrongs committed at lower levels. Rather than revealing their faith in the Party's benevolence, they were trying to compel it to be benevolent.[84] Moreover, for reasons we have noted above, the center did not necessarily disappoint those who addressed it, thereby acknowledging errors and deviations from the Party line. In two of the above examples, the petition was successful—but, we might add, even then the person could remain in the records not as a "middle peasant" but as a "former chiabur," with some of the same stigma attached (though no longer the excessive quotas).[85] While we do not mean to imply that contestation generally led to satisfaction of one's claims, we do want to underscore that situations were not always as black and white as some might assume. A host of factors contributed to the resolution of disputes, some of which were favorable to petitioners.

We emphasize particularly, however, that filing contestations engaged a per-

[83] See DJAN HD, Fond Sfat Popular al Raionului Orăştie, file 7/1954, n.p. Redefining or repositioning oneself took work, especially in this man's case, as he was one of Vlaicu's most influential men from one of its most influential families. At his funeral in the 1970s, his courtyard was packed.

[84] Nonetheless, bypassing commune and district committees did have the political advantage of alerting the hierarchy to potential abuse, putting the lower committees on notice that their review of the case(s) in question would be "watched." Of course, those who submitted contestations might henceforth find themselves watched too, by the Securitate.

[85] ANIC, Fond C.C. al P.C.R.–Cancelarie, file 43/1955, 1–2, 4–6.

son directly in class war as pedagogy. To write a contestation was to rewrite one's own local biography. If a chiabur's signing of a prepared petition to join the collective farm was an act of submission to the Party's authority, contesting classification as a chiabur was a purposeful act aimed at reshaping a person's identity. In arguing that a person who appeared to be a servant really was not (as in the case just above) or why using extra labor at harvest made the petitioner like any ordinary peasant, people labeled chiaburs (and this included many a "middle peasant") sought to erase what had once made them visible in the village in order to pass themselves off as being just like everyone else. They were learning the official categories and how to use them for their own interests: for example, they claimed that they owned less land than they actually did; divided it into several plots attributed to other family members; or pointed out that their land was inherited or was their wife's dowry (i.e., they had not purchased it) and thus should not qualify them for chiabur status. Peasants who questioned their designation as chiaburs were not only relinquishing their status honor to avoid class stigma, but also actively trying to redefine themselves in the Party's terms. Of particular importance, they were absorbing the notion of "exploitation," performatively relating themselves to it, and relinquishing the notion of wealth in people as a viable basis for social position. And so were the cadres engaged in verifying their status.

As a result of the Party's instructions regarding the chiabur lists and verification practices, the number of chiaburs varied over time. Some were reclassified, while others remained on the lists and still others were added. These changes were themselves related to the situation with food supplies and the changing rhythm of forming collectives. In general, when the pace was stepped up, class war intensified, even if its manifestation varied locally, regionally, and nationally. Where there was strong political resistance, class war was more vehement and prolonged, regardless of local conditions for agricultural production (see Kligman 2009; Stoica 2009). When the leadership pulled back on collectivization, class war seemed to subside in its ferocity as well. After 1962, as Romania's leaders began distancing themselves from Soviet policy, the concern with class origins faded away.

Responses to Class War

What reception did peasants give the idea of class exploitation? Did it succeed? Did all these sources of harassment turn fellow villagers against the chiaburs? For some, undoubtedly yes—those who jeered as a chiabur passed by pushing the mayor in a wheelbarrow, or who repeated ugly slogans and rhymes; those whose former disadvantaged status had now been bettered. The idea's resonance among villagers depended largely on their socioeconomic position at the time. Some poor peasants who had been servants spoke bitterly about wealthy peasants and social inequalities in the period before socialism.[86] They were among those who embraced class war and saw wealthy peasants for what the Party said they were: chiaburs, exploiters. Other poor peasants noted that while some persons labeled chiaburs had worked hard alongside their workers, there were indeed "bad" chiaburs who had maltreated them—a point with which some former chiaburs concurred.[87] Poor peasants who were sent to Party school reminisced about learning of class exploitation and class consciousness, then returning to their villages motivated to seek justice through promoting class war. A man in his eighties who had been a servant asked rhetorically, "What did wealthy peasants ever do for the world? Nothing. . . . Everything they did, they did for themselves." The communists, he added, created schools and encouraged education for all. We heard a number of stories like the following, from a schoolteacher of chiabur origin:

> Because of the new ideology, the tensions among groups in the village had sharpened slowly but steadily. The idea of class struggle had been assimilated by the gentlest of people, and they tried to put it into practice. Propaganda managed to instill hatred between people—co-villagers, neighbors—who had been on the best of terms before. When I was a student at the Odorhei high school, I wanted to send word home to my parents. I looked for people from the village at Csiszár Restaurant, where they used to stop with their carts to rest their horses. I met old B. S. there over a glass of wine. We talked, and when I mentioned the favor I needed, he raised his voice and—somewhat under the influence of alcohol—told me loud and clear, "We're not in the same camp, we don't belong together, I'm not passing on any message for you." That's how he showed me what he'd taken in from the activists' propaganda.[88]

Sympathy for the Chiaburs

Nonetheless, many villagers supported the chiaburs: the class war that cadres sought to foment sometimes inspired expressions of social solidarity. In Dobro-

[86] Some people still use the term chiabur after 1989, though it no longer carries the pejorative meanings of those times. This is reminiscent of MacLean's point that categories have their own biographies over time and cultural milieu (2005: 79–80).

[87] One former servant recounted how, as a poor youth in Ieud, he was forced to work off a fine that should have been levied against the wealthy peasant who employed him and whose orders he was following when he was caught illegally sawing wood in the forest. He also referred to a wealthy peasant who hired a poor person to serve a prison term in his stead (D. V., Kligman interview). A Gypsy, now old, remembered the chiabur who maltreated him, never letting him take a break for a cigarette, telling him that if he wanted to smoke, to do so on the road, not at work (Chelcea 2003b: 17). Back in Bucharest, Vasile Luca noted in an Orgburo meeting of the C.C. on June 6, 1950: "The kulak is not the one who's going to set fire to the crop, but he'll have some miserable agricultural worker do it" (ANIC, Fond C.C. al P.C.R.–Cancelarie, file 41/1950, 19 [RLA]).

[88] 2, Oláh interview.

gea, Iordachi observes, "The strategy of dividing the village community by class war did not work as hoped. All those interviewed said that in Jurilovca there were no true chiaburs, only chiaburs 'made' by political criteria who were just peasants like them" (Iordachi 2003: 42). He quotes a landless fisherman: "One or another had a couple of hectares of land, or a still for making brandy, or a windmill. And they made him a chiabur. But basically they were pretty poor people. . . . We were glad to have somewhere to earn a piece of bread, a kilo of flour. If we didn't have these people, it would have been even worse."[89] Similarly, in the Hungarian region, one night a man was handcuffed and taken from one police station to the next, all the way to Csikszereda, and beaten at every stop; then they brought him home and asked people what such an exploiter deserved. Many villagers shouted at them to leave him alone, saying that he had always been very respected, was elected to the village leadership, helped build a birthing home and a medical center, and did many good things. Angry, the Party leaders told them they had been misled and would eventually learn that he was in fact an enemy of the people (Kristó 1999: 159–60). In Odorhei county, leaders were dismayed to find that one entire commune "joined in solidarity with the chiaburs, coming with 100 horse-drawn carts to the county capital to demand justice. This created a difficult atmosphere; the poor peasantry does not agree with our methods."[90]

Under cover of darkness, loyal poor peasants risked bringing food to the families of chiaburs whose stocks had been demolished by exaggerated requisitions, or risked hiding what they could of grain and flour for them, ever mindful of the consequences they would suffer should they be caught.[91] Such support is understandable: chiaburs had been the ones who gave people loans of money or food to tide them over, offered protection as godparents, etc. Even though it was risky, many peasants nonetheless manifested some sympathy for their "class enemies."[92] Some did so in broad daylight:

> We had seven hectares and would have some produce left after they took our quotas. (*Could you hide some?*) Yes. Deiu lui Pîca [a very poor man] was part of a group that went around checking to see if people had stuff hidden in the loft. He'd climb up the ladder, look around, and say, "Nothing here." But there would be a lot there! Guys below trusted him and didn't check. He saved several people this way.[93]

[89] V. Z., Iordachi interview.

[90] Reported by Teohari Georgescu in a meeting with county Party secretaries in 1950; the minutes are quoted in Cătănuş and Roske 2000: 166.

[91] Interviews corroborate archival reports about poor peasants and others hiding grain for chiaburs. See, for example, ANIC, Fond C.C. al P.C.R.–Cancelarie, file 6/1952, 24 (RLA).

[92] The same social support occurred during Soviet collectivization as well. Viola writes that peasants would try to protect kulaks from deportation, insisting when asked, "We have no kulaks here" (a refrain heard in Romania as well). After some kulaks were deported from one area, four thousand peasants took communion at church, and three thousand wore black mourning armbands; villagers refused to take orders about destroying kulak property (1987: 87, 89).

[93] 59, Verdery interview.

For all the Party's efforts, the model of comportment and values underlying chiaburs' former elite status was not completely overthrown. The fact that for the most part, unlike Soviet kulaks, they remained in their natal villages (perhaps following a few years' deportation) doubtless contributed to this continuity. Thus, whereas the Soviet model removed or "liquidated" kulaks altogether (see Viola 2007), Romania's communists preferred to keep them alive and in place. The difference would prove important in patterns of peasants joining the collectives.

Lamenting One's Fate

As for people named chiaburs, they responded in numerous ways we have already described—hiding their quotas, encouraging others to resist collectivization, filing repeated contestations, sabotaging production plans, engaging in violence, joining partisan bands in the mountains, and so forth—all amply documented in the existing literature. We augment these with other ways of struggling with all the pain and torment to which they were subjected. Many did so in silence, protecting their children from the horrors as much as they could and saying nothing that could get them into further trouble. Some, however, took solace in their cultural repertoires for expressing suffering, with poetic laments over the misfortunes that had turned their lives upside down.[94] Such poetic laments, like the written petitions submitted to authorities to seek redress of a grievance, represent distinct cultural forms of expression, each constructed to chronicle affliction *and* to gain sympathy for the aggrieved's position.[95] In the former, the lamenter presented her- or himself as the victim of suffering and hardship, and appealed to emotional sensibilities; in the latter, the petitioner, drawing on the new socialist vocabulary, re-presented her- or himself as a "new socialist person" and appealed to socialist norms of justice. We underscore, however, that the poetic lament was produced mainly for its author—in oral or written form—and at most, for a few trusted kin or friends, whereas the petition was directed to a Party official. Some villagers made use of both of these cultural forms—for catharsis, on the one hand, and possible resolution, on the other. The following are two such poetic laments, composed by a chiabur couple, husband and wife respectively.[96] Not all areas of Romania have these poetic forms; the two below come from Maramureş.

[94] The lament form is drawn from funeral traditions. In addition to emotional catharsis, this form allows the lamenter to embed other grievances into her expression of pain and sorrow. Funeral laments are customarily a female genre; otherwise, the poetic lament is not gendered. See Kligman 1988.

[95] See further comments on the lament form in appendix 2.

[96] Kligman collected these in 1990 during summer fieldwork in Ieud, Maramureş. Such texts are difficult to come by.

Chiabur's Lament

So I had to leave
Despite all I had to do in the village.
I got home late.
I remember it well
I'd been in the house for just a little while
When they came and took me.
They took me, they arrested me
They threw me in jail
Because I didn't turn in all my quotas
Of meat and of milk.
But, God, how could I
When I had nothing left?
They put me in jail, they jailed me
Without being guilty
Because all the livestock I had
I went to the market and sold them
I sold them and then gave them the money,
What I had left they took
The crops I harvested
I gave it to them whole.
I was in jail for three months
And after that they let me go
I was supposed to be in jail longer
And I don't know what happened
But after three months I was out.
I came home in May
And went plowing
I plowed for three weeks
My lot and other people's.
When I finished with the corn
I still had the buckwheat to plow.
I went to Trunchi to plow
So I could finish quickly
I got up really early
And I drove the horses to death
By breakfast time I was done
Plowing the whole lot
I still had to harrow.
And then . . . came to me
And told me, Ste, there's trouble
They're here for you again

Leave the plow, leave everything
And go as far as you can
So that nobody knows
Where you are from and what's with you.
Woman, I'm leaving right now
And I went to Porceanu
A bit of bread I took
And I left that very moment,
I went to the Iza train station
And left for the wide world again
I went far away in the wide world
Where no one would know my name.

Chiabura's Lament

And when I got married too
I chose a young man from our village
Handsome and wealthy
Young and to my liking
Handsome and pleasing
And as tall as a fir tree;
There was no other like him in the village.
And filled with goodness
I hadn't seen another like him in the villages around here
And so kind-hearted
There was no one like him.
But the world changed
And we came in harm's way a lot.
It changed so that
Those at the bottom came out on top
The last came to rule
The first suffered
The first, jailed
The last, head of the village
Since the world changed,
They took all my family
And put them in jail
They took everything in our home
They swept my attic clean
They left no wheat, nor straw,
No sheep in the sheepfold
No oxen left, no horses,
Not even a mug of cornmeal.

They didn't take them all at once
Today a horse, tomorrow a cow,
Today forty sheep,
The day after tomorrow a pair of oxen.
Until there was nothing left
They took everything to the collective.
We kept hearing rumors
That it was soon to be over,
That in a month
The Americans would come to our country.
In a month, in a year,
They'd come across the ocean
They'd come and save us
Things would be as they used to.
But years and years passed
And we ended up poor
Without cows and oxen,
Nothing but troubles.
We lived to see a time
When we had nothing to eat.
Quotas and taxes kept growing,
No one cared
That you didn't have anything to eat
And you couldn't pay.
They kept coming,
Coming to force you
To give them your share.
But, God, how can you give them
When you don't have anything?
Stables, barns, and attic, empty
And in the house not even a blanket
No cover on the bed
Oh God, what am I to do?
Because my husband's in jail,
My children ask me for food
And you don't have anything to give them
There's no cornmeal left
There's no milk because there are no cows
Because they took everything from us
Wheat, potatoes they took away,
They swept my attic clean
I ran through the village
And I got all sorts of things

From the people in the village
Who didn't have heavy taxes
And who had paid already.
I fed my children,
I didn't let them starve.
But when it was the hardest
I didn't know what to do
But it was God's almighty will
That evil Stalin
Evil and cursed
The devil came and took him.
I think he threw him in hell. . . .
And we joined the collective,
God, how upset I was.
Because I found myself poor again,
Without horses and with one cow in the stable
Poor me, I have no wealth
No land and no power
To turn the tables again
To make the world as it used to be. . . .
And they don't see, damn them,
How hard our life is now.

This woman, like others, sighed, "What I made in a lifetime, they destroyed in an instant."

The Attenuation of Social Ties

Notwithstanding our examples of peasants supporting their unfortunate chiaburs, the effects of class war on village social organization were devastating. Merle Fainsod (1958), writing of the Soviet Union, commented on the extraordinary capacity of the socialist system to remake social relations; we have shown here the centrality of class war in that process. In many respects, it provided the torque for organizational breakthrough. Although kinship relations remained basic to villagers' lives, class war had altered the meanings of these relations, and their colonization by the Party had bled out some of the trust necessary to sustaining them. The persecution of wealthy peasants who had been key nodes in village networks thinned those networks, thus weakening the social ties that rooted people in their communities.[97] When villagers manifested solidarity in support of their chiaburs, they did so in fear. And when this

[97] So, too, did emigration from rural communities, which we discuss further in chapter 8.

solidarity took the form of revolt against collectivization, as in Vadu Roşca, the ensuing repression so destroyed solidarity that even those arrested informed on one another (Stoica 2009).[98] This is not to say that traditional Romanian villages had been conflict-free: solidarity had not been their primary trait. But where it had existed, class war along with broad repression reduced the solidary unit from the village as a whole to its constituent households and smaller kin networks. Social relationships had been attenuated.

This thinning of relationships has another source underappreciated in the literature on collectivization: the effects of food shortages and their implications for the collectivization drive.[99] Food everywhere is essential to the reproduction not just of people's physical bodies but also of their social ties. As is more widely true, in Romania before collectivization there was no social occasion without abundant supplies of food.[100] Preparing and serving it engaged the energies of many women who were kin and neighbors, and the activities both strengthened those ties and made them manifest. In addition, consuming the food cemented the ties of those who ate together. The higher one's social status, the more important was the display of one's capacity to mobilize both food and eaters. When food became scarce, those occasions diminished: consequently, the social relations they forged were diminished as well.[101]

Reduced food supplies opened the way for collectivization by precipitating threats to social reproduction, which the Party's assault on village social structures would only exacerbate. In Romania, the causes of food shortage were primarily the quota system, which diverted food from the peasantry to the cities, and the country's war-reparations debt to the Soviet Union, which drained away thousands of tons of grain each year. These shortages helped to prepare the way for transforming village social relations; the policies related to class warfare were part of the process. The steeply progressive quotas placed on chiaburs had the effect of forcing them to increase production and thwarting both their accumulation of capital and their reproduction of social ties, so essential

[98] The revolt in Vadu Roşca was partially attributed, at least retrospectively, to the villagers' strong social solidarity (see Stoica 2009).

[99] Thanks to Kenneth MacLean for conversations on this theme. Food shortages and famine loom large in the global experience of collectivization. They include the terrible famine in Ukraine (1932–33), famines and repeated food shortages in Vietnam right through the 1970s, and famine in China (1958–61). In Romania, there was a devastating famine in Moldavia in 1944–46 and serious food shortages elsewhere in the country as well, into the mid-1950s. As Conquest (1986) has argued for Ukraine and MacLean (2005) for Vietnam, some of these famines were man-made—the main cause being excessive food requisitions at prices that did not permit families to procure food otherwise.

[100] We note that there is an important cultural element in defining what counts as "food." We often heard from our respondents that quotas left them with nothing to eat—yet no one spoke of people starving to death. One respondent indicated this cultural element in saying that collectors took all the best wheat and left them with only brown flour.

[101] Verdery (1996: chapter 2) made this same argument for Romania in the 1980s.

to signifying and maintaining their status. Whether cadres intended it or not, quotas served to reduce the occasions for hospitality among kin and to neutralize the chiaburs not just economically but also socially, by making it impossible for them to feed others.

A telling sign of endangered social relations is the silence that many respondents associate with the time of collectivization, as we observed at the end of chapter 5: people tell us they spoke less both to their kin and to other villagers, to prevent being overheard and reported on. Siblings who disagreed on whether to join would communicate less often; those who had joined would retreat from public spaces to avoid commentary. Reducing communication automatically reduces sociality, and, as we discussed in our introduction, it helped set the stage for post-1989 battles over historical truth and claims to authentic social memory.

Conclusion

The processes unleashed by class war reconfigured both village social relations and individuals' relations with the state, creating the mechanisms of power by which the Party both ruled and legitimated its authority. In concluding chapter 5, we suggested a parallel between persuasion work and the actions of a virus: like a virus, communist cadres first entered their host, then used its mechanisms of reproduction to develop their own, for their own ends. This image is equally apposite to the fomenting of class warfare. For people in village communities, the status hierarchy and social organization were themselves a form of power, resting on the embeddedness of persons in their relationships. Villagers used these resources to respond to the power of the Party, which in turn colonized these very relations, recognizing their strength. If at first peasants delayed entering collectives in the name of family relations, they finally entered in the name of those same relations: to enable a child to stay in school or a kinsman to hold on to a job. Even when they justified joining "because everyone else has done it," as we will show in the next chapter, they were invoking their community relations, not their responsibility to the state. It would be their last such opportunity, for with their entry petitions they made the Party the ultimate network, the patron, the generative site of social relationships. They entered into a set of bureaucratic relations in place of the community ones that had contained them hitherto—the result of organizational breakthrough.

At the same time, however, we must remember that for many villagers, precommunist social organization had been very oppressive, with multiple forms of social, gender, and ethnic inequity. In emphasizing the violence the communists wrought upon these structures and the pathos of the fate of wealthy peasants (who include some of our best respondents), we can too easily overlook the question of whether those structures should indeed have been preserved.

One of the ironies of collectivization is that as cadres strove to wipe out the existing social organization by fomenting class war, villagers were compelled to defend relations that were harsh and brutal.[102] Not all were willing to do so. Only thus can we understand why the Party was able to recruit from those groups disadvantaged in the traditional order: the poor, Roma, Jews, migrants in villages that regarded them as "foreigners," and so on—a point we will return to in chapter 7. Such allies were essential to collectivizing, and, as chapter 8 will show, they were among its main beneficiaries.

[102] We thank an anonymous reviewer for insisting on this point.

Part III

OUTCOMES

Chapter 7

The Collectives Are Formed

> Either you hang yourself, or you drown yourself, or you join the collective.[1]

> Comrade M. V., the cousin of a chiabur, goes around telling people that if they join the GAC with Roma they'll work until their eyes pop out because [Roma] don't like to till the land . . . and they don't want to have someone telling them what to do when they go to work.[2]

> Some people said that the Americans would come—yes, the Americans would come. But others said, "By the time the Americans come we'll be destroyed by the colhoz! They'll kill us with the colhoz before the Americans come to take us out." And people were discouraged, no one knew any more what to think.[3]

THE TECHNOLOGIES OF persuasion we have detailed in the preceding chapters—the propaganda, mimesis, denunciations, enlightenment work by cadres, class war, and so on—had one express goal: that peasants would join the collectives "of their own free will." They did so throughout the period under consideration, from 1949 to 1962, but with greatly increased frequency once the final campaign got underway in 1957. Can we discern any patterns in how that occurred? Aside from the more or less uniform application of the same technologies, were there general similarities in the manner of peasants' signing up? Were there significant differences? In this chapter we summarize what we were able to learn about these questions.

Their path to this outcome involved finally relinquishing at least two persistent fantasies that inspired resistance from 1945 on: the fantasy that cadres would get tired of trying to collectivize and would go away, and the fantasy that the Americans would come to the rescue. This latter dream of the liberating Americans was well entrenched in all the East European countries, even as far east as Ukraine, long part of the Soviet Union.[4] Throughout the early to mid-1950s, the fantasy of American liberation sustained groups of partisans hiding in the mountains and enspirited peasant resistance to joining the collectives. A popular subversive rhyme captured this enduring hope: "Mother in heaven, give strength to the partisans until the Americans come!" (Roske 2003: 100; see also below). Romanians finally began to surrender this hope with the Hungarian revolution of 1956. At the time of the revolution, hope had been high. To

[1] V.C.T., Dobrincu interview.
[2] DJAN HD, Fond CR PMR, file 103/1951, 252.
[3] V.T.T., Dobrincu interview.
[4] Adriana Petryna, personal communication.

take only two of many examples: as reported in an information bulletin from Stalin region, people were going around saying things like, "In Hungary the people opened their eyes and rose up to protest the misdeeds of the communists," and "What happened in Hungary will be in Romania in a week at most."[5] But when the Americans did not come to help Hungarians, who rose up in such numbers, how could anyone expect them to come to Romania, even farther away? One respondent commented, "Lots of people were saying, 'How long have I heard the Americans are coming! They're coming on foot! They're not coming here ever—from now on, we're stuck with these [communists]!"[6] Although the events in Hungary produced a brief delay in the "second wave" of the collectivization drive, by early 1957 it was resumed with determination and carried through to completion in 1962. By this time, the arguments that people "had no choice" and would have to sign up must have seemed much more convincing than was true in the early '50s, when there were not so many cadres insisting on it. Moreover, by the second wave, villagers had repeatedly experienced or witnessed the Party's violence and repression of anticollectivization revolts. The temporal compression that followed is remarkable: in the space of a couple of weeks or months, whole villages signed up that had resisted for years.

Following several years of practices, then, that drew people into a process increasingly determined by the authorities and eroded their will and confidence, collectivization was brought to completion. In this chapter, we argue (furthering our argument in chapter 5) that although peasants eventually capitulated to the assault on their way of life, in some respects cadres themselves had to capitulate to that way of life in order to win: they had to acknowledge the importance of village status systems, bringing chiaburs into the collectives instead of excluding them. After that, the process went much more quickly. Then we survey some of the social variables that affected patterns of forming the collectives. Among these are religious and ethnic composition, colonization, ecological/economic adaptation, local politics, and historical differences by region. Our findings are tentative, for our team's research in one or another settlement of the country's major regions can hardly provide definitive evidence concerning these variables. Nonetheless, we present them as suggestions for further work.

The First Shall Be Last? Patterns of Joining

In our interviews, we asked respondents if they could remember who had signed up first. The replies almost always characterized early joiners in something like these terms: "the poor," "landless peasants," "alcoholics," "those who

[5] ANIC, Fond C.C. al P.C.R.–Organizatorică, file 43/1956, 17.

[6] D.V.H., Dobrincu interview.

didn't like to work," "lazy people," "fools," "illiterates," "Gypsies," "communists," "tractor drivers," and "*their* people." A typical instance:

> Right away they flocked to become secretary and mayor and executive committee members and whatnot, all the rascals, the worst people in the village grabbed a leadership position and all that. And they all gathered together and they were the ones who then oppressed people. [They claimed] this one's a chiabur, that one's a chiabur, but they didn't leave [to work] for six years like I did, to make [enough to buy] one hundred or two hundred sheep. . . . They didn't leave the village to go and earn something. They stayed put. All the bad people in the village were there [in the beginning]. Those who became Party members later, in the '70s, after the '70s, then there were more well-to-do people who started to join, you know? But in the beginning, we saw all sorts of bad things happening here.[7]

Some elaborated caustically on their answers, especially with respect to Party and GAC members' illiteracy and lack of preparation for the work. Others used the characterizations to justify their own refusal to join: for instance, Vultur reports for Tomnatic that wealthier families did not join because "[t]hey didn't want to get mixed up with 'just anybody,' since at first there were only miserable wretches [*prăpădiți*] in it."[8] This opinion is widely held, many respondents affirming that in the GAC there were only "lazy people, drunks, Gypsies. . . . To join in with them could only be a form of punishment or social degradation" (Vultur 2003: 42). Naturally, such descriptions depended on one's social position—middle and wealthy peasants would speak dismissively of "the poor," who in turn would find other expressions of abuse. The answers also depended on the terms under which one had joined: Party and former collective farm members who had not been coerced into joining or had positive views about the model collectives, such as early joiners in Sântana or Pechea (see Goina 2003; Şandru 2003), tended to avoid the derogatory terms used by late joiners, former chiaburs, and status-conscious middle peasants.

Stoica (2003: 9) insightfully cautions that pejorative descriptors are leitmotifs of a present-day, postcommunist discourse that moralizes the "first wave" of collectivization as the work of undesirable social elements; thus, these ways of talking are at least partly an artifact of retrospective interviews. Supporting this is that respondents discussing who joined first usually answered with *categories* of people ("the laziest," "the worst people"—in short, the morally reprobate) rather than with individual names. Lățea proposes (2003: 24) that the widespread attribution of early joining to people seen as poor or morally inferior indicates how our respondents, a decade after the collapse of socialism, were trying to resolve the then-pressing question of who was responsible for collectivization. Since our formerly wealthy or middle peasant respondents of course

[7] N. I., Stan interview for M. Stewart.

[8] See Vultur 1997: 258.

saw themselves as morally upright, blaming the poor and the "bad" took the responsibility from their own shoulders.

Logically speaking, we might expect certain patterns. Aside from the "Party line" that invited the poor first and the rich last, the poor could be expected to be first, for they had the most to gain and virtually nothing to lose. Having eked out a marginal existence for many years, they might now draw salaries and enjoy lording it over the wealthier who once lorded it over them. Yet because the poor also had the least material wealth to contribute, cadres were not always eager to take them and sometimes preferred to bring in those chiaburs who sought membership so as to lighten their burdens, until the Party leadership prohibited this practice. Cadres would press the poor to join when they needed numbers, but otherwise the poor were not their preferred targets. Poor peasants were actually in a very delicate position. Expected to join for ideological reasons, they were fearful of the consequences of not joining, having noted the bruised bodies of fellow villagers. As one older peasant from Reviga remarked, "Those who were poorer said that it was better to go to the local council to sign up than to be beaten" (Chelcea 2003b: 34). On the other hand, they were subject to intimidation by more powerful villagers, who might beat them up as well.

Another group likely to enter early—a rather small proportion of the total where they were present—were colonists who had been settled in villages being collectivized (such as Sântana, Reviga, and Jurilovca, in our sample). As outsiders, their positions were vulnerable. They had little social or material capital, meaning that they could not count on others coming to their aid, hiding grain for them, or helping them pay their quotas (e.g., Goina 2003: 21). They did not have local networks that embedded them in reciprocal social obligations on which they could potentially draw in times of need. As one report about successful collectivization in Constanța observed, "the people are not tied to the land; there, they are colonists" (Iordachi 2003: 21). Others in similar binds—"rehabilitated" Germans whose property had been confiscated after the war, Roma who did not have land, and poor or landless peasants—all had good reason to renounce what little they might have possessed and join the collectives. We return below to the matter of colonization.

In several of our communities (such as Vlaicu, Măgina, Sântana, and Tomnatic) we found a related pattern involving not colonists but other kinds of nonlocals. Often, the local residents who pushed for the formation of a collective or were active in it were not from locally born village families but had moved or married into it. In Romanian villages, as we noted in chapter 2, "outsiders" were viewed with disfavor and accorded marginal status. Such inmigrants might have neither the extended networks of kin nor the deep attachment to ancestral parcels that would incline them to resist collectivizing. Moreover, since postmarital residence in Romanian villages was usually virilocal, the disadvantage was greater if the in-marrying person was a man who moved into his wife's household (as opposed to acquiring a separate house), known as "son-in-law in the house" [*ginere în casă*]—a somewhat lowly status.[9] A man like this might well be drawn to the new statuses available to him in the collective farm, just as the poor peasants were. Creed has noted this same pattern in Bulgaria (1998: 57–58). The cultural logic involved in "outsiderness" made it a strong candidate for respondents speculating about who joined early. For example, in Domaşnea, some people believed that the district-level Second Party Secretary, Comrade Toma, had implemented collectivization there

> because he was a newcomer [pejorative]. Puşcaş—who was the first secretary—was one of us, from the Banat, and in principle wasn't quite in agreement. . . . There are also witnesses who say that Toma A. was "some sort of a Jew, who came from around Timişoara," in the logic of the stereotype attributing an exclusively or predominantly foreign character to communist power in Romania. (Vultur 2003: 71)

Both in people's imaginaries, then, and in actual fact, the non-locally-born may have played a disproportionate part in creating a given village's collective.

On the basis of our documentary evidence, however, the answer to the question of who joined early is very complex. First, despite the forces favoring the poor, in some of our villages such as Domaşnea and Rimetea, people recalled that those who joined first were among the better off (e.g., Ţărâu 2003: 49). (Such joiners in the first wave of collectivization were usually expelled in the first wave of "dechiaburization.") Among the early joiners might be people from respected families with a "problem," such as prior membership in the fascist organization or having a father involved in commerce; this might be combined with personal ambition. In Vlaicu, one man whose father ran a tavern was among the first to join because (according to his relatives) "he wanted them to make him president."[10] Thus, a number of better-off families might well sign up before many of the poor. Second, people of any status who had entered into state employment (such as the schoolteacher, postal employees, and workers on the railway or in industry) or local structures of power would have to join early. Lăţea refers to these people as "captives":

> [A]ccording to some of my interlocutors, the first collective members from Dobrosloveni were those who, in their capacity as functionaries, members of commissions and sub-commissions, salaried workers or simply "volunteers," had to understand that if they didn't wish to overly complicate their future, they had to join the GAC. Nevertheless, the dominant local recollection is wholly different: those who joined among the first were the "poor." (2009: 335–36)

A close examination of the entry petitions to the GAC convinces him that figuring in an administrative position was a better predictor of early joining than was membership in the "poor" category.

[9] In Romanian, the verb for "to marry" differs according to whether the person marrying is male or female: a man *se însoară*, a woman *se mărită*. A son-in-law who moves into his wife's home is described with the female form of the verb.

[10] 59, Verdery interview.

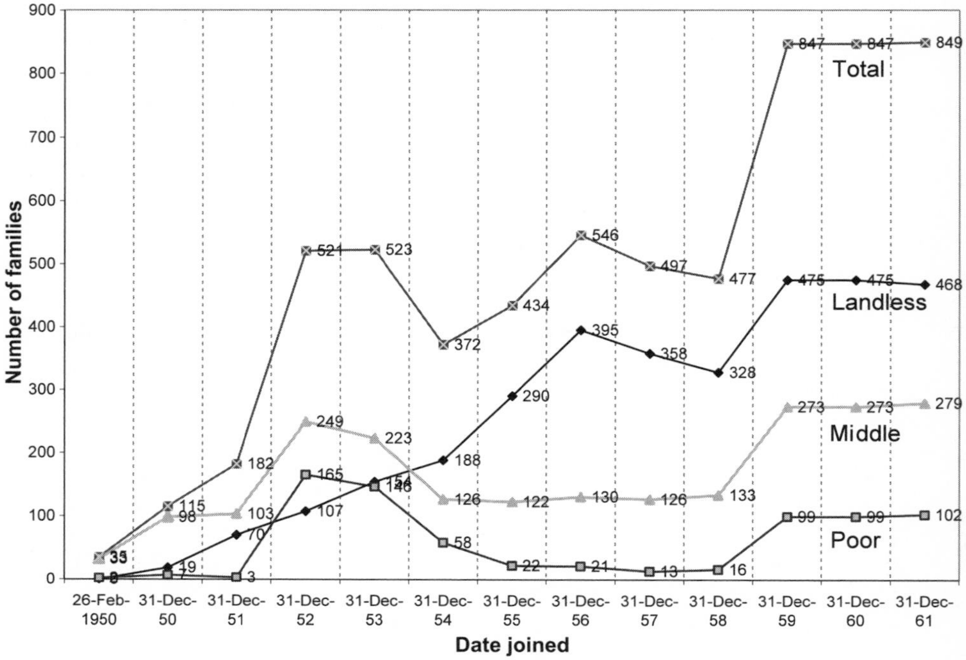

Figure 7.1. Families joining the Sântana "New Life" GAC to 1961, by socio-economic status. *Source:* Goina, personal comunication. (The category "chiaburs" is absent from the statistics on which the table is based.)

Third, patterns of joining differed in villages of different social, ethnic, or religious composition and of different forms of livelihood. They differed also according to the time at which their "big push" occurred: those collectivizing in the first wave of GAC formation (1949–50) when material endowments to the GACs were high might attract more middle peasants, as Goina shows in his graph of those joining the "New Life" GAC, begun in 1950 with minimal coercion (see figure 7.1). For the first three years, middle peasants considerably outstripped the poor and landless. Because the GAC at Sântana was a model farm, however, unusually rich in resources, we would not expect to find this pattern in GACs formed later without these advantages.

Finally, we note that respondents' memories on the question of who joined early are not reliable: people tend to "remember" that they themselves joined late, after "most of the village" had already signed up, but the dated lists we found belie that recollection.[11] It was the rare respondent who acknowledged having joined early. One of Lățea's respondents made this point clearly, in dis-

[11] For example, Arhiva CAP-ului Aurel Vlaicu, "Opisul Dosarului din cererile de înscriere în G.A.C. Victoria."

cussing how people justified to the activists their refusal to join: "They were afraid to be the first to do it: 'Why should I be the first to sign up? Let others do it, not me!'" (Lățea 2009: 342).

One statistic that is sometimes thought to prove that early joiners were poor—namely, the rather small amounts of land that appear in the records when collectives were initially formed—is misleading, for it proves only that those who joined *brought in* small amounts, not that they *had* small amounts; many middle peasants who joined kept out or hid part of their land for themselves when they signed up. Overall, however, it is probably fair to say that the majority of early joiners were poor, for cadres mainly kept out wealthy peasants during the first wave, and the middle peasants they targeted held back. Moreover, if we recall the property structure of Romania prior to collectivization, over half of all farms had less than three hectares and three-quarters had less than five hectares. Inevitably, then, people of modest means would form the bulk of new collective farms. Respondents tend to "forget" those who were not poor, retrospectively preserving the dignity of higher-status people.

The Pace of Collectivizing

Another finding concerns the pace and trajectory of the process. In the early years and stretching on into the late 1950s, many peasants dawdled and evaded the inevitable, finding rich sources of delay in manipulations of time and kinship. People blamed wives, husbands, parents, and in-laws for preventing them from joining the collective; they invented innumerable excuses to postpone signing up. They waited for the Americans to come; they fled into the woods. After all the postponing, however, many of our team members found that once people began to join (which might be some years after activists had begun persuasion work), most of the village signed up fairly fast: in Dobrosloveni, two weeks; in Vlaicu, three weeks; in Domaşnea, one month; in Corund, three months; in Poiana Sibiului, "practically overnight," etc.[12] The main exceptions were in collectives that had been established early in the 1950s and that embraced only a subset of villagers, such as in Sântana, Pechea, or Ieud; then, in the second wave in the late 1950s, everyone else joined—rapidly. Figure 7.1 above shows that in Sântana there were two spurts of joining; in the first spurt, nearly half joined in the short space of six weeks. In Ieud, some three hundred petitioned to join the GAC "Scânteia" (sic) between February and April 1962 (but here, about half the village never signed up at all, the village remaining only partially collectivized throughout the communist period).[13]

[12] Speed did not necessarily indicate the same thing in all places. For instance, in Darabani, two-thirds joined in the last two days before the GAC was launched, but this doubtless reflected extreme coercion. See table 5.1, p. 321.

[13] Arhiva Primăriei Vişeu de Jos, Maramureş, Fond 335, file 18/1962. A combination of Ieud's

What determined this pattern? Why should it be that after many years of refusing to sign up, everyone all of a sudden would sign up en masse? Bodó suggests that this may be a false problem: lengthy preparation, including wearing people down by constant assaults to their dignity, had laid the groundwork for a rapid conclusion (2003: 2–4). Although she is certainly right, we can say more. To do so, we invoke our earlier discussion about the village status hierarchy and note that decisions to join are probably best seen as collective, not individual, ones—even if it was individuals who had to sign the enrollment petitions.

One reason for the pacing (aside from the slowdown after Stalin's death in 1953) is that until late 1956, many peasants had avoided joining because they expected the regime to fall, whether by the coming of the Americans or by something else. A report from some recalcitrant villages in Hunedoara region as late as spring 1957 (this was *after* the suppression of the 1956 Hungarian uprising) claimed, "People think this will all disappear in 2–3 years."[14] In a sense, Țârău suggests, they did not take the new government seriously, villagers in upland locations in particular (2003: 19n48). We also see this possibility in fiction of the period, such as Preda's novel *Moromeții*. Although peasants continued to revolt against the regime's reinvigorated efforts to complete collectivization, when they finally saw that there was little hope of an alternative, when they saw violence around them or experienced it themselves, and when it began to appear that the regime was now institutionalized, they reasoned that if everyone else was doing it, they should too (Țârău 2003: 19n48).

Second, as the campaign drew to a climax and activists knew time was running out, they began making promises that drew people in, as we saw with the conditions written on the back of entry petitions to the GACs (see chapter 5; Lățea 2009). Strategic arrests, beatings, and deportations also produced an atmosphere of communal anxiety that predisposed people to join. Activists were under pressure to hasten the creation of GACs and bring the process to a "successful" conclusion. In Maramureş, for example, between November 1, 1961, and March 9, 1962, there was a mad rush to establish new GACs. On March 9, 1962, there were reportedly 370 GACs, representing an increase of 140 over the four months, and a total of 46,629 families had joined old and new GACs. Two days later, a telephoned memorandum increased that number to 48,648. Moreover, it claimed that the 95,342 families in GACs as of March 1 had grown to 113,690 families by March 12.[15]

Third, let us consider some comments from our interviews concerning when people had joined: "I didn't have any more choice: I kept hiding, and when I saw that almost everybody had joined . . ." "[My father-in-law] said, 'We have to join

poor soil quality and the villagers' recalcitrance contributed to its not being fully collectivized (Kligman 2009).

[14] DJAN HD, Fond CR PMR, file 2431/1957, 140.

[15] See DJAN MM, Fond Comitetul Regional al PMR-Maramureş, file 42/1962, 32, 40.

too, 'cause look, so-and-so and so-and-so have joined.'" "I'd go to the meetings and come home and tell my husband, 'Look, X joined, and Y.'" "Others have joined and they haven't died, so I won't either." "After more than half of the village had signed up." "My father-in-law said to me, 'Sign up, Gheorghe, we don't have any choice. Everyone has joined and they'll end up making fun of you! Instead of having them make fun of you, . . . sign up, 'cause look, everyone else is in it.'" These reasons echo similar ones given earlier for not giving quotas or joining: "if no one goes to work on the collective they can't do anything to us, and if everyone joins I will too."[16] We will further document this pattern below.[17]

In people's comments, note that the emphasis is always on the signer *in relation to others*—half the village, specific people, etc. Early in the process, social pressure was felt against joining. Those who signed up would be mocked: "You're so impotent that you can no longer manage 100–200 sheep and be your own master? Now you're a servant at the CAP?" (Stewart and Stan 2009: 266). Lățea documents another form of this in Dobrosloveni, where several of his respondents said that no one wanted to sign up because their peers threatened to burn their house down if they joined. For instance:

(*Some signed up earlier than others. Why?*)

I. B.: Do you know the policy at that time, when very few signed up? They would say: "Look, I'll sign up, but don't tell anyone, because they'll set my house on fire!" and that's why very few signed up!

(*Well, and who set houses on fire?*)

I. B.: Nobody did, people weren't hateful, but they were afraid to be the first to do it. (Lățea 2009: 342)

This reply reveals beautifully the sense of collective pressure, even though no one was actually burning houses down. But at a certain point, the tide turned: people would use collective pressure to explain why they had to join, as in the respondent above whose father-in-law tells him to sign so people won't make fun of them any more. In Darabani, as the campaign progressed, rumors spread that those who refused to sign up for the "new way" would be socially isolated (they would be barred from work, from sending their children to school, from buying things or from leaving their courtyards, etc.). Indeed, fear of social ostracism, of being alone as most others entered the GAC, recurs in many ac-

[16] DJAN HD, Fond CR PMR, file 2426/1957, 41–52. See also the scene in Preda's *Moromeții* (1967, vol. 2: 260) in which peasants refuse en masse to give their quotas, saying that if nobody does it, then "[t]hey can't do anything about it." And concerning signing into the GAC, they say, "If everyone does, I will" (261).

[17] Two weeks of "persuasion" in Măgina to form an association (*întovărășire*) proceeded thus: between January 30 and February 4, 1960, ten entry petitions were signed; in the subsequent five days, another twenty-one were signed; in two more days, another thirty-three; and on the final two days, ninety-eight (DJAN AB, Fond Sfatul Popular al Comunei Cacova (Livezile), file 84. Courtesy of Țârău 2003: 31–32.).

counts about the end of resistance: "What happened to others would happen to me, too!"; "Why should I be different?" (Dobrincu 2009: 294).

Fourth, and especially important, as the "final assault" of the collectivization campaign ramped up, desperate cadres all over Romania began to court the wealthy and visible peasants of the former status order—those neutralized former enemies of the people–rather than the poor and marginal types of before.[18] What mattered was a person's having previously enjoyed high status, whether or not labeled a chiabur.[19] Cadres resorted to local cultural knowledge, turning to respected godparents in the village who were likely to have been wealthier, with many relatives and godchildren. Here is how one cadre involved in collectivizing explained it, telling how he tried to persuade the local Party Secretary to stop persecuting a chiabur:

> I said to them, "He's not against the regime. This is a prosperous guy who minds his own business and doesn't get involved in politics against the Party, so leave him alone. When we start trying to make a collective there, he's the kind of person we'll have to appeal to." . . . A well-to-do man had a lot of ritual kin, a lot of friends, had workers he worked with, and influenced the atmosphere in the village. And this was the kind of person we would have to use for collectivizing. If this kind of fellow signed up, the chain would break [*se rupe lanțul*]; after him all resistance would fall apart.[20]

"Courting" of chiaburs could take less benign forms. Another activist put the matter succinctly: "To hell with 'of my own free will!' It was from fear! —'cause they took two or three of the most outstanding people and did them harm."[21] Or, hoping to capitalize on the social trust such families still enjoyed, the Securitate tried to entrap them, though this was not easy. Thus, in the middle of the night—as was their wont—a local official came to escort B. S., a highly respected chiabur from Ieud, to a meeting, where he was made the following offer:

> Do you cherish your family? Your wife? If so, then you should do as we tell you and you'll be happy. . . . We want you to go to the forest, as if running away. We'll have taken you in a car from which you'll pretend to escape. We'll fire a shot—not at you—in the air, not to frighten you. You then join the others hiding in the woods and come back weekly to report to us. We'll give you a house, everything you need, your family won't lack for anything.[22]

[18] This was not a new strategy but it had been suppressed earlier in the decade.

[19] By the mid-to-late 1950s, the term "chiabur" was less frequently used in official documents, but for clarity's sake we continue to refer to them as chiaburs rather than the more correct "wealthy peasants." Goina, for instance, notes that most of the families named chiabur in Sântana had not owned a great deal of land; most of them were classified chiabur because they owned a shop or a brandy still. Such people would not have been especially respected. And in his village, people did not sign up in relation to when chiaburs joined.

[20] M. H., Verdery interview.

[21] 186, Verdery interview.

[22] B. S., Kligman interview.

He refused this generous offer, saying he was a fearful sort, not suited for such a mission. His refusal earned him a kick in the pants and a prison stay of three months. (It was his first stay of several until he finally joined the collective in February 1962; the authorities made clear that his children and extended family members would suffer the consequences of further refusal on his part. Relatives of his spent much longer, harder years in some of Romania's most notorious prisons and labor camps, where the authorities actively exploited their vulnerabilities to try to recruit them as informers.)[23] In Ieud, not many chiaburs joined the GAC, mainly those who had been subjected to extreme pressure, like this man; a number of them simply fled the village until Dej announced the successful end of collectivization. When they did join, they were immediately given positions of responsibility—B. S. was made brigade leader, another became secretary. This seems to have contributed to the rapid joining of Ieudeni in their wake.

Villagers themselves recollected the effectiveness of these tactics. One woman, the daughter of chiaburs in the Miercurea Ciuc region, observed that the comrades in charge of organizing the collective thought their work would be easy if they could convince her father to sign because the whole village would then follow suit (Kristó 1999: 212). In that same area, after accepting chiaburs into the GAC who were considered the most upstanding persons in their communities, the number of villagers who joined tripled in the course of three days.[24] Similarly, a man from Dobrosloveni: "And who did they try to break down, who did they force? The wealthiest and the worthiest people in the village. They figured if they got these people to join, the simpler ones would follow suit: 'Hey, if Fănică son of Bancu joined . . . if Titu son of Ghiţă joined. . . . Worthy people joined; why shouldn't I join? Hey, let's join too!' and they did, one by one. . . . Like sheep to be milked!"[25] A respondent from Tomnatic used the same animal imagery: "You take the sheep with the bell, then everything else will follow."[26] Finally, there is the testimony of one G. C., who happened to live next door to the house where the signing-up took place. He would sit outside and tell people as they went in, "Don't sign up!"

[23] Securitate reports detail how individuals were to be recruited: the goal of so doing, information about the intended recruitee, the method to be used, and so on. The cynicism with which human vulnerabilities were manipulated is one of the more disturbing features of these reports, the techniques of which are widespread throughout the world. Under "method of recruitment," the reporting officer noted: "We established co-interests. . . . the subject would appreciate better medical treatment because he is in poor health and when he is released from prison, wants to return to his family to put his children through school. Relatedly he would like a better dietary regime to improve his health. With these considerations in mind, we recommend that he be recruited as an agent on the basis of co-interests." (See ACNSAS, FR, file 985, 5.)

[24] See DJAN MU, Fond Comitetul PMR, file 12/1950, 97–98, cited in Márton 2005. Also see Kristó (1999: 38) for a different form of broken promises to chiaburs.

[25] S. A., Lăţea interview.

[26] R. A., Vultur interview.

> And then they took me and sentenced me to twenty years in jail. And they went through the village to get people to sign into the collective.
>
> (*So more people joined after they arrested you?*)
>
> Yes, of course. Only after they arrested me did they make the collective. They took me because they couldn't do it. . . . Here's what those guys said, "If you don't take C. you'll never ever get a collective in Vlaicu!"[27]

He was not alone in his view of his importance. In February 1958, activist Florescu from Orăştie gave a declaration against two men who had assaulted him (G. C. being one), concluding, "I want to add that if both of them had signed up, the [GAC] would have been inaugurated a long time ago because they have a lot of influence over the village population."[28]

In other words, during the final campaign after 1957, cadres had to relax the policy that had excluded chiaburs from the collectives as part of class war, shifting the emphasis to including them, and this brought in villagers from the other social groups. By the late 1950s, the word "chiabur" disappeared from documents and actions to demonize them declined. Once chiaburs were allowed to sign up, others began to sign up en masse. Cătănuş and Roske observe (2000: 21) that in Dolj, as soon as chiaburs joined the GAC, "the peasants showed themselves eager to join it. As soon as measures were taken to exclude chiaburs, the number of G.A.C. members fell by half." Additional documents show us this possibility in even more detail. By April 1962, when the campaign was declared complete, about 250 households in Vlaicu had joined the "Victory" collective farm; a few others joined later. According to two lists from the farm office,[29] the first people joined in early February 1959; over the next month a total of 21 households signed up, some being of good reputation and the rest poor or landless (significantly, the majority were not from long-standing local families).[30] On March 3 a more concentrated blitz began: 26 signatures were recruited in that week, 89 in the next, and 63 in the third. In less than three weeks (between March 3 and 21), nearly three-fourths of the village joined the collective farm. Particularly interesting is what was happening as the numbers picked up. As of March 3, a widow from an influential family joined; four days later three very visible men were arrested for disturbing public order. One of them was a former mayor, whose wife then joined the collective that very day.

[27] 195, Verdery interview.

[28] ACNSAS, FI, file 3936/1, 10ff.

[29] One is a summary list that gives a file number, a name, the date of signing, and the animals and inventory brought into the farm (Arhiva CAP-ului Aurel Vlaicu, "Opisul Dosarului din cererile de înscriere în G.A.C. Victoria."). The first nine entries are missing. The second (untitled) is a more detailed listing without dates but seemingly in the order of joining. There is rough consistency in the two sets of dates, but a number are very discrepant. In those cases, we have used the date as given in the summary list, to arrange all households by time of joining. It is likely that the dates are not all accurate, so the exercise should be seen as an approximation.

[30] They had married in, moved in for work, or come with parents who had moved in earlier. The two most respected in that group were the schoolteacher and the postal employee.

Figure 7.2. Inaugurating a new GAC in Bonțida. Courtesy of Artexpo Foundation.

The numbers shot up for the next several days, bringing in others from wealthy and important families. On March 17 (by which time just under half the village households had joined), the single most influential person in Vlaicu signed up, along with three others of high renown; together they had a large number of kin and ritual kin. The following day had the highest total of any: 34 (14 percent of all those who joined). A full 20 percent of the village signed up in the next four days. On March 23, 1959, the collective was inaugurated, with the fanfare that always accompanied this event.[31]

These data appear to confirm the view, then, that when activists concentrated on either jailing or persuading the most influential families, the rewards were very gratifying for them. And activists were not above faking a persuasion: in Poiana Sibiului, word went out that D. I, a much-respected person, had signed up—someone had even seen the paper at the People's Council office. "Others then said, 'If he's signed, how could I not sign?' After that people joined in droves, 222 all at once. All night long they were at the People's Council signing up." But it turned out that the paper with D. I.'s signature was forged.[32]

In short, forming a collective farm was an event with network properties. It was not a series of individual decisions but emerged from a dense web of connections among households in a community (see also Creed 1998: 67–68). In particular, it seems that when the most respected families had been "persuaded" to join, then everyone else fell into line, paradoxically at last giving the Party the

[31] DJAN HD, Fond CR PMR, file 104/1959, 13.

[32] L. M., Budrală interview for M. Stewart.

"mimesis" and emulation it had sought all along, but from the opposite direction.[33] Once the linchpins of the system of status honor had renounced the basis of their position, then so could everyone else: "If [rich] X has joined, then so can I." Similarly, once a family's kin had given up the "self" that rested on land, then others could too (see chapter 2). In this sense, villagers are right when they say that they joined "about when everyone else did." They signed up all at the same time, then, because it was not an individual but a collective decision, influenced by kin, neighbors, friends, and above all the former village elite.[34] Exemplifying what Schelling refers to as contingent behavior (1978: 17)—behavior that depends on what others are doing, often a critical mass of others—these peasants showed that a "critical mass" may concern not just how many are behaving a particular way (94), but *who* is behaving that way.[35] The village elite continued to exercise social power despite the Party's concerted attack on local status systems, a significant difference from the Soviet experience, where that elite was effectively removed. As Jowitt observed, in their efforts to redefine society Marxist-Leninist regimes paradoxically and "unintentionally strengthen many traditional postures in what for the regime are often priority areas" (1974: 1126). To succeed in collectivizing the country, activists were obliged to accommodate these "traditional" aspects of local social organization. Even if chiaburs had lost status in practical, material terms, they retained it in social and spiritual ones: throughout the communist period, the funerals of former chiaburs were conducted not by the usual one or two priests but by many, out of respect, and hundreds of mourners pressed into their courtyards.

Axes of Variation

We have suggested two important similarities in how collectives were formed across Romania: the speed with which a given community's members signed up once the process began, and the likely role of preexisting social hierarchies in that outcome. But what of intercommunity variation?[36] Romania's villages differed significantly from one another in a number of ways. The country's population was heterogeneous with respect to religion and ethnonational identification; some of its settlements had existed continuously for centuries, whereas others had been settled late or included people brought in as colo-

[33] Many thanks to Virgiliu Țărău for this insight. We note similar findings from other collectivizing situations: Ross (2000: 123) reports for East Germany that many poorer peasants made joining the collective contingent on the entry of larger farmers they had worked for, revealing both paternalism and village solidarity. See also Lampland 1995: 179–80, for Hungary.

[34] Thanks to Puiu Lățea for helpful conversation on this point.

[35] Thanks to Rogers Brubaker for this reference.

[36] We are indebted to Stuart Plattner for forcing us to think more systematically about these sources of variation, and to Dumitru Șandru for extensive comment on this section.

nists—in the late nineteenth century, or even as collectivization itself was proceeding; villages differed in their topography, ecology, and economic adaptations; some parts of the country were more strategic than others (see chapter 2); and the main regions (Transylvania, the Banat, Oltenia, Muntenia, and Moldavia) had divergent histories. All these variables might affect how collectivization took place.

Although our data are neither comprehensive enough nor detailed enough to permit firm conclusions, we will indicate some of the tendencies we were able to observe within our sample, which we intentionally shaped to include these variables (see table 0.1 in the introduction). We briefly discuss the role played by religious and national composition and recency of settlement, then treat at greater length political composition and differences in ecological niche, both locally and nationally. The grounds for exploring variation are the compositions of our communities: Iordachi's Jurilovca, an ethnically mixed fishing community with a history of colonization; Chelcea's Reviga, also containing colonists; Goina's Sântana and Verdery's Vlaicu, both mixed German-Romanian agricultural communities; Vultur's comparison of multiethnic lowland Tomnatic with monoethnic upland Domaşnea; Stewart and Stan's shepherd populations in Poiana Sibiului; Kligman's Ieud and Dobrincu's Darabani, both of which contained religious differences; and the four communities studied by Bodó and Oláh (Armăşeni/Csíkmenaság, Corund/Korond, Lueta/Lövéte, and Sânpaul/Homoródszentpál) as well as Ţărău's Rimetea/Torockó, which were distinctive from the rest both religiously and in their ethnic composition, consisting primarily of Hungarians. Contrasting with these are Lăţea's Dobrosloveni and Şandru's Pechea, both religiously and ethnically uniform agricultural villages. The details of these cases show that despite overall similarities in the experience of Romania's communities with collectivization, there was extensive local variation in whether, how, how early, and how thoroughly collectivization took place. We emphasize that these are not simply abstract variables selected for their possible significance but variables that counted in the Romanian case.

General Patterns: Space, Time, and Difference

In brief, here are the main points we wish to emphasize to frame the rest of the discussion.

1) Spatial location and ecology were everything. As we explained in chapter 2, the communities most vulnerable to being collectivized were lowland settlements dependent entirely on grain farming, with animal husbandry as an auxiliary activity. Those nearer large towns and along transportation routes were readily accessible to Party activists, more susceptible to surveillance,

and crucial for the urban food supply. Therefore, they were more likely to be targeted early and subjected to a lengthy barrage of persuasion. Certain regions of the country were seen as highly strategic and given top priority. The more distant a community and the more marginal to settled agriculture, the greater the room for maneuver its residents enjoyed. Shepherds, as we will see, were particularly privileged in this regard. It is possible that in hill villages where agriculture was less productive and collectives less likely to succeed, idiosyncratic features might affect whether the village was collectivized or not, and how violently. In such contexts, the political ambitions of a handful of people could determine the fate of an entire village. Therefore, belonging to a hill community may have given peasants an advantage in being less susceptible initially and better endowed with resources for resistance (including flight into the forests). This rule was not firm, however, for if Party activists set a priority on collectivizing a more remote village, as happened with Ieud, its marginality did not protect it.

2) Timing was also crucial. The very earliest collectives formed in 1949 (in our sample, Pechea and Sântana) received huge investments and experienced little or no coercion: their first round of members joined willingly and were well rewarded for it. Thereafter, as we indicated in chapter 5, force of some kind was almost inevitable, but its forms varied over time and space. Earlier in the process, following a spate of physical brutality in 1950 and again in 1952, threats of job loss or expulsion of children from school were more common; a period of relative relaxation in the mid-1950s gave way to modifications of the penal code and increased physical violence in the early 1960s—alongside promises and negotiations—as the campaign drew to a close. In other words, *all* forms of persuasion, from physical force through negotiation, intensified toward the end (differentiated, of course, by social status). In our discussion below we will not dwell on these differences in timing, but they should be kept in mind.

3) Solidarities and divisions, as suggested in chapter 4, significantly shaped the experience of collectivization. Exactly how that happened, however, is complex. If the village population were relatively homogeneous and stable over time, more persuasion work and different techniques would be required than if it were of more recent colonization or were divided by significant class, religious, national, or other differences. On the one hand, important internal divisions of any kind offered Party activists fault lines to exploit in promoting GAC membership, but on the other, enhanced solidarity *within* each such division provided grounds for resistance that could retard success. The more general point is that *any* grounds for heightened solidarity among most or some subset of villagers might potentially slow the progress of collectivizing them. Neo-Protestants or Greek Catholics in mixed communities, for instance, or communities in which religious and ethnic difference coin-

cided (e.g., Hungarians who were Unitarian) might hang together against joining despite additional pressures exerted by cadres determined to collectivize them. Whatever might contribute to polarizing officials and organizers against village households would work to villagers' advantage. Particularly complex were settlements of recent colonization, in which the diverse origins of the residents would fragment internal solidarity against cadres and thus facilitate collectivizing, yet at the same time such settlements lacked the large and influential kin groups that cadres could target to speed things up.

Thus, there were multiple causes that could distinguish any given household's or village's experience of being collectivized from the experience of another household in the same community or village in the same district and region, as well as countrywide. In the remainder of this section we will illustrate some of these contentions from our specific cases, beginning with religion and nationality.

Religious Diversity

What were the effects of not belonging to the majority religion, Romanian Orthodoxy? We must recall, first, that because the Communist Party promoted atheism as its official stance, people of *all* religious faiths were potentially in danger. As it happened, some proved more secure than others. Historically, Eastern Orthodoxy has held closer relations to secular powers than was true of other Christian denominations, especially Protestant ones, and the Romanian Orthodox hierarchy indeed achieved a fairly stable accommodation with the communists.[37] To promote collectivization, for example, Orthodox priests often engaged in persuasion work and submitted reports, including which members of the church hierarchy belonged to GACs, which were cooperative or not, etc.[38] On the other hand, the Party saw denominations having a clearly transnational character (Roman Catholics, Baptists, etc.) as special threats and organized them within a Ministry of Cults, exercising close surveillance over them and outright banning some of them, such as the Greek Catholics and Jehovah's Witnesses. One of our cases shows us a religious minority targeted for special treatment. The community of Darabani, researched by Dobrincu, contained a minority of neo-Protestants, including Baptists and Seventh-Day Adventists. In 1958 the authorities received an order that these people should be

[37] There is debate on the extent to which its priests served as secret police informers, relative to priests of other faiths. Many Orthodox priests had been involved in the Legionary movement, which would have made them uniquely vulnerable to pressure to report on others in exchange for their freedom (Şandru, personal communication). See also Vasile 2005; Tismăneanu et al. 2007: 259

[38] See, for example, DJAN MM, Fond Parohia Ortodoxă Română—Carei, Baia Mare, file 32/1961, 6–10; file 17/1956, 20, notes the helpful support of a Roman Catholic priest, for collectivization also.

kept under surveillance en bloc and strong pressure was placed on them to join the collective. Despite this heightened attention, they joined—along with most others in the village—only at the last minute, in March 1962, having displayed a high level of internal solidarity and mutual assistance that earned the grudging envy of fellow villagers. In most other communities in our sample, religious affiliation per se does not seem to have been important in collectivization, except possibly for contributing to *ethnic* solidarity, as with the Unitarians in Hungarian communities such as Corund and Sânpaul, also collectivized late. (In these places, however, there was no religious division: all belonged to the same sect.)

One exception to that statement concerns religious division in communities containing Greek Catholics (Uniates)—in our sample, Ieud, researched by Kligman, whose members were predominately Uniates. In 1948 the Party suppressed Greek Catholicism, forcibly merging its properties and followers with the Orthodox Church. Many of its priests and bishops proved especially difficult to subdue, however, refusing to serve the Securitate and preferring prison and death to revoking their faith. Kligman's 2009 study shows the effects of this on collectivization. Where Uniate priests like those in Ieud or Călineşti (in the neighboring Mara valley) resisted the merger, the Party not only persecuted them and their faithful but also pursued collectivization aggressively, despite the generally poor quality of the soil in mountainous Maramureş.[39] Indeed, the first collective in the region was created in Ieud as a means to suppress its religious and political "reactionaries," who actively agitated first against communism and then against collectivization. One of Ieud's either most revered or reviled (depending on which "camp" one associated with) Greek Catholic priests was also the regional Vice President of Iuliu Maniu's Peasant Party. The secret police, as we mentioned in chapter 4, viewed him not only as a retrograde religious and political leader, but also as the "spiritual leader" of the Popşa terrorist group operating in the area, which earned him the classification of a "mortal enemy of socialism" in his penal file.[40] Local communist authorities and adherents of the Orthodox Church blamed the Greek Catholics for much of the repression that Ieud endured, especially during the first wave of collectivization. As a former president of the GAC noted, "If it hadn't been for those priests. Father Joldea did the most harm. All of Ieud suffered because of him."[41]

This example shows us, then, that religious affiliation might result in the collectivization of a community that from an economic point of view was otherwise unsuited to it. Technically speaking, it was not the religious difference it-

[39] DJAN MM, Fond 274, file 17/1951, 138, presents the soil quality of seventeen villages in the Vişeu district: all but two were category V (poor; the other two were IV).

[40] See Kligman 2009; Duică 2005; and ACNSAS, FP, file 84/v. 12, 273; also Pleşa 2006, on Greek Catholic priests and the Şuşman group in Apuseni.

[41] D.V.D., Kligman interview. Greek Catholics did not agree, of course. For them, that same priest was a moral and courageous man.

self that was significant but its political implications and the resistance to communist power implicit in them. Doubtless there were other features of this community that contributed to the result—not every upland Transylvanian community containing Greek Catholics was collectivized, although this was more likely in those in which the Greek Catholic priests refused to become Orthodox. But the religious difference was critical. Otherwise, it seems that the principal effect of religious difference in collectivization was to provide a wedge for cadres in villages that were divided among faiths, and a potential basis for greater solidarity both there and in religiously homogeneous communities.

Ethnonational Identity

When Communist Parties took power in Eastern Europe, the Soviet line on national identity still held that it was epiphenomenal and would ultimately disappear. National*ism* (or "chauvinism") was problematic for communist internationalism, but national difference per se was not. In Romania, with its multinational population, the communist project would seek to engage people of all nationalities. Party organizations were expected to ensure that minorities held leadership positions proportional to their numbers in any given community and to combat chauvinism whenever it arose.[42] High proportions of Jews, Hungarians, and other minorities in Romania's Communist Party (driven there in part by the discriminatory policies of the interwar Romanian state) indicated that these groups would play an active part in the new environment—and would be blamed by Romanians for "causing" communism.[43] The most numerous minority, likely to be the best organized, was the Hungarians in Transylvania, but Soviet dominance and the fact that there were top party officials of Hungarian origin (Moghioroş, Luca) made it clear that communism was not a Romanian product being imposed upon that group. There were at first only two forms of system-wide discrimination by national identification. One was against the resident German minority, as representatives of a "bourgeois" people who were tainted by wartime associations with Hitler (see below).[44] By contrast, for the Roma (Gypsy) minority, the regime offered positive discrimination in the form of new employment opportunities.

Our sample of communities revealed rather little influence of ethnonational difference other than in the German case to be discussed shortly. In the Hun-

[42] DJAN HD, Fond CR PMR, file 93/1951, 207.

[43] Although some Romanians still like to blame communism on the Jews, we note that after World War II, owing to the country's wartime alliance with Hitler, the numbers of Romania's Jews had plummeted; many then emigrated to Israel. We therefore do not discuss this group further.

[44] In some communities in western Romania, Hungarians were at least temporarily subjected to surveillance and punishment for suspected sympathies with the activities of Hungary's fascist government during the war.

garian settlements studied by Bodó, Țârău, and Oláh, nothing happened that was not also typical of Romanian villages, and Oláh cites work in mixed communities to the same effect. According to him:

> The data from this period make it clear that ethnicity was not an important variable in these campaigns, as Party activists and State officials were all Hungarian, persuasion campaigns were conducted in Hungarian, as were written propaganda materials. Historian László Márton reached the same conclusion in his comparative work on Romanian and Hungarian villages in the Mureș district. The Hungarian elite of the HAR [Hungarian Autonomous Region] implemented Party instructions faithfully not only in the collectivization campaigns, but also in the areas of educational and cultural policies. For example, at the Regional Party Conference of January 6–7, 1962, Hungarian Party cadres requested that Romanian-speaking sections be set up at the Târgu Mureș Medical School and a Romanian-language section created at the Târgu Mureș Theater. One can therefore conclude that the HAR's elites construed its formal autonomy as a means to express Party loyalty, and not to defend the social and ethnic interests of their subordinates. (Oláh 2009: 245–46)

Thus, it is at the micro level in mixed communities that we should look for the consequences of ethnonational difference. Unfortunately, we had no mixed Romanian-Hungarian communities in our sample. In the mixed Romanian-Lipovan community of Jurilovca, Iordachi claims, the situation was somewhat atypical because Romanians were quite marginal; since there was no competition over resources or political power, interethnic tensions were minor and therefore not prominent in collectivization. This may explain why nationality never appeared spontaneously as an issue in his respondents' accounts of the process.[45] Nevertheless, it does figure in some of our data, in the following forms.

First, we have numerous instances of interethnic cooperation, with peasants of different nationality combining to oppose the collectivizers. This occurred in Jurilovca, and it also appears in our documents. For instance, a Securitate report for Trei Scaune county in 1950 noted, "In the villages of Bățanii Mari and Beliu it has been found that the Romanian peasants have completely abstained from joining the collective farms, so no one has signed up yet, and the Hungarians say that if the Romanians don't sign up, they won't either; consequently, the work of organizing the collective has been suspended."[46] Likewise, in February 1957, Hungarians in the village of Jeledinți (Hunedoara) began to withdraw en masse from their GAC, an action soon imitated by Romanians in that and other villages in the same commune.[47] In Darabani, Jews who had entered the police

[45] Iordachi, personal communication.

[46] ACNSAS, FD, file 5, 197.

[47] DJAN HD, Fond CR PMR, files 2426 and 2431/1957. In 1920 (the closest date for which we have village-level statistics by nationality), there were 204 Romanians and 398 Hungarians in Jeledinți, and members of both withdrew from the GAC; the two other villages in the commune

force helped prevent Soviet authorities from requisitioning the belongings of their Romanian friends.[48] Sometimes the cooperation might be between subsets of different national groups, as in Tomnatic, where conflicts between wealthy and poor Germans created room for alliances between some of them and Romanians.

Second, however, we find that prior ethnic tensions and stereotypes retained their force in daily interactions. Sometimes the stereotypes were positive: for example, according to Goina, nearly everyone he interviewed in Sântana attributed their collective's success in good measure to its large number of Germans, a people Romanians view as exceptionally hardworking and honest (2003: 5, 35); Verdery found similar attitudes among Romanians in Vlaicu concerning that village's German minority. But more often the stereotypes were negative, and in consequence "chauvinism" at this level was a frequent problem. A 1950 regional "situation report" described chauvinist attitudes among the coinhabiting nationalities of Maramureş: in Rona de Jos, the president of the GAC "openly told a Jewish woman that she should return where she came from, 'Auschşitz,'" a policeman who had been drinking with some former "reactionaries" in Vişeu de Sus beat up a Jew in the street, individual railway workers complained about Hungarians and Jews in leadership positions, and the chief accountant of the "Centrala IPEIL [Central Plant for the Exploitation and Industrialization of Wood] in Sighet expressed his hostility against salaried Hungarian workers, referring to them as 'filthy Hungarians [*unguri spurcaţi*].'" Meanwhile, Hungarians continued to show their national solidarity: "In Ocna Şugatag, using the inauguration of Petőfi's statue as a pretext, they readied Hungarian flags." While Ukrainians allegedly felt "inferior" to other groups, they also expected "exceptions" to be made for them.[49]

Aggravating these chauvinist tendencies was the association of specific local minorities with communist power. In the words of a 1958 refugee from Dobrogea, the order for recruiting Party cadres was this: "In the districts the first-line recruits to Party membership are from the Tatar and Lipovan minorities, who are entrusted with missions requiring loyalty and with leadership posts, for which fact they are hated everywhere, in both towns and villages."[50] The idea that the minorities, especially the Lipovan "Old Believers" (who held a special status with the Russians), were responsible for collectivization appears in the

(Magura and Mărtineşti) contained Romanians only, but their GACs too began to fall apart along with that in Jeledinţi. Interestingly, none of the reports on this matter mentioned the Hungarian revolution, which had occurred four months earlier, even though Securitate reports make it clear that the effects of this revolution in villages were being closely followed.

[48] I. D., Dobrincu interview.

[49] Why they expected exceptions and of what sort are not detailed. See DJAN MM, Fond PMR Comitetul Judeţean Maramureş, file 88/1950, 50.

[50] After them came the poorest villagers (servants, cowherds, etc.), and then collectivists and intellectuals; see Iordachi 2003: 20 (from OSA, Rl 2632/1959, "The Rumanian Workers Party, Finance, Cadres, Education," 25 June 1958, 3).

work of local historians as well, who point to their overrepresentation in the local Party apparatus. In that same region Armenians also sided actively with the communists, winning the hostility of Romanians they persecuted (although this was not the case with the more prosperous Armenians in Bucharest, who took the opposite position).[51] Similarly, a Romanian respondent from Vlaicu recalled with distaste the Hungarian quota collectors who spoke only Hungarian and with whom you couldn't try to strike any deals: "They were the stuff of the devil! They were Hungarians! What could we do with them?! He spoke Hungarian, and we didn't know what he was saying."[52] (Unlike this respondent, another from the same village remembered with affection the two Hungarians who served in the commune administration for a couple of years and whom he befriended; they were responsible for removing his father from chiabur status.)

Especially likely to attract negative feeling as they took on political positions were the Roma. As Stewart and Stan put it:

> [A]t a moment when the Romanian local authorities were unable to attract popular support they managed to find allies only among categories of people who were excluded from the community, like the Roma. In Jina village, with a population of shepherds and foresters, popular history still recalls the early period of communism, when the only person willing to be a mayor was a Gypsy [*băieș*] from the Gypsy settlement at the outskirts of the village. For people unfamiliar with the local setting it is perhaps worth stressing the truly shocking upset such a reversal of the clearly established local hierarchy entailed. So much of the lives of these villagers, shepherds and others alike, is defined by contrast to hierarchically lower others, such as the Gypsies, whose whole way of life offers a kind of moral parable in inappropriate behaviour, that for the villagers to suddenly find themselves ruled by those they had ruled (and at times trampled on) was no small shock to the system. (2003: 28)

Given widespread and long-standing Romanian prejudice against Roma, it could be expected that Roma might have many grudges to settle in their new positions or as denouncers of people who had treated them ill in the past.

Tense daily interactions around nationality issues could spill over into the local Party organization. For example, a report to the Hunedoara regional leadership concerning places where different groups were and were not getting along noted:

> Localities where there are bad relations between Romanians and Hungarians include Turdaş where even the Party Secretary has manifested against Romanian Party members because she is Hungarian and has to defend Hungarians' interests and they don't agree with certain actions taken by Romanians. In Turdaş there is no collabora-

[51] Dumitru Şandru, personal communication, and 1995.

[52] 23, Verdery interview.

> tion between Hungarian and Romanian Party members, but no misunderstandings are mentioned for other localities. . . . The Party organization there is not working to combat chauvinism.[53]

In another location, owing to the negligence of the district Party organization, a local Party branch was "not preoccupied with assuring good relations among the nationalities because they got instructions about it only in Hungarian."[54] More revealingly, "District organizations have not given the necessary help to these brigades, as is evident from the fact that . . . there has not been the slightest reduction in the nationalism that exists among Romanians, Hungarians, and Roma, given the tendency of these to make Party cells on the basis of nationality."[55]

The most serious consequences of national identifications, from the Party's point of view, were that they might produce solidarities that would disrupt class struggle and the broader collectivization process. For example, a 1950 meeting of the Party Secretariat discussed deviations from the Party line with activists from a predominantly Hungarian (Szekler) area manifesting precisely this problem. When the activists maintained that in general, their area had only "good farmers" and not chiaburs (whom they considered, remarkably, to be households with over thirty-five hectares), they were told that they were favoring national unity over class unity.[56] The same accusation was made concerning Hungarians in Câmpulung, Maramureş, who were manifesting chauvinism by not unmasking their chiaburs.[57]

That ethnic minority status could produce solidarity against collectivization is undoubted, but equally certain is that it did not *necessarily* do so. (We referred above to divisions among the Germans in Tomnatic, for instance.) Such an outcome might have been more likely in communities of mixed composition than in homogeneous ones. But there were many possible grounds for a community's developing solidarity against activists intent on collectivizing it; nationality was one of them, just as it was one means by which cadres could seek to divide community members against one another to facilitate the collectivization process. Other bases for solidarity included religion (as mentioned above), extensive endogamy that led to a high degree of kin relatedness among villagers, long-standing settlement (as opposed to recent colonization, or in-migration from upland areas), relatively low social differentiation, and so on. What made a difference to both collectivizers and collectivized was anything that produced sayings of the following kind, noted in Party reports: "If

[53] DJAN HD, Fond CR PMR, file 103/1951, 53.

[54] Ibid.

[55] DJAN HD, Fond CR PMR, file 309/1951, 106.

[56] ANIC, Fond C.C. al P.C.R.–Cancelarie, file 59/1950, 74. Courtesy of O. Roske.

[57] DJAN MM, Fond Comitetul Județean Maramureş, file 88/1950, 50.

everyone joins the GAC, I'll join too," and "If none of us joins the GAC, they can't do anything to us."[58] This last slogan was attributed to peasants who had left the GAC in Jeledinți, both Hungarians and Romanians.

The matter of Romania's ethnic Germans deserves a separate discussion. Here, the issue is not whether identity provided a basis for anticollective solidarity but the particulars of interethnic relations. In 1945, the property of Germans was confiscated and some seventy thousand of them were deported from numerous communities for war-reparations labor in the Soviet Union. In addition, after their return entire families and communities of them were deported internally to the Bărăgan plains; those who remained in their natal communities were subject to often-brutal repression by local authorities, being thrown out of their homes to the benefit of Romanians colonized from poorer areas. Three of our project's settlements (Vlaicu, Sântana, and Tomnatic) contained German populations, all of which suffered deportation to either the Soviet Union or other parts of Romania. As we observed in chapter 2, the expropriation of Germans was the first act of collectivization, producing land for founding new state farms and for distributing to numerous Romanian peasants, whether those already living in the same villages (as in Vlaicu) or others brought in from elsewhere (as in Sântana and Tomnatic).

In Sântana, studied by Goina, Germans were deported to the Soviet Union but not to the Bărăgan. Romanians took over local politics from these Germans, who had dominated up to that time, and in 1949 they founded the first GAC, largely with newly impropriated colonists who were having trouble working their land. Initially, Germans and the generally younger Romanian colonists, who came from hill villages and had fairly backward agricultural practices the Germans were quick to disdain, did not get on well; the Germans resented having to live in a small corner of their large houses while colonists they regarded as uncivilized occupied the rest. But the leaders of the GAC had cleverly evaded the Party's formal rules about not allowing Germans into collectives and were thus able to establish a farm with a heavily German labor force that, having few alternatives, worked hard and contributed greatly to the organization's early success, winning the admiration of Romanian collectivists. By the mid-1950s, conflicts had begun to die down, as many of the colonists either moved into their own houses or returned to their natal villages. One German respondent answered Goina's question about whether ethnic identity made a difference in the collective farm: "No. At lunchtime, the Germans sat over here, the Romanians there next to them, and each ate what they had brought in their lunch bags."[59] Similarly, a colonist recalled the two groups as complementary from the time the Germans entered: "And from then on the collective went even better! It went well before but even better after that! And

[58] DJAN HD, Fond CR PMR, file 2426/1957, 47.

[59] Z. S., Goina interview.

then. . . . You had to work on holidays too. You weren't allowed to have a break. When it was the Germans' holidays, the Romanians would go, when it was the Romanians' holidays, the Germans would go."[60]

The situation in Vlaicu was somewhat different, for there, the Romanians who received Germans' land were not colonists but had been living side by side with them since the 1890s. Verdery's Romanian respondents, in her research in both the 1970s and for this project, attributed the relative prosperity of their village to the presence of Germans. For example:

> Around here [the people in] Vlaicu were considered by those from the villages around us to be brighter, smarter. As I see things now and as my father used to tell me, "It's the Germans who civilized us." My father used to say this. I say, "How so?" He says, "They're very correct, honest, and very clean. And it's from them that we learned to plant flowers in our yards and whatnot."[61]

According to their reports, although after the war some Romanians derided the Germans for their loss of status, others were quick to help them, in a few cases offering back small pieces of the land they had received so the former owners could have a garden. Similarly, a German respondent recalled, "In '45 I'd already been expropriated. But still, the wheat we had sown, that is, my uncle and my aunt and my mother. . . . Uncle Ion [who had been given the speaker's land] said, 'Take your wheat because it's yours; you sowed it, you worked for it.' But others didn't do this. But then he was expropriated too, they didn't let him keep his land either."[62]

The situation of Germans in Tomnatic, researched by Vultur, was the same as that in Sântana: they were expropriated, some were deported to the Soviet Union, and Romanian colonists from all across the country were brought into their houses, producing situations of tremendous conflict. The conflict was not only between Romanians and Germans, however, but among the Romanian colonists themselves: a November 1946 report reveals that "in villages of colonists, Macedonians, Transylvanians and Bukovinans [from Romania] clashed, with each group struggling to control the commune's leadership in order to redistribute the best farms to their regional group."[63] Unlike Germans in Sântana, some of Tomnatic's Germans were also deported to the Bărăgan plains—but so were some of the recently impropriated Romanian colonists.

60 G. A., Goina interview.

61 206, Verdery interview. See also Verdery 1983: chapter 5.

62 258 #2, Verdery interview. A respondent born near Brașov, which had a large number of Germans, reported that most of those in his natal village were to be deported to Russia after 1945; his grandfather, who as a young man had been a servant to a German family, was called upon to round them up for deportation, but he "didn't want them on his conscience" and simply disappeared for a while (N. C., Verdery interview, Geoagiu).

63 Râmneanțu 1996: 179; cited in Vultur 2009a: 147.

In fact, proportionately more Romanians were deported than Germans.[64] To account for this discrepancy, Vultur invokes the complex ethnic history of this region, where Habsburg authorities in the early eighteenth century had settled French- and German-speaking immigrants from Alsace-Lorraine. Thoroughly Germanized by the late nineteenth century, they nonetheless retained the memory of "French" ancestry and seem to have availed themselves of both identities during subsequent decades, as Romanian government policy veered first toward France, then toward Germany. Population figures from 1928 record nearly equal numbers of French and German speakers; French speakers are absent from 1930 and 1941 census figures (when Germany was ascendant), and there are no German speakers in statistics from 1947, by which time deportations of Germans were well underway. It is likely that Tomnatic's Germans were reasserting French identity, if they could, thus avoiding the fate intended for them—and indeed, Vultur shows, there were fewer Germans deported from Tomnatic than from other areas (2009a: 144). To facilitate claims of French identity, the local priest had made each claimant a genealogy from the parish archives, showing their ancestors with French names. Some of them even argued that they should be exempt from expropriation; thus: "The citizens of this commune are of French nationality, as established by the Timişoara Administrative Court and the Supreme Administrative Court" (144). Here, then, is a surprising use of national identity, available to only a few "Germans" in Romania—and its use diminished the solidarity of the group of Germans in that settlement. In this instance we see once again the bases for variability that differentiated the experience of one Romanian settlement from another.

Colonization

We should briefly mention another basis for differentiation that we have already seen in the discussions of Tomnatic and Sântana: the presence of colonists. This variable had several possible effects on collectivization. First, it prevented the use of certain techniques, such as exerting pressure on the heads of the most respected and largest kin groups (of which there were few or none among the colonists) to bring numerous family members into the collective. But second, the relative lack of solidarity among the colonists inhibited their opposing the formation of the GAC as a group, making villages with many recent colonists easier to collectivize. Indeed, it seems that cadres purposely brought in colonists on the land of deportees for precisely this reason.[65] Be-

[64] See figures in Vultur 2003a: 32–33. For more on this case, see Vultur 2003b.

[65] Both Goina and Vultur, who worked in communities with large numbers of colonists brought in 1945, are of this opinion.

cause they were bound together by few networks, they were more susceptible to activists' inducements. Other aspects of their situation increased this susceptibility, as Goina reports: "The colonized Romanians were mostly poor young people who had no roots in the village, cut off from the conservative influence of their extended families. They also lacked adequate means to work the land. Many of them sympathized with the new regime, seeing it as the ally of the peasant for having given them land" (Goina 2009: 377). Iordachi believes that in another of our colonized settlements, Jurilovca, this feature contributed to its rapid collectivization by weakening the social fabric of the village in two ways. First, those more recently colonized were in a precarious situation and were not able to resist state pressures. Their diverse origins and meager resources had prevented them even from building their own church to shore up their minority status. Second, although the settlement's main ethnic groups were not openly antagonistic and even cooperated against outsiders to some degree, these groups' spatial and linguistic segregation created a cleavage that made the village de facto more vulnerable.[66] The strategy of colonizing to collectivize did not always work out as planned, however: in Tomnatic, the diverse colonists brought in on expropriated German land proved very resistant to giving their land back, and the subsequent deportation of a number of them in 1951 may have been a response.[67]

Recency of arrival and places of origin were also significant variables. In Sântana and Tomnatic, the colonists had come recently from all across the country in the space of a year or two; they were certainly not interconnected through durable social networks, and substantial early GACs (1949, 1950) were formed with them. By contrast, in one village of Reviga commune studied by Chelcea (Mircea, colonized 1921–29, collectivized in 1959), the colonists had come from just two upland settlements near each other and therefore already had networks of relations among themselves. Once collectivization began, a number of them returned to their two natal communities, with which they had maintained ties. (The same thing happened in Sântana.) A second Reviga village, Rovine (colonized in 1893–1921), was more diverse, its members coming from six other settlements; it was collectivized by 1957. But the example of Reviga shows that other characteristics could outweigh the fact of colonization: Chelcea concludes that the area was so isolated and the possibilities for class struggle in this impoverished population so limited that it was left until late in the process (2009: 399). Therefore, a history of colonization might affect the pace and form of collectivizing, but not necessarily, and other variables could intervene.

[66] Iordachi, personal communication.

[67] Vultur, personal communication.

Ecology/Economy

A variable of fundamental importance in any village's collectivization experience was its local economy and ecological niche, closely linked with its location. Plains villages entirely based on grain farming were the most vulnerable; mountain settlements engaged in animal husbandry had the greatest freedom. Settlements with multiple sources of income (trades, crafts production) were better able to resist the collectivizers than those limited to cultivation. Part of the reason for these patterns was that the Party cared most about feeding the population and would target the most productive grain areas first. Within the lowlands, villages near urban markets might have advantages over those farther away: instead of giving their produce as quotas, wealthier peasants could take it to market, where it was much better paid, earning enough money to buy their assigned amounts and even, as some Party documents complained, to pay wages that would attract day laborers away from working for the ill-paying GACs.[68]

Villages in marginal locations, however, had advantages of other kinds, at least initially.[69] Because the costs of collectivizing the uplands were greater for a lower return, numerous hill villages were left until very late in the process or never collectivized at all.[70] As Gheorghiu-Dej put it, "Don't start making collective farms there [in mountainous areas], because they'll be accursed. The Bulgarian comrades hastened to do it and then tried to back off, but they couldn't."[71] Initially the apparatus of repression was inadequate to collectivizing them all, and by the time it became more efficient, the villagers might have made special arrangements with authorities and were left alone in consequence. Such settlements tended to be very cohesive, their marginal economies making them unlikely targets of the in-migration and colonization that disrupted solidarity in settlements farther down. Kinship connections were tighter than in more diverse lowland communities—Vultur reports this for Domaşnea, for instance, generalizing the point to other hill villages (2003a: 78). We might say that there was "more kinship" in the hills, and this could pose obstacles to the collectivizers. In addition, men there could be absent for long periods, either fleeing into the forests to escape the collectivizers or engaging in forms of livelihood other than agriculture. During their absence, their wives would refuse to sign

[68] For example, ACNSAS, FD, file 7/v. 1, 176, 370, and ACNSAS, FD, file 7/v.2, 219, for the industrializing Hunedoara region.

[69] Over time, however, the center allocated so few resources to hill settlements (such as educational and health care facilities) that they gradually became depopulated.

[70] See the dissertations by Beck (1979) and Randall (1983), based on fieldwork during the mid-1970s in two uncollectivized hill villages.

[71] Plenary of the Central Committee of the Romanian Workers' Party, November 26–28, 1958; reference courtesy of Dumitru Şandru.

up, on the grounds that the men were away. Only if these villages became sites of organized resistance—the celebrated "terrorist bands" (see Duică 2005; Kligman 2009)—would the authorities go after them.

Owing to the country's topography, upland-lowland ecological distinctions are to be found throughout Romania and therefore are not region-specific. Other sorts of adaptation are more localized, such as with the fishing community of Jurilovca (Dobrogea). This community was multiethnic, including so-called Lipoveni (Russian Old Believers) and a minority of Romanian war veterans colonized in the early twentieth century. Lipoveni were primarily fishermen, although they followed other occupations too; cultivation, practiced by the Romanians, was decidedly secondary, in part because the state had accorded the colonists so little assistance. As a former fisherman put it to Iordachi (2003: 52–53):

> In the neighboring villages there were people who were real farmers. The Lipoveni didn't even know how to work the land, they were not farmers originally. They worked, brought in money from all over the place. Construction sites, unskilled workers, simple folk. And they'd leave [to find work] around the country. The Danube–Black Sea Canal—when it was made, all the Lipoveni were there. Or other construction sites, building projects, there were the Lipoveni. Or sea fishing—Lipoveni. Any kind of fishing, Lipoveni were there. From this point of view, this village got richer. [But] the collective was like an add-on, a burden for everyone, our collective wasn't good for anything.[72]

The Romanians were the more attached to land, their only source of livelihood. Collectivizers targeted both groups, but their experiences differed correspondingly; because the Romanians' precarious economic equilibrium was easily destroyed, they succumbed to collectivization early (Iordachi 2003: 54).[73]

By far the most distinctive adaptation was shepherding, represented in our project by the community of Poiana Sibiului (see Stewart and Stan 2003, 2009).[74] These shepherds developed multiple strategies to avoid delivering their produce to the state, taking advantage of the weak points in the centralized collecting system. Because they were permitted to deliver their quotas to any collection center in the country—as lowland villagers could not—they could identify the centers that collected more than the plan required and then use

[72] V. Z., Iordachi interview.

[73] Another special adaptation consisted of villages in the former "Border Regiments" established by the Habsburgs in Transylvania, many of which were in heavily forested areas administered as joint property. In 1956, when Party cadres tried to collectivize the thirty-one thousand families of the former Border Regiment 13 from Caransebeş, the inhabitants sent a letter to Dej arguing that they had already been collectivized since the mid-eighteenth century under Empress Maria-Theresa and were still (in 1956) holding and exploiting their land in common (even though the Border Regiments had been disbanded by imperial patent in the late nineteenth century). Thanks to Dumitru Şandru for this information.

[74] The following paragraphs are based on the report and paper by Stewart and Stan (2003, 2009).

reciprocity or bribery to convince the collectors to register the surplus in their names. According to one interviewee, "They had this surplus and you had to give him something to declare that it was the quota you delivered. And you came to the Local Council with the proof 'I delivered the quota.' But in fact you hadn't delivered anything. You just got the certificate from the collector."[75] In this way, they managed to amass significant fortunes for themselves (and their preferred officials), to the detriment of the state. Poiana Sibiului was a source of amusing stories from the 1980s, about villagers who wanted to install elevators in their homes or who asked the permission of the authorities to purchase helicopters for better surveillance of their flocks. Small wonder, then, that there were few chiaburs in Poiana: as we showed in chapter 6, they had enough money to bribe their way off the lists.

An important fact distinguishing Poiana from other shepherding communities was that it had relatively little land. Unlike their neighbors, who could eke out a living from agriculture alongside their sheep, Poienari had long been forced to adapt and to "negotiate" with state officials in a creative manner. They developed relationships that functioned both at the local level and countrywide, both horizontally (with other shepherds) and vertically (with the authorities). Their informal relations were much more effective and flexible than the structures of state domination. Paradoxically contributing to their success were various forms of collective mutual aid that had functioned in the past, in which several families managed their sheep in joint property. Now they would help each other by hiding one another's sheep when cadres came around to count them for quota and taxation purposes. We might almost say that both Party and shepherds had the structure of nomadic empires based on far-flung networks of exploitation, but the shepherds were more successful.[76]

After the collectives were well established, they hired some shepherds to administer the collectives' "sheep plan." They received good salaries and were also allowed to bring their own sheep to the farm, which then covered the costs of grazing and wintering the animals as well as giving the shepherd impressive quantities of grain. In other words, shepherds would use collective farm property to their own benefit (as would other farm members, but on a smaller scale). Through bribes and informal relations with the farms' leaders, they reduced surveillance over their activity, enabling a permanent conversion of resources from the collective to themselves. Unlike most lowland peasants, who joined the collective farms because they had no other viable survival options and be-

[75] D. I., Stan interview for Stewart.

[76] An additional reason for the prosperity of these populations was that from very early times, they had been administered as part of the Saxon lands, rather than the Magyar-dominated counties where most Transylvanian Romanians lived (see Verdery 1983: 83–86), and thus benefited from privileges (such as tax exemption) that other Romanians in Transylvania did not enjoy. The wealth they had been able to amass gave them an advantage in dealing with the communist authorities from the very outset.

cause they had been pauperized through burdensome taxes and repressive measures, when the shepherds of Poiana finally joined the collective farms they did so freely. In contrast to most of the collectivized peasants, their marginality gave them a privileged position and even power.

This is not to say that control over them was wholly impossible. Had the authorities been determined to bring the shepherds under their control, they could probably have done so, even if at considerable cost. But the motivation for it was lacking, in comparison with the motives for gaining control over similarly marginal communities such as Ieud in Maramureş or Domaşnea in the Banat. Stewart and Stan conclude (2009: 268–71) that unlike Maramureş villages, with their "subversive" Greek Catholic religion and overt resistance to the state (such as by resisting military service), the shepherding villages near Sibiu posed no serious threats to the regime while providing valuable resources such as meat, cheese, and milk to local Party representatives.[77] Nothing justified there the "special treatment" accorded Ieud, owing to its reputation as "a center of reactionaries." The haste of the authorities in implementing the reforms in cities and agricultural villages, and the absence of negative cultural or political attitudes in transhumant villages like Poiana Sibiului, gave their inhabitants freedom enjoyed by few others.

Shepherds prospered because they could identify the limits of the communist apparatus, which was rigid and resource-poor, and learned to benefit from the system's shortcomings. They illustrated to a high degree the more general truth that anyone who managed to retain control of some means of production or had resources to distribute could profit from the system. While the Party's control structures could put pressure on the settled population in the lowlands, they were quite inadequate for the territorially mobile shepherds, whose property was portable, easy to conceal, and in most cases invisible to the eyes of the control agents. It was precisely the relative marginality and geographical, political, and economic isolation of villagers like those in Poiana Sibiului that enabled them, unlike most of Romania's rural population, to resist the oppression of the communist authorities and even to turn the oppressive measures to their advantage (Stewart and Stan 2009: 269–71).[78]

National Political and Economic Factors

This outcome, however, was partly the product of ecology in a broader sense: the political ecology that determined which parts of the country would be targeted first for "model collectives" and early, intensive persuasion work. A vil-

[77] One form of negotiation between the regime and shepherds was for the latter to inform on "bandits" hiding in the mountains in return for the authorities' turning a blind eye to shepherds' concealing the number of their sheep.

[78] Recall that infrastructural constraints discouraged cadres from seeking out shepherds.

lage's position in this space-time of collectivization significantly affected how its inhabitants would fare in the process as a whole. We have already presented, in chapter 2 (table 2.5), some evidence of spatial differentiation, explaining the early collectivization of the Dobrogea/Constanța region, for example, by the presence of Soviet troops there and in the Banat by its contributions to the food supply. To illustrate the effects of early collectivization in a highly strategic region, we will present the case of Pechea (Galați region), researched by Dumitru Șandru.[79] This community—one of the largest in our sample, with 7,585 inhabitants in 1956—was in the first group of twenty-one in which collectivization was launched in 1949 and the very first in its region. As a result, the GAC formed in that year benefited from privileges and state assistance (such as donations of state land and sizable investments in machinery and infrastructure) that produced high incomes not enjoyed by any other GAC founded later. The approximately 100 families who first joined this GAC—with no form of coercion—consisted almost entirely of poor peasants. Many soon acquired leadership positions that further consolidated their economic advantage. Their example drew additional recruits, and within a year the GAC had 251 member households, still from among the more modest households. For the next six years, however, few additional households signed up; the remainder continued to work on their own as before. In 1957, the Party leadership determined to complete the collectivization of this region. Against considerable peasant resistance, activists exerted extensive pressure, intimidation, and brutality to get everyone into GACs, expanding the initial one and forming a second in the space of only a month; by the end of 1957, the total number of collectivized households for Pechea is given as 1,955, with 5,700 hectares.[80] The methods used to achieve this included beating up those who resisted and calling selected members of the village's three associations to assemblies at which they would vote to convert the entire association into a GAC. Peasants who fled to avoid having to sign up were subjected to forms of torture by specialists brought in from the regional capital. Abandoning their land, some left the village altogether rather than sign up. Although the leadership reported upward that collectivization was complete, in fact a number of households continued to resist, joining only two years later.

The story of Pechea's collectivization shows the two distinctly different approaches to it: the initial period of free consent Ana Pauker initiated in 1949 before she was purged, and the later period of "free consent." Șandru draws attention to two consequences: the different degrees of resistance and the different recollections of peasants from these two periods. There was no resistance to

[79] The following paragraphs are drawn from Șandru's final report for the project (2003).

[80] There is some doubt about this number, which yields a larger number of households for the population than seems warranted by the normal family size. Thus, we cannot securely provide a percentage that the number of collectivized households would represent of all village households (D. Șandru, personal communication).

collectivizing in the first wave, and those who had joined then remembered it in largely glowing terms, whereas those from the second phase had resisted with determination and remembered both the experience and the collective itself negatively. The latter held the view that collectivization had not improved their standard of living but rather worsened it; the former, who had once been poor and whom collectivization had endowed with office jobs, heartily disagreed. At least for them, Pauker's strategy had paid off.

Local Politics

If decisions at the center created the broad patterns of variation we have just noted, patterns in the local politics of collectivization are harder to discern. We will need many more local studies before it is possible to generalize concerning the kinds of people who took on leadership posts, their local conflicts, and how they behaved. Our sample of villages indicates that there were wide disparities; here are three brief examples. First, as we indicated above, no Germans were deported from the community of Sântana to the Bărăgan in the 1950s. The reason, Goina was told, was that the first GAC president refused to execute the deportation orders, since he depended on the "work ethic" of Sântana's Germans to develop the "model" collective farm he was told to create (Goina 2003: 51). Other communities of Germans, such as those in Tomnatic, were not so lucky (see Vultur 2003a). Second, in Maramureş, a district Party activist in Sighet was reported to have set the course of collectivization in that area, declaring, "In the heart of the reactionaries, we are going to create the first collective" (Kligman 2009: 165). Although the first target, Ieud, was not best suited for large-scale agricultural production, as we have indicated above its ongoing political and religious anticommunist resistance made it a hotbed of "enemies." District-level and national political-ideological interests readily coincided, and Ieud became a "model" of a sort very different from that in Sântana. Where resistance against communist policies was high, considerations other than political-economic ones might serve as the basis for forced collectivization. Third, Bodó (2003) has evidence that the village of Corund, which was not suited to forming a GAC, was collectivized nonetheless owing to the political ambitions of local leaders who were eager for the jobs that would come their way. Initiating this, it was said, was the local doctor, who had good relations with the district: "hoping to attract praise, he personally requested that higher authorities include this village, too, in the process of collectivization" (Bodó 2003: 2). We suspect that these kinds of ambition by a handful of local people may have generated requests to collectivize a specific village fairly often. The point should be kept in mind lest we always think of collectivization as having come from above, as our respondents tended to suggest.

Another variable affecting the course of collectivization was the number of local Party members, and here again the communities in our sample differ considerably. In the two communities Oláh researched, Lueta and Sânpaul, the former had a substantial number of communists; their principal occupation was not agriculture but mining and factory work, a consequence of the village's relatively poor soil. These nonpeasant insiders were the ones who initiated collectivization and carried it through.[81] The same thing holds for the village of Rimetea, which had a large number of communists; many residents were engaged in nonagricultural occupations, and the collective was formed early through local initiative (Țârău 2003: 38–40). In Sânpaul, by contrast, with good soil and excellent agricultural productivity, the initiative came from without—the village was targeted as a "model GAC"—and collectivizing it required concerted and often brutal activity by activists from elsewhere. Lest we conclude that nonagricultural occupation predisposed villagers to collectivization, however, we have the example of Corund (Bodó 2003), a village of potters, who resisted precisely because they needed their marginal farms to complete their livelihood.

The village of Rimetea, just mentioned, offers further evidence of how variable local politics could be when compared with neighboring Măgina, both studied by Țârău.[82] To begin with, several villages nearby were never collectivized even though district and commune authorities had taken the first steps to do so, in an abusive manner. Through family connections, those villagers managed to obtain an audience with Chivu Stoica, president of the Council of Ministers, and complained about the abuses, which were then rectified. In the wake of this success, district authorities ceased their work and the villages remained uncollectivized. Țârău notes that the minuscule number of Party members in those communities probably contributed to the outcome. Rimetea, by contrast, was unusual in the number of its Party members and sympathizers and the degree of its overall politicization.[83] In June 1952 a delegation of its Party members went to visit a model GAC that had been running for two years. They returned convinced to set up their own collective, despite the fact that Rimetea had not been planned for one at that point, and they soon launched their own GAC with forty-two member families. Thus, local initiative was wholly responsible for creating this farm. Nonetheless, it took another nine years and much external intervention before the majority of villagers were persuaded to join it. District authorities were sufficiently dismayed by the slow progress, and they got rid of the initial Party leadership and put in place local activists of their own choosing (including a woman so hell-bent on collectivizing that she was nick-

[81] Even so, Oláh notes, a couple of wealthy peasants also backed the new organization.

[82] The following paragraphs are drawn from Țârău's final report for the project (2003).

[83] "In 1952, there were 82 members of the Romanian Workers' Party, 35 of the Plowmen's Front, 55 of the Union of Young Workers, 200 women in the Union of Democratic Women of Romania, and 276 people in the Hungarian Popular Union; compared with both Măgina and other collectivized villages in the Turda district, these percentages make Rimetea stand out" (Țârău 2003: 39).

named "Ana Pauker"). When results did not improve, the entire GAC leadership was replaced.

Whereas Țărău presents this process as one in which the local initiators were fairly united in their purposes (even if the outside authorities were not pleased with the outcome), in neighboring Măgina, by contrast, precisely the opposite was true. There, the Party organization was very small and was under the sway of three brothers from a family that had moved into the village from some distance away several decades before; one of the brothers reportedly worked for the Securitate. They began to form a GAC with a number of poorer families, but their brutal methods won them wide opprobrium. As a result, a faction arose within the tiny Party branch around a longtime Party member from the village, who proceeded to expand the number of Party members and thereby his own political base. One of his acolytes explained his techniques for recruiting villagers into the Party, so different from that of the other group:

> We'd go through the village with this old guy from time to time to persuade people. This Mărginean was really, really honest and really correct. He didn't harm anyone! He'd say: Hey, sign up, come on! Let's take these guys down! Because they're good for nothing! These aren't communists! He kept explaining that these guys were just using people and what not. . . . And so we too somehow went and registered as Party members. (Țărău 2009: 215)

For the collective farm, an effect of the shift in the balance of power within the Party was this: "The process of collectivization was initiated in the form of an association and fully subordinated to the small Party chapter of the village's RWP comprised of poor peasants, which was, according to some, receptive to certain clan interests. It concluded with wealthy peasants at the forefront of the GAC's leadership, under whose direction the collective managed to function" (Țărău 2009: 217). From these examples we can see that at the level of local communities, collectivization might engage the political energies of diverse people in highly variable ways. Any history of the process must delve into these variations, more easily uncovered through oral histories (with all their limitations) than through documents, from which local scheming and machinations are generally erased.

Variations Based in History

One final source of variation must at least be mentioned, even if not fully fleshed out: that relating to historical differences from one province to another. As of 1945 Romania's territory included areas that had been part of three historical empires—the Russian, Habsburg, and Ottoman. Each of these had left its mark as late as 1918 on the structures of property and inequality in the territories under its domination. In some areas the population density was high, in others sparse. Agricultural productivity varied widely, as did the amounts that peasants received from the land reforms of 1921 and 1945. Owing to wars and depopulation, Romanian authorities in the twentieth century had colonized immigrants in some places and created huge state reserves in others; in one place or another they had promoted industry or pushed for ethnic and religious homogenization; they had implemented land reforms differentially by region; and in general they had presided over a richly varied national landscape. These disparities are integral to the process of collectivization, affecting among other things the bases for resistance. With further research, we might find many interesting variations related to such historical differences. For instance, Transylvania differed from eastern and southern Romania in having much smaller latifundia, which meant that Transylvania may have had more people to convince per square kilometer. Did this mean proportionately more violence? Were more cadres required there proportionately than in those other historical regions?

Lacking the space to summarize all the relevant historical factors by region, we cite at length Iordachi's summary of collectivization in Dobrogea, which mentions many of the variables we think most important in accounting for its timing and pace.

> Dobrogea displayed peculiar characteristics as compared to other Romanian regions: it had a marked multi-ethnic character, was exposed to waves of state-organized colonization to increase the ethnic Romanian presence and experienced a subordinate administrative status between 1878 and 1913. Its ethnic composition was strongly affected by the Romanian-Bulgarian and Romanian-German population exchanges of 1940, and by the Lipoveni emigration to the USSR in the early postwar years.
>
> At the onset of collectivization, the economy of the small Dobrogean households was marked by low productivity, owing to the scarcity of farming tools and equipment and the 1945–1946 drought. Consequently, peasants felt compelled to form associations to work the land more effectively. The expropriation of great estates by the new communist regime further weakened the inherited social structure of the province, as farm laborers who had worked for large landlords were left without income and turned into protest groups that could be easily manipulated by the new regime. Furthermore, the fact that the Romanian state inherited vast expanses of arable land from the Ottoman Empire facilitated the early consolidation of the socialist sector in the region's agriculture, a development that increased pressure on privately-owned farms and further limited market competition.
>
> The armed anticommunist resistance in Dobrogea (1948–1952) led to increased political repression throughout the province. As an important Iron Guard stronghold, . . . the province was an important target of the communists' defascization cam-

> paigns. Waves of political purges consolidated the role of the Party. Armed confrontations between authorities and anticommunist partisans caused a high degree of mobilization among communist elites and fueled the zeal with which the Party wrought its socio-political changes throughout the province. As in other historical provinces of Romania, . . . there was a strong correlation between the intensity of anti-communist resistance movements and the state-organized violence that accompanied collectivization.
>
> The fast pace of collectivization in Dobrogea at the beginning of the 1950s drew the attention of Bucharest authorities, who realized that, given the small size of the province, they could turn Dobrogea into a showcase for collectivization. Consequently, the central government provided Dobrogean authorities with special political, organizational and financial support to launch the unprecedented 1956–1957 campaign that succeeded in making Dobrogea the first completely collectivized historical province of Romania.
>
> The strong Soviet military presence and geo-political interests in Dobrogea prompted the province's rapid Sovietization. In 1959, when collectivization was complete, Nikita Khrushchev visited Dobrogea to inspect the results of socialist agriculture. . . . The "Dobrogean collectivization model" thus appears as a contingent combination of Soviet geo-political interests and involvement, national and local variables. (Iordachi 2009: 130–31)

Elsewhere he notes that early demographic changes had modified the numerical balance of and relations among ethnic groups in the province, undermining the internal cohesion and autonomy of the different groups and weakening their tie with land. In the absence of legislation, some of the colonists settled in the region were in an uncertain juridical position, lacking both full property rights over their houses and a powerful attachment to the pieces of land they had recently received (Iordachi 2003: 62). In addition, the peasants held much larger surface areas than usual, as many as thirty to forty hectares—and that caused problems with fulfilling their quotas, set according not to productivity but to surface area; thus, they were more eager to unload their land than the majority of peasants would have been. These factors distinguished Dobrogea significantly from other major areas of Romania.[84] We could adduce comparable distinguishing features for every region.

This said, we underscore that all these variables crosscut one another, and timing was perhaps the most significant of them all. Regional and historical differences weighed less heavily in distinguishing the experience of two villages than did the time of their collectivization. A village in Oltenia and one in Moldavia both collectivized in 1950 had more in common than two Oltenian villages collectivized in 1950 and 1960. During the period we treat, a great deal changed in Romania. If those collectivized early had great difficulty imagining

[84] Our thanks to Dumitru Şandru for his comments on this section.

what a collective was, that was no longer true a few years later, when villages nearby might have had a collective for some time. Cadres who initially had no commitment to communist ideology and could not envision a GAC were in a much different place after a couple of years of figuring out how to make their way in the system.

Conclusion

We leave this chapter emphasizing the variability rather more than the general patterns of Romania's collectivization. The state of research to date does not permit greater synthesis—concerning, for instance, where violence and brutality prevailed over more bureaucratic solutions, or what proportion of the peasantry benefited from collectivization as opposed to being undone by it. These weighty questions await the completion of the many studies Romanian scholars have undertaken. For the present, rather than seek a premature synthesis we find it more instructive to decompose the process, while resisting the common tendency to default to a single, Soviet-inspired model of communist society by emphasizing how Romanians variously appropriated it.

If the grounds for variation within Romania were extensive, they were all the more so for collectivization across the Soviet empire as a whole. To be sure, the Soviet model provided a hegemonic set of guidelines, but in no two countries were either the process or the outcome identical. The same can be said of the colonial encounter more broadly, as the dominant power strives to "modernize" the people whose lives it invades: the blueprint runs up against variant local conditions and political calculations that prevent it from being perfectly replicated. Thus, even as none of our settlements is "typical" (a problematic construct) of the process as a whole but can at best provide a sense of the possibilities and constraints inherent in the Romanian context, neither is the story of Romanian collectivization "typical" of the experience in the Soviet bloc as a whole. With this observation, we might return to the notion with which we began this book: the Soviet blueprint. Although certain features of the process were indeed laid down by the Soviet experience, our research makes clear how wrong is the assumption—such as that of the old totalitarian model—that to understand Eastern Europe, one need only know what happened in the Soviet Union. The Soviet technology came to them as a script; once transferred out of the capital city into daily life in the provinces, it was inevitably subjected to multiple readings, improvisation, negotiation, and outright rejection. The form of the script was consequential, but it was not determinative.

Collectivization was a uniform policy dictated by an external power having little familiarity with local conditions—whether Romanian, Ukrainian, Caucasian, or even Russian—implemented by a Party leadership largely ignorant of agriculture and not much interested in understanding the peasants on their own terms. Without the use of compelling force to shoehorn such diversity into a single one-size-fits-all model, collectivization would not have been possible. But as our historical ethnography reveals, the texture of the experience for individuals, households, and communities varied widely. The same was true of the results of collectivization, as we will show in our final chapter.

Chapter 8

The Restratification and Bureaucratization of Rural Life

> And I, for one, if it weren't for this regime, wouldn't be an engineer, maybe I wouldn't even be a mechanic, I wouldn't be a colonel, I wouldn't be anything.
> —*Secret police officer, railway engineer*[1]

> You know, we say it was bad, but it wasn't bad! If your son finished high school, he got a job. And with bread in hand. There wasn't so much vagabondage, people didn't know about drugs, they didn't smoke as much, or [drink] so much coffee. . . . Since the revolution, there's nothing but discord. . . . Now, brother and sister don't get along, mother and daughter don't talk.
> —*Wife of middle peasant*[2]

> The tremendous significance of the collectives, comrade Stalin teaches us, consisted precisely in the fact that they are the principal basis for the use of machines and tractors in agriculture, the chief basis for transforming the peasant, for changing his psychology in the spirit of socialism.[3]

> Hey, Stalin, what have you done? From horses you've made sausages and from Gypsies, deputies!
> —*Popular rhyme*[4]

THE FORMATION OF collectives had far-reaching consequences. Chief among them were a greatly changed village social organization, the overturning of older status hierarchies and the emergence of new ones, and the infusion of everyday life with politics. A new relationship arose between citizens and the Party-state, the Party's institutionalization bringing the political center permanently into villages to a much greater degree than before. We might characterize this new relationship as the bureaucratization and politicization of the rural world. With collectives, villages ceased to be primarily sources of community and became segments of formal organizations that reached upward into higher administrative levels. We conclude our analysis of collectivization by describing what this meant.

[1] From Rostás and Momoc 2007: 210.

[2] Fürtös and Bârlea 2009: 312.

[3] ANIC, Fond C.C. al P.C.R.–Agrară, file 18/1949, 2.

[4] "*Măi, Staline, ce ai făcut? Din cai ai făcut cârnati, Şi din ţigani, deputaţi!*" For a longer, formalized text, see Dobeş et al. 2004: 67.

The message we wish to convey in this chapter owes much to Ken Jowitt's treatment of Leninism (1978). Jowitt singles out two aspects of Leninist strategy that made it distinctive. First, it relied on collectivization "as a particular means of undermining the peasant extended household and village—not so much as work units or social references, but rather as *units and models of social, economic, and political power*" (63, our emphasis). Second, although as in liberal regimes its orientation is to impersonal norms, "impersonality is not expressed in procedural values and rules (i.e., due process), but rather in the charismatic impersonality of the party organization. The novelty of Leninism as an organization is its substitution of charismatic impersonality for the procedural impersonality dominant in the West" (34). Following Weber, he suggests that this kind of charismatic organization might "routinize" over time in the direction of either "traditional" or "modern" systems (or a mix of the two). Specifically, traditional status-based peasant systems share with charismatic organizations a "stress on personal (not abstract) and substantive (not formal) considerations. Both forms of social action are 'hostile' to the impersonal-rational calculation that typifies modern organization" (45). Concerning Romanian communism, he briefly explores the place of traditional "familism" in it but does not pursue the point further.

Jowitt's argument is relevant to our discussion here in the following way. In chapter 6, we suggested that to promote class struggle, the Communist Party first had to create classes, moving from status-based hierarchies to class-based ones so as then to eradicate them. Here, we examine the subsequent process of a move from status and class to Party, in Weber's terms, as village life becomes bureaucratized and politicized. Instead of communities electing their mayors we find organizations staffed by political appointees; instead of work in families, work organized in brigades. Villages and households no longer circumscribe the life plans of their members. What brings status and privilege is not landed wealth (precluded by the creation of bureaucratic farming organizations) but Party position, even if many villagers refuse to accord real deference to this new elite. At the same time, however, these developments do not bring modern bureaucracy of the *impersonal* type, the Bolsheviks' aims notwithstanding: rather, we see a flourishing of *personal* relations—a routinization toward "traditional" organizational principles characteristic of precommunist Romanian society, based on extensive clientelism. Collective farm members strove endlessly to personalize their relations, "making friends" with those whose power position might prove useful to them. Thus, much as we argued in chapter 3 concerning cadres, villagers' adaptations to the new system populated it with a kind of relationship inimical to its design.

In this chapter we briefly review the effects of these changes. Because our team's research did not extend beyond the early 1960s, we cannot offer a full assessment of the economic effectiveness of collective farms. Instead, we focus our discussion on the years of the collectivization campaign—1949–62—and limit ourselves to the following four topics. We begin with the remarkable social and geographical mobility that accompanied the communist transformation. Industrial development and the bureaucratization of society meant the proliferation of new jobs for people in villages, even as they lost the land that had rooted them in their communities. Among the consequences were a restratification of village life, as prior hierarchies based on owning means of production gave way to new ones based on political position and other bases of inequality. Additional changes affected family and household, including new patterns of authority and modifications in kinship, which receded in importance as against new kinds of personalistic ties. Especially significant were changes in gender roles and generational expectations. Moreover, the bureaucratization of work changed that basic daily reality for peasants, along with the personhood ideals that had been tied to it. "Persons" defined through landownership, self-directed work effort, and "wealth in people" gave way to bureaucratic state subjects oriented to getting by. All these changes were interconnected; we begin with mobility and move on to kinship, restratification, work, and concepts of person.

Mobility and the Transformation of Work

Peasants into Bureaucrats

For the poor and landless who entered early, joining the collectives offered upward mobility: they had little to lose but potentially much to gain. Not least among the benefits of joining the GACs in the first wave of collectivization was stability, with respect to both employment (even if it was part-time) and salary (even if it was minimal). This reduced the precariousness of everyday existence that previously had been the lot of such people.[5] Poor peasants used to privation became the recipients of "cheese, onions, oil and even olives, items that were otherwise hard for most people to procure" (Chelcea 2003b: 34). Some of them gained additional benefits: starting in the early 1950s, village residents were increasingly employed in local offices, ranging from bureaucratic positions to jobs as drivers, night watchmen, cleaners, and so forth. As we indicated in chapter 6, one of the most significant changes in Romanian village social structure was the expansion of positions of authority, compared with prewar times. Before, there had been a small number of administrative positions and these had been either ratified by the villagers (who elected the mayor) or imposed from without (police, notary). Now, the number of positions increased. For example, Lățea finds in Dobrosloveni that from a local administration that totaled nine to ten people at most in the 1930s (including the schoolteachers),

[5] There was considerable variation across the country regarding how people were paid—in currency or goods—and the adequacy of payment relative to promises. Also, payment varied over time. Contrary to general assumptions, collectivization was not uniformly considered negative.

in the 1950s about eighty people came to have salaried "functions" of some kind, from delegates supervising aspects of the quota requisitions, to committee members who oversaw farm inventory and set payments, to various kinds of communal guards, and so forth (2009: 335).

Many of these people who now became spokesmen for power—mayors, Party secretaries, collective farm chairmen, and brigade leaders—were neither locals legitimized by the esteem of other villagers nor outsiders imposed by the state: they were locals and outsiders ratified by the Party. As we indicated in chapters 3 and 7, they came disproportionately from once-devalued categories: in-migrants, in-marrying sons-in-law, the formerly poor and landless, and members of national minorities, all of whom saw in the new order a chance for social influence and mobility that had long been denied them. (Precisely these social origins, however, meant that they did not always enjoy among their fellow villagers the prestige their positions were supposed to bring.) Their good fortune came at the expense of the previous village elite, the wealthy peasants, who had lost all their land and were largely excluded from positions in the agricultural bureaucracy, at least initially.

For those whom the old system had disfavored, the collectives offered some unprecedented opportunities—something our largely negative postsocialist interviews tended to obscure. For example, in his interviews with former collectivists in Pechea, which had been the first GAC established in the Galaţi region, our colleague Dumitru Şandru was suspicious of the primarily laudatory evaluations he heard of it. On closer inspection, however, he realized that most of the people offering them had not only benefited from the privileges accorded this early collective farm but also long held leadership positions of one kind or another in the farm's organization; in addition, they had completed short training courses that qualified them for higher earnings. A poor peasant who had been a brigade leader in the wine-growing sector added a twist to his positive assessment of collectivization: "We were afraid, but the people who collectivized us did us a favor by forcing us in" (Şandru 2003: 24). The complaints they did offer concerned the 1980s, when things deteriorated considerably. (Not surprisingly, the Pecheans with negative views were those who had opposed collectivization and joined the GAC only by force in the final campaign; they had received none of its benefits.)

The various forms of upward mobility had a gendered dimension, in keeping with communist tenets promoting gender equality. The Party promoted the political advancement of women, giving them positions in the GAC leadership and Party hierarchy. Recall that in Ieud, a poor peasant woman was thrilled that she could learn to write; she then served as one of the village council's scribes, copying out many of the petition forms for people to sign even though she was unable to read what she had copied.[6] Women were named to positions of responsibility as members of GAC leadership councils, brigade leaders, and Party secretaries. A collectivization poem celebrated a GAC president:

[6] See chapter 4. P. N., Kligman interview.

The president, a good lady
Took the village in her hands
To improve, to fix . . .
When her face smiles
Everyone loves her.
But when she says something
Everyone falls in line.
Falls in line and makes haste
Not to be absent.[7]

In Lueta, at the end of the 1950s a woman became GAC president, though not everyone was pleased about women's acquiring this kind of authority: some commented that "women were the most dangerous organizers," carrying out their roles zealously (Oláh 2003: 58). Women's advancement went beyond the strictly political: they were hired in the postal service along with men, and as telephone operators, cleaners, or sales clerks at the local store. They were professionally trained to be midwives, displacing the now-unacceptable traditional practice of learning by apprenticeship to other midwives (Kligman 1998)—and they became doctors too, as well as teachers and other educated professionals.

As is apparent, accompanying the occupational mobility that an expanded bureaucracy generated was a remarkable expansion of higher education and democratization of access to it for those previously unable to afford schooling. With the formation of collectives, many peasant families opted to educate children who might otherwise have been kept at home to tend sheep and cattle or to work on and inherit the farm. (Until the early 1960s, however, children of chiaburs were handicapped in access to university.) The growth of industry and industrialization of agriculture required tens of thousands of engineers in particular. Many village youth entered the urban labor force as managers in the industrial bureaucracy or agronomists in the rural one. Village families with children in higher education and in the professions gained prestige independent of their political status, adding complexity to the politicized village hierarchy.

New Social Divisions

This initial wave of upward mobility, then, brought some villagers into elite positions and moved others out of them in accord with the institutionalization of Party rule and the politicization of village status systems. Although the Party pushed its ideology of social equality and the term "Comrade" aimed linguistically to erase prior social differentiations, it did not mask the hierarchy that distinguished "Comrades" from "comrades." Within these broad categories,

[7] Iordachi 2003: 51–52.

power struggles were fought, manipulated, and negotiated. Moreover, the new local leadership developed its own hierarchy of evaluation, which was based not on a family's prior status but on "social origin" and membership in the socialist agricultural organizations (GACs and associations). Now, the rich were to be despised and the poor promoted. All community members—both those who benefited from the changes and those who did not—had to develop attitudes and self-concepts in response to the new hierarchy.

As people began to join collectives, new forms of social division also appeared, crosscutting that of class war: those for and against collectivization, or those enjoying upward social mobility and those suffering the reverse. An elderly peasant who chronicled Ieud's tumultuous history observed:

> With collectivization, our village was divided in two: collectivists and non-collectivists. Those who joined escaped from all debts, but they also lost the land they had inherited from their parents, remaining with nothing but their two hands with which they worked to earn their existence. For those who didn't join, they suffered all the consequences, having none of the rights that all Romanian citizens should have. . . . The question—"are you a collectivist or not"—sorted [us], so those in leadership positions would know how to treat each individual.[8]

People who joined the Party or collectives might scoff at and taunt those outside it. In Apoldu de Jos, among the first villages collectivized in its area, an older peasant recalled the reaction of his neighbors when he and a few others joined the GAC:

> Our community was divided into neighborhoods, twenty-one neighborhoods, and in each, up to thirty families. . . . And from my neighborhood, only two of us [joined]. . . . The others wanted to remove us from the neighborhood, to throw us out because to join the collective then, they said, you had made a fool of yourself, and they hassled you, as if you had done something shameful, something outrageous, by joining the collective.[9]

Another peasant, from Săpânța, Maramureș, acknowledged that those who did not join the collective had a very rough time, "but they refused to join from their own vanity [*prostia lor*], not from anything else. They said they wouldn't join, they wouldn't submit to the communists."[10] The scoffing could go both ways, and mockery of the airs put on by parvenus was standard fare:

> In Poiana, there was a Gypsy mayor. The guy was a blacksmith. Wasn't he cocking his nose?! There was the stable where they kept the bulls at one end of the village. . . . There was a stud [horse] in the stables. A stud was really something in those times, like a Mercedes. And the mayor was riding the stud through the main street, wearing

[8] Pleș-Chindriș n.d.: 7.

[9] G. N., Budrală interview for M. Stewart.

[10] Fürtös and Bârlea 2009: 311.

> gloves on his hands. I saw him myself, I was a child then. The villagers in Poiana, who liked to pull people's leg, some of them would ask: Look at him! Why is he wearing those gloves? And another would answer: Well, it's cold up there on horseback, don't you realize? (Stewart and Stan 2009: 256)

Further divisions arose between those who brought property into the GAC and those who did not. As one respondent observed, "There was this woman whose brandy distillery was taken to the GAC courtyard, and when she was in the field hoeing with other women she would lash out at those who brought nothing and would say things like: 'You, you brought nothing to the GAC, whereas I gave them the distillery, my horse, everything!'" (Iordachi 2009: 128). In addition, despite official talk of the worker-peasant alliance, villagers might perceive their interests as contrary to those of industrial workers, such as the Hunedoara chiabur who supposedly complained that the police would not allow him to sell his cow (presumably, he ought to give it to the GAC). He fumed, "We toil only for the workers and nothing remains for us; everything is meant for the workers!"[11] Other divisions separated collectivists and peasants who remained in the private sector, whom collectivists often saw as becoming rich from commercializing their products (brandy, wool, cheese, hay, fruit) while others suffered. Conflicts between these groups could be felt as late as the austerity-ridden 1980s (not to mention after 1989), as in this example from Lueta:

> We were standing in line to buy bread. There were a lot of us, old, young, women, men, and the bread hadn't been delivered yet. An old collectivist and a younger man, who wasn't in the collective, were standing in line next to each other. And the old man was disgruntled, I don't remember exactly, he said something about lousy food, to which the young man replied, furious: "Shut up! You shouldn't even be standing in line, you don't deserve any bread, when you made the collective you took all the good land, including ours, so how come you don't have bread now?"[12]

If families from uncollectivized villages migrated down to live in collectivized ones, this perceived division of fortunes reinforced the split between "locals" and "outsiders." Such divisions were present not only within villages but also among them: despite the perception of their advantage, isolated and mountainous villages rarely benefited from the new order (access to education, clinics, etc.), which led gradually to their depopulation.

That same local-outsider split divided villages to which colonists had been brought, especially if (as was often the case) the colonists then joined the collectives. Within the collectives themselves there were divisions between simple members, on the one hand, and white-collar workers and other salaried employees, on the other—and among these, differences between those with higher

[11] DJAN HD, Fond CR PMR, file 888/1953, 148.

[12] 5, Oláh interview.

education, such as agronomists, and those without, such as brigade leaders. Overall, these divisions reflected the extent to which households and individuals were drawn into the processes of bureaucratization and Party institutionalization and thus into the embrace of the Party-state.

Geographical Mobility and Labor Force Requirements

As is evident, the communists' development plan created an active internal labor market and promoted extensive geographical mobility, starting even while the collectives were still forming.[13] At first the migrants were likely to be chiaburs and middle peasants who could not provide for their families while paying the exorbitant requisitions and taxes levied against them; a family member might head for work elsewhere. It was not long, however, before low pay in the collectives pushed GAC members into the ranks of migrants as well. Urban opportunities drew people—especially young and male—away from the villages in droves. Men left to join building crews that were literally "building socialism" by constructing its infrastructure: apartment complexes for the working classes, roads and railways, communication systems, and so on. Or they went to work in factories, often commuting on a daily or weekly basis, depending on available transportation. For some, this was an exciting period, as they pursued education and previously unimagined possibilities. There was seemingly infinite room for factory labor, in Romania's once-agrarian economy, and the movement heightened the interdependencies between rural and urban milieux.

The outflow left the labor force in agriculture increasingly feminized and elderly, however, and low pay produced lax work and rampant absenteeism. As a peasant from Săpânţă (Maramureş) commented, "People no longer did quality work."[14] Aggravating the problem during the 1950s were bouts of exodus from the GACs, as members withdrew because promises or payments had not been respected, because they could not make ends meet working in the GAC, because of the political relaxation between 1953 and 1957, and so on. Moreover, according to Securitate reports, chiaburs "agitated" poor and middle peasants not to participate in planting, harvesting, and the like, promoting work stoppages and significant losses.[15] Expansion of the bureaucracy worsened the situ-

[13] Internal labor migration existed before the communists came to power, but on a less extensive scale.

[14] Fürtös and Bârlea 2009: 335. B. S., a former brigade leader in Ieud, elaborated: [in the collective] "a person was paid by the norm, so he tried to work more, and, of course, working a lot, he also worked badly" ("*Cum s-o colectivizat Ieud*," unpublished MS., n.d.).

[15] In addition, peasants refused to bring their livestock and inventory into the collective, or they began taking their cows home to work their former land (ANIC, Fond 1, file 748/1952, 41).

ation: a number of people who had joined the collectives did not perform their agricultural labor because they had taken salaried positions. For example, out of five hundred members of the GAC "Filimon Sîrbu" in Sona, Făgăraş region, only fifty to sixty showed up regularly for work, and in the village of Jupa, Caransebeş, not one member did.[16] It seems that many salaried workers who signed up assumed that family members in the village would do the work for the GAC, but according to archival documents, most of them did not.[17] This is not surprising, given that those expected to carry out agricultural labor were mainly women and the elderly. Women had many other household tasks to perform and the elderly were often infirm.

These difficulties with the agricultural labor force (which persisted throughout the communist period) yielded yet another migrant stream, as people from the poorer, less industrialized, or uncollectivized areas of the country migrated for seasonal agricultural work in the more fertile, industrialized, and collectivized areas where collectivists commuted to nearby factories and farm labor was short. People went from Moldavia, Maramureş, and Oaş to the Danube Delta to cut reeds, or to work in mines or on state farms in Romania's more developed or more fertile regions (Dobrincu 2003a: 48–50). They would return home periodically, paid in wheat, grain, and cash, depending on how they had negotiated their contracts. It was rumored that they were better paid than locals: by most accounts, these "outsiders" drove hard bargains, though they also committed themselves to long, hard hours.[18] A former GAC president from Ieud noted that he once sent some forty people to work in a collective in Arad, where "they earned more in a summer than did our entire collective farm"; he added, "People lived well *because* they worked as migrant laborers" (their earnings from the GAC in Ieud being inadequate).[19] Not surprisingly, the arrival of "outside" work teams in a village generated social conflicts with the locals. Outsiders generally meant additional costs for the GAC in question, for temporary laborers had to be housed and fed (Iordachi 2003: 49).

Labor hunger throughout the economy set up a constant tension between people's mobility aspirations and local labor requirements. To counter the drain of workers from GACs and make up for absenteeism (as well as to increase GAC property holdings), Party officials tried a variety of stratagems. Villagers who sought work in industry, perhaps to escape their obligatory deliveries and

[16] ACNSAS, FD, file 7/v. 1, 78.

[17] See ANIC, Fond 1, file 58/1951, 3 (RLA).

[18] From many years of observation in Maramureş, Kligman corroborates the rumor and would include people from Oaş in the category of migrant laborers despised by locals for their willingness to work hard and live in harsh conditions (typical of migrants the world over).

[19] He himself eventually left for work elsewhere, noting that Ieud should never have been collectivized, since it lacked appropriate terrain: of its five thousand hectares, only four hundred were arable. "What could be produced from that? There was no way to make a go of it there."

contracts, were required to donate their land to the collectives or village councils, or to be members of and work in their collectives despite their other jobs.[20] GAC members who went to work in the cities to supplement family income during the winter months received notices like this one, reminding them of their local obligations when spring planting time came around:

> We, the Governing Council of the GAC "Red Dawn," call to the attention of comrade Pál Lajos that he should kindly take his place in the collective farm on April 1, 1956, recognizing that the farm needs a male work force and has a real need for [its] comrade, because the work force is small and we have a lot to build and we request that, in the interest of developing the farm [our] comrade give his full support. (Oláh 2003: 25)

Jobs and GAC participation were intertwined in other ways. For example, in Corund, a well-known center for ceramics, potters were allowed to continue their work in pottery only if they contracted to do thirty to sixty units of work per year for the GAC. While they considered this arrangement a form of blackmail, they nonetheless had to fulfill their contractual agreement. Many did so by paying others to carry out the work (Bodó 2003: 13), just like the shepherds in Poiana Sibiului, who had to agree to similar conditions (Stewart and Stan 2009: 258). The fishermen of Jurilovca, also bound by such stipulations, frequently found themselves escorted by armed police to make good on their agricultural obligations (Iordachi 2003: 49).

At the same time, industry had its own labor force needs that might come into conflict with those of agriculture, further conditioning migration streams and mobility. For instance, one skilled and valued worker from Lueta received numerous "requests" from the village council that he return to work in the collective, but his factory leadership protected him. Rather than relinquish him, they advised him to return home every few weeks so that he would be seen working in the fields, even paying his salary from time to time during such absences (Oláh 2003: 61). After each two-week stint, the factory would send a car to bring him back to work.

Tying labor contracts for workers in mining, industry, shepherding, ceramics, the railroads, forestry, fishing and the like to membership in and work for the collectives was nevertheless not enough to cover labor requirements in agriculture, especially in view of its seasonal exigencies. After all, planting and harvesting can be delayed only so long before the crop is compromised. To address this ongoing issue, cadres set up yet another migratory stream, of short duration: they brought in outsiders—soldiers, factory workers, students, mem-

[20] That workers who had agricultural property of any kind had to be reminded repeatedly that they could not receive salaries from the state if they were not also members of the "socialist agricultural sector" speaks to the problems of that sector, not to mention people's lack of conviction regarding its superiority. See Oláh 2003: 42.

bers of youth organizations, and so on—to carry out "patriotic labor" at peak periods in the agricultural cycle (see, for example, Márton 2005: 34).[21]

How institutions and persons accommodated labor-force needs demonstrates the complexity of the situation that GACs and the Party leadership confronted. Where sticks were attached to carrots, coercive methods did not, on the whole, yield the desired results. By contrast, where "flexible accommodation" prevailed (Goina 2003, 2009), more consensual relations emerged, leading to more willing participation, as we see from the model GAC "New Life" in Sântana. This GAC had acquired land without adequate labor, since the German chiaburs from whom much of its land was confiscated were not supposed to be allowed into GACs. As noted in chapter 7, the leadership successfully argued for permission to accept the Germans as members. In this way, local interethnic tensions were ameliorated, costly "outsiders" were unnecessary, and the GAC benefited from the Germans' superior work experience and habits (Goina 2009).

In this section we have shown that the institutionalization of Party rule in the villages broke open their borders, bureaucratized their employment structure, and created new opportunities for work, particularly beneficial to those who had previously occupied marginal statuses. The formation of collectives proletarianized the peasants and sprang them free of their natal communities, launching them into migratory flows around the country. The weak performance of most GACs provided an incentive for movement that then created perennial labor-force problems for them. We now turn to some effects of these changes on another fundamental aspect of life in Romania's villages: kinship and family.

From Patriarchal Households to the Paternal Party

The formation of collectives altered patterns of family, work, and cooperation, as Mihail Cernea showed in his work in the 1970s (1974, 1978). Whereas household heads had previously determined who would do what kind of work and when, choosing the kin or neighbors with whom they would cooperate, collective farm leaders took over those decisions. They set up cooperation in brigades and teams, often formed not on kinship but on territorial or other principles (e.g., different neighborhoods forming different brigades). Kinship

[21] Local Party cells were also supposed to mobilize various local branches of mass organizations, such as the Union of Young Workers (UTM) or women's organizations, who, in turn, were to mobilize their constituencies; they did so with varying success. In Ieud, for example, they were chastised for not being effective (DJAN MM, Fond Comitetul Raional PMR Vişeu, file 334/1961/v. 5, 84–90). The state also made extensive use of forced labor, deploying prisoners and the deported to labor camps, the canal, and so on.

retreated in importance, and households ceased to function as work units, replaced by bureaucratic organizations. Party officials in the regional or national capital might determine a person's work patterns in a given village. (Only in the 1970s, as problems with collectives led to major changes, did households regain some of these functions; see Kideckel 1993). These changes dealt a major blow to patriarchally based authority relations in families, into which Party institutions began to insert themselves. Launching collectives also launched a bureaucratization of family life, a process that villagers enhanced by trying to domesticate the new forms through personal ties.

Changing Configurations of Generation and Gender

A group who suffered a particularly devastating reversal of fortune with collectivization was the elderly, in particular male household heads over about age fifty-five. As Goina puts it:

> The loss of land had the most radical impact of all on the village elderly. Control over the land was one of the most effective mechanisms through which household heads exercised control over their families. As children received their share of the land only at marriage, and sometimes not even then, the loss of land resulted in the weakening of paternal authority. Often, after collectivization, a young man working in town or as a brigade leader at the collective had more money and more influence than his still-active father. (2003: 46)

Thus, collectivization diminished the power of parents over their children. Signing their land over to the GAC, they also surrendered the basis of security in their old age. What had once been a world in which children obeyed their parents began to give way to the reverse. Moreover, a privilege of older men with land had been to monopolize village leadership, but now a man thirty years old could become president of the GAC or the People's Council. Very disturbing to elderly people was the loss of the respect and deference they had always received in village society, regardless of their social status. For example, instead of addressing an elderly man with terms meaning "uncle" (*nene*, *bade*) and the honorific second-person pronoun (*dumneata*), Party activists might use "hey you!" or "you there!" (*mă*, *bă*), maybe even with the man's first name—wholly unacceptable behavior for a decent person. Cadres pushed old people around, made them stand rather than offering them a chair—in short, humiliated them in front of others. These sudden changes in their social status were quite as upsetting to them and to other villagers as were the reversals of fortune of chiaburs.

Indeed, the two reversals might coincide. A possibility we do not have the data to prove is that elderly people were disproportionately named chiaburs.

On the one hand, this could be expected since they were the ones controlling the land. More subtly, however, their place in the domestic cycle would have made them more vulnerable to class war than younger ones, much as Chelcea argues for the owners of nationalized houses (2003a). If they lived alone and their grown children were settled in another household or even in town, they would not have sufficient labor for working their land, and owing to decrepitude or ill health they might have to hire day laborers or servants. This made them "exploiters of others' labor" and, hence, chiaburs. Many of the chiabur contestations—especially those of widows—make precisely this argument: we are old and frail, our children are gone, we have no one to work our land and had to hire some help. But we're not exploiters, merely elderly. In the lists of chiaburs, differences in household demographics may help to explain otherwise puzzling inclusions. This permutation of class war would have been unusually galling in that, as we showed in chapter 3, over three-fourths of communist cadres were under forty years of age. Thus—as in China's Cultural Revolution—class war was generational war, in several senses.

Work in collectives also undermined husbands' control over wives, who took their orders from brigade leaders and earned their own pay separately from their spouses (Cernea 1978). As we mentioned above, the Party actively promoted gender equality, changing the balance of relations and responsibilities in families and bringing women into the work force. Collectivization liberated them to become not just mothers but paid employees. Reform of the domestic sphere and gender roles came not just from altering property relations and the labor process but also from centralizing domestic services. Party institutions took on many of the service aspects of women's work (at least in theory), providing food, medical assistance, and care of children and the elderly, as well as developing the household-appliance industry for labor-saving devices. These became increasingly essential when husbands (and sometimes even the women themselves) began commuting for factory work. Of necessity, then, village women acquired more authority in their households.

Party organizations such as the Union of Democratic Women of Romania (UDFR) actively taught women to expect and defend their rights. Here is what Şoimuş villager Susana Ciortea told Party leaders Gheorghiu-Dej and Pauker, in a meeting held in 1951 (they were discussing cadres' abusive behavior in collectivizing the village):

> Some time went by and they had a meeting at the farm offices and we women went too, to find out what's happening in our country and how the collective is being made, because at the UDFR they told us that we too have rights. But when we got to the meeting, we were told, "We don't need you, go home, who told you to come here?" We didn't go to the meeting again for fear they would throw us out.[22]

[22] ANIC, Fond C.C. al P.M.R.–Cancelarie, file 19/1951, 2 (RLA), and published in Moraru et al.

Instead, they went straight to the top to complain about their treatment. In short, the Party bureaucratized and politicized its relation to women, who then used what they had learned to contest ongoing forms of patriarchal behavior. Lest one think that with all this their status was uniformly improved, however, we note that all the transformations we have been discussing led to a feminization of agriculture. Although that meant greater authority for women in household decisions, counterbalancing it was the relegation of agriculture to the lowest status in both prestige conceptions and budgetary allocations. Moreover, in the collective farms a gendered division of labor and authority persisted for quite some time, as the above quotation nicely illustrates.

Transformations of Kinship

Changes in gender and generational roles were part of a more thoroughgoing transformation in ideas concerning kinship, which "recast the family's internal definition and its place in the social system" (Jowitt 1978: 68). In chapters 5 and 6, we showed how both peasants and cadres manipulated kinship, modifying its meanings in the process. The bureaucratization of work in the collectives diminished cooperation among kin, narrowing the range of effective kinship (even though it remained significant) and, in many places, gradually inducing "genealogical amnesia" (Chelcea 2003a: 715). The changes extended further into family life with the end of private ownership, though in complex ways. On the one hand, many of our respondents claimed that collectives brought bad relations among family members (e.g., "The collective brought only hatred, rancor between families"[23]). Indeed, at the time of collectivization, when one spouse or sibling joined, the result was often quarrels with the remaining spouse or siblings. On the other hand, after collectives were formed there was no longer any motive—at least in theory—for rancor over unequal inheritance, once common among siblings or between the generations. Class warfare might either exacerbate conflict among kin or increase solidarity.[24]

Moreover, the Party-state gradually asserted itself as a kind of surrogate family. Much has been written of the ostensible "alliance" struck between communist parties and women in socialism (e.g., Gal and Kligman 2000; Goven 1993; Fitzpatrick 2005) as Party institutions took over some of the work formerly done by women, encouraged their aspirations, and defended them against abusive kin. Fitzpatrick writes of "Wives' Tales" in the Soviet Union, describing how men contemplating divorce might be denounced by their wives, who

2004: 541–46. See also Buckley (2006: 278) on Soviet debates about women's paid labor and housework.

[23] "Colhozu n-o adus dicât uri, duşmănii, ş-intri familii" (G. D., Dobrincu interview).

[24] Hooper (2006) illustrates the dynamics of divided loyalties between the Party and family members.

would appeal to the Party to help them hang onto their wayward spouses (2005: chapter 12). We find similar patterns in Romania. Family members, particularly women with alcoholic husbands, might turn to GAC leaders to adjudicate their problems. Just such a case was discussed in a meeting of the leadership council of the GAC "New Life" in Sântana. The husband claimed he could no longer get along with his wife, who did not take care of the house properly. He wanted the council to steer her in the right direction. His wife, on the other hand, complained that not only was he drunk much of the time, but he also beat her repeatedly, leaving serious lesions on her body; furthermore, his drinking caused the usual host of household budgetary problems associated with alcoholism in families. She insisted that it was impossible to continue the marriage unless he changed. The council weighed in, attributing responsibility for this sorry family situation to both parties and adding that if the husband did not seriously mend his ways, he would lose his position (Goina 2003: 36).[25]

Such events participated in a much larger colonization of family and kinship by Party policy. Casting itself as the paterfamilias of everyone in the "household" defined by national territorial boundaries, the Party leadership created a deeply paternalistic relationship with Romania's citizens. It demanded of them the kind of filial respect and responsibility that parents expected of their children, exercising judgment and control over their activities and disciplining them as it deemed necessary.[26] Those who benefited from its largesse were expected to manifest their loyalty and appreciation. In these ways, the Wise Leader-Party would supplant parental functions, and biological families would give way to political ones, such as the GAC and other Party institutions. Romanian communism would become a "great family," linked in fraternal relations with other socialist states (see Hooper 2006, for the Soviet case). Thus, the Party sought to naturalize itself in the kinship idiom basic to village life.

Another change affected ritual kinship or godparenthood, to which we have referred in earlier chapters. A highly developed institution in precommunist Romania, ritual kinship involved sponsoring couples at marriage and their children at baptism. Ritual kinship had always had an instrumental aspect, but under socialism this aspect took on much greater significance. It became one of several means by which villagers sought to domesticate the Party through creating personalistic ties with it, refusing its supposedly impersonal, bureaucratic norms. This was a favored way of trying to shape an institutional, instrumentalized relationship through affective, culturally grounded ties aiming to personalize it.

In the past, villagers selected as godparents had come almost exclusively from prominent, that is, land-rich, families (including, in some areas, large

[25] Haney (2002) also reports on women calling upon social welfare case workers to intervene or mediate their abusive family relationships (e.g., alcoholic partners who beat them).

[26] On state paternalism, see Verdery 1996; Kligman 1998. For a related discussion on Hungary, see Lampland 1995: 180–86.

landowners who might be absentee). In some parts of the country this relation was inherited: the children of my parents' godparents would sponsor my own marriage, and so on (see also Hammel 1968, for Serbia). With socialism these patterns changed: each generation made its own choices rather than inheriting its parents', and people increasingly selected sponsors from outside the community, basing their selections not on land-owning prominence but on other characteristics that might make them useful—a former classmate with a powerful administrative job, or one's factory foreman, in a sort of industrialization of kinship. Villagers might socialize their relationship to the GAC by inviting the president and his spouse to serve as godparents, hoping that the ritual-kin relation would work to their advantage when they needed assistance or favors (see Kideckel 1993: chapter 6). Such godparents found themselves caught, of course, between the expectations of the Party and those of their godchildren—a tension that ramified throughout the society and compromised the intended results. For that very reason, cadres who agreed to serve as godparents might be roundly criticized in the press (see Jowitt 1978: 70–71). They could also make good use of the institution, however, utilizing it to amass "wealth in people" that might cushion labor shortages in the farm (see Humphrey 1983). In yet another colonizing of kinship practices, Party cadres sometimes created fictive kin relations between socialist enterprises, especially between factories and collective farms, thereby casting the "peasant-worker alliance" in a traditional, if incongruous, idiom.[27]

Making Friendship

All over the world, people use personal ties to create security in the face of insecure conditions. Conditions in socialist Romania were highly insecure and remained so; personalizing relationships was a logical reaction, as we suggested in chapter 3 concerning cadres. Aside from strategic selection of ritual kin, villagers sought to create as many connections as possible with people who had resources of some sort to distribute, seeking links through shared acquaintances, shared localisms or school ties, or gifts and bribes. The various ways of "making friends" with people who possessed political or economic capital became so common that according to a 1970s joke, the initials for the Romanian Communist Party (PCR) actually meant *pile, cunoştiinţe, şi relaţii*, or "connections, acquaintances, and relations." Early in the socialist period, such connec-

[27] For example: "On August 13, 1950, an Agricultural Collective Farm came into being, in Buznea commune [Iaşi], under the name 'GAC Ion Creangă,' having as its godfather [*naş*] the 'August 23' factory in the city of Iaşi" (ASRI, Fond D, file 4470, 64–66. Courtesy of O. Roske). Less striking but in the same vein is another instance from Odorhei: "The Party leadership assigned the weaker collectives industrial enterprise 'patrons' that helped them with accounting, harvesting, and certain equipment" (Oláh 2003: 19).

tions could be crucial to survival. For example, one man recounted the story of his grandfather, a chiabur against whom a penal case had been opened. But he had a connection at the courthouse who kept putting his dossier at the bottom of the pile; each time it rose to the top, his connection would put it back down at the bottom. In this way the case was postponed for several months until the hysteria of the moment faded.[28]

After collectivization was completed the stakes became less dire—and personalism even more rampant. It was a fundamental means for getting by in the unpredictable world of socialism. There was always some ill-defined area that offered room for maneuver, and maneuver people did, instrumentalizing relations to their own ends, never certain whether they would manage or not. Whether sooner or later, many accommodated to the exigencies of hard times with compromises that enabled them and their families to survive. If the Party made chiaburs, people responded by "making a bit of friendship." That is, they paid the collector or other local officials "with cheese, plum brandy, whatever I had, and they lowered my quotas. What else could I do?"[29] This same person elaborated further on what he meant: "I managed as best I could. I made a little friendship with V. and he helped me. There wasn't much else you could do. Others asked me, 'How did you arrange that?' I'd say, 'As best I could.' If you made friends, you know, you gave him a little something, then he gave you a break." The instrumentalism of these "friendships" was generally more naked than that of godparenthood, especially when it involved making bribes. Here is another example, from Ieud (the respondent is quoting his approach to a requisitions collector):

> Isn't there something you could do to get me out of giving this quota? I can't pay it. You can see I don't have anything. He says, "if you give me a nice tip, I'll let you off." We reached an agreement. "You give me 300 lei and I'll let you off." I don't have it now but I'll come up with something and I'll pay you. . . . In those days 300 lei was a lot of money, it was a good [month's] salary. With great difficulty I managed to get the money and I gave him 200 once and then he waited until I was able to give him the other 100. [After that] no one asked me again if I have my quotas or not.[30]

Although making friends could be a means of making a profit, as with the shepherds who were so gifted at it, for most villagers it was a necessary survival strategy that enabled them and their families to get by. "Getting by" was itself dictated in large measure by the failings of an underdeveloped command economy that had to satisfy both war reparations and its own modernization plans. The bottom line for those who survived by "making a little friendship" was, as

[28] N. C., Verdery interview, 2009.

[29] I. S., Kligman interview. Fellow villagers suspected that wealthier peasants who somehow managed were informers, though there is little to substantiate that claim. Bribery was effective, in any event.

[30] Ibid.

one canny peasant put it, "Come on, let's be honest. If you knew how to get by, then you screwed someone else."[31] Uncertainty had become the *modus vivendi* of the times and required creative individual responses that put social solidarity at risk, fraying the ties that had bound village social relations and replacing them with ties more useful to making one's way in a new bureaucratized system. It was precisely this dynamic that gave the Party bureaucracies of socialism their special stamp: they were thoroughly penetrated with personal relations (Horváth and Szakolczai 1992). Thus, when we argue that an effect of collectivization was to bureaucratize rural society, we are not claiming the triumph of a rational-legal "iron cage." Quite the contrary.

Status Reversal

The two previous sections have underscored a fundamental change that accompanied collectivization: the overturning of status hierarchies. Contributing to this outcome were not only the developments we have been discussing—social mobility, the creation of bureaucratic positions in villages, and the quest for new targets of friendship—but also the practice of class war, described in chapter 6, which ravaged community stratification systems. Large landowners who had served as patrons were removed through confiscations and imprisonment; the wealthier peasants who had served as mayors, godparents, employers of wage labor, and linchpins of village status were stripped of their possessions, offices, and dignity. Schoolteachers and priests who had once formed a highly respected village intelligentsia were co-opted into the Party's projects; priests became salaried employees of an atheist state bent on eliminating their influence. In place of these elites came new ones, many from families or social groups that had once been looked down upon, as well as new categories of communist status honor, such as *fruntaș* (leader), awarded to villagers who worked hard in the collective.

Because status ideas had entered into people's deepest self-conceptions, the overturning of previous hierarchies had momentous effects. People accustomed to being disconsidered and treated with scorn now had an opportunity for revenge. Here is a Comlăușan describing the new social order: "Those who had ten to twelve hectares or more, they were viewed badly. The poor people were glad they got to grind those people under their heel a bit, . . . they were glad that *you*, rich person, come and mow with a scythe instead of just standing and watching *me* do it."[32] In Dobrosloveni after the GAC's first harvest, members of a family who had previously "eaten polenta with onions" (connoting relative poverty) received more corn than they could store and were able to buy

[31] Ibid.

[32] O. M., Goina interview. Nevertheless, in many regions, chiaburs worked together with those they may have taken on to assist them.

a radio. "In an outburst of joy, they organized a small family party where the neighbors heard shouts and cries of exultation among which the following: 'I'd kiss the soles [others say "the ass"] of the collective, for it made us human! [*oameni*, that is, respectable people]'" (Lațea 2009: 336). These reactions notwithstanding, our interviews show that some poor people felt sorry for the rich—godparents to most of them—and did not gloat at their tribulations. Previous hierarchies were not fully obliterated; as we saw in chapter 7, it was chiefly the inclusion of chiaburs that enabled collectivization to be completed.[33] Therefore, those who rejoiced too openly at the misfortune of others might find themselves ostracized and subjected to moral shaming by those defending the older status order. The once-poor family with their boisterous party and others like them earned the contempt of other Dobrosloveni villagers; to this day, the episode serves there as an example of unacceptable behavior (336).

For peasants in the middle and upper status groups, the loss of their status was a source of ongoing distress, leaving them permanently scarred. Collectivization not only tore away their possessions: it shattered their self-image as persons of substance. Those accustomed to receiving deference were routinely humiliated by those accustomed to giving it; the devastating effects of these assaults cannot be overestimated. Quoting a former chiabur's recollections from Corund, Bodó writes: "We were like exiles. We didn't even have permission to watch a play presented in the village. They wouldn't give us tickets for it" (2003: 22). It was not just in farming communities that this reversal was acutely felt. We noted in chapter 7 a similar experience for the shepherds of Poiana Sibiului, as reported by Stewart and Stan (2003). There, being ruled by long-despised Roma who had become local officials was a profound shock to the system (28).[34]

In extended interviews, our project member Julianna Bodó explored this sense of shock for two Hungarian communities, Corund/Korond and Armașeni/Csíkmenaság in central Transylvania. Because her interpretation seems more widely relevant, we will present it at some length. The changes in village structures of influence and status, Bodó argues, destabilized people's self-conceptions, as they were forced to call into question their accustomed interpretations of their own and others' behavior. Daily public encounters with the new authorities produced discomfort and confusion for many villagers, for

> at the formal level these meetings contained a marked asymmetry: the villagers held a lower position than the representatives of power. On the other hand, at the level of

[33] On the intersection of old and new status hierarchies, see Verdery 1977: chapter 5.

[34] Nevertheless, these scholars find that aside from having to accept a "Gypsy" mayor, shepherds did not suffer the overturning of their status order for long. They write, "While in other villages the practice of declaring people exploiters had reached most of its goals . . . the shepherds of Poiana Sibiului to a great extent succeeded in preserving their material position and their status as members of the economic elite. . . . In this way the class relations between the 'exploiters,' the 'poor peasants' and 'middle peasants' were actually not reversed for very long" (Stewart and Stan 2003: 32–33).

> informal interactions, the asymmetry was reversed: villagers were fully aware that they themselves were "somebodies," whereas the group members were "nobodies." When villagers were called to the town hall, the situation was humiliating for precisely this reason. They believed the new leadership was purposely humiliating them by sending these nobodies to their houses. The respondents I interviewed expressed outrage even now at having been forced to muffle their views when they received visits from the "local organizers," were ordered around by them or were openly threatened, without being able to argue back. It was not force or the imposition of authority that was perceived as humiliating, but the distorted logic of promoting unworthy individuals into positions of power in society. (Bodó 2009: 363)[35]

What Bodó's respondents recalled most vividly in their interviews was not the abuses of the communist leadership (there is nothing new in this, they would say: power always abuses its subjects) but these trivial humiliations by local nobodies. They felt the repeated silencing of their reactions as a deep insult—a sentiment we suspect was widespread. In addition, villagers found themselves constantly brought up short by the unpredictable dispositions of the new authorities. It was not only the content that was confusing or troubling but the form in which it was expressed, often using modes of address that would earlier have been judged disrespectful and coarse. Such encounters assaulted villagers' sense of self-esteem, forcing them to ask themselves, "Who am I, that they can do these kinds of things to me?" "What have I come to, that these nobodies can behave like this with me?" (Bodó 2003: 37).[36]

In response, Bodó contends, villagers did everything possible to protect their self-conception from these assaults, resorting to several stratagems. One was to curtail the frequency and length of contacts with local officials, so as to minimize the number of potential injuries to their self-esteem. Another was linguistic practices that symbolically degraded the new authorities, such as according them nicknames—a time-honored village practice all over Romania—that referred unflatteringly to their new occupations. In addition, in her community parents communicated their disdain to their children at home by deriding people who were in positions of authority.[37] Finally, she suggests, people spoke as seldom as possible about collectivization, not just because it was an unpleasant subject but because discussion of it called a person's self-image into question.

Lățea, too, explores, to rather different effect, the question of how people

[35] We emphasize that this characterization pertains to everyday interactions in a changed village social organization. Where villagers had suffered ongoing violence (e.g., through incarceration), the affronts to their senses of self were embodied, as we discuss in the "Methods" section of the introduction.

[36] The form of these questions might suggest that the people whose self-concept she is describing were people of some means, not the more modestly or poorly endowed. Bodó (personal communication) believes, however, that the experience was common to most villagers where she worked, confronted with ideas from without that were upsetting their way of life.

[37] Parents nonetheless had to be careful about what they communicated to their children, lest they repeat criticisms of the Party at school or in public, at great risk to their families.

strove to protect a self-image in the face of status decline. He suggests that people who in the past had made a habit of being on good terms with the authorities might do the same with the new power, thereby coming to fill some of the new positions. Instead of seeing this behavior as (merely) opportunist, he sees it as an effort "to resituate oneself inside what appeared to be a new local configuration of authority, or . . . a set of attempts to remain, to the extent possible, true to oneself" (2003: 28). In other words, seeing themselves as about to lose a social position that grounded a particular self-image, they did what they could to relocate themselves socially in keeping with that self-image. Thus, not all who adhered to the new power were the former poor: they might be men of some means who regretted being reduced in status and whose wealth was not—or no longer—so great as to have them excluded from political positions.

Underlying this discussion, ultimately, is the politicization and bureaucratization of the local status system, as landed wealth ceased to be the basis for social position. With that change came alterations in the ideology and practices of personhood that had sustained the earlier status order. In our final section we further explore the destruction of village status ideologies, as "persons" gave way to bureaucratic subjects.

From Persons to Subjects

> Much still remains to be learned about the creation, development, and impact of collectivized agriculture. Perhaps the greatest gap in our knowledge occurs in the social realm: What kinds of people did such a farming system produce?[38]

If the person-ideal of the prewar Romanian peasantry emphasized possession, wealth in people, and self-directed hard work, we should expect many of these villagers to experience collectivization as an assault upon values fundamental to the person. It is clear from our interviews that they did. First and most obviously, the loss of their land deprived them of the personhood associated with possession, which some felt as a complete overturning of values. A respondent from Darabani offered this assessment:

> The peasant doesn't own anything anymore. The peasant was disowned. . . . As if this wasn't Romania anymore, [as if there weren't] Romanians in this country! As if there were people brought in from somewhere and no one owned anything anymore. I mean they gave something, they did give them something, but [they couldn't own anything.] We were raised here, here was our inheritance from our parents, from our forefathers! [Now] you didn't have any rights![39]

[38] Pryor 1992: 357.

[39] V.T.T., Dobrincu interview.

From having been a free person with rights who was master of his possessions, this man says, the peasant became a slave who was not even a Romanian but was "brought in from somewhere," unrooted to the soil.[40] The loss of land was at the same time a severe blow to the social and familial connections that had accompanied it, including connections to children through the promise of inheritance, to ancestors from whom one's land had come, and to kin and friends with whom work had been shared. As we have seen, in these ways, collectivization threw both "wealth in people" and possession-based personhood into complete disarray. We will not elaborate further upon these points but turn to the third aspect of personhood, self-directed hard work and the values associated with it—an area emphasized by many of our respondents. Dobrincu summarizes it succinctly (2003a: 77): "Most of my interlocutors mentioned the negative consequences of collectivization: dispossession of property, poor-quality work and even encouraging people not to work, diminishing correctness almost to the point of its disappearance, the creation of dependence on the state for an important part of the population."

The Changing Nature of Work

Work is the defining constant of peasant life the world over, and it was basic to Romanian villagers' sense of human worth. With collectivization, this most fundamental of their activities was modified almost beyond recognition. Forms of so-called work appeared that cheapened the meaning of the word—like "persuasion work" and "political work," which cadres did not by physical exertion (except when beating people) but by blather, lies, and threats.[41] Work rhythms changed, in keeping with the new bureaucratic regimen: "In comparison with the strenuous work of before collectivization, when periods of working non-stop and sleeping in the fields alternated with periods of relative inactivity, the standardized, rationalized work introduced by the new institutional structure of the GAC meant a revolution in the way of life" (Goina 2003: 34). The working day was defined not from dawn to dusk or by agricultural tasks but according to hours. Peasants reported to work by the clock, a new experience for them, and their performance was assessed in abstract "workdays," "points," or "norms" that made little sense to villagers and were open to unfair manipulation. As a former chiabur later turned brigade leader observed, "It was very hard in the collective as people weren't used to working as the GAC [leadership] expected," that is, according to predetermined norms.[42] There seemed to be no clear link between the work they did and improvements in their material

[40] In some areas of Romania, *viță*, or "root," refers to a family branch. Its "quality" is inherited through the family line and is in keeping with the notion of being unrooted. See Kligman 1988: 328.

[41] Most villagers esteemed intellectual work, not equated with "persuasion" or "political" work.

[42] B. A., "Cum s-o colectivizat Ieudul," unpublished manuscript, n.d.

situation, as there had been before. Officials seeking to rationalize labor found it difficult to get peasants to work on a schedule rather than at their own speed or convenience.[43]

The collectives' new work arrangements made encounters with bureaucracy an everyday affair. Like all other workers, villagers now had to have a work card (*cartea de muncă*). As we see from Iordachi's description of the bureaucratization of work for Jurilovca's fishermen, the change did not affect only farmers:

> Being a state employee meant more vulnerability to administrative pressure and the loss of one's independence in the organization of work. The state exerted firm control on fishing methods: the labor force was dramatically reorganized, older fishermen were forced into retirement and family fishing teams were replaced with so called "fishing brigades" which the state kept on a tight leash. Prohibition on alcohol was imposed even during the cold wintertime and poaching was severely punished. Most importantly, fishermen felt heavily exploited, as the state paid them only for 10 to 20 percent of the harvested fish, whereas in the interwar years the [fishing association] used to pay them up to 50 percent. Officials used state control over labor to turn Jurilovca's predominantly fishing economy into a predominantly agricultural economy. (2009: 130)

Villagers did not see all the changes as bad, however. For instance, they no longer had to get up at 3:00 or 4:00 a.m. to trek to distant fields, and respondents recall that work became less arduous, since machines took over many tasks (after all, the mechanization of agriculture had been one of the promises of collectivization): "From a farm worker, man became an industrial worker because he no longer had reason to work in the field, where the tractor took his place, as did the seeder with which seeding was finished in three days."[44] Concerning the new team-based labor, opinions were mixed. Some found it contrary to nature (e.g., "Work in common! There hasn't *ever* been anything like that!" [Vultur 2003a: 90]) or objected to the "free-rider problem" ("In a team, you couldn't know how others were doing their job. I weeded the corn thoroughly, but I wasn't sure if the person who did the second weeding was doing it well" [Chelcea 2009: 417]). Because this group work was not part of ongoing relations of reciprocity, did not involve one's own land, and was not driven by ideological commitment to the communist project, some people reported less motivation for working well. Moreover, as mentioned above, individuals were paid according to set production norms, which motivated them to work more rather than better. Others, however, enjoyed working in a team, like this man

[43] DJAN MM, Fond Comitetul Raional Vişeu–Secţia Economico-Agrară. file 8/1951/vol. V, 64, notes that not all collectivists fulfilled their required seasonal workdays; Fond PMR Maramureş–Organizatorică, file 77/1956–1961, 45 (uncatalogued, GAC-Ieud records), complained that collectivists are not "disciplined enough" and fail to show up for work regularly.

[44] F. W, Pătraşcu interview for Vultur. Mechanization was not uniformly developed across Romania, however.

from Reviga: "You didn't even notice how fast time went by during the day. As a private farmer, it was just me and my woman working together" (417). A former middle peasant from Vlaicu told of the fun she had had working on the collective with her team; they would take food and drink to the fields, have a good time, and laugh a lot: "If we'd just been working our own land it wouldn't have been as much fun because we would have been only a few kin, but here there were a lot more of us."[45]

As the measure of work shifted toward bureaucratic forms, ceasing to be an activity directed at household reproduction and assessed by household members, and especially as pay for it became unsatisfactory, people ceased to work as hard as they had before. This was one of the changes most frequently mentioned by our respondents. For example, to a question whether the collective had changed the village: "People got softer with their work. Those who still worked got softer: no point in having anything, 'cuz tomorrow they'll take it."[46] Indeed, "people encouraged each other to work slower, and children were taught . . . that 'in the collective you don't have to rush,' 'you don't have to do a perfect job,' 'you don't have to push yourself,' etc. These discursive practices undermined work at the collective. In contrast, to work on your own farm, you ought to get up early, prepare yourself well, and carry out all the tasks as correctly as possible" (Bodó 2003: 50). In many Romanian collectives, this pattern persisted throughout the socialist period.

The same picture emerges from the archives. Across the country, in both the first and second waves of collectivization, reports continually noted that collective members showed up for work either rarely or not at all. Those forcibly drawn into the GACs refused to work the collective fields, instead working on their old parcels.[47] Minutes of meetings of the General Assembly and of the Leadership Council of Lueta/Lövéte often assessed the work of members with complaints such as "the collectivists get up late, don't want to go out to work in a timely way, each morning comrade president has to go from person to person to get them out for sowing, they do few work-days per year, they leave the collective farm and hire on at the mines or factories, etc." (Oláh 2003: 42). Admittedly, these kinds of complaints varied widely from farm to farm. In contrast to cases like the above were collectives in which people worked very hard and were well rewarded, especially in the early years (for instance, Sânpaul and Sântana, in our sample). Lax work habits, however, were far more common.

Motivating the labor force became a constant preoccupation of farm managers, requiring creative solutions. In Domaşnea during the GAC's first year (1963), when almost no one went to work in the farm, a brigade leader had the idea of sending people to cultivate the land they had previously owned. This

[45] 164, Verdery interview.

[46] Z. S., Goina interview. The verb used was *s-au muiat*.

[47] ACNSAS, FD, file 7/v. 1 (passim) and ASRI, Fond D, file 4638, 199–200, n.d (RLA).

seemed to help, and Vultur explains why: "Because in people's minds working at random, on anyone's land was nonsense, while working one's own land, even after joining the collective, still had some logic to it, resting on the peasant's mental representation of the tie joining land, property, family, and identity." She adds the following from a respondent: "Well how can you like it when you see you're taken to a place you shouldn't be working. I wanted to go work on my land but I didn't want to work in other places where the land wasn't mine. There are some things that separate people from each other" (Vultur 2003a: 90). Although the brigade leader's solution succeeded at the time, it was not viable in the long-term for mechanized agriculture on consolidated fields. As we indicated above, another (more costly) solution was to bring in workers from elsewhere.

All these changes struck a blow against ideas of the person based on identification with work. Collectivization reduced not just the commitment to work but the self-directed initiative that had accompanied possession in rural ideology, for self-direction could no longer define the person if direction came from the farm leaders. Villagers' work in the collective was the most menial, with decision making reserved for the "experts," trained agronomists who were rarely locals. Until the reforms of the mid-1970s, collectivists could neither direct their own labor process nor exercise control over their pay, which was notoriously bad throughout the communist period.[48] As a respondent from Sântana who had long resisted joining the GAC put it, "How can I go and let them tell me what to do, as if I can't tell myself what to do? Can't I do what they do? I can do even better than they!" (Goina 2003: 50).[49] This aspect of collectivization was perhaps the most widely remarked in our interviews: that collectivization had destroyed peasants' love of work, their work ethic. Because of the manner of its creation, socialist agriculture confronted self-respecting persons with an awkward dilemma: those who thought of themselves as estimable wanted to be hardworking, but not in the context of the farm. A continual flight of labor from collectives was one response. Another was to redefine work not as an integral part of the self-respecting person but in terms of "getting by," often by stealth rather than effort.[50]

[48] This was less true of the remuneration system that evolved in the 1970s, the "global accord" system (see Kideckel 1993: 109–15), but even there, the farm leadership placed severe limits on how much authority the household head might have over the labor process.

[49] An East German collectivist similarly remarked, "As a private farmer I was my own boss, now I'm just a farmhand [*Knecht*] and have to let myself be pushed around by every fop" (Port 2007: 232).

[50] Consider a respondent's comment after the collective farm in Vlaicu was dismantled and private owning restored. Asked if she felt that regaining her land had changed her in any way, this woman replied: "*Yes*! I feel more powerful, prouder, because it's mine, because I'm rich, because things are going well. I hold my head up higher. I'm different now, completely different!" (151, Verdery interview). Both she and others saw the return of their land as a return of their dignity, enabling them to feel like *respectable persons*.

Challenges to the Ethical Person: Theft and Getting By

If it was no longer possible to be a respectable person through the virtues associated with owning and work, then what were the alternatives? Our interviews as well as our long experience in socialist Romania make it clear that this was a problem. Both before and after 1989, villagers complained that it was difficult to be an ethical person under socialism without resorting to a dual system of values, engaging in unseemly behavior such as lying and stealing to support one's family. Before collectivization, respondents maintained, honesty was prized (doubtless in part a retrospective romanticization): for example, "Your word was your word, a promise was a promise" (Lațea 2003: 15). Village status hierarchy was mediated through obligations that bound people such as godparents and godchildren together in the rhythms of social exchange based on an ethic of reciprocity. By contrast, villagers saw the Party's methods of dealing with people—its own included—as having eroded honesty and social trust. Cadres did not honor promises they made, especially to a class enemy. Lying, stealing, and falsifying the facts became customary practice, in what respondents view as a general debasement of moral personality. In a memoir written after 1989, a man from Ieud explained how this happened:

> They came down from the District [offices], all sorts of people, workers and intellectuals, but mostly Party activists, who would try to persuade you, nicely but with all kinds of threats too, depending on the situation of each family, because if they couldn't talk you into it they'd [do it by force] . . . they'd lie to us, saying that they'd give us [something] . . . [they'd lie to us] in one form, the people would lie to them in another form. Then the stealing began because they'd promise we'd get [something] and we didn't and the people, seeing that they wouldn't get what they'd been promised, to make ends meet, they started stealing from the collective. . . . And now theft is number one. It's all come down to the saying "because he knows how to get by." So a person who would lie and steal could scrape together something around the house. But a person who knows how to get by is a two-faced liar and thief. Honest work won't get you very far, you can get by, but you can't even do that properly. We've become a people [nation] that doesn't seem to be able to tell the truth anymore.[51]

Owing to the low level of pay in the collective, people found it difficult to make ends meet without stealing, an activity they presented to us as acceptable so long as the theft was from the collective rather than from an individual. A widespread view was that "[h]e who doesn't steal from the state is stealing from his family." Respondents preferred to say they were "taking" rather than "stealing" from the collective farm, and they justified doing so because the farm used their land, or paid them too little for their labor. Bodó offers an example: "On

[51] B. S., "Cum s-o făcut colectivul la Ieud," unpublished memoir, n.d.

the way back from work in the fields, the head of the household picks up ears of corn and urges the children to do the same, to look for the larger and riper ones and take home 'as much as we can, because they took them from us anyway'" (2003: 50; see also Verdery 2003: 65–69). Theft was one of the forms of agency available to people who felt they had been expropriated of their capacity for initiative and self-direction in work.

Besides stealing from the collective, villagers had to learn to get by in other ways different from before. As indicated in the quotation above from Ieud, they placed increasing value on the ability to cope, to fend for oneself and one's family (*a se descurca*), the person thus gifted being called *descurcăreț*, "resourceful" or "clever." Usually implying shrewdness and a certain hesitation in applying scruples, this ideal was silent on the values of hard work and honesty, which might be insufficient for family welfare in the new conditions. Ruefully though our respondents might admit it, such resourcefulness could now win greater admiration than did honesty. It was not, of course, a new quality, merely one whose valence had shifted.

Party workers had to combat such resourcefulness right from the start—in response to 1950s food requisitions, for instance. Although ostensibly quotas were unavoidable, in fact this was not so. A former collector gave Kligman an example: "I had two cows in the barn but I declared only one, and with the other I could manage my quotas better, since your quota was set for one cow but you were milking two, so you could get by better."[52] A particularly clever peasant from Măgina got his total reduced in the following manner. According to a villager, one day comrade Újvárosi, the district head of collections, came into the village and went to the residence of Han Vasile, demanding that he (in the words of a witness)

> give pork, beef, or grain, whatever he was asked to give, and he—it was just him and his wife, they didn't have children—said, "I won't, I won't give [anything] and right now I'm going to go hang myself." He was clever in a way, he was clever . . . and he went to look for some rope and he went toward a tree rope in hand, and Újvárosi got scared, and he got so scared he started saying never mind, never mind, it's not that bad . . . and he got up and took off.[53]

A final example from Ieud shows comparable talent:

> I had two cows when I lived in the village, and I would yoke them because I didn't have any oxen. As I was going down the road with the cart, Grigore the collector saw me. I go home and put the cows in the barn. It was noon. My brother-in-law comes and says, "Hey Ștefan, come outside." And there he asks: "How many cows do you have?" And he sends one of the guards to see how many cows I have in the barn.

[52] V.P.T., Kligman interview. This practice depended on having successfully declared fewer animals than one actually had, when officials took the farm census.

[53] FI01, Țărău interview.

> Because the guy who saw me plowing with the cows reported me. They told me to give several thousand liters of milk from the two cows. "Fine," I say. "You won't taste any milk from me!" Grigore, Pintuoaiă's son, also lived here and we were friends so I told him about my problem. I'd need a barren cow, one that doesn't give any milk and isn't about to calve. So I can take the cow to the vet and get an exemption from the milk quota. So the guy gave me his cow and I went to [the village of] Rozavlea to see the vet. The vet examined it and gave me a certificate and I got them off my back.[54]

This kind of cleverness was a vital means of getting by and manipulating the system. It might include cooperating with local officials, perhaps reporting on or even denouncing one's fellow villagers, and engaging in other forms of behavior hardly consonant with the old person-ideal. Villagers became fearful, and that led them to do things they might otherwise have thought unworthy. Threats that their children would be expelled from school or lose urban jobs generated anxiety, leading to compromises.

Our experience in Romania confirms that theft and these various survival strategies were in reality a major problem for collectives, but it is worth dwelling for a moment on respondents' continually insisting on theft and lying, in their discourse about the past. We noted above that for peasants, the old status ideals emphasized visibility. People with land, many relatives, and control of the labor process had been *visible people* (*oameni văzuți*), central to village social and political life. Everyone could *see* the crowds of workers on the fields of high-status villagers at peak periods, that their cattle were numerous and fat, their crops well tended; everyone could see how many times their carts toiled through the village at harvest time, groaning with produce; they had something to *show* for their work and possessions (see also Verdery 2003: chapter 4).[55] Their social embeddedness was evident in displays of hospitality, in the size of their weddings, the numbers of people at their funerals. The emphasis on honesty speaks to the same preoccupation with visibility, with surfaces, with transparency, in their representation of precommunist times. The communist preoccupation with hidden enemies and states of mind, however, negated the premise of visibility as the test of worth, moving the evaluative gaze from surfaces to interiors. Communism was about things that were hidden, that were not as they seemed—anonymous denunciations, deceit, taking things under cover of darkness, hiding in the mountains, ferreting out sabotage. Visibility, it had turned out, was perilous; it marked one, drawing unwelcome attention. The talents necessary to survival involved staying out of view and, as we discuss elsewhere, remaining silent. Accordingly, practices of personhood would migrate inward, toward resourcefulness and coping.

[54] I. S., Kligman interview.

[55] This language of "showing" comes from Bodó, personal communication, concerning the Odorhei district. Fully aware of the context, local Party leaders understood that villagers could also see these same "visible" people visibly humiliated through public unmaskings, beatings, and so on.

We have been discussing various ways of getting by, many of them seen as morally questionable. The preoccupation with getting by was an effect of the bureaucratization of rural life, in which resources became a function of one's position in a far-flung organizational system. No longer available to be mobilized by families through their own endowments, resources were caught in the Plan. Villagers would have to get by through finding their way to crumbs in the interstices of the Plan, gaining access to them via the connections and friendships we described above. Could they experience "getting by" as a form of agency, in comparison to the self-directed initiative of before?

In our interviews and conversations with villagers, we were struck by the frequency with which their language suggested, precisely, a lack of agency. Large numbers of them denied, for instance, that it was possible to influence the authorities—that there was any way of avoiding one's quotas, even in a village where one collector did jail time for having helped people reduce their obligations. More generally, we noted in our discussions a tendency for respondents to depict themselves as passive, as people to whom things happened. This image conflicts with the energetic and inventive strategies we have just described, revealing a sharp divergence between representation and reality. Far from seeing themselves as self-directing agents, our respondents tended to characterize themselves as lacking in agency and to attribute responsibility elsewhere.

Action and Responsibility

Many people represented themselves to us as helpless victims, having no choice. Vultur expresses it thus: "It is fairly typical and frequent for respondents to report the actions of power at an impersonal level, as an indeterminate 'them,' in relation to which the victims are passive receptacles, like objects" (2003a: 40). Passerini (1992: 11) expresses the more general point, noting the "impact on memory of feelings of guilt and complicity. A widespread attitude of victimization can be found in testimonies of people who lived under totalitarian regimes, expressed by laying the blame on power and on their own helplessness, as if nothing could be done to resist domination." In our interviews we found a number of retrospective images of "passivity." These include the large majority of our respondents who affirmed that quotas had to be paid and there was no way of getting around them, even though others had told us precisely how to do so: "They took *everything*, there was nothing we could do [*Au luat TOT, n-aveai ce face*]." "It could get to the point that you didn't have anything left to eat! You had to buy things at the market. . . . You had to give X amount, you had to. Done! You had to give it. You couldn't bargain!"[56] They tended to pass over or

[56] II01, Țărău interview.

to have forgotten important possibilities for action, and this suggests the work of a certain codification of memory. For example, especially in the early and mid-1950s, it was possible to withdraw from collectives, but most of our respondents did not mention it and, when we asked, did not remember it (e.g., Goina 2003: 27). Many also did not recall that people labeled chiaburs could file contestations, often successfully: once a chiabur always a chiabur, they seemed to think.[57]

Another representation of themselves as without agency comes in descriptions of what happened to their belongings once the collective was formed. Again, "They took everything"—carts, plows, horses, cattle, and land. Often the phrasing was in passive or reflexive verb forms: everything was taken from us (*ni s-a luat tot*). But as the following quotations show, such expressions understated agency:

> In one week almost the whole village signed up. We kept our cattle until spring, . . . until they built the stables. Then one day, after they made the stables, they came and took them and put them in the stables. (*Did they come and take them there, or did they have you take them?*) They had us take them. The mayor came and the CAP president and they took them away.[58]
>
> It took about two weeks until everyone joined, the whole village. . . . From then on, "Come on, everyone, tomorrow . . . whatever you have in your yard, oxen, a cow. . . load them in the cart. . . . Get the hoe, get the cart—I had bought a new cart—go with the cart, go with the harrow, go with the plow, go with the spade . . . we put them all in the cart and went and unhitched them there. It made a huge pile [*grămadă*] there.[59]
>
> At collectivization they told a farmer to hitch the cart and get it out of the courtyard. He said he wouldn't. The man, although he wasn't a wheelwright or a carpenter, had made a cart for himself, old-style but a new cart with iron fittings. Two horses with colts, two cows with calves, and three oxen he had to take out of his courtyard! The man said he wouldn't, even if they shot him, they could take them but he wouldn't hand them over himself. He cried after his horses, so the leaders had to send another man to hitch the horses and get them out of the courtyard, cart and all.[60]

In the first passage, the respondent is so wedded to the idea of his possessions being *taken away* that even after he has just said he himself took them, he repeats that officials took his things from him. The next speaker distances himself from the event differently, acknowledging that they took things but then switching from the first to the second person. In these passages, what actually happened—they themselves had to take their things to the farm headquarters—in-

[57] Among the few who remembered otherwise was one whose grandfather had been reclassified owing to the respondent's friendship with the local Party secretary, who had told him outright that they would resolve his petition favorably.

[58] 72, Verdery interview.

[59] D. T., Lățea interview.

[60] 9, Oláh interview.

creases the poignancy of the story, for as the third quotation confirms, it is one thing if people sat passively in their courtyards while someone else took their animals away, and quite another for them to be ordered to remove their animals and other possessions by their own hand. The latter is the more pedagogical practice, training people in obedience to the Party-state.

A number of our respondents represented their relations with the authorities as if they were animals: they were led into collectives "like an ox to the slaughter," "like a pig to be stuck," "like sheep to be milked"; "they put the bridle over our head."[61] Another recalled that the GAC had initially given out a lot of produce, "to attract the others, like when you give corn to a sheep" (Chelcea 2009: 413). Still another used animal imagery to represent helplessness in a different way. "Father didn't want to join. They took his horses from his cart, and he got very angry. It was like they'd taken his hands when they took his horses. He was really fond of them." This suggests both a loss of agency and a somatization of the idea of "donating" to the collective (439).

Still other representations of inaction come from how respondents described the process of signing up, which usually involved lengthy periods of waiting. As we noted in chapter 5, peasants and authorities were working with different temporalities: the authorities were in a hurry to make deadlines and win competitions for signing people up, whereas the peasants were in no hurry at all and could gain a great deal by postponing, waiting for the "Americans to come," etc., in hopes that if people could hold out a while, perhaps the whole communist nightmare would end. Even those who told us they planned to join would "wait and see" first. After waiting and seeing, they said, they finally signed up when they realized they "had no choice," "we had to do it," "there was no escaping it." "Waiting," however, was decidedly a form of action, which might involve subtle verbal strategies. In a particularly striking example, the respondent shows how people might actively manipulate passive imagery:

(*What did you do when they would come to you for persuasion? Did you allow them into the courtyard? How did you talk to them, what did you tell them? Could you talk straightforwardly with them?*)

S. A.: Do you know how it was? You had to look for some reasons, so that you wouldn't say "I don't want to," you'd say "I can't want to" . . . because I'm determined by some . . . I'm determined by something![62]

Here he makes himself passive and works to displace responsibility from himself to some higher level—"determined by something"—the goal being to euphemize personal responsibility and resignify it as necessity, insofar as possible (Lățea 2009: 339). Even local cadres we interviewed might diminish their own

[61] The first three are from several interviews by Lățea in Dobrosloveni (see Lățea 2003), the fourth from M.G., interviewed by Vultur in Domașnea.

[62] S.A., Lățea interview (see Lățea 2009: 338–39).

responsibility, such as the former CAP president who described most of his actions by saying "they sent me," "they put me there," "they made me go," with himself as always recalcitrant,[63] or the local activist who claimed to have hidden in his barn and written his reports without actually going to the villages he'd been assigned.[64]

The allocation of responsibility elsewhere appears, as well, in people's replies to our questions about who signed up early and who late, discussed in chapter 7. Many put themselves among the last, after "most of the village" had already signed up—that is, others had taken the first step. Moreover, as we showed, those others were seen as morally inferior. By claiming that they joined only after everyone else had signed up, respondents displaced responsibility from the individual to the collective, lodging initiative and agency in the community. This way of putting the matter may be preferable to speaking of "passivity" and adds an interesting footnote to our discussion of signing up, in chapter 7. Although persuasion work initially targeted individual household heads, in the end it succeeded only when respectable families—repositories of wealth in people and representatives of community—were allowed to join. The community, not individuals, held the agency that formed the collectives.

* * *

In this section we have been indicating how respondents represent themselves as lacking in personal agency—as recipients of action, as targets rather than agents—and attribute responsibility to outside forces or the community. How might we interpret these representations? Are they an effect of socialism, of the postsocialist years, or perhaps merely of the interview situation? Are the passivity-and-victimhood tropes simply an established form of emplotment in East European "cultures of complaint"? In official history telling in Romania (as in much of the region more broadly), the narrative position of victim is well established—we see it, for instance, in history textbooks. Perhaps it is a more attractive position for people to take with us than presenting themselves as failed small-scale heroes ("we resisted but lost"). Do these images suggest the ravages of old age on the capacity for action (nearly all our respondents were over seventy)—especially when the end of socialism had opened possibilities for action that their age prevented them from taking? Alternatively, do people find the post-1989 possibilities for action best highlighted by a past presented as lacking in such possibilities? Do the images show us how our villagers were striving to allocate responsibility for the wretched policies of a now-failed regime they had suffered through and then "got used to"? Would their answers to us have been the same if the communist system had not in the meantime collapsed as mor-

63 186, Verdery interview.
64 197, Verdery interview.

ally bankrupt? (We generally doubt it: after 1989, they would be understandably loath to admit having helped to build the now-failed system; the new default position was more likely to be condemnation than resignation.)

On the basis of our research in the 1970s and '80s, we can say that representations of powerlessness and individual inaction were common then as well. Thus, while not denying the intricacies of the post-1989 interview situation, we wish to suggest that these images have roots in the realities of life under socialism, which promoted a relentless "democratic centralism" in place of autonomous personal initiative. Horváth and Szakolczai observe (1992: 141), "The real strength of the party . . . resided not in institutions or structures, but in keeping individuals in a state of personal dependence." In the Party's ideology of "rational redistribution" (Konrád and Szelényi 1979), subjects would be not active participants but grateful recipients of benefits their rulers decided upon for them—like small children in a family (Verdery 1996: 63). Among the techniques Horváth and Szakolczai identify that undercut people's sense of independent initiative was turning their attention away from daily-life issues they cared about, making them accept that they had no control over these, and encouraging their interest in distant events they could not control, such as the Korean war (1992: 127).[65] Another was to nullify initiative while claiming to promote it—a classic example being the very process of joining the collective, as authorities repeatedly insisted that people were to join only through "willing consent" while in fact forcing them in.

The subject disposition such techniques produced was dependency, rather than the autonomous self-direction of the "modern subject." The "vanguard Party" attitude of Romanian communism cultivated a disposition that would root action in initiative from above, where knowing was lodged in experts rather than in lowly peasants. Increasingly dependent on the state for their well-being, socialism's subjects had become wards of the bureaucracy (Kligman 1998: chapter 1). Lățea (2009) suggests that this kind of dependency made them "captives" of the Party-state, a "captivity" that applied to all citizens, regardless of their relation to the Party (see chapter 7). One of Lațea's key respondents, himself a retired middle peasant, commented, "Those who were empowered [by the Party] were, at the same time, obligated to it."[66]

Beyond this, however, we note that the language of blaming and evasion of responsibility coursed through the entire socialist system, not just the ex-post-facto comments of our respondents. What else was the Party's obsession with

[65] This could backfire: for example, some peasants refused to join until they could see how the Korean War turned out (ACNSAS, FD, file 5/1950, 57).

[66] Lățea 2003: 29. The sense of *luați la putere* (those who were integrated into the Party whether as apparatchik or employee) simultaneously signifies *luați la întrebări* (available to be questioned, or having responsibilities to the Party) and captures the reciprocal dynamic between the state and its citizens. Lățea uses "captive" more restrictively than we do here (see our discussion of joining the GACs, in chapter 7), but we find the concept more broadly useful.

sabotage, with hidden enemies, with chiaburs and "politicals"; what else the motivation for show trials and for sacrificing "unmasked" comrades, for rituals of verification and self-criticism? Installing socialism in a recalcitrant country produced upheaval and massive unintended consequences, so things rarely went well; someone had to be blamed, then purged. As the society became ever more bureaucratized, with employment and resources gathered up into the Plan, everyone was potentially vulnerable. Moreover, the practice of purging wrought havoc on personal responsibility. "The system" or "they" made me do it: us/them, a fractal distinction that could be applied at any level, became a prime means of allocating responsibility elsewhere. (Was this in part the effect of a bureaucratic organization immobilized by crosscutting clientelism and personalistic ties?) Yet, as our examples of "getting by" have amply shown, personal initiative was in rich supply, especially in the figure of the clever and resourceful (*descurcăreț*) person whom villagers regarded with such ambivalence. If the main ways of exercising initiative were morally suspect, perhaps thinking ex post facto of oneself as passive was preferable.

In discussing passivity and initiative we do not intend a paean to the autonomous actor of western individualism as the social-scientific model for agency, a notion decisively rebutted by Asad (2000), Mack (2008), and many others. That was not the kind of self-directed initiative the older person-ideal upheld, for such persons were always also embedded in their socialities. Our aim has been to explore the effects of collectivization on those ideals. In so doing, we believe we see traces of everyday life under socialism, with the new dependent subject disposition it cultivated. Within the resulting political and bureaucratic subordination, a certain kind of action emerged, one dedicated to getting by and to promoting the welfare of one's household, however one could.

Conclusion

We have described in this chapter the consequences of subsuming village communities within formal organizations that bureaucratized relations of family, social status, and work. The organizational scheme of collective farms provided new kinds of work as well as a grid for the location of resources; villagers sought to appropriate this grid by cultivating personal ties to those located within it. In this way they shaped the Romanian Party in a "traditional" rather than a "modern" direction, to use Jowitt's terms, refusing its charismatic impersonality and insisting on something more personal.

This chapter has shown even more of a process we have emphasized throughout concerning the Soviet blueprint: its susceptibility—like all comparable designs—to extensive modification and negotiation as it moved out into the Romanian countryside. Collectivization was intended to provide the basis for a more productive, industrialized agriculture and for raising the level of civilization in the countryside so as to give birth to a rural "new socialist person." The material we have presented shows the bureaucratization of village families, work, and senses of self, with unfortunate effects on labor motivation and possibilities for ethical living. People's attempts to make do within the confines of their politicized existence included not only domesticating their bureaucratic organization personalistically but also engaging in various practices they saw as having dubious morality. One might say that Romanian collectivization took the Soviet blueprint to its logical conclusion. The Romanian peasantry bore the heavy costs of that experiment.

Subduing the peasantry remained a constant struggle for Party leaders until they announced the campaign's "successful" completion in 1962, though in reality this struggle continued for many more years. Because none of the changes accompanying it happened smoothly, they had repeatedly to adjust their policies and tactics to accommodate unforeseen circumstances, both internal and external. Conditioning their accommodation, as we have seen, were multiple crosscutting variables: ecology, location, religion, nationality, local politics, and so on. In all circumstances, cadres had to work not only *against* "traditional" village organization but also *with* it, if the pedagogies for learning new ways of thinking, acting, and being were to hold sway. The new system disrupted the old in fundamental ways, introducing a new mentality, morality, and work ethic that proved (surprisingly, for some) difficult to dislodge after 1989. To the extent that learning these new socialist ways entailed "forgetting" former practices (such as celebrating secular rather than religious holidays, or privileging Comrades—with a capital C—rather than chiaburs), we have nevertheless seen that the *habitus* of traditional social organization was not readily eradicated. Peasants did learn to speak a new language and to work in brigades (effectively or not), but they as readily relied on kin relations to make their way in the ever-expanding socialist bureaucracy. Despite divesting chiaburs of economic capital, cadres failed to corrode their social capital fully and could complete the collectivization campaign only by acknowledging their status. In the end, cadres' efforts to break through village organization succeeded only by recourse to many of the community's own organizing principles; this, in turn, compromised the result.

These kinds of conclusions enable us to nuance the question of "resistance" so important to discussions of the end of communism. During the socialist period, Romanians were often represented as "passive" by people who wanted more overt signs of resistance to tyranny from them—something more like Hungary in 1956 or Poland in 1980—and as not to have offered substantial resistance to their regime. The history of Romania's collectivization provides irrefutable evidence to the contrary: Romanian peasants engaged in constant resistance to collectivization, in multiple forms, confounding the Party's projects and causing it to modify its plans. Despite the exercise of massive force and the undeniable disruption of social relations and practices in the countryside, the communists had to reckon with the peasantry. Given the will of both Romanian and Soviet Party leaders to collectivize, as well as the forces arrayed against the peasantry, there was no way they could have escaped it. Nevertheless, within a communist rule much more oppressive than those of Hungary or Poland, Romanians found ways of first struggling valiantly against collectivization and then pursuing their own life projects within its confines. (That some of the means conflicted with their sense of moral behavior only sharpened their dilemmas.) Even if the Party's power was authoritatively established by the time the campaign ended, the diverse repertoire of challenges that so many peasants posed to the regime dogged its footsteps for the rest of its existence. Their violent opposition had compelled reciprocal levels of violence detrimental to the desired outcome, and their less visible forms of resistance as collective farmers reduced the effectiveness of Romania's socialist agriculture. In this sense, we can align Romania with Fainsod's judgment, in *How Russia Is Ruled*: "The peasantry is the Achilles heel of Soviet Communism" (1953: 442).

Conclusion

> The regime was someone else's doing. This was Russian communism. We were not in control of our destiny; Stalin was the leader.[1]

> They wanted to change the spiritual and economic views and economic power of the population precisely because a person without a solid economic base can be more easily manipulated in every way.[2]

> Taking full responsibility, we meet today to lay to rest a somber chapter in our country's past. . . . For Romanian citizens, communism was an imposed regime . . . a totalitarian regime both begun and ended through violence. It was a regime of oppression, which stole five decades of Romania's modern history, trampled the law and obligated citizens to live with lies and in fear. . . . We have the necessary data to condemn Romania's communist regime without right of appeal. A democracy without memory is one in a state of grave suffering. We must not forget, so that we do not repeat the mistakes of the past.
> —*Traian Băsescu, President of Romania, December 18, 2006*[3]

On December 18, 2006, at a joint session of the two chambers of Romania's Parliament, President Traian Băsescu officially condemned the former communist regime and its assault on Romania's people and history. This formal condemnation—for many, long overdue, for others, unfounded—added political ballast to the fierce struggles over history and memory that the collapse of communism unleashed.[4] Lest President Băsescu's words have silencing effects, scholarship must continue to explore the possibilities for historical understanding that the regime's collapse has opened and must strive to prevent their premature foreclosure—a goal we hope to promote with this book.

Our research benefited enormously from the window of opportunity in which

[1] I. S., Kligman interview.

[2] B. S., Kligman interview.

[3] Tismăneanu et al. 2007: 11–12.

[4] It is not our interest to assess the Final Report on which President Băsescu's condemnation was based, or the debates that have ensued. Nonetheless, although we are fully aware of the moral impetus for the president's declaration, we believe that a sweeping condemnation of communism as a system—rather than a sustained examination of its crimes—may inadvertently undermine the nuanced chronicling of that era's complexity. Signs of the heated responses it would evoke erupted during the Parliamentary session when Cornel Vadim Tudor, then head of the ultranationalist Greater Romania Party (and former Ceauşescu-era sycophant), along with others, disrupted the proceedings. On the opposing positions, see, for example, Ernu et al. 2008 and Tismăneanu forthcoming).

we conducted it: older respondents who were adults during the collectivization campaign were still alive, archives were being opened, and the codification of memory was less formalized than it soon became through the influence of print, visual, and oral memory markers, including President Băsescu's condemnation. Indeed, as we have shown, access both to those who lived through the period and to increasingly available documentation has given rise to a greatly enriched, multivocal—some might say, cacophonous—history of the recent past, which had for the most part been an ideologically scripted, black and white rendering of events. Employing multiple methods, we have sought to build knowledge of collectivization by presenting it as a massive social engineering project whose technologies were mediated through daily practices of kinship, rural temporalities, and status ideals. The tensions and confusion that project aroused as people contested it, negotiated their way through it, and adapted to it made the process far from straightforward—as are all state and nation-building endeavors, in fact. Rather than ask whether the process succeeded or failed, our aim has been to reveal the complexities of the process and the nuances that individual and community relations brought to it. In these concluding remarks we summarize our main points and seek to extend our analysis, addressing broader comparative questions about the socialist variant of modern state-making and the connections we have found among the Party-state, persons, and property forms.

Of Blueprints and Cadres

The Soviet Union exported the revolutionary technology of collectivization to its satellites, providing the blueprint along with Soviet advisors to guide them. This blueprint set out the parameters for establishing collectives: new methods to improve agricultural production, a new institutional infrastructure, and an arsenal of pedagogical techniques with which cadres were to enlighten peasants and discipline dissenters. Yet, as we have seen, collectivization was not carried out in a uniform manner anywhere. Blueprints may provide a plan, but social practices are not so easily hammered or welded into place. We have shown here the limits of the Soviets' attempt to impose a technology even more unsuited to Romania than it had been in the Soviet Union, and we have emphasized forces modifying the blueprint. Romania's small and weak Communist Party, dependent on the Soviet Union, faced a largely agrarian population that offered heavy resistance. Complicating their task was the ongoing strength of the country's interwar fascist movement in both rural and urban areas, among all social strata. Inherent in the Party's small size was its inadequate supply of trained cadres, necessitating some reliance on personnel brought over from the bourgeois era and on others whose loyalty to the Party was untested. These facts distinguish Romania from countries with smaller rural populations (e.g., Czechoslovakia, Poland, Hungary), larger communist parties (e.g., Czechoslovakia, East Germany), and different agrarian politics (e.g., Bulgaria, where the popular Agrarianists led a significant cooperative movement).

Although the structural features of Romania's collectivization may have followed the Soviet architecture, the above characteristics caused its interior design to vary greatly over time and place. Where people lived (in agricultural flatlands, fishing or remote mountain villages), what social positions they inhabited (class, nationality, political, gender, and generation), and how cadres carried out the mission of creating GACs (cajoling or coercing consent) together shaped the contours of variation. The impossibility of imitating Soviet practice required compromises of many kinds. Because collectivization involved such a large percentage of Romania's populace—in contrast to, say, Hungary or Czechoslovakia—it was the single most far-reaching policy the Party undertook, and its compromises thus ramified widely throughout society.

Central to our account have been Party cadres, tasked with enlightening peasants about the virtues of collectivizing. It was primarily they who mediated the struggle between the Party's idealistic goals and peasants' self-understandings, embedded in the changing rhythms and social organization of everyday life in the villages; it was they who had to translate the Party's utopian vision to a largely recalcitrant, uncomprehending audience. Our chapters show the mundaneness of revolutionary practice, as cadres went about the daily work of overturning a rural social order against often-determined opposition. Gradually learning that they could not impose upon peasants an imported language, set of categories, and social agenda but had to insert their intentions into existing idioms, they improvised ways of drawing peasants into discourse with them. Certain idioms took pride of place: kinship and status inequality, which became objects of mutual appropriation utilized by activists and villagers alike, frequently to contrary ends. Cadres understood these idioms well: whether or not they were members of the communities in which they carried out their revolutionary work, many were products of the very social organization they sought to change.

Vital to the outcome of the campaign were cadres' understanding and implementation of central directives. Given the pressures from the Soviet Union and other quarters, the challenge of fascist strength in the countryside, the influence of the historical parties, and other conditions that favored collectivizing, Party leaders needed results from their cadres. But they could not provide what was most likely to guarantee success: investment funds, agricultural machinery, and other resources to set up collectives that would work well and attract new members without coercion. Moreover, because many cadres lacked the conviction that would make them persuasive to the peasants, they resorted instead to false promises, threats, and physical force. Leaders kept asking cadres to produce the impossible—to bring in unattainable quotas, to triple their peasant recruits—which caused activists to complain repeatedly that they simply could not cope.[5] Once Party leaders realized that they must utilize activists who were local and not just those sent out from Party headquarters, they were forced to delegate the capacity for action downward (though they might also give orders). Even if they did not, overstretched cadres would seize for themselves the opportunity to act, sometimes violently. Cadres could obtain results only by exercising initiative—which many had neither the training nor the ideological commitment to use properly.

In the early years above all, owing to inexperience, lack of administrative capacity, and insufficient infrastructure, the center could not control its cadres. They would under- or overexecute their instructions—in part to manage local conditions for which the center could not adequately plan, in part to cultivate their own careers, and in part because many neither understood nor were truly convinced of the benefits of collectivization. They abused their authority and misinterpreted Party directives, evading or outright subverting proper implementation. For this they might be rewarded, or punished. With the resources accorded them, however, the task was near impossible without violence. Whether or not the center ordered repression is less important than the structural situation of the cadres for whom it proved indispensable—be that in Romania, the Soviet Union, Bulgaria, or elsewhere.

These processes were not planned as such. In all likelihood, not planning but confusion and improvisation prevailed at the outset. Until Gheorghiu-Dej firmly consolidated his power by ousting the Pauker faction, the contradictions at the center resulted in contradictory messages lower down, contributing to turmoil in the countryside. No leadership can maintain full control while simultaneously creating new institutions and its own authority, especially when the leadership itself is divided. Cadres were not thinking strategically about "creating new subjectivities": they were trying desperately to figure out how to get things done in a fluid situation. If, following communism's collapse in 1989, tremendous confusion reigned while political authority, practices, and institutions were being transformed, we can only imagine how much more chaotic were the years of its beginnings in the early 1950s. The 1990s too were a period of technology transfer in an unpropitious setting, with "experts" and unprepared cadres acting in a relative power vacuum, as factions at the top fought over the direction of change. Then, too, improvisation and abuses carried the day, as those implementing *de*collectivization in the countryside adapted instructions to local conditions and their own advantage, compromising the new property order in the process, just as had happened before (see Verdery 2003).

Unfortunately, the Party's weakness relative to its Soviet mentors and its peasantry set up constant pressure for the leadership to regain control, hindering the development of more effective solutions. Goina (2009) observed, for instance, that where local officials engaged in "flexible accommodation" to in-

[5] Thanks to Dorin Dobrincu and Constantin Iordachi for suggesting these points.

ternal and external opportunities and constraints, the result was more consensual relations and greater participation in the Party's project. In his research site, Sântana, even if collectivists remembered the collectivization process unhappily, they recalled their experiences with their model collective "New Life" in largely positive terms. The GAC president was an adroit leader who skillfully developed a flexible stance that enabled him to exploit local resources to the collective's benefit, and he won members' willing participation by providing them with greater access to health care, diverse educational and leisure opportunities, and so forth. Such benefits were tangible and enduring, not simply rhetorical flourishes. Evidence of his effectiveness was that these villagers were loath to disband their collective after 1989.[6]

This example suggests that had the Party provided more resources to the GACs and allowed farm officials greater autonomy in setting up and running their farms, the outcome might well have been more positive.[7] But instead, Party leaders pushed to maintain control, within a more or less uniform, coercive Soviet model. It is hardly surprising, then, that the majority of Romania's peasants did not embrace the collectives with enthusiasm. What might have happened, we wonder, if Party leaders had heeded Pauker's advice against "us[ing] methods of forcefully pressuring the peasants to enter the collective farms" (Levy 2001: 109) and had set aside the coercive blueprint in favor of flexible accommodation?

For social science, there is nothing new in observing that blueprints rarely conform to how they are implemented, whether the location be the Soviet bloc, postsocialist transformation, Iraq after Saddam, or colonial situations elsewhere in the world (e.g., Sahlins 1994; Stoler 2009). More interesting is to ask how the effort to impose the model spurred improvisation and innovation, and how the encounter of different social orders and their accompanying cultural templates transformed history. The question applies to the Soviets' attempt to enforce the blueprint not only on Romania but also on their own rural world. Among the outcomes we have emphasized for Romania is the "personalization" of socialist society. Its sources were ubiquitous: peasants attempting to "make a bit of friendship" by creating kinship from their bureaucratic relation to a local official, and cadres creating personalistic ties with the peasants, among themselves, and with their superiors. If in theory the Party was to be based (as Jowitt argued) on charismatic impersonalism—an intermediary step to achieving an alternate form of western rational-legal authority—then the personalization of state-society relations challenged any such development. The goal was ostensibly a classless society dedicated to equality among subjects who were commit-

[6] Throughout the 1990s, fewer than 10 percent returned to individual farming in Sântana (Goina, personal communication).

[7] Collectivization was more successful in Bulgaria in this regard (see Creed 1998) and in Hungary (Swain 1985).

ted to the revolution, under the guidance of an impersonal Party bureaucracy. Instead, what emerged was a new system of privilege, an apparatus of cadres dedicated to personalistic connections, and subjects who performed compliance while seeking connections of their own to bypass the Party's dictates. This leads us to ask further about the nature of the bureaucracy and form of modernity peculiar to Soviet-style socialism, at least in its Romanian variant. What kind of modern state did it produce?

An Alternative Bureaucratic Modernity?

In certain important respects, socialist modernity was like familiar Western European forms, with an emphasis on building up infrastructure, educating a citizenry, modernizing means of production, and facilitating capital accumulation through guarantees of property forms, even if these were of a noncapitalist kind. Partisans of Foucault's work on modern governmentality (1991) would find much to recognize as well: government as the right disposition of things, targeted at populations and favoring apparatuses of security; an emphasis on knowledge (here epitomized in historical materialism and its scientific laws of social progress); the creation of disciplines for managing populations; and so on. As for the kind of power proper to these systems, as in other modern states it "is exercised on immediate everyday life, it categorizes individuals and distinguishes them through their individuality, it attaches them to their identity, and it imposes on them a law of truth" (2002: 331). Despite their much-vaunted collectivism, these regimes also individualized through assignment to categories—the "political," the chiabur or poor peasant, the "enemy of the people"—which became truth-bearing identities.

In seeking what might have been distinctive in Soviet-style socialism as we have seen it in Romania, we find ourselves drawn specifically to the nature of its bureaucracy. From Weber on, bureaucracy has been considered a key feature of the modern state and of modernizing projects. Weber saw bureaucracy as "*the* means of transforming social action into rationally organized action. . . . [It] was and is a power instrument of the first order for one who controls the bureaucratic apparatus" (Weber 1978: 987). Scott (1998) elaborated on modern statecraft, focusing on practices that make individuals "legible" or visible, thereby enabling state agents both to "know" and to maintain surveillance over their populations. Legibility enabled "the capacity for large-scale social engineering" (5). To accommodate this process, the growth of institutional and communication infrastructures accompanied expanded bureaucratization with practices that "inscribed, codified, verified, and documented" individual identity (Caplan and Torpey 2001: 3). Yet, as Caplan and Torpey observed (6), such documentary forms "also furnish people with the means . . . to 'write' themselves into life and history. In this, they do not just behave in accordance with the requirements of bureaucratic categories, but create themselves as 'legible' subjects of their own lives."[8]

Here, Lefort's insistence (1986: 119–20) on viewing bureaucracy as a "social formation" and bureaucratization as the "reordering of a system of domination" is also pertinent to our analysis of the fate of the Soviet blueprint in Romania. What distinguished the modernizing strategies of totalizing regimes such as Romania's from those of western democracies was the scope of the former's intentions, if not always their realization. Institutions across the country, whether in villages, towns, or cities, lacked organizational autonomy and had to hew to Party-dictated goals (although often using very unorthodox means). Party leaders sought to monopolize the public domain and to control the bureaucratic apparatus as well as the accumulation and redistribution of resources. They demanded adherence to the rule of Party law and "consent" to its policies (e.g., individuals joining the collectives of their own free will). The creation of cadres and pedagogies of persuasion set the bureaucratization of social relations in motion; the authority of the Party-state and its mechanisms of rule were shaped through their practices. A new classification system recast former social role models into enemies of the people; new devices for "legibility" created multiple means for identifying and tracking individuals (ranging from employment registers to secret police and penal files); and the authorities extended the state's reach by encouraging vigilant citizens to denounce and inform on family and friends.

Nevertheless, bureaucracy is not only a means of domination but also, as Caplan and Torpey indicate, a site of conflict. The political center could not fully dictate people's daily actions, despite the centralized edifice of bureaucratized relationships it erected to do so. In the early years, it simply lacked the infrastructure to achieve such control either over local authorities, who often managed to exercise a degree of autonomy, or over citizens, who contested their classification as enemies, wrote petitions, or engaged in revolts and other oppositional acts. By the end of the collectivization campaign, however, Party leaders had established extensive discipline and command over both groups. The forms of this subordination were more overt, and more overtly constraining, than those of modern western bureaucratic states.

The effect of increased bureaucracy and bureaucratization was consequential for the Party-state, dramatically extending its penetration into everyday life. Perhaps another feature distinguishing these regimes among contemporary state forms was their mixture of distance and intimate invasion. From the rural point of view, authority was increasingly exteriorized, its center far removed from the village institutions that had previously served as the loci of rule. While there is nothing unusual about exteriorizing authority—it is a general aspect of

[8] See Jochen Hellbeck's excellent work on this point (2006).

modernization—in Romania that authority was simultaneously distant yet omnipresent. Whether in the form of cadres or secret police, insiders or outsiders, the Party-state invaded private life, colonizing and bureaucratizing it. Activists targeted the family and kin relations; cadres forced their way into peasant homes to carry out their persuasion work; collectors ransacked them in search of hidden flour; and so on. Such invasions sowed disharmony or promoted solidarity among family members, reconfiguring their relations.

It is worth dwelling further on the police function in these societies, which we believe was overdeveloped relative to other modern states. Indeed, according to Hungarian sociologists Horváth and Szakolczai (1992) in their study of Hungarian Party cadres, characteristic of these systems was that they extended to the whole of civil society the police function of harmonizing individuals with the common good—a function developed first in early modern France (165ff.; see also Martin n.d.). We would go further, underscoring the role of surveillance in socialist states. Because the ideological commitment of cadres, state officials, and Party members was always in doubt, the dual Party/state structure adopted in the Soviet Union to accommodate a similar lack of trained cadres fit Romania's situation rather well. This dual structure institutionalized the twin practices of surveillance and vigilance, exercised throughout Romanian society. The Soviet KGB maintained surveillance over the Romanian Party leadership, who maintained surveillance over cadres at all levels, who maintained surveillance over one another and over the population. Although surveillance had its specialists (the Securitate), it was doubled by vigilance from people of all kinds, who were expected to exercise it lest an enemy attempt sabotage or sneak into a position of responsibility. If their vigilance uncovered suspicious behavior, they should proceed with unmaskings and denunciations. In fundamental contrast to the liberal state's ideal of trust and transparency, these practices simultaneously engaged citizens in the repressive apparatus of the state and institutionalized mistrust at the heart of the political system.

We have pointed to several contradictory consequences of this institutionalization of systemic mistrust. One was that the doubling of state and Party bureaucracies produced immense organizational problems, with multiple overlapping controls and huge duplication of effort—very costly for a system lacking resources and reliable political workers. A second was that while Party leaders strove to create a ruling class with no social ties—a class of eunuchs[9]—wholly dependent on the Party, the "eunuchs" strove in turn to cover their backs by creating precisely these kinds of ties by various means. A third was to create new opportunities for agency, new subject relations, and new kinds of persons, as everyone from elites to ordinary citizens was handed the instruments for bringing the repressive apparatus down upon their fellows—that is, all were made the Party's accomplices (see Gross 1988). The incitement to vigilance

[9] Thanks to James Scott for this wording.

formed new sensibilities, encouraging citizens to "see with the eyes and act with the heart of the party" and thereby extend its reach (Lampland n.d.: 25). But at the same time, the Bolshevik idea of the vanguard party diminished agency for all but cadres and ranking Party members, rendering the others largely dependents of the Father Party—a less agentive subject relation. In brief, these societies mobilized citizen energies differently from other modern states.

If we follow Foucault in seeing modern governmental forms as leading citizens to internalize the norms guiding conduct, then socialist governmentality was distinctive in that citizens learned not only to watch themselves but also to watch and be watched by others. They learned to participate directly in the repressive apparatus, in ways that western states began to approximate only after 2001, with efforts to contain the "terrorist threat." The image of the panopticon popularized by Bentham and Foucault places the observer unseen at the center, with the observed arrayed around him visibly. Perhaps a better image for socialist systems is that the citizen is placed at the center with multiple kinds of observers arrayed around him vigilantly. Both forms place all citizens under surveillance, individualizing them. The difference is a matter of the intensity of that surveillance, the extent to which it enters into the individual psyche (rather than being lodged in multiple social relations external to the individual, as in socialism), and the implications for subjects' behavior in response. Some enter into the policing of others, thickening the web of surveillance; some seek to protect themselves by cultivating relations with others they hope will prove loyal; but either way, socialism's individualization of its citizens proceeds through network embeddedness, rather than through rendering them autonomous of social connections. It is not by chance that socialist citizens see the world in terms of "us" and "them," rather than "me" and "you." To clarify this, we return to the issue of changed property regimes and the connection of property with personhood and Party-state.

Property, Persons, and Party-State

In exporting their revolutionary ideals and practices, Soviet leaders intended not only to modernize production but also to transform the organization and exercise of power. Throughout this book we have emphasized the intersection of state, property, and person and have contended that collectivization was instrumental in constituting Romania's Party-state. We might now draw together the strands of that argument. The communists began by parasitizing the state apparatus of "bourgeois" Romania, first gaining control of key ministerial portfolios (justice, transportation), then with Soviet assistance installing a bogus coalition government. From this vantage point they built up parallel Party structures and altered institutions: education, justice, the media, and so on. The 1945 land reform and subsequent nationalizations of land and industry took them into the institution of property. Collectivization intensified that move, drawing them further down the organizational scale from ministries and national organizations into villages. There, they began trying to convert status groups into classes so as to foment class war. Divergences from Russian communal village forms, however, made the Soviet experience unhelpful as a guide for cadres dealing with villages of smallholders. Creating chiaburs and agitating among poor peasants did not produce the expected class struggle or a poor-peasant groundswell in favor of GACs; Romania's cadres had to try to persuade individual families, one at a time, to sign up. But in taking on this task, they had less guidance not only from the Soviet past but also from preexisting patterns in their own country, for previous Romanian governments had not intervened intensively at the household level.

That level, however, was precisely where "property" was lodged: in relations within and among households. There lies the land necessary to forming collectives, but even households that owned no land were deeply implicated in property, which concerns broad patterns of appropriation within social and cultural relations. Among the most critical of these relations are those involving self and person. Rural Romanian status ideals held that a complete and worthy person must control his labor process and its product, facilitated by having land and animals and by wealth in people—that is, by centrality in extended social networks. Collectivization meant losing possession of one's land and animals, losing the resources that attracted other people into one's networks, losing control over one's work and harvest and, perhaps most important, losing the ability to provide adequately for one's family. Quotas upset peasants by diminishing their control of the product, and joining the collective deprived them of control over their work. They were particularly angered by having to sign petitions that said they were joining because they couldn't manage on their own, which struck a blow to both their pride and their personhood. Because matters of control over land, labor, and its product were mediated by networks and kinship groups—that is, because Romania's rural property relations centered on embeddedness in social networks rather than on individuals—cadres found they had to intervene in kinship relations. This led them into the heart of community reproduction, where they sought to decouple land from personhood and to remake village life. The consequence was multiple forms of peasant resistance.

How is this related to the creation of the Party-state? The answer to that question depends partly on how one understands the concept of "state." The more or less standard conception of the state has long seen it as a bounded entity controlling a territory and behaving as a unitary, autonomous actor through the decisions of leaders, who exercise "legitimate violence" in its interest. Using this, we can connect the Party-state to collectivization as the arena par excellence within which the Dej faction consolidated its position against its rivals. Because the fate of agriculture was so central to the Party's designs for Romanian communism, the positions carved out in debating it became the pivot for defining the identity of the Party-state. Or, using a similar conception, we could point to the combination of a weak political center with few reliable cadres facing a large rural population; this inevitably meant that the center would lose control over lower levels, producing tendencies to feudalization (which Jowitt has seen as characteristic of Romanian communism).[10] An institutionalist conception of the state brings some alternative insights. For example, if cadres' attacks on village reproduction generated peasant resistance that provoked ever-greater repression, this would shape the Party-state by increasing the preponderance of the police and security wings in the political apparatus. Both conceptions, although dynamic, say nothing about the social and cultural relations of rural property that collectivization affected.

The conception we have employed here, by contrast, understands the state as a contradictory ensemble of institutions, projects, and practices rather than an organized actor, and as a cultural and relational (rather than largely institutional) phenomenon in which subjectivities are a central element. From this vantage point, it is easier to see how dismantling property at the level of peasant households changed the Bolshevik project that Romania imported. In the Soviet Union, peasant smallholding had only shallow roots, and communal forms had proved very resilient against efforts to undo them.[11] There, peasant resistance to collectivization was a defense of community, elites, and church. In Romania, with its predominantly smallholding peasantry, resistance was largely a defense of households and family livelihood. Thus, collectivization required new practices and technologies, such as colonizing kinship, forms of house-to-house persuasion that magnified the need for scarce cadres, and other techniques less necessary in the Soviet context.

This view of state formation meshes with a relational and cultural view of property. Collectivization drew the Party away from law and policing into the rhythms of village life and its forms of sociality: ties of kinship, long-standing practices of hospitality and mutual aid, ritual kinship linking households of unequal means, forms of feeding the ancestors whose substance descendants shared with the land they worked. It brought cadres face to face with peasant senses of personhood, with a *habitus* of giving or receiving deference, with the attendant feelings of inferiority in the unpropertied and of competence and dignity in those who controlled their own work or that of others. It was in dealing with these aspects of property—with property as kinship and personhood—that Party-state creators found their greatest challenge. Collectivization could *only* be a localized and relationally embedded process; the organizational and cultural forms it encountered and the resistances they entailed modified the project and thereby the Party-state that attempted it.

As we have shown throughout this book, for the peasantry the rural status

[10] Jowitt, personal communication.

[11] See, for example, Fitzpatrick 1994b; Viola 1986.

order permeated social being. This and the other main features of village social organization we have emphasized constituted forms of power, which rested on social hierarchy and on people's embeddedness in social relationships. These forms of power flowed upward against the downward flow of instructions and repression; the ensuing resistance altered the practices of power. In launching a frontal assault on these village institutions, Romania's communists were compelled to adopt practices that affected the *modus operandi* of the state apparatus they were building. Although they were able to "break through" village social organization, they had to make compromises, such as becoming drawn into personalistic relations with peasants. Most important, because a Party leadership desperate for agricultural output had chosen not to liquidate the chiaburs as the Soviets had largely done, Romania's cadres found themselves in retreat before peasant status norms: they had to change tactics to make use of village elites having extensive kinship ties. If whole villages then joined the collectives after months and years of resistance, perhaps it was not just because they "gave up" but rather because they accepted a negotiated solution that had tacitly recognized their values. Only thus could cadres finally recruit them into the project.

We can perhaps see the ongoing effects of the cultural aspects of property in rural status systems even with those villagers who became agents of collectivization. Poor and marginalized people entering the Party's service as cadres took on work of extreme difficulty and danger. How was the Party leadership able to mobilize their energies, for good or ill? Plan targets and socialist competitions may have been enough to motivate some of them, but a more compelling motivator lies in matters of status and personhood: the improved life chances the Party offered those it recruited from among the disadvantaged. The communists *made them somebody*—and for people who had been "nobody" before, retaining their new status was a powerful stimulus. Village status hierarchies had accorded dignity and deference to peasants who had land and "wealth in people"; disdain and psychic injury fell to those who lacked them. Although not every communist functionary or activist came from the latter category, many did. In their work as collectivizers, these cadres had cause every day to be reminded of who they had been. The embodiment of their changed circumstances was the chiabur, that epitomal village "somebody." If poor-peasant cadres sometimes pursued class war too harshly, perhaps that was because those village elites were the people most likely to organize others against the new order—and were thus the prime threat to local cadres' position. Chiaburs represented everything that such people could lose, especially their newfound authority and upward mobility into the ranks of "somebody." For these cadres, failure was not an option: if they did not get results, they would become nobody once again. How they got those results was less important than getting them. The effects of their actions ramified throughout the whole country as well as across the political landscape and entered into the new mechanisms of authority being constituted.

How they got results had substantial implications, however, for rural subjectivities—and thus for the nature of the Party-state, because subjectivities are an essential aspect of state forms. Collectivization affected 77 percent of Romania's population and alienated a significant part of it. Attacking property relations, it attacked the foundations of village life. Because cadres had difficulty persuading peasants with argument, performing consent became persuasion's proxy. We have repeatedly drawn attention to the seminal role of such performances, best exemplified by their being "obligated" to join the collectives of their own "free will." "Truth" generally lay in performing conviction, the result of applying whatever array of persuasive pedagogies proved "convincing"—from more benign forms of propaganda to public humiliation, beatings, or imprisonment. To avoid imitating such negative examples, peasants imitated conviction. We might say that to a Party that introduced imitation (mimesis) as a form of persuading, peasants responded by imitating consent.

Thus began their disaffection with collectivized agriculture, and with it the growth of alienated and performative subjectivities that were a hallmark of Romanian socialism. Performing consent as they joined the collectives led to broader patterns of performing allegiance (see also Yurchak 2006), which eroded the Party's projects. Such performances, we might add, were practiced not only by peasants but by virtually everyone—Party leaders or members compelled to confess their failings in show trials or self-criticism sessions, cadres preparing endless reports in which they paid lip service to the Party's priorities, and later on, everyone in the labor force who acted in accord with the mock slogan, "They pretend to pay us, and we pretend to work." Performing consent became a key survival strategy for all, which drew them into relationships with the state that were both complicitous and duplicitous.

The ways in which peasants performed consent set the stage for the ubiquitous "we-they/us-them" dichotomies that characterized communist rule until its collapse in 1989. As various analysts have shown (e.g., Kharkhordin 1999; Kligman 1998), such dichotomies entered into socialist forms of subjectivity, inscribing an oppositional *habitus* at the core of the Party-state. We agree with Yurchak (2006), however, who argues that to see life under socialism as a matter of "us" versus "them" grossly oversimplifies. This dichotomy is best viewed as a fractal distinction (see chapter 5), whose terms are not strictly differentiated but interpenetrate as they are reproduced at different hierarchical levels. The story of collectivization is complex because it separated people's fates in a complexly layered process. Depending on the context, "we's" could become "they's." "We-villagers" became subdivided into "we" and "they": "we" victims of collectivizing and "they" who perpetrated it. "They-cadres" split into "we" cadres from the village and "they" from outside, or into those who denounced their fellow cadres and those who were purged, as "they" replicated in ever-wider circles upward to Bucharest.

Further complicating these dichotomies were techniques that drew people into dialogue with the Party, whether through denouncing others or defending themselves—contesting the assignment of unfair quotas, writing petitions to dispute their classification as chiaburs, and so on. Such actions complicated individuals' relationships both to the Party-state and to themselves as well. In representing themselves through dichotomous subjectivities, people were able to evade responsibility for what happened in their midst, to see themselves as victims of forces beyond their control and to blame things on an indeterminate "them." In understanding such representations, however, we must again bear in mind that those considered to be "them" were nonetheless related to, often part of, "us."

Given how difficult it is to talk about subjectivities, a complex topic rendered even more so by the static of retrospective interviews, we cannot offer more decisive conclusions on this point, but only indicate its significance. To talk of performative subjectivities is not simply to use a trendy jargon but to indicate questions we might raise about exterior and interior, about how persons or selves become divided and how power both produces and colonizes this division.[12] We indicated in chapter 8 that collectivization ended the "visible" economy on which status and personhood had rested—large and well-tended holdings, carts moving through the village laden with crops, numerous workers on one's fields. During the 1950s it became dangerous to be too visible. As a result, practices of personhood tended to turn inside, toward coping and resourcefulness. They had lost their external material grounding in ownership. Instead, the Party's emphasis on hidden loyalties and motivations, on enemies to be unmasked, created a new kind of interior space hospitable to new forms of subjection to authority—as well as new forms of contesting it.

These remarks bring us back to the links between property and personhood, inviting further speculation. Western property theory sees property as a relation between persons and things, attaching singular items to singular owners. As Marilyn Strathern puts it, "The fact of possession constructs the possessor as a unitary social entity, true whether the owner is acting as an individual or a corporation" (1988: 104). Thus, a unitary relation to things creates unitary personhood. A version of this view underlies an important strain of European political philosophy, as described (using slightly different terms) by John Pocock (1985), according to which property is the foundation of both personality and government. Pocock identifies an ongoing eighteenth-century debate as to which kind of property, landed or commercial, was thought to provide the better material anchor for unified personality. For some, the best anchor of a stable civic personality was land, and commerce threatened that stability with the "hysterical" and "flighty" personality it generated. The debate, which was partly about the proper balance between possession and exchange in society, entered into the thinking of Marx, among others.

[12] The subordination of the self to the power of the state is a general feature of modern state-society relations. Here, we draw attention to the particular forms such subordination took in Romania. Also see Kligman 1998.

The property actions of communist parties amounted to a gamble that transforming property forms would create new kinds of persons, defined less by commerce than by possession—and by possession of new kinds. By collectivizing land, the Bolsheviks and other parties hoped to set up a unitary relation to it that superseded particularistic or individualized (household) interests. Moving the locus of proprietary identity from households to collective- and state-farm entities was to create units of identification and coactivity among the joint owners. The result would not detach property from personhood but would reconfigure their relationship on a larger scale: bearing a unitary relation to supraindividual socialist property would endow collective farmers with a collective consciousness. The Bolsheviks never intended to destroy property. They understood that it is a central political-economic relation, which in complex societies guarantees certain forms of appropriation backed by state power. Launching their rule with confiscations and nationalizations, they signaled only that the new Party-state would not guarantee *bourgeois* property, then inaugurated new forms of *socialist* property that it would back instead. These new forms would support appropriation (and expropriation) by and for the Party toward its redistributive goals, anchoring identities and forms of personhood that were collective. Moreover, the new forms would exclude commerce from personhood by decommodifying land and thereby creating noncommodified relations among the persons defined through it.

This project of creating new socialist persons through socialist property encountered a number of difficulties, however. First, as we have suggested, the forceful manner of collectivization produced not unitary but divided personhood. Second, while renouncing their possessions, middle and well-to-do peasants also renounced their commitment to personhood based on labor—a real cost for a Party that both privileged labor ideologically and needed it developmentally. And third, the assumption that collective consciousness would come from ramping upward the "unitary person" of socialism—by linking it to larger socialist (state and collective) farms—fell afoul of the practices developed to run them. Devolving downward the authority to create those farms also created the "hierarchy of estates of administration" essential to how socialist property worked, as different levels of the political hierarchy acquired competing interests in how to manage it (see Humphrey 1983; Verdery 2003). By working against the desired collective consciousness of socialist property, these competing interests finally helped to bring the system down.

* * *

The experiment with Soviet-style collectives has ended. The rural poverty they hoped to ameliorate, however, has not; if anything, twenty-first-century processes of accumulation and dispossession worldwide have intensified it. New blueprints imported by ambitious experts promise liberation through privatization or microcredits; development consultants ply their pedagogies to break through community structures in the name of prosperity for all. The hope for a better future—that source of so much benefit to humankind, and so much harm—will be more wisely pursued, we believe, if informed by the kinds of analysis we have offered here. Then the painful collectivization of Romania's peasants will at last have borne some fruit.

Appendix I

Project and Participants

Collectivization is a very complex subject, one far exceeding our joint capacities. Therefore, we formulated the project as a multidisciplinary, collaborative endeavor and invited a number of Romanian colleagues to join us, as well as Robert Levy (historian, Academy for Jewish Religion, Los Angeles), Michael Stewart (anthropologist, University College, London),[1] and Linda Miller (legal consultant, New York and Bucharest). The disciplines included history, anthropology/ethnography, sociology, law, and literary criticism. Our main objectives in selecting our research team were to foster cooperation that was not only international and interdisciplinary, but also intergenerational. Toward this end, alongside well-known university professors and senior researchers, we also invited a number of younger researchers. First, we included five Romanians from doctoral programs in the United States or at the Central European University, Budapest. Three were studying with us: Liviu Chelcea and Puiu Lățea with Verdery at the University of Michigan, and Călin Goina with Kligman at UCLA. We added to these Cătălin Stoica, then studying at Stanford University, and Constantin Iordachi, from the Central European University.[2] Our remaining members were (with their affiliations as of 2011):

Julianna Bodó, Professor at Sapientia, Hungarian University of Transylvania, Department of Social Sciences, and Scientific Researcher, WAC (Center for Regional and Anthropological Research), Miercurea-Ciuc;

Dorin Dobrincu, Director, Romanian National Archives (2007–), and Researcher, A. D. Xenopol Institute of History, Iași;

Eugen Negrici, Professor of Literature, University of Bucharest;

Sándor Oláh, Scientific Researcher, WAC;

Marius Oprea, President, Center for the Investigation of the Crimes of Communism in Romania, Bucharest;

Octavian Roske, Associate Professor, University of Bucharest, Faculty of Foreign Languages and Literatures, and Scientific Director/Senior Researcher, National Institute for the Study of Totalitarianism, Bucharest;

[1] Michael Stewart hired additional researchers for his part of the project: Răzvan Stan, Andrea Varga, and Dumitru Budrală. These researchers did not participate in any of the group's meetings, however, although Stan is coauthor of Stewart's final report for the project (2003).

[2] An early member, Zsuzsanna Török, was a doctoral student at the Central European University who had initiated research in Odorhei; she proposed withdrawing in favor of Sándor Oláh, whose research experience in that region was much greater.

Dumitru Şandru, Professor of History, University of Iaşi, and Senior Researcher, A. D. Xenopol Institute of History, Iaşi;
Virgiliu Ţârău, Associate Professor, History Department, Babeş-Bolyai University, and Institute of History, Cluj-Napoca; Vice President, National Council for the Study of the Securitate Archives (2008–);
Smaranda Vultur, Professor of Ethnology, University of the West, Timişoara.

Our researchers' sites were distributed as follows (present-day counties in parentheses): (1) for *Transylvania*: Julianna Bodó, Corund/Korond and Armăşeni/Csíkmenaság, two Hungarian villages from the area inhabited by Szeklers (Harghita); Călin Goina, Sântana commune (Arad); Gail Kligman, Ieud commune (Maramureş); Sándor Oláh, the former district (*raion*) of Odorhei (Harghita); Michael Stewart, Poiana Sibiului commune (Sibiu); Virgiliu Ţârău, the former district of Aiud (Cluj); Katherine Verdery, the village of Aurel Vlaicu (herein, Vlaicu) and parts of Orăştie district (Hunedoara); Smaranda Vultur, Tomnatic commune (Timiş) and Domaşnea commune (Caraş-Severin); (2) for *Moldavia*: Dorin Dobrincu, Darabani commune (Botoşani); Cătălin Stoica, the villages of Vadu Roşca and Năneşti (Vrancea); Dumitru Şandru, Pechea commune (Galaţi); and (3) for *southern Romania*: Liviu Chelcea, Reviga commune (Ialomiţa); Constantin Iordachi, the village of Jurilovca (Tulcea), with a synthetic overview of Dobrogea region; Puiu Lăţea, Dobrosloveni commune (Olt). Additional information about our sites appears in table 0.1 in the introduction.

Our methods combined techniques and sources from all the disciplines represented, with particular emphasis on archival documents, official statistics, legislation, and oral history interviews. In using these sources, we profited greatly from the different experiences and skills of our team members. The historians provided instruction on how to use archives—where to find the various collections, how they were created, what problems to anticipate. The anthropologists, sociologists, and ethnographers provided instruction on oral-historical research—how to devise and conduct semistructured interviews, what issues to anticipate—and underscored the necessity of careful research preparation within a shared conceptual framework.

We held several meetings over the course of five years. An initial planning meeting at UCLA was followed by three working meetings in Timişoara (September 2000) and Bucharest (September 2001 and February 2003). For each meeting, participants prepared summaries of their research, which helped us to develop and maintain a shared approach throughout the project. The Timişoara meeting was essential in consolidating the multidisciplinary character of our research. Over several days, we discussed both the theoretical framing of the project and the two principal methodologies each participant would employ: intensive interviewing and archival research. We also discussed ethical requirements, as governed by the Human Subjects Review protocols of US funding agencies. The second project meeting was disrupted by the events of September 11, 2001, which prevented the attendance of Verdery and Levy, but we were nonetheless able to discuss everyone's progress at this midpoint of the project and resolve some of the methodological problems our team members were encountering. At our final meeting in February 2003, we discussed preliminary versions of papers for an edited volume (Dobrincu and Iordachi 2005; Iordachi and Dobrincu 2009).

Appendix II

Methodology

In our introduction, we briefly raise a number of issues concerning the reliability of our interview and archival data. In this appendix we discuss some of these issues at greater length. We organize them in four sets of points, concerning access to archives, linguistic forms affecting circulation of documents, "heroes and victims," and our relationships with the communities where we worked.

Concerning Access to Archives

Access to documents was an arduous, often serendipitous process. Our experiences varied by the type of archive, for example, national, regional, local, Securitate. Some of us were welcomed and given whatever we asked for; others were treated more warily, perhaps with hints that a small bribe might lubricate access. Some had no difficulty xeroxing documents, yet others found obstacles placed in our way. The differences transcended customary assumptions about "foreign" and "native" researchers, for Verdery had good access while some of the Romanians did not. Access to archives was largely a function of each researcher's personal relations, either with personnel at the archives in question or with well-connected individuals having the authority to open doors, whose attitudes toward our work varied widely. Verdery attributes her ease with access in the Hunedoara branch of the State Archives to long familiarity with the man who became director after 1989, as well as with his predecessor. Kligman, by contrast, had repeated difficulties acquiring material in both the central National Archives and various regional branches.[1] Both Verdery and Kligman received permission to use the archive of the Securitate, probably through their personal connections. Others found archivists to be inappropriately possessive of the materials whose circulation they controlled, far exceeding professional bounds.[2] In the postcommunist era, many researchers believe such interventions are intentional, in the interest of preventing hidden histories from coming to the fore.

Once approved, researchers encountered a range of infrastructural prob-

[1] Kligman is especially grateful to Marius Oprea, Andrei Pleşu, and Virgiliu Ţârău for their assistance. Her experiences with archival access did not markedly improve even as a member of the Presidential Commission to Investigate the Crimes of Communism.

[2] Researchers in Romania (whether Romanian or foreign) frequently encounter this type of administrative abuse.

lems—from inadequate storage, poor preservation, and documents not yet or unsystematically catalogued (largely from lack of personnel), to selective access to those that were.[3] Some archives suffered significantly during World War II, their inventories destroyed during bombing campaigns or depleted through fire and theft. After the collapse of communism, archives again suffered damage, if differently. Valuable Party documents disappeared, for example, having been confiscated, thrown out, buried, burned, or shredded. Local archives, including those of former collective farms, had disappeared or were too damaged to use, or they were not systematically transferred to the regional branches of the Romanian National Archive as mandated by law. Stoica, for example, found critical transcripts missing: no one could account for the disappearance of documents covering the period just before and after the 1957 peasant revolt in Vadu Roşca, where he conducted his research.[4] He does not attribute their absence to the archivists, who were cooperative and forthcoming, themselves eager to see the missing documents he sought.

Two Notes Concerning Linguistic Aspects of Documents

Penal files, particularly those associated with political cases, show especially clearly the relationship among standardization, repetition, the performative, and the ritualization of discursive forms (Connerton 1989; Kligman 1998; Hull 2003).[5] They also point to another important dimension of textual production, namely, its scripted character, perhaps best exemplified in the transcripts of communist-era show trials of political figures and intellectuals,[6] and, further down the hierarchy, the trials of anticommunist "terrorists."[7] In mounting such cases, defendants were repeatedly interrogated as well as tortured until they "learned" their roles, that is, until their declarations fit the scripts they were expected to enact (see chapter 3 on ritual sacrifice). Hence, when reading such files, it is crucial to read the fullest set of documents that pertain to a case or situation.[8]

Internally circulated documents additionally draw attention to the Party's

[3] See the list of archives in the front of this book.

[4] On the 1957 revolt, see Stoica 2009, among others. Levy (2001: 11) notes that Gheorghiu-Dej "ordered archival documents destroyed on a least one occasion."

[5] Levy (2001) distinguishes the transcripts of Party meetings and commissions from penal interrogations, arguing that the former tend to be less scripted.

[6] See, for example, Hodos (1987) on show trials in Eastern Europe; Giugariu 1996; Giugariu and Cantacuzino (1996) on Romania's Pătrăşcanu trial; Brent and Naumov (2003) on the Soviet Doctors' Plot. To further the scripting of declarations for Party purges, Levy (2001: 12) notes that a list of "leading questions provided to the declarants has been found in the archives."

[7] See, for example, ACNSAS, FP, file 84, about subversive groups in Maramureş, discussed in chapter 4.

[8] Reading only one penal file gives a limited, distorted picture of what happened or what was at

control of information and its dissemination. The designation "Top Secret" distinguished from other documents those meant only for a restricted circle of recipients because the information in them was considered sensitive. As Stoler observes, such a designation accords a document "sacred status"; "codes of concealment," she writes, "are the fetishes of the state itself" (2009: 26). Secret status limits access and promises confidences. Through it, information was not only kept from the public, but created a kind of underground within the Party hierarchy itself and underscored communist regimes' obsession with secrecy, a fact often more important than the precise items so classified (see Martin n.d.; Viola 2000: 11). We can also see how that obsession filtered down into the population, which reproduced it in their own everyday practices out of fear. We have found the information in such documents generally to be more credible, precisely because it was intended for a circumscribed audience.[9]

Concerning Heroes and Victims

Two methodological points concern our discussion of memories of victimization. First, in a post-1989 era that has glorified resistance to communism, those who cannot draw on such former exploits may more readily claim victimization by forces more powerful than they. Passerini and others have noted this kind of memory mechanism at work in the oral histories of people "who lived under totalitarian regimes, expressed by laying the blame on power and on their own helplessness" (1992: 11).[10] She observed that rationalizing passivity in this way is recent in Russia and heavily influenced by media coverage of the communists' overwhelming domination. We do not mean to suggest that people should or could have effectively resisted the regime's attempts to subjugate their ways of life; we merely call attention to this effect on oral-historical narrative.

Related to this point is another concerning the form such narratives often take. Observers such as Nancy Ries (1997) and Golfo Alexopoulos (1997) have noted that Russians past and present make frequent use of a speech genre they call the "ritual lament," a cultural form also familiar to us from our work in Romania. Found in speech ranging from written petitions to informal conversation over coffee, this form enlists the sympathy of the listener, presenting the speaker

stake; by contrast, reading the declarations of all accused brings to light the scripted nature of the "legal" proceedings.

[9] A "top secret" label did not necessarily correlate with how many people read the document. Such files also detail the crimes of communism, presenting statistics (aggregate and stratified) on the number of people arrested, incarcerated, killed, etc.

[10] Passerini also noted that some who suffered in prisons and labor camps resent the claims of victimization by those who did not fare nearly so badly. Kligman found that the former commented on such "victims," although not with resentment.

as a victim of suffering and hardship. Because the subject of the grievance can be fairly trivial or—as in our respondents' accounts of their collectivization experiences—deeply disturbing, the lament genre can pose interpretive problems for the interviewer. We do not mean to minimize the suffering that people endured but only to indicate a mode of expression in which their memories were often cast. This mode could take on very specific forms: when a respondent from Maramureş communicated the misery of collectivization to Kligman by means of a versified funeral lament, she was using a cultural form particular to that region to shape her communication. In Romania, the funeral lament and what is known as the *doina*—a folksong of sorrow and longing—provide cultural referents for various other forms of "laments" (see, for example, Kligman 1988).

Concerning Interviewer Relationships

Members of our research team had very different relationships to their research sites, and this had an impact on the kinds of oral information they were able to obtain. Five members did not have extensive prior familiarity with the communities in which they worked (Chelcea, Iordachi, Şandru, Stoica in Vadu Roşca, Vultur in Domaşnea), though most had contacts of some sort who led them there. Two (Oláh and Vultur) had conducted previous research in their research sites during the 1990s. Five members (Bodó, Dobrincu, Goina, Lăţea, Stoica) were born in the communities they researched for our project or have close kin there (grandparents, affines). Goina, for instance, grew up in Sântana, where his mother still lives. Importantly for this project, his paternal grandfather had been a founding member of the first "model" collective farm in Sântana and was its first president. His family's role in collectivization was largely advantageous for his research, with respect to access to respondents. At the same time, he suspected that they may have censored their criticisms of the collective precisely because of his relation to his influential grandfather. Nonetheless, his maternal grandfather had opposed collectivization and held out from joining until 1960. In this regard, Goina could probe the pros and cons of collectivization through his own family's experiences.

Dorin Dobrincu is also a native of the settlement in which he worked, Darabani, from a long-standing and respected family, but his situation is quite different from Goina's. Instead of being descended from a founder of the collective, he is a member of a religious minority that resisted collectivization (though many of his relatives belong to the Orthodox majority), and his parents were among the last to enter the collective; this may have encouraged co-villagers to accentuate the negative side of the process. Lăţea found that his local knowledge from growing up in the community he studied facilitated his research in important—and time-saving—ways: he knew "names, genealogies, conflicts, past and present feuds." Armed with local knowledge of this kind, he could, in effect, use relationships to his project's advantage, playing naïve, pretending he didn't know about something, and then following his interlocutors' reactions. He could also share family stories to stimulate conversation further.[11] Lăţea also stated that having pursued this particular project resulted in the deepening of his relationships with people in his natal community.

Bodó's relationships with her research sites were somewhat different. One of them (Corund/Korond) is her husband's natal village, and she has affines and friends there, as well as neighbors who know her. One relative was particularly helpful in introducing her to possible interviewees (some of whom were relatives). Because she and her husband have conducted other research projects in Corund over the years, her familiarity with the village is almost "native." Concerning Armăşeni/Csíkmenaság, her mother held a teaching post there in the 1950s. Even though she stayed only two years, some villagers still remember her, a connection reinforced by ongoing friendship with two other teachers who worked in that village. These people introduced Bodó to a number of respondents. In addition, Bodó's husband commuted to work there as a teacher for a few years before 1989. These connections gave her an unusual kind of entrée into the village.

Other than those born in their research sites, however, none of the Romanians equaled our own longevity in the field: spanning over twenty-five years, in stays sometimes lasting a year. This familiarity helped transform our potentially problematic identities as "foreigners" into "familiars"[12] and enabled us to benefit from the local knowledge and dense relationships we had formed and maintained both before and after 1989. Without these opportunities, we would have had much more difficulty doing this kind of work, with the trust it required.[13] Whether one is a foreigner or a "national," lengthy exposure allows ethnographers to interpret responses from 2000 to 2003 according to the social relations and attitudes of villagers in the 1970s and 1980s, thereby correcting to some extent for the effects of the rupture of 1989 (see Bodó 2009; Vultur 2009b; and Lăţea, above). In singling out ethnographic research, we should distinguish between ethnographic and more strictly interview-based work: the latter is less privileged than the former, in that oral histories or repeat interviews do not allow the researcher to evaluate responses in broader discursive fields of daily communication and interaction over time in the way that long-term ethnographic research does. As our discussion thus far suggests, getting at the complexities of usable pasts is akin to "peeling the onion," layer by layer.[14]

[11] Lăţea, personal communication, 2008.

[12] We note that recognition of our scholarly work also helped open access to archives for others in our team, notably at the CNSAS.

[13] Romanians who lack ties to a community (as kin, through networks or experience) are considered nearly as "foreign" as those of us from abroad.

[14] We draw from Günter Grass (2007), whose revelations about his own hidden history during his youth under the Nazis sparked heated debate regarding generational and moral responsibilities, among many issues. His account resonates with problematic issues we discuss here.

Verdery's relations to the community of Vlaicu began in 1973, with her dissertation research. She continued to visit the village periodically throughout the communist period, returning there for an extended project between 1993 and 1997. Its topic, the restitution of land that had been given to the collective in the 1950s, involved her in lengthy conversations and data gathering that contributed to this project, but more importantly, her ongoing relationships facilitated her interviews for it and provided a check on her respondents' recollections. As already mentioned, Kligman's long experience in Ieud, further enriched by her access to hidden histories in the form of peasant memoirs and poetry, similarly allowed her to assess what respondents said after 1989 with what she knew from the 1970s and 1980s. Discrepancies accentuated the importance of interpreting in appropriate context what people said in the 1990s and being sensitive to their efforts to make their pasts more palatable. Kligman witnessed a dramatic case of revisionist history that drove this point home. Before 1989, she listened to an oral poetic version of tragic events that happened because of the respondent's actions back in the 1950s, in consequence of which men who had been hiding in the surrounding hills were rounded up and arrested. In that version, the respondent was a well-meaning but unwitting dupe of the Securitate. But after 1989, Kligman went to record her verses with another local poet who had heard this poem many times in the past. Much to their astonishment, the respondent denied ever having composed them. In the more open political environment, her past actions no longer seemed so innocent to some. To maintain her status as victim, she engaged in an unexpected form of self-serving strategic forgetting. Without Kligman's extensive field research in Ieud, she would have been none the wiser. Again, such instances underscore why what is said when and to whom is essential to assessing whether it is a reliable version of what happened.

Studying the Recent Past: Methodological Considerations for Future Research

The breadth of structural and experiential variation we have documented is instructive for future research. Our multimethodological approach to studying Romania's recent communist past has yielded, we believe, a multifaceted, nuanced picture of the collectivization process. Nevertheless, we recognize the limitations inherent in uneven access to respondents and archives, which may be yet more problematic for researchers beginning oral-historical or ethnographic research a decade or more after ours. Had we begun our "salvage" historical ethnography today, we could not have conducted the number of interviews that we did, and the results of our ethnographic interviews would be less rich and diverse.

One of the effects of the pedagogical techniques we reviewed in part 2 was people's resort to silence, the absence of talk, which Bodó (2003) posited as a means of self-protection. In villages, what we might refer to as "politicized silence" quieted the ubiquitous public "gossip of the village." In consequence, Bodó argues, the village community was unable to fashion a collective version of what was happening (which we would further qualify in terms of its fashioning collective *versions*). Silence of the kind that collectivization produced was a social silence, reflecting villagers' social embeddedness. Meanwhile, Party scribes formulated the collective history. In the postsocialist period, collective histories were increasingly shaped by researchers and others who did not live through that period, making attention to the methodological issues we have raised ever more urgent. The explosion of oral histories since 1989, for example, compels us to emphasize that memories are as variable in the present as people's experiences were in the past. Some villagers, such as those in "model" GACs like Sântana and Pechea, hold positive views of their collectives, but—like most others elsewhere—decidedly not of the collectivization *process*. Pechea provides a cautionary methodological lesson: respondents who had joined its GAC during the first wave have very different recollections of collectivization from those who entered in the second wave when sticks (coercion) rather than carrots (incentives) were wielded to get them to sign on (Şandru 2003; see also Khubova et al. 1992; Passerini 1992). Analysts must be sensitive to temporal variation when assessing retrospective accounts, many of which collapse such variation into a single time frame.

Other gaps in the study of collectivization include paralleling the kind of study we have done with generationally stratified studies of the children of previous collectivists and their grandchildren as well, to examine the collectives between 1962 (the end of the campaign) and the collapse of communism in 1989.[15] Another is that of noncollectivized villages, located in both lowland and peripheral areas. How did peasants in these locales fare during the years of the campaign? How did the Party exact loyalty from them, even though they were not "captives" in the same way as those who were collectivized? We know that marginal communities or populations with means of production and resources to redistribute, such as the shepherds of Poina Sibiului, managed to make the new system work to their advantage. We also know that many peripheral communities, while left to their own devices, were simultaneously the victims of the Party's neglect, meaning they did not enjoy the infrastructural improvements (infirmaries, schools, electrification) that others did. To survive, their residents had to migrate, whether permanently or seasonally.

Since we began our research, access to archival material has increased exponentially.[16] Indeed, the volume of available documents can overwhelm re-

[15] On decollectivization after 1989, see Verdery 2003. Another gaping chasm in the study of collectivization pertains to the Securitate, especially interviews with them. Few are willing to talk, and we must evaluate with great care anything said by the few who do.

[16] Several members of our research team have contributed importantly to the ever-increasing availability of or access to archival documents: Dorin Dobrincu (Director, National Archives of

searchers, proving both a blessing and a curse. Because these materials are now better catalogued in local, regional, and national archives (although much remains to be done), scholars can more readily and systematically conduct case studies of how the Party's mechanisms of rule took shape, following the tracks of power up, down, and across the Party hierarchy. Furthermore, use of the Soviet archives will provide new insight into how relations between the Soviet and Romanian leaders affected collectivization, particularly following the deaths of Stalin and Gheorghiu-Dej. We need more comparative studies within Romania itself and with the other countries in the Soviet sphere. Wherever collectivization occurred, it was a dynamic process marked by coercion, consent, and contestation to varying degrees within and between the Party and the peasantry; the diversity of these experiences warrants historical ethnography.

Romania); Marius Oprea (Center for the Study of Communist Crimes in Romania); Octavian Roske (Institute for the Study of Totalitarianism); and Virgiliu Țârău (National Council for the Study of the Securitate Archives).

Appendix III

List of Interviewers and Respondents

THIS LIST INCLUDES only those respondents quoted in the text, not all those interviewed. All interviews took place in 2000–2 and in the site given, except where noted. Categories noted are birth year or approximate age at the time of the interview, sex, "social origin," principal occupation.

LIVIU CHELCEA (Reviga):
V.S.: 71, male, middle peasant, former president of Reviga collective farm.

DORIN DOBRINCU (Darabani):
C.I.D.: 81, male, middle peasant, collective farmer.
C.S.C.: 68, male, chiabur origin, collective farmer.
D.S.: 82, male, middle peasant, collective farmer.
G.D.: 71, male, middle peasant, collective farmer.
G.D.B.: 72, male, middle peasant, collective farmer.
I.D.: 80, female, middle peasant, collective farmer.
I.F.: 78, male, son of a chiabur, uncollectivized farmer (did not join the GAC).
M.I.D.: 86, male, middle peasant, collective farmer.
M.V.I.: 72, male, middle peasant, former GAC president.
V.A.R.: 81, male, middle peasant, uncollectivized farmer.
V.D.A.: 70, male, middle peasant, collective farmer.
V.T.T.: 77, male, son of middle peasant and chiabur, collective farmer.

CĂLIN GOINA (Comlăuş, Caporal Alexa, and Sântana):
B.A.: 70, male, wealthy peasant, mechanic, local Party secretary; Comlăuş (1995, 2002).
G.A.: 82, male, poor peasant, former GAC president; Caporal Alexa (2003).
G.C.: 58, male, wealthy-peasant mother and worker father, teacher; Comlăuş (2003).
M.M.: 81, male, colonist of poor-middle status, former GAC vice president and Party secretary; Sântana (2001, 2003).
O.M.: 80, male, wealthy peasant, factory worker and collective farmer; Comlăuş (1995, 2002).
S.A.: 80, female, poor peasant, collective farmer; Sântana.
V.B.: 64, male, colonist of poor-peasant origin, former chauffeur for the GAC; Sântana.
Z.S.: 75, male, German of poor-peasant origin, construction worker in collective farm; Sântana.

CONSTANTIN IORDACHI (Jurilovca):

L.B.: b. 1938, female, daughter of lower-middle-status fisherman, former GAC worker, widow.

M.T.: b. 1927, male, poor peasant, former GAC chairman.

V.Z.: b. 1933, male, son of landless fisherman, former tractor driver and GAC chairman between 1970 and 1980.

GAIL KLIGMAN (Ieud):

B.G.: b. 1920, male, middle-wealthy peasant, Uniate priest.

B.P.: b. 1942, female, wealthy peasant, agricultural worker.

B.S.: b. 1922, male, middle-wealthy peasant, collective farm member and brigade leader.

C.G.: b. 1929, male, middle-wealthy peasant, agricultural worker.

C.I.: b. 1949, male, wealthy peasant, collective farm member.

C.V.: b. 1927, male, middle-wealthy peasant, former political prisoner, factory worker.

D.I.: b. 1933, male, wealthy peasant, former political prisoner, accountant.

D.M.: b. 1953, female, wealthy peasant, collective farm member.

D.V.: b. 1919, male, wealthy peasant, collective farm member.

D.V.D.: b. 1923, male, poor peasant, former GAC president; Giulvăz, Timiş.

H.D.: b. 1911, male, middle wealthy, agronomist (cadre); Sighetu Marmaţiei.

H.V.: b. 1930, middle peasant, shepherd employed by the collective farm.

I.S.: b. 1914, male, middle peasant, collective farm member, miner.

P.C.G.: b. 1922, male, middle-wealthy peasant, agricultural worker.

P.G.: b. 1922, male, poor-middle peasant, former regional Party Secretary; Baia Mare.

P.G.R.: b. 1941, male, middle-wealthy peasant, collective farm member.

P.N.: b. 1932, female, poor peasant, collective farm member.

P.S.: b. 1921, male, poor peasant (Ruthenian), prison guard; Tisa.

P.V.: b. 1927, poor peasant, collector.

T.S.: b. 1949, male, middle peasant, teacher.

DANIEL PUIU LĂŢEA (Dobrosloveni):

A.B.: ca. 75, male, middle peasant, collective farmer.

D.T.: 81, female, middle peasant, housewife (did not work in the collective farm; husband a skilled worker) (2002, 2003).

I.B.: 75, male, middle peasant, former accountant in Dobrosloveni collective farm (2002, 2003).

I.D.: 79, male, middle peasant, equipment manager in the collective farm (2002, 2003).

M.D.: 74, female, middle peasant, collective farmer (2003).

M.T.: 76, female, chiabur family, housewife (did not work in the collective farm) (2002, 2003).

S.A.: 77, male, middle peasant, postman (2003).

OLÁH SÁNDOR (Lueta/Lövéte and Sânpaul/Homoródszentpál):
2: 75, female, chiabur family origin, retired intellectual; Sânpaul.
3: 72, male, middle peasant, retired collective farmer; Sânpaul.
5: 49, male, uncollectivized peasant family, factory worker; Lueta.
6: 72, male, middle peasant, retired factory worker and uncollectivized peasant; Lueta.
9: 75, female, chiabur family, collective farmer (initially excluded); Sânpaul.
10: 85, male, middle peasant, retired collective farmer; Sânpaul.

MICHAEL STEWART (Apoldu de Jos and Poiana Sibiului):
(Note: Interviews conducted by R. Stan and D. Budrală)
A.Ţ.: b. 1922, male, chiabur sheep owner, shepherd in collective farm; Apoldu de Jos (R. S., 2004).
B.L.: b. 1918, female, poor origin, former staff member of mayor's office and party activist; Poiana Sibiului (R. S., 2005).
D.I.: b. 1924, chiabur sheep owner, shepherd in collective farm; Poiana Sibiului (R. S., 2004).
G.N.: b. 1924, male, middle peasant, wheelwright in collective farm; Apoldu de Jos (D. B.).
L.M.: b. 1919, male, chiabur origin, collective farmer; Apoldu de Jos (D. B.).
N.I.: b. 1923, chiabur sheep owner, shepherd in collective farm; Poiana Sibiului (R. S., 2004).
P.N.: b. 1921, male, middle peasant, collective farmer; Apoldu de Jos (D. B.).

CĂTĂLIN STOICA:
15: 63, male, middle peasant, retired construction worker; participated in the revolt in Vadu Rosca and sentenced to prison.

VIRGILIU ŢÂRĂU (Rimetea and Măgina):
BA01: b. 1923, male, poor peasant, collective farmer.
FI01: b. 1914, male, middle peasant, former functionary; Aiud.
II01: b. 1920, male, poor peasant, collective farmer, former functionary in collective.
SA01: b. 1923, male, poor peasant, craftsman and collective farmer.

KATHERINE VERDERY (Aurel Vlaicu except where otherwise noted):
7: b. 1929, male, poor-middle peasant, railway worker.
23: b. 1923, male, poor-middle peasant, collective farmer.
24: b. 1923, male, poor-peasant, factory worker.
56: b. 1921, female, poor peasant, husband a shoemaker.
59: b. 1931, wealthy peasant, collective farmer.
72: b. 1924, male, middle peasant, collective farmer and petty functionary.
108: b. 1926, female, poor in-migrant, collective farmer.

130: b. 1930, male, middle peasant, functionary.
151: b. 1923, female, middle peasant, collective farmer.
154: b. 1926, male, middle peasant, railway worker.
164: b. 1935, female, middle peasant, collective farmer and factory worker.
186: b. 1931, male, poor-middle peasant, collective farm functionary and president.
194: b. 1925, male, middle peasant, factory worker.
195: b. 1922, male, wealthy peasant, factory worker.
197: b. 1920, male, poor peasant, factory worker and activist (briefly).
206: b. 1952, female, middle peasant, clerk.
213n: b. 1953, female, wealthy peasant, agronomist.
213Z: b. 1948, female, wealthy peasant, teacher.
217, b. 1926, female, middle peasant, collective farmer.
258: b. 1925, male, German, factory worker.
258 I2: b. 1933, female, daughter of schoolteacher, white-collar worker.
261: b. 1924, male, poor peasant, factory worker.
A.D.T.: b. ca. 1928, functionary's wife; Orăştie.
C.D.: b. 1924, male, from a family of railway workers, functionary; Orăştie.
G.Z.: b. ca. 1928, male, wealthy peasant, collective farmer; Geoagiu.
K.L.: b. ca. 1930 near Gherla, male, middle peasant, retired functionary; Cluj (1999).
M.H.: b. ca. 1929, male, wealthy peasant, functionary and teacher; Geoagiu (1993, 1999, 2000, 2002).
N.C.: b. ca. 1950, male, agronomist; Geoagiu (2009).
R.A.: b. ca. 1938, male, son of notary, university professor; Cluj.

SMARANDA VULTUR (Domaşnea and Tomnatic)
(Note: Code numbers for each refer to the number in the online database of the Oral History Archive of the Fundaţia a Treia Europa, in which these interviews are publicly available [www.memoriabanatului.ro]):
F.W: b. 1910, male, father functionary, employed in commerce, German origin, code 235.
M.G.: b. 1924, female, poor peasant, collective farmer; Domaşnea, code 328.
M.I.: b. 1922, wealthy peasant, collective farmer; Domaşnea, code 315.
N.W.: b. 1919, middle-peasant family declared chiabur, collective farmer; ethnic German, former Bărăgan deportee; Tomnatic (1996, 2001), code 329.
P.C.: b. 1932, male, middle peasant, accountant and store clerk; participated in persuasion work; Domaşnea, code 323.
R.A.: b. 1927, male, wealthy peasant, president of association and collective farm, later chauffeur; Domaşnea, code 313.
V.D.: b. 1927, male, wealthy peasant, former collective farm brigadier; Domaşnea, code 314.

BIBLIOGRAPHY

A link to many of the project's Final Reports (2003) can be found at www.press.princeton.edu/titles/9615.html.

Adair, Bianca L. 2001. "The Agrarian Theses and Rapid Collectivization: Accommodation in Hungarian Agriculture, 1956–60." *Journal of Communist Studies and Transition Politics* 17 (2): 131–47.

Alexopoulos, Golfo. 1997. "The Ritual Lament: A Narrative of Appeal in the 1920s and 1930s." *Russian History/Histoire russe* 24 (1–2): 117–29.

———. 1999. "Victim Talk: Defense Testimony and Denunciation under Stalin." *Law and Social Inquiry* 24 (3): 637–54.

———. 2008. "Stalin and the Politics of Kinship: Practices of Collective Punishment, 1920s–1940s." *Comparative Studies in Society and History* 50: 91–117.

Anderson, Benedict. 1983. *Imagined Communities: Reflections on the Origins and Spread of Nationalism*. London: Verso.

———. 1990. "The Idea of Power in Javanese Society." In *Language and Power*, 17–77. Ithaca: Cornell University Press.

Anderson, David. 1998. "Property as a Way of Knowing on Evenki Lands in Arctic Siberia." In *Property Relations*, edited by C. M. Hann, 64–84. Cambridge: Cambridge University Press.

Anghelache, Camelia. 1999. "Aspecte selectate din documentele deţinute de arhivele naţionale din fosta arhivă a C.C. al P.C.R. privind colectivizarea." *Analele Sighet* 7: 615–25.

Anisescu, Cristina. 2002. "Dinamica de structură şi rol a reţelei informative în perioada 1948–1989." In *Arhivele Securităţii*, edited by Marian Stere, Consiliul Naţional pentru Studierea Arhivelor Securităţii, 10–50. Bucureşti: Pro Historia.

Appadurai, Arjun, ed. 1986. *The Social Life of Things: Commodities in Cultural Perspective*. Cambridge: Cambridge University Press.

Arhivele Naţionale ale României. 2004. *Stenogramele şedinţelor Biroului Politic şi ale Secretariatului Comitetului Central al P.M.R.* Vol. 3, 1950–1951. Bucureşti: Arhivele Naţionale ale României.

Asad, Talal. 2000. "Agency and Pain: An Exploration." *Culture and Religion* 1: 29–60.

Assmann, Jan, and John Czaplicka. 1995. "Collective Memory and Cultural Identity." *New German Critique* 65 (Spring–Summer): 125–33.

Bakhtin, Mikhail M. 1981. "Discourse in the Novel." In *The Dialogic Imagination*, 259–422. Austin: University of Texas Press.

Băileşteanu, Jean. 1987. *Drum în tăcere*. Craiova: Scrisul Românesc.

Bălan, Ion. 2000. *Regimul concentraţionar din România 1945–1964*. Bucureşti: Fundaţia Academia Civică.

Barany, Zoltan. 1994. "Soviet Takeovers: The Role of Advisers in Mongolia in the 1920s and in Eastern Europe after World War II." *East European Quarterly* 28 (4): 409–34.

Bărbulescu, C. 1952. "Creaţia nouă de cântece populare." *Studii şi cercetări de istorie literară şi folclor* 1 (104): 193–220.

Bateson, Gregory. 1936. *Naven: A Survey of the Problems Suggested by a Composite Picture of the Culture of a New Guinea Tribe Drawn from Three Points of View*. Cambridge: Cambridge University Press.

Beck, Sam. 1979. "Transylvania: The Political Economy of a Frontier." Ph.D. diss., University of Massachusetts, Amherst.

Benison, S. 1971. "Oral History: A Personal View." In *Modern Methods in the History of Medicine*, edited by E. Clark, 286–305. New York: Oxford University Press.

Berdahl, Daphne. 2010. *On the Social Life of Postsocialism: Memory, Consumption, Germany*. Bloomington: Indiana University Press.

Bertaux, Daniel, ed. 1981. Introduction to *Biography and Society: The Life History Approach in the Social Sciences*, 5–18. Beverly Hills: Sage.

Binns, Christopher. 1979–80. "The Changing Face of Power: Revolution and Accommodation in the Soviet Ceremonial System." 2 parts. *Man* 14 (4): 170–87; 15 (1): 585–606.

Bodeanu, Denisa, and Cosmin Budeancă, eds. 2004. *Rezistenţa armată anticomunistă din România: Grupul Teodor Şuşman (1948–1958), mărturii*. Cluj-Napoca: Argonaut.

Bodó, Julianna. 2003. Final Report, Collectivization Project, authors' files. Published in 2004 in Hungarian as *"Így kollektivizáltak minket . . .": Kulturalis antropológiai elemzés két székelyföldi településről ("Aşa ne-au colectivizat . . .": Analiză antropologică despre două sate din Secuime)*. Miercurea-Ciuc, Romania: Pro-Print.

———. 2009. "Persuasion Techniques and Community Reactions in the Village of Corund (the Autonomous Hungarian Region)." In Iordachi and Dobrincu 2009: 355–68.

Bonnell, Victoria. 1997. *Iconography of Power: Soviet Political Posters under Lenin and Stalin*. Berkeley: University of California Press.

Boris, Eileen, and Angélique Janssens, eds. 1999. "Complicating Categories: Gender, Class, Race and Ethnicity." *International Review of Social History*, supplement 7, special issue.

Bossy, Raoul. 1955. "Religious Persecutions in Captive Romania." *Journal of Central European Affairs* 15 (2): 161–80.

Bourdieu, Pierre. 1977. *Outline of a Theory of Practice*. Cambridge: Cambridge University Press.

———. 1990. *In Other Words: Essays Towards a Reflexive Sociology*. Cambridge: Polity Press.

Bowker, Geoffrey, and Susan Leigh Star. 2000. *Sorting Things Out: Classification and Its Consequences*. Cambridge, MA: MIT Press.

Bozgan, Ovidiu. 2000. *România versus Vatican. Persecuţia Bisericii Catolice din România comunistă în lumina documentelor diplomatice franceze*. Bucureşti: Sylvi.

Braham, Randolph, ed. 1994. *The Tragedy of Romanian Jewry*. New York: Columbia University Press.

Brauner, Harry. 1979. *Să auzi iarba cum creşte*. Bucureşti: Eminescu.

Brent, Jonathan, and Vladimir Naumov. 2003. *Stalin's Last Crime: The Plot Against the Jewish Doctors, 1948–1953*. New York: Harper Collins.

Brown, Kate. 2004. *A Biography of No Place: From Ethnic Borderland to Soviet Heartland*. Cambridge, MA: Harvard University Press.

Brown, Keith. 2003. *The Past in Question: Modern Macedonia and the Uncertainties of Nation*. Princeton: Princeton University Press.

Brown, Michael F. 2003. *Who Owns Native Culture?* Cambridge, MA: Harvard University Press.

Brown, Peter. 1981. *The Cult of the Saints: Its Rise and Function in Latin Christianity*. Chicago: University of Chicago Press.

Brubaker, Rogers, and Frederick Cooper. 2004. "Beyond 'Identity.'" *Theory and Society* 29 (1): 1–47.

Brubaker, Rogers, Margit Feischmidt, Jon Fox, and Liana Grancea. 2006. *Nationalist Politics and Everyday Ethnicity in a Transylvanian Town*. Princeton: Princeton University Press.

Brus, W. 1986. "Postwar Reconstruction and Socio-economic Transformation." In *The Economic History of Eastern Europe, 1919–1975*, edited by M. C. Kaser and E. A. Radice, 564–641. Oxford: Clarendon Press.

Buckley, Mary. 2006. *Mobilizing Soviet Peasants: Heroines and Heroes of Stalin's Fields*. Lanham, MD: Rowman & Littlefield.

Budeancă, Cosmin, Florentin Olteanu, and Iulia Pop, eds. 2006. *Rezistența anticomunistă: Cercetare științifică și valorificare muzeală*. 2 vols. Cluj-Napoca: Argonaut.

Burawoy, Michael. 1985. *The Politics of Production: Factory Regimes under Capitalism and State Socialism*. London: Verso.

Burke, Peter. 1989. "History as Social Memory." In *Memory: History, Culture, and the Mind*, edited by Thomas Butler, 97–113. New York: Basil Blackwell.

Câmpeanu, Pavel. 1988. *The Genesis of the Stalinist Social Order*. Armonk, NY: M. E. Sharpe.

———. 1990. *The Origins of Stalinism*. Armonk, NY: M. E. Sharpe.

———. n.d. Lecturi arhivistice. Ana Pauker (I): căderea. MS, authors' files.

Caplan, Jane, and John Torpey, eds. 2001. *Documenting Individual Identity: The Development of State Practices in the Modern World*. Princeton: Princeton University Press.

Caravia, Paul, Virgiliu Constantinescu, and Flori Stănescu. 1998. *Biserica întemnițată: România, 1944–1989*. București: Institutul Național pentru Studiul Totalitarismului.

Carrithers, Michael. 1985. "An Alternative Social History of the Self." In *The Category of the Person*, edited by Michael Carrithers, Steven Collins, and Steven Lukes, 234–56. Cambridge: Cambridge University Press.

Cătănuș, Dan, and Octavian Roske. 2000. *Colectivizarea agriculturii în România: Dimensiunea politică*. Vol. 1, *1949–1953*. București: Institutul Național pentru Studiul Totalitarismului.

———. 2004. *Colectivizarea agriculturii în România: Represiunea*. Vol. 1, *1949–1953*. București: Institutul Național pentru Studiul Totalitarismului.

———. 2005. *Colectivizarea agriculturii în România: Dimensiunea politică*. Vol. 2, *1953–1956*. București: Institutul Național pentru Studiul Totalitarismului.

Cernea, Mihail. 1974. *Sociologia cooperativei agricole*. București: Academiei.

———. 1978. "Macrosocial Change, Feminization of Agriculture, and Peasant Women's Threefold Economic Role." *Sociologia Ruralis* 18: 107–24.

Cesereanu, Ruxandra, ed. 2006. *Comunism și represiune în România: Istoria tematică a unui fratricid național*. Iași: Polirom.

Chelcea, Liviu. 2003a. "Ancestors, Domestic Groups and the Socialist State: Housing

Nationalization and Restitution in Romania." *Comparative Studies in Society and History* 45 (4): 714–40.

Chelcea, Liviu. 2003b. Final Report, Collectivization project, authors' files.

———. 2009. "'Here in Reviga, There Was Nobody to Wage the Class Struggle': Collectivization in Reviga, Bărăgan Plain (Bucharest Region)." In Iordachi and Dobrincu 2009: 399–422.

Chiper, Ioan, and Florin Constantiniu. 1995. "Modelul stalinist de sovietizare a României, II." *Arhivele Totalitarismului* 3: 28–29.

Cîrstocea, Ioana. 2002. "Eşalonul de mijloc al partidului unic." In *Securiştii partidului*, edited by Marius Oprea, 46–79. Iaşi: Polirom.

Ciuceanu, Radu, and Corneliu Mihai Lungu, eds. 2003. *Stenogramele şedinţelor conducerii P.C.R., 23 septembrie 1944–26 martie 1945*. Bucureşti: Institutul Naţional pentru Studiul Totalitarismului.

Climo, Jacob, and Maria Cattell. 2002. "Introduction: Meaning in Social Memory and History: Anthropological Perspectives." In *Social Memory and History: Anthropological Perspectives.* Walnut Creek, CA: AltaMira Press.

Cohen, David William. 1994. *The Combing of History*. Chicago: University of Chicago Press.

Cojoc, Marian. 2001. *Dobrogea de la reforma agrară la colectivizarea forţată (1945–1957)*. Constanţa: Muntenia şi Leda.

Colas, Dominique. 2002. "Säubernde und gesäuberte Einheitpartei: Lenin und der Leninismus." In *Ein Gespenst geht um in Europa, Das Erbe kommunistischer Ideologien*, edited by Uwe Backès and Stephane Courtois. Köln: Böhlau.

Collier, Jane, and Michelle Rosaldo. 1981. "Politics and Gender in Simple Societies." In *Sexual Meanings*, edited by Sherry Ortner and Harriet Whitehead, 275–329. Cambridge: Cambridge University Press.

Confino, Alon. 1997. "Collective Memory and Cultural History: Problems of Method." *American Historical Review* 102 (5): 1386–403.

Connerton, Paul. 1989. *How Societies Remember.* Cambridge: Cambridge University Press.

Conquest, Robert. 1986. *The Harvest of Sorrow: Soviet Collectivization and the Terror-Famine*. New York: Oxford University Press.

Constante, Lena. 1990. *L'évasion silencieuse: trois milles jours seule dans les prisons roumaines*. Paris: Éditions La Découverte.

———. 1995. *The Silent Escape: Three Thousand Days in Romanian Prisons*. Berkeley: University of California Press.

Constantinescu-Iaşi, Petre. 1954. *Arta plastică în Republica Populară Romînă, 1944–1954*. Bucureşti: Editura de Stat pentru Literatură şi Artă.

Constantiniu, Florin, and Mihail C. Ionescu. 1993. "Planul sovietic de comunizare a României (martie 1945)." *Revista istorică* 4 (7–8): 657–61.

Crampton, Richard. 1994. *Eastern Europe in the Twentieth Century—and After*. London: Routledge.

Creed, Gerald. 1998. *Domesticating Revolution: From Socialist Reform to Ambivalent Transition in a Bulgarian Village*. University Park: Pennsylvania State University Press.

Crişan, Gheorghe. 2004. *Piramida puterii: Oameni politici şi de stat, generali şi ierarhi din Romania (23 august 1944–22 decembrie 1989)*. Bucureşti: Pro Historia.

Cutler, William, III. 1970. "Accuracy in Oral History Interviewing." *Historical Methods Newsletter* 3: 1–7.

Damian, Anca, Florin Vreazu, and Ion Bălan, eds. 2002. *Colectivizare în Vlaşca, 1949–1950: Documente*. Bucureşti: Vinea.

Dăncuş, Mihai, ed. 2005. *Satul maramureşean 1945–1989: Viaţa socială, economică, politică, culturală şi religioasă. Studii şi documente*. Sighetu Marmaţiei: Muzeul Maramureşului.

Daniel, E. Valentine. 1996. *Charred Lullabies: Chapters in an Anthropography of Violence*. Princeton: Princeton University Press.

Davies, R. W. 1980. *The Socialist Offensive: The Collectivisation of Soviet Agriculture, 1929–1930*. London: Macmillian.

de Coppet, Daniel. 1985. "Land Owns People." In *Contexts and Levels*, edited by R. H. Barnes, Daniel de Coppet, and R. J. Parkin, 78–90. Oxford: JASO.

Degeratu, Claudiu, and Octavian Roske. 1994a. "Colectivizarea agriculturii. Modelul sovietic: Ridicarea necontenită a nivelului de trai." *Arhivele Totalitarismului* 2 (1–2): 80–91.

———. 1994b. "Colectivizarea agriculturii. Modelul sovietic: Drumul belşugului." *Arhivele Totalitarismului* 2 (3): 54–68.

———. 1994c. "Colectivizarea agriculturii. Modelul sovietic: Ştiinţa biruitoare." *Arhivele Totalitarismului* 2 (4): 47–59.

Deletant, Dennis. 1995. *Ceauşescu and the Securitate: Coercion and Dissent in Romania, 1965–1989*. Armonk, NY: M. E. Sharpe.

———. 1998. *Romania under Communist Rule*. Bucharest: Civic Academy Foundation.

———. 1999. *Communist Terror in Romania: Gheorghiu-Dej and the Police State, 1948–1965*. New York: Hurst.

———. 2006. *Hitler's Forgotten Ally: Ion Antonescu and His Regime, Romania 1940–44*. New York: Palgrave Macmillan.

Diac, Florin. 2004. *O istorie a învăţământului românesc modern. Vol 2., 1944–1989*. Bucureşti: Oscar Print.

Dobeş, Andrea. 2003. "Mărturii despre drama femeii române în perioada 1950–1964." *Anuarul Institutului de Istorie Orală* 4: 215–34.

Dobeş, Andrea, Gheorghe Mihai Bârlea, and Robert Fürtös. 2004. *Colectivizarea în Maramureş: Contribuţii documentare (1949–1962), vol. 1*. Bucureşti: Fundaţia Academia Civică.

Dobre, Florica, ed. 2003. *Bande, bandiţi şi eroi: Grupurile de rezistenţă şi Securitatea (1948–1968)*. Bucureşti: Enciclopedică.

———. 2004. *Membrii C.C. al P.C.R., 1945–1989: Dicţionar*. Bucureşti: Enciclopedică.

———. 2006. *Securitatea: Structuri—Cadre: Obiective şi metode*. Vol. 1, *(1948–1967)*. Bucureşti: Enciclopedică.

Dobrenko, Evgeny, and Eric Naiman, eds. 2003. *The Landscape of Stalinism: The Art and Ideology of Soviet Space*. Seattle: University of Washington Press.

Dobrincu, Dorin. 2000–1. "Ajutorul marelui frate: Consilierii sovietici în România lui Gheorghe Gheorghiu-Dej." *Analele Ştiinţifice ale Universităţii "Alexandru Ioan Cuza" din Iaşi, Istorie* 46–47: 211–48.

———. 2002. "Colectivizarea, cote şi revolte ţărăneşti în vestul Romaniei (1949)." *Anuarul Institutului Român de Istorie Recentă* 1: 282–318.

———. 2002–3. "Transformarea socialistă a agriculturii, răscoalele ţărăneşti şi deportările din nordul Moldovei (1949)." *Anuarul Institutului de Istorie "A.D. Xenopol"* 39–40: 459–87.

Dobrincu, Dorin. 2003a. Final Report, Collectivization project, authors' files.

———. 2003b. "Libertate religioasă şi contestare în România lui Nicolae Ceauşescu: Comitetul Creştin Român pentru Apărarea Libertăţii şi de Conştiinţă (ALRC)." *Analele Sighet* 10: 203–27.

———. 2004. *Proba infernului. Personalul de cult în sistemul carceral din România potrivit documentelor Securităţii, 1959–1962.* Bucureşti: Scriptorium.

———, ed. 2008. *Listele morţii: Deţinuţi politici decedaţi în sistemul carceral din România potrivit documentelor Securităţii, 1945–1948.* Iaşi: Polirom.

———. 2009. "Persuasion, Delay and Coercion: Late Collectivization in Northern Moldova: The Case of Darabani (Suceava Region)." In Iordachi and Dobrincu 2009: 274–304.

Dobrincu, Dorin, and Constantin Iordachi, eds. 2005. *Ţărănimea şi puterea: Procesul de colectivizare a agriculturii în România (1949–1962).* Iaşi: Polirom.

Duica, Camelia. 2005. *Rezistenţa anticomunistă din Maramureş: Gruparea Popşa.* Bucureşti: Institutul Naţional pentru Studiul Totalitarismului.

Dumitrescu, G. St. 1960. "The Rumanian Peasantry's Resistance to Agricultural Collectivization." *RFE Report, Open Society Archives* 202/11.

Dumitriu, Petru. 1950. *Nopţile din iunie.* Bucureşti: Editura pentru Literatură şi Artă.

Dunca, Ioan. 2004. *Aur şi noroi.* Constanţa: Metafora.

Dunn, Elisabeth. 2004. *Privatizing Poland: Baby Food, Big Business, and the Remaking of Labor.* Ithaca: Cornell University Press.

Duţu, Maria. 1994. "Aspecte ale obligaţiilor financiare impuse României prin Convenţia de Armistiţiu din 12 septembrie 1944." *Revista istorică* 9–10: 899–905.

Easter, Gerald. 2000. *Reconstructing the State: Personal Networks and Elite Identity in Soviet Russia.* Cambridge: Cambridge University Press.

Eidelberg, Phillip G. 1974. *The Great Rumanian Peasant Revolt of 1907: Origins of a Modern Jacquerie.* Leiden: Brill.

Enyedi, György. 1967. "The Changing Face of Agriculture in Eastern Europe." *Geographical Review* 57 (3): 358–72.

Ernu, Vasile, Costi Togozanu, Ciprian Şiulea, and Ovidiu Ţichindeleanu, eds. 2008. *Iluzia anticomunismului: Lecturi critice ale Raportului Tismăneanu.* Chişinău: Cartier.

Eyal, Gil. 2004. "Identity and Trauma: Two Forms of the Will to Memory." *History and Memory* 16 (1): 5–36.

Fainsod, Merle. 1953. *How Russia Is Ruled.* Cambridge, MA: Harvard University Press.

———. 1958. *Smolensk under Soviet Rule.* Cambridge, MA: Harvard University Press.

Ferry, Elizabeth Emma. 2005. *Not Ours Alone: Patrimony, Value, and Collectivity in Contemporary Mexico.* New York: Columbia University Press.

Fitzpatrick, Sheila. 1990. "Introduction: Sources on the Social History of the 1930s." In *A Researcher's Guide to Sources on Soviet History in the 1930s*, edited by Sheila Fitzpatrick and Lynne Viola, 3–25. Armonk, NY: M. E. Sharpe

———. 1994a. *The Practice of Denunciation in Stalinist Russia.* Washington, DC: National Council for Soviet and East European Research.

———. 1994b. *Stalin's Peasants: Resistance and Survival in the Russian Village after Collectivization.* New York: Oxford University Press.

———. 2000. *Stalinism: New Directions.* London: Routledge.

———. 2005. *Tear off the Masks! Identity and Imposture in Twentieth-Century Russia*. Princeton: Princeton University Press.

Fitzpatrick, Sheila, and Robert Gellately. 1996. "Introduction to the Practices of Denunciation in Modern European History." *Journal of Modern History* 68 (December): 747–67.

———, eds. 1997. *Accusatory Practices: Denunciation in Modern European History, 1789–1989*. Chicago: University of Chicago Press.

Foucault, Michel. 1991. "Governmentality." In *The Foucault Effect: Studies in Governmentality*, edited by Graham Burchell, Colin Gordon, and Peter Miller, 87–104. Chicago: University of Chicago Press.

———. 2002. "The Subject and Power." In *Essential Works of Foucault, 1954–1984*, vol. 3:327–48. New York: New Press.

Fürtös, Robert, and Gheorghe Mihai Bârlea, eds. 2009. *Colectivizarea în Maramureş: Mărturii de istorie orală*. Bucureşti: Fundaţia Academia Civică.

Gal, Susan, and Gail Kligman. 2000. *The Politics of Gender after Socialism: A Comparative Historical Essay*. Princeton: Princeton University Press.

Geertz, Clifford. (1966) 1973. "Person, Time, and Conduct in Bali." In *The Interpretation of Cultures*, 360–411. New York: Basic Books.

Getty, J. Arch, and Oleg V. Naumov. 1999. *The Road to Terror: Stalin and the Self-Destruction of the Bolsheviks, 1932–1939*. New Haven: Yale University Press.

Gheorghiu-Dej, Gheorghe. 1955. *Articole şi cuvântări*, 4th ed. Bucureşti: Editura de Stat pentru Literatură Politică.

———. 1962. "Raport cu privire la încheierea colectivizării şi reorganizării conducerii agriculturii." In *Articole şi cuvântări, iunie 1961–decembrie 1962*. Bucureşti: Politică.

Gillet, Olivier. 2001. *Religie şi naţionalism: Ideologia Bisericii Ortodoxe Române sub regimul comunist*. Bucureşti: Compania.

Giugariu, Mihai, ed. 1996. *Principiul bumerangului: Documente ale procesului Lucreţiu Pătrăşcanu*. Bucureşti: Vremea.

Giugariu, Mihai, and Cristina Cantacuzino. 1996. *Prigoana: Documente ale procesului C. Noica, C. Pillat, N. Steinhardt, Al. Paleologu, A. Acterian, S. Al-George, Al. O. Teodoreanu, etc*. Bucureşti: Vremea.

Giurchescu, Anca. 1987. "The National Festival 'Song to Romania': Manipulation of Symbols in the Political Discourse." In *Symbols of Power*, edited by C. Arvidsson and L. E. Blomquist, 163–72. Stockholm: Almquist and Wiksell International.

Glaeser, Andreas. 2011. *Political Epistemics: The Secret Police, the Opposition, and the End of East German Socialism*. Chicago: University of Chicago Press.

Gluckman, Max. 1943. *Essays on Lozi Land and Royal Property*. Rhodes-Livingston papers, no. 10.

———. 1965. *The Ideas in Barotse Jurisprudence*. New Haven: Yale University Press.

Goina, Călin. 2003. Final Report, Collectivization project, authors' files.

———. 2009. "'Never leave 'til tomorrow what you can do today!'": A Case Study of a Model Collective Farm, 'New Life' Sântana (Arad Region)." In Iordachi and Dobrincu 2009: 369–98.

Goven, Joanna. 1993. "Gender Politics in Hungary: Gender and Anti-feminism." In *Gender Politics and Post-Communism: Reflections from Eastern Europe and the Former Soviet Union*, edited by Nanette Funk and Magda Mueller, 224–40. New York: Routledge.

Grama-Neamțu, Emanuela. 2010. "Building Politics, Searching for Heritage: Architecture, Archeology and Imaginaries of Social Order in Romania (1947–2007)." Ph.D. diss., University of Michigan.

Grass, Günter. 2007. *Peeling the Onion*. Orlando: Harcourt.

Gregory, Paul R. 2004. *The Political Economy of Stalinism: Evidence from the Soviet Secret Archives*. Cambridge: Cambridge University Press.

Grele, Ronald J. 1985. *Envelopes of Sound: The Art of Oral History*. Chicago: Precedent Publishing.

Gribincea, Mihai. 1996. *Agricultural Collectivization in Moldavia: Bessarabia During Stalinism, 1944–1950*. Boulder, CO: East European Monographs.

Gross, Jan. 1982. "A Note on the Nature of Soviet Totalitarianism." *Soviet Studies* 34 (3): 367–76.

———. 1988. *Revolution from Abroad: The Conquest of Poland's Western Ukraine and Western Belorussia*. Princeton: Princeton University Press.

Grzymała-Busse, Anna. 2001. "The Organizational Strategies of Communist Parties in East Central Europe, 1945–1989." *East European Politics and Societies* 15 (2): 421–53.

Gump, Brooks, and Karen Matthews. 1998. "Vigilance and Cardiovascular Reactivity to Subsequent Stressors in Men: A Preliminary Study." *Health Psychology* 17 (1): 93–96.

Halbwachs, Maurice. (1925) 1992. *On Collective Memory*. Chicago: University of Chicago Press.

Halfin, Igal. 2007. *Intimate Enemies: Demonizing the Bolshevik Opposition, 1918–1928*. Pittsburgh: University of Pittsburgh Press.

Halfin, Igal, and Jochen Hellbeck. 1996. "Rethinking the Stalinist Subject: Stephen Kotkin's 'Magnetic Mountain' and the State of Soviet Historical Studies." *Jahrbücher für Geschichte Osteuropas* 44: 456–63.

Hallowell, A. Irving. 1955. "The Nature and Function of Property as a Social Institution." In *Culture and Experience*, 236–49. Philadelphia: University of Pennsylvania Press.

Hammel, Eugene A. 1968. *Alternative Social Structures and Ritual Relations in the Balkans*. Englewood Cliffs, NJ: Prentice-Hall.

Haney, Lynne. 2002. *Inventing the Needy: Gender and the Politics of Welfare in Hungary*. Berkeley: University of California Press.

Hann, C. M. 1980. *Tázlár: A Village in Hungary*. Cambridge: Cambridge University Press.

———, ed. 1998. *Property Relations: Renewing the Anthropological Tradition*. Cambridge: Cambridge University Press.

Harris, Grace. 1989. "Concepts of Individual, Self, and Person in Description and Analysis." *American Anthropologist* 91: 599–612.

Harvey, David. 2005. *A Brief History of Neoliberalism*. Oxford: Oxford University Press.

Heinen, Armin. (1986) 1999. *Legiunea "Arhanghelului Mihail": Mişcarea socială şi organizaţia politică*. Bucureşti: Humanitas.

Helin, Ronald A. 1967. "The Volatile Administrative Map of Rumania." *Annals of the Association of American Geographers* 57 (3): 481–502.

Hellbeck, Jochen. 2006. *Revolution on My Mind: Writing a Diary under Stalin*. Cambridge, MA: Harvard University Press.

Hindus, Maurice Gerschon. 1988. *Red Bread: Collectivization in a Russian Village*. Bloomington: Indiana University Press.

Hodos, George. 1987. *Show Trials: Stalinist Purges in Eastern Europe, 1948–1954*. New York: Praeger.

Holquist, Peter. 1997. "'Information is the Alpha and Omega of Our Work': Bolshevik Surveillance in Its Pan-European Context." *Journal of Modern History* 69 (3): 415–50.

Hooper, Cynthia. 2006. "Terror of Intimacy: Family Politics in the 1930s Soviet Union." In *Everyday Life in Early Soviet Russia*, edited by Christina Kiaer and Eric Naiman, 61–91. Bloomington: Indiana University Press.

Horváth, Ágnés, and Árpád Szakolczai. 1992. *The Dissolution of Communist Power: The Case of Hungary*. London: Routledge.

Hughes, James. 1996. *Stalinism in a Russian Province: A Study of Collectivization and Dekulakization in Siberia*. New York: St. Martin's Press.

Hull, Matthew. 2003. "The File: Agency, Authority, and Autography in an Islamabad Bureaucracy." *Language and Communication* 23 (3): 287–314.

Humphrey, Caroline. 1983. *Karl Marx Collective: Economy, Society, and Religion in a Siberian Collective Farm*. Cambridge: Cambridge University Press.

———. 2002. *The Unmaking of Soviet Life: Everyday Economies after Socialism*. Ithaca: Cornell University Press.

Huyssen, Andreas. 1995. *Twilight Memories: Marking Time in a Culture of Amnesia*. New York: Routledge.

Iancu, Gheorghe, and Virgiliu Ţârău. 2000. "The Peasants' Uprisings in the Counties of Arad and Bihor in 1949." In *Romanian and British Historians on the Contemporary History of Romania*, edited by George Cipăianu and Virgiliu Ţârău, 153–66. Cluj-Napoca: Cluj University Press.

Iancu, Gheorghe, Virgiliu Ţârău, and Ottmar Traşcă. 2000. *Colectivizarea agriculturii în România: Aspecte legislative, 1945–1962*. Cluj-Napoca: Presa Universitară Clujeană.

Ilie, Oana. 2001. "Canalul Dunăre şi Marea Neagră în presa anilor 1949–1953." *Arhivele Totalitarismului* 1–2: 79–93.

Ioanid, Ion 1999. *Închisoarea noastră cea de toate zilele*. Vol. 1, *1949, 1952–1954*. Bucureşti: Humanitas.

Ioanid, Radu. 2000. *The Holocaust in Romania: The Destruction of Jews and Gypsies under the Antonescu Regime, 1940–1944*. Chicago: Ivan R. Dee.

Ionescu, Ghiţa. 1964. *Communism in Rumania, 1944–1962*. New York: Oxford University Press.

Ionescu-Gură, Nicoleta. 2000. "Categoria socială a 'chiaburului' în concepţia PMR din anii '50." *Analele Sighet* 8: 284–98.

———. 2005. *Stalinizarea României: Republica Populară Română, 1948–1950, transformări instituţionale*. Bucureşti: ALL.

———. 2006. *Nomenclatura Comitetului Central al Partidului Muncitoresc Român*. Bucureşti: Humanitas.

Iordachi, Constantin. 2003. Final Report, Collectivization project, authors' files.

———. 2004. *Charisma, Politics, and Violence: The Legion of the "Archangel Michael" in Interwar Romania*. Trondheim Studies on East European Cultures and Societies, no. 15.

———. 2009. "Constanţa, the First Collectivized Region: Soviet Geo-political Interests, National and Regional Factors in the Collectivization of Dobrogea (1949–1962)." In Iordachi and Dobrincu 2009: 3–140.

Iordachi, Constantin, and Dorin Dobrincu, eds. 2009. *Transforming Peasants, Property and Power: The Collectivization of Agriculture in Romania, 1949–1962*. Budapest: Central European University Press.

Jowitt, Kenneth. 1971. *Revolutionary Breakthroughs and National Development: The Case of Romania, 1944–1965*. Berkeley: University of California Press.

———. 1974. "An Organizational Approach to the Study of Political Culture in Marxist-Leninist Systems." *American Political Science Review* 68: 1171–91.

———. 1978. *The Leninist Response to National Dependency*. Berkeley: IAS.

———. 1992. *New World Disorder: The Leninist Extinction*. Berkeley: University of California Press.

Judt, Tony. 2002. "The Past Is Another Country: Myth and Memory in Post-war Europe." In *Memory and Power in Post-War Europe*, edited by Jan-Werner Müller, 157–83. Cambridge: Cambridge University Press.

Kansteiner, Wulf. 2002. "Finding Meaning in Memory: A Methodological Critique of Collective Memory Studies." *History and Theory* 41 (2): 179–97.

Kantorowicz, Ernst. 1957. *The King's Two Bodies: A Study in Medieval Political Theology*. Princeton: Princeton University Press.

Keane, John. 1988. "More Theses on the Philosophy of History." In *Meaning and Context*, edited by James Tully, 204–17. Cambridge: Polity.

Kenedi, János. 1981. *Do It Yourself: Hungary's Hidden Economy*. London: Pluto.

Kenez, Peter. 1985. *The Birth of the Propaganda State: Soviet Methods of Mass Mobilization, 1917–1929*. Cambridge: Cambridge University Press.

Kharkhordin, Oleg. 1995. "The Soviet Individual: Genealogy of a Dissimulating Animal." In *Global Modernities*, edited by Mike Featherstone, Scott Lash, and Ronald Robertson, 202–26. Thousand Oaks, CA: Sage.

———. 1999. *The Collective and the Individual in Russia: A Study of Practices*. Berkeley: University of California Press.

Khubova, Darie, Andrei Ivankiev, and Tonia Sharova. 1992. "After Glasnost: Oral History in the Soviet Union." In Passerini 1992: 89–103. New Brunswick, NJ: Transaction.

Kideckel, David A. 1982. "The Socialist Transformation of Agriculture in a Romanian Commune, 1945–62." *American Ethnologist* 9: 320–40.

———. 1993. *The Solitude of Collectivism: Romanian Villagers to the Revolution and Beyond*. Ithaca: Cornell University Press.

———. 2008. *Getting By in Postsocialist Romania: Labor, the Body, and Working-Class Culture*. Bloomington: Indiana University Press.

King, Robert R. 1980. *History of the Romanian Communist Party*. Stanford: Hoover Press.

Klein, Kerwin Lee. 2000. "On the Emergence of Memory in Historical Discourse." *Representations* 69: 127–50.

Kligman, Gail. 1981. *Căluș: Symbolic Transformation in Romanian Ritual*. Chicago: University of Chicago Press.

———. 1988. *The Wedding of the Dead: Ritual, Poetics, and Popular Culture in Transylvania*. Berkeley: University of California Press.

———. 1998. *The Politics of Duplicity: Controlling Reproduction in Ceaușescu's Romania*. Berkeley: University of California Press.

———. 2009. "Creating Communist Authority: Class Warfare and Collectivization in Ieud (Maramureş Region)." In Iordachi and Dobrincu 2009: 165–202.

Kligman, Gail, and Katherine Verdery. 2006. "Social Dimensions of Collectivization: Fomenting Class Warfare in Transylvania." In *World Order after Leninism*, edited by Vladimir Tismaneanu, Marc Morjé Howard, and Rudra Sil, 127–48. Seattle: University of Washington Press.

Konrád, George, and Ivan Szelényi. 1979. *The Intellectuals on the Road to Class Power*. New York: Harcourt Brace Jovanovich.

Kopeček, Michal. 2008. *Past in the Making: Historical Revisionism in Central Europe after 1989*. Budapest: Central European University Press.

Kotkin, Stephen. 1995. *The Magnetic Mountain: Stalinism as a Civilization*. Berkeley: University of California Press.

Kravchenko, Victor. 1946. *I Chose Freedom: The Personal and Political Life of a Soviet Official*. New York: Charles Scribner's Sons.

Kristó, Tibor, ed. 1999. *Kuláksors: Székely kulákok történetei*. Csíkszereda: Státus Könyvkiadó.

Kundera, Milan. 1981. *The Book of Laughter and Forgetting*. New York: Penguin.

Lampland, Martha. 1995. *The Object of Labor: Commodification in Socialist Hungary*. Chicago: University of Chicago Press.

———. N.d. "Divining the Secrets of Class Warfare: Intuiting Menace and Building Vigilance in Stalinist Hungary." Unpublished paper.

Lane, Christel. 1981. *The Rites of Rulers: Ritual in Industrial Society, the Soviet Case*. Cambridge: Cambridge University Press.

Lăţea, Daniel. 2003. Final Report, Collectivization project, authors' files.

———. 2009. "Revolution in Bits and Pieces: Collectivization in Southern Romania (Craiova Region)." In Iordachi and Dobrincu 2009: 329–54.

Lee, Ching Kwan, and Guobin Yang. 2007. *Re-envisioning the Chinese Revolution: The Politics and Poetics of Collective Memories in Reform China*. Washington, DC: Woodrow Wilson Center Press.

Lefort, Claude. 1986. *The Political Forms of Modern Society: Bureaucracy, Democracy, Totalitarianism*. Cambridge, MA: MIT Press.

Le Goff, Jacques. 1992. *History and Memory*. New York: Columbia University Press.

Lévesque, Jean. 2006. "Exile and Discipline: The June 1948 Campaign against Collective Farm Shirkers." *Carl Beck Papers in Russian and East European Studies*, no. 1708.

Levy, Robert. 2001. *Ana Pauker: The Rise and Fall of a Jewish Communist*. Berkeley: University of California Press.

———. 2002. *Gloria şi decăderea Anei Pauker*. Bucureşti: Polirom.

———. 2009. "The First Wave of the Collectivization Campaign: Central Policies and their Regional Implementation, 1949–1953." In Iordachi and Dobrincu 2009: 27–48.

Lewin, Moshe. 1968. *Russian Peasants and Soviet Power: A Study of Collectivization*. New York: Norton.

———. 1985. *The Making of the Soviet System: Essays in the Social History of Interwar Russia*. New York: New Press.

———. 2005. *The Soviet Century*. London: Verso.

Leys, Ruth. 2000. *Trauma: A Genealogy*. Chicago: University of Chicago Press.

Liiceanu, Aurora. 2000. *Nici alb, nici negru: Radiografia unui sat românesc, 1948–1998.* București: Nemira.

———. 2003. *Rănile memoriei: Nucșoara și rezistența din munți.* Iași: Polirom.

Luca, Vasile. 1949. *Expunere asupra legii impozitului agricol: Legea impozitului agricol.* București: PMR.

Lummis, Trevor. 1987. *Listening to History.* London: Hutchinson.

Mack, Phyllis. 2008. *Heart Religion in the British Enlightenment: Gender and Emotion in Early Methodism.* Cambridge: Cambridge University Press.

MacLean, Kenneth A. S. 2005. "The Arts of Disclosure: Peasant-Bureaucrats, Historiography, and State Socialism in Viet Nam." Ph.D. diss., University of Michigan.

———. 2007. "Manifest Socialism: The Labor of Representation in the Democratic Republic of Vietnam (1956–1959)." *Journal of Vietnamese Studies* 2 (1): 27–79.

Maine, Henry Sumner. 1863. *Ancient Law: Its Connection with the Early History of Society, and Its Relation to Modern Ideas.* London: J. Murray.

Malinowski, Bronislaw. 1935. *Coral Gardens and Their Magic.* London: Allen and Unwin.

Manning, Roberta T. 2001. "The Rise and Fall of 'The Extraordinary Measures,' January-June, 1928: Toward a Reexamination of the Onset of the Stalin Revolution." *Carl Beck Papers in Russian and East European Studies*, no. 1504.

Manoliu-Furnică, Vladimir. 1997–98. "Lupta anticomunistă a unui țăran maramureșean pe nume Chindriș." *Revista de Istorie Socială* 2–3: 253–61.

Marino, Adrian. 1972. "Great Figures in the History of Romanian Genius." *Times* [London] 29, special supplement, December 29, 1972.

Martin, I., C. Anderca, C. Neuman, A. Sitaru, and V. Uibaru. 1959. *10 ani de realizări în GAC "Victoria" din Lenauheim.* București: Editura Agro-Silvică de Stat.

Martin, Terry. 2001. *The Affirmative Action Empire: Nations and Nationalism in the Soviet Union, 1923–1939.* Ithaca: Cornell University Press.

———. n.d. *The Politics and Sociology of Information in the Soviet Union, 1918–1954.*

Márton, László. 2003. *A kollektivizálás Székelyudvarhely rajonban.* Hargita: Kalendárium.

———. 2005. *Acțiunile împotriva gospodăriilor colective în regiunea Mureș (septembrie 1950–decembrie 1951).* Cluj: UBB (MS, authors' files).

Mauss, Marcel. 1954. *The Gift: Forms and Functions of Exchange in Archaic Societies.* Glencoe, IL: Free Press.

Mendelson, Sarah, and Theodore Gerber. 2006. "Failing the Stalin Test: Russians and Their Dictator." *Foreign Affairs* 85 (1): 2–8.

McDonald, Tracy. 2002. "A Peasant Rebellion in Stalin's Russia: The Pitelinskii Uprising, Riazan, 1930." In *Contending with Stalinism: Soviet Power and Popular Resistance in the 1930s*, edited by Lynne Viola, 84–108. Ithaca: Cornell University Press.

———. 2009. "From Physical to Symbolic Violence: Villagers Remember Collectivization." Paper presented at the Annual Convention of the American Association for the Advancement of Slavic Studies, Boston.

Miller, Linda. 2009. "Law and Propaganda: Rural Land Ownership, Collectivization and Socialist Property in Romania." In Iordachi and Dobrincu 2009: 81–100.

Miłosz, Czesław. 1953. *The Captive Mind.* New York: Knopf.

Mitrany, David. 1930. *The Land and the Peasant in Rumania: The War and Agrarian Reform (1917–21).* London: Oxford University Press.

Moisa, Gabriel. 1999. *Colectivizare, rezistență și represiune în vestul României (1948–1951)*. Oradea: Muzeul Țării Crișurilor.

Montias, John Michael. 1967. *Economic Development in Communist Rumania*. Cambridge, MA: MIT Press.

Moraru, Camelia, Constantin Moraru, and Veronica Vasilov, eds. 2004. *Stenogramele ședințelor Biroului Politic și ale Secretariatului Comitetului Central al PMR*. Vol. 3, *1950–1951*. București: Arhivele Naționale ale României.

Morgan, Lewis Henry. 1877. *Ancient Society*. Calcutta: Bharati Library.

Mosely, Philip E. 1958. "Collectivization of Agriculture in Soviet Strategy." In *Collectivization of Agriculture in Eastern Europe*, edited by Irwin T. Sanders and Enno E. Kraehe, 49–66. Lexington: University Press of Kentucky.

Müller, Jan-Werner. 2002. "Introduction: The Power of Memory, the Memory of Power and the Power over Memory." In *Memory and Power in Post-War Europe*, edited by Jan-Werner Müller, 1–35. Cambridge: Cambridge University Press.

Mungiu-Pippidi, Alina. 2010. *A Tale of Two Villages: Effects of Coerced Modernization on the East European Countryside*. Budapest: Central European University Press.

Murașko, Galina P. 1998. "Represiunile politice în țările Europei de est la sfîrșitul anilor '40: Conducerea sovietică și nomenclatura națională de partid și de stat." *Analele Sighet* 6: 339–49.

Năstase, Andreea, and Stejărel Olaru. 2002. "În perioada construirii socialismului, cadrele hotărăsc totul." In *Securiștii partidului: Serviciul de Cadre al P.C.R. ca poliție politică*, edited by Marius Oprea, 95–112. Iași: Polirom.

Neagoe, Elisabeta. 2002. "Situația trupelor MAI la sfârșitul anului 1949." In *Arhivele Securității*, edited by Consiliul Național pentru Studierea Arhivelor Securității, 130–39. București: Pro Historia.

Negrici, Eugen. 1995. *Poezia unei religii politice: Patru decenii de agitație și propaganda*. București: Fundației PRO.

———. 1997. *Literature and Propaganda in Communist Romania*. București: Romanian Cultural Foundation Publishing House.

———. 2003. *Literatura română sub comunism*. București: Fundației PRO.

———. 2005. "Rolul literaturii în campania de colectivizare." In *Țărănimea și puterea: Procesul de colectivizare a agriculturii în România (1949–1962)*, edited by Dorin Dobrincu and Constantin Iordachi, 154–73. Iași: Polirom.

Nelson, Daniel N. 1980. *Democratic Centralism in Romania: A Study of Local Communist Politics*. Boulder, CO: East European Monographs.

Nietzsche, Friedrich. (1887) 1989. "On the Genealogy of Morals." In *On the Genealogy of Morals and Ecco Homo*, edited by Walter Kaufman. New York: Vintage.

Nikolaevsky, Boris. 1965. *Power and the Soviet Elite*. New York: Praeger.

Nora, Pierre, ed. 1984–92. *Les lieux de mémoire*. 7 vols. Paris: Edition Gallimard.

———. 1989. "Between Memory and History: Les lieux de mémoire." *Representations* 26: 7–24.

Oláh, Sándor. 2001. *Csendes csatatér: Kollektivizálás és túlélési stratégiák a két Homoród mentén (1949–1962)*. Miercurea-Ciuc: Pro-Print.

———. 2003. Final Report, Collectivization project, authors' files.

———. 2009. "Collectivization in the Odorhei District (The Autonomous Hungarian Region)." In Iordachi and Dobrincu 2009: 229–50.

Olick, Jeffrey. 1999. "Collective Memory: The Two Cultures." *Sociological Theory* 17: 333–48.

Olick, Jeffrey, and Joyce Robbins. 1998. "Social Memory Studies: From 'Collective Memory' to the Historical Sociology of Mnemonic Practices." *Annual Review of Sociology* 24: 105–50.

Oprea, Marius. 2001. "Ghidul arhivelor comunismului." *Revista de Istorie Militară* 2: 5–12.

———, ed. 2002. *Securiştii partidului: Serviciul de cadre al PCR ca poliţie politică*. Iaşi: Polirom.

———. 2003. Final Report, Collectivization project, authors' files.

———. 2009. "The Final Offensive: 'The Socialist Transformation of Agriculture' from Slogans to Reality (1953–1962)." In Iordachi and Dobrincu 2009: 49–80.

Păiuşan, Cristina, and Radu Ciuceanu. 2001. *Biserica Ortodoxă Română sub regimul comunist*. Bucureşti: Institutul Naţional pentru Studiul Totalitarismului.

Passerini, Luisa, ed. 1992. *Memory and Totalitarianism*. Vol. 1, *International Yearbook of Oral History and Life Stories*. New Brunswick, NJ: Transaction Publishers.

Pateman, Carole. 1988. *The Sexual Contract*. Stanford: Stanford University Press.

Penner, D'Ann. 1995. "Pride, Power, and Pitchforks: Farmer-Party Interaction on the Don, 1920–1928." Ph.D. diss., University of California, Berkeley.

Pleş-Chindriş, Gavrilă. n.d. *Colectivizaria la Ieud: Mărturisiri din celea petrecute*. Ieud, Maramureş, manuscript.

———. 2009. *Pe drumul amintirilor: poezii*. Sighetu Marmaţiei: Asociaţiunea pentru Cultura Poporului Român din Maramureş.

Pleşa, Elis Neagoe. 2006. "Motivaţie religioasă în mişcarea de rezistenţă anticomunistă: Rolul preoţilor Greco-catolici Grigore Jaflea şi Simion Roşa în grupul 'Leon Şuşman.'" In *Rezistenţa anticomunistă: Cercetare ştiinţifică şi valorificare muzeală*, edited by Cosmin Budeancă, Florentin Olteanu, and Iulia Pop, 90–104. Cluj-Napoca: Argonaut.

Pocock, John G. A. 1985. "The Mobility of Property and the Rise of Eighteenth-Century Sociology." In *Virtue, Commerce, and History*, 103–23. Cambridge: Cambridge University Press.

Poledna, Rudolf. 2001. *Sint ut sunt, aut non sint? Transformări sociale la saşii ardeleni după 1945*. Cluj-Napoca: Presa Universitară Clujeană.

Pope, Earl. 1992. "Protestantism in Romania." In *Protestantism and Politics in Eastern Europe and Russia*, edited by Sabrina Ramet, 157–208. Durham, NC: Duke University Press.

Port, Andrew I. 2007. *Conflict and Stability in the German Democratic Republic*. Cambridge: Cambridge University Press.

Portelli, Alessandro. 1991. *The Death of Luigi Trastulli and Other Stories: Form and Meaning in Oral History*. Albany: State University of New York Press.

Poznanski, Kazimierz Z. 1992. *Constructing Capitalism: The Reemergence of Civil Society and Liberal Economy in the Post-Communist World*. Boulder, CO: Westview Press.

Prager, Jeffrey. 1998. *Presenting the Past: Psychoanalysis and the Sociology of Misremembering*. Cambridge, MA: Harvard University Press.

Preda, Marin. 1952. *Desfăşurarea*. Bucureşti: Editura pentru Literatură şi Artă.

———. 1955. *Moromeţii*. Vol. 1. Bucureşti: Editura pentru Literatură şi Artă.

———. 1967. *Moromeţii*. Vol. 2. Bucureşti: Editura pentru Literatură şi Artă.

Procesul unui grup de spioni, trădători şi complotişti în slujba Vaticanului şi a centrului de spionaj Italian, Bucureşti, 10–17 septembrie 1951. 1952. Bucureşti: Editura de Stat pentru Literatură Ştiinţifică.

Prodan, David. 1979. *Răscoala lui Horea*. Bucureşti: Ştiinţifică şi Enciclopedică.

Pryor, Frederic. 1992. *The Red and the Green: The Rise and Fall of Collectivized Agriculture in Marxist Regimes*. Princeton: Princeton University Press.

Radosav, Doru, Valentin Orga, Almira Ţenţea, Florin Cioşan, Cornel Jurju, and Cosmin Budeancă. 2003. *Rezistenţa anticomunistă din Apuseni: Grupurile Teodor Şuşman, Capotă-Dejeu, Cruce şi Spadă*. Cluj-Napoca: Argonaut.

Râmneanţu, Vasile. 1996. "Activitatea organizaţiei judeţene Timiş-Torontal a Frontului Plugarilor în perioada 1944–1946." *Analele Banatului (Serie nouă istorie)* 4 (2): 173–86.

Randall, Steven Gale. 1983. "The Household Estate under Socialism: The Theory and Practice of Socialist Transformation and the Political Economy of Upland Peasant Workers in Romania." Ph.D. diss., University of Massachusetts, Amherst.

Rappaport, Joanne. 1998. *The Politics of Memory: Native Historical Interpretation in the Columbian Andes*. Durham, NC: Duke University Press.

Republica Populară Română. 1948. "Constituţia Republicii Populare Române." *Monitorul Oficial* part 1, no. 87.

———. 1952. "Constituţie a Republicii Populare Române." *Buletin Oficial al Marii Adunări Naţionale a Republicii Populare Române* (septembrie, no. 1 [27]).

Republica Populară Română, Direcţia Centrală de Statistică. 1956. *Recensămîntul populaţiei din 21 februarie 1956: Structura demografică a populaţiei*. Bucureşti: Direcţia Centrală de Statistică.

Republica Socialistă România. 1984. *Anuarul statistic al Republicii Socialiste România 1984*. Bucureşti: Direcţia Centrală de Statistică.

Rév, István. 1987. "The Advantages of Being Atomized: How Hungarian Peasants Coped with Collectivization." *Dissent* 34: 335–50.

Ries, Nancy. 1997. *Russian Talk: Culture and Conversation During Perestroika*. Ithaca: Cornell University Press.

Roberts, Henry. 1951. *Rumania: Political Problems of an Agrarian State*. New Haven: Yale University Press.

Ronnås, Per. 1984. *Urbanization in Romania: A Geography of Social and Economic Change Since Independence*. Stockholm: Economic Research Institute, Stockholm School of Economics.

Roske, Octavian. 1992. *Dosarul colectivizării agriculturii în România 1949–1962*. Bucureşti: Parlamentul României.

———, ed. 2001. *Mecanisme represive în România, 1945–1989: Dicţionar biografic, A–C*, Bucureşti: Institutul Naţional pentru Studiul Totalitarismului.

———. 2003. Final report, Collectivization project, authors' files.

———. 2005. "Colectivizarea şi mecanismul colectărilor: istorii paralele." In Dobrincu and Iordachi 2005:113–35.

———. 2009. "Radiografia unui eşec: Colectivizarea agriculturii în România." In *Transformarea socialistă: Politici ale regimului comunist între ideologie şi administraţie*, edited by Ruxandra Ivan, 77–107. Iaşi: Polirom

Roske, Octavian, Florin Abraham, and Dan Cătănuş. 2007. *Colectivizarea agriculturii în Romania: Cadrul legislativ, 1949–1962*. Bucureşti: Institutul Naţional pentru Studiul Totalitarismului.

Ross, Corey. 2000. *Constructing Socialism at the Grass-Roots: The Transformation of East Germany, 1945–1965*. New York: St. Martin's Press.

Rostás, Zoltán, and Antonio Momoc. 2007. *Activiştii mărunţi: Istorii de viată*. Bucureşti: Curtea Veche.

Rotman, Liviu. 2004. *Evrei din România în perioada comunistă, 1944–1965*. Iaşi: Polirom.

Rowbotham, Sheila. 1973. *Hidden from History: 300 Years of Women's Oppression and the Fight against It*. London: Pluto Press.

Sachelarie, Ovid, and Nicolae Stoicescu, eds. 1988. *Instituţii feudale din Ţările Române: Dicţionar*. Bucureşti: Academiei.

Sadoveanu, Mihail. 1959. *Mitrea Cocor*. Bucureşti: Editura pentru Literatură şi Artă.

———. 1952. *Aventură în Lunca Dunării*. Bucureşti: Tineretului.

Sahlins, Marshall. 1994. "Cosmologies of Capitalism." In *Culture/Power/History*, edited by N. Dirks, G. Eley, and S. Ortner. Princeton: Princeton University Press.

Salameh, Sławomira. 1997. "Bitter Harvest: Antecedents and Consequences of Property Reform in Postsocialist Poland, 1989–1993." Ph.D. diss., University of California, Berkeley.

Şandru, Dumitru. 1995. "Ukrainian Nationalists, the Maramureş and Bucovina." *Transylvanian Review* 4 (4): 68–85.

———. 2003. Final report, Collectivization project, authors' files.

———. 2005. *Reforma agrară din 1945 în România*. Bucureşti: Institutul Naţional pentru Studiul Totalitarismului.

Sapolsky, Robert M. 2004. *Why Zebras Don't Get Ulcers*. New York: Henry Holt/Owl Books.

Schelling, Thomas C. 1978. *Micromotives and Macrobehavior*. New York: Norton.

Schneider, Jane. 1980. "Trousseau as Treasure: Some Contradictions of Late Nineteenth Century Change in Sicily." In *Behind the Myth of Culture*, edited by Eric Ross, 323–59. New York: Academic Press.

Schnell, Felix. 2009. "Rapine, Revenge, Redistribution—Scenarios from Ukraine, 1928–1932." Paper presented at the Annual Convention of the American Association for the Advancement of Slavic Studies, Boston.

Schuman, Howard, and Jacqueline Scott. 1989. "Generations and Collective Memories." *American Sociological Review* 54: 359–81.

Scott, James. 1985. *Weapons of the Weak: Everyday Forms of Peasant Resistance*. New Haven: Yale University Press

———. 1998. *Seeing Like a State: How Certain Schemes to Improve the Human Condition Have Failed*. New Haven: Yale University Press.

Semelin, Jacques. 2003. "Toward a Vocabulary of Massacre and Genocide." *Journal of Genocide Research* 5 (2): 193–210.

Seriot, Patrick. 2002. "Officialese and Straight Talk in Socialist Europe of the 1980s." In *Ideology and System Change in the USSR and East Europe*, edited by Michael Urban, 202–12. New York: St. Martin's Press.

Sharma, Aradhana, and Akhil Gupta. 2005. *The Anthropology of the State*. Oxford: Blackwell Publishing.

Shearer, David R. 1998. "Crime and Social Disorder in Stalin's Russia: A Reassessment of the Great Retreat and the Origins of Mass Repression." *Cahiers du monde russe* 39: 119–48.

———. 2001. "Social Disorder, Mass Repression, and the NKVD during the 1930s." *Cahiers du monde russe* 42: 505–34.

———. 2009. *Policing Stalin's Socialism: Repression and Social Order in the Soviet Union, 1924–1953*. New Haven: Yale University Press.

Sherbakova, Irina. 1992. "The Gulag in Memory." In Passerini 1992: 103–15. Oxford: Oxford University Press.

Shue, Vivienne. 1988. *The Reach of the State: Sketches of the Chinese Body Politic*. Stanford: Stanford University Press.

Siegelbaum, Lewis, and Andrei Sokolov. 2004. *Stalinism as a Way of Life: A Narrative in Documents*. Abridged ed. New Haven: Yale University Press.

Slama-Cazacu, Tatiana. 1991. "Limba de lemn." *România literară* 17 octombrie: 4–5.

———. 2000. *Strategeme comunicaționale și manipulare*. Iași: Polirom.

Slezkine, Yuri. 1994. "The USSR as a Communal Apartment, or How a Socialist State Promoted Ethnic Particularism." *Slavic Review* 53 (2): 414–52.

Smuts, B. 1992. "Male Aggression against Women: An Evolutionary Perspective." *Human Nature* 3: 1–44.

Sokolovsky, Joan. 1990. *Peasants and Power: State Autonomy and the Collectivization of Agriculture in Eastern Europe*. Boulder, CO: Westview.

Somers, Margaret. 1992. "Narrativity, Narrative Identity, and Social Action: Rethinking English Working-Class Formation." *Social Science History* 16: 591–630.

Spulber, Nicolas. 1958. "Collectivization in Hungary and Romania." In *Collectivization of Agriculture in Eastern Europe*, edited by Irwin T. Sanders and Enno E. Kraehe, 140–65. Lexington: University Press of Kentucky.

Stahl, Henri H. 1958–65. *Contribuții la studiul satelor devălmașe romînești*. București: Academiei Republicii Populare Romîne.

———. 1980. *Traditional Romanian Village Communities: The Transition from the Communal to the Capitalist Mode of Production in the Danube Region*. Cambridge: Cambridge University Press.

Stalin, I. V. 1948–52. *Opere*. Vol. 10. București: Editura Partidului Muncitoresc Român.

Stan, Sabina. 2001. "'Making up people': Classifications étatiques, categories locales et gestion des identités dans la collectivisation des campagnes roumaines." *Cahiers de sociologie économique et culturelle* 36: 91–112.

Stancu, Zaharia. 1968. *Desculț*. București: Editura pentru Literatură.

Stănescu, N. S. 1957. *Cooperativizarea agriculturii în R.P.R.* București: Editura de Stat pentru Literatură Politică.

Stark, David, and László Bruszt. 1998. *Postsocialist Pathways: Transforming Politics and Property in East Central Europe*. Cambridge: Cambridge University Press.

Stephens, Sharon. 1986. "Ideology and Everyday Life in Sami (Lapp) History." In *Discourse and the Social Life of Meaning*, edited by Phyllis Pease Chock and June R. Wyman, 205–32. Washington, DC: Smithsonian Institution Press.

Stere, Anca. 2002. "Câteva aspecte ale ideologizării culturii populare." *Sympozia: Caiete de etnologie și antropologie* 1: 147–55.

———. 2003. "The Social Dimensions of the Folkloric Text in the Post War Totalitarianism." *Symposia: Caiete de Etnologie și Antropologie*: 83–93.

———. 2009. "The Use of Folk Compositions in Conveying Ideological Messages: The Collectivization Process." *New Europe College Yearbook* 2005–06, edited by Irina Vainovski-Mihai, 321–51. București: New Europe College.

Stewart, Michael, and Răzvan Stan. 2003. Final Report, Collectivization project, authors' files.

———. 2009. "Collectivization and Resistance in the Shepherding Village of Poiana Sibiului (Sibiu Region)." In Iordachi and Dobrincu 2009: 251–74.

Stillman, Edmund O. 1958. "The Collectivization of Bulgarian Agriculture." In *Collectivization of Agriculture in Eastern Europe*, edited by Irwin T. Sanders and Enno E. Kraehe, 67–102. Lexington: University Press of Kentucky.

Stoica, Cătălin Augustin. 2003. Final Report, Collectivization project, authors' files.

———. 2006. "Once upon a Time There Was a Big Party: The Social Bases of the Romanian Communist Party." *East European Politics and Societies* 19 (4): 686–716.

———. 2009. "One Step Back, Two Steps Forward: Institutionalizing the Party-State and Collective Property in Two Romanian Villages (Galați Region)." In Iordachi and Dobrincu 2009: 432–54.

Stoler, Ann Laura. 2009. *Along the Archival Grain: Epistemic Anxieties and Colonial Common Sense*. Princeton: Princeton University Press.

Storm-Clark, C. 1971. "The Miners, 1870–1970: A Test Case for Oral History." *Victorian Studies* 15 (1): 49–74.

Strathern, Marilyn. 1988. *The Gender of the Gift: Problems with Women and Problems with Society in Melanesia*. Berkeley: University of California Press.

Sulițeanu, Ghizela. 1952. "Viața cântecului popular in comuna Ieud." *Revista Uniunii Compozitorilor din RPR*. 44–56.

Swain, Geoffrey. 2003. "Deciding to Collectivise Latvian Agriculture." *Europe-Asia Studies* 55: 39–58.

Swain, Nigel. 1985. *Collective Farms which Work?* Cambridge: Cambridge University Press.

Szalontai, Balázs. 2003. "The Dynamics of Repression: The Global Impact of the Stalinist Model, 1944–1953." *Russian History/Histoire Russe* 29 (2–4): 415–42.

———. 2005. *Kim Il Sung in the Khrushchev Era: Soviet-DPRK Relations and the Roots of North Korean Despotism, 1953–1964*. Stanford: Stanford University Press; Washington, DC: Woodrow Wilson Center Press.

Szelényi, Iván. 1988. *Socialist Entrepreneurs: Embourgeoisement in Rural Hungary* (with Robert Manchin, Pál Juhász, Bálint Magyar, and Bill Martin). Madison: University of Wisconsin Press; Cambridge: Polity Press.

Tănase, Stelian. 1998. *Elite și societate: Guvernarea Gheorghiu-Dej, 1948–1965*. București: Humanitas.

———. 2002. *Acasă se vorbește în șoaptă*. București: Compania.

———, ed. 2003. *Anatomia mistificării*. București: Humanitas.

———. 2005. *Clienții lu' Tanti Varvara: Istorii clandestine*. București: Humanitas.

Tănăsescu, Bogdan. n.d. *Colectivizarea între propagandă și realitate*. București: Globus.

Țârău, Virgiliu. 2003. Final Report, Collectivization project, authors' files.

———. 2009. "Collectivization Policies in the Cluj Region: The Aiud and Turda Districts." In Iordachi and Dobrincu 2009: 203–228.

Taylor, Charles. 1994. "The Politics of Recognition." In *Multiculturalism*, edited by Amy Gutmann, 25–75. Princeton: Princeton University Press.

Ten Dyke, Elizabeth. 2001. *Dresden: Paradoxes of Memory in History*. New York: Routledge.

Thelen, Tatjana. 2005. "Violence and Social (Dis)continuity: Comparing Collectivization in Two East European Villages." *Social History* 30 (1): 25–44.

Thom, Françoise. 1987. *La langue de bois*. Paris: Julliard.

Tismăneanu, Vladimir. 2003. *Stalinism for All Seasons: A Political History of Romanian Communism*. Berkeley: University of California Press.

———. 2008. "Democracy and Memory: Romania Confronts Its Communist Past." *Annals, AAPSS* 617: 166–80.

———. forthcoming. *Democracy, Memory, and Moral Justice: Romania Confronts Its Communist Past*.

Tismăneanu, Vladimir, Dorin Dobrincu, and Cristian Vasile, eds. 2007. *Raport final, comisia prezidențială pentru analiza dictaturii comuniste din România*. București: Humanitas.

Tonkin, Elizabeth. 1992. *Narrating Our Pasts: The Social Construction of Oral History*. Cambridge: Cambridge University Press.

Tribe, Keith. 1995. *Strategies of Economic Order: German Economic Discourse, 1750–1950*. Cambridge: Cambridge University Press.

Trouillot, Michel-Rolph. 1995. *Silencing the Past: Power and the Production of History*. Boston: Beacon.

Turnock, David. 1986. *The Romanian Economy in the Twentieth Century*. New York: St. Martin's Press.

Vansina, Jan. 1965. *Oral Tradition: A Study in Historical Methodology*. Translated by H. M. Wright. London: Routledge & Kegan Paul.

Vasile, Cristian. 2003a. *Între Vatican și Kremlin: Biserica Greco-Catolică în timpul regimului comunist*. București: Curtea Veche.

———. 2003b. *Istoria Bisericii Greco-Catolice sub regimul comunist, 1945–1989: Documente și mărturii*. Iași: Polirom.

———. 2005. *Biserica Ortodoxă Română în primul deceniu comunist*. București: Curtea Veche.

———. 2007. "Secția de propagandă și agitație și 'îndrumarea' culturii române, 1948–1953: Câteva considerații." *Studii și materiale de istorie contemporană* 6: 52–54.

Verdery, Katherine. 1977. "Ethnic Stratification in the European Periphery: The Historical Sociology of a Transylvanian Village." Ph.D. diss., Stanford University.

———. 1983. *Transylvanian Villagers: Three Centuries of Political, Economic, and Ethnic Change*. Berkeley: University of California Press.

———. 1991. *National Ideology under Socialism: Identity and Cultural Politics in Ceaușescu's Romania*. Berkeley: University of California Press.

———. 1994. "The Elasticity of Land: Problems of Property Restitution in Transylvania." *Slavic Review* 53 (4): 1071–109.

———. 1995. "Faith, Hope, and *Caritas* in the Land of the Pyramids, Romania 1991–1994." *Comparative Studies in Society and History* 37 (3): 623–69.

———. 1996. *What Was Socialism, and What Comes Next?* Princeton: Princeton University Press.

———. 1999. *The Political Lives of Dead Bodies: Reburial and Postsocialist Change*. New York: Columbia University Press.

———. 2003. *The Vanishing Hectare: Property and Value in Postsocialist Transylvania*. Ithaca: Cornell University Press.

———. 2009. "Exploiters Old and New: Making and Unmaking 'Rich Peasants' in Aurel Vlaicu (Hunedoara Region)." In Iordachi and Dobrincu 2009: 307–28.

Viola, Lynne. 1986. "Bab'i Bunty and Peasant Women's Protest during Collectivization." *Russian Review* 45 (1): 23–42.

Viola, Lynne. 1987. *The Best Sons of the Fatherland: Workers in the Vanguard of Soviet Collectivization*. New York: Oxford University Press.

———. 1996. *Peasant Rebels under Stalin: Collectivization and the Culture of Peasant Resistance*. New York: Oxford University Press.

———. 2000. "The Role of the OGPU in Dekulakization, Mass Deportations, and Special Resettlement in 1930." *Carl Beck Papers in Russian and East European Studies*, no. 1406.

———, ed. 2002. *Contending with Stalinism: Soviet Power and Popular Resistance in the 1930s*. Ithaca: Cornell University Press.

———. 2007. *The Unknown Gulag: The Lost World of Stalin's Special Settlements*. Oxford: Oxford University Press.

Viola, Lynne, V. P. Danilov, N. A. Ivnitskii, and Denis Kozlov, eds. 2005. *The War Against the Peasantry, 1927–1930: The Tragedy of the Soviet Countryside*. New Haven: Yale University Press.

Voicu-Arnăuţoiu, Ioana Raluca. 1997. *Luptătorii din munţi: Toma Arnăuţoiu, grupul de la Nucşoara. Documente ale anchetei, procesului, detenţiei*. Bucureşti: Vremea.

Volokitina, Tat'iana Vladimirovna. 2002. *Moskva i Vostochnaia Evropa: Stanovlenie politicheskikh rezhimov sovetskoga tipa, 1949–1953. Ocherki istorii*. Moscow: Rosspen.

Vultur, Smaranda. 1997. *Istorie trăită, istorie povestită: Deportarea în Bărăgan 1951–1956*. Timişoara: Amarcord.

———. 2000. *Germanii din Banat prin povestirile lor*. Bucureşti: Paideia.

———. 2002a. *Lumi în destine: Memoria generaţiilor de început de secol din Banat*. Bucureşti: Nemira.

———. 2002b. *Memoria salvată: Evreii din Banat, ieri şi azi*. Iaşi: Polirom.

———. 2003a. Final Report, Collectivization project, authors' files.

———. 2003b. "Les avatars identitaires des Français du Banat." In *Visibles mais pas nombreux: Les circulations migratoires roumaines,* edited by Dana Diminescu, 99–115. Paris: Editions de la Maison des sciences de l'homme.

———. 2009a. *Din radiografia represiunii: Deportarea în Baragan, 1951–1956*. Timişoara: Mirton.

———. 2009b. "The Role of Ethnicity in the Collectivization of Tomnatic/Triebswetter Village (Banat Region) (1949–1956)." In Iordachi and Dobrincu 2009: 141–64.

Watson, Rubie S., ed. 1994. *Memory, History, and Opposition under State Socialism*. Santa Fe, NM: School of American Research Press.

Weber, Max. 1978. *Economy and Society: An Interpretive Outline of Sociology*. Vol. 1. Edited by Guenther Roth and Claus Wittich. Berkeley: University of California Press.

Wedel, Janine. 1986. *The Private Poland*. New York: Facts on File.

Weiner, Annette. 1992. *Inalienable Possessions: The Paradox of Keeping-While-Giving*. Berkeley: University of California Press.

Wertsch, James. 2002. *Voices of Collective Remembering*. Cambridge: Cambridge University Press.

White, Geoffrey. 2006. "Epilogue: Memory Moments." *Ethos* 34: 325–41.

Wood, Elizabeth. 2005. *Performing Justice: Agitation Trials in Early Soviet Russia*. Ithaca: Cornell University Press.

Woodward, Susan. 1995. *Socialist Unemployment: The Political Economy of Yugoslavia, 1945–1990*. Princeton: Princeton University Press.

Yaney, George L. 1971. "Agricultural Administration in Russia from the Stolypin Land

Reform to Forced Collectivization: An Interpretive Study." In *The Soviet Rural Community*, edited by James R. Millar, 3–35. Urbana: University of Illinois Press.

Yates, Frances. 1966. *The Art of Memory*. Chicago: University of Chicago Press.

Yurchak, Alexei. 2006. *Everything Was Forever Until It Was No More: The Last Soviet Generation*. Princeton: Princeton University Press.

Zerubavel, Eviatar. 2003. *Time Maps: Collective Memory and the Social Shape of the Past*. Chicago: University of Chicago Press.

Zub, Alexandru, and Flavius Solomon. 2003. *Sovietization in Romania and Czechoslovakia: History, Analogies, Consequences*. Iaşi: Polirom.

Index